ANNUAL REVIEW OF SOCIOLOGY

ANNUAL REVIEW OF SOCIOLOGY

VOLUME 11, 1985

RALPH H. TURNER, *Editor*

University of California, Los Angeles

JAMES F. SHORT, JR., *Associate Editor*

Washington State University

ANNUAL REVIEWS INC.   4139 EL CAMINO WAY   PALO ALTO, CALIFORNIA 94306 USA

ANNUAL REVIEWS INC.
Palo Alto, California, USA

International Standard Serial Number: 0360–0572
International Standard Book Number: 0–8243–2211–8
Library of Congress Catalog Card Number: 75–648500

Annual Review and publication titles are registered trademarks of Annual Reviews
Inc.

Annual Reviews Inc. and the Editors of its publications assume no responsibility
for the statements expressed by the contributors to this *Review*.

Typesetting by Kachina Typesetting Inc., Tempe, Arizona; John Olson, President
Typesetting coordinator, Janis Hoffman

PRINTED AND BOUND IN THE UNITED STATES OF AMERICA

PREFACE

In 1969 the Sociology Panel of the joint Behavioral and Social Science Survey of the National Academy of Sciences and the Social Science Research Council formally recommended publication of an annual review of sociology as a step toward strengthening sociological knowledge. The Council of the American Sociological Association agreed, and ASA entered into a collaborative enterprise with Annual Reviews, Inc. to publish the *Annual Review of Sociology*. This volume begins the second decade of publication. The *Annual Review of Sociology* has become the indispensable record of trends and developments in the discipline.

As originally conceived, the purpose of the *Annual Review of Sociology* was to provide authoritative surveys of recent important sociological theory and research in specialized fields (or of recent literature from other disciplines that is important for the development of a specialty in sociology). The reader with a general background would be brought up-to-date on the nature and status of rival points of view and the variety of empirical work in the field. In addition, reviews were to be interpretative and critical.

In order to ensure a proper diversity of topics in each volume, the Editorial Committee uses the 12 broad categories that appear in the cumulative title index as an organizing framework and checklist. These categories serve as a heuristic device rather than a rigid structure. Within this loose framework, the specific topics for review change each year. The rate of accumulation of sociological knowledge and the pattern by which the discipline advances could not justify reviewing the same topics in successive years. Many problems and seminal ideas in sociology stimulate a flurry of relatively transient interest and may justifiably be reviewed only once. Others produce a slow accumulation of knowledge and—more importantly—a slow change in perspective that would merit recurrent review, but only perhaps at five- to ten-year intervals. Our editorial policy is to reassess specific topics about five years after publication of the initial review so as to decide which ones ought to be reviewed again.

Only the topic of mass communications, first reviewed in Volume 5, is being reviewed again in the current volume. But the way in which sociology grows by constantly branching is documented through many continuities with earlier work. A comprehensive review of race and ethnic relations in Volume 1 was followed by "Black Identity and Self-Esteem" in Volume 5, "Black Students in Higher Education" in Volume 7, and "New Black-White Patterns," "Urban Poverty," and "The Impact of School Desegregation" in the current volume. Reviews of "Ethnic Mobilization" and "America's Melting Pot Reconsidered" in Volume 9 are followed by a chapter on "Ethnicity" in this volume. Exploration of subjective processes in organizations, developed first in Volume 3, was followed by "Negotiated Orders and Organizational Cultures" in Volume 10

(continued)   v

and by "Organizational Culture" in this volume. A review of "The Social Organization of the Classroom" in Volume 4 is complemented in this volume by a more macrosociological examination of "The Organizational Structure of the School."

Whenever feasible our authors base their reviews on international literature rather than solely United States sources. In addition, four chapters in this volume were written by scholars outside of the United States, each covering research from abroad in greater depth than might otherwise have been possible. These chapters deal with "The Petite Bourgeoisie in Late Capitalism" (authors from Scotland), "White Collar Crime" (author from Australia), "The Organizational Structure of the School" (author from England), and "The Sociology of Mass Communication" (author from the Netherlands).

We continue the practice begun last year of including abstracts with all chapters. And we include a complete subject index for the current volume and cumulative indexes of chapter titles and authors for Volumes 1–11.

The Editorial Committee is never satisfied that the articles appearing in a volume are perfectly representative of the most vital recent developments in sociology. We therefore invite specific proposals from all members of the discipline. What areas of activity have we overlooked? What specialized developments may not otherwise come to the Committee's attention on a timely basis? It is especially helpful to the Committee when a recommendation is accompanied by a paragraph describing the proposed topic, some key bibliographic examples, and the names of persons qualified to prepare the review. In a few instances, sociologists who have proposed topics and volunteered themselves as expert reviewers have been commissioned to prepare chapters.

THE EDITORS AND THE EDITORIAL COMMITTEE

Annual Review of Sociology
Volume 11, 1985

CONTENTS

viii   CONTENTS   (*continued*)

RELATED ARTICLES FROM OTHER *ANNUAL REVIEWS*

From the *Annual Review of Anthropology*, Volume 14 (1985)

Text and Discourse, Aaron V. Cicourel
Status and Style in Language, Judith T. Irvine
Chicano Studies, Renato Rosaldo
Peasant Ideologies in the Third World, Joel S. Kahn

From the *Annual Review of Energy*, Volume 10 (1985)

A Decade of United States Energy Policy, Mark D. Levine and Paul P. Craig

From the *Annual Review of Psychology*, Volume 36 (1985)

Sex and Gender, Kay Deaux
Personality: Current Controversies, Issues, and Directions, Lawrence A. Pervin
The School as a Social Situation, Seymour B. Sarason, Michael Klaber
The Psychology of Intergroup Attitudes and Behavior, Marilynn B. Brewer and
   Roderick M. Kramer
Social Factors in Psychopathology: Stress, Social Support, and Coping Processes,
   Ronald C. Kessler, Richard H. Price, Camille B. Wortman

From the *Annual Review of Public Health*, Volume 6 (1985)

*The Community-based Strategy to Prevent Coronary Heart Disease: Conclusions
   from the Ten Years of the North Karelia Project*, Pekka Puska, Aulikki Nissinen,
   Jaako Tuomilehto, Jukka T. Salonen, Kaj Koskela, Alfred McAlister, Thomas E.
   Kottke, Nathan Maccoby, and John W. Farquhar
Symposium on Occupation Health:
   Introduction, David H. Wegman
   The Study of Stress at Work, Dean B. Baker
   The "Right to Know": Toxics Information in the Workplace, Nicholas A.
      Ashford and Charles C. Caldart
   Fatal and Nonfatal Injuries in Occupational Settings: A Review, Jess F. Kraus
   Surveillance for the Effects of Workplace Exposure, William E. Halperin and
      Todd M. Frazier

Ann. Rev. Sociol. 1985. 11:1–25

WHITE COLLAR CRIME

John Braithwaite

Senior Research Fellow, Department of Sociology, Research School of Social Sciences, The Australian National University, Canberra 2601, Australia

Abstract

Only banal generalizations are possible in answer to questions of who engages in white collar crime and why. Doubt is cast on the common assertion that firms in financial difficulty are more likely to offend than profitable ones. Qualitative studies of how white collar offenses are perpetrated and how regulatory agencies seek to control offenses constitute the most illuminating part of the literature. This literature depicts consistent pressure for blame for white collar crime to be passed downwards in the class structure, widespread use of international law evasion strategies, and a preference of control agencies for informal, "direct action" modes of social control over litigious regulation. The thesis that the latter reflects "capture" by ruling class interests is critically examined. It is contended that community attitudes toward white collar crime have become increasingly punitive. The review concludes that theoretical progress is most likely via organization theory paradigms, but that partition of white collar crime into "corporate (or organizational) crime" and "occupational crime" is necessary to facilitate such progress.

INTRODUCTION

The number of scholars who have worked on white collar crime has been modest, and the impact of white collar crime research on mainstream sociological theory unimportant. But we will see that white collar crime research marks a rare case of sociological scholarship having a substantial impact on public policy and public opinion. Even more unusual, this impact is largely attributable to the work of one great sociologist—Edwin H. Sutherland.

1

0360-0572/85/0815-0001$02.00

WHITE COLLAR CRIME RESEARCH BEFORE SUTHERLAND

There were great scholars on whose shoulders Sutherland could stand. The Dutch Marxist, Willem Bonger, in his *Criminality and Economic Conditions* (1916), was the first to develop a theory of crime which incorporated both "crime in the streets" and "crime in the suites". Bonger's contention was that capitalism "has developed egoism at the expense of altruism". Bonger argued that a criminal attitude is engendered by the conditions of misery inflicted on the working class under capitalism, and that a similar criminal attitude arises among the bourgeoisie from the avarice fostered when capitalism thrives.

Influential criminological theory between Bonger and Sutherland continued to focus on class as the critical variable, but it was a truncated focus concerned with explaining why the poor seemed to commit more crime than the rest of us. Bonger's insight—that to assume poverty causes crime is to neglect the widespread nature of ruling class crime—was largely ignored until Sutherland revived it.

The important American antecedents in the early part of the century were the sociologist E. A. Ross (1907) and the muckrakers—e.g. Tarbell (1904); Steffens (1904); Norris (1903); Sinclair (1906). In journalistic exposés and fictionalized accounts, these writers laid bare the occupational safety abuses of mining magnates, the flagrant disregard for consumer health of the meat packing industry, the corporate bribery of legislatures, and many other abuses. The muckrakers were responsible for some of the important statutes, like the US Federal Food, Drug, and Cosmetic Act of 1906, which criminalized many forms of corporate misconduct that Ross had been forced to label as "criminaloid". Sutherland's mission was to turn muckraking into sociology.

SUTHERLAND

White collar crime became part of the English language when Edwin Sutherland gave his Presidential Address to the American Sociological Society in 1939 (Sutherland 1940). Sutherland's talk, "The White Collar Criminal", scorned traditional theories of crime which blamed poverty, broken homes, and disturbed personalities. He noted that many of the law breakers in business were far from poor, from happy family backgrounds, and all too mentally sound. After ten years of further research, Sutherland published *White Collar Crime* (1949). The book was a devastating documentation of crimes perpetrated by America's 70 largest private companies and 15 public utility corporations. His publisher, Dryden, insisted that all references to the companies by name be deleted for fear of libel suits. It was another 34 years before the uncut version was published (Sutherland 1983).

Sutherland (1983:7) defined white collar crime as "a crime committed by a person of respectability and high social status in the course of his occupation." The definition has its problems. The concept of "respectability" defies precision of use. The requirement that a crime cannot be a white collar crime unless perpetrated by a person of "high social status" is an unfortunate mixing of definition and explanation, especially when Sutherland used the widespread nature of white collar crime to refute class-based theories of criminality.

These deficiencies have rendered white collar crime an impotent construct for theory building in sociology. No influential theory of white collar crime has developed, let alone an attempt to link such work to wider sociological theory. Sutherland's theory of differential association in *White Collar Crime* was a general theory of all crime, one whose generality borders on a platitudinous restatement of social learning theory (cf Mathews 1983; Albanese 1984).

As Farrell & Swigert (1983) point out, while there have been those who dabbled with differential association (e.g. Clinard 1946), anomie theory (Sherwin 1963), labelling theory (Waegel et al 1981; Swigert & Farrell 1980), and social psychological and personality theories (Stotland 1977; Monahan & Navaco 1980), theoretical progress began only in the late 1970s when the individualistic theorizing spawned by the Sutherland tradition was rejected in favor of applying organization theory paradigms to the phenomenon. Ironically, it was lawyers (Stone 1975, Coffee 1977) who led this theoretical reorientation rather than sociologists (but note the important roles of Cohen 1977, Schrager & Short 1978, Ermann & Lundman 1978, and Gross 1978). The reorientation became possible only when ties to the Sutherland definition were cut in favor of a focus on the narrower domains of organizational or corporate crime.

The only justification for locating contemporary research in the white collar crime construct is phenomenological. The concept is shared and understood by ordinary folk as more meaningful than occupational crime, corporate deviance, commercial offenses, economic crime or any competing concept. Moreoover, as Geis & Goff (1983:xi–xii) point out, Sutherland's Americanism soon became "crime en col blanc" in France, "criminalita in colletti bianchi" in Italy and "weisse-kragen-kriminalität" in Germany.

Most researchers have dealt with the problem of definition by simply studying violations of particular laws (tax, environmental, antitrust, consumer protection, fraud). Patterns and processes of violations of such laws are all phenomena worthy of study in their own right, yet it is a pity that the phenomena do not comfortably sit as building blocks for theorizing around a more all-encompassing concept. In the conclusion to this review, I argue that we should cling to Sutherland's overarching definition, but then partition the domain into major types of white collar crime which do have theoretical potential.

Sutherland's operationalizing of the new concept also came under attack from lawyers. Sutherland was content to consider illegal behavior as white collar crime if it were punishable, even if not punished, and if the potential penalties for infringement were civil rather than provided for in a criminal code (Sutherland 1983:51). Tappan (1947) led a tradition insisting on proof beyond reasonable doubt in a criminal court before anything could be called a crime (Burgess 1950; Orland 1980). Sutherland's counter is today accepted by most sociologists—that to do this would be to sacrifice science to a class-biased administration of criminal justice that neglects the punishment of white collar offenders, often giving them the benefit of civil penalties for offenses that in law could equally be punished criminally. Sutherland was right in principle, but in practice he and his disciples often counted actions that were not violations of law (e.g. recalls of hazardous consumer products) as instances of white collar crime.

THE LEGACY OF SUTHERLAND

Two young scholars who later became preeminent in criminology quickly followed in Sutherland's footsteps—Marshall Clinard and Donald Cressey. Clinard produced a book on price control violations during World War II (Clinard 1952), and Cressey wrote *Other People's Money*, a study of embezzlement (Cressey 1953). There followed a twenty year hiatus during which a few diehards, notably Gilbert Geis and Herbert Edelhertz, kept the flickering flame of white collar crime research alight (Geis 1962, 1967, 1968; Edelhertz 1970). As a result, white collar crime continued to penetrate criminological textbooks and sociological teaching on crime.

When Watergate and then the foreign bribery scandal took America and the world by storm in the mid 1970s, a generation of students had been educated in the vocabulary of white collar crime. Public interest in the subject overflowed; American research dollars were for the first time unleashed in significant quantities. By the late 1970s, an international community of white collar crime scholars had been established.

STYLES OF CONTEMPORARY RESEARCH
The Search for Generalizations

Who engages in white collar crime and why? An unimpressive tradition of positivist criminology has developed around these two questions. The only generalizations that can reasonably be made about the characteristics of white collar criminals are banal. White collar criminals are not likely to be juveniles and are not likely to be female or poor. These generalizations are virtually true by definition, since juveniles, women, and the poor do not generally occupy the occupational roles required for white collar offending.

The only answers to "why" questions that can be made safely are also of no explanatory power. As Shichor (1983:1) suggests, "The most obvious explanation—that greed is the major causal factor of white collar crime—is very probable but it is too general". The same can be said of Sutherland's (1983:240) differential-association explanation, that "criminal behavior is learned in association with those who define such criminal behavior favorably and in isolation from those who define it unfavorably."

What of more tantalizing questions about which cultures, which periods of history, what types of organizations are associated with high rates of white collar crime? There is a tradition of comparative politics which persuasively concludes that as nations become more economically developed, corruption of public officials decreases (Wraith & Simpkins 1963; Scott 1972). These scholars interpret the historical decline of corruption in countries such as Britain in essentially Weberian terms—as legitimacy shifts from loyalty to family and tribe to authority for a national administrative order, new national elites mobilize public disapproval against the determination of administrative priorities by bribes.

But few other credible claims to this kind of generalization can be made, largely because of the elusiveness of adequate data. The nature of white collar crime—its complexity, the power of its perpetrators—means that only an unrepresentative minority of offenses is detected and officially recorded. Not only is the problem of nonreporting less severe with regard to common offenses, but there are alternative measures—self-reports and victim surveys. The latter are ruled out because victims of white collar crime are rarely aware that they have been so victimized (but see McCaghy & Nogier 1982), the former because company directors do not respond to questionnaires about their criminal activities. Reiss & Biderman (1980) in their encyclopedic study for the US Justice Department have demonstrated the enormous difficulties of assessing the level of white collar crime in one country at one point in time.

Questions as to which types of organizations generate greater white collar criminality are somewhat more manageable and consequently have attracted significant empirical work. I am aware only of one data set in the world that would be adequate to address such questions and this is a very narrow one. Approximately 140,000 health and safety violations are recorded each year against American coal mining companies. Systematic bias is less than in other data sets because the US Mine Safety and Health Act requires four random inspections of each coal mine per year and, unlike most regulatory statutes, it requires the inspector to cite every violation observed. Since the source of data is semirandom patrol by the agency rather than nonrandom reporting to the agency, and since the policy of nondiscretionary citation, while frequently ignored in practice, at least substantially reduces selective bias by inspectors, the US Mine Safety and Health Administration data are the closest we can approach to an indication of offending rates for organizations of different types. While there has been work on which kinds of companies have lower accident rates (DeMichiei et al 1982; Braithwaite 1985), no criminologist has yet explored the characteristics of companies with high violation rates and the settings and other variables that seem to bear on such rates.

Use of other, more doubtful data sets has failed to yield a crop of generalizations about criminogenic organizations. It has been common for reviews, on the basis of limited studies by Lane (1953), and Staw & Szwajkowski (1975), to assert that firms in financial difficulty are more likely to offend than profitable ones. However, the two studies on the most substantial samples both found no association between company profitability and corporate crime (Perez 1978:124; Clinard et al 1979:304). The latter found a slight negative association between firm liquidity and corporate crime. Review of the literature on industry concentration, company size, and similar economic variables yields highly conflicting findings (Clinard & Yeager 1980:50–1). Moreover, there is some evidence suggesting that regulatory stereotypes of large firms as law-abiding leads to less punitive treatment of them in comparison to smaller companies (Lynxwiler et al 1984). Contrary to the perceptions of many casual readers of the white collar crime literature, we may ultimately find that Aristotle (Book II:65, from Greek) was right all along, that "The greatest crimes are caused by excess and not by necessity".

It may seem odd to argue that quantitative comparisons of offending rates for different companies are the kinds of research least needed when the two most influential studies of white collar crime—those of Sutherland (1983) and Clinard & Yeager (1980)—were precisely of this kind. There are three answers to this. First, the quantification of white collar crimes in both works was important in demonstrating to a disbelieving world that the biggest and best companies are widely involved in criminality; it was not, however, very important for correlational analysis. Second, the major intellectual contributions of both works concerned their syntheses of theory and qualitative data. Third, even if the quantitative aspect of their work did have substantial intellectual as opposed to polemical significance, it is doubtful, given the problems outlined above, that future scholars will be able to advance much upon it.

It is remarkable that a reviewer can say so little about what quantitative and motivational studies of white collar crime have established. Ideas that at first seemed fruitful, such as Cressey's (1953) explanation of embezzlement in terms of "nonsharable financial problems", have failed to attract a body of literature to support them (Nettler 1974). American sociologists have dominated the first forty years of white collar crime research, and their continued attachment to "who" and "why" questions has slowed progress. "In their obsession with the motivational issues surrounding why people do what they do, criminological theorists have tended to neglect the equally (if not more) important issue of *how* they are able to do what they do" (Levi 1984).

There may be some further progress with motivational research. To make strides, however, this work would have to stop asking "Why do people commit white collar crime?" and begin to ask, "Given the great rewards and low risks of detection, why do so many business people adopt the 'economically irrational' course of obeying the law?"

Modus Operandi Studies

A number of recent studies, both scholarly and journalistic, of how people and organizations offend have enhanced our understanding of white collar crime (e.g. Carson 1982, Knightley et al 1979, Doig 1984, Boulton 1978, Vandivier 1982, Stone 1977, Parker 1976, Waters 1978). Levi's (1981) study of long-firm fraud showed the low likelihood of legal control when frauds cross several national boundaries; it also showed the trade-offs enforcement agencies must make between stopping fraud to protect creditors and waiting until there is evidence for a conviction. The modus operandi literature repeatedly demonstrates international law evasion strategies that utilize Swiss banks, tax havens, pollution havens, or international dumping of banned products. This points up the limitations of both research and control strategies confined to behavior within one set of national boundaries (Sheleff 1982, Delmas-Marty 1980, Edelhertz 1980, Delmas-Marty & Tiedemann 1979).

The modus operandi literature demonstrates the existence of consistent pressures to pass blame for white collar crime downward in the class structure. It is not difficult for powerful actors to structure their affairs so that all of the pressures to break the law surface at a lower level of their own organization or in a subordinate organization. Examples include company presidents appointing "vice-presidents responsible for going to jail", respectable companies engaging contractors to do illegal dirty work such as disposing of toxic wastes or producing fraudulent scientific data about the safety of a product, or hiring agents to pay bribes (for a review of such studies, see Braithwaite, 1982a:71–5).

Combined with the recurrent demonstration of the capacity of organizations to manufacture an impression of confused accountability for wrongdoing, the scapegoating literature has underpinned a tradition of legal scholarship defending the need for a capacity to impose criminal liability on corporations (Yale Law Journal 1979, Harvard Law Review 1979, Coffee 1984, Stone 1980, Fisse 1978, 1983, 1984; Leigh 1977; Schudson et al 1984).

Vaughan's (1983) study of Medicaid fraud by the Revco drug store chain illustrated how complexity in a regulatory system can increase risks of noncompliance. It also showed how organizations are less easily controlled when governments are dependent on them for a service, more easily controlled when the organization is dependent on the government. Reisman's (1979) work on corporate bribery showed that while bribes are deviations from a "myth system", they may be deemed appropriate under the "operational code"—the private and unacknowledged set of rules that selectively tolerates bribery as an ordinary and necessary form of business. Reisman warns that unless we realize that not only business people but also Presidents of the United States subscribe to both the "myth system" and the "operational code", we will never understand the social realities of bribery. Studies of the Ford Pinto homicide prosecution have illuminated how intra- and inter-organizational struggles occur between those who wish to put human lives into a cost-benefit calculus and those who wish to treat human life as sacrosanct (Strobel 1980, Kramer 1982, Cullen et al 1984).

The literature documents criminality on such a scale among public organizations (Douglas & Johnson 1977)—from corruption of police departments (Duchaine 1979, Sherman 1978), to massive illegal mail interception programs by the CIA (Ermann & Lundman 1982:144–54), to the US army intentionally exposing soldiers to fallout from nuclear explosions (Stone 1982:1459–60)—that the profit motive must be questioned as the supreme cause of white collar crime. All organizations, capitalist or socialist (Los 1982), experience pressure to resort to illegitimate means of goal attainment when legitimate means are blocked. As Gross (1978:72) points out: "Some organizations seek profits, others seek survival, still others seek to fulfill government-imposed quotas, others seek to service a body of professionals who run them, some seek to win wars, and some seek to serve a clientele. Whatever the goals might be, it is the emphasis on them that creates the trouble".

Sherman's (1978) study of corruption in police departments concluded that a scandal might cause corruption to be submerged while media coverage of the scandal runs its course, but that the corruption resurfaces unless the adverse publicity produces internal organizational countermeasures, such as a proactive internal affairs branch which uses anticorruption techniques verging on entrapment.

The modus operandi literature merges with a literature on what organizations do when their misconduct reaches public attention. This research has significant implications. Demonstrating the importance of adverse publicity as a control mechanism raises the question of regulatory strategies that mobilize adverse publicity and of publicity orders by courts that are used as sanctions against white collar offenders. Empirical findings that newspapers often do not take up stories of white collar crime (Dershowitz 1961, Evans & Lundman 1983, Randall & DeFillippi 1984, cf Brants & de Roos, in press) imply reliance on formal court-ordered rather than informal publicity. And Sherman's finding that white collar crime just bobs up again once the heat is off unless internal controls are introduced suggests consideration of management restructuring orders to guarantee that the impact of reforms is enduring (Mathews 1976, Solomon & Nowak 1980).

On the other hand, Fisse & Braithwaite (1983) showed with their 17 case studies that white collar crime scandals often produced substantial preventive reform prior to or even in the absence of conviction. Waldman's (1978, 1980) studies of the impact of antitrust prosecution showed that some of the most dramatic changes in the competitiveness of markets occurred where the government failed to secure convictions. When companies had the threat of divestiture or prosecution hanging over their heads throughout the many years during which an antitrust case incubates, they generally improved their antitrust compliance. To be able to present themselves more favorably to the court they may, for example, pull down barriers to entry, cease retaliating (as by predatory pricing) against competing firms, or even become industry leaders in the development of antitrust compliance codes, as IBM did during its years of antitrust litigation (Fisse & Braithwaite 1983:204–12). They may even actively recruit a competitor into the industry. Thus, du Pont, acquitted in 1956 for monopolizing the cellophane market, during the nine-year court battle recruited the Olin corporation to enter the industry as a competing cellophane manufacturer. Substantial white collar crime control often occurs in cases prosecutors lose.

Similarly, qualitative empirical studies of regulatory agencies (to be reviewed in the next section) show that most of the compliance with the law achieved by such agencies is without recourse to criminal conviction. Qualitative research of a variety of kinds therefore suggests the need for a theory of organizational crime control without conviction—a theory which incorporates the significance of the reaction of white collar offenders to informal publicity, prosecutorial threats, and negotiation with inspectors. This would involve a major shift from the current preoccupation with deterrence and incapacitation following conviction.

Control Agency Studies

Until the 1970s, sociologists had a simplistic conception of business regulatory agencies as "captured" law enforcement bodies, the members of which were responsible for the inequality of a justice system which turned a blind eye to the crimes of the powerful while bludgeoning those of the poor. The only systematic empirical investigations of the "capture" thesis (Quirk 1981, Freitag 1983) lend little support to this conception (see also Weaver 1977).

A proliferation of studies since 1970 tend to show that from the top administrator to the junior inspector, most officers of regulatory agencies never saw themselves as law enforcers (Kagan 1978, Cranston 1979, Richardson et al 1982, Carson 1970, Shover et al 1983, Gunningham 1984; cf Katzmann 1980, Weaver 1977). Beyond the control agency studies mentioned in this review, Hawkins (1984:3) has cited an additional 35 which sustain the conclusion that regulatory agencies that deal with pollution, occupational health and safety, consumer protection, housing, discrimination, wage and price control, forestry, meat inspection, and agriculture all tend to conciliatory compliance styles rather than a punitive law enforcement approach (cf Bardach & Kagan 1982). Regulators are mystified by the sociologists' charge that their role creates structural inequality in the criminal justice system because they had never thought of themselves as part of the criminal justice system. Some of them have a tougher, more adversarial stance toward business than their critics in criminology textbooks. It is just that often they reject prosecution as the best way of getting tough.

Perhaps the most powerful of the early control agency studies was Schrag's (1971) account of what happened when he took over the enforcement division of the New York City Department of Consumer Affairs. When Schrag began in the job he adopted a prosecutorial stance. In response to a variety of frustrations, however, especially the use of delaying tactics by company lawyers, a direct action model was eventually substituted for the judicial model. Nonlitigious methods of achieving restitution, deterrence, and incapacitation were increasingly used. These included threats and use of adverse publicity, revocation of licence, writing directly to consumers to warn them of company practices, and exerting pressure on reputable financial institutions and suppliers to withdraw support for the targeted company.

The studies of business regulatory agencies cited above showed that regulatory officials view their primary objective as achieving substantive regulatory goals (safer factories, cleaner air, stronger competition); the fact that they were creating an inequitable criminal justice system by rejecting prosecution as the way to achieve those goals hardly occurred to them. Reiss (1983, 1984) dubbed the predominant regulatory strategy revealed in the literature as "compliance" rather than "deterrence" law enforcement systems: "The principal objective of a compliance law enforcement system is to secure conformity of law without the necessity to define, process, and penalize violations." (Reiss 1983:93–4). Optimism about the efficacy of compliance systems should be tempered by McCormick's (1977) conclusions concerning nonenforcement of US antitrust law. He argues that the lack of a continuously identifiable body of criminal violations symbolizing and reinforcing reaction has led to a "neutralization of indignation", which in turn has permitted some legitimation of illegality.

If the regulators are right and the public best protected when regulators deal with most business crime by negotiation, bluff, adverse publicity, and other informal sanctions, then what of sociological theories which assume that nonprosecution reflects the unwillingness of the state to confront ruling class interests? What of jurisprudential theories that insist it is right to deploy the criminal law equally against rich and poor? Will it still be right if it is shown that the poor are left worse off in more dangerous factories, marketplaces, and environments when compliance strategies are rejected in favor of less effective retributive strategies? Should resources for policy evaluation research now be directed away from the effectiveness of law reform, of various court-ordered sanctions and remedies, in favor of evaluating different regulatory negotiation strategies (DiMento 1984)?

It will be some time before we are ready to hazard answers to these policy questions. The point here is that the qualitative studies of control agencies have prompted a fundamental rethinking of theory and policy implied by the questions. I suspect that some of the sociologists enraptured with the proposition that regulatory agencies opt for compliance law enforcement systems because this is the only way to achieve their mission are too quick to explain away capture. Nor is there really any evidence to support the reverse-capture views of scholars such as James Q. Wilson who see regulatory agencies as captured by "the new class" (Weaver 1978). As I have argued elsewhere, no matter what view one has of the efficacy of compliance law enforcement systems, that efficacy might be enhanced when it is complemented by criminal punishment (Braithwaite 1985).

We need more studies of what regulatory agencies actually do. In addition to the intensive single agency studies that have been so important in beginning to reshape our thinking about crimes of the powerful, we need some more adventurous studies that paint a broad canvas, comparing a large number of agencies. Cross-cultural studies are also needed, given what we already know about how much regional cultures can affect the enforcement strategy of a single agency (Shover et al 1984). Kelman's (1981) research, which showed a more negotiated style of occupational health and safety enforcement in Sweden, compared with a more punitive style in the United States, is a promising beginning to this type of work.

Another dimension coming into focus from the control agency studies is the importance of private justice systems. As Reiss (1983:81) points out, we know more about the way the Securities and Exchange Commission controls illegal behavior in marketing securities (Shapiro 1984) than we know about the role of the New York Stock Exchange in detecting such behavior. It is becoming clear that many regulatory agencies attempt to maximize their impact for the tax-payer's dollar by effectively delegating important areas of enforcement to private justice systems, some of which may be puny in the extreme, others of which may invoke draconian sanctions such as withdrawing a doctor's right to practice with minimum due process protections. A few scholars are now beginning to grapple with the implications of the staggering growth of private law enforcement systems in modern societies (Shearing & Stenning 1981).

THE WIDER IMPLICATIONS OF WHITE COLLAR CRIME RESEARCH

The literature on white collar crime has contributed significantly to our understanding of how enormous class inequalities are maintained even in welfare states with nominally progressive taxation systems. The billions of dollars transferred annually from the poor to the rich by antitrust offenses (Barnett 1979, Shepherd 1970, 1975; Goff & Reasons 1984) and tax evasion (Levi 1982:37; Barnett 1984; cf Long 1982) are particularly important. For example, some data suggest that illegal returns to monopoly power may account for perhaps one-quarter of the total value of corporate stock held by the four million top wealth holders in the United States (Barnett 1979:184).

The study of white collar crime probably also contributed a little to rendering some reality to the sociology of law. There was a time when it was common for Marxists to argue that "law is a tool of the ruling class" (Quinney 1974:52). The reified class interest analysis that one sees in the earlier work of scholars like Quinney has been demolished by both liberal and Marxist scholars who grant some autonomy to social control agencies (e.g. Chambliss & Seidman 1971, O'Malley 1980). In modern capitalist societies there are many more statutes which criminalize the behavior of corporations (anti-pollution laws, occupational health and safety laws, antitrust laws, laws to enforce compliance with standards for everything from elevators to cleaning animal cages in laboratories) than there are laws which criminalize the behavior of the poor. Moreover, under many of the business statutes, mens rea is not required for proof of guilt; self-incrimination can be forced on defendants; search and seizure without warrant are provided for; and due process protections are generally weak (cf. Hopkins 1981).

None of this is to deny the existence of profound class bias in the way laws are often administered. The common disjunction between tough laws against business and weak enforcement of them indicates a need to separate the instrumental and symbolic effects of legislation (Edelman 1964, Gusfield 1967, Carson 1975, O'Malley 1980, Hopkins & Parnell 1984). Edelman is undoubtedly correct that unorganized and diffuse publics tend to receive symbolic rewards, while organized professional ones reap tangible rewards. Equally, it is true that traditionally unorganized interests—consumers, women, environmentalists, workers—are becoming organized. Even if the failure of regulatory agencies to mobilize available laws against business can be justified on grounds that this is not the most effective way of safeguarding the public, the fact of unequal enforcement of the law in ruling class interests cannot be escaped. Note also Hagan's (1982) findings that the justice system gives greater assistance to corporate than to individual victims of crime.

The fundamental class bias in the criminal justice system is that white collar offenders, if they get to court at all, are punished less severely than traditional criminals (Snider 1982). Notwithstanding that, two major studies have now found that higher status individuals who are white collar offenders do not tend to be treated more leniently by US courts than lower status white collar offenders (Hagan et al 1980; Wheeler et al 1982). Indeed, the study by Wheeler et al surprisingly found a positive correlation between the socioeconomic status of white collar offenders and the probability of imprisonment (cf Geis 1984).

The white collar crime literature does have important implications for jurisprudence. Three elements of the literature come together to establish this relevance. The first of these is the literature demonstrating the massive numbers of unpunished white collar offenders in the community and the enormous damage to persons and property caused by their offending (e.g. Goff & Reasons 1984, Sutherland 1983, Saxon 1980, Clinard & Yeager 1980; Meier & Short 1982). Second is the literature arguing that protection of the public from white collar crime is better achieved by compliance law enforcement systems than by deterrence law enforcement systems. The third is the literature showing that ordinary citizens have had remarkably punitive attitudes recently toward white collar crime (Frank et al 1984; Cullen et al 1982, 1983a; Jones & Levi 1983; Salas et al 1982:512–4; and earlier studies reviewed in Braithwaite 1982b:731–42).

This third stream of the literature is most interesting because it refutes a major plank of Sutherland's original work—that white collar crime is allowed to flourish because of permissive community attitudes toward it. Sutherland of course probably was correct in saying that community attitudes were tolerant in his time. Public interest crusades against white collar crime that drew inspiration from Sutherland possibly were responsible for changing the very community tolerance toward the phenomenon that Sutherland lamented. What this literature shows, in summary, is that the community perceives many forms of white collar crime as more serious and deserving of longer prison sentences than most forms of common crime. There are exceptions to this pattern. Tax offenses and false advertising in most studies are not viewed as serious crimes, and most types of individual homicide are perceived as more serious than all types of white collar crime. Nevertheless, white collar crimes that cause severe harm to persons are generally rated as more serious than all other types of crime and even some types of individual homicide. Meier & Short (1984) have shown that not only do citizens view white collar crime as serious, they rate being victimized by white collar offenses as more likely than being victimized by other life hazards, including common crime.

The importance of these three elements of the literature for jurisprudence is that they show the political, fiscal, and moral impossibility of fidelity to a pure retributive philosophy of punishment. Whether the deserved punishment is determined by community attitudes toward the offense or by objective harm, retributivists, because of this literature, must judge white collar crimes to deserve heavy punishment. Add this fact together with the literature that concludes there are more white collar offenses and offenders in the community than common criminals, and it follows that equitable application of a retributive philosophy would see more white collar offenders in prison than common criminals. Given the minuscule numbers of prison spaces currently occupied by white collar criminals and the enormous costs of incarceration, this would be a fiscal and political impossibility. Moreover, if the devotees of compliance law enforcement systems for business crimes are even partially right, a policy of consistent administration of just deserts to convictable offenders would undermine compliance and jeopardize more lives and cost millions of dollars. Equal retributive justice would have been achieved over the bodies of victims of those white collar crimes that cause physical harm (the very white collar crimes toward which the community is most punitive).

Thus, the white collar crime literature implies that if equitable retributivist philosophies are to be relevant to moral choices in the real world, they must be tempered with utilitarian considerations, including those of crime control and fiscal restraint. Retributivists can reject this, as von Hirsch (1982) has done, by denying these conclusions from the white collar crime literature—by denying that white collar crime is subjectively and objectively more serious than common crime, by disputing that white collar crime is more pervasive than common crime, by scoffing at suggestions that consistent, proportional punishment could be less effective in preventing crime than compliance or mixed compliance/deterrence law enforcement systems—see also van den Haag (1982 a,b). How these differing streams of white collar crime literature develop should have important implications for those who seek a philosophy of punishment that can be equitably implemented in the real world, rather than in some possible or impossible world.

THE WHITE COLLAR CRIME LITERATURE AND PUBLIC POLICY

The first two sentences of the 1949 edition of *White Collar Crime* read, "This book is a study of the theory of criminal behavior. It is an attempt to reform the theory of criminal behavior, not to reform anything else" (Sutherland 1949:v). Sutherland's book did not reform the theory of criminal behavior; its significance in the way it influenced people like Ralph Nader was more profound than its impact on any criminological theorist.

It has already been speculated that there may have been an element of self-defeating prophecy in Sutherland's observation about "the unorganized resentment of the public toward white collar crimes" (Sutherland 1983:59). Without the impact Sutherland has had on criminolological and legal education, one wonders whether governments would be under pressure in the Western democracies to "do something" about at least the most visible kinds of white collar crime. In some measure, governments have responded. Pointing to examples like Abscam, some would even argue they have overreacted (Marx 1982). Under the Carter administration, the crusade against white collar crime, with high profile endorsement by the President, reached the point where the FBI to some degree downgraded efforts to solve offenses such as bank robbery in order to concentrate more intensively on fraud, corruption, and other white collar crime (Geis & Goff 1983:xxxi). Much of this, though not all, has changed under the Reagan administration. Coffee (1983:24) recently pointed out that 17% of the criminal cases handled by US Attorneys' office in 1981 were classified by the Attorney as "White Collar Crimes." Another 8 percent were classified either as "Government Regulatory Offenses" or "Official Corruption". This of course means that considerably more than 25 percent of federal prosecutorial resources were involved because white collar cases are more complex than average. Admittedly, the bulk of these numbers consist of small-time white collar criminals. So numerous have been the corruption convictions of New York politicians that one study found members of the state legislature during the 1970s to have four times the probability of a criminal record as other citizens (Katz 1980:162).

Sutherland would be surprised to see the appearance since his death of agencies such as the Environmental Protection Agency, the Consumer Product Safety Commission, the Occupational Safety and Health Administration, the Office of Surface Mining Reclamation and Enforcement, and the Mine Safety and Health Administration.

The number of fatalities from coal mining accidents is today less than a tenth of its level earlier in the century for the United States, United Kingdom, Australia, France, and Japan (Braithwaite 1985). [For the more skeptical views on the impact of occupational safety enforcement, see Smith (1979), Viscusi (1983).] In Japan, where criminal pollution convictions number over 6,000 a year, the rate of noncompliance with water quality standards for lead, cyanide, cadmium, arsenic, and PCBs by 1980 was at a tenth of the levels prevailing at the beginning of the 1970s (Japanese Environment Agency 1981). Even in the United States (Gallese 1982, Bardach & Kagan 1982:94) and Britain (Storey 1979) with their less rigorous environmental enforcement, the fish are returning to many rivers that were once heavily polluted (cf MacAvoy 1979, Barnett 1981, 1983). Modest consumer product safety enforcement in the United States during the 1970s produced a 40 percent drop in ingestion of poisons by children, a halving of crib deaths of babies, and virtual elimination of children's sleepwear as a cause of flameburn injuries [Costle 1979, see also Consumers' Federation of America (1983) for an estimate of 5 million disabling injuries prevented by the Consumer Product Safety Commission].

In a recent work, I have become persuaded that reforms whereby governments give bargaining clout to regulatory agencies, and companies give top management backing to internal compliance groups, can reduce and have substantially reduced white collar crime (Braithwaite 1984, 1985; cf Vaughan 1983). Interestingly, Ralph Nader, the world's most celebrated cynic on regulatory agencies, has also experienced some transition in view. His organization recently reviewed the evidence of the hundreds of thousands of lives saved by the Occupational Safety and Health Administration, Environmental Protection Agency, National Highway Traffic Safety Administration, Food and Drug Administration, and the Consumer Product Safety Commission (Green & Waitzman 1981).

As Chambliss (1967) has argued, white collar criminals are among the most deterrable types of offenders because they satisfy two conditions: they do not have a commitment to crime as a way of life and their offenses are instrumental rather than expressive. White collar criminals are also more deterrable than working class criminals because they have more of those things that can be lost by criminal conviction or informal means of stigmatization—status, respectability, money, a job, a comfortable home and family life. This view is supported by some quasi-experimental time series and interview studies, which suggest that white collar offenders are deterred by prosecution (Hopkins 1978, Holland 1982, Fisse & Braithwaite 1983; Lewis-Beck and Alford 1980; Perry 1981; Stotland et al 1980, Block et al 1980, Boden 1983, Epple & Visscher 1984, cf Jesilow et al 1980).

Indeed, Geis and I have argued that not only deterrence, but also two other discredited doctrines of traditional criminology—rehabilitation and incapacitation—are effective when applied to white collar crime (Braithwaite & Geis 1982). Incapacitation of criminal doctors or mine managers can be achieved by withdrawing their licence to practice their profession or stopping production at a work site rather than by imprisonment; rehabilitation does not occur on the psychiatrist's couch, but at the hands of the management consultant. State-imposed rearrangements of criminogenic organizational structures are easier to effect than state-imposed rearrangements of individual psyches.

On the other hand, the literature also supports the view that proving the guilt of white collar suspects is more difficult, particularly because of the complexity of the evidence and the capacity of wealthy defendents to mobilize legal talent (Levi 1981, Sutton & Wild 1978, 1979; Rider & Ffrench 1979; Ogren 1973; Green 1978). This reality is a major plank of those who argue for compliance over deterrence law enforcement systems.

Empirical observation of organizational crimes also indicates considerable scholarly agreement on a few additional matters of policy relevance. With large corporations, rarely do the boards of directors become involved in preventing, participating in, or even knowing about corporate offenses (US Senate 1976, De Mott 1977, Coffee 1977, Eisenberg 1976, Mace 1971). This raises doubts about the Ralph Nader proposal of public interest directors for major corporations as a white collar crime countermeasure.

Case studies of crimes committed on behalf of large organizations repeatedly document either orchestrated or negligent communication blockages that prevent knowledge of white collar crime from reaching the desks of top management (Geis 1967, Stone 1975, Conklin 1977, Coffee 1977, Katz 1979). This can be functional for the organization; it allows top management to say to underlings, "I want you to achieve this result, but I don't want to know how you do it", and it protects the corporation as a legal person from the taint of knowledge necessary to prove corporate crime. It can also be dysfunctional in depriving top management of knowledge of white collar crimes pursued to achieve subunit goals or personal ambitions that are at odds with the overall goals of the organization. Governmentally mandated compliance auditing and reporting, corporate ombudsmen and other free routes of communication to the top, staff rotation and laws to protect whistle blowers are among the policy options that have been suggested by this strand of the literature.

Finally, interview research with company executives consistently elicits the view that it is top management attitudes, most particularly those of the chief executive, which determine the level of compliance with the law in a corporation (Clinard 1983, Brenner & Molander 1977, Baumhart 1961, Cressey & Moore 1980:48; cf Kantor 1978, Schelling 1974). Moreover, middle managers are frequently reported as squeezed by a choice between failing to achieve targets set by top management and attaining the targets illegally (Getschow 1979). In other words, while it is middle management who perpetrate the criminal acts, it is top management which set the expectations, the tone, the corporate culture that determines the incidence of corporate crime. These findings again imply reforms to ensure that top management will be tainted with knowledge of illegalities, as well as reforms to facilitate prosecution of chief executives who are willfully blind (Fisse 1973, Wilson 1979) to the creation of criminogenic corporate cultures.

PUTTING WHITE COLLAR CRIME ON A SOUNDER CONCEPTUAL FOOTING

Some of the deficiencies of white collar crime as a concept have become clear in this review. But what are the alternatives? Many Marxists, following the tradition of Taylor, Walton, and Young (1973) would have us abandon the laws of capitalist societies for defining our domain. Yet by accepting the laws of the capitalist state, sociologists hardly legitimate ruling class interests when they deal with that subset of laws that criminalize predominantly the behavior of the ruling class. Survey data show that the critical criminologists of the 1970s were essentially wrong in arguing that there is no consensus around the laws of capitalist societies [see the fifteen studies cited in the reference Braithwaite (1982b), but note the methodological caveats of Miethe (1982) and Cullen et al (1983b)].

If it is false consciousness which drives working class people toward this consensus, then it is an odd sort of false consciousness which, inter alia, consensually supports draconian penalties against ruling class crimes. Liberal and Marxist sociologists alike should feel no embarassment at taking the considerable progressive democratic support for laws prohibiting white collar crime as the basis for their research. Those who choose to study violations of "politically defined human rights" (Schwendinger & Schwendinger 1975), or some other imaginative definition of deviance, will deserve to be ignored for indulging their personal moralities in a social science that has no relevance for those who do not share that morality.

The alternative influential definition of white collar crime was formulated by Edelhertz (1970) as "an illegal act or series of illegal acts committed by non-physical means and by concealment or guile, to obtain money or property, to avoid the payment or loss of money or property, or to obtain business or personal advantage". The first drawback of this alternative is that it turns attention away from white collar crimes that do physical harm to persons, which, as we have seen, are the kinds of crime that arouse greatest concern in the community. Second, the Edelhertz definition deletes the Sutherland requirement that the offenses be perpetrated in the performance of occupational roles. The practical consequences for empirical research have been that most white collar criminals end up having blue collars (e.g. Hagan et al 1980). This is because the offenders who use concealment or guile to obtain money illegally and who are most likely to be convicted by courts are welfare cheats. A white collar crime literature dominated by studies of welfare offenders would require a very different theoretical orientation than that which has developed. On the other hand, as Edelhertz and Rogovin (1980:3) point out, a definition which is neutral concerning the social standing of the offender is imperative for public policy because it is unacceptable for the state to target enforcement that is contingent on the status of the offender.

Bloch & Geis (1970:307), seeking clearly homogeneous types of offenses, suggested the following distinctions: offenses committed by (1) individuals as individuals, (2) employees against their employers, (3) policymaking officials for the corporation, (4) agents of the corporation against the general public, and (5) merchants against customers. A variety of such classifications have been proposed (Shichor 1983), none of them with the force to command an authoritative partition of the field.

The most influential partition has been that of Clinard & Quinney (1973) which divides white collar crime into occupational and corporate crime. "Occupational crime consists of offenses committed by individuals for themselves in the course of their occupations and the offenses of employees against their employers." Note that this brings in many "blue collar" occupational crimes. Corporate crime, in contrast, is defined as "the offenses committed by corporate officials for the corporation and the offenses of the corporation itself". A variation is Schrager & Short's (1978) definition of "organizational crime"; this has the advantage over corporate crime of making it clearer that crimes committed on behalf of public as well as private organizations are within the ambit of the concept. The Clinard & Quinney partition is now supported by Geis (1982:x), Kramer (1984), and Grabosky (1984).

Probably the most sensible way to proceed with organizing work in this area is first to stick with Sutherland's definition. This at least excludes welfare cheats and credit card frauds from the domain. Second, following Clinard & Quinney, occupational crimes should be separated from corporate or organizational crime.

Corporate crime, as the core area of concern, is then left as a broad but reasonably homogenous domain for coherent theorizing. While useful theories of white collar crime have proved elusive, influential corporate or organizational crime theory is a possibility. Occupational crime is a much less homogenous category—employees who offend against employers engage in a very different activity from doctors who rip off their patients. General theories of occupational crime might be as difficult as theories of white collar crime. Progress here might be confined to studies of specific types of occupational crime (e.g. Quinney 1963; Pontell et al 1982).

ACKNOWLEDGMENTS

I wish to thank Gilbert Geis, James F. Short, Jr., Marshall Clinard, Frank Jones, Peter Grabosky, and Philip Petit for comments on an earlier draft of this paper.

Literature Cited

Albanese, J. S. 1984. Corporate criminology: explaining deviance of business and political organizations. *J. Crim. Justice* 12:11–19

Aristotle. *Politics.* Transl. J. E. C. Welldon, 1932. London: Macmillan. 412 pp

Bardach, E., Kagan, R. A. 1982. *Going by the Book: the Problem of Regulatory Unreasonableness.* Philadelphia: Temple University Press. 375 pp

Barnett, H. C. 1979. Wealth, crime and capital accumulation. *Contemp. Crises.* 3:171–86

Barnett, H. C. 1981. Corporate capitalism, corporate crime. *Crime Delin.* 27:4–23

Barnett, H. C. 1983. *Hazardous waste cleanup: the benefit and cost of the Reagan Economic Recovery Program.* Presented to Ann. Meet. Am. Soc. of Criminol., Denver

Barnett, H. C. 1984. Tax evasion by proxy: the gray market in welfare capitalism. *Contemp. Crises* 8:107–23

Baumhart, R. C. 1961. How ethical are businessmen? *Harv. Bus. Rev.* 39:5–176

Bloch, H., Geis, G. 1970. *Man, Crime and Society.* New York: Random House. 552 pp., 2nd ed.

Block, M. K., Nold, F. C., Sidak, J. G. 1980. *The deterrent effect of antitrust enforcement: a theoretical and empirical analysis.* Technical Report ISDDE-1-78, Hoover Institution, Stanford University. 98 pp

Boden, L. I. 1983. *Government regulation of occupational safety: underground coal mine accidents 1973–1975.* Unpublished manuscript. Boston, Harvard School of Public Health

Bonger, W. A. 1916. *Criminality and Economic Conditions.* Boston: Little, Brown. 706 pp

Boulton, D. 1978. *The Grease Machine: The Inside Story of Lockheed's Dollar Diplomacy.* New York: Harper & Row. 289 pp

Braithwaite, J. 1982a. Paradoxes of class bias in criminal justice. In *Rethinking Criminology,* ed. H. E. Pepinsky, 61–84. Beverly Hills: Sage. 160 pp

Braithwaite, J. 1982b. Challenging just deserts: punishing white-collar criminals. *J. Crim. Law Criminol.* 73:723–63

Braithwaite, J. 1984. *Corporate Crime in the Pharmaceutical Industry.* London: Routledge & Kegan Paul. 440 pp.

Braithwaite, J. 1985. *To Punish or Persuade: Enforcement of Coal Mine Safety.* Albany: State Univ. of New York Press.

Braithwaite, J., Geis, G. 1982. On theory and action for corporate crime control. *Crime and Delinquency* 28:292–314

Brants, C. H., de Roos, Th. 1984. Pollution, press and penal process. *Crime and Social Justice.* In press

Brenner, S. N., Molander, E. A. 1977. Is the ethics of business changing? *Harv. Bus. Rev.* 55:59–70

Burgess, E. W. 1950. Comment. *American Journal of Sociology* 56:34

Carson, W. G. 1970. White-collar crime and the enforcement of factory legislation. *Br. J. Criminol.* 10:383–98

Carson, W. G. 1975. Symbolic and instrumental dimensions of early factory legislation: a case study in the social origins of criminal law. In *Crime, Criminology, and Public Policy,* ed., R. Hood. Glencoe: Free. 650 pp.

Carson, W. G. 1982. *The Other Price of Britain's Oil: Safety and Control in the North Sea.* New Brunswick, N.J.: Rutgers Univ. Press. 320 pp.

Chambliss, W. J. 1967. Types of deviance and the effectiveness of legal sanctions. *Wisc. Law Rev.* Summer:703–19

Chambliss, W. J., Seidman, R. B. 1971. *Law, Order, and Power.* Reading, Mass.: Addison-Wesley. 533 pp

Clinard, M. 1946. Criminological theories of violations of wartime regulations. *Am. Sociol. Rev.* 11:258–70

Clinard, M. 1952. *The Black Market: A Study of White-Collar Crime.* New York: Holt, Rinehart. 392 pp.

Clinard, M. 1983. *Corporate Ethics and Crime: The Role of Middle Management.* Beverly Hills: Sage. 189 pp.

Clinard, M., Quinney, R. 1973. *Criminal Behavior Systems: A Typology.* New York: Holt, Rinehart & Winston. 274 pp.

Clinard, M., Yeager, P. C. 1980. *Corporate Crime.* New York: Free. 386 pp.

Clinard, M., Yeager, P. C., Brisette, J., Petrashek, D., Harries, E. 1979. *Illegal Corporate Behavior.* Washington D.C.: National Institute of Justice. 314 pp.

Cohen, A. K. 1977. The concept of criminal organization. *Br. J. Criminol.* 17:97–111

Coffee, J. C., Jr. 1977. Beyond the shut-eyed sentry: toward a theoretical view of corporate misconduct and an effective legal response. *Virgin. Law Rev.* 63:1099–1278

Coffee, J. C., Jr. 1983. The metastasis of mail fraud: the continuing story of the "evolution" of a white-collar crime. *Am. Crim. Law Rev.* 21:1–28

Coffee, J. C., Jr. 1984. Corporate criminal responsibility. In *Encyclopedia of Crime and Justice,* ed. S. H. Kadish, Vol. 1:253–64. New York: Free

Conklin, J. E. 1977. *"Illegal But Not Criminal."* Englewood Cliffs: Prentice-Hall. 153 pp.

Consumers' Federation of America. 1983. *On the Safe Track: Deaths and Injuries Before and After the Consumer Product Safety Commission.* Consumers' Federation of America: Washington, D.C. 11 pp.

Costle, D. M. 1979. Innovative regulation. *Econ. Impact* 28:8–14

Cranston, R. 1979. *Regulating Business: Law and Consumer Agencies.* London: Macmillan. 186 pp.

Cressey, D. 1953. *Other People's Money: The Social Psychology of Embezzlement.* New York: Free

Cressey, D., Moore, C. A. 1980. *Corporation Codes of Ethical Conduct.* New York: Peat Marwick and Mitchell Foundation. 101 pp.

Cullen, F. T., Clark, G. A., Mathers, R. A., Cullen, J. B. 1983a. Public support for punishing white-collar crime: blaming the victim revisited? *J. Crim. Justice* 11:481–93

Cullen, F. T., Link, B. G., Polanzi, C. W. 1982. The seriousness of crime revisited: have attitudes toward white-collar crime changed? *Criminology* 20:83–102

Cullen, F. T., Link, B. G., Travis, L. F., Wozniak, J. F. 1983b. *Consensus in crime seriousness: empirical reality or methodological artifact?* Presented to Ann. Meet. American Society of Criminology, Denver

Cullen, F. T., Maakestad, W. J., Cavender, G. 1984. The Ford Pinto case and beyond: corporate crime, moral boundaries, and the criminal sanction. In *Corporations As*

Criminals, ed. E. Hochstedler, 107–30. Beverly Hills: Sage. 168 pp.

Delmas-Marty, M. 1980. White-collar crime and the EEC. In *Economic Crime in Europe*, ed. L. H. Leigh, 78–105. London: Macmillan. 211 pp.

Delmas-Marty, M., Tiedemann, K. 1979. La criminalité, le droit penal et les multinationales. *La Semaine Juridique* 2935, March: 21–8

DeMichiei, J. M., Langton, J. F., Bullock, K. A., Wiles, T. C. 1982. *Factors Associated With Disabling Injuries in Underground Coal Mines*. Washington D.C.: Mine Safety and Health Administration. 72 pp.

De Mott, D. A. 1977. Reweaving the corporate veil: management structure and the control of corporate information. *Law Contemp. Prob.* 41:182–221

Dershowitz, A. 1961. Increasing community control over corporate crime. *Yale Law Journal* 71:281–306

DiMento, J. 1984. *Getting compliance: environmental law and American business.* Unpublished manuscript, University of California, Irvine. 230 pp.

Doig, A. 1984. *Corruption and Misconduct in Contemporary British Politics*. Harmondsworth: Penguin. 437 pp.

Douglas, J. D., Johnson, J. M., eds. 1977. *Official Deviance: Readings in Malfeasance, Misfeasance, and Other Forms of Corruption*. Philadelphia: J. B. Lippincott. 429 pp.

Duchaine, N. 1979. *Literature of Police Corruption*. New York: John Jay. 200 pp.

Edelhertz, H. 1970. *The Nature, Impact and Prosecution of White Collar Crime*. Washington, D.C.: National Institute of Law Enforcement and Criminal Justice. 77 pp.

Edelhertz, H. 1980. Transnational white-collar crime: a developing challenge and a need for response. *Temple Law Quarterly* 53:1114–26

Edelhertz, H., Rogovin, C. eds. 1980. *A National Strategy for Containing White-Collar Crime*. Lexington: Lexington Books. 138 pp.

Edelman, J. M. 1964. *The Symbolic Uses of Politics*. Urbana: Univ. of Ill. Press. 201 pp.

Eisenberg, M. A. 1976. Legal models of management structure in the modern corporation: officers, directors and accountants. *Calif. Manag. Rev.* 63:363–439

Epple, D., Visscher, M. 1984. Environmental pollution: modeling occurrence, detection and deterrence. *J. Law Econ.* 27:29–60

Ermann, M. D., Lundman, R. J. 1978. Deviant acts by complex organizations: deviance and social control at the organizational level of analysis. *Sociol. Q.* 19:55–67

Ermann, M. D., Lundman, R. J., eds., 1982.

Corporate and Governmental Deviance. New York: Oxford Univ. Press. 2nd ed., 294 pp.

Evans, S. S., Lundman, R. J. 1983. Newspaper coverage of corporate price-fixing. *Criminology* 21:529–41

Faberman, H. A. 1975. A criminogenic market structure in the automobile industry. *Sociol. Q.* 16:438–57

Farrell, R. A., Swigert, V. L. 1983. *The corporation in criminology: new directions for research*. Presented to Ann. Meet. American Sociological Association

Fisse, B. 1973. Responsibility, prevention, and corporate crime. *New Zealand Universities Law Review.* 5:250–79

Fisse, B. 1978. The social policy of corporate criminal responsibility. *Adelaide Law Rev.* 6:361–412

Fisse, B. 1983. Reconstructing corporate criminal law: deterrence, retribution, fault, and sanctions. *Southern California Law Review* 56:1141–1246

Fisse, B. 1984. The duality of corporate and individual criminal liability. In *Corporations as Criminals*, ed. E. Hochstedler, 69–84. Beverly Hills: Sage. 168 pp.

Fisse, B., Braithwaite, J. 1983. *The Impact of Publicity on Corporate Offenders*. Albany: State University of New York Press. 393 pp.

Frank, J., Cullen, F. T., Travis, L. F. 1984. *Sanctioning corporate crime: public support for civil and criminal intervention*. Presented to Ann. Meet Midwest. Crim. Justice Assoc.

Freitag, P. J. 1983. The myth of corporate capture: regulatory commissions in the United States. *Soc. Prob.* 30:480–491

Gallese, L. R. 1982. Connecticut's Naugatuck River became a sewer; now even its polluters are cheering the cleanup. *Wall Street J.* 16 July:36–7

Geis, G. 1962. Toward a delineation of white-collar offenses. *Sociol. Inq.* 32:160–71

Geis, G. 1967. The heavy electrical equipment antitrust cases of 1961. In *Criminal Behavior Systems*, eds., M. Clinard, R. Quinney. New York: Holt, Rinehart & Winston. 498 pp.

Geis, G., ed. 1968. *White-Collar Criminal: The Offender in Business and the Professions*. New York: Atherton. 448 pp.

Geis, G. 1982. *On White-Collar Crime*. Lexington, Mass.: Lexington. 217 pp.

Geis, G. 1984. White-collar and corporate crime. In *Major Forms of Crime*, ed. R. F. Meier, Beverly Hills: Sage

Geis, G., Goff, C. H. 1983. Introduction. In *White Collar Crime: The Uncut Version*, E. H. Sutherland. New Haven: Yale Univ. Press. 291 pp.

Getschow, G. 1979. Some middle managers cut corners to achieve high corporate goals. *Wall Street J.* November 8

Goff, C. H., Reasons, C. E. 1984. Organizational crimes against employees, consumers and the public. In *The Political Economy of Crime: Readings for a Critical Criminology*, ed. B. D. MacLean. Toronto: McClelland and Stewart

Grabosky, P. N. 1984. Corporate crime in Australia: an agenda for research. *Australian and New Zealand J. Criminol.* 17:95–107

Green, M. 1978. *The Other Government: The Unseen Power of Washington Lawyers*. New York: Norton. 340 pp.

Green, M., Waitzman, N. 1981. *Business War on the Law: An Analysis of the Benefits of Federal Health/Safety Enforcement*. Washington, D.C.: Ralph Nader. 162 pp., 2nd ed.

Gross, E. 1978. Organizational crime: a theoretical perspective. In *Studies in Symbolic Interaction*, ed. N. Denzin, 55–85. Greenwich, Conn: JAI

Gunningham, N. 1984. *Safeguarding the Worker: Job Hazards and the Role of Law*. Sydney: Law Book. 426 pp.

Gusfield, J. 1967. *Symbolic Crusade*. Urbana: Univ. Ill. Press. 198 pp.

Hagan, J. 1982. The corporate advantage: a study of the involvement of corporate and individual victims in a criminal justice system. *Soc. Forc.* 60:993–1022

Hagan, J., Nagel, I., Albonetti, C. 1980. The differential sentencing of white-collar offenders in ten federal court districts. *Am. Sociol. Rev.* 45:802–20

Harvard Law Review, 1979. Corporate crime: regulating corporate behavior through criminal sanctions. *Harv. Law Rev.* 92:1127–375

Hawkins, K. 1984. *Environment and Enforcement: Regulation and the Social Definition of Pollution*. Oxford: Clarendon. 253 pp.

Holland, P. A. 1982. The effectiveness of prosecutions under the Environment Protection Act. *Environmental Paper No. 2*, Melbourne: Graduate School of Environmental Science, Monash University. 55 pp.

Hopkins, A. 1978. The anatomy of corporate crime. In *Two Faces of Deviance: Crimes of the Powerless and Powerful*, ed. P. R. Wilson, J. Braithwaite, 214–31. Brisbane: Univ. Queensland Press. 309 pp.

Hopkins, A. 1981. Class bias in the criminal law. *Contemp. Crises* 5:385–94

Hopkins, A., Parnell, N. 1984. Why coal mine safety regulations in Australia are not enforced. *Int. J. Sociol. Law* 12:179–84

Japanese Environment Agency. 1981. Unpublished data available from the author on request

Jesilow, P., Geis, G., O'Brien, M. J. 1980. *The importance of experimental research in deterrence studies*. Presented to Ann. Meet. Am. Soc. Criminol. San Francisco

Jones, S., Levi, M. 1983. *Police-Public Relationships*. Unpublished research report, University College, Cardiff

Kagan, R. 1978. *Regulatory Justice: Implementing a Wage-Price Freeze*. New York: Russell Sage. 200 pp.

Kantor, R. M. 1978. *Powerlessness corrupts: effects of structural variables on organizational behavior—as seen from the top*. Presented to Ann. Meet Am. Sociol. Assoc., San Francisco

Katz, J. 1979. Concerted ignorance: the social construction of cover-up. *Urban Life* 8:295–316

Katz, J. 1980. The social movement against white-collar crime. In *Criminology Review Yearbook, Vol 2*, ed. E. Bittner, S. L. Messinger, 161–81. Beverly Hills: Sage. 733 pp.

Katzmann, R. A. 1980. *Regulatory Bueaucracy: The Federal Trade Commission and Antitrust Policy*. Cambridge: MIT Press. 223 pp.

Kelman, S. 1981. *Regulating America, Regulating Sweden: A Comparative Study of Occupational Safety and Health Policy*. Cambridge: MIT Press. 270 pp.

Knightley, P., Evans, H., Potter, E., Wallace, M. 1979. *Suffer the Children: The Story of Thalidomide*. New York: Viking. 309 pp.

Kramer, R. C. 1982. Corporate crime: an organizational perspective. In *White-Collar and Economic Crime*, ed. P. Wickman, T. Dailey, 75–94. Lexington: Lexington. 285 pp.

Kramer, R. C. 1984. Corporate criminality: the development of an idea. In *Corporations as Criminals*, ed. E. Hochstedler, 13–38. Beverly Hills: Sage. 168 pp.

Lane, R. E. 1953. Why businessmen violate the law. *J. Crim. Law, Criminol. Police Sci.* 44:151–65

Leigh, L. H. 1977. The criminal liability of corporations and other groups. *Ottawa Law Rev.* 9:246–302

Levi, M. 1981. *The Phantom Capitalists: the Organisation and Control of Long-Firm Fraud*. London: Heinemann. 346 pp.

Levi, M. 1982. The powers of revenue agencies: an overview. *Br. Tax Rev.* 1:36–51

Levi, M. 1984. Giving creditors the business: dilemmas and contradictions in the organisation of fraud. *Int. J. Sociol. Law* 12:321–33

Lewis-Beck, M., Alford, J. R. 1980. Can government regulate safety? The coal mine example. *Am. Polit. Sci. Review* 74:745–56

Long, S. 1982. Growth in the underground economy? An empirical issue. In *White-Collar and Economic Crime*, ed., P. Wickman, T. Dailey, 95–120. Lexington: Lexington. 285 pp.

Los, M. 1982. Crime and economy in the Communist countries. In *White-Collar and Economic Crime*, ed. P. Wickman, T. Dailey, 121–38. Lexington: Lexington. 285 pp.

Lynxwiler, J., Shover, N., Clelland, D. 1984. Determinants of sanction severity in a regulatory bureaucracy. In *Corporations as Criminals*, ed. E. Hochstedler, 147–65. Beverly Hills: Sage. 168 pp.

McCaghy, C. H., Nogier, J. M. 1982. *A pilot survey on exposure, victimization, and susceptibility to consumer frauds*. Presented to Ann. Meet. Am. Soc. Criminol. Toronto

McCormick, A. E., Jr. 1977. Rule enforcement and moral indignation: some observations on the effects of criminal antitrust convictions upon societal reaction processes. *Soc. Prob.* 25:30–39

MacAvoy, P. W. 1979. *The Regulated Industries and the Economy*. New York: W. W. Norton

Mace, M. L. 1971. *Directors: Myth and Reality*. Boston: Harvard Business School Division of Research. 207 pp.

Marx, G. T. 1982. Who really gets stung? Some issues raised by the new police undercover work. *Crime and Delin.* 28:165–93

Mathews, A. F. 1976. Recent trends in SEC requested ancillary relief in SEC level injunctive actions. *Bus. Lawyer* 31:1323–52

Mathews, M. C. 1983. *Corporate crime: self-regulation vs. external regulation*. Presented at Ann. Meet. Am. Sociol. Assoc., Detroit

Meier, R. F., Short, J. F., Jr. 1982. The consequences of white-collar crime. In *White-Collar Crime: An Agenda for Research*, ed. H. Edelhertz, T. D. Overcast, 23–49. Lexington, Mass.: Lexington. 235 pp.

Meier, R. F., Short, J. F., Jr. 1984. *White-collar crime as hazard: perceptions of risk and seriousness*. Unpublished paper, Washington State University

Miethe, T. D. 1982. Public consensus on crime seriousness: normative structure or methodological artifact? *Criminology* 20:515–26

Monahan, J., Navaco, R. W. 1980. Corporate violence: a psychological analysis. In *New Directions in Psychological Research*, eds. P. Lipsitt, B. Sales, 3–25. New York: Van Nostrand Reinhold. 336 pp.

Nettler, G. 1974. Embezzlement without problems. *Br. J. Criminol.* 14:70–77

Norris, F. 1903. *The Pit*. New York: Doubleday Page. 421 pp.

Ogren, R. W. 1973. The ineffectiveness of the criminal sanction in fraud and corruption cases: losing the battle against white-collar crime. *Am. Crim. Law Rev.* 11:959–88

O'Malley, P. 1980. Theories of structural versus causal determination: accounting for legislative change in capitalist societies. In *Legislation and Society in Australia*, ed. R.

Tomasic, 50–65. Sydney: Allen & Unwin. 420 pp.

Orland, L. 1980. Reflections on corporate crime: 'law in search of theory and scholarship'. *Am. Crim. Law Rev.* 17:501–20

Parker, D. B. 1976. *Crime by Computer*. New York: Charles Scribner. 308 pp.

Perez, J. 1978. *Corporate criminality: a case study of the one thousand largest industrial corporations in the U.S.A.* PhD thesis. Univ. Penn.

Perry, C. S. 1981. *Safety laws and spending save lives: an analysis of coal mine fatality rates 1930–1979*. Unpublished, Department of Sociology, University of Kentucky

Pontell, H. N., Jesilow, P. D., Geis, G. 1982. Policing physicians: practitioner fraud and abuse in a government medical program. *Soc. Prob.* 30:117–25

Quinney, R. 1963. Occupational structure and criminal behavior: prescription violations by retail pharmacists. *Soc. Prob.* 11:179–85

Quinney, R. 1974. *Critique of Legal Order: Crime Control in Capitalist Society*. Boston: Little, Brown. 206 pp.

Quirk, P. J. 1981. *Industry Influence in Federal Regulatory Agencies*. Princeton, N.J.: Princeton Univ. Press. 260 pp.

Randall, D., DeFillippi, R. 1984. *Media coverage of corporate malfeasance: a comparison of media source coverage of corporate violations in the oil industry*, Unpublished paper, Washington State University

Reiss, A. J., Jr. 1983. The policing of organizational life. In *Control in the Police Organization*, ed. M. Punch, 78–97. Cambridge: MIT Press. 346 pp.

Reiss, A. J., Jr. 1984. Selecting strategies of social control over organizational life. In *Enforcing Regulation*, ed. K. Hawkins, J. M. Thomas, 23–35. Boston: Kluwer-Nijhoff. 198 pp.

Reiss, A. J., Biderman, A. 1980. *Data Sources on White-Collar Law Breaking*. Washington, D.C.: USGPO (LXXXVI) 486 pp.

Reisman, W. M. 1979. *Folded Lies: Bribery, Crusades, and Reforms*. New York: Free. 277 pp.

Richardson, G., Ogus, A., Burrows, P. 1982. *Policing Pollution: A Study of Regulation and Enforcement*. Oxford: Clarendon

Rider, B., Ffrench, L. 1979. *The Regulation of Insider Trading*. New York: Dobbs Ferry

Ross, E. A. 1907. *Sin and Society: An Analysis of Latter-Day Iniquity*. Boston: Houghton Mifflin

Salas, L., Solano, S. N., Vilchez, A. I. G. 1982. Comparative study of white collar crime in Latin America with special emphasis on Costa Rica. *Revue Internationale de Droit Penale* 53:505–21

Saxon, M. 1980. *White Collar Crime: The*

Problem and the Federal Response. Washington, D.C.: Congressional Research Service. 98 pp.

Schelling, T. C. 1974. Command and control. In *Social Responsibility and the Business Predicament,* ed. J. W. McKie, 79–108. Washington, D.C.: Brookings. 361 pp.

Schrag, P. G. 1971. On Her Majesty's secret service: protecting the consumer in New York City. *Yale Law J.* 80:1529–1603

Schrager, L. S., Short, J. F., Jr. 1978. Toward a sociology of organizational crime. *Soc. Prob.* 25:407–19

Schudson, C. B., Onellion, A. P., Hochstedler, E. 1984. Nailing an omelet to the wall: prosecuting nursing home homicide. In *Corporations as Criminals,* ed. E. Hochstedler, 131–46. Beverly Hills: Sage. 168 pp.

Schwendinger, H., Schwendinger, J. 1975. Defenders of order or guardians of human rights? In *Critical Criminology,* ed. I. Taylor, P. Walton, J. Young, 113–46. London: Routledge & Kegan Paul. 268 pp.

Scott, J. C. 1972. *Comparative Political Corruption.* Englewood Cliffs: Prentice-Hall

Shapiro, S. P. 1984. *Wayward Capitalists: Target of the Securities and Exchange Commission.* New Haven: Yale Univ. Press. 248 pp.

Shearing, C. D., Stenning, P. C. 1981. Modern private security: its growth and its implications. In *Crime and Justice: An Annual Review.* ed. M. Tonry, N. Morris. Chicago: University of Chicago Press. 353 pp.

Sheleff, L. 1982. International white-collar crime. In *White-Collar and Economic Crime,* eds. P. Wickman, T. Dailey, 39–58. Lexington: Lexington Books. 285 pp.

Shepherd, W. G. 1970. *Market Power and Economic Welfare.* New York: Random House. 302 pp.

Shepherd, W. G. 1975. *The Treatment of Market Power.* New York: Columbia Univ. Press. 326 pp.

Sherman, L. 1978. *Scandal and Reform: Controlling Police Corruption.* Berkeley: Univ. Calif. Press. 273 pp.

Sherwin, R. 1963. White-collar crime, conventional crime and Merton's deviant behavior theory. *Wis. Sociol.* 2:7–10

Shichor, D. 1983. *On corporate deviance and corporate victimization: some elaborations.* Presented to Ann. Meet. American Society of Criminology, Denver

Shover, N., Clelland, D. A., Lynxwiler 1983. *Developing a Regulatory Bureaucracy: The Office of Surface Mining Reclamation and Enforcement.* Washington, D.C.: National Institute of Justice. 118 pp.

Shover, N., Lynxwiler, J., Groce, S., Clelland, D. 1984. Regional variation in regulatory law enforcement: the Surface Mining

Control and Reclamation Act of 1977. In *Enforcing Regulation,* eds. K. Hawkins, J. M. Thomas, 121–46. Boston: Kluwer-Nijhoff. 198 pp.

Sinclair, U. 1906. *The Jungle.* New York: Doubleday and Page. 413 pp.

Smith, R. S. 1979. The impact of OSHA inspections on manufacturing injury rates. *J. Hum. Res.* 14:145–70

Snider, L. 1982. Traditional and corporate theft: a comparison of sanctions. In *White-Collar and Economic Crime,* ed. P. Wickman, T. Bailey, 235–58. Lexington: Lexington. 285 pp.

Solomon, L. D., Nowak, N. S. 1980. Managerial restructuring: prospects for a new regulatory tool. *Notre Dame Lawyer* 56:120–40

Staw, B. M., Szwajkowski, E. 1975. The scarcity-munificence component of organizational environments and the commission of illegal acts. *Admin. Sci. Q.* 20:345–54

Steffens, L. 1904. *The Shame of the Cities.* New York: McClure, Phillips. 406 pp.

Stone, C. 1975. *Where the Law Ends: The Social Control of Corporate Behavior.* New York: Harper & Row. 273 pp.

Stone, C. 1977. A slap on the wrist for the Kepone mob. *Bus. Soc. Rev.* Summer:4–11

Stone, C. 1980. The place of enterprise liability in the control of corporate conduct. *Yale Law J.* 90:1–77

Stone, C. 1982. Corporate vices and corporate virtues: do public/private distinctions matter? *Univ. Penn. Law Rev.* 130:1441–509

Storey, D. J. 1979. Has economics of environmental law enforcement or has the prosecution of polluters led to cleaner rivers in England and Wales? *Environ. Plan. A* 11:897–918

Stotland, E. 1977. White-collar criminals. *J. Soc. Iss.* 33:179–96

Stotland, E., Brintnall, M., L'Heureux, A., Ashmore, E. 1980. Do convictions deter home repair fraud? In *White-Collar Crime: Theory and Research,* ed. G. Geis, E. Stotland, 252–65. Beverly Hills: Sage. 320 pp.

Strobel, L. P. 1980. *Reckless Homicide? Ford's Pinto Trial.* South Bend, Ind.: And Books. 286 pp.

Sutherland, E. H. 1940. The white collar criminal. *Am. Sociol. Rev.* 5:1–12

Sutherland, E. H. 1949. *White Collar Crime.* New York: Dryden 272 pp.

Sutherland, E. H. 1983. *White Collar Crime: The Uncut Version.* New Haven: Yale Univ. Press. 291 pp.

Sutton, A., Wild, R. 1978. Corporate crime and social structure. In *Two Faces of Deviance: Crimes of the Powerless and Powerful,* ed. P. R. Wilson, J. Braithwaite, 177–98. Brisbane: Univ. Queensland Press. 309 pp.

Sutton, A., Wild, R. 1979. Companies, the law and the professions. In *Legislation and Society in Australia*, ed. R. Tomasic, 200–12. Sydney: Allen & Unwin. 420 pp.

Swigert, V. L., Farrell, R. 1980. Corporate homicide: definitional processes in the creation of deviance. *Law Soc. Rev.* 15:101–22

Tappan, P. W. 1947. Who is the criminal? *Am. Sociol. Rev.* 12:96–102

Tarbell, I. M. 1904. *The History of the Standard Oil Company*. New York: Macmillan

Taylor, I., Walton, P., Young, J. 1973. *The New Criminology: For a Social Theory of Deviance*. London: Routledge & Kegan Paul. 325 pp.

U.S. Senate 1976. *Report of the Securities and Exchange Commission on Questionable and Illegal Corporate Payments and Practices; Hearings of Banking, Housing and Urban Affairs Committee*, 94th Cong., 2nd Sess.

van den Haag, E. 1982a. Comment on "Challenging just deserts: punishing white collar criminals". *J. Crim. Law Criminol.* 73:764–9

van den Haag, E. 1982b. Reply to Dr. John Braithwaite. *J. Crim. Law Criminol.* 73: 794–6

Vandivier, K. 1982. Why should my conscience bother me? In *Corporate and Governmental Deviance: Problems of Organizational Behavior in Contemporary Society*, ed. M. D. Ermann, R. J. Lundman, 102–22. New York: Oxford Univ. Press. 294 pp.

Vaughan, D. 1983. *Controlling Unlawful Organizational Behavior: Social Structure and Corporate Misconduct*. Chicago: University of Chicago Press. 174 pp.

Viscusi, W. K. 1983. *Risk by Choice: Regulating Health and Safety in the Workplace*. Cambridge: Harvard Univ. Press. 200 pp.

von Hirsch, A. 1982. Desert and white-collar criminality: a response to Dr. Braithwaite. *J. Crim. Law Criminol.* 73:1164–75

Waegel, W., Ermann, M. D., Horowitz, A. M. 1981. Organizational responses to imputations of deviance. *Sociol. Q.* 22:43–55

Waldman, D. E. 1978. *Antitrust Action and Market Structure*. Lexington, Mass.: Lexington Books. 182 pp.

Waldman, D. E. 1980. Economic benefits in the IBM, AT&T, and Xerox Cases: government antitrust policy in the 70s. *Antitrust Law Econ. Rev.* 12:75–92

Waters, J. A. 1978. Catch 20.5: corporate morality as an organizational phenomenon. *Organ. Dynam.* Spring: 3–19

Weaver, P. H. 1978. Regulation, social policy and class conflict. In *Regulating Business: The Search for an Optimum*, ed. D. P. Jacobs, 193–218. San Francisco: Institute for Contemporary Studies. 261 pp.

Weaver, S. 1977. *Decision to Prosecute: Organization and Public Policy in the Antitrust Division*. Cambridge: MIT Press. 196 pp.

Wheeler, S., Weisburd, D., Bode, N. 1982. Sentencing the white-collar offender: rhetoric and reality. *Am. Sociol. Rev.* 47:641–59

Wilson, L. C. 1979. The doctrine of wilful blindness. *Univ. New Brunswick Law J.* 28:175–94

Wraith, R., Simpkins, E. 1963. *Corruption in Developing Countries*. London: Allen & Unwin

Yale Law Journal 1979. Structural crime and institutional rehabilitation: a new approach to corporate sentencing. *Yale Law J.* 89:353–75

Ann. Rev. Sociol. 1985. 11:27–47

EFFECTS OF SIBLING NUMBER ON CHILD OUTCOME

David M. Heer

Population Research Laboratory, Department of Sociology, University of Southern California, Los Angeles, California 90007

[The cartoon shows four young children. The oldest speaks.] *Mommy, my baby book is stuffed full of pictures and cards and dates and writing and baby teeth, and hair and stuff . . . Dolly's just has some junk shoved in between the pages . . . Jeffy's hasn't been opened yet . . . and PJ doesn't even have a baby book!*

Bil Keane, "The Family Circus" (1970).
Reprinted by courtesy of the Register and Tribune Syndicate.

Abstract

This article reviews studies concerning the impact of sibling number on a selected series of outcomes including IQ, educational attainment, status of current job, and current earnings. Sibling number is a variable over time and cannot be properly measured unless data are available on the number and timing of all births and the age at which each child in the family ceases to be dependent. Unfortunately, existing research is too much based on secondary analysis of data sets for which all of the requisite information is not available. Controversies surround the question whether there is a causal impact of sibling number on IQ and, if so, how it can be explained; these are reviewed in detail. Research on the impact of sibling number on the other three dependent variables is reviewed, particularly where it contributes to our knowledge of the impact on educational attainment net of IQ, on job status net of education attainment, and on current earnings net of job status. It is concluded that decisions on the number and spacing of children are among the most important decisions parents can make. Therefore the large amounts of funds needed for data collection will be funds well spent.

27

0360-0572/85/0815-0027$02.00

INTRODUCTION

One of the most important decisions facing married couples is how many children to have and when to have them. A very important consideration in making these decisions is the tradeoff between the number of children and the potential quality of each child's life. Parents need to know how an increase in the number of their children and/or a particular spacing between them will affect the outcome for each child. Social science research ought to be able to help parents make these decisions intelligently. Unfortunately, to date research on how the number and spacing of siblings affects the outcome for each child does not provide parents with the information they ought to have. A major reason for this is that almost all attempts to answer these questions have involved the secondary analysis of data sets collected by agencies for whom these questions were not of paramount importance.

Social scientists have three theories for explaining the facts observed thus far concerning the relationship between the number and spacing of children and outcomes for the children. The oldest theory states that an increase in the number of siblings or a decrease in the spacing between them dilutes the time and material resources that parents can give to each child and that these resource dilutions hinder the outcome for each child. A relatively new theory states that account must be taken not only of parental resources but also of the resources given to each child by his siblings. A third theory contends that there is no causal relationship between number and spacing of children and child outcomes and that any apparent relationships are spurious.

Before beginning the discussion of the impact of sibling number on specific outcomes, I want to spend some time in considering how, in light of these theories, the independent variable should be measured. The most important aspect of sibling number is that it is a variable over time. Consider first an eldest child who will eventually have six siblings. He will begin his life as an only child; perhaps only by adolescence will he have six siblings. The spacing between the various siblings will determine the total number of years in which this firstborn has each given number of siblings from none to six.

Now consider the lastborn child in this same family. He will begin his life with six siblings. If none die, he will continue to have six siblings. However, the number of his siblings who remain financially dependent may decrease with time. To determine the sibling number at each point in the child's life, we must know—in addition to the final sibling number—the child's birth order, the spacing between each birth, and the age at which each child in the family became financially independent or died. All of the information about the sibling number of each child in the family will be contained in a graph in which we plot the number of financially dependent siblings against the age of the child.

Table 1   Matrix of number of financially dependent siblings for the firstborn among five children, each child spaced exactly three years apart.

Exact age of given child	Financially dependent siblings by age group					Total sibling number
	Under 3	3–6	6–12	12–18	18–21	
0	0	0	0	0	0	0
3	1	0	0	0	0	1
6	1	1	0	0	0	2
12	1	1	2	0	0	4
18	0	0	2	2	0	4

However, the proper measurement of sibling number has additional complications. First of all, according to all existing theories, the ages of the other siblings are relevant for the outcome for the given child. All of the relevant information is available only when it is possible to construct a matrix in which the rows present the age of the given child and the columns the age grouping of the siblings for whom a count of sibling number will be made. Many such matrices could be developed, some much more elaborate than others. Perhaps only a small amount of information would be lost if a matrix were constructed in which the rows would present the age of the given child as follows: 0, 3, 6, 12, and 18, and the columns would present the number of financially dependent siblings whose age was one of the following: under 3, 3 to 6, 6 to 12, 12 to 18, and 18 and over.

An illustration should be helpful. Table 1 presents the matrix of the number of siblings for a child who is the firstborn among five children, all of whom are spaced exactly three years apart and all of whom are financially dependent only up to exact age 21. Table 2 presents the matrix for the lastborn child among five children with characteristics identical to those in Table 1. It can be inferred

Table 2   Matrix of number of financially dependent siblings for the lastborn among five children with characteristics identical to those in Table 1.

Exact age of given child	Financially dependent siblings by age group					Total sibling number
	Under 3	3–6	6–12	12–18	18–21	
0	0	1	2	1	0	4
3	0	0	2	2	0	4
6	0	0	1	2	1	3
12	0	0	0	1	1	2
18	0	0	0	0	0	0

from these tables that the oldest child in this family, as compared to the youngest child, will probably suffer from a diminution of parental resources (probably financial resources) in adolescence. The youngest, on the other hand, will likely suffer, as compared to the oldest, from a reduction of parental resources (probably time resources) in infancy and early childhood.

Finally, it is also possible that the sex of each sibling must be taken into account as well as the age, at least for certain outcomes such as educational attainment. To do this would create a three-dimensional matrix with double the number of cells of the original matrix, unless some further reduction were made in the number of ages to be presented for the given child or in the number of age groupings for his siblings.

I shall henceforth use the term *sibling-number matrix* to denote any matrix that presents the number of financially dependent siblings of defined ages (and defined sex) at defined ages of a given child. I consider that research concerned with the consequences of the number and spacing of children should be based on data sets for which some version of this matrix can be constructed.

Unfortunately, most of the data sets used to study the effect of sibling number on various child outcomes have only contained information on birth order and sibling number at time of interview; almost none contains data on birth spacing. For data sets without information on birth spacing no version of the sibling-number matrix can be constructed. Moreover, of those few data sets for which there is information not only on birth order and sibling number at time of interview but also on age differences between siblings, none has been analyzed by means of a sibling-number matrix.

What measures have been used for data sets in which only birth order and sibling number at time of interview were known? Sometimes, as in Blake (1981b) or Lindert (1978), a matrix of variables has been created from the cross-classification of the two variables. More frequently, the two variables have simply been added separately and additively into a multiple-regression equation.

What measures have been used in data sets that additionally contain data on the age differences among siblings? Waldrop & Bell (1964) invented and first used a measure they labelled *sibling density*. This measure has also been used by Kidwell (1981). Sibling density is defined as the summation over all siblings of the inverse of the difference in age between a given sibling and the reference child. Thus it weights the impact of each sibling on the given child by the inverse of the age distance between them. The measure cannot distinguish a firstborn child from a lastborn (but will distinguish each from a middle child). Hence it should probably be used only along with a measure of birth order. Lindert (1978) utilized a series of 12 dummy variables simultaneously depicting number of siblings and birth order, which also differentiated middle children with sibship sizes of four or five according to the average spacing between consecutive siblings.

Kidwell (1981) also used a set of the following three variables: sibling number at time of interview, birth order, and the average age difference between the reference child and all siblings. Obviously, the three variables used by Kidwell can be utilized with a relatively small sample whereas construction of a sibling-number matrix demands a large sample. Moreover, it is possible that Kidwell's three variables contain most of the information that could be obtained from a sibling-number matrix. However, until the results with respect to child outcome of a sibling-number matrix can be compared to the results from the three variables used by Kidwell (1981) we cannot be sure how much information is lost by the utilization of these three variables rather than the full set of variables embodied in a sibling-number matrix.

Since the previous literature does not consider sibling number to be a variable over time, as I believe it should be defined, I shall in my review of previous literature conform to existing custom and denote sibling number as number at the time of the interview. In addition I shall use the term *sibling position variables* to denote the set of variables including as a minimum both birth order and sibling number at interview and as a maximum both of these variables plus summary variables concerned with sibling spacing.

Before I continue further, it is also necessary to define the dependent variable of this essay more precisely. *Child outcome* is potentially a very broad and encompassing term. It can and should include outcomes measured when the child is still a minor and also outcomes when the child has reached adulthood. Due to space limitations, this review will not consider such outcomes as life expectancy, height, and weight. [The research concerning the negative effect of sibling number on these outcomes was well reviewed by Wray (1971).] Nor shall I consider such outcomes as relationships with parents or peers; delinquency; subjective well being; or mental health. Reviews by Terhune (1974) and Clausen & Clausen (1973) found the research on most of these topics inconclusive. My review will focus only on three variables that I consider crucial in determining the socioeconomic status of the child after reaching maturity. Specifically, in the next section I shall discuss the impact of sibling position variables on intelligence; following that, their impact on educational attainment; and in a further section, their impact on current job status and earnings.

EFFECT ON INTELLIGENCE

A fairly large number of distinctly different tests have been developed over the years to measure intelligence. The correlations between results of these tests are not perfect but are always substantial. For the sake of simplicity, in this review I shall make no distinction between different IQ tests.

It has been well established for at least 35 years that there is a substantial inverse relationship between an individual's IQ score and the number of his or her siblings at the time of testing. The inverse relationship was documented with a sample of 70,805 Scottish 11-year old children (Scottish Council for Research in Education 1949, 1953) and with a sample of 95,237 French school children aged from 6 to 12 (Heuyer et al 1950; Gille et al 1954). In the Scottish study a group IQ test showed a correlation of $-.28$ with the number of siblings; the individually administered Stanford-Binet test showed a correlation of $-.32$. The mean score on the Stanford-Binet test fell from 113 for only children to 91 for those with five siblings. Even before these two large-scale studies, however, the negative relationship between the two variables had been shown to occur with moderately large samples. More complete details on the several studies conducted prior to or soon after World War II are presented in Anastasi (1956).

The large sample size in the Scottish and French studies allowed for a test of whether the inverse relationship between number of siblings and IQ would hold when the sample was subdivided by major occupation group of the child's father. In the Scottish data, the inverse relationship between sibling number and IQ held regardless of the occupation of the father. In the French study, the inverse relationship between the number of siblings and intelligence held among the children whose fathers were in the lower occupational groups but was much less pronounced or nonexistent among children with fathers in managerial or professional occupations. The Scottish study also presented results for IQ cross-classified by both sibling number and birth order. Among children with the same number of siblings, children of a middle birth order were shown to have the lowest IQ.

Since the publication of the Scottish and French studies, numerous other large data sets have been examined to look at the association between sibling number and IQ. Among the large United States data sets that have been analyzed are the 88,000 high school seniors interviewed for Project Talent in 1960 (Burton 1968); 794,859 National Merit Scholarship participants in 1965 (Breland 1974); 3428 children aged 6–11 who participated in the National Health Examination Survey in 1963–1965 (Steelman & Mercy 1980); 6031 survivors in 1975 of a sample of Wisconsin High School seniors first interviewed in 1957 (Sewell et al 1980); and the 1912 tenth-grade boys in 1966 of the Youth in Transition Study (Bachman 1970; Blake 1981b). Among the more important studies conducted outside the United States is a second study of 100,000 French school children 6–14 years old examined in 1965 (Institut National d'Etudes Demographiques 1973); a study of 400,000 19-year-old males in the Netherlands born in 1944–1947 (Belmont & Marolla 1973); a study of 4195 British children examined at either age 8 or 11 (Douglas 1964); and a study of 4031 British children aged 11 (Eysenck & Cookson 1970).

Two generalizations emerge from these various studies. First, the association of sibling number with IQ usually appears to depend upon social class. The lower the social class of the father, the more pronounced the association between sibling number and IQ. (An article by Marjoribanks & Walberg (1975) reanalyzing the data on the 400,000 19-year-old males in the Netherlands is perhaps the most comprehensive and sophisticated analysis of the interactions between social classes, sibling position variables, and IQ in the extant literature.) Second, if birth order is held constant, the larger the number of siblings, almost invariably the lower is the IQ. However, it is extremely important to note that no generalizations can be made about the impact of birth order when the number of siblings is held constant. In some of the studies the higher the birth order, the lower the IQ, when sibling number is held constant, while in other studies, the relationship between birth order and IQ is in the form of a U-shaped distribution or may even be positive.

Research Issues

The most important issue about these data is whether sibling position variables have a causal impact upon IQ or whether the relationships established in previous research may be spurious or at least seriously misspecified. To settle this question, we must be able to control for all other variables that might affect the relationship. Let us now examine the validity of some hypotheses that assume that the observed relationships between sibling position variables and IQ may be spurious.

A major alternative hypothesis is that the observed relationships may occur only because of failure to control for the IQ of the mother and father of the child. As Anastasi (1956) pointed out, the IQ of the parents may be relevant to the IQ of the child either through hereditary mechanisms or because high-IQ parents are more effective in providing an environment that will facilitate their child's intellectual development. We do know that there is a substantial correlation between the IQ of each parent and the IQ of the child. Higgins et al (1962) studied 1016 families of presumably completed fertility in Minnesota; for them the IQ of the mother, the father, and the children had been ascertained. The father-child IQ correlation was .43 and the mother-child IQ correlation .45. Moreover, it would appear that to account for the child's IQ it is necessary to know both the mother's IQ and the father's IQ since there appears to be a correlation of only .33 between these two variables (Higgins et al 1962).

At least two important studies have shown the patterns by which the IQ scores of the parents vary with the number of children that the mother bears. The aforementioned study by Higgins et al (1962) is the first of these. For mothers and fathers with from one to five children there were no substantial differences in mean parental IQ depending on number of children. However, among families where the number of children was at least five, the parental IQ descended rapidly with number of children. Cliquet & Balcaen (1981) examined the effect of IQ on a variety of fertility-related dependent variables for a sample of 619 ever-married women in Belgium who were patients at a Ghent University hospital. The relationship between IQ and present number of children was in the form of an inverse U-shaped distribution. Women with two children had the highest IQ; for women with at least two children there was a pronounced inverse linear relationship between IQ and number of children. The relationship between IQ and expected family size was also in the form of an inverse U-shaped distribution, with a peak IQ among women expecting three children.

The two above-mentioned studies are based on samples either of mothers or of fathers. Properly, we ought to correlate the two parental IQ's with sibling number among a sample of children. Preston (1976) has shown that there is a large discrepancy between the average number of children borne by women of completed fertility and the average sibship size (defined as the number of siblings plus one) of offspring of those women. For example, women in the United States aged 45 to 49 years old in 1970 had an average of 2.705 children. However, the average sibship size of offspring of these women was 4.461. Accordingly, since the inverse relationship between parental IQ and number of offspring is found only for men and women of moderate fertility or higher, we might expect a more negative linear correlation between parental IQ and sibship size for a sample of children than the linear correlations we find between IQ and number of offspring for samples of men and women past reproductive age. Some of the latter correlations are positive, e.g. one reported by Bajema (1963) for both sexes combined, and one reported by Waller (1971a) for women only. I have been able to find only one study in which children were the unit of analysis. This is a study by Waller (1971b) that relates data concerning the father's IQ to number of siblings for a sample of 170 male children now adults. Waller (1971b) found that for this sample the linear correlation between father's IQ and the son's sibling number was $-.104$. The exact magnitude of this coefficient must be considered unreliable since it is subject to a high degree of sampling error. In addition, it is not likely that the relationship between parental IQ and number of siblings is linear; rather it would appear to be in the shape of either an inverse L-shaped or an inverse J-shaped distribution.

Moreover, it should be noted that although studies that control for parental social-class variables may help to control for parental IQ, they do so only imperfectly because correlations between mother's and father's IQ and their social-class characteristics are only moderate. For example, according to the study by Waller (1971a), based on a sample of 699 men and women who were presumably past reproductive age, the correlation between IQ and educational attainment for men was only .57 and that for women only .46; similarly, the correlations between IQ and the Hollingshead Two-Factor Index of Social Position were only .53 and .27 respectively.

To my knowledge the only study with a substantial sample size that does relate number of siblings to IQ while holding constant the IQ of each parent is that of Olneck & Bills (1979) who reanalyzed the data set previously used by Higgins et al (1962). In a very cursory report, they stated that the zero-order correlation of − .300 between number of siblings and IQ previously reported by Higgins et al (1962) was reduced to a standardized regression coefficient of − .240 when the IQ scores of each parent were used as control variables. However, the analysis of Olneck & Bills (1979) suffers from their assumption that the number of siblings was linearly related to IQ; in this sample it was not (Higgins et al 1962).

In summary, it would appear that we have good evidence that any equation that relates number of siblings to IQ without holding constant the IQ of each parent will be misspecified. This misspecification may be greatest among children with six or more siblings. However, the exact magnitude of the specification error is simply not knowable at this time.

A second alternative hypothesis is that the observed relationships between sibling position variables and IQ are misspecified because of a failure to take into account whether a child was wanted at time of conception and/or birth. Pohlman (1965) has done the most to popularize the contention that children unwanted at time of conception suffer damage to their physical and mental well-being. Pohlman (1965) did not explicitly hypothesize that an unwanted child would suffer in his cognitive development; however, as I have pointed out earlier (Heer 1975), the hypothesis is certainly reasonable. Moreover, Bumpass & Westoff (1970) have shown that there is a strong negative relationship between the number of existing children a mother has borne and whether she wants a given child at time of conception. Thus it is reasonable to conclude that relationships between sibling position and IQ may not be accurately specified unless account is taken of whether the child has been wanted.

Let us now pay attention to those hypotheses that presume that the relationships between sibling position variables and IQ are not spurious. Anastasi (1956) was one of the first persons to advance the hypothesis that sibling position variables might be causally related to IQs of children. Anastasi postulated that with an increasing number of children parents would be able to provide fewer material resources to facilitate each child's mental development and also would be able to devote less time to contact with their children. The fact that the association between number of siblings and IQ has been shown to be strongest in the lower socioeconomic status groups is consistent with the hypothesis that material constraints among large families in such groups are detrimental to a child's intellectual development. In further support of her hypothesis, Anastasi cited the findings of the large-scale Scottish and French studies (Scottish Council for Research in Education 1953; Gille et al 1954) that twins always had lower IQ scores than singletons even when number of siblings was held constant. In addition, Anastasi cited as support for such an hypothesis the findings from the large-scale French study (Gille et al 1954). This study showed that among 1244 families with exactly two children, after control for social-class origin, the longer the spacing between a child and its sibling the higher the IQ. Finally, Anastasi postulated that parental contact should affect verbal IQ more than nonverbal IQ. She cited evidence gathered by Nisbet (1953) on several thousand Scottish schoolchildren that showed that number of siblings had a higher correlation with a child's verbal IQ tests than with nonverbal. Anastasi concluded that a definitive test of the hypothesis of a nonspurious effect of sibling position variables on IQ could be conducted only if the relationships between sibling position variables and IQ held after controls for the IQ of each parent were instituted.

In this essay, I shall follow Blake (1981b) in referring to Anastasi's hypothesis as the dilution hypothesis to distinguish it from a slightly different hypothesis advanced more recently.

Are all data gathered thus far consistent with the dilution hypothesis? Perhaps the most serious objection to the hypothesis is the inconsistency of results that relate birth order to IQ within subgroups that have the same sibling number. According to the dilution hypothesis one might expect birth order always to be negatively related to IQ when the number of siblings at time of interview is held constant. This expectation would follow from the assumption that the amount of parental contact in early childhood is more important for the child's IQ than contact at older ages. What factors might cause the relationship between birth order and IQ to be other than negative? Zajonc (1976) has emphasized the possible importance of differences in birth spacing. For data sets where later-born children had higher IQ's than middle-born or early-born children, it might be that the birth spacing between later-born siblings was considerably longer than the spacing between the earlier born. This factor might be important because only the presence of other very young siblings (and not older siblings) might affect the cognitive development of the child in the first five years of its life. Zajonc (1976) has also pointed out that the relationship between birth order and IQ within subgroups of identical sibship size appears to be much more frequently negative the older the individual at time of testing. For example, the data for male 19-year-olds in the Netherlands show a consistently negative relationship whereas the data for 11-year-old schoolchildren in Scotland (Scottish Council for Research in Education 1949) do not. Zajonc (1976) has also emphasized that a child who is young at time of testing, e.g. age 11, and is also the first child out of a total sibship of six must be closely spaced with his other siblings. On the other hand, he points out that a child who is young at time of testing and who is the last of six children does not necessarily come from a family in which all of the children are closely spaced. In contrast, if testing occurs when the child is already grown, there is no necessity that either the firstborn or the lastborn be closely spaced with other siblings.

In this connection, recent research by Lindert (1978) is quite relevant. Lindert reanalyzed the data from the 1296 families in Syracuse, New York, who had been interviewed in 1967–1968 in the Cornell-Syracuse time-use survey. He estimated the total additional number of hours of childcare time given by the mother per additional child for various combinations of numbers and ages of children and for working and nonworking mothers. A striking feature of the table was the tremendous difference in additional hours of childcare time per each additional child depending on the age of that child; the older the child, the fewer the additional hours. Also noteworthy were fairly substantial differences in additional childcare time per additional child in each defined age group in relation to the total number of children in the family; the greater the number of children, the fewer the additional hours.

Although Zajonc has been instrumental in pointing out how birth-spacing effects may operate in such a way that the dilution hypothesis is made more plausible, he himself is best known for his advocacy of an alternative to dilution theory which he calls confluence theory (Zajonc & Markus 1975; Zajonc 1976; Zajonc et al 1979). In explaining a child's intellectual development, confluence theory takes into account not the dilution of parental resources but the absolute level of intellectual ability of each member of the family at each point in time in the child's life. Zajonc et al (1979) postulate that the yearly gain in absolute intelligence of a given child is affected by the root mean square of the absolute level of intelligence of everyone in the family: parents, adult relatives, siblings, and the reference child included. Thus according to this theory one should find a negative relationship between IQ and sibling number when birth order is held constant but varying relationships between IQ and birth order when sibling number is held constant. One should also find that a child with siblings considerably older than himself will attain a higher IQ than a child of the same age with the same number of siblings but for whom the average age of siblings is lower. Zajonc also postulated that a child's yearly gain in absolute intelligence would be raised if he had the chance to teach younger siblings. Lastborn children (including only children) who had no chance to teach younger siblings would thus be disadvantaged. Zajonc, although claiming that his theory fit the data collected by Belmont & Marolla (1973) well, nevertheless admitted that these data could be explained by other theories as well.

Let us now contrast Zajonc's theory with the classic dilution theory. Essentially the dilution theory says that sibling-position variables affect the amount of time and material resources that parents can give children; further it says that variation in the amount of these resources received by each sibling affects that child's IQ. Classic dilution theory thus allows for no direct effect of sibling-position variables on IQ, only for indirect effect through parental resources bestowed on the child. In contrast, confluence theory predicts that there should be a direct effect of sibling-position variables on IQ when the amount of parental resources invested in the child is held constant. Obviously, the validity of confluence theory vis-à-vis dilution theory cannot be tested until a data set has been collected that explicitly includes a set of variables indicating the monetary and time resources invested in the child at each point during his childhood. No such data have yet been gathered. Nevertheless, Lindert's analysis (1978) dealing exclusively with time inputs is again relevant. Lindert analyzed not only the time input of the mother into childcare but also that of all other members of the family. Older siblings were found to play an important role in the care of younger siblings. Thus it is no longer possible to argue that Zajonc is wrong simply because older siblings do not have a significant impact on the life of the reference child.

However, to test confluence theory certain other variables will also have to be considered. Blake (1981a) has been very critical of Zajonc's hypothesis that lastborn and only children suffer from not being able to teach younger siblings. She pointed out that only children were more likely to come from broken homes than other children and that the experience of a broken home probably served to reduce IQ. She cited the research done by Claudy et al (1979) that makes use of the Project Talent data; these showed that among children in unbroken homes the only children had higher IQ's than the children in two-child families. Moreover, Zajonc's teaching hypothesis can be criticized on another ground: It is possible that there is a selectivity bias for only and other lastborn children— namely, if parents have a mentally defective child, they may decide that they cannot both care for that child and have additional children.

Needed Research

How can we go about improving our knowledge of how sibling-position variables affect IQ? In my opinion, the most important step to be taken is the thorough analysis of a data set that includes not only sibling-position variables but also the IQ of each parent. One such data set currently exists, namely the set used by Higgins et al (1962), Waller (1971a, 1971b), and Olneck & Bills (1979) consisting of 1016 Minnesota families; this set is under the control of the Dight Institute of Human Genetics at the University of Minnesota.

Are there other extant data sets the analysis of which would further our understanding of the impact of the sibling-number matrix on IQ? The most promising is the data set for the study of high school seniors in Wisconsin in 1957. Sewell & Hauser (1977) described a 1975 follow-up survey designed to obtain a large amount of information on the siblings of the original respondents. The age, sex, and educational attainment of each living sibling was ascertained, and one sibling was designated to be the subject for further inquiries in the 1975 interview and to be a candidate for interview in a survey conducted in 1977. The 1977 survey, consisting of interviews with about 2000 of the designated siblings, collected a large amount of data on details of educational attainment, labor force and work experience, and earnings in 1976. It also collected data on IQ as measured during the high school years. Included in the 1975 survey were more than 9000 individuals, for whom there is now apparently available all of the information needed to create a sibling-number matrix. Thus this sample can show us the separate impact of each variable within this matrix, albeit in a sample in which neither the IQ of the mother nor of the father can be controlled. In addition, the 1977 survey makes possible the analysis of intrafamily differences in IQ that are dependent on birth order and birth spacing. Such analysis, now under way, permits an automatic control for the IQ of each parent and will thus allow an excellent test of the effect of these two variables on IQ.

EFFECT ON EDUCATIONAL ATTAINMENT

Studies concerned with the effect of sibling-position variables on educational attainment can be based on samples of the total adult population or on special subgroups of that population. Such differences in type of sample have implications for the relationships observed. For example, a study looking at the later educational attainment of high school seniors can tell us nothing about the effect of sibling number on the chances of reaching at least 11 years of completed schooling. With this methodological note in mind let us proceed to substantive issues.

Educational attainment has been shown to be strongly affected by measures of intelligence. However, it may also be affected directly by variables associated with the sibling-number matrix. A large number of siblings or close spacing between the child and his siblings may dilute the parental resources of time and money bestowed upon a given child. These resource dilutions may have an adverse impact upon educational attainment among children with the same IQ. Accordingly, in this review I shall emphasize those studies that at least hold IQ constant. However, I shall first mention two studies that do not hold IQ constant but are the only studies employing a large sample that look at birth-order effects as well as sibship-size effects. I shall then examine a study based on sibling pairs which automatically holds constant the effect of parental IQ.

Blake (1981b) analyzed data from the 1970 National Fertility Study separately for 3868 ever-married females 23 years of age and over and for 3782 husbands 25 and over. At interview, 27 separate variables were created by cross-classifying sibling number with birth order. The impact of each of these 27 variables on educational attainment was examined while six background variables, excluding IQ, were held constant. For both men and women there appeared to be a rather direct negative impact of sibship size on educational attainment, but, according to Blake, birth order was not an important variable.

Using the data set mentioned earlier that included not only respondents who had been high school seniors in Wisconsin in 1957 but all of their siblings, Hausek & Sewell (1983) investigated the effects of birth order on educational attainment for each sibship size, while controlling for age and various characteristics of the parents. Although sibship size had an important effect, they concluded that among persons with the same sibship size birth order itself had no statistically significant effect on educational attainment.

Lindert (1978) studied the impact of sibling position variables on a sample of 767 sibling pairs in which one sibling was a senior male employee in a New Jersey utility company. Although this study does not control for the IQ of either member of the sibling pair, it does provide an automatic control for the IQ of the parents. Lindert's dependent variable was the schooling advantage of the firstborn in a sibling pair that included the firstborn and some other sibling. As mentioned previously, for a different data set Lindert had examined the effect of sibling-position variables on average time inputs into each child from other members of the family. Lindert used these averaged time-input data in his analysis of the sibling pairs. Holding constant other background variables, he found that the degree of advantage of the firstborn in educational attainment was a statistically significant positive function of the difference in average time input. However, since the average time inputs for each sibling position may have been associated with average material inputs for each sibling position and these average material inputs were not measured, it is uncertain whether the time inputs or the material inputs were the responsible agent for the sibling-pair differences obtained.

Other studies examine the effects of sibling number on educational attainment holding constant IQ and/or grade point average. Four of these deserve mention here.

The classic study in this category was Duncan (1968). Duncan worked mainly with data on a sample of white males 25–34 years old collected from a supplement to the October 1964 Current Population Survey. However, data on early intelligence were not available from this sample. Accordingly, correlation coefficients between early intelligence, educational attainment, and the other variables were obtained from other studies. A model was presented in which the effect of the number of siblings on educational attainment was estimated while early IQ, father's education, and father's occupation were held constant. The standardized path coefficient between number of siblings and educational attainment was estimated to be $-.15$. This was comparable in magnitude to either the standardized coefficient from father's education to educational attainment or from father's occupation to educational attainment.

Olneck & Bills (1979) analyzed data for a sample of 1033 males interviewed by telephone in 1973; the data had been gathered as completely as possible from a population of 2782 boys who had had their IQ tested in the sixth grade in the Kalamazoo, Michigan public schools sometime between 1928 and 1950.

Holding constant IQ, age, and other socioeconomic background variables, Olneck & Bills found that the number of siblings had a statistically significant negative effect on educational attainment.

Behrman et al (1980) analyzed data from the National Research Council's twin registry. The basic sample consisted of white male twins born 1917–1927 who had both been in military service. The subsample analyzed by Behrman et al (1980) included 609 males for whom a score on an intelligence test (GCT) was available; both members of these twin pairs had served as enlisted men in the Navy. Thus the sample censored out both those twin pairs not able to meet the cognitive standards of the Navy and those pairs where at least one member became a Naval officer. Sibling number was measured according to the number of siblings alive in 1940. Holding constant IQ and eight other background variables, the regression of sibling number on years of schooling was − .066, not statistically significant at the .05 level.

Finally, let me describe the results obtained by Sewell et al (1980) from the panel study of high school seniors in Wisconsin in 1957. With IQ and seven other background variables held constant, they found for males a statistically significant unstandardized regression coefficient of − .043 between number of siblings reported in 1975 and educational attainment. For females, with the same set of variables held constant, the unstandardized regression coefficient between number of siblings and educational attainment was − .050, also statistically significant. Holding constant the above-mentioned variables plus the normalized grade point average, Sewell et al found for males a statistically significant coefficient of − .028 between sibling number and educational attainment. The identical coefficient for females was − .038, also statistically significant.

Needed Research

To date no research has been conducted relating the variables of a sibling-number matrix to educational attainment while IQ was held constant. This situation can easily be remedied since the Wisconsin data set analyzed by Sewell et al (1980) contains both the necessary information to construct a sibling-number matrix and the necessary sample size to make the results from such a matrix useful. Existing results from the Wisconsin study suggest that such a matrix may need to include the sex as well as the age of the respondent's siblings.

Future research with this dependent variable should also hold constant whether a child was wanted at conception or birth.

In my opinion, it will be necessary to have studies of the relationship between sibling position variables and educational attainment for many different cohorts, because I believe the coefficients linking these two variables will vary considerably by time and by place. Educational attainment is not only affected by the magnitude of parental financial resources invested in the child but also by the magnitude of resources invested in the child by state and local governments and by the federal government. It is highly probable, in my opinion, that the coefficients obtained in the Wisconsin study for persons who were high school seniors in 1957 are more negative than would be obtained in a study of a more recent cohort of high school seniors who have been exposed to the tremendous increase in federal funding of college scholarships dating from President Johnson's administration of the 1960s.

EFFECT ON STATUS OF CURRENT JOB AND ON CURRENT EARNINGS

The conventional model of the socioeconomic status process assumes that educational attainment affects the status of the current job and that the status of the current job affects current earnings. Most commonly, occupational status is measured by Duncan's SEI score (Duncan 1961), which provides a numerical score for each detailed occupation defined by the U.S. Bureau of the Census based on the distribution of earnings and educational attainment among persons in the occupation. I shall follow this conventional model and present in two separate sections research relating these to sibling-position variables. I shall only include studies in which IQ is one of the independent variables. This will avoid a misspecification problem with respect to the impact of the sibling-position variables. Unfortunately, the only sibling-position variable in any of these studies is the sibling number at one specific point in time.

Effect on Status of Current Job

The results from four studies will be cited. Duncan (1968) in his study of white males 25–34 years old, reported a standardized coefficient of −.04 between number of siblings and the Duncan SEI score of the current occupation, after controlling for background variables including early and late IQ scores and educational attainment.

Olneck & Bills (1979), analyzing data for 1004 males from their previously mentioned Kalamazoo study, found no statistically significant effect of the number of siblings on occupational status after controlling for educational attainment, IQ, age, and background variables.

In the sample of 609 former Navy enlisted men, Behrman et al (1980) analyzed the impact of the number of siblings alive in 1940 on the SEI score of the respondent's occupation in 1967. Holding constant background variables including IQ, educational attainment, and the SEI score for the first job, Behrman et al (1980) found that the unstandardized coefficient relating the number of siblings to the SEI score for the current job was negative but not statistically significant. However, holding constant all of the above-mentioned variables other than the SEI score for the first job, they obtained a statistically significant coefficient of $-.073$.

Sewell et al (1980) in their study of Wisconsin high school seniors of 1957 obtained the following results with respect to the current job, 18 years after high school graduation. If background variables including IQ, educational attainment, and the Duncan SEI score for the first job are held constant, males obtained a statistically significant positive unstandardized coefficient of .250. If all of the above-mentioned variables save the SEI score for the first job are held constant, they obtained a positive coefficient of .164, which was not statistically significant. Holding constant all of the variables mentioned above except grade point average and variables relating to educational attainment, Sewell et al obtained a statistically significant negative coefficient of $-.248$. For women the first two of the corresponding coefficients were $-.091$ and $-.155$, neither of which was statistically significant; the third corresponding coefficient was a statistically significant $-.443$.

The results obtained by Sewell et al (1980) for men are particularly noteworthy because they show a positive advantage to having many siblings when one is in the transition from the first job to the current job. These results might be explained by an hypothesis that under certain circumstances a large number of siblings may enhance job information networks and thereby enhance occupational mobility from first to current job. Nevertheless, it should again be emphasized that all of the coefficients relating the number of siblings to current occupational status are substantively small compared to the standard deviation in the Duncan SEI score, which for the Wisconsin males was 24 and for the Wisconsin females 20.

Effect on Current Earnings

Three studies are available for analysis. In his study of white males 25–34 years old Duncan (1968) found that the number of siblings had no statistically significant effect on current earnings when the Duncan SEI score for the current job, educational attainment, IQ, and other background variables were held constant.

Olneck & Bills (1979), analyzing data for 919 males from the Kalamazoo study, found no statistically significant effect of number of siblings on the natural log of earnings, either for an equation in which only age and other background variables were controlled or for an equation in which IQ and educational attainment were also controlled.

Behrman et al (1980) obtained two interesting results in their analysis of 609 former Navy enlisted men born 1917–1927. Holding constant background variables including IQ, educational attainment, and the Duncan SEI score for the job held in 1967, they found a coefficient of −.015 between the number of siblings and the natural log of earnings in 1973. This coefficient was not quite high enough to be statistically significant. Holding constant only initial background variables and IQ, with no control for educational attainment or occupational status, they found a statistically significant coefficient of −.019 between number of siblings and the natural log of 1973 earnings.

Let me spell out in more detail the exact import of the coefficient of −.019, obtained by Behrman et al, relating number of siblings to the natural log of 1973 earnings net, of the effects of initial background variables and IQ. Assume a sample of men who had the average value expressed on all of the background variables with the exception of number of siblings. Among such men those with only one sibling alive in 1940 would have average 1973 earnings of $15,902. Among such men with six siblings, the average 1973 earnings would be $14,461. One may also calculate from the data of Behrman et al (1980) an estimate of the effect of sibling number on earnings from an equation in which IQ was not included among the initial background variables held constant. In this equation the coefficient for the effect of the number of siblings alive in 1940 on the natural log of earnings in 1973 was −.025. Among a sample of men at the mean of all of the other background variables, those with one sibling would have had earnings of $16,075 and those with six siblings earnings of $14,186. These estimates are subject to two opposing biases. First of all, because of the failure to include in the equation the mother's IQ, father's IQ, or whether the child was wanted at time of conception, the effect of sibling number on earnings through its influence on IQ is probably overstated. Secondly, because the sample is censored to exclude disproportionately both those of very low and perhaps very high IQ (it is limited to twin pairs both members of which were former Naval-enlisted men), its estimate of the effect of sibling number on earnings through its impact on IQ is probably underestimated.

Needed Research

I have been able to find only a few studies that examine the effect of sibling number, net of IQ, on the status of current job or on current earnings. In my opinion, many more studies are needed since I suspect that the relationships obtained may vary by time and by place. Moreover, none of the studies include any sibling position variables other than sibling number at a specified point in time. Further research should remedy this lack. It should also be able to hold constant whether a child was wanted at conception or birth.

CONCLUSIONS

All of the research conducted so far on the impact of sibling-position variables on child outcomes has been from data sets collected by agencies that did not have a primary interest in investigating such relationships. Most of these data sets have contained information on birth order and the number of siblings at time of interview, but not data on age differences between siblings. Research has, however, clearly established that child outcomes depend not only on birth order and on number of siblings at interview but also on the age differences between siblings. Thus, to be most informative, research should be conducted from data sets capable of creating a sibling-number matrix in which each cell of the matrix represents the number of siblings of a defined age range (and sex) at each of several defined ages of the child. Since the number of variables in such a matrix is potentially numerous, research on the effects of sibling number is optimally conducted with large samples, which, of course, are also costly.

In my opinion, our factual knowledge concerning the effect of sibling-position variables on IQ is only marginally superior to what it was at the time Anastasi (1956) wrote her much-cited review. I have to repeat Anastasi's plea that we gain the opportunity to analyze thoroughly a data set containing not only the child's IQ but that of each parent as well. I only add that we also ought to have the opportunity to include a measure as to whether the child was wanted at time of conception and/or birth.

I have also emphasized my belief that future studies should be such as to provide a substantial number of cases within subgroups, divided by time and place of late adolescence, because differences by time and by area in the degree of governmental subsidies to college students have strong effects on the relation between educational attainment and sibling-position variables.

These negative comments aside, there is no doubt that in recent years we have gained a much better idea of how sibling-position variables affect the time resources devoted to each child and of how they affect educational attainment, current job status, and current earnings. We have also profited by development of confluence theory as a challenge to the classical dilution theory with respect to the impact of these variables on IQ.

Despite the fact that further research on the effects of sibling number may be costly, I feel that it is very much worthwhile. Choosing the number and spacing of children is one of the most important ways a married couple can affect child outcomes. Thus parents should have access to a very accurate knowledge of how these decisions will affect their children's future. If such knowledge demands a considerable expenditure of funds, these funds will be well spent.

ACKNOWLEDGMENTS

I would like to thank Judith Blake, Robert Hauser, Peter Lindert, and William Sewell for valuable comments on the first draft of this essay.

Literature Cited

Anastasi, A. 1956. Intelligence and family size. *Psychol. Bull.* 53:187–209

Bachman, J. G. 1970. *Youth in Transition,* Vol. 2, *The Impact of Family Background and Intelligence on Tenth-Grade Boys.* Ann Arbor, MI: Inst. Soc. Res.

Bajema, C. J. 1963. Estimation of the direction and intensity of natural selection in relation to human intelligence by means of the intrinsic rate of natural increase. *Soc. Biol.* 10:175–87

Behrman, J. R., Hrubec, Z., Taubman, P., Wales, T. J. 1980. *Socioeconomic Success: A Study of the Effects of Genetic Endowments, Family Environment, and Schooling.* Amsterdam: North-Holland

Belmont, L., Marolla, F. A. 1973. Birth order, family size and intelligence. *Science* 182:1096–1101

Blake, J. 1981a. The only child in America. *Pop. Dev. Rev.* 7:43–54

Blake, J. 1981b. Family size and the quality of children. *Demography* 18:421–42

Breland, H. 1974. Birth order, family configuration, and verbal achievement. *Child Dev.* 45:1011–19

Bumpass, L., Westoff, C. F. 1970. The "perfect contraceptive" population. *Science* 169:1177–82

Burton, D. 1968. Birth order and intelligence. *J. Soc. Psychol.* 76:199–206

Claudy, J. G., Farrell, W. S. Jr., Dayton, C. W. 1979. *The Consequences of Being an Only Child: An Analysis of Project Talent Data.* Palo Alto, Calif: Am. Inst. Res.

Clausen, J. A., Clausen, S. R. 1973. The effects of family size on parents and children. In *Psychological Perspectives on Population,* ed. J. T. Fawcett, pp. 185–208. New York: Basic

Cliquet, R. L., Balcaen, J. 1981. *Intelligence, Family Planning and Family Formation.* Presented at Int. Pop. Conf., Manila

Douglas, J. B. 1964. *The Home and the School.* London: Macgibbon & Kee

Duncan, O. D. 1961. A socioeconomic index for all occupations. In *Occupations and Social Status,* ed. A. Reiss et al, pp. 109–61. New York: Free Press of Glencoe

Duncan, O. D. 1968. Ability and achievement. *Soc. Biol.* 15:1–11

Eysenck, H. J., Cookson, D. 1970. Personality in primary school children. 3. Family Background. *Br. J. Educ. Psychol.* 40:117–31

Gille, R., Henry, L., Tabah, L., Sutter, J., Bergues, H., et al. 1954. Le niveau intellectuel des enfants d'age scolaire: la determination des aptitudes; l'influence des facteurs constitutionnels, familiaux, et sociaux. *Inst. Natl. Etudes Demographiques: Trav. Doc.,* Cahier 23

Hauser, R. M., Sewell, W. H. 1983. Birth order and educational attainment in full sibships. *Center for Demography and Ecology, Univ. Wis.-Madison, Work. Pap. 83–31.* 44 pp.

Heer, D. M. 1975. *Society and Population.* Englewood Cliffs, NJ: Prentice-Hall. 2nd ed.

Heuyer, G., Pieron, H., Pieron, Mme. H., Sauvy, A. 1950. Le niveau intellectuel des enfants d'age scolaire: une enquete nationale dans l'enseignement primaire. *Inst. Natl. Etudes Demographiques: Trav. Doc.,* Cahier 13

Higgins, J. V., Reed, E. W., Reed, S. C. 1962. Intelligence and family size: a paradox resolved. *Soc. Biol.* 9:84–90

Institut National d'Etudes Demographiques. 1973. *Enquete Nationale sur le Niveau Intellectuel des Enfants d'Age Scolaire,* Cahier 64. Paris: Presses Univ. France

Kidwell, J. S. 1981. Number of siblings, sibling spacing, sex, and birth order: their effects on perceived parent-adolescent relationships. *J. Marriage Fam.* 43:315–32

Lindert, P. H. 1978. *Fertility and Scarcity in America.* Princeton: Princeton Univ. Press

Marjoribanks, K., Walberg, H. J. 1975. Birth order, family size, social class, and intelligence. *Soc. Biol.* 22:261–68

Nisbet, J. D. 1953. *Family Environment: A Direct Effect of Family Size on Intelligence.* London: Cassell

Olneck, M. B., Bills, D. B. 1979. Family configuration and achievement: effects of birth order and family size in a sample of brothers. *Soc. Psychol. Q.* 42:135–48

Pohlman, E. 1965. Results of unwanted conception: some hypotheses up for adoption. *Soc. Biol.* 12:11–17

Preston, S. H. 1976. Family sizes of children and family sizes of women. *Demography* 13:105–14

Scottish Council for Research in Education. 1949. *The Trend of Scottish Intelligence.* London: Univ. London Press

Scottish Council for Research in Education. 1953. *Social Implications of the 1947 Scottish Mental Survey.* London: Univ. London Press

Sewell, W. H., Hauser, R. M. 1977. On the effects of families and family structure on achievement. In *Kinometrics: Determinants of Socioeconomic Success Within and Between Families,* ed. P. Taubman, pp. 255–83. Amsterdam: North-Holland

Sewell, W. H., Hauser, R. M., Wolf, W. C. 1980. Sex, schooling, and occupational status. *Am. J. Sociol.* 86:551–83

Steelman, L. C., Mercy, J. A. 1980. Unconfounding the confluence model: a test of sibship size and birth-order effects on intelligence. *Am. Sociol. Rev.* 45:571–82

Terhune, K. W. 1974. *A Review of the Actual and Expected Consequences of Family Size.* Buffalo: Calspan Corp.

Waldrop, M., Bell, R. 1964. Relation of preschool dependency behavior to family size and density. *Child Dev.* 35:1187–1195

Waller, J. H. 1971a. Differential reproduction: its relation to IQ test score, education, and occupation. *Soc. Biol.* 18:122–36

Waller, J. H. 1971b. Achievement and social mobility: relationships among IQ score, education, and occupation in two generations. *Soc. Biol.* 18:252–59

Wray, J. D. 1971. Population pressure on families: family size and child spacing. In *Rapid Population Growth: Consequences and Policy Implications,* ed. Natl. Acad. Sci. pp. 403–61. Baltimore, Md: Johns Hopkins Press

Zajonc, R. B. 1976. Family configuration and intelligence. *Science* 192:227–36

Zajonc, R. B., Markus, G. B. 1975. Birth order and intellectual development. *Psychol. Rev.* 82:74–88

Zajonc, R. B., Markus, H., Markus, G. B. 1979. The birth order puzzle. *J. Pers. Soc. Psychol.* 37:1325–41

Ann. Rev. Sociol. 1985. 11:49–73

THE ORGANIZATIONAL STRUCTURE OF THE SCHOOL

William B. Tyler

Department of Sociology, Darwin Institute of Technology, P.O. Box 40146, Casuarina, N. T., Australia 5792

Abstract

The sociology of school organization is today fragmented by a bewildering variety of theoretical perspectives—interactionist, neo-Durkheimian, phenomenological, to name a few. Central to the development in this field over the past decade has been the rejection of the ideal-type of bureaucratic organization as formulated by Weber and the attempt to locate formal structures of the school within the strategies and motives of teachers, pupils, and administrators. The result has been, however, a certain loss of theoretical focus and a failure to think through the contradictions of particular perspectives and to formulate their partial insights into more rigorous and embracing conclusions. The ascendant model of school structure is now that of the loosely coupled system, in which technologies are uncertain, goals unclear, and the formal structures of which tend towards anarchy. This model contrasts markedly with other dominant perspectives, notably those in the structuralist tradition (e.g. Bernstein, Foucault) that describe school organization in terms of a close theoretical relationship between pedagogy, ideology, and the apparatus of control and surveillance. This review explicates these tensions and contradictions in contemporary accounts of school structure and suggests ways in which they may be reconciled.

INTRODUCTION

Despite the number of authoritative reviews of the school as a formal organization (Bidwell 1965, Dreeben 1973, Davies 1973, 1981; Boyd & Crowson 1981), the sociological study of the school as an institution has proven to be lacking in both depth and specificity (Corwin 1974, Bell 1980, Allison 1983).

49

0360-0572/85/0815-0049$02.00

Although the school was organizationally mature and culturally ubiquitous before schooling assumed its age-specific, bureaucratic, and obligatory features in the late nineteenth century (Reimer 1971), it has somehow managed to remain at the margins of sociological interest. This is not to say that the structural features of school *systems* have lacked extensive theoretical or sociohistorical analysis (Durkheim 1977, Hopper 1971, Archer 1979), but rather that the formal properties of the school—the localized administrative entity concerned with the face-to-face instruction of the young—have tended to be ignored within the mainstream sociological enterprise. Apart from the lively interest shown by administrative theorists in school organization, social-scientific focus has been on the whole polarized—whether towards such macrosociological questions as the correspondence between school and work organization (Bowles & Gintis 1976) or towards the micro or interactional aspects of control in classrooms (Woods 1983). The aim of this review therefore is to identify and to expose the rich though often hidden veins of sociological enquiry that treat the school as an institution in its own right.

This apparent neglect may result from the schools' lack of a technology that links inputs to a rationally-deducible index of performance—or even of a clear and unambiguous set of procedures by which such a criterion could be defined. Indeed the school has most often been conceptualized in the past decade as a 'loosely coupled' set of events and personnel and functions (Weick 1976), analogous to a football game played on a sloped field with numerous goals and a rather anarchic system of scoring (J. March, personal communication quoted by Weick 1976:1). Though schools may possess many of the formal properties of the Weberian ideal-type of bureaucracy [such as a hierarchy of offices, a fixed and official division of labor, formalized procedures, and promotion by expertise (Weber 1946: 196–244)], it is the indeterminacy of their decision-making processes that appears to characterize their organizational structures—a feature they share with other educational institutions such as colleges (March & Olsen et al. 1976). Some theorists have gone so far as to claim that school organization is shaped more by the logic of public confidence surrounding the myths and ceremonies of certification than by any internal relationship between their official goals and their instructional practices (Meyer & Rowan 1983).

Inherent within these post-Weberian models of school organization are some unresolved theoretical problems. If schools are loosely coupled or anarchic organizations, what can one give as the reasons for this, within a more general and comparative perspective? Is it possible to produce a theoretical scheme which might generate an entirely different set of empirical forms, which are nevertheless recognizable as schools? Secondly, if the formal requirements of system-oriented theory of school structure could be met, what might be the implications of this for the interactive order of this institution—that is to say, the realm of face-to-face communication and experience so central to our definition of the school? How tight are the links between the formal and interactional spheres of schooling and how might one draw lines of causation between them? According to Goffman (1983:11) this relationship is, typically for modern societies, another example of loose coupling, which he defines precisely as "a nonexclusive linkage between interactional practices and social structures". He suggests that this linkage may be compared to "a set of transformation rules, or a membrane selecting how various relevant social distinctions will be managed within the interaction." Do these insights however merely compound the special difficulties of constructing a theoretical model of the school that implies at least some degree of unity, integration, and consensus?

The rejection of a holistic approach to school organization implied by loose coupling (Willower 1982:93) may be a less adequate response than first appears. Although schools are ostensibly autonomous from the pressures of the market (and consequently perhaps further enjoy a degree of subunit independence), the loose coupling metaphor has only heuristic value unless it is embedded more precisely within a general perspective that constitutes the sociohistorical context of the apparently autonomous actor within a specific theoretical tradition or paradigm (Morgan 1980). Two diverse fields associated with school organization may serve to illustrate the need for some kind of theoretical synthesis, despite the apparently high levels of indeterminacy, discontinuity, and autarchy typical of organizational analysis of schools at the empirical level. The first of these is seen in the renaissance in recent years of the school effectiveness debate (Reynolds 1982) in which certain aspects of internal organization are taken as causal influences on a school's behavioral and academic performance. The second problem area is defined by the role played by the ostensibly meritocratic and rationalized forms of schooling within theories of social reproduction, Marxist and non-Marxist (Bourdieu & Passeron 1977, Bernstein 1977, Sharp, 1980), as well as by those who follow the archaeological method of institutional analysis of Foucault (Jones & Williamson 1979). In neither of these two opposed fields of enquiry—the one prescriptive and unashamedly empiricist, the other intensely theoretical—is the apparent looseness of school organization anything more than a starting point.

Within the school effectiveness research, for example, there are increasing applications of econometric methods that employ latent variables (the linear combination of the manifest or observed variables) which are assigned weights according to a prespecified model, in order to better estimate the contribution that school and home make to individual levels of performance (Noonan & Wold 1977). Such methods are considerably more sophisticated than earlier approaches that attribute causal significance by the increment in variance explained (Coleman 1966; Peaker 1975). They are, in addition, more theoretically justifiable than the rather inductive derivation of a composite process or climate variable from a host of indices of the school's internal state (e.g. Rutter et al 1979 and critiques by Goldstein 1981, Cuttance 1981). Whatever the methodological orientation of this tradition of research, however, its apparent aim is to identify the processes and structures that reduce the unexplained variations in outcomes, to construct much tighter models of the school as a social system than those of contemporary sociological theories of school organization. Indeed the search for the effective school appears to reinforce in practice the unidimensionality of such constructions, notably in the recommendations of the Rutter group for the tight ship approach to school management (1979:186–94).

The search for less apparent sources of structuring beneath the surface of empirical data also characterizes the theorists of models of social reproduction. Here the attention is guided, not by some predictive model that links theoretically opaque but quantifiable processes to a desired effect, nor by any hypothesized interdependence among such variables as organizational goals, instructional methods and administrative arrangements, but rather it is guided by the invisible positioning effects of ideology which systematically maintains a particular construction of the teaching and learning process (Bernstein 1982). In this instance any apparent looseness of the system, whether in pockets of autonomy at the lower level of the hierarchy, or in the absence of causal interdependence among abstracted indices of context, structure, and outcomes, may eventually be interpreted as a covert form of class domination rather than as a functionally significant strategy.

The ritual classifications that seem to allow for the decoupling of activities and outcomes from formal controls (Meyer & Rowan 1983) could, for example, contain within them ideological messages that may facilitate the reproduction of class power in indirect and subtle ways.

Any review of the literature on school organization therefore will need to explain why both the prescriptive and critical approaches to school structure depend on rather tighter explanatory models than do conventional organizational theories. In order to clarify the paradoxes and difficulties associated with metaphors of loose coupling and organized anarchy, an attempt will therefore be made to provide the grounds for discovering theoretical affinities within what have been rather disparate and often contending approaches to the school as an organization. First of all the organizational and administrative literature offers a rich source of empirical inquiry into schools and it will be used to trace the changing interpretations of the Weberian approach up to the point of its rejection. Secondly an attempt will be made to underscore the inadequacies of the post-Weberian model by pointing to the contributions that have been made to an understanding of school structures by the *verstehende* and interactionist stream of Weberian sociology. Finally, the review will return to consider the points of contact between these two so-called normative and interpretive approaches (Karabel & Halsey 1977) and from there, the possible grounds for their synthesis in some of the recent structuralist and neo-Durkheimian treatments of the school as an institution.

THE SCHOOL AS A COMPLEX ORGANIZATION

Much of the organizational literature on the school appears to aim to demonstrate the negative case. Although it is granted that the coordination and administration apparatus of schools has many features of the bureaucratic ideal-type, it is agreed by most analysts that the more interesting aspects of the social structure of schools elude such a construct. Public or state schools appear moreover to be relieved from many of the more routine functions and activities by virtue of their being administered by larger units that are in the main responsible for the negotiation of salary levels, the certification and recruitment of staff, the maintenance of plant, and the procurement of resources. These are usually a far remove from the instructional activity of the school and so appear not to be of great day to day interest to teachers (Lortie 1969:35–6, Hanson 1976, 1977:31). The attractiveness of explanations of school structure that begin with the task of instruction (as characterized by the contingency model reviewed below) rather than with administrative systems and public accountability is therefore understandable. However, even this model has been rejected by many sociological and administrative theorists recently because of its poor predictive and explanatory power. The tendency to debunk any hyper-rational model of organization (Wise 1979) has led to some exciting but not yet fully realized insights into the unique features of school structure.

The Bureaucratic Model

Most of the empirical study of organization that has employed the Weberian ideal-type as an instrument of comparative analysis has indicated that bureaucracy should be conceived as a number of independently-varying dimensions rather than as a unitary construct. Schools appear to be no exception to this pattern, despite the relative paucity of empirical study. Although Bidwell could claim in fact as late as 1965 that there was "no existing study of the prevalence or incidence either of bureaucratic structures or processes in school systems" (p. 992) there have been a number of studies that are of interest. These inquiries owe a good deal to the theoretical and empirical contributions of Corwin (1968, 1970, 1975, 1981), who has done much to synthesize the administrative and the sociological perspective in the study of the school as a bureaucracy. The dominant theme of Corwin's—and of other researchers'—inquiries into bureaucratic/professional conflict at the school level has been to explore some of the insights of the Parsonian theory of organization which locates a central tension in the Weberian model between the normative demands of hierarchy and of expertise (Parsons 1947, 1956).

There are two fairly distinct methodological traditions in the study of bureaucracy and these are well represented in the research on schools. The first is the perceptual approach associated with Hall's Organizational Inventory (Hall 1963). The second is the Aston approach, which uses more descriptive, less subjective data (Pugh et al 1968). Despite their differences, each provides data to challenge the earlier postwar research that assumed bureaucracy is a unitary type, either present or absent (Gouldner 1954). Each of these methodologies attempts to capture a similar set of bureaucratic characteristics (centralization of decision-making, functional specialization, procedural specification). The Hall approach relies on the responses of subordinates (teachers) to a range of perceptual items scored as a Likert-type scale (e.g. the division of labour item is: "One thing people like around here is the variety of work"). The Aston strategy on the other hand is to obtain detailed descriptive data from a lengthy interview with the chief executive (usually the principal or headteacher). Here each aspect or dimension is measured by the presence or absence within the organization of various types of functions, documentary controls and standardized procedures and by an indication of the location in the hierarchy where a set of decisions are taken.

Empirical research supports the claim that there are two axial principles of school organization, irrespective of the methodology employed or of the tension between them. The first adaptations of the Hall Organizational Inventory to schools were carried out in Canada (MacKay 1964a, 1964b; Robinson 1966, McKague 1969). These showed that the dimensions of bureaucratic control (hierarchy of authority, presence of rules and procedural specification, and impersonality) tended to be positively intercorrelated among themselves but correlated negatively with measures of complexity (technical expertise and division of labour). Punch (1969), also using the Hall methodology, isolated two distinct factors (authority and expertise) in a sample of Canadian schools. In the United States, Hage & Aiken (1970) employed the Hall inventory as part of a wider comparative inquiry into the hypothesized effect of bureaucratic control on rates of change in several types of organization, while J. G. Anderson (1966, 1968) also carried out extensive research into innovation at the school level. Later B. D. Anderson (1973) used a modification of MacKay's scale in a sample of Canadian high schools as part of an investigation into the effects of bureaucracy on student alienation, although the factorial pattern he discerned was somewhat different from that obtained in the earlier studies.

Using a version of the Aston schedule, Kelsey (1973) undertook a comparative study of secondary schools in England and in Canada but was apparently limited in his analysis by the narrow definition of specialization in the original schedule. Heward (1975) also used a version of the Aston schedule in an inquiry into the organizational background to innovation in sample English primary and secondary schools. She found—in common with many of the replications of the original Aston study (Pugh & Hinings 1976)—that centralization was negatively related to nearly all of the main measures of bureaucratic structure. Sousa & Hoy (1981) used both methodologies in a study of fifty-two secondary schools in the United States. Their findings indicate a high degree of correlation between the two sets of measures, although the low relationship between hierarchy of authority (Hall inventory) and centralization (Aston schedule) indicates that they "clearly were not measuring the same thing" (1981:34). These researchers then carried out a principal-components analysis which yielded four factors whose interpretation was relatively straightforward: organizational control, rational specialization (accounting together for about a half of the total variance in the two sets of measures), system centralization, and formalization of routine.

The multidimensionality of measures of organizational structure in schools appears therefore to provide some support for the theoretical tradition that has attempted to modify the Weberian ideal-type in the direction suggested by Parsons, whether for professional organizations in general (e.g. Litwak 1961) or for schools in particular (Katz 1964, Bidwell 1965, Corwin 1974, Lortie 1969, 1975). Hanson (1975; 1976–1977) has reformulated the bureaucratic model to take account of some of these complexities embodied in what he calls 'Lortie's tangle'—the "several strands of hierarchical control, collegial control and autonomy" (Lortie, 1969:1). Hanson sets out a conceptual framework (the Interacting Spheres Model), which delineates two zones of influence, authority, and power that interact in a fragile and delicate balance. Because of this separation, the bureaucratic model taken by itself is held to "range from weak to inadequate as a conceptual tool in the affairs of management and analysis" (1976–1977:37). One may perhaps extend this distinction upwards as is suggested by Sousa & Hoy's factorial separation of the control apparatus within the school from the overall degree of centralization in the surrounding system. In their analysis it appeared that the loci of power "can be high within the school building or high within the educational system or high or low within both" (1981:36).

There seems to be some disagreement, however, within these analyses as to the source of the principle of separation between the two spheres of influence— power or authority. Does it lie in the collegiate norms and values of the teaching profession, in the physical separation of the teacher's workspace, or in the internal elaboration of the school system as it grows? The first of these explanations is stressed by Hanson. Limited as their sphere of influence may be, teachers do have a "degree of autonomy surrounding the conduct of affairs in the classroom, as well as the discretion to make curricular decisions within well-defined limits" (1976:37). This is one of the main sources of the tendency towards debureaucratization attributed to schools by Bidwell (1965:1012)—a normative strain between the nurturant ideology of teachers and universalistic demands of the administrative system, in addition to the more familiar source of conflict noted by Parsons (1947). In contrast with this, one could advance the contingency explanations of school organization that would follow Lortie (1964:274) in treating the physical separation of the teacher's workspace (sometimes referred to as the egg-crate model of the school) as one of the most important determinants of intraschool variation.

One cannot however rule out a third possibility, based on research into school systems, that suggests a more cautious, evolutionary explanation of the emergence of a loosely coupled professional subsystem. A study of educational innovations in school systems by Daft & Becker (1978:144) indicates that organizational complexity, the seedbed of later professional activity, is itself a 'consequence not a cause' of innovations originating in the administrative system. These researchers propose a dual core model of innovation that would indicate that the association found among professional activity, high complexity, and low centralization in many of the studies of bureaucratic structure reviewed above may be spurious and limited only to an emergent technical core that is loosely coupled both internally and externally to the administrative system. Conversely, structural innovation is most successful "when the technical core is tightly coupled to the administrative core and when authority is centralized with administrators" (Daft 1978:208). Such a conclusion would indicate that the reported multidimensionality of organizational structure could be an artefact of the level of analysis chosen (i.e. schools instead of their parent systems) and of the research design (cross-sectional rather than longitudinal). Certainly this developmental model would give another perspective on the rather disparate and often curvilinear relationships between bureaucratization and other variables such as teacher satisfaction (Moeller & Charters 1966; Musgrove 1970:104; Allison 1983:25) and level of innovation (Corwin 1975:25).

The Contingency Model of School Organization

Of the three possible explanations of the bifurcated nature of authority in schools, the one which lends itself most readily to a rigorous testing by survey methods is the contingency model, which posits a close interdependence between the task environment and patterns of administration and governance. This model has implications for the other two as well. If, in the first instance, collegiality is nothing more than a collective response to the fairly routine demands of a craft technology, then it would appear to be a rather shaky basis for claims towards professional autonomy. In the second place, the high importance that contingency theorists place on the structural imperatives arising from the task may enable the analyst to specify rather more precisely where the motor of organizational change resides; it could thereby provide an empirically testable set of causal propositions as to organizational growth and differentiation.

The contingency model, which has its origins within a technical-functionalist theory of the firm, has enjoyed a wide and continuing following in the comparative study of organizations (Lawrence & Lorsch 1967:185–210; Perrow 1972:50–91; 1973:145–76) and can be seen as a concurrent development to the multidimensional interpretation of the Weberian ideal-type. It proposes that organizational features are best explained as functional responses to the uncertainty, variability, and interconnectedness of the task environment, which is often constituted as a function of organizational size. When this environment is stable and predictable, something like the classical bureaucratic type is most appropriate (particularly for a large concern); but when the raw material that people work with is poorly understood and variable, then a more effective strategy is to delegate authority to specialists and to coordinate activities through flatter and more participatory administrative systems.

In the secondary school field the contingency approach has been used both as a theoretical foundation for programs of organizational development and innovation (Fullan 1982, Moon 1983) and as an analytical model for explaining administrative adaptation (Derr & Gabarro 1972, Tyler 1973, Hanson & Brown 1977). Researchers and commentators have consistently stressed the advantages of participatory collaborative structures, particularly in the technical core, as a response to the increased diversity of intake and the rapidity of curricular change. At the higher levels of school management, however, the case for implementing such strategies is less categorical, and the patterns of organizational change appear to be more indirect and gradual. Richardson's (1973) detailed case study of a large English comprehensive school over a period of several years, inspired by a sociotechnical systems model (which shares many features of the contingency approach but is somewhat less deterministic), provides a rich source of evidence for this more complex view of administrative response to school-wide changes in the technical core. The headteacher in this school appeared able to incorporate a participatory and consultative form of management within a strictly differentiated and hierarchical structure. This strategy indirectly reinforced the lines of command yet at the same time rendered them more responsive and supple. Such an account resonates with Perrow's hypothetical example (1972:73–4) of the process by which a traditional bureaucratic public school accepted a major innovation in the form of a new instructional unit, thereby preserving its overall stability and continuity.

If applications of the contingency model to the secondary school have tended to be partial, fragmentary, and ambiguous, the same does not hold for the research in the primary or elementary school, where applications have been rigorous, sustained, and theoretically aware. This is so not only at the classroom level (Bossert 1979; Cohen et al 1979a) but also by extension at the organizational level, largely as a result of the introduction of more informal, integrated, and pedagogically sophisticated methods associated with team teaching and the open-space classroom. The most important research in this area was carried out during the 1970s by US federal educational research and development centers at Stanford University (Meyer et al 1971; Bredo 1975, 1977; Cohen et al 1979b, 1981) and at the University of Oregon (Pellegrin 1970; Packard et al 1978; Charters & Packard 1979). These research groups both explored and tested some of the fundamental propositions of the contingency model in large samples of elementary schools over a number of years. The research design enabled these groups to determine the extent to which changes in instructional technology (teaming and open space) affected patterns of task structure (interdependence and collaboration) as well as the more general features of school administration (the degree of collegial influence, principal's style of supervision).

Although it is not possible to do justice here to the large volume of materials produced by these interrelated projects, it may be fair to say that the contingency model has met here with only patchy and qualified support. The studies each fall into two parts: the first cross-sectional surveys, which indicated that many of the hypothesized effects did take place following teaming; and the second, more painstaking and cautious longitudinal follow-up studies which showed just how fragile and impermanent instructional innovation in school can be and how indeterminate its measurable effects. Not only did it appear that "instructional interdependence tends to be transitory, emerging and disappearing in the course of school year" (Cohen 1981:172), but the content of team decisions did not accord with the high uncertainty/problem-solving orientation of the model; decisions were concerned largely with routine and mechanistic functions such as cross-grouping (Bredo 1975). Regression analyses of structural ('work and governance') variables on the more technological ones, showed rather low levels of prediction, with explained variance ranging between 20 and 50% (Charters & Packard 1979:43, Table 2). It would appear from these and associated studies that consistent and predictable changes in the organizational structure of elementary schools do not occur unless there is a high degree of teacher interdependence over a number of different task areas—an effect which appears to be reinforced by the increased visibility afforded by open-space architecture.

The School as a Loosely Coupled System

In the light of these findings it is perhaps no surprise that many researchers who were associated with contingency and Weberian models should in the 1970s have been attracted to alternative perspectives on school organization, particularly to those that provide a less determinate and rationalized picture of the school as a social system. Reviving some of Bidwell's insights into the endemic looseness of coordinative processes in school, several theorists have attempted to reconceptualize educational organization in terms more in keeping with ambiguity of goals and uncertainty of technology than with models borrowed from the study of commercial and business enterprises. There have been several varieties of this post-Weberian approach, all deceptively similar and cross-fertilizing, but in many respects epistemologically and theoretically diverse.

The first alternative to Weberian approaches to be proposed was the so-called garbage can/organized anarchy model of Cohen et al (1972), developed for colleges and universities but considered by many to be applicable to schools (Bell 1980:187; Allison 1983:17–18). In fact the term 'loose coupling' was used in this context and later extended by Weick in the seminal paper cited above as a general metaphor for research into all forms of educational organizations (1976). In this paper the concepts of rational planning and hierarchical control were rejected in favour of a model that stressed the loose connections between stable subassemblies, which Weick considers to be "the crucial elements in any organization or system" but which maintain their own identity at all times (1976:3). Meyer & Rowan (1983) have made a further contribution by using the term 'decoupling' to imply not merely the empirical responsiveness of these subassemblies to one another, but the disconnections in the theoretically-constituted elements of goals, technology, and organization—"Loose coupling implies a disconnection of bureaucratic structure from technical activity and of this activity from its effects" (Meyer & Rowan 1983:71). The forces of cohesion in educational systems in this approach are not internal but external, deriving from their collective effort to manage the "societally agreed-on rites defined in societal myths (or institutional rules) of education" (p. 76). Tight coupling exists only at the level of control over the ritual classifications, which are so important for legitimation processes in the schooled corporate society.

This rather rapid transition from contingency and functionalist theories of the school to revisionist or conflict interpretations thus exposes by implication many of the problems of the model of the school as a loosely coupled system. Although there have been some studies inspired directly or indirectly by this model (Abramowitz & Tenenbaum 1978; Hannaway & Sproull 1979; Bell 1979, 1980; Rowan 1982), it seems to have generated a good deal of confusion and is perhaps responsible to a large extent for the amorphous state of theorizing in this area. The central theoretical problem is the status of the events, units, or subassemblies that are loosely coupled. If Weick wishes to "convey the image that each loosely coupled event preserves its own identity and some evidence of its physical and logical separateness" (1976:3), then it must be asked, according to what criteria (e.g. power, authority, or expertise) is any identity to be constituted? Does the physical separateness of the buildings of a split-site school always provide a given basis for some kind of dual identity, or is it a mere administrative detail? Is the 'logical' basis of separation between subject departments to be found in the formal structure of the official statements or in the 'logic of confidence' invested in academic disciplines by public attitudes and beliefs (Meyer & Rowan, 1983:90–2).

So many difficulties arise in applying this model that it appears to be both vacuous and confusing. Nevertheless it is instructive to unravel some of the problems it raises in order to see a way ahead. Three main sources of ambiguity can be discerned in the loose-coupling literature. It will be argued that these can only be understood in terms of the functionalist theories of the school and the unresolved problems rooted in the legacy from the contingency model.

1. What kinds of environments promote loose coupling? Although the review of the innovation literature suggests that loose coupling occurs most often in the professionalized technical core of this school and would therefore be typical of the rapidly changing, even turbulent environment, Weick in a more recent paper (1980) has argued that this view is mistaken and that it is a strategy more characteristic of environments with low variability and high homogeneity. This would contrast loose coupling, as Willower (1982:94) has pointed out, with the type of environmental contexts for which the organized-anarchy model was developed, characterized by their extreme fluidity and intractability. In the terms of the sociotechnical typology of Emery & Trist (1965) in which environments are classified by their 'causal textures', one might ask whether loose coupling is promoted by the placid, randomized environment or by the more unpredictable disturbed-reactive type. This confusion permeates the literature. While some theorists of school organization have pointed out the advantages of loose coupling as a strategy for turbulent conditions (Turner 1977; Bell 1980), others such as Meyer & Rowan have stressed its advantages for maintaining stable and institutionalized relations in the sociopolitical environment. This ambiguity is probably more acute because loose coupling theorists tend to ignore or dismiss the sociotechnical and functionalist framework.

2. Does a decentralist strategy imply loose or tight coupling? Just as the question of environmental strategy brings with it difficulties, so does the classification of the internal interdependencies of the school system by the loosely coupled model. Weick's recent paper is consistent in that it considers discretion and decentralization as more typical of a tightly coupled system—as a more sophisticated organizational response demanded by greater uncertainty—but there are still problems in identifying the incidence of such tightness in the internal life of schools. If one were to follow the low-variability/low

discretion/loose-coupling causal sequence, then it would appear that the authoritarian, formalized regimes typical of the one-room schools of yesteryear are in fact more loosely coupled than the open space, informal elementary schools of today. This may be so in terms of a more general model of regulation, but it is a difficult argument to sustain within a perspective that is attempting to revise if not demolish conceptions of rationality and efficiency associated with the classical bureaucratic model.

3. What role do values play in a loosely coupled system? When one replaces a technical-rational model of school organization with one somewhat more amorphous, there is a strong possibility, following the four-function paradigm of Parsons, that societal values will become a more salient feature of subsequent functionalist explanations. Despite the full elaboration of this paradigm by Hills for public schools (1976), there still remains the difficulty within the Parsonian theory of organization of constructing a model that asserts the primacy of values (in the societal sense) over the more precisely defined, externally referenced functions that pertain to the managerial, the technical, and the institutional spheres. This difficulty fails to arise not because, as Willower (1982:93) claims, loose coupling (which refers to internal and not external relations) is a logical consequence of such functional differentiation, but rather because societal values seem to have very tenuous causal links with empirical variations in school structure. It is perhaps more useful therefore, as Dreeben (1976:871) argues, to begin with the organizational activities scheme rather than with the values-goals-functions scheme (though both are to be found in Parsons' writings on organizations); it is within these areas that most of the problematics of the distribution of authority reside. However, when the role of societal values is downgraded into the maintenance of consensually derived norms of performance and mechanisms of public accountability, it has the paradoxical consequence of producing an explanation of school structure very similar to that found in revisionist literature. From a Parsonian perspective, Dreeben sees the mechanisms of administrative control in schools in much the same terms as Meyer & Rowan. He argues that control is exercised through quasi-feudal administrative structures whose zones of authority and interest are defined in terms of administrative task, rather than by the normative elements that one might infer from a societal function such as pattern maintenance.

The rather bizarre uses by conflict theorists of the symbolic apparatus of mechanical solidarity (ritual, ceremony, myth) may therefore be explained to some extent by the normative vacuum created when functionalist theorists failed to bridge the gap between societal values on the one hand and the primitive segmentations of task and interest on the other. The Durkheimian affinity between the quasi-feudal units of school structure and the ritual classifications of certification and performance implies a pre- rather than a post-bureaucratic model of the school. Such a marriage of structure and symbol seems nevertheless to have little to do either with the models of the innovative organization that found such currency in the 1960s, with the classical statements of the school as an agent of moral regulation (Durkheim 1977), or as a central institution in a society dominated by legal-rational modes of authority (Weber 1946:240–4). Since this stream of organizational literature has led to what seems to be a theoretical impasse, it may be well to view the school not as a set of causally related functions, but rather as an emergent property of the interests, interpretations, and face-to-face interactions of its members.

THE INTERACTIVE ORDER AND SCHOOL ORGANIZATION

The conception of the school as a site where individuals and groups interact rather than as an externally-defined system of functions and activities does not necessarily detract from a sociological interest in its organizational forms. The ideographic, interactionist, and phenomenological accounts of school organization have been given forceful support in recent organizational literature (Greenfield 1975, 1980). These approaches attempt to demonstrate that, far from being a collection of segmented functions, schools are problematic and tension-ridden formations whose structural variations are best explained through the meanings, negotiations, and strategies of individual actors. The school in other words can be conceived not as a given structure but as a product of the collective and often implicit accommodations among teachers, students, and administrators (as well as of parents, supervisory personnel, and ancillary staff). This structure is far from being rock-solid. Indeed it is a rather precarious arrangement where negotiated rules and not collective rituals are the stuff of everyday social encounter and where the relationship between actions and their effects is only infrequently ambiguous or unclear from the perspective of students or teachers themselves.

It is possible in this approach to recapture the interpretative traditions so important to the Weberian perspective on organizations (King 1980). In so doing one can discover a normative system that has proven not only to be remarkably resilient but to have itself undergone some profound transformations in its patterns of involvement, communication, and control. Many of these more fundamental changes often elude the more episodic and situational type of analysis offered by an interactionist perspective and are enriched by some of the attempts at synthesis with the macro concerns of classical sociology (as discussed in the following section). The central question here however is to review recent research into the nature of the interdependence of the everyday experience of students and teachers on the one hand and the formal structures in which they find themselves on the other. Are these links, as Goffman suggests, also loosely coupled, or can one detect some greater degree of determinacy here than in the case of organizational components themselves? What is the nature of the relationship between the formal structure of the school and the motives, strategies, and actions of everyday life for teachers and students?

The dominant feature of interactionist approaches to school organization appears to be the discovery of the conflict between teachers and student; thereby they trace the roots of institutional power to the competing interests of these two groups. In Waller's important and original contribution to the sociology of school organization, mutual hostility and perpetual conflict characterize the relations between students and staff. Even the most orderly school is "a despotism in a state of perilous equilibrium" (1932:10). Bidwell claims that the matrix of forces acting on the administrative system is such as to reinforce the repressive character of the classroom and to push the social system of the school in the direction of what Gouldner (1954) calls a punishment-centered (rather than a representative) bureaucracy (1965:980). Bidwell locates Gordon's participant observation of a high school (1957) in this tradition, particularly for his evidence of classroom conflict deriving from the incompatibilities between the teacher's academic demands and those of the student culture. One way out of this dilemma for Gordon's teachers (which Bidwell sees as having the ultimate effect of debureaucratizing the authority structure of the school) was to allocate grades in order to disrupt the social structure of the student group and then to step in with affective support when students began to conform. The bureaucratic structure of the school seems therefore to be often no more than a shell in which a variety of ploys and stratagems for getting by are enacted.

Substantively, very little seems to have changed in schools since these early studies. The research of Woods (1979) within an interactionist perspective is of particular interest since it explores, in an English secondary modern school in the early 1970s, a model of student adaptation developed by Wakeford (1969) which incorporates elements both from Merton's (1957) functionalist theory of deviance and from Goffman's typology of inmate strategies in *Asylums* (1961). Student subcultures are seen by Woods to be neither pro nor anti school in the simple terms suggested by a good deal of this literature (e.g. Hargreaves, 1967) but rather in terms of their strategic adaptations to the educational bureaucracy. Woods (1979:18–19) identifies two primary paths to conformity—'instrumental compliance' and 'ritualism'; there is another which he characterizes as a form of 'secondary adjustment' typical of the nonacademic student. This is colonization, a term indirectly taken from Goffman's work on total institutions, which means 'working the system' and 'getting by'. Here there is a parallel with the Waller-Gordon tradition; in order for control to be exercised at all, many of the bureaucratic strictures have to be removed or negotiated into an operable form. The same capacity to devise strategies of coping also characterizes the teacher perspective in Woods' study. Following Becker's study of the Chicago schoolteacher in the early 1950s (1976), Woods sets out a range of possible survival strategies, only one of which comes anywhere near an officially approved definition of the teacher's role (1979:146–69).

Are school routines and procedures to be understood as instruments of collective control and domination (cf. Waller 1932:312), or do they have some consensual basis? According to Cusick, who carried out with his associates a number of remarkable participant-observer investigations into the student perspective in high schools in the United States (Cusick 1973; Cusick et al 1976), the formal structure of the school merely provides a loose structure for the containment and minimal instruction of a student body divided along the lines of race, class, and gender. Confronted with what is essentially a holding operation, administrators divide and rule. In the school studied by Cusick, a very repressive structure denied students any real power by absorbing much time in routine activities and waiting about in groups. From this perspective, conflict is managed not so much through direct hierarchical control and punishment or through collective rituals (as in Waller's schools) but rather by administrative strategies of suppression and fragmentation. The complexities, intentional or not, of these global methods of control provide some context for understanding the debureaucratizing strategies of teachers and the colonization of the system by disaffected groups of pupils.

Against the organizational model which stresses the softness of the schools' technology, its imprecision of goals, and looseness of administrative mechanisms, one could in the light of this conflict-interactionist approach discern a quite determinate model, where the room for structural variation is strictly constrained by the 'perilous equilibrium' of control. Such a model does not need be a coercive despotism, however, but can be maintained by a variety of implicit and calculative forms that have considerably greater refinement and flexibility. One such mechanism is explored by King & Ripton (1970) in a study of what they call 'collective reciprocity'. True to the interactionist tradition, these researchers questioned the consensual view of school organization and suggested instead a dynamic model of control based on a kind of contract emerging out of "the near congruency between teachers' career needs and the students' conception of education as an instrumental process" (p. 46). The dynamic of collective reciprocity in this study of Canadian high schools in the late 1960s bears a remarkable similarity to the 'primary mode' of adaptation identified by Woods; it could be usefully complemented by the latter's expansion of the interactionist model to the lower-ability groups. Another mechanism for the containment of conflict has been identified by Reynolds (1976) in the idea of 'the truce' between teachers and pupils. This implies that if teachers will not try to interfere in the expressive domain (e.g. by enforcing rules about smoking, uniforms and chewing gum) then pupils are likely to be more cooperative in the classroom, with apparently desirable effects on the school overall rates of delinquency, truancy, academic failure, and behavior.

It is however difficult to put forward a model of conflict and the strategies for its containment and dispersal in schools without taking into account the rich or even dense network of rules through which this is mediated. The systemic or even consensual aspects of the modalities of control are perhaps as important as its substantive realization in any one school. One of the consensual aspects appears to be the acute awareness of students of principles of fair play and of rule violation that do not apparently arise out of specific negotiations or contexts. Werthman's 1963 study of delinquent boys shows that even among a deviant group evaluation procedures are rigorously scrutinized and that any signs of bias were met with disruptive behavior. However much Woods' students appeared to dislike schools they appeared to operate according to their own core of institutional norms, which were constant across classrooms (1979:111). A study of 'trouble' in an English comprehensive school by Marsh et al (1978) identified a number of teacher offences deserving of retribution; the most unforgivable was when a 'soft' teacher unsuccessfully tried to assert authority (1978:38). The phenomenological study of deviance in classrooms carried out by Hargreaves et al (1975) called into question the centrality of 'role' in the interactionist and conflict framework by showing the fundamental importance of the rule system by which teachers and pupils establish order through the construction of normal behavior. At this deeper level, notwithstanding the individual and collective strategies of accommodation and of conflict resolution, one could argue that the interactive sphere is not entirely at odds with the universalistic norms of the formal bureaucratic framework, but rather it shares the same stock of taken-for-granted knowledge.

It is noteworthy that the problem of classroom order should reemerge from a tradition that initially was obsessed with strategies of control. That the functionalist concern with boundary, order, and normative consensus should emerge from the study of the minute details of rule-maintenance may not however be so surprising. When an action theorist takes an interest in rules-in-use, it almost inevitably leads to consideration of the consensual basis of common-sense knowledge in institutions, and it may even suggest that teachers and pupils experience these rules as social facts in the Durkheimian sense. Indeed Hargreaves (1979) argues that many of Durkheim's ideas on order in schools have been misunderstood by the labelling theorists who have taken a naive and superficial antifunctionalist interpretation of the notion of social pathology. In his view, egoism and anomie, if applied strictly in the Durkheimian sense, "prove to be rather unconvincing explanations of school counter-cultures or teacher-designated deviants, but are more persuasive in relation to 'indifferent' or 'instrumentalist' pupil types". In other words the 'typical' or 'primary' forms of adaptation are those most pathological or unhealthy, while the counter-school groups such as Willis' 'lads' (1977) are by no means the true deviants. Hargreaves' applications of a Durkheimian perspective resonate with Testanière's (1968, 1972) distinction between 'traditional' and 'anomic' forms of misbehavior in French secondary schools. It would seem that sociological explanations of particular instances of disruption must sooner or later come to terms with such transformations of the moral order in schools and the dislocations that these generate in the apparatus of control.

The reemergence of interest in frameworks of internal cohesion more general than those created and sustained in particular encounters does not of course resolve the very vague question as to how loosely coupled the formal and the interactive orders of the school may be. However it does suggest that the strength of any link may itself be indicative of a particular stage of institutional evolution and may be inaccessible by purely interpretative methodologies. This leads us then to consider the final and most ambitious theoretical project in the sociology of school organization—the attempt to provide a framework which synthesizes the organizational and the interactionist perspectives on the school. Although the problem of synthesis is a general one, the most notable attempt to resolve it in the sociology of the school has been that of Bernstein. In recent years also some of the followers of Foucault's theory of discourses have attempted a very similar task—to locate the hidden regulative principles of institutional transformation in terms which embrace both objectivity and subjectivity, power as well as knowledge. It will be of some interest therefore to review these two projects briefly and to suggest points of contact between them.

TOWARDS SYNTHESIS: BERNSTEIN AND FOUCAULT

One of the underlying themes of this review has been that partial insights generated by organizational models and by interactionist approaches have each proven unsatisfactory as general sociological explanations of school structure. In the first instance the recent emphasis of the first tradition on the role of ritualized and prebureaucratic elements of formal control is inadequate to deal with the dense and sophisticated, rule-based systems of regulation found in the internal life of the school. In the second place the interactionist perspective has proven to lack a sociohistorical dimension that might explain the normative transformations of school life and the cultural shifts that affect the methodologies of investigation themselves; neither of these are directly available to the consciousness of individual actors. How can these two traditions be combined to provide an understanding in greater depth of the formal patterns of control and authority in educational institutions?

Bernstein's attempt to synthesize these two levels of analysis is based on a

theory of communication that ultimately stems from the Durkheimian opposition between mechanical and organic solidarity (1977). This opposition has
been developed over the past two decades in the form of several polarities of
school types (stratified/differentiated; open/closed) or of the dominant principles of moral regulation (collection code/integrated code). As a normative or
moral response (and not a primarily adaptive one, as a Parsonian theorist might
claim) to changes in the division of labour, there has been a significant shift in
the modalities of control that characterize the socialization process in late
capitalist societies—away from visible and hierarchical forms towards invisible, indirect, and personalized forms. However, because they represent a form
of privilege associated with access to the institutions of cultural innovation and
reproduction that tend to flourish in mature and late capitalist societies, these
more ostensibly open and less coercive modalities are just as likely to be the
instrument of class repetition and of cultural domination as were the older
individualized forms of rationality that gave a cultural advantage to the prop-
ertied classes in earlier phases of capitalism.

It is not the intention here to give a detailed critique of this complex and
evolving framework (see Cherkaoui 1977, Gibson 1977), which owes as much
to Weber as it does to Durkheim, but rather to evaluate its uses as an instrument
of institutional analysis. The main advantage of Bernstein's theory of school
structure is that it liberates the Durkheimian framework from a fixation with
function, consensus, and solidarity and focuses instead on the formal features
or modalities through which power and control (roughly 'classification' and
'framing' respectively) are realized. It is therefore entirely compatible with a
conflictual and interactionist perspective (indeed the Meadian framework is
embodied in the differentiation of role options available in the more evolved
structures) and leads to a critical awareness of the regulative properties of
communication in which research traditions themselves are located.

Although the potential of this synthetic theory is enormous for providing
unique insights into the deritualization of the culture of the schools and into the
bonds between the formal and the interactive order, its empirical validation has
been fraught with some difficulty. King carried out a number of empirical tests
(1976; 1981) of Bernstein's framework in a sample of secondary schools in the
southwest of England and concluded that his results gave "only limited support
for some of the propositions of Bernstein's sociology of the school"
(1976:439). More recently Tyler (1983) has argued that King's conclusions are
premature, because the methodology employed (versions of the Aston schedule) was probably affected by the way the probabilistic features of the
principle of coding necessarily intrude into the empirically observable patterns
of association among scale items and dimensions of organizational structure.
He recommends a canonical (or latent variable) approach to the analysis of the

association between indices of classification and of framing. He demonstrates the power of this method to reveal strong and significant indices of correlation in comparative samples of work organizations. One might conclude therefore that a fair and adequate test of Bernstein's theory on school organizations has yet to be carried out.

Foucault's concern has been with the nexus between power and knowledge in the form of what he calls 'the discourse' as it is worked out in the changing technologies of practice in various institutional and disciplinary domains including the school (Foucault 1977; see Sheridan 1980 for a review of Foucault's work). A central feature of his method is to uncover the regulative principles whereby behavior is defined and normalized through microtechnologies of physical control. In the realm of school organization, this method leads not to the role of pedagogy as a vehicle of class reproduction but to the techniques of surveillance and punishment that enable institutional power to be made both diffuse and invisible. One of these methods is embodied in the architectural arrangement, devised by the English utilitarian philosopher Bentham, known as the Panopticon; it did not find wide use in its original form yet embodied an important aspect of design in prisons, schools, asylums, and factories. This building, consisting of a number of insulated chambers around a central observation tower, had the effect of inducing in the inmate "a state of conscious and permanent visibility that assures the permanent functioning of power" (Foucault 1977:201). The theory of discourse that gives rise to such practices is at the same time both specific and synthetic (in the terms of the orientations to school structure presented in the earlier sections). Popular schooling in its discursive sense is not simply an instrument of socialization nor an agent of class domination but rather a set of practices which only in certain historical instances takes on these meanings and functions. Although some authors (Musgrove 1970:55–57; Wallace 1980:137) have commented on the panopticist features of the open-space classroom, the fullest treatment of popular schooling using Foucault's 'archeological' method to discover its discursive and nondiscursive properties and transformations is that of Jones & Williamson (1979). From an analysis of early nineteenth century English schooling, these authors argue that schooling existed as means of securing public morality and of preventing crime—a practical embodiment in its architecture and structure of the two disciplines of bodily discipline and of the regulation of population science that emerged at this time.

Atkinson (1981) draws some lines of intellectual lineage between Foucault's work and that of Bernstein by placing both in the tradition of French structuralism. This is an important insight elaborated by Diaz (1984) as part of a larger project on the nature of pedagogic discourse. This author concludes that Bernstein's work can be situated in a structuralist perspective because of his attempt to isolate the fundamental patterning (or 'grammar') of the power and control by which cultural reproduction is realized; it is however more difficult to place Foucault, whose analysis is less systematic in this sense. Power in Foucault's writings is not derived from macroforces such as state and class but is its own basis and can only be approached through microsituations (Diaz, 1984, p. 11).

One important point of comparison resides in the parallels one might draw between Foucault's claim that there has been an institutional shift from traditional forms of the exercise of power from visibility towards invisibility (as say in the Panopticon), and the transition from mechanical to organic solidarity where the institutional authority is itself invisible but the objects of power (e.g. the teachers and students in the open-space classrooms, researched in the team teaching studies reviewed above) are highly visible and continually supervised (Diaz 1984: 17). There is a twist to this analogy that has not been adequately treated either by Diaz or by other commentators such as Musgrove, who in fact sees the open-space classroom as a threat to the power of assistant teachers. On the contrary, however, Bernstein's invisible pedagogy or integrated code (typical of the highly evolved form of organic solidarity) depends not on the hierarchical control of a principal or headteacher but on the internalization of abstract principles of orientation and action by teachers and students themselves. The arrangement of the various elements of these two theoretical approaches—knowledge, power, control and subject—in such a discursive transformation has yet to be explicated.

CONCLUSION

This review of attempts at theoretical synthesis would indicate an image of the school as a more tightly-coupled system than organizational and administrative approaches now suggest. The way ahead for the sociological study of the school organization therefore appears to be through a cross-fertilization of the various approaches and perspectives discussed, rather than the dismissal or rejection of any one either because of its apparent abstruseness or its lack of theoretical sophistication.

Three major themes have now appeared that have to be common to all three sections on the sociology of school organization—(a) the competition, not always clearcut, between spheres of professional activity and bureaucratic authority; (b) the dialectic between externally produced societal constraints and internal processes of differentiation and sociotechnical change; and (c) the transformation of the regulative basis of order and control away from the condensed symbolic forms such as the ceremonies and visible hierarchies familiar to Waller (1932) into more indirect and invisible modalities of control and surveillance represented by such devices as the complex timetable, the unit for disruptive students, and the permissive course option scheme. Implicit in this review therefore is an agenda for future research into the school as a social system that could direct lines of inquiry along one or more of these axes of theoretical tension. Such a redirection might serve both to reverse the polarization of research perspectives that characterizes contemporary literature on the school and to enliven and revive the central concerns of the classical sociological tradition in the organization of social reproduction.

Literature Cited

Abramowitz, S., Tennenbaum, E. 1978. *High School '77*. Washington, D.C.: National Institute of Education

Allison, D. J. 1983. Towards an improved understanding of the organizational nature of schools. *Educ. Admin. Q.* 19:7–34

Anderson, B. D. 1973. School bureaucratization and alienation from high school. *Sociol. Educ.* 46:315–34

Anderson, J. G. 1966. Bureaucratic rules: bearers of bureaucratic authority. *Educ. Admin. Q.* 2:7–34

Anderson, J. G. 1968. *Bureaucracy in Education*. Baltimore: Johns Hopkins Univ. Press

Archer, M. 1979. *Social Origins of Educational Systems*. London: Sage

Atkinson, P. 1981. Bernstein's structuralism. *Educ. Anal.* 3:85–95

Becker, H. 1976. The career of the Chicago public schoolteacher. See Hammersley and Woods, 1976, pp. 68–74

Bell, L. A. 1979. The planning of educational change in a comprehensive school. *Durham Newcastle Res. Rev.* 42:1–8

Bell, L. A. 1980. The school as an organization: A reappraisal. *Brit. J. Sociol. Educ.* 1:183–9

Bernstein, B. 1977. *Class, Codes and Control*, Vol. 3. *Towards a Theory of Educational Transmissions*. London: Routledge Kegan Paul. 2nd ed.

Bernstein, B. 1982. Codes, modalities and the process of cultural reproduction: a model. In *Cultural and Economic Reproduction in Education: Essays on Class, Ideology and the State*, pp.304–55. London: Routledge Kegan Paul

Bidwell, C. E. 1965. The school as a formal organization. In *Handbook of Organizations*, ed. J. G. March, pp. 972–1022. Chicago: Rand-McNally

Bossert, S. T. 1979. *Tasks and Social Relationships in Classrooms*. Cambridge: Cambridge Univ. Press

Bourdieu, P., Passeron, J. C. 1977. *Reproduction in Education, Society and Culture*. Transl. R. Nice. London: Sage (From French)

Bowles, S., Gintis, H. 1976. *Schooling in Capitalist America: Educational Reform and the Contradictions of Economic Life*. London: Routledge & Kegan Paul

Boyd, W. L., Crowson, R. L. 1981. The changing conception and practice of public school administration. In *Review of Research in Education*, ed. C. Berliner, 9:311–73. Washington, DC: Am. Educ. Res. Assoc.

Bredo, E. 1975. Collaborative relationships on teaching problems: implications for collegial influence, team morale and instructional practices. *Stanford University, Calif. Technical Report No. 45*

Bredo, E. 1977. Collaborative relationships among elementary school teachers. *Sociol. Educ.* 50:300–9

Charters, W. W. Jr., Packard, J. S. 1979. *Task Interdependence, Collegial Governance and Teacher Attitudes in the Multiunit Elementary School*. Eugene, OR.: Center for Educational Policy and Management

Cherkaoui, M. 1977. Bernstein and Durkheim: two theories of change in educational systems. *Harv. Educ. Rev.* 47:556–64

Cohen, E. G., Intili, J. K., Robbins, S. H. 1979a. Tasks and authority: a sociological view of classroom management. In *Classroom Management: Seventy-eighth Yearbook of the National Society for the Study of Education*, ed. D. L. Duke, 2:116–43. Chicago: Univ. Chicago Press

Cohen, E. G., Deal, T. E., Meyer, J. W., Scott, W. R. 1979b. Technology and teaming in the elementary school. *Sociology of Education* 52:20–33

Cohen, E. G. 1981. Sociology looks at team teaching. See Kerckhoff & Corwin, 1981, pp. 116–43

Cohen, M. D., March, J. G. & Olsen, J. P. 1972. A garbage can model of organizational choice. *Admin. Sci. Q.* 17:1–25

Coleman, J. S. 1966. *Equality of Educational Opportunity*. Washington, DC: US Dept. HEW

Corwin, R. G. 1968. Education and the sociology of complex organization. In *On Education—Sociological Perspectives*, ed. D. A. Hansen, J. E. Gerstl, pp. 156–223. New York: Wiley

Corwin, R. G. 1970. *Militant Professionalism:*

a *Study of Organizational Conflict in High Schools*. New York: Appleton-Century-Crofts

Corwin, R. G. 1974. Models of educational organization. In *Review of Research in Education*, ed. F. N. Kerlinger, J. B. Carroll, 2:274–95. Itasca, Ill.: Peacock

Corwin, R. G. 1975. Innovation in organizations: the case of schools. *Sociol. Educ.* 48:1–37

Corwin, R. G. 1981. Patterns of control and teacher militancy: theoretical continuities in the idea of "loose coupling". See Kerckhoff & Corwin, 1981, pp. 261–91

Cusick, P. A. 1973. *Inside High School*. New York: Holt

Cusick, P. A., Martin, W., Palonsky, S. 1976. Organizational structure and student behavior in secondary school. *J. Curr. Stud.* 8:3–14

Cuttance, P. F. 1981. Post hoc rides again: a methodological critique of "Fifteen Thousand Hours: Secondary Schools and their Effects on Children". *Qual. and Quant.* 15:315–34

Daft, R., Becker, S. W. 1978, *The Innovative Organization: Innovation Adoption in School Organization*. New York: Elsevier

Daft, R. 1978. A dual-core model of organizational innovation. *Acad. Mgmt. J.* 21:193–210

Davies, B. 1973. Organizational analysis of educational institutions. In *Knowledge, Education and Cultural Change*, ed. R. Brown, pp. 249–95. London: Tavistock

Davies, B. 1981. Schools as organizations and the organization of schooling. *Educ. Anal.* 3:47–67

Derr, C. B., Gabarro, J. J. 1972. An organizational contingency theory for education. *Educ. Admin. Quart.* 8:26–43

Diaz, M. 1984. On pedagogical discourse: Bernstein and Foucault. Unpublished manuscript, Univ. of London Inst. of Educ.

Dreeben, R. 1973. The school as a workplace. In *Second Handbook of Research Teaching*, ed. R. Travers, pp. 450–73. Chicago: Rand-McNally

Dreeben, R. 1976. The organizational structure of schools and school systems. See Loubser et al., 1976, 2:857–73

Durkheim, E. 1977. *The Evolution of Educational Thought*. Transl. P. Collins, London: Routledge & Kegan Paul. (From French)

Emery, F. E., Trist, E. L. 1965. The causal texture of organizational environments. *Human Relations*. 18:21–32

Foucault, M. 1977. *Discipline and Punish: the Birth of the Prison*. Transl. A. Sheridan. Middlesex, Eng.: Penguin (From French)

Fullan, M. 1982. *The Meaning of Educational Change*. New York: Teachers College Press

Gibson, R. 1977. Bernstein's classification and framing: a critique. *Higher Educ. Rev.* 9:23–46

Goffman, E. 1961. *Asylums*. Garden City, NY: Doubleday

Goffman, E. 1983. The interaction order. *Am. Sociol. Rev.* 48:1–17

Goldstein, H. 1981. The statistical procedures. In *Fifteen Thousand Hours a Discussion*, ed. B. Tizard et al., pp. 21–5. Univ. of London Inst. of Education

Gouldner, A. 1954. *Patterns of Industrial Bureaucracy*. New York: Free

Gordon, C. W. 1957. *The Social System of the High School*. Glencoe, Ill.: Free

Greenfield, T. B. 1975. Theory about organization: a new perspective and its implications for schools. In *Administering Education: International Challenge*, ed. M. Hughes, pp. 71–9. London: Athlone

Greenfield, T. B. 1980. The man who comes back through the door in the wall: discovering truth, discovering self, discovering organizations. *Educ. Admin. Q.* 16:41–2

Hage, J., Aiken, M. 1970. *Social Change in Complex Organizations*. New York: Random House

Hall, R. 1963. The concept of bureaucracy: an empirical assessment. *Am. J. Sociol.* 69:32–40

Hammersley, M., Woods, P., eds. 1976. *The Process of Schooling*. London: Routledge & Kegan Paul.

Hannaway, J., Sproull, L. S. 1979. Who's running the show: coordination and control in educational organizations. *Admin. Notebook* 27

Hanson, M. 1975. The modern bureaucracy and the process of change. *Educ. Admin. Q.* 11:21–36

Hanson, M. 1976–7. Beyond the bureaucratic model: a study of power and autonomy in educational decision-making. *Interchange* 7:27–38

Hanson, M., Brown, M. E. 1977. A contingency view of problem solving in schools: a case analysis. *Educ. Admin. Q.* 13:71–91

Hargreaves, D. 1967. *Social Relations in a Secondary School*. London: Routledge & Kegan Paul

Hargreaves, D., Hestor, S. K., Mellor, F. 1975. *Deviance in Classrooms*. Routledge & Kegan Paul

Hargreaves, D. 1979. Durkheim, deviance and education. In *Schools, Pupils and Deviance*, ed. L. Barton & R. Meighan, pp. 17–31. Driffield, Eng.: Nafferton

Heward, C. M. 1975. *Bureaucracy and Innovation in Schools*. PhD thesis. Univ. of Birmingham, Eng.

Hills, R. J. 1976. The public school as a type of

organization. See Loubser et al., 1976, 2:829–856

Hopper, E. ed., 1971. *Readings in the Theory of Education Systems.* London: Hutchinson

Jones, K., Williamson, K. 1979. The birth of the schoolroom. *Ideol. and Consciousness* 1:58–110

Karabel, J., Halsey, A. H., eds. 1977. Educational research: a review and an interpretation. Editors' introduction to *Power and Ideology in Education,* pp. 1–85. New York: Oxford Univ. Press

Katz, F. E. 1964. The school as a complex social organization. *Harv. Ed. Rev.* 34:428–55

Kelsey, J. G. 1973. *Conceptualization and Instrumentation for the Comparative Study of School Operation.* PhD thesis. Univ. Alberta, Edmonton

Kerckhoff, A., Corwin, R. G. eds. 1981. *Research in Sociology and Socialization: Research on Educational Organizations, Vol. 2.* Greenwich, Conn.: Jai

King, A. C., Ripton, R. A. 1970. Teachers and students: a preliminary analysis in collective reciprocity. *Can. Rev. Sociol. & Anthropol.* 7:35–48

King, R. A. 1976. Bernstein's sociology of the school: some propositions tested. *Brit. J. Sociol.* 27:430–43

King, R. A. 1980. Weberian perspectives on the sociology of the school. *Brit. J. Sociol. Educ.* 1:7–23

King, R. A. 1981. Bernstein's sociology of the school—a further testing. *Brit. J. Sociol.* 32:259–65

Lawrence, P. R., Lorsch, J. W. 1967. *Organization and Environment: Managing Differentiation and Integration.* Boston: Harvard Univ. Press

Litwak, E. 1961. Models of organization which permit conflict. *Am. J. Sociol.* 67:177–84

Lortie, D. C. 1964. The teacher and team teaching: Suggestions for long-range research. In *Team Teaching,* ed. J. T. Shapin & H. F. Olds, Jr., pp. 270–305. NY: Harper & Row

Lortie, D. C. 1969. The balance of control and autonomy in elementary school teaching. In *The Semi-Professions and their Organization,* ed. A. Etzioni, pp. 1–53. New York: Free Press

Lortie, D. C. 1975. *The Schoolteacher: a Sociological Study.* Chicago: Univ. of Chicago Press

Loubser, J. J., Baum, R. C., Effrat, A., Lidz, V. M., eds. 1976. *Explorations in General Theory in Social Science: Essays in Honor of Talcott Parsons, 2 Vols.* New York: Free

McKague, T. R. 1969. *A Study of the Relationship between School Organization and the Variables of Bureaucratization and Leader Attitudes.* PhD thesis. Univ. of Alberta, Edmonton

MacKay, D. A. 1964a. *An Empirical Study of Bureaucratic Dimensions and their Relationships to Other Characteristics of School Organization.* PhD thesis. Univ. of Alberta, Edmonton

MacKay, D. A. 1964b. Should schools be bureaucratic? *Can. Admin.* 4:5–8

March, J. G., Olsen, J. P. et al. 1976. *Ambiguity and Choice in Organizations.* Olso: Universitetsforlaget

Marsh, P., Rosser, E., Harre, R. 1978. *The Rules of Disorder.* London: Routledge & Kegan Paul

Merton, R. 1957. *Social Theory and Social Structure.* Chicago: Free

Meyer, J., Cohen, E. G., Brunetti, F., Molnar, S., Lueders-Salmon, E. 1971. The impact of the open space school upon teacher influence and autonomy. *Technical Report No. 21* Center for Res. and Dev. in Teaching, Stanford Univ., Calif.

Meyer, W., Rowan, B. 1983. The structure of educational organizations. In *Organizational Environments: Ritual and Rationality,* ed. J. W. Meyer, W. R. Scott, pp. 71–98. London: Sage

Moon, B. ed. 1983. *Comprehensive Schools: Challenge and Change.* Windsor, Eng.: NFER-Nelson

Moeller, G. H., Charters, W. W. Jr. 1966. Relation of bureaucratization to sense of power among teachers. *Admin. Sci. Q.* 10:444–55

Morgan, G. 1980. Paradigms, metaphors and puzzle-solving in organizational theory. *Admin. Sci. Q.* 25:605–22

Musgrove, F. 1970. *Patterns of Power and Authority in English Education.* London: Methuen

Noonan, R., Wold, H. 1977. NIPALS path modelling with latent variables. *Scand. J. Educ. Res.* 21:33–61

Packard, J. S., Charters, W. W. Jr., Duckworth, K., Jovick, T. G. 1978. *Management Implications of Team Teaching: Final Report.* Eugene, OR. Univ. of Oregon

Parsons, T. 1947. Introduction. In M. Weber, *The Theory of Social and Economic Organization,* pp. 3–86. Transl. A. M. Henderson, T. Parsons. New York: Free (From German)

Parsons, T. 1956. Suggestions for a sociological approach to the theory of organization. I. *Admin. Sci. Q.* 1:63–85

Peaker, G. F. 1975. *An Empirical Study of Education in Twenty-Two Countries.* Stockholm: Almqvist & Wiksell

Pellegrin, R. J. 1970. Professional satisfaction and decision making in the multiunit schools. *Technical Report No. 7.* Center for the Advanced Study of Educ. Admin., Eugene, Ore.: Univ. of Oregon

Perrow, C. 1972. *Organizational Analysis: a Sociological View*. London: Tavistock

Perrow, C. 1973. *Complex Organizations: a Critical Essay*. Glenview, Ill.: Scott, Foresman.

Pugh, D. S., Hickson, D. J., Hinings, C. R., Turner, C. 1968. Dimensions of organization structure. *Admin. Sci. Q.* 13:65–106

Pugh, D. S., Hinings, C. R. eds. 1976. *Organizational Structure: Extensions and Replications—the Aston Programme II*. Farnborough, Eng.: Saxon House

Punch, K. F. 1969. Bureaucratic structure in schools: towards a redefinition and measurement. *Educ. Admin. Q.* 5:43–57

Reimer, E. 1971. *School is Dead*. Middlesex, Eng.: Penguin

Reynolds, D. 1976. The delinquent school. See Hammersley & Woods, 1976, pp. 217–229

Reynolds, D. 1982. The search for effective schools. *School Organization* 2:215–37

Richardson, E. 1973. *The Teacher, the School and the Task of Management*. London: Heinemann

Robinson, N. 1966. *A Study of the Professional Role Orientation of Teachers and their Relationship to Bureaucratic Characteristics of School Organizations*. PhD. thesis. Univ. of Alberta, Edmonton

Rowan, B. 1982. Organizational structure and the institutional environment: The case of the public schools. *Admin. Sci. Q.* 27:259–79

Rutter, M., Maugham, B., Mortimore, P., Ouston, J., Smith, A. 1979. *Fifteen Thousand Hours: Secondary Schools and their Effects on Children*. London: Open Books

Sharp, R. 1980. *Knowledge, Ideology and the Politics of Schooling: Towards a Marxist Analysis of Education*. London: Routledge & Kegan Paul

Sheridan, A. 1980. *Michel Foucault: the Will to Truth*. London: Tavistock

Sousa, D. A., Hoy, W. K. 1981. Bureaucratic structure in schools: a refinement and synthesis in measurement. *Educ. Admin. Q.* 17:21–39

Testanière, J. 1968. Le chahut traditionnel et le chahut anomique. *Rev. Franc. Sociol.* 8:17–33 (Suppl.)

Testanière, J. 1972. Crise scolaire et revolte lyceenne. *Rev. Franc. Sociol.* 13:3–34

Turner, C. M. 1977. Organizing educational institutions as anarchies. *Educ. Admin.* 5:6–12

Tyler, W. 1973. The organizational structure of the secondary school. *Educ. Rev.* 25:223–36

Tyler, W. 1983. *Organizations, Factors and Codes: a Methodological Enquiry into Bernstein's Theory of Educational Transmissions*. PhD thesis. Univ. of Kent at Canterbury, Eng.

Wakeford, J. 1969. *The Cloistered Elite: a Sociological Analysis of the English Boarding School*. London: Macmillan

Wallace, G. 1980. The constraints of architecture on aims and organization in five middle schools. In *Middle Schools: Origins, Ideology and Practice*, ed. A. Hargreaves, L. Tickle, pp. 125–140. London: Harper & Row

Waller, W. 1932. *The Sociology of Teaching*. NY: Wiley

Weber, M. 1946. *From Max Weber: Essays in Sociology*. Transl. H. H. Gerth, C. W. Mills. New York: Oxford Univ. Press. (From German)

Weick, K. 1976. Educational organizations as loosely coupled systems. *Admin. Sci. Q.* 21:1–19

Weick, K. 1980. Loosely coupled systems: relaxed meanings and thick interpretations. Unpublished manuscript, Cornell University, Ithaca, NY

Werthman, C. 1963. Delinquents in school: a test for the legitimacy of authority. *Berkeley J. Sociol.* 8:39–60

Willower, D. J. 1982. School organizations: perspectives in juxtaposition. *Educ. Admin. Q.* 18:89–110

Willis, P. 1977. *Learning to Labour*. Farnborough: Saxon House.

Wise, A. 1979. Why educational policies often fail; the hyper-rationalization hypothesis. *J. Curr. Stud.* 9:43–5

Woods, P. 1979. *The Divided School*. London: Routledge & Kegan Paul

Woods, P. 1983. *Sociology and the School: an Interactionist Viewpoint*. London: Routledge & Kegan Paul

Ann. Rev. Sociol. 1985. 11:75–91

THE IMPACT OF SCHOOL DESEGREGATION:
A Situational Analysis

Douglas Longshore

US General Accounting Office, Washington, DC

Jeffrey Prager

Department of Sociology, University of California, Los Angeles, California 90024, and Institute for Advanced Study, Princeton, New Jersey 08540

Abstract

The effects of school desegregation will become clearer as we develop a more comprehensive awareness of variability in the desegregation "situation." In this paper, we distinguish three dimensions of a situational analysis: macro/micro, objective/subjective, and proximal/distal. We use these dimensions to evaluate the research on students' academic achievement, self-esteem, and intergroup relations, identifying points along each dimension where research seems well advanced and points where more research is needed.

INTRODUCTION

Desegregation research has suffered because it is atheoretical. The preponderant concern has been with the impact of desegregation. But without sound theoretical guidelines research produces no consensus on how to conceptualize either desegregation itself or its possible effects on achievement, self-esteem, and other variables. For this reason, many commentators have suggested that research move away from the preoccupation with effects and concentrate instead on the desegregation process. There is a pressing need, they argue, to conceptualize and take into account variability in the desegregation "situation" (e.g. Cohen 1975, Hawley & Rist 1975, Longshore 1982a, Prager et al 1986, Schofield 1978, Stephan 1978). In our view, if we could comprehend theoreti-

0360-0572/85/0815-0075$02.00

cally the parameters of the situation, we would be closer to understanding what we mean by desegregation and why it has been successful in some settings but not in others.[1] To demonstrate this point, we offer in this paper a situational analysis of research on three outcomes—academic achievement, self-esteem, and intergroup relations.

THE SITUATION IN SOCIAL SCIENCE

Our need to comprehend variability in the desegregation situation derives from a more general failure among social scientists to acknowledge the *situation* as an arena for social action. The situation has a long history in the fields of sociology, social psychology, and psychology, but only recently has it been the object of renewed interest (e.g. see Magnusson 1981). Yet no other concept seems better suited to provide clarity and insight to disparate approaches in the study of school desegregation.

To speak of the situation is to acknowledge that behavior is a product of a particular field of action with its own unique qualities. Lewin's (1935) field theory, heavily influenced by Gestalt psychologists, viewed the person and the environment as parts of a single field. Rather than observing the person as a separate entity, divorced from the field, Lewin argued that one should study individuals in their field of forces—in a group and in light of their roles within the group. However, field theory cannot fully satisfy a sociologist's interest, one concerned more with identifying the situational features relevant to an analysis than with understanding the cognitive and perceptual processes of individuals.

Yinger, a sociologist sympathetic to field theory, has argued that behavior must be conceived as simultaneously situational and personal. His approach would focus on individual behavior in its social context and would, therefore, incorporate both psychological and sociological factors. To neglect either, Yinger insists, leads to less accurate predictions of individual behavior. "A person's perceptions are a function not only of his sensitivities but also of the available stimuli, many of them derived from culture and social structure" (Yinger 1963:583).

From a somewhat different angle, symbolic interactionism also points to the significance of situational analysis. Blumer (1969), for example, is sharply critical of analyses that treat social structure, cultural norms, and the like as determinants of social action. At the same time, he insists that those exogenous

---

[1]This approach also guided the development of original articles on theory and methods in school desegregation research (Prager et al 1986) for a project funded by the National Institute of Education (Contract 400-80-0039). The situational theme for that project was conceived by Melvin Seeman, and we gratefully acknowledge his guidance.

variables are not irrelevant to understanding social processes but are mediated through a collective definition within settings. To take another example, Turner's (1970) role theory argues that cooperative action is more likely when actors share a similar repertoire of roles and can define one another's behavior in terms of that shared repertoire. Glaser & Strauss's (1964) discussion of awareness contexts and Scheff's (1967, 1970) work on consensus, while not focusing on role repertoires, examine how different distributions of information can generate situations characterized by varying levels of consensus.

This attention to the situation represents a general appreciation of the variability and significance of context. Yet the fact remains that, certainly with respect to desegregation studies, the situation has not been accorded the theoretical centrality it needs if we are to understand and predict outcomes. In this paper, we consider school desegregation research with the situation as our focal point. In our view, it is important to appreciate and make vivid the fact that, regardless of theoretical orientation, outcomes are a function of the variation in context and process that occurs in the real world. We offer the situation less as a theory of outcomes than as an insistence that causality cannot be established without identifying the conditions that bring it to life.

If no single theoretical perspective will do, what are the dimensions of a situational analysis? We suggest an approach that takes cognizance of three dimensions: macro/micro, objective/subjective, and proximal/distal. First, the chasm between macro and micro orientations is wide, and there is little evidence of convergence. Large-scale studies, with aggregated data from metropolitan, state, or even national sources, are seldom linked explicitly with micro experimental or ethnographic studies of single classrooms or schools. Nor are findings compared across levels of analysis—individual to classroom to school. But, adopting a situational approach, we propose attention to the contextual and process variables that define desegregation situations in both macro and micro terms.

Likewise, the situational approach serves to reconcile studies concerned with the objective world of institutional constraints and those concerned with the subjective world of "meaning making." The consequentiality of either one cannot be understood apart from the other. For example, as Rosenberg notes, sample surveys treat each member of the sample as an isolated atom, unconnected with other members of the sample. This overlooks the fact that objective demographic variables can have different meanings in different contexts. "It may be a very different experience to be black in a white context than to be black in a black context, to be rich in a rich context than to be rich in a poor context, to be Hispanic in an Hispanic context or an Anglo context, etc." (Rosenberg 1986).

Finally, explanations that view social events distally remain sharply counterposed to the more proximal phenomenological orientation of some research.

Distal variables like folkways or community climate extend our perspective, but often they seem only weakly related to day-to-day behavior. On the other hand, if we focus on more proximal variables because they seem more salient, we will miss the distal elements that give experience its full meaning and that may, under some conditions, become quite salient for people after all.

These dimensions of the situation, as it is broadly conceived in social science, provide a useful structure for reviewing the outcomes of school desegregation. By locating studies within these parameters, we can develop a more systematic picture of what we know and do not know about desegregation. By emphasizing the situational variability of outcomes, we also bypass the factional debates over whether desegregation per se does or does not show some measurable impact.

THE IMPACT OF SCHOOL DESEGREGATION

Several reviews of desegregation research (Epps 1981, Prager et al 1986, St. John 1975, Stephan 1978) report weak and inconsistent effects on student achievement, self-esteem, and intergroup relations—the outcomes of perennial interest since *Brown*. For this reason, as we have noted, reviewers argue that future work should be more situational, i.e. should pay attention to the contextual and process variables that characterize particular desegregated settings. Some scholars have proposed lists of variables that seem to operate as key situational features of desegregated settings and should therefore be included in future research (e.g. Hawley & Rist 1975, Schofield 1978). Empirical findings can tell us what variables to add to, or delete from, our lists. We can also catalogue positive and negative outcomes under conditions representing various combinations of these variables. But such lists do not promise a systematic awareness of situational variability. The approach is inductive, and we can never be sure we have found all the important variables.

Some studies have been guided explicitly by models in which variation in the desegregation situation is conceptualized as a set of antecedent or intervening variables that produce direct, indirect, and/or interactive effects. Ogbu's (1986) macro-level model posits job ceilings and other factors as determinants of a minority group's response to desegregation. In studies of cooperative learning, Webb (1982) and Johnson et al (1983) have formulated micro-level models for the effects of several variables (e.g. on-task behavior and goal interdependence) on achievement and intergroup relations. Such models are more productive than mere lists, since models postulate causal chains for particular outcomes at particular levels of analysis. But even this approach does not necessarily fill out the parameters of a situational analysis. Those cited above apply to one level of aggregation, excluding contextual features and processes that may predict the same outcome at others. Of course, models can include macro and micro variables, with distal and proximal, objective and subjective variables as well (e.g. Blalock 1986). But such models are difficult to conceptualize and to test empirically, since they incorporate such disparate sorts of data. Recognizing that "meticulous research on a few variables is preferable to sloppy research on many" (Longshore 1982a), we have relied instead on models incorporating only some variables, usually within a single theoretical framework and at a single level of analysis. For these reasons, even the use of causal models has not fully explicated the important dimensions of the desegregation situation.

Our strategy is to review the empirical desegregation research along the macro/micro, proximal/distal, and objective/subjective dimensions. Using this strategy, we can assess more systematically the research on school desegregation. For instance, explicit attention to the objective/subjective dimension reminds us to look both for direct effects of objective variables and for effects mediated by subjective perceptions. The proximal/distal dimension reminds us that distal variables may not predict outcomes in some micro or subjective models but may still loom large in macro or objective models. In this review, we first offer an interpretive summary of the research, citing contextual and process variables relevant to each outcome. We include some research on topics other than desegregation (e.g. tracking and cooperative learning), since that research helps to account for the effects of desegregation itself. We then evaluate outcomes in situational terms and identify points along each dimension where research seems well advanced and points where research is sorely needed.

Achievement

Studies of desegregation have turned up more positive than negative effects on minority achievement and, in general, no effect on white achievement (Crain & Mahard 1978, St. John 1975). But according to major literature reviews, methodological problems render many studies worthless (Bradley & Bradley 1977, St. John 1975). In two recent meta-analyses, Crain & Mahard (1981, 1983) sorted studies by their methodological quality and found that better research on minority achievement is more likely to turn up positive results. Black achievement seems most enhanced when desegregation occurs at the earliest grades. Their 1981 meta-analysis suggests two contextual features of desegregated schools that may enhance achievement. First, desegregation plans with a metropolitan scope show greater black achievement gains, perhaps because metro plans reach more middle-class whites and desegregation is therefore socioeconomic as well as racial, or because metro plans assign more blacks to high-quality suburban schools. Second, black achievement improves most when blacks are in schools that are mostly white. Again, the socioeconomic mix is probably more thorough in such schools.

But why should desegregation across socioeconomic status (SES) be important? The answer depends partly on in-school processes that seem related to
minority achievement. These include the lateral transmission of values and
staff expectations. According to some research (e.g. Coleman et al 1966,
Lewis & St. John 1974), desegregation boosts minority achievement because
acceptance by higher-SES whites facilitates the transmission of their proachievement values and skills. More recent research has found that white
acceptance is not necessarily higher for minority students whose achievement
improves with desegregation (Gerard & Miller 1975, Miller 1981, Patchen
1982). Of course, desegregation does not generally improve intergroup relations, and when it does, intergroup ties usually remain superficial and tentative
(see below). But a large body of research on cooperative learning suggests that
desegregation can, under certain conditions, produce more intimate and lasting
cross-race acceptance. When students work together in small mixed-race
groups, they are more likely to help each other and less likely to feel threatened
socially by other-race students. Whites and nonwhites also do better on subsequent measures of achievement (Johnson & Johnson 1975, Rosenholtz &
Wilson 1980, Slavin 1978a,b, Webb 1982). Johnson et al's (1980) research has
demonstrated further that high-ability students do not simply provide answers
to other students. Regardless of ability, students learn superior problem-
solving skills in small groups.

Another process that affects achievement involves the staff expectations for
different SES levels and racial groups. These expectations apparently impinge
on track placement decisions and teacher/student interaction. Expectations are
not necessarily unrealistic or biased (e.g. see Natriello & Dornbusch 1983), but
they can sustain an achievement gap that might otherwise be narrowed (Cooper
1979, Luge & Hoge 1978). First, placement in a noncollege track restricts
student access to peers with superior learning skills and reduces student
exposure to multitask classroom organization—conditions that tend to restrict
achievement (Bossert 1979, Karweit & Hansell 1983). Second, teachers seem
to use praise for different purposes, depending on students' race or ability.
With high-ability and white students, teachers use praise to reward academic
effort; with low-ability and nonwhite students, teachers use it to reward quiet,
passive behavior, whether students are on task or not (Cooper 1979, Massey et
al 1975, Harvey 1980).

How are these patterns related to the effect of desegregation? First, tracking
is a structural feature of a school and can vary across schools (Karweit &
Hansell 1983). Placement of students in college and noncollege tracks depends
on the number of slots available in each track and each student's relative
position in the pool of applicants for these slots. In turn, the number of available
slots depends on the presence of qualified teachers and community pressure for
college-preparatory education (Sorensen 1978). Desegregated schools often

have better qualified teachers (Gifford 1978, McIntire et al 1982) and, on the average, get more community pressure for college-track education than do segregated minority schools. Thus, more college-track slots may be available for nonwhites in many desegregated schools. Second, if some teacher behaviors are directed at the class as a whole, teachers with more white or high-ability students will communicate higher standards and provide more praise for time on task—actions that shape the behavior of minority as well as white classmates (Veldman & Sanford 1984). Hawley (1981) reports that teachers in desegregated classrooms are in fact more demanding of, and more responsive to, minority students than teachers in segregated schools (see also Crain 1978). These two processes may also help to account for the importance of SES implied by the contextual factors cited above—metro desegregation and school racial composition. Minority students in classrooms with more high-SES peers may acquire skills and experience patterns of interaction with the teacher that enhance achievement.

MACRO/MICRO   First, we clearly need more macro-level research on achievement. Much of the empirical work on curricular tracking is at the individual level, i.e. track placement is analyzed as an attribute of individual students (Karweit & Hansell 1983). But, as noted above, placement also depends on structural features of schools, which in turn depend on resources and community pressure. The opportunity for college-track placement may also vary at the district level (Alexander & Cook 1982:631n). Yet we know little about variation at these higher levels of analysis or about how desegregation affects tracking at any level.

Similarly, if certain teacher/student interaction styles enhance minority achievement, we need research beyond the individual level. Many studies on teacher praise and criticism record discrete interactions between teacher and students and then aggregate by race or ability (e.g. Gay 1975, Jackson & Cosca 1974, Massey et al 1975). Some studies have aggregated discrete interactions to the classroom level and correlated those with class-level racial composition or ability (e.g. Harvey 1980, Cooper 1979, Martin et al 1980). But we also need research on teacher/*class* interaction, to find out whether the effect of desegregation on minority achievement operates at least partly through teachers' higher expectations for, and responsiveness to, desegregated classes over minority classes.

PROXIMAL/DISTAL   Research on cooperative learning provides our most detailed analyses of proximal variables' effect on achievement. As noted, students in cooperative groups more often help each other with academic tasks, but the effect does not rest solely on the transfer of information from high- to low-ability students. Webb (1980) has found that students who give more explanations for a task show higher achievement than those who give fewer, even with ability held constant. Receiving help from peers seems to improve achievement only when students actually ask for help and get an explanation of the task, not simply the solution (Webb 1982). Working further toward the conditions under which cooperative groups enhance achievement, Perret-Clermont (1982) has reported favorable effects when students are just beginning to grasp the concepts required for mastery of an assigned task. Error and disagreement in the group (arising because students have different bits of relevant information or different skill levels) lead to "cognitive restructuring" among students at all skill levels and ultimately to their "discovery of the logic of a concept" (1982:112). In short, we seem to be getting a good grasp on the more proximal factors affecting achievement in small groups.

Research suggests the importance of more distal factors as well. Track placement seems contingent on individual and school characteristics quite distinct from these more proximal effects. Alexander & Cook (1982) found that high school track placement is due mainly to demonstrated ability but argued that ability may itself be a function of more distal variables, namely, teacher behavior and tracking decisions in earlier grades (see also Eder 1981, Haller & Davis 1981).

More generally, Ogbu (1974, 1978) has argued that job ceilings imposed on some groups foster school policies (such as tracking) and a particular "folk epistemology" regarding the value of school among group members. Suttles (1986), in a less structural but still distal approach, notes that culturally based "myths of national membership" regarding the group's right to inclusion and esteem affect real and perceived prospects for academic success. These complementary views both represent a claim for the importance of variables more removed from the day-to-day experience of students. Yet direct connections can be drawn between distal factors such as these and the more proximal ones. Proximal tracking decisions and teacher behavior are in part a response to student racial and SES characteristics and to actual student behavior. These decisions and behaviors are themselves a response to more distal group-specific epistemologies and expectations. If, during the early school years, these causal sequences are set in motion, later events (e.g. less minority persistence, higher dropout rates) sustain and justify educational outcomes (see Evertson et al 1980, Brophy & Good 1970, Martin et al 1980). Teachers in low-ability and noncollege-track classrooms will show less warmth to their students, make less rigorous demands, and keep class activities highly structured (Hansell & Karweit 1983, Metz 1978, Miller 1983)—all of which restrict achievement. To the extent that desegregation reverses or at least weakens these connections, minority achievement improves.

OBJECTIVE/SUBJECTIVE   Some inconsistencies in the literature on teacher behavior may be due to differences between objective and subjective measures.

Teachers often report that expectations do not influence their behavior toward students, but Mangold (unpublished, cited in Gay 1975) collected both observations and teachers' self-reports. Teachers said their behavior was the same toward white and black pupils, but observers found that whites received more praise and more opportunities for sustained interaction with teachers. Moreover, we do not know whether students respond more to absolute frequencies of teacher behavior or to frequencies relative to other students in the room. Martin et al (1980) reported that the relative frequency of opportunities to interact with the teacher predicted student achievement; the absolute frequency did not. But do students respond similarly to the relative frequency of praise for academic work, praise for proper behavior, criticism, and so on? If so, we may have here a direct link to folk epistemologies and "myths" of exclusion. Relative frequencies favoring whites would confirm minority expectations for opportunity within mainstream institutions. More equitable frequencies might lead minority pupils to revise their expectations and efforts upward, and thus set in motion a causal sequence likely to raise achievement.

Finally, we need more research on the subjective aspects of track placement in desegregated schools. Dimaggio (1982) has found that students' "cultural capital" (interest in symbolic-status pursuits such as art and classical music) predicts track placement, apart from SES. Others have argued that tracking creates a consciousness among students—a set of aspirations, habits, and dispositions that widens the difference across tracks (Coser 1975, Persell 1977). Are these subjective predictors and subjective outcomes of tracking implicated in the positive effects of desegregation on minority achievement? On the other hand, since cooperative learning groups seem to promote closer contact and reduce social threat, use of these groups in the early school years may create certain subjective realities that undercut later class- and race-linked tracking decisions by spreading the cultural capital around or by raising proachievement skills and aspirations.

Self-Esteem

Findings on the relationship between desegregation and self-esteem are so inconsistent that no overall conclusion can be drawn. Based on her review, St. John (1975) believes that desegregation may actually have harmed minority self-esteem, especially academic self-esteem (see also Miller 1983). But Weinberg (1977) reported more favorable than unfavorable effects. And Epps (1978, 1981) preferred not to generalize at all.

Results from cooperative learning groups suggest that, as with achievement, desegregation under certain conditions can enhance the self-esteem of white and minority students. Aronson et al (1978) have described favorable effects on general and academic self-esteem, for blacks, Hispanics, and whites. From their review, Johnson et al (1983) concluded that cooperative groups promote self-esteem, perhaps with peer acceptance as the intervening factor. Sharan

(1980) has added that increased self-esteem may result when students serve as a valuable learning resource for others.

MACRO/MICRO   Much of our research on self-esteem, especially the research showing a favorable impact of desegregation, is at the micro level. The intervening processes may be peer acceptance, achievement, and success in the role of learning resource for the group. But these possibilities have not been tested.

A more macro view will have to incorporate the effects of tracking on self-esteem. Placement in noncollege tracks is said to stigmatize pupils and lower their self-esteem (Karweit & Hansell 1983). Yet Ogbu reminds us that folk epistemologies can include system blame, or his words "a sense of enduring collective institutionalized discrimination" (Ogbu 1986), and this may forestall any negative effect on self-esteem. Outside cooperative groups, we do not know the conditions under which desegregation raises or lowers self-esteem among either white or minority children.

PROXIMAL/DISTAL   The difficulty of isolating the effects of desegregation itself becomes clear when we view the research along this dimension. Rosenberg (1986) has traced much of the confusion to neglect of a more proximal "child's-eye view." Self-esteem is a consequence of reflected appraisals, i.e. the reactions of significant others. But, as Rosenberg puts it, "some others are more significant than other others." For nonwhites, as for whites, the most significant others are "mostly or exclusively" same-race (see also Epps 1981, Hare 1980, Taylor & Walsh 1979). For this reason, desegregation is unlikely to produce dramatic effects on self-esteem. Yet some studies suggest that desegregation may damage minority self-esteem. If it does, the preponderance of same-race significant others may not offset entirely the negative impact of minority exposure to whites. On the other hand, with cooperative learning, desegregation enhances minority and white self-esteem. Apparently, in these groups, distal others somehow have a positive effect.

A more distal view also emerges in Crain et al's (1982) finding that greater controversy in the early stages of desegregation is associated with higher academic self-esteem among black students a few years later. To explain this, Crain et al noted that controversy spurred considerable local civil rights activity and that successful activity enhanced racial pride. Consequently, "it is not surprising that academic self-esteem should be high when racial pride is high" (Crain et al 1982:151). The argument is plausible, but further research should trace the causal sequence more carefully, identifying links between this quite distal predictor and blacks' self-esteem some years later.

OBJECTIVE/SUBJECTIVE   Rosenberg (1986) has argued that social science mistakenly views desegregation symbolically, rather than experientially. Segregation symbolizes stigma and rejection; desegregation, equality and acceptance. Yet "the concrete experience of segregated living" is not filled with inferiority and rejection. Similarly, social science takes attitudes toward one's race as a symbol of attitudes toward one's self. But subjectively, these attitudes are scarcely related at all (Rosenberg 1979, Cross 1978). "This does not mean that race is not important to the child—it is—but many other features of the self are of equal or greater importance in determining the child's feelings of self-worth" (Rosenberg 1986; see also Pettigrew 1978).

The need for a subjective view is apparent also in the research linking academic self-esteem and ability to general self-esteem. For middle-class whites, those links may be fairly strong. But peer acceptance, social skills, and the ability to assume adult roles may contribute more to the general self-esteem of minority children and lower-class whites (Hare 1977, 1980).

Intergroup Relations

Like that on self-esteem, research on intergroup relations does not support a general conclusion on the effect of desegregation (see reviews by St. John 1975, Schofield 1978, Stephan 1978). Findings become more clear when certain contextual and process variables are identified. Following Allport (1954), we can classify these by the elements in contact theory they seem to represent: equal-status contact, norms favorable to intergroup relations, close cross-race exposure, the presence of individuals who counteract racial stereotypes, and task interdependence.

The status of various groups in desegregated schools may be partly a function of contextual features like racial composition and SES. Some studies have suggested that equal racial proportions are conducive to intergroup relations (e.g. Gottlieb & Ten Houten 1965, St. John & Lewis 1975), but these were based on very few schools. Other studies, based on Southern or nationwide school samples, have found intergroup relations least favorable in racially balanced schools (Bullock 1976, Crain et al 1982, Longshore 1982b,c). The interpretation of these results assumes that students form a sense of turf or control at school (Suttles 1968). When proportions are roughly equal, the issue of control remains salient and disruptive.

Another possible contextual source of status in school is SES. When minority and white students are more similar in SES, intergroup relations can be better (Rosenfield et al 1981, St. John & Lewis 1971). But Patchen (1982) found no relationship between SES similarity and intergroup relations. And in Iadicola's (1980) research, when white and Hispanic SES levels were more similar, Hispanics' intergroup attitudes were less favorable, reportedly because Hispanics felt less pressure to assimilate.

In schools where principal and teacher norms are supportive, student intergroup relations are better (Crain et al 1982, Gerard & Miller 1975, St. John & Lewis 1975). What specific behaviors are at work here? Teacher warmth (pleasant interaction, acceptance) seems positively related to intergroup relations (Serow & Solomon 1979), as does teacher fairness as perceived by students (Patchen 1982, St. John 1975).

Evidence on three other contact conditions—task interdependence, close exposure, and the breakdown of stereotypes—appears in the literature on cooperative learning. Task interdependence is of course the essence of cooperative groups. Students in such groups develop more friendships across racial and ability groups (Bossert 1979, Hallinan 1976, Johnson et al 1983, Slavin & Hansell 1983). Moreover, friendships appear stronger, i.e. more intimate and lasting (Hansell & Slavin 1981), and the small-group experience seems to generalize, leading to more cross-race friendships outside the group as well (Lazarowitz et al 1980, Markovsky et al 1984, Ryan & Wheeler 1977, Slavin & Hansell 1983). Finally, while there is no direct evidence that cooperative groups undercut racial stereotypes, that linkage seems plausible. Cooperative groups enable students to develop and display a wider range of cognitive and social skills than is possible in most traditional classrooms, and where achievement disparities do exist they are less obvious (Rosenholtz & Wilson 1980).

Cooperative learning seems to set up equal-status contact and favorable intergroup norms as well. Cohen (1982) has argued that racial contact will not be equal-status unless group members' expectations for racial differences in ability are deliberately reversed. But in some cooperative learning arrangements, students can contribute equally to the group score, regardless of their ability. Since cooperative groups do promote favorable intergroup relations, this method of equalizing status appears strong enough to generate some success. Cooperative groups also "clearly legitimize positive interracial contact" (Slavin & Hansell 1983:109). Direct research on this claim is scanty. But Morris (unpublished, cited in Cohen 1982) found that prior exposure to norms for friendly interaction (listening to others, giving everyone a chance to talk) equalized actual rates of interaction in cooperative groups.

MACRO/MICRO   At the macro level, we have some indication that favorable staff norms promote intergroup relations among students. But the macro research on equal-status contact is quite inconsistent. Neither racial composition nor SES has shown a clear pattern of association with student intergroup outcomes. We can say only this: Intergroup relations are not necessarily better when SES or racial proportions are equal, and they may actually be worse.

At a more micro level, all five of Allport's contact conditions are approached in cooperative groups. White and minority students in such groups consistently show gains in intergroup ties, including stronger and more lasting ones. The most pressing need may be for research on intervening variables, i.e. research linking macro context variables to intergroup outcomes and linking micro intergroup processes to overall school-level outcomes. If racial composition or SES does affect intergroup relations under some conditions, we must trace the processes by which that occurs. If elements of folk epistemologies or "myths" of exclusion vary across racial/ethnic groups or schools, we need to trace the processes through which those beliefs are acted out or, in schools with a favorable intergroup climate, revised. Similarly, we have some evidence that small-group experiences generalize, but we need to explore the social and cognitive processes by which mere acquaintances develop closer ties despite having no first-hand cooperative contact.

PROXIMAL/DISTAL   When we evaluate the research along this dimension, one problem with assessing the impact of equal-status contact becomes clear. Racial composition and SES are more distal proxies for in-school status. Quite possibly, these variables are inconsistent predictors of intergroup relations because they are not particularly salient for students in many schools. But while the effect of racial composition is inconsistent, the effect of race itself is not. Perhaps, above the individual level of analysis, race does not represent status for students (see below). Or perhaps it is a more salient variable in face-to-face interaction than as a feature of school context.

Staff norms are another relatively distal element of school context, yet norms do seem to have consistent effects on student intergroup relations. Evidently the school climate is favorable when teachers are more supportive and fair with students. Similar processes seem at work in small groups, enhanced by the cooperative nature of group tasks. It seems safe to conclude that school climate, in both a distal and a more proximal sense, is important to student intergroup relations.

OBJECTIVE/SUBJECTIVE   Effects of cooperative groups have been assessed both subjectively and objectively. Most studies have relied on sociometric self-reports to measure intergroup outcomes, but Johnson & Johnson's (1981) positive findings were based on actual observation. Interaction was "aimed at supporting and regulating efforts to learn and ensuring that everyone was actively involved in the group's work" (Johnson et al 1983:32).

Attention to the objective/subjective dimension also pinpoints another problem with macro equal-status variables. Social scientists have viewed status objectively, as a function of symbolic variables like racial composition. But from Rosenberg's child's-eye view, school racial composition may have little to do with status and more to do with power. Intergroup relations vary across schools in ways quite consistent with a conceptualization of racial composition as a resource for claiming turf (Longshore 1982b,c, 1984). So our problem is not just with the level of analysis or with the more distal quality of racial composition. Instead, we may be mistaken in assuming that the subjective meaning of equal proportions is equal status (see also Robinson & Preston 1976).

CONCLUSION

Most striking is the consistently favorable impact of cooperative learning. This technique seems to promote conditions (e.g. equal-status contact, favorable norms) otherwise very difficult to achieve in desegregated schools (see Cohen 1975, Schofield 1982, Scherer & Slawski 1979). Considerable research shows that, under these conditions, desegregation does improve achievement, self-esteem, and intergroup relations for both minority and white children.

Beyond these empirical results, our review also identified parameters for a situational analysis. The purpose was to distinguish, in a systematic way, what we do and do not know about the desegregation situation. Along the macro/ micro dimension, micro research suggested that the favorable impact of desegregation on achievement may be due to teachers' expectations and, at least in cooperative groups, to a transmission of pro achievement values and skills. But our review suggested that more macro research is needed on teacher behavior toward the class as a whole. We also need more macro research on track placement—the circumstances under which desegregation raises the number of college-track slots for minority students, and the processes by which tracking affects self-esteem. Research on intergroup relations requires attention at both levels—the relevance of race and SES at the macro level, and the micro processes by which the experience in cooperative groups generalizes to peers outside one's group.

Along the proximal/distal dimension, we have a fairly good sense for the proximal (small-group) experiences affecting achievement. We also know that more distal variables (e.g. past community controversy, school climate, other-race peers) can affect outcomes, yet we know very little about the processes underlying these effects. Finally, attention to the objective/subjective dimension revealed differences between self-reports and observations. But we cannot simply rely on objective data. This review highlighted issues for which a subjective viewpoint would contribute much—how do students react to relative frequencies of teacher behavior in its different aspects, what are the relevant components of self-esteem for various racial and SES groups, and what is the subjective meaning of more distal variables like race and track placement?

We have quite deliberately reached across theoretical lines and academic disciplines to define and demonstrate the usefulness of a situational analysis. While we cannot know what future issues may arise, we believe it will be easier to recognize them, develop applicable models, and evaluate findings if we maintain sensitivity to the parameters of the desegregation situation. A situational approach will help us develop a more subtle and comprehensive appreciation of the conditions that define the experience of students and staff in desegregated schools.

Literature Cited

Alexander, K. L., Cook, M. A. 1982. Curricula and coursework: a surprise ending. *Am. Sociol. Rev.* 47:626–40

Allport, G. W. 1954. *The Nature of Prejudice*. Boston: Addison-Wesley

Aronson, E., Bridgeman, D. L., Geffner, R. 1978. Interdependent interactions and prosocial behavior. *J. Res. Dev. Educ.* 12:16–27

Blalock, H. M. 1985. A model for racial contact in schools. See Prager et al 1986

Blumer, H. 1969. *Symbolic Interaction*. Englewood Cliffs: Prentice-Hall

Bossert, S. T. 1979. *Tasks and Social Relationships in Classrooms*. New York: Cambridge Univ. Press

Bradley, L., Bradley, G. 1977. The academic achievement of black students in desegregated schools. *Rev. Educ. Res.* 47:399–449

Brophy, J. E., Good, T. L. 1979. Teachers' communication of differential expectations for children's classroom performance. *J. Educ. Psychol.* 61:365–74

Bullock, C. S. 1976. Interracial contact and student prejudice. *Youth Soc.* 7:271–309

Cohen, E. 1975. The effects of desegregation on race relations. *Law Contemp. Probl.* 39:271–299

Cohen, E. 1982. Expectation states and interracial interaction in school settings. In *Ann. Rev. Sociol.* 8:209–35

Coleman, J. S., Campbell, E. Q., Hobson, C. J., McPartland, J., Mood, A. M., et al. 1966. *Equality of Educational Opportunity*. Washington, DC: US GPO

Cooper, H. M. 1979. Pygmalion grows up: a model for teacher expectation communication and performance influence. *Rev. Educ. Res.* 49:389–410

Coser, R. 1975. The complexity of roles as a seedbed of individual autonomy. In *The Idea of Social Structure*, ed. L. Coser. New York: Harcourt

Crain, R. L. 1978. *Report to the Honorable Paul Egly on the Crawford Remedy*. Los Angeles: Calif. Superior Court

Crain, R. L., Mahard, R. E. 1978. Desegregation and black achievement. *Law Contemp. Probl.* 42:17–56

Crain, R. L., Mahard, R. E. 1981. Minority achievement: policy implications of research. See Hawley 1981, pp. 55–84

Crain, R. L., Mahard, R. E. 1983. The effect of research methodology on desegregation-achievement studies: a meta-analysis. *Am. J. Sociol.* 88:839–54

Crain, R. L., Mahard, R. E., Narot, R. 1982. *Making Desegregation Work*. Cambridge: Ballinger

Cross, W. E. 1978. Black families and black identity. *Western J. Black Stud.* 2:111–24

Dimaggio, P. 1982. Cultural capital and school success. *Am. Sociol. Rev.* 47:189–201

Eder, D. 1981. Ability grouping as a self-fulfilling prophecy: a microanalysis of teacher-student interaction. *Sociol. Educ.* 54:151–62

Epps, E. 1978. The impact of school desegregation on the self-evaluation and achievement orientation of minority children. *Law Contemp. Probl.* 42:57–76

Epps, E. 1981. Minority children: desegregation, self-evaluation, and achievement orientation. See Hawley 1981, pp. 85–106

Evertson, C. M., Anderson, C. W., Anderson, L. M., Brophy, J. E. 1980. Relationship between classroom behaviors and student outcomes in junior high mathematics and English classes. *Am. Educ. Res. J.* 17:43–60

Gay, G. 1975. Teachers' achievement expectations of and classroom interactions with ethnically different students. *Contemp. Educ.* 46:166–72

Gerard, H. B., Miller, N. 1975. *School Desegregation*. New York: Plenum

Gifford, B. R. 1978. *Toward a Workable Remedy: Maximizing Integrated Educational Settings and Equalizing Resource Allocation Policies in the Los Angeles Unified School District*. Los Angeles: Calif. Superior Court

Glaser, B., Strauss, A. 1964. Awareness contexts and social interaction. *Am. Sociol. Rev.* 29:669–79

Gottleib, D., Ten Houten, W. 1965. Racial composition and the social system of three high schools. *J. Marriage Family* 27:204–12

Haller, E. J., Davis, S. A. 1981. Teacher perceptions, parental social status, and grouping for reading instruction. *Sociol. Educ.* 54:162–74

Hallinan, M. 1976. Friendship patterns in open and traditional classrooms. *Sociol. Educ.* 49:254–64

Hansell, S., Karweit, N. 1983. Curricular placement, friendship networks, and status attainment. See Karweit & Epstein 1983, pp. 141–61

Hansell, S., Slavin, R. E. 1981. Cooperative learning and the structure of interracial friendships. *Sociol. Educ.* 54:98–106

Hare, B. 1977. Racial and socioeconomic variation in preadolescent area-specific and general self-esteem. *Int. J. Intercultural Rel.* 1:31–51

Hare, B. 1980. Self-perception and academic achievement: variations in a desegregated setting. *Am. J. Psychiatry* 137:683–89

Harvey, M. R. 1980. Public school treatment of low-income children: education for passivity. *Urban Educ.* 15:279–323

Hawley, W. D. 1981. Equity and quality in education: characteristics of effective desegregated schools. In *Effective School Desegregation: Equity, Quality, and Feasibility*, ed. W. D. Hawley, pp. 297–308. Beverly Hills, Calif.: Sage

Hawley, W., Rist, R. C. 1975. On the future implementation of school desegregation. *Law and Contemporary Problems* 39:412–426

Iadicola, P. 1980. *School Characteristics and Assimilation*. Presented at the Annual Meeting of the Society for the Study of Social Problems, New York

Jackson, G., Cosca, C. 1974. The inequality of educational opportunity in the Southwest. *Am. Educ. Res. J.* 11:219–29

Johnson, D., Johnson, R. 1975. *Learning Together and Alone*. Englewood Cliffs: Prentice-Hall

Johnson, D., Johnson, R. 1981. Effects of cooperative and individualistic experiences in interethnic interaction. *J. Educ. Psychol.* 73:444–9

Johnson, D., Skon, L., Johnson, R. 1980. Effects of cooperative, competitive, and individualistic conditions on children's problem-solving performance. *Am. Educ. Res. J.* 17:83–94

Johnson, D., Johnson, R., Maruyama, G. 1983. Interdependence and interpersonal attraction among heterogeneous and homogeneous individuals: a theoretical formulation and a meta-analysis of the research. *Rev. Educ. Res.* 53:5–54

Karweit, N., Epstein, J. 1983. *Friends in School.* New York: Academic

Karweit, N., Hansell, S. 1983. School organization and friendship selection. See Karweit & Epstein 1983, pp. 29–38

Lazarowitz, R., Sharan, S., Steinberg, R. 1980. Classroom learning style and cooperative behavior of elementary school children. *J. Educ. Psychol.* 72:97–104

Lewin, K. 1935. *A Dynamic Theory of Personality.* New York: McGraw-Hill

Lewis, R., St. John, N. 1974. Contribution of cross-racial friendship to minority group achievement in desegregated classrooms. *Sociometry* 37:79–91

Longshore, D. 1982a. Social psychological research on school desegregation. In *New Directions for Testing and Measurement,* No. 14, ed. D. Monti, pp. 39–52. San Francisco: Jossey-Bass

Longshore, D. 1982b. Race composition and classroom hostility. *Social Forces* 61:73–78

Longshore, D. 1982c. School racial composition and blacks' attitudes toward desegregation. *Soc. Sci. Q.* 63:674–687

Longshore, D. 1984. School control and intergroup relations. *Soc. Sci. Q.* 65:150–7

Luge, S. R., Hoge, R. D. 1978. Relations among teacher rankings, pupil-teacher interactions, and academic achievement. *Am. Educ. Res. J.* 15:489–500

Magnusson, D. 1981. *Toward a Psychology of Situations: An Interactional Perspective.* Beverly Hills: Sage

Markovsky, B., Smith, L. F., Berger, J. 1984. Do status interventions persist? *Am. Sociol. Rev.* 49:373–82

Martin, J., Veldman, D. J., Anderson, L. M. 1980. Within-class relationships between student achievement and teacher behaviors. *Am. Educ. Res. J.* 17:479–490

Massey, G. C., Scott, M. V., Dornbusch, S. M. 1975. Racism without racists. *Black Scholar*:10–19

McIntire, R. G., Hughes, L. W., Say, M. W. 1982. Houston's successful desegregation plan. *Phi Delta Kappan* 63:536–8

Metz, M. H. 1978. *Classrooms and Corridors.* Berkeley: Univ. Calif. Press

Miller, N. 1981. Changing views about the effects of school desegregation. In *Scientific Inquiry in the Social Sciences,* ed. M. Brewer, B. E. Collins, pp. 413–53. San Francisco: Jossey-Bass

Miller, N. 1983. Peer relations in desegregated schools. See Karweit & Epstein 1983, pp. 201–17

Natriello, G., Dornbusch, S. 1983. Bringing behavior back in: the effects of student characteristics and behavior on the classroom behavior of teachers. *Am. Educ. Res. J.* 20:29–43

Ogbu, J. 1974. *The Next Generation: An Ethnography of Education in an Urban Neighborhood.* New York: Academic

Ogbu, J. 1978. *Minority Education and Caste.* New York: Academic

Ogbu, J. 1985. Structural constraints in school desegregation. See Prager et al 1985

Patchen, M. 1982. *Black-White Contact in Schools.* West Lafayette: Purdue Univ. Press

Perret-Clermont, A. N. 1982. Approaches in the social psychology of learning and group work. In *Confronting Social Issues: Applica-*

tions of Social Psychology, Vol. 2., ed. P. Stringer, pp. 97–122. New York, NY: Academic

Persell, C. 1977. *Education and Inequality.* New York: Free Press

Pettigrew, T. F. 1978. Placing Adam's argument in a broader perspective. *Soc. Probl.* 41:58–61

Prager, J., Longshore, D., Seeman, M. 1986. *School Desegregation Research: New Approaches to Situational Analyses.* New York: Plenum. In press

Robinson, J. W., Preston, J. D. 1976. Equal-status contact and modification of prejudice. *Soc. Forc.* 54:911–24

Rosenberg, M. 1979. Group rejection and self-rejection. *Res. Commun. Mental Health* 1:3–20

Rosenberg, M. 1985. Self-esteem research: a phenomenological corrective. See Prager et al 1985

Rosenfield, D., Sheehan, D. S., Marcus, M. M., Stephan, W. G. 1981. Classroom structure and prejudice in desegregated schools. *J. Educ. Psychol.* 73:17–26

Rosenholtz, S. J., Wilson, B. 1980. The effect of classroom structure on shared perceptions of ability. *Am. Educ. Res. J.* 17:75–82

Ryan, F., Wheeler, R. 1977. The effects of cooperative and competitive background experiences of students on the play of a simulation game. *J. Educ. Res.* 70:295–9

St. John, N. 1975. *School Desegregation: Outcomes for Children.* New York: Wiley

St. John, N., Lewis, R. 1971. The influence of school racial context on academic achievement. *Soc. Probl.* 19:68–78

St. John, N., Lewis, R. 1975. Race and the social structure of the elementary classroom. *Sociol. Educ.* 48:346–68

Scheff, T. 1967. Toward a sociological model of consensus. *Am. Sociol. Rev.* 32:32–45

Scheff, T. 1970. On the concepts of identity and social relationship. In *Human Nature and Collective Behavior,* ed. T. Shibutani. Englewood Cliffs: Prentice-Hall

Scherer, J., Slawski, E. J. 1979. Color, class, and social control in an urban desegregated school. In *Desegregated Schools,* ed. R. C. Rist, pp. 117–154. New York: Academic

Schofield, J. 1978. School desegregation and intergroup relations. In *Social Psychology of Education,* ed. D. BarTal, L. Saxe, pp. 329–63. New York: Wiley

Schofield, J. 1982. *Black and White in School.* New York: Praeger

Serow, R. C., Solomon, D. 1979. Classroom climates and students' intergroup behavior. *J. Educ. Psychol.* 71:669–676

Sharan, S. 1980. Cooperative learning in small groups. *Rev. Educ. Res.* 50:241–271

Slavin, R. E. 1978a. Student teams and achievement divisions. *J. Res. Devel. Educ.* 12:39–49

Slavin, R. E. 1978b. Student teams and comparisons among equals. *J. Educ. Psychol.* 70:532–8

Slavin, R. E., Hansell, S. 1983. Cooperative learning and intergroup relations. See Karweit & Epstein 1983, pp. 93–114

Sorensen, A. 1978. *The Organizational Differentiation of Students in Schools.* Presented at the National Invitational Conference on School Organization and Effects, San Diego

Stephan, W. G. 1978. School desegregation: an evaluation of predictions made in Brown v. board of education. *Psychol. Bull.* 85:217–38

Suttles, G. 1968. *The Social Order of the Slum.* Chicago: Univ. Chicago Press

Suttles, G. 1985. School desegregation and "the national community." See Prager et al 1985

Taylor, M. C., Walsh, E. J. 1979. Explanations of black self-esteem. *Soc. Psychol. Q.* 42:242–52

Turner, R. H. 1970. *Family Interaction.* New York: Wiley

Veldman, D. J., Sanford, J. P. 1984. The influence of class ability level on student achievement and classroom behavior. *Am. Educ. Res. J.* 21:629–44

Webb, N. H. 1980. Group process: the key to learning in groups. *New Directions for Methodology of Social and Behavioral Science* 6:77–87

Webb, N. H. 1982. Student interaction and learning in small groups. *Rev. Educ. Res.* 52:421–45

Weinberg, M. 1977. *Minority Students: A Research Appraisal.* Washington, DC: National Institute of Education

Yinger, J. M. 1963. Research implications for a field view of personality. *Am. J. Sociol.* 68:580–92

Ann. Rev. Sociol. 1985. 11:93–111

SOCIOLOGY OF MASS COMMUNICATION

Denis McQuail

University of Amsterdam, Oude Hoogstraat, 24, CE 1012, Amsterdam, Netherlands

Abstract

Mass communication has always been an object of interdisciplinary study, but it is currently gaining a greater degree of autonomy. The paradigm that is emerging has probably been more influenced by sociology than by any other discipline. This review deals with literature, mainly published during the last five years, chosen according to the significance or representativeness of the main themes. Among these is media theory, where the field has proved very sensitive to wider debates within the social sciences, especially those provoked by the advocacy of more critical theory and research and by attacks on positivism. The cultural studies approach has gained ground, and there has been more interchange between humanistic and scientific approaches. The question of media power has remained very much at the center of debate. The critical-cultural developments mentioned have made some contribution to a reconceptualization of the problem and to the adoption of new research strategies that pay more attention to long-term, institutional effects of media. The range of social issues associated with the study of mass communication has widened, with special attention given to questions of women in society, international communication, and the social consequences of new information technology.

INTRODUCTION

The route between sociology and the study of mass communication sometimes appears to be a one-way street. A flow of people, concepts, and methods has come from sociology and contributed especially to a development of theory and a greater degree of autonomy and identity for what has always been a multidisciplinary enterprise. Yet mass communication appears within mainstream

93

0360-0572/85/0815-0093$02.00

sociology as no more than a peripheral and optional subfield. The situation is somewhat surprising, given the fact that the principal organizing themes of the subject are more than ever rooted in sociological ways of thinking about the exercise of social power, the mediation of social relations, the reproduction of society and culture, and the organization of social experience.

Following the custom of this *Annual Review* and the precedent of Holz & Wright (1979), attention will be concentrated on work published during the last five years, with such earlier references as are necessary for sense or continuity. The literature is discussed under a set of conventional headings that have been in use in one guise or another since Lasswell long ago described the study of communication as an attempt to answer the question "Who says what, in which channel, to whom and with what effect?". Despite the convenience of this formulation for indicating the concerns of the field, there has been a more or less continuous shift away from the model of mass communication that it implies, so as to render it misleading about the prevailing ways of thinking about mass media (McQuail & Windahl 1982). Lasswell here reflects a view of mass communication as primarily the planned application of certain technologies for purposes of mass persuasion, information, or control. The formulation directs attention to matters of avowed purposes, overt meaning, and communicative efficiency.

The decline of this (applied social psychology) model has been one of the main effects of a more sociological approach, which offers in exchange: a greater emphasis on the determining part played by the structure of society and external social forces in defining and allocating the roles of "sender" and "receiver" and in relating these to each other. Secondly, this model proposes the view that media messages are at least as much received as sent and that choice and perception, and the determinants of these, are at least as significant as the motives for "sending" and the degree of efficiency achieved. Thirdly, the media are not merely neutral channels, freely available for the purpose of sending messages, but instead are complex social institutions whose theories, traditions, norms, practices, and self-chosen objectives all exert an influence on the messages they transmit. Fourthly, messages as sent are much more than a set of rational acts of transmission; they belong to much broader systems of social and cultural meaning, with many possible interpretations of origin and function.

While this is not everyone's version of the field of study, most of the recent developments that go beyond the practicalities of data collection have either presumed elements of this broad view or have been in debate with it. A number of recent texts provide an overview of the field consistent with this view, including DeFleur & Ball-Rokeach (1982), Davis & Baran (1981), McQuail (1983), as well as several readers, including Curran et al (1977) and Gurevitch et al (1982). There is also a set of compilations of ongoing research published as

Mass Communication Review Yearbooks (Wilhoit & de Bock 1980, 1981; Wartella, Whitney & Windahl 1982, 1983).

DEVELOPMENTS OF THEORY

Some indications have already been given of directions of change in media theory; in general, the field has been touched by the same currents and conflicts that have marked the rest of sociology and the social sciences more widely. An insight into the nature of recent debates can be obtained from several contributions to a special issue of *The Journal of Communication* entitled "Ferment in the field," among which the article by Rosengren (1983) provides the most coherent and original view of what has been happening. Borrowing from an analysis of organizational sociology by Burrell & Morgan (1979), he plots the main approaches in communication research according to two crosscutting dimensions; one separates the 'sociology of radical change' from the 'sociology of regulation' (functionalism), and the other separates more 'subjective' from more 'objective' approaches. Crudely summarized, this yields a four-fold typology of radical-subjective; radical-objective; subjective-functionalist; and objective-functionalist. According to Rosengren, this last could hold the great majority of empirical studies of communication. At the same time, he points out that criticisms and questions raised about objective functionalism have been mainly raised in the other three, 'dissident' cells, which are characterized by critical thinking, more qualitative methods, and attention to knowledge and culture rather than to society and behavior. Yet they have mainly been framed in non-testable terms. Rosengren argues that many of the questions could be tested empirically within the objective-functionalist paradigm. While the oppositions are overstated for heuristic purposes, this scheme does help to sum up the state of the art and to identify the main conflicts of theory.

There are alternative ways of describing the issues raised by Rosengren, and other implications to note. For instance, the objective/subjective opposition is not only a separation according to choice of method—interpretive vs. positivistic; but it also separates holders of an instrumental view of communication from those who conceive of it more as expression and ritual (Carey 1977). Communication can be seen as an integral part of a culture and consciousness, as well as a tool of human activity (Carey 1977). The radical/functionalist division is also familiar in other contexts and has a long history, reflecting the distinction made by Lazarsfeld forty years ago between 'critical' and 'administrative' research, a subject more recently revisited by Blumler (1978). It finds another current expression in the terms "Marxist" and "liberal-pluralist" used by Gurevitch et al (1982), where the former identifies the tradition in which media are seen mainly as forgers of (false) consciousness in the interests of those with economic power and control, while the latter applies to those for whom media systems in liberal democracies are largely the outcome of an adjustment between demand and supply for information and cultural services. The research of the one aims to be critical and demystifying, first of all, and of the other, descriptive, analytic, and often reformist. This opposition is especially evident in Britain (Becker 1984). The critical school contains within it a more objective, materialist wing, which stresses the political economy of media (Garnham 1979) and determination by class structures; it has a more subjective variant that places emphasis on ideology in content and on consciousness-forming processes (Barrett et al 1979, Hall 1982).

Within the functionalist or pluralist tradition there are also divergent tendencies in defining the objects of study and in choosing a method. Subjective approaches favor case studies, description, ethnography, and interpretation applied especially to questions of culture and audience experience. More objective approaches favor extensive data collection and multivariate analysis and go more into studies of media reach and effect. The subjective-objective division also parallels a more fundamental theoretical division between a media-centered and a society-centered approach. The view that changes in communication are a primary cause of social change has a long history and finds its best case in the social history of printing, but it exerts a perennial attraction for some sociologists and arouses the ire of others. Thus, Gouldner (1976) attributed certain distinctive features of post-Enlightenment society and politics to print media, especially newspapers, and the more recent "decline of ideology" to new electronic media. Golding & Murdock (1978) strongly advocated the alternative view of the media-society relationship, as likely to explain more and as more appropriate for sociologists. Rosengren (1980) dealt with the essential underlying question in a somewhat different way, by crosstabulating the alternative propositions "Culture influences social structure" and "Social structure influences culture" (including mass media within culture). He labels the four possible outcomes as "idealism," "materialism," "autonomy," and "interdependence"; these in turn can stand for the main varieties of theory about mass media and social change.

The issues discussed briefly in this section provide the context for more focused debate about the direction and strength of mass media influence and the interpretation of media content. The challenge of critical research has itself stimulated a good deal of writing (Gitlin 1978, Lang 1979, Haight 1983). Gitlin attacked what he termed the dominant paradigm of media sociology that, by concentrating on personal influence, has obscured the true power of media in society. Lang (1979) points to some roots of critical theory in Germany, but the continuing tendency to identify critical theory with a European rather than an American tradition, while partly really does less than justice to the diversity of American work and overestimates the unity of European. A fascinating glimpse into relevant intellectual history is provided by Hardt's

(1979) account of early German theories concerning the press, in which functionalist perspectives predominated.

MEDIA AS ORGANIZATION AND INSTITUTION

One of the ways out of the seeming impasse and the sterility of research on media effects was a redirection of attention toward the media as a social institution, in which formally organized work takes place, directed toward the production of knowledge and culture. As Hirsch (1977) and others have emphasized, the media share important features with other complex and institutionalized work settings, although they differ mainly in the extent to which the product of media work is supposed to be creative, novel, original, or unexpected (news) and yet produced with extreme regularity and often against much more demanding time schedules than apply in other industries. In addition, questions of political freedom and artistic autonomy are often central in relating individual workers to media organization and media organization to society. Overviews of some of these issues are to be found in Elliott (1977) and Gallagher (1982); the most relevant readers are Christian (1980) and Ettema & Whitney (1982).

Research has uncovered a complex, sometimes private or enclosed world in which people solve the practical problems of producing culture to order, routinely providing news of the unexpected and maintaining some kind of stable relationship to a largely unknown audience. Since most media work is part of show business it should not be too surprising that illusions have to be protected. The many strategies and routines for achieving the ends mentioned have been described in a number of studies, especially those dealing with news, and they show a high measure of agreement (Tuchman 1978a, Schlesinger 1978, Gans 1979, Altheide & Snow 1979, Golding & Elliott 1979; Fishman 1980, 1982; Lester 1980). Several of the studies emphasize that news is a manufactured version of reality, a view that also permeates much work on news content. While a conceptual distinction can be drawn among individual communicator, the specific work organization, and the institution as a whole, some of the best work has shed light on different levels. A good example is Burns's (1977) study of the BBC, which looked at several different occupational specialties within a public broadcasting organization that happened also to be a national institution and a model for institution-building elsewhere. He was especially interested in the interplay between the total ethos, the professionalism of broadcasters, and the demands of career, management, and practical tasks.

A study of comparable range is that which Gans (1979) conducted over a number of years into the work of news personnel of major American networks and news magazines. His findings lend support to the view that such elite media and media elites are inclined to reinforce rather than weaken the established social order and reigning consensus, although not out of cynical self-interest or subservience to ruling class interests. They are more likely to be moved by a self-sufficient professionalism to reflect the world as they believe it is, or by a liberal-reformist tradition that accepts the system as improvable, or by a view of the world that they genuinely share with other middle-class beneficiaries of the same system.

Interestingly, a rather different kind of inquiry by Dreier (1982) into the connections between press and corporate power concluded that the main US elite newspapers were both the most integrated into the capitalist power structure and most inclined to adopt a corporate-liberal perspective—an attitude of "responsible capitalism." This finding belongs at the institutional level of analysis, and Dreier argues that one is more likely to find the factors that differentiate between news organizations at this level, rather than through studies of news rooms. This is an important pointer to a direction for research, on the basis of a now fairly adequate picture of how news is made on a day-to-day basis. In this context, the work of Dimmick & Coit (1982) deserves citation, since they identify a set of different levels—ranging from the supranational to the intraindividual—at which influences on story selection may operate; they suggest that most pressure or constraint originates at levels remote from the place of actual story-writing, thus allowing the ideal of professional autonomy for journalists to survive.

The work of Engwall (1978) on newspaper organizations has also shed light on the occupational diversity associated with what has been called a nonroutine bureaucracy. He distinguished four main work cultures, each associated with a different goal or work task: the news-oriented culture; the politically oriented; the economically oriented; the technically oriented. While conflicts inevitably arise between cultures, an ultimate reference to what will please the public and thus sell newspapers may provide a final basis for agreement. The issue of freedom and creation within the constraints of institution and organization has continued to attract attention. A valuable collection of articles edited by Ettema & Whitney (1982) provides evidence of problems experienced in a wide range of media contexts and of solutions adopted. There continues also to be attention to such established topics as professionalism (Tuchman 1978b), the response to time constraints (Gellis & Faulkner 1978) and to objectivity norms of the press, especially in historical perspective (Schudson 1978, Schiller 1981).

The sociology of media organizations is gradually being extended and consolidated theoretically by attention to: the variety of roles in media industry as a whole (Hirsch 1978); different kinds of media, for instance news agencies (Boyd-Barrett 1980), popular music (Frith 1983), and book publishing (Coser et al 1981); and some occupations previously neglected, such as that of screen actor (Peters & Cantor 1982) or fiction writer (Cantor & Jones 1983, Kingston

& Cole 1983). In this work, there is also an increased focus on economic and industrial aspects of cultural production and news dissemination. Film has also regained some of its status as a medium deserving serious institutional analysis despite the decline of the cinema (see Jowett & Linton 1980).

MEDIA CONTENT AND CULTURE

The systematic analysis of content was one of the earliest applications of survey techniques to the study of mass communication, and the output of media continues to be subject to sampling, categorization, enumeration, and statistical manipulation for a variety of purposes. Among these are to shed light on the character and (possibly hidden) aims of the originators; to assist in interpreting social functions and potential effects; to see evidence of wider changes in culture and society; and to illuminate or characterize audience composition. There have been several comprehensive reviews of methods and evidence, most recently that by Krippendorf (1980). One recent trend is the harnessing of content analysis to the evaluation of media performance for either critical or reformist purposes, as distinguished above. Thirdly, the prominence of agenda-setting inquiries in effects research has also stimulated content analysis. Finally, intensive, qualitative analysis of content has gained ground, aided by concepts and methods drawn from semiology and structuralism (Woollacott 1982). The line between extensive, numerical analysis and intensive, qualitative analysis has become blurred as a result of moves from each side to borrow from the other.

The tradition of comparing a media reality with a relevant version of social reality remains strong. A number of studies concern, as in the past, various minorities or minority activities that either involve direct comparisons with reality or point to distorted or negative representation of a systematic kind. Examples include research on the portrayal of women and sex roles (Tuchman 1978b, Ferguson 1983); trade unions (Glasgow Media Group 1980); crime (Graber 1980; Fishman 1978); political deviants (Shoemaker 1984). The general line of interpretation in most such research has been that the reality represented or reported deviates from other possible "objective" versions of reality, mainly as a result of the media's own needs and working procedures. The result is at best a somewhat ritualistic and top-heavy version of the world and, at worst, a confirmation of popular stereotypes and an unwitting (usually) but active form of social control.

Golding & Middleton (1982) contributed to the latter version by showing that British news media are no better disposed in their reporting practice to welfare recipients than to other deviants and tend to invoke Poor-Law attitudes. According to Hall et al (1978), the same media played an active part in stigmatizing political deviants as extremists at a time when domestic social and economic crisis might have made them a danger to the state. Other British research on television news treatment of industrial matters (Glasgow Media Group 1980) also lent support to the argument that established media tend to take an implicitly official point of view in respect even of legitimate activities that seem to threaten an assumed national interest or to violate majority opinion. This particular study is a good example of work that has combined exhaustive enumeration with attention to implied meaning contained in verbal and visual codes and cues. It is also an example of work that has provoked antagonism in the media and academic controversy (Anderson & Sharrock 1979, Murdock 1980).

However, the thesis that majority media tend to favor majority opinion and established interests has always tended to receive more support from content analysis than has another long-standing view—that media encourage a breakdown of social control (Janowitz 1981). One of the most impressive long-term research projects of the period, that of Gerbner et al (1979, 1980) involving a systematic study of the putative message of American network television over the years seems, paradoxically, to offer support for both interpretations. Television seems to offer a view of the social world as disordered and dangerous, especially for the weak and disadvantaged; at the same time, it endorses moderate or consensual political solutions (Gerbner et al 1984). Content analysis alone, unconnected with evidence of social correlates or consequences, is almost impossible to interpret and existing studies of effects are both scarce and open to challenge (see below).

The trend toward using content analysis for evaluative purposes has already been illustrated, but it is most noteworthy in two particular areas not yet directly discussed—one having to do with objectivity or its opposite, bias, another with balance in the selection and flow of international news and other kinds of content. There has been some useful attention to the meaning of objectivity and the criteria for assessing its presence or absence (Rosengren 1979; Boyer 1981) and an especially welcome translation of a conceptual scheme developed in Sweden by Westerståhl (1983) that distinguishes between balance and impartiality on the one hand and information quality aspects, such as accuracy and relevance, on the other. Some addition to the tradition has been achieved by testing a concept of diversity against content (McQuail & van Cuilenburg 1983) and by developing methods for analyzing bias in visual portrayals (Kepplinger 1982).

Research on the flow of news and other content continues to be supplemented by findings confirming established tendencies, e.g. for content to flow globally from North to South and West to East, to follow patterns of trade and politics, to be qualitatively more negative as well as quantitatively more scarce in relation to poorer countries and regions (Adams 1982, Varis 1984,

Sreberny-Mohammadi 1984). There have been some developments in relating news coverage to foreign policy interests and interpreting some of the patterns of systematic omission. Golding (1980) argues that what is left out most significantly are the dimensions of social-economic process (long-term change) and of power, resulting in a view of the world as unchanging and unchangeable. The literature has also been lightened by a move to show the results graphically (e.g. Womack 1981), but the findings, as with studies of objectivity, mainly redirect attention to questions of why news content is the way it is, rather than give clear answers about purpose and effect.

The trend toward more qualitative, intensive research has certainly been stimulated by cross-fertilization between social scientific media study and humanistic, now often semiological, approaches. The result is usually a hybrid, in which systematic, analytic descriptions of content and genres are made with the aim of uncovering deeper or relatively hidden meaning and of explicating the manner in which messages are encoded and might be decoded. Examples are found in relation to advertisements (Williamson 1978), television serial fiction (Fiske & Hartley 1978), and current affairs television (Brunsdon & Morley 1978). Several studies of news sought to un-cover its 'rules of discourse' (van Dijk 1983) and its mythic or ritual elements (Smith 1979, Knight & Dean 1982, Chaney 1983, Davis & Walton 1983). The impetus behind work of this kind is divided between a commitment to cultural models of communication and a concern with uncovering ideology at work.

There has been a wider tendency to break down the boundaries between the study of communication, of knowledge, and of culture; and boundaries be-tween mass culture and culture in general. It has also become more common to view media production as an aspect of more general cultural production (Curran & Schudson 1982). The notion of a consciousness industry (Tuchman 1983) has been widely adopted as a description of the media, and the develop-ment of qualitative methods for systematic analysis has helped to open up visual media for analysis (Thomas 1982). It has also become easier to bring fiction and entertainment within the same frameworks of study that have long been applied to information and easier to analyze the latter in terms of its ritual, mythic, story-telling, and expressive functions. There has been some progress in distinguishing key features of different media languages and component genres, for instance the work of Ellis (1982), which subtly differentiated the output of film and broadcast television according to elements of content, production, reception, and social history. Snow (1983) sketched the main features of a number of 'media cultures', with their own grammars appropriate to some institutional features of the media concerned. Lastly, we should attend to another rediscovery—of the relation between media style and life-style.

Hebdige (1979), for instance, explores the way in which media culture imping-es on and overlaps with the culture of dress and behavior.

THE MEDIA AUDIENCE

Several aspects of the audience that are potentially of most interest to sociolog-ists have remained largely unrepresented, except indirectly, in research—a matter also regretted by Holz & Wright (1979) in their review of the field. Among these aspects are the structure of social relations within aggregate audiences; the wider functions of media behavior for the rest of social life; the degree to which media use is structured by norms and conventions; the degree to which audiences have a conscious social identity or act as an audience in relation to others and toward communicators.

Nevertheless, there continues to be no shortage of evidence that the size and composition of aggregate audiences vary predictably according to familiar social-demographic factors, which are, in turn, related to cultural background and time availability. The importance of these has been underlined in a major study of the US television audience (Comstock et al 1978) that identified five "highly attracted" publics—of women, children, blacks, the elderly, and low-income people. A sophisticated study of the attitudes and dynamics of the (declining) American newspaper public is also one of the gains of the period (Bogart 1981); this shows again the extent to which media use reflects sensi-tively the varying, changing needs and social circumstances over the life cycle, as well as the changing pattern of what media offer. The dominant feature of the recent past has been the continued inroads of television into newspaper use (Robinson & Jeffres 1979; Tunstall 1980), but the future also carries an imminent challenge for television as we know it. What has been termed an era of "media abundance" (Blumler 1979a) is bound to alter habits and destabilize familiar audience patterns. We can expect, if anything, a less social and more individualized audience experience.

On the broad and related question of whether the media audience is, general-ly, passive and unthinking, there continue to be inconsistent answers. Barwise et al (1982) report very modest levels of selectivity by the television audience, according to the criterion of repeat viewing of similar or serial content. Himmelweit et al (1981) found quite a high degree of discriminating choice by the British television audience, which appeared able to apply some consistent criteria of judgment to programs. A rather different picture of the American television public has been painted by Neuman (1982), returning to a much older sociological interest in the relation between education, occupation, and media use. He found little evidence that education helped to make members of the audience more critical or selective and concluded that the television audience is effectively culturally homogeneous and soporific. Sahin & Robinson (1981) see the domination of leisure time by commercial television as a form of colonization, somewhat in line with Smythe's (1977) theory that the main product of the media is the audience, which can be sold to advertisers.

Nevertheless, more consistent support exists for a view of the audience as showing significant features of sociability in its behavior. Lull (1980) provides a useful inventory of social uses of television, based on observations of family viewing. These comprise structural uses—for background, companionship, regulating activities and talk; relational uses—mainly providing topics and occasions for conversation; social learning—use in in self-socialization; affiliation/avoidance uses—for gaining or avoiding social contact and to increase or decrease solidarity; competence/domination—aiding the role of opinion leader or first informant. The evidence of Hedinsson (1981) is that peer group relations among adolescents are not harmed by extensive use of television and generally the social or parasocial functions of this medium may well be as prominent as their antisocial effects. According to research on children reported in Brown (1976), books are much more likely to be guilty on the latter count. It should not be a matter for surprise that not only media content but also media use contributes to solidarity and socialization.

Much recent research on the audience has been carried out within what has been called the uses and gratifications tradition, which assumes an interactive connection between external social pressures and individual selection of and response to media. Its main concerns have been to identify the purposes of media choice, relate these back to social circumstances and forward to media choice, to assessment of the media experience, and to other possible effects. It has been advocated both as an empirical approach to studying culture and an audience-oriented way of studying media effects. There has been much research as well as some methodological and conceptual development during the period (to be reviewed by Rosengren et al 1985) and also a continuing controversy over what the approach can really tell us about the motives for media use and, especially, the connections between the various stages or levels indicated.

Some research (e.g. Kippax & Murray 1980) casts doubt on the value of evidence about motive and expectation in actually differentiating mass media use; the suspicion has been voiced that media expectations have more to do with broadly disseminated images of the media and their contents than with specific and valid individual goal-directed choices (Lichtenstein & Rosenfeld 1983). In any case there has been much anxious search for clarification of concepts and explication of method (Becker 1979, Rubin 1981, Windahl 1981). The question of relation between audience motive and effect is also a central one for exploration (Gantz 1978, Blumler 1979b, Weaver 1980), with no real agreement on how far and under what conditions audience expectations help to differentiate or predict effects.

Despite the problems associated with the approach, it continues to produce useful studies of particular audiences and particular content types, for instance in relation to television news (Levy 1978), soap operas (Miyazaki 1981), and the elderly audience (Rubin & Rubin 1982). It also provides a method for studying inter-media differences (Weaver & Buddenbaum 1980) and for making sense of the functions of various kinds of entertainment (Tannenbaum 1981) that otherwise elude investigation. The most ambitious research of the period in the uses and gratifications tradition is probably the Swedish Media Panel, a long-term inquiry into children and media use that is beginning to yield results (Hedinsson 1981, Johnsson-Smaragdi 1983, Roe 1983). Future research may well require methods for the study of specially profiled audiences and those attracted to particular content types, rather than audiences for media channels, "senders," or organizations, as in the past. The development of a concept of taste culture (Lewis 1980) seems also more appropriate to the new media era than do earlier models of the media public, involving as it does a notion of an aggregate of similar content appealing to a set of persons sharing the same taste and, possibly, life-style, but not necessarily the same class or demographic identification. Such taste cultures will also be difficult to reconcile with older notions of cultural stratification.

MEDIA EFFECT AND INFLUENCE

The topic of media effect is central to the field and continues to attract research and periodic reviews of research (Katz 1980, McLeod & Reeves 1980, Roberts & Bachen 1981, Lang & Lang 1981), although there may have been some relative decline in research activity. During the 1970s, it appeared that theory and research were reverting to an earlier view of powerful media, a view that had in its time been weakened by lack of empirical confirmation. Noelle-Neumann's (1973) seminal paper entitled "Return to the concept of powerful mass media" both encapsulated the spirit of the change and gave it impetus. Her theory of the spiral of silence (Noelle-Neumann 1977, 1984)—according to which mass media tend to disseminate self-fulfilling impressions about what is the dominant (or consensual) opinion—has been controversial but has acquired more theoretical support than otherwise (Taylor 1982, Katz 1983).

There were several reasons why theories of dominant media should have regained ground, among them the growing centrality and apparent homogenization of the media, according to several criteria. It only required some shifts of conceptualization of the nature of media effects to accomplish a change of scholarly emphasis, especially on matters to do with long-term opinion change (Lemert 1981). In what is perhaps the most authoritative of the reviews of research cited above, Lang & Lang (1981) argued that there was never any good reason to doubt the power of mass media. According to their analysis, most evidence for the limited effects position came from research conducted according to only two of four possible research strategies. The first of these they call 'study of the audience', where direct effects of 'exposure' on individuals are sought. The second is the 'search for correspondences', which involves relating trends in media content to aggregate changes in society. The third strategy Lang & Lang call the 'concern with refraction', by which they mean that the media tend to create a symbolic environment, to originate their own version of social reality, which becomes influential in its own right. Finally, they point to the study of outcomes, in which the media play a part in the unfolding of major social events, especially at times of critical events. Lang & Lang believe that when the two latter strategies are employed, important effects for the media are to be found, although they are complex, interactive, and not very predictable.

Research belonging to the first strategy is still conducted, because individuals and institutions still continue to believe that media have direct effects on people. Many familiar kinds of research are represented: on elections (Blumler 1983); on advertising (Roloff & Miller 1980); on children and young people, especially on matters to do with crime, aggression, and pornography (Eysenck & Nias 1978); on public information campaigns (Rice & Paisley 1981); on socialization (Adoni 1979); on the adoption of innovations (Rogers 1982); on learning from news and information (Katz et al 1977, Findahl & Hoijer 1981). This last named area is attracting especial attention, along with other aspects of television news, and evidence is accumulating of the rather low effectiveness of the genre, for reasons that are partly built into its traditional format. Substantial evidence exists now that short-term individual effects do occur, especially where favorable conditions obtain—such as relevant and positive motivation, attention, novelty, repetition, and environmental support.

Under the label "study of correspondences," we can include work on cultural indicators (Rosengren 1980, 1981), which concerns long-term relations that exist among media content, social change, and opinion change. Evidence relating to Sweden, where much work has been done, is somewhat ambiguous about the direction of effect (Rikardsson 1981, Carlsson 1981). The 'cultivation analysis' work of Gerbner and colleagues (1979, 1980, 1984) has suggested that the more people view television, the more they adopt features of the mainstream television view of the world. Doubts have been expressed about the causal nature of the relationship (Hughes 1980, Hirsch 1980, 1981) and about the applicability of the findings in other countries (Wobor 1978). It is quite possible that the relationship between society and systematic features of content are too complex for any conventional means of proof to demonstrate the strength and degree of direction in the relationship. Research on media agenda-setting follows the logic of the search for correspondences, although it has conceptual affiliations to refraction theory. Its main proposition—that people derive their views of what are current and salient issues and topics for opinion from the relative weight given in mass media to various topics—has found some limited support in research evidence (Weaver et al 1981, Shaw et al 1981), but other assessments (e.g. Becker 1982) are very cautious. Unfortunately for the thesis, there are alternative ways in which influence can flow in the three-cornered relationship of politics-people-media, and the requirements for proof are stringent. Detailed study of opinion formation in varying local contexts shows that many factors apart from quantity of media coverage influence opinion and opinion about opinion (Tichenor et al 1980). Research on knowledge gaps (Olien et al 1982) has an affinity with that on agenda-setting, since it also concerns correspondences between media use and information levels and the process by which the gap between the information-rich and information-poor may close or widen over time. Work has continued in this area (Genova & Greenberg 1979, Gaziano 1983), sometimes with references to a long-standing concern—the relative advantages of television and the print media (Clarke & Fredin 1978). We are reminded by Gandy (1982) that if media do shape a view of the world, this view is likely to reflect the concerns, if not views, of those who have most power to gain access to media—especially governments and corporate pressure groups, as well as other wealthy and organized interests.

The concern with 'refraction' as a kind of effect covers the 'spiral of silence' theory, mentioned above, which has been tested in respect of media and opinion in Germany (Noelle-Neumann 1980). Many studies of media bias and consciousness-forming invoke the logic of refraction when positing effects, although empirical confirmation is not easy to come by. Hartmann (1979) offered some evidence of the effects of media treatment of trade union matters in Britain, and studies of socialization seem to support the broad line of thought (Hawkins & Pingree 1980). Paletz & Entman (1981) offer an account of the way in which media have disseminated a conservative myth concerning the deradicalization of America in the 1970s. The last strategy recommended by Lang & Lang—the study of outcomes—has probably its best example in the work of the Langs themselves (1983). They studied the unfolding of the Watergate affair from break-in to resignation and concluded that the media were a powerful factor, not for their direct effect on public opinion, but because they were used by the major actors and eventually helped to legitimize the social pressures that led to Nixon's fall. Gitlin's (1981) study of the New Left student movement in America in the 1960s shows that the movement both depended on the media for access to public attention and became trapped by the image the media created of it. There has been recent attention to a not dissimilar phenomenon—the relationship of interdependence and mutual antagonism between media and civil terrorists (Schmid & de Graaf 1982, Schlesinger et al 1983). Whether the media actually stimulate terrorism or civil disorder remains in dispute, but the possibility of imitation and contagion cannot be ruled out (Phillips 1980). There is little doubt, however, that the critical events framework probably offers the most promise for future sociological study of media effects, however demanding the requirements of method.

CONCLUSION

The sociology of mass communication has always been stimulated by and concerned with issues of wider social relevance and we can see some extension of the range of issues that are raised in relation to mass media. Most prominent among the newer issues are media and the position of women; international media flow and its consequences; the consequences for society of media change. Each of these has now developed its own literature, cutting across the boundaries adopted in this review, and out of which only a few titles can be cited. In respect of the first-named issue there are useful overviews in Butler & Paisley (1980) and Smith (1982), and attention is being redirected from matters of sex-role socialization to matters of media production and to sexism in media research (McCormack 1978, 1983). On the question of global media flow, recent work, both academic and polemical, has focused on the outcome of a Unesco Commission (McBride 1980), for instance Hamelink (1981). Conceptual matters have also received attention (Boyd-Barrett 1982). Changes in media, mainly as a result of technologies of cable and satellite transmission, are too recent and rapid to have produced a definitive literature or evidence about consequences, but sociological concerns center on the implications of these technologies for the distribution of knowledge and power (Woodward 1980) and the potential threat to the public sphere (Elliott 1982). Local community life also may not benefit from the potential inherent in abundant, small-scale, and interactive media. The heralded information society is thus being greeted at its dawn by social analysts with a mixture of optimism and pessimism comparable to that which greeted the first age of mass media.

Literature Cited

Adams, W. C., ed. 1982. *Television Coverage of International Affairs*. Norwood, NJ: Ablex
Adoni, H. 1979. The functions of mass media in the political socialization of adolescents. *Commun. Res.* 6:84–106
Altheide, D. L., Snow, R. A. 1979. *Media Logic*. Beverly Hills, Calif: Sage
Anderson, D., Sharrock, W. 1979. Biassing the news: technical issues in 'media studies.' *Sociology* 30:367–85
Barrett, M., Kuhn, P., Wolff, J., eds. 1979. *Ideology and Cultural Production*. London: Croom Helm

Barwise, T. P., Ehrenberg, A. S. C., Goodhart, G. J. 1982. Glued to the box? Patterns of television repeat-viewing. *J. Commun.* 32(4):22–29
Becker, L. B. 1979. Measurement of gratifications. *Commun. Res.* 6:54–73
Becker, L. B. 1982. The mass media and citizen assessment of issue importance. See Wartella et al, 1982, pp. 521–36
Becker, S. L. 1984. Marxist approaches to media studies. *Crit. Stud. Mass Commun.* 1(1):66–80
Blumler, J. G. 1978. The social purposes of

mass communication research: a transatlantic perspective. *Journ. Q.* 55:219–30

Blumler, J. G. 1979a. Looking at media abundance. *Communication* 5:125–58

Blumler, J. G. 1979b. The role of theory in uses and gratifications research. *Commun. Res.* 6:9–36

Blumler, J. G. 1983. *Communicating to Voters*. London and Beverly Hills, Calif: Sage

Bogart, L. 1981. *Press and Public*. Hillsdale, NJ: LEA

Boyd-Barrett, O. 1980. *The International News Agencies*. London: Constable

Boyd-Barrett, O. 1982. Cultural dependency and the mass media. See Gurevitch et al, 1982, pp. 174–95

Boyer, J. H. 1981. How editors view objectivity. *Journ. Q.* 58:24–28

Brown, J., ed. 1976. *Children and Television*. London: Collier-Macmillan

Brunsdon, C., Morley, D. 1978. Everyday television: "Nationwide." London: British Film Institute

Burns, T. 1977. *The BBC: Public Image and Private World*. London: Macmillan

Butler, M., Paisley, W. 1980. *Women and Mass Media*. New York: Human Sciences

Cantor, M. G., Jones, E. 1983. Creating fiction for women. *Commun. Res.* 10(1):111–37

Carey, J. W. 1977. Mass communication research and cultural studies. See Curran et al, 1977, pp. 409–25

Carlsson, G., Dahlberg, A., Rosengren, K. E. 1981. Mass media content, public opinion and social change: Sweden 1967–74. See Rosengren, 1981, pp. 227–40

Chaney, D. 1983. A symbolic mirror of ourselves: civic ritual in mass society. *Media Cult. Soc.* 5:119–35

Christian, H., ed. 1980. The sociology of journalism and the press. *Sociol. Rev. Monogr.* No. 20

Clarke, P., Fredin, E. 1978. Newspapers, television and political reasoning. *Public Opin. Q.* 42:143–60

Comstock, G., Chaffee, S., Katzman, N., Roberts, D. 1978. *Television and Human Behavior*. New York: Columbia Univ. Press

Coser, L. A., Kadushin, C., Powell, W. W. 1981. *The Culture and Commerce of Publishing*. New York: Basic

Curran, J., Gurevitch, M., Woollacott, J., eds. 1977. *Mass Communication and Society*. London: Arnold

Curran, J., Schudson, M., eds. 1982. The production of culture. *Media Cult. Soc.* 4(1)

Davis, D. K., Baran, S. J. 1981. *Mass Communication and Everyday Life*. Belmont, Calif: Wadsworth

Davis, H., Walton, P., eds. 1983. *Language Image Media*. Oxford: Blackwell

DeFleur, M., Ball-Rokeach, S. 1982. *Theories of Mass Communication*. London and New York: Longman. 4th ed.

Dimmick, J., Coit, P. 1982. Levels of analysis in mass media decision-making. *Commun. Res.* 9(1):3–32

Dreier, P. 1982. The position of the press in the U.S. power structure. *Soc. Probl.* 29(3):298–310

Elliott, P. 1977. Media organisations and occupations. See Curran et al, 1977, pp. 142–73

Elliott, P. 1982. Intellectuals, the 'Information Society' and the disappearance of the public sphere. *Media, Cult. Soc.* 4(3):243–53

Ellis, J. 1982. *Visible Fictions*. London: Routledge

Engwall, L. 1978. *Newspapers as Organisations*. Farnborough Hants.: Saxon House

Ettema, J. S., Whitney, D. C., eds. 1982. *Individuals in Mass Media Organizations*. Beverly Hills, Calif: Sage

Eysenck, A. J., Nias, D. K. B. 1978. *Sex, Violence and the Media*. New York: St. Martins

Ferguson, M. 1983. *Forever Feminine*. London: Heinemann

Findahl, O., Höijer, B. 1981. Media content and human comprehension. See Rosengren, 1981, pp. 111–32

Fishman, J. 1978. Crime waves as ideology. *Soc. Probl.* 25:531–43

Fishman, M. 1980. *Manufacturing the News*. Austin, Tex: Univ. of Texas Press

Fishman, M. 1982. News and non-events: making the invisible visible. See Ettema & Whitney, 1982, pp. 219–40

Fiske, J., Hartley, J. 1978. *Reading Television*. London: Methuen

Frith, S. 1983. *Sound Effects*. New York: Pantheon

Gallagher, M. 1982. Negotiation of control in media organisations and occupations. See Gurevitch et al, 1982, pp. 149–73

Gandy, O. 1982. *Beyond Agenda-Setting: Information Subsidies and Public Policy*. Norwood, NJ: Ablex

Gans, H. J. 1979. *Deciding What's News*. New York: Pantheon

Gantz, W. 1978. How uses and gratifications affect recall of television news. *Journ. Q.* 55:664–72, 681

Garnham, N. 1979. Contribution to a political economy of mass communication. *Media Cult. Soc.* 1(2):123–46

Gaziano, C. 1983. The knowledge gap: an analytical review of media effects. *Commun. Res.* 10(4):447–86

Gellis, R., Faulkner, R. 1978. Time and TV news: task temporalization in the assembly of unscheduled events. *Sociol. Q.* 19:89–102

Genova, B. K., Greenberg, B. S. 1979. Interest in the news and the knowledge gap. *Public Opin. Q.* 43:79–91

Gerbner, G., Gross, L., Morgan, M., Signorielli, N. 1979. The demonstration of power: violence profile No. 10. *J. Commun.* 29:177–96

Gerbner, G., Gross, L., Morgan, M., Signorielli, N. 1980. The mainstreaming of America: violence profile No. 11. *J. Commun.* 30:10–27

Gerbner, G., Gross, L., Morgan, M., Signorielli, N. 1984. The political correlates of TV viewing. *Public Opin. Q.* 48:283–300

Gitlin, T. 1978. Media sociology: the dominant paradigm. *Theory Soc.* 6:205–53

Gitlin, T. 1981. *The Whole World is Watching.* Berkeley: Univ. Calif. Press

Glasgow Media Group. 1980. *More Bad News.* London: Routledge

Golding, P. 1980. The missing dimensions—news media and the management of social change. See Katz & Szecsko, 1980, pp. 63–81

Golding, P., Elliott, P. 1979. *Making the News.* London: Longman

Golding, P., Murdock, G. 1978. Theories of communication and theories of society. *Commun. Res.* 5:339–56

Golding, P., Middleton, S. 1982. *Images of Welfare.* Oxford: Basil Blackwell

Gouldner, A. V. 1976. *The Dialectics of Science and Technology.* New York: Seabury

Graber, D. 1980. *Crime News and the Public.* New York: Praeger

Gurevitch, M., Bennett, T., Curran, J., Woollacott, J. 1982 *Culture, Society and the Media.* London: Methuen

Haight, T. 1983. The critical research dilemma. *J. Commun.* 33(3):226–36

Hall, S., Critcher, C., Jefferson, T., Clarke, J., Roberts, B. 1978. *Policing the Crisis.* London: Macmillan

Hall, S. 1982. The rediscovery of ideology: return of the repressed in media studies. See Gurevitch et al, 1982. pp. 56–90

Hamelink, C. J., ed. 1981. *Communication in the Eighties: a Reader on the McBride Report.* Rome: IDOC International

Hardt, H. 1979. *Social Theories of the Press.* Beverly Hills, Calif: Sage

Hartmann, P. 1979. News and public perception of industrial relations. *Media Cult. Soc.* 1:225–70

Hawkins, R., Pingree, S. 1980. Some processes in the cultivation effect. *Commun. Res.* 7:193–226

Hebdige, D. 1979. *Subculture: the Meaning of Style.* London: Methuen

Hedinsson, E. 1981. *Television, Family and Society.* Stockholm: Almqvist & Wiksell

Himmelweit, H. T., Swift, B., Jaeger, M. E. 1981. The audience as critic: a conceptual analysis of television entertainment. See Tannenbaum, ed., 1981, pp. 67–106

Hirsch, P. M. 1977. Occupational, organizational and institutional models in mass communication. In *Strategies for Communication Research,* ed. P. Hirsch, P. V. Miller, F. G. Kline, pp. 13–42. Beverly Hills, Calif: Sage

Hirsch, P. M. 1978. Production and distribution roles amongst cultural organisations. *Soc. Res.* 45:315–30

Hirsch, P. M. 1980. The "scary world" of the non-viewer and other anomolies. *Commun. Res.* 7(4):403–56

Hirsch, P. M. 1981. On not learning from one's mistakes. *Commun. Res.* 8(1):3–38

Holz, J. R., Wright, C. R. 1979. Sociology of mass communications. *Ann. Rev. Sociol.* 5:193–217

Hughes, M. 1980. The fruits of cultivation analysis: a re-examination of some effects of television viewing. *Public. Opin. Q.* 44(3):287–302

Janowitz, M. 1981. Mass media: institutional trends and their consequences. In *Reader in Public Opinion and Mass Communication,* ed. M. Janowitz, P. M. Hirsch, pp. 261–85. New York: Free

Johnsson-Smaragdi, U. 1983. *TV Use and Social Interaction in Adolescence.* Stockholm: Almqvist & Wiksell

Jowett, G., Linton, J. M. 1980. *Movies as Mass Communication.* Beverly Hills, Calif: Sage

Katz, E., Adoni, H., Parness, P. 1977. Remembering the news: what the picture adds to recall. *Journ. Q.* 54:231–40

Katz, E. 1980. On conceptualizing media effects. In *Studies in Communication,* Vol. 1, ed. T. McCormack, pp. 119–41. Greenwich, Conn: JAI

Katz, E. 1983. Publicity and pluralistic ignorance. See Wartella et al, 1983, pp. 89–99

Katz, E., Szecsko, T., eds. 1980. *Mass Media and Social Change.* Beverly Hills, Calif: Sage

Kepplinger, H. M. 1982. Visual biases in TV campaign coverage. *Commun. Res.* 9(3):432–46

Kingston, P. W., Cole, J. R. 1983. Economic and social aspects of the literary situation. *Public Opin. Q.* 47:361–85

Kippax, S., Murray, J. P. 1980. Using the mass media: need-gratification and perceived utility. *Commun. Res.* 7(3):335–60

Knight, G., Dean, T. 1982. Myth and the structure of news. *J. Commun.* 32(2):145–61

Krippendorf, K. 1980. *Content Analysis.* Beverly Hills, Calif: Sage

Lang, K. 1979. The critical function of empirical communication research. *Media Cult. Soc.* 1:83–96

Lang, G., Lang, K. 1981. Mass communication and public opinion: strategies for research. In *Social Psychology: Sociological Perspectives,* ed. M. Rosenberg, R. H. Turner, pp. 653–82. New York: Basic

Lang, G., Lang, K. 1983. *The Battle for Public Opinion.* New York: Columbia Univ. Press

Lemert, J. B. 1981. *Does Mass Communication Change Public Opinion After All?* Chicago: Nelson Hall

Lester, M. J. 1980. Generating newsworthiness: the interpretive construction of public events. *Am. Sociol. Rev.* 45:984–94

Levy, M. R., 1978. The audience experience with television news. *Journ. Monog.* 55

Lewis, G. H. 1980. Taste cultures and their composition. See Katz and Szecsko, 1980. pp. 201–17

Lichtenstein, A. L., Rosenfeld, L. B. 1983. Uses and misuses of gratifications research. *Commun. Res.* 10(1):97–109

Lull, J. 1980. The social uses of television. *Hum. Commun. Res.* 6(3):197–209

McBride, S. 1980. *Many Voices, One World.* Paris: Unesco

McCormack, T. 1978. Machismo in media research: a critical view of research on violence and pornography. *Soc. Probl.* 25(5):544–55

McCormack, T. 1983. Male conceptions of female audiences: the case of soap operas. See Wartella et al, 1983, pp. 273–83

McLeod, J. M., Reeves, B. 1980. On the nature of mass media effects. In *Television and Social Behavior,* ed. S. B. Withey, R. P. Ables, 17–54. Hillsdale, NJ: Erlbaum

McQuail, D. 1983. *Mass Communication Theory.* London and Beverly Hills, Calif: Sage

McQuail, D., Windahl, S. 1982. *Communication Models for the Study of Mass Communication.* London: Longman

McQuail, D., van Cuilenburg, J. J. 1983. Diversity as a media policy goal. *Gazette* 31(3):145–62

Miyazaki, T. 1981. Housewives and daytime serials in Japan. *Commun. Res.* 8(3):323–41

Murdock, G. 1980. Misrepresenting media sociology. *Sociology* 14:457–68

Deleted in proof

Neumann, W. R. 1982. Television and American culture: the mass media and the pluralistic audience. *Public Opin. Q.* 46:471–87

Noelle-Neumann, E. 1973. Return to the concept of powerful mass media. *Stud. Broadcasting* 9:66–112

Noelle-Neumann, E. 1977. Turbulences in the climate of opinion: methodological applications of the spiral of silence theory. *J. Commun.* 24:143–58

Noelle-Neumann, E. 1980. Mass media and social change in developed societies. See Wilhoit & de Bock, 1980, pp. 657–78

Noelle-Neumann, E. 1984. *The Spiral of Silence.* Chicago: Univ. Chicago

Olien, C. N., Donohue, G. A., Tichenor, P. J. 1982. Structure, communication and social power: evolution of the knowledge gap hypothesis. *Massacommunicatie* 10(3):81–87

Paletz, D. L., Entman, R. M. 1981. *Media, Power, Politics.* New York: Free

Peters, A. K., Cantor, M. G. 1982. Screen acting as work. See Ettema & Whitney, 1982, pp. 53–68

Phillips, D. P. 1980. Airplane accidents, murder and the mass media: towards a theory of imitation and suggestion. *Soc. Forc.* 58(4):1001–24

Rice, R. E., Paisley, W. J., eds. 1981. *Public Information Campaigns.* Beverly Hills, Calif: Sage

Rikardsson, G. 1981. Newspaper opinion and public opinion. See Rosengren, 1981, pp. 215–26

Roberts, D. F., Bachen, C. M. 1981. Mass communication effects. *Ann. Rev. Psychol.* 32:307–56

Robinson, J. P., Jeffres, L. W. 1979. The changing roles of newspapers in the age of television. *Journ. Monogr.* No. 63

Roe, K. 1983. *Mass Media and Adolescent Schooling.* Stockholm: Almqvist & Wiksell

Rogers, E. M. 1982. *Diffusion of Innovations.* New York: Free. 3rd ed.

Roloff, M. E., Miller, G. R., eds. 1980. *Persuasion.* Beverly Hills, Calif: Sage

Rosengren, K. E. 1979. Bias in news: methods and concepts. *Stud. Broadcasting* 15:31–45

Rosengren, K. E. 1980. Mass media and social change. See Katz & Szecsko, 1980, pp. 247–63

Rosengren, K. E., ed. 1981. *Advances in Content Analysis* Beverly Hills, Calif: Sage

Rosengren, K. E. 1983. Communication research: one paradigm or four? *J. Commun.* 33(3):185–207

Rosengren, K. E., Wenner, L. A., Palmgreen, P., eds. 1985. *Media Gratification Research: Current Perspectives.* Beverly Hills, Calif: Sage.

Rubin, A. M. 1981. An examination of television viewing motivation. *Commun. Res.* 8(2):141–66

Rubin, A. M., Rubin, R. B. 1982. Older persons' TV viewing patterns. *Commun. Res.* 9(2):287–313

Sahin, H., Robinson, J. 1981. Beyond the realm of necessity: TV and the colonization of leisure. *Media, Cult. Soc.* 3(1):85–95

Schiller, D. 1981. *Objectivity and the News.* Philadelphia: Univ. Penn. Press

Schlesinger, P. 1978. *Putting Reality Together: BBC News.* London: Constable

Schlesinger, P., Murdock, G., Elliott, P. 1983.

Televising Terrorism. London: Comedia; New York: Marion Boyar

Schmid, A. P., de Graaf, J. 1982. *Violence as Communication*. Beverly Hills, Calif: Sage

Schudson, M. 1978. *Discovering the News*. New York: Basic

Shaw, D. L., McCombs, M. E., eds. 1981. *The Emergence of American Political Issues: the Agenda-Setting Function of the Press*. St. Paul, Minn: West

Shoemaker, P. J. 1984. Media treatment of deviant political groups. *Journ. Q.* 61(1):66–75, 82

Smith, R. R. 1979. Mythic elements in TV news. *J. Commun.* 29:51–7

Smith, M. Yodelis. 1982. Feminism and the media: research retrospectives. *Commun. Res.* 9(1):145–60

Smythe, D. W. 1977. Communication: blindspot of western marxism. *Can. J. Pol. Soc. Theory.* 1:1–27

Snow, R. P. 1983. *Creating Media Culture*. Beverly Hills, Calif: Sage

Sreberny-Mohammadi, A. 1984. The "World of the News" study. *J. Commun.* 34:121–34

Tannenbaum, P. H. 1981. *The Entertainment Functions of Television*. Hillsdale, NJ: LEA

Taylor, D., Garth, 1982. Pluralistic ignorance and the spiral of silence. *Public Opin. Q.* 46:311–55

Thomas, S., ed. 1982. *Film/Culture*. Metuchen NJ: Scarecrow

Tichenor, P. J., Donohue, G. A., Olien, C. N. 1980. *Community, Conflict and the Press*. Beverly Hills, Calif: Sage

Tuchman, G. 1978a. *Making News*. New York: Free

Tuchman, G. 1978b. The symbolic annihilation of women. In *Hearth and Home*, ed. G. Tuchman, A. K. Daniels, J. Benet, pp. 3–29. New York: Oxford Univ. Press

Tuchman, G. 1978c. Professionalism as an agent of legitimation. *J. Commun.* 28:106–13

Tuchman G. 1983. Consciousness industries and the production of culture. *J. Commun.* 33(3):330–41

Tunstall, J. 1980. The British press in the age of TV. See Christian, 1980, pp. 19–36

van Dijk, T. A. 1983. Discourse analysis: its development and the application to the structure of news. *J. Commun.* 33(3):20–43

Varis, T. 1984. The international flow of television programs. *J. Commun.* 34(1):143–52

Wartella, E., Whitney, D. C., Windahl, S., eds. 1982, 1983. *Mass Communication Review Yearbook*, Vols. 3, 4. Beverly Hills, Calif: Sage

Weaver, D. 1980. Audience need for orientation and media effect. *Commun. Res.* 7(3):361–76

Weaver, D., Buddenbaum, J. M. 1980. See Wilhoit & de Bock, 1980, pp. 371–89

Weaver, D., Graber, D., McCombs, M. E., Eyal, C. 1981. *Media Agenda-Setting in a Presidential Election*. New York: Praeger

Westerståhl, J. 1983. Objective news reporting. *Commun. Res.* 10(3):403–24

Wilhoit, G. C., deBock, H., eds. 1980, 1981. *Mass Communication Review Yearbook*, Vols. 1, 2. Beverly Hills, Calif: Sage

Williamson, J. 1978. *Decoding Advertisements*. London: Marion Boyars

Windahl, S. 1981. Uses and gratifications at the crossroads. See Wilhoit & de Bock, 1981, pp. 174–85

Wobor, J. M. 1978. Televised violence and paranoid perception: the view from Great Britain. *Public Opin. Q.* 42:315–21

Woollacott, J. 1982. Messages and meaning. See Gurevitch et al, 1982, pp. 91–111

Womack, B. 1981. Attention maps of ten major newspapers. *Journ. Q.* 58(2):260–65

Woodward, K., ed. 1980. *The Myths of Information Technology and Post-Industrial culture*. Madison, Wis: Coda

REFERENCE ADDED IN PROOF

Burrell, G., Morgan, G. 1979. *Sociological Paradigms and Organizational Analysis*. London: Heinemann

Ann. Rev. Sociol. 1985. 11:113–27

MACROSOCIOLINGUISTICS AND THE SOCIOLOGY OF LANGUAGE IN THE EARLY EIGHTIES[1]

Joshua A. Fishman

Ferkauf Graduate School of Psychology, Yeshiva University, Bronx, New York 10461

Abstract

The topics, journals, and languages of publication for articles and books on sociolinguistic matters listed in *LLBA* and in *Sociological Abstracts* in 1981–82 are reviewed. It is clearly necessary to examine a large number of journals regularly and to have a reading knowledge of several languages in order to follow recent work in the sociology of language. Recent work on a number of macrosociolinguistic topics (e.g. diglossia, language maintenance, bilingual education) is reviewed in detail. Macrosociolinguistics is integrated conceptually as is macrosociology as a whole. Macrolevel studies not only contribute to the entire sociolinguistic enterprise but contribute significantly to the development of sociology per se.

THE STATE OF THE UNION

Twenty years ago the Social Science Research Council's Committee on Sociolinguistics sponsored a seminar on sociolinguistics, at Indiana University (Bloomington). Participants were faculty members with an active interest in that area of specialization. The seminar itself was one of the large number of academic activities that made up the Summer Linguistic Institute, an annual summer event for advanced students and faculty, conducted by the Linguistic Society of America and rotated from one university campus to another. Some of the seminar participants also taught at the Institute; most of the participants,

---

[1] As its title implies, this review does not purport to cover work in microsociolinguistics, a focus that has been reviewed in several previous issues of the *Annual Review of Sociology*.

0360-0572/85/0815-0113$02.00

however, spent the full eight weeks of their stay in Bloomington in private study and active interaction with each other at daily sessions. All in all, this was a memorable and productive launching of the field as a visible entity.

The 10–12 seminarists were drawn from a variety of academic disciplines—linguistics and anthropology, as might be expected for a topic focusing on language, and sociology, which was well represented. The interdisciplinary nature of the field was generally (although not universally) accepted, not only as a self-definitional characteristic but as a programmatic one in terms of interests to be elicited in others. Nevertheless, the focus on language was newer for sociology than for linguistics/anthropology, and it quickly became apparent that the latter would have to lead the way, whereas sociology could only slowly develop into a position of copartnership. Between the two fields, "the state of the union" within sociolinguistics/sociology of language has long been rather unbalanced. Sociolinguists have continued to be far more often trained in linguistics than in sociology, the latter often being considered useful only for informal exposure and orientation rather than as a substantive and formal body of technical skills and theoretical propositions.

It is to selected aspects of this union, the interdisciplinary field variously referred to as sociolinguistics or sociology of language, that this review turns in order to provide a progress report on "the state of the union" as of the early 1980s. By this period the founding fathers, who participated in the Bloomington seminar of 1964, were joined by a large number of others; their enterprise had yielded worldwide results in courses, conferences, and publications; and a new generation of scholars and practitioners had arisen whose work fully merits careful attention.

Data Under Review

Owing to the cooperation of *Sociological Abstracts* and *Language and Language Behavior Abstracts* (to both of which thanks are gratefully expressed), all items abstracted from 1980 to 1982 and coded as "linguistics" in the former or as "sociolinguistics" in either source were identified to constitute the universe for this review. This yielded 466 items (journal articles, chapters in collective volumes, books) almost equally divided between the two sources. This itself is a noteworthy development. That *Sociological Abstracts* should yield as many (actually six more) abstracts coded either "linguistics" or "sociolinguistics" than does the abstract journal covering the language field per se is an indication of a growing role for and awareness of the study of language within the total sociological enterprise. It is also instructive that the amount of overlap between these two sources is negligible—only some 20 items out of 466—strongly suggesting that both sources, the sociological one and the more

Table 1 Non-English items, abstracted 1980–82, pertaining to sociolinguistics/sociology of language

Language	SOURCE		Total
	SA[a]	LLBA[b]	
French	29	30	59
Spanish	13	3	16
German	6	13	19
Italian	6	7	13
Russian	2	11	13
Other	2[c]	3[d]	5
Total	58	67	125

a = *Sociological Abstracts*; b = *Language and Language Behavior Abstracts*; c = 1 Finnish and 1 Hungarian; d = 2 Dutch and 1 Finnish

linguistic one, are needed in order to keep fully abreast of work in the total interdisciplinary field.

LANGUAGES OF PUBLICATION

Of the 466 items that constitute our universe, slightly more than a quarter (26.82%; see Table 1) were published in languages other than English. Almost half of the non-English items were in French, with German, Spanish, Italian and Russian each accounting for between 13% and 15% of the whole. The total number and the proportion of listed and abstracted non-English items are each large enough to argue powerfully for advanced reading mastery in at least one of the major continental languages (preferably two) as a prerequisite skill for sociolinguistic specialization (above and beyond the non-English language requirement of empirical fieldwork per se which often involves learning a vernacular that may be unencumbered by literacy).[2]

Even more important, however, is the realization that the sociolinguistic enterprise has truly become an international one rather than the primarily Anglo-American pursuit that it was as recently as a decade ago. Even the clear predominance of English publications cannot mask the fact that many of the scholars publishing in English live, work, and are involved in non-Anglo-American contexts, thereby contributing to the international nature of the field.

[2]My own impression is that the non-English literature pertaining to sociolinguistic matters is actually somewhat larger than that indicated by Table 1, particularly insofar as Spanish and Russian are concerned. There is also a small but continuous stream of literature in Catalan, Dutch, Hebrew, Japanese and other languages (e.g., Serbo-Croatian and Swedish) that seems not to have reached the abstracting services that define our universe. Thus, the functional argument for advanced literacy in one or more non-English languages is even stronger than Table 1 would imply.

JOURNALS OF PUBLICATION

The publications in which sociolinguistic items appear constitute a very large and diversified set. In 1980–82 this set consisted of 223 separate publications for a total of 466 items or, roughly, no more than 2 items per publication. Books, of course, count as one item (unless they contain separately authored articles) and serve to depress the overall item per publication average but, by and large, the low overall average to which we are referring is only negligibly due to books (20 in all). This low average of items to publications reflects the huge number of different journals in which articles of sociolinguistic content are published each year. In order to provide access to even half of this worldwide literature, a library would need to carry over a hundred journals. Actually, the problem is even more severe since these journals are not only many in number but they are very diversified as to disciplinary affiliation: education, psychology, political science, history, distinct language and literature specializations, distinct language and area study specializations, law, philosophy, religion, medicine and numerous other fields, not even to mention sociology, linguistics, anthropology and sociolinguistics/sociology of language per se.

The top baker's dozen among sociolinguistic publications, all of which published at least seven sociolinguistic articles from 1980 to 1982, were (in alphabetic order): *Anthropological Linguistics, English World-Wide, Etudes de linguistique appliquée, Georgetown University Round Table on Languages and Linguistics, International Journal of the Sociology of Language, Journal of Multilingual and Multicultural Development, Language in Society, Languages, Language Problems and Language Planning, Language Sciences, Revista Paraguaya de Sociología, Voprosy Yazykoznaniya* and *Women's Studies International Quarterly. Only one of these 13 (Revista Paraguaya de Sociología)* may be considered atypically overconcerned with sociolinguistic matters during the particular period we are reviewing. However, more impor-

Table 2 Publications for sociolinguistic/sociology of language items, abstracted 1980–82, by number of items published

Number of items published	Number of publications
Twenty or more items	3
Ten to nineteen items	4
Five to nine items	13
Two to four items	64
One item	139
Total	223

tantly, the remaining dozen outlets[3] most reliably sociolinguistic account for a total of only 133 items, i.e. for only roughly 29% of the total output. This underscores the need to read not only voluminously but also very widely and to utilize abstracting sources regularly in order to follow the sociolinguistic literature. For sociologists in particular, it implies the need to constantly follow journals outside of their own field and, indeed, outside of those that are usually carried in social science libraries alone.

TOPICAL CONCENTRATIONS

It is obviously more difficult to review the topical emphases within our universe of items, if for no other reason than the difficulty of specifying topics for those articles (the lion's share) that have relevance to a variety of topics. Data on mother tongue of kindergarteners, for example, may be related to a variety of other variables: educational, psychological, political, social, economic, ethnic self-identification and/or attitude. In order to avoid a very complex (even if possibly more accurate) topical classification, an assistant and I jointly classified all of the 466 items constituting the universe of this review, assigning each item to a single topic only. The topical distribution in Table 3 (which deals only with topics dealt with by at least 10 items) is the result of our classification efforts. Although this table must be interpreted cautiously, particularly due to the macrolevel topical interests of the classifiers themselves, it does have some instructive value.

Clearly, the most frequently encountered topics include a good number that are distinctly and uniquely sociolinguistic, e.g. attitudes toward languages and their users, dialect/standard differences or the societal functions related to each, language planning, multilingualism/diglossia and the characteristics and/or functions of spoken language acts/events. On the other hand, a goodly number of the most frequently encountered topics deal squarely with classical sociological topics, e.g. ethnicity/national identity, sex role–related behaviors, minorities, political processes, and social stratification, not to mention such applied sociology fields or neighboring disciplines as education, law, language learning, or literary analysis. Sociologists interested in any of these topics or fields would do well to consult the sociolinguistic literature regularly for new perspectives and, even more frequently, for new data pertaining to them.

[3]The above list is shaped, of course, both by the journals abstracted and the topical coding practices of LLBA and SA. Some additional journals that should probably be added to any short list of most frequent sociolinguistic outlets are *Child Language, Semiotics* and *Text*. A very recent addition to this list would be the *Journal of Social Psychology of Language*.

Table 3 Largest topical concentrations among sociolinguistic items abstracted 1980–82

Topic	Number of items
Language planning (status and/or corpus)	26
Ethnicity/national identity	24
Sex role–linked language behavior	22
Multilingualism (including diglossia)	19
Minorities	16
Social stratification (social class, social status)	13
Education	12
Language learning/teaching	12
Politics/political issues	11
Attitudes toward languages/language users	10
Dialect/standard differences/functions	10
Law/legal processes	10
Literary analysis	10
Spoken language characteristics/functions	10
Other topics (82)	261
Total	466

SELECTED SOCIOLINGUISTIC CONTRIBUTIONS TO SOCIOLOGICAL TOPICS

The first half of this review will be devoted to mentioning and briefly discussing some selected sociolinguistic items that were abstracted during 1980–82 and that dealt with sociological topics, with preference given to items that did not appear in standard sociological journals. The underlying message in this selection is that sociologists will often miss considerable relevant research if they fail to check through the sociolinguistic literature in connection with their particular topics of interest.

Sex-Related Roles and Expectations

Sociolinguists/sociologists of language have contributed considerably to the general conclusion that women are more concerned for societally defined "propriety" in interpersonal behavior. The language counterpart to such "restriction to propriety" has been explored in several studies. In many instances, women have been found to use nonstandard ("incorrect") speech less frequently and to engage in hypercorrect speech (i.e. speech that is more "proper" than the situation calls for) more frequently than do men. In the American context, Maynor (1981) has now added a historical dimension to "feminine = propriety proneness" by going into the 1930 files of *The Linguistic Atlas of New England*.

On the basis of the direct responses of 297 males and 119 females on grammatical items (both usage and acceptability), the expected female propriety proneness was corroborated for respondents of similar age, occupation, and education. The author speculates that women may have felt a greater need to indicate their social aspirations through speech since they were less likely than men to achieve occupational status. This interpretation would lead us to expect a decrease in female propriety proneness in recent years as greater equalization and even identity of male-female roles is achieved.

Alpatov & Kryuchkova (1980) provide confirmatory evidence for expectations that large-scale social changes in male-female relationships are leading to an attenuation of female politeness behavior in speech. Japanese culture is well known to have traditionally required special politeness behaviors for females. Similarly, the Japanese language is particularly rich in gender differentiations, both morphophonologically and morphosyntactically. In the past, females have been expected to use more polite personal pronouns and diminutives as well as to adopt politeness formulas indicating an exaggeratedly lower status vis-à-vis male interlocutors. Such usages have all been decreasing rapidly in recent years among the younger generation for whom egalitarian role relationships have generally become increasingly common.

Canadian data pertaining to bilingualism (English/French) among francophones in Quebec long revealed that males learned English more frequently, and used it more often and for more years than did females. This finding has been interpreted as revealing a lesser tendency for francophone females to obtain higher education, to enter the workforce, to work away from home, to seek job mobility, and to interact with governmental agencies compared to francophone males. During the 1960s and 1970s, these differences in inter-sex roles and experiences began to grow smaller in Montreal, just as they have also lessened in Puerto Rico. Accordingly, Angle & Hesse-Biber (1981) no longer found different rates of learning and using English between younger males and females in these two settings.

The fact that differences in sex-role behavior and expectations have decreased among the young still leaves us unenlightened as to just how such widespread but generationally patterned social change takes place. Young people, after all, have been socialized, at least initially, by adults, that is by the very generations among whom less change has occurred in relation to sex-role behaviors and expectations. As far as language socialization is concerned, there continues to be ample evidence that to this very day American parents and other adults speak differently to boys than to girls. Greif (1980) has reported that both fathers and mothers interrupt daughters more than sons (during ages 2–5) and that they speak simultaneously more often when their daughters speak than when their sons speak. Similarly, in Sweden children still learn sex-specific speech characteristics at an early age (3–7 years), and boys and girls are quite predictably spoken to differently by adults (Fichtelius, Johansson, & Kerstein 1980). Thus, any adolescent or postadolescent equalization of sex roles and expectations may very well be a product of the youth culture (i.e. of the greater interaction of young folks with each other, without adult intervention, as well as of their greater selective interaction with certain categories of adults who support youth culture values and behaviors).

Obviously, sociolinguistic data can be quite sensitive for monitoring social change, as Cooper has demonstrated both in connection with use of the so-called "generic he" (1984) as well as in more general theoretical terms (1982).

Ethnicity/Nationality Issues

Few topics have received as much general sociological attention in recent years as has ethnicity. Given the urgency of the social problem that attends this topic, it need come as no surprise that ideological, political, and philosophical biases are quickly revealed by scholars who turn their attention in this direction. The sociolinguistic literature has certainly not been immune in this connection. Just as sociolinguistics/sociology of language had been "put to use" on behalf of Nazism during the dark days of Hitler's Germany (Weinreich 1946), so it has "proven itself to be useful" in the USSR (Isayev 1977) and has found its services "to be of value to the state" in francophone Africa today (Turcotte 1979). None of this is surprising, nor is it in any way a more likely occurrence vis-à-vis sociolinguistics/sociology of language than with respect to sociology (or even with respect to linguistics) more generally. Since ethnicity-and-nationality are themselves frequently matters of contention, ethnicity and nationality-related scholarship that can avoid such contention and focus on genuine intellectual problems is all the rarer and all the more praiseworthy.

One such intellectual problem is concerned with arriving at an improved theoretical conceptualization of the link between language and ethnicity. A careful review of articles in the *Harvard Encyclopedia of American Ethnic Groups* (Thernstrom et al 1980) reveals an emphasis, on the part of writer after writer, on language as a prime marker of ethnicity. On the other hand, the *Encyclopedia* carries a long article explicitly on this topic that stresses the detachability of the two and the recurring realignments between them that have transpired throughout history (Fishman 1980a). Obviously, we are dealing with both a very frequent and yet not an indissoluble relationship.

Among sociolinguists, Paulston & Paulston (1980) have investigated the role of language in the maintenance of ethnic boundaries. Their analysis focuses upon revitalization movements and upon minority groups—that is, upon groups characterized by stress, rapid social change, heightened elitist awareness of group needs, identity activization, and political efforts. Eastman & Reese (1981) stress that under the foregoing circumstances it is not the knowing, speaking, or claiming of the group language that leads to ethnic self-ascription but, rather, the association of the language with all ongoing community processes of problem definition and solution in daily life. Obviously, the primary symbol system of the species is both best capable and most likely to become symbolic of the entire society with which it is associated. The associated language is, therefore, more than part of culture per se (neither religion, law, education, nor customary interaction being possible without it). Furthermore, it serves as a powerful index to its associated culture. As a result of both of the foregoing, it is also most naturally symbolic of that culture, as well as most useful to heighten awareness of it. As such, although language rightfully claims a special relationship with culture (Fishman 1980b), the relationship is far more detachable and more widely sharable than elitist or proto-elitist consciousness raisers are likely to admit or recognize.

While the lion's share of language and ethnicity exploration continues to deal with varying aspects of the link, widely presumed to be indissoluble, between language and ethnicity/nationality (see Lefevre 1979 and Pool 1979 for two outstanding examples of sociolinguistic work along these lines), the previously mentioned issues of detachability and sharability have also come in for some additional consideration, long overdue. Dorian (1980) has presented considerable detail about "fisherfolk ethnic identity" in East Sutherland, Scotland. Four different "languages" have distinguished this group from its neighbors during the past century: pure Gaelic when their neighbors were already speaking English-impacted Gaelic; English-impacted Gaelic when their neighbors were already Gaelic/English bilinguals; persistent Gaelic/English bilingualism when their neighbors had become English speaking monolinguals; and, finally, Gaelic-influenced English when their neighbors had long since learned to speak English with little if any Gaelic lexical or grammatical interference. Thus, the long-standing linguistic component of fisherfolk ethnicity is the lag in their language usage relative to the rest of the population, rather than any consistent language all their own. (For further development of this theme, see Fishman 1985.) A long-term process of dynamic pluralism in ethnocultural and ethnolinguistic behaviors is implied by most of the above research as well as by that of Grandguillaume (1979) on the Maghreb and that of Boulding (1979) on international ethnocultural perspectives.

It should be quite clear from the foregoing that even such a burgeoning field as ethnicity/nationality, a field that has long attracted thousands of sociologists throughout the world, can find stimulating new concepts and provocative data in the sociolinguistic literature.

PROGRESS IN SELECTED SOCIOLINGUISTIC TOPICS

The remainder of this review will be devoted to three topics within macrosociolinguistics. These are topics that might very well be of interest to most sociologists but, thus far, they have primarily interested sociolinguists. Here again, preference will be given to work appearing in journals other than those usually encountered by American sociologists and sociolinguists.

Diglossia

Diglossia (bilingualism that is widespread, stable, functionally complementary, and societal rather than individual) continues to be attested to, studied, and found theoretically provocative, perhaps to the point of becoming the keystone of the macrosociolinguistic enterprise. While it remains true, as heretofore, that most studies of diglossia deal with less developed or less modernized settings and, therefore, with Third World contexts (see, e.g., Chaudenson 1979, Gardy & Lafont 1981, Prudent 1981, Parasher 1980, Zughoul 1980), this is by no means exclusively so. Indeed, Jacob (1981) goes to considerable pains to demonstrate that diglossia neither requires economic stagnation nor prevents economic development. Several other investigators stress the dynamic nature of diglossia phenomena. Gardy & Lafont (1981) point to the possibility of social conflict polarizing around each of the languages involved, as well as language interference and mixture between them. Prudent (1981), in particular, points to code switching that may be so frequent, and to lexical as well as syntactic hybridization that is so widespread, that a new variety (an interlect) may be considered to have arisen, either extending or replacing the former diglossia pattern. Kremnitz (1981) perceptively points out that the co-presence of two or more languages or varieties in a community does not necessarily imply diglossia. (Widely accepted, long lasting, and functionally complementary language use is far less common than bilingualism.) Indeed, mere co-presence may be far more conflicted (and, therefore, require both individual and societal analysis for its illumination) than is typical of diglossia.

In many Third World contexts, where social change—including economic modernization—may be far from negligible, former colonial languages may still retain their long-standing control over formal literacy-related pursuits. Nevertheless, some educational use of the vernaculars associated with the less high status and more informal everyday rounds of common folk can, at times, be attained (Chaudenson 1979) without disrupting the overall diglossia system. On the other hand, there may be considerable reluctance to detract from the status and formality of the written language (Parasher 1980), or, even more, to appear to question the superiority of a sanctified classical language (Zughoul 1980).

It need hardly be pointed out that diglossia settings both require and contribute to the sociological study of social change. To reject diglossia on ideological grounds that it supposedly restricts literacy or social mobility (a suggestion that ignores the Swiss or Luxembourgian examples to the contrary) is to politicize the epistemological foundations of sociolinguistics (for further comments along these lines, see Guiora 1984).

Maintenance of Minority Languages

This topic flows directly from the prior one. Without diglossia within their own speech communities, minority languages lose their functional uses and, therefore, their users as well. The topic also has many additional ramifications in educational and governmental policy that have given it greater professional and public recognition. This is also true outside of the United States; sociolinguists abroad having been widely attracted to this topic (see e.g. Anderson 1981 reviewing several dozen papers; Tabouret-Keller & Lucket 1981).

Within the United States the maintenance of Spanish and Black English and the use of bilingual education for "illicit" maintenance purposes (not intended by the Bilingual Education Act) have received the largest share of both scholarly and public attention. The Chicano case has been well studied earlier by Skrabenek (1970), more recently by Hudson-Edwards and Bills (1982), and most particularly by Lopez (1982). Insofar as Spanish is concerned, all of them find a decreasing degree of intergenerational ethnolinguistic continuity, as well as growing constriction to oral use within the family domain even among those who do maintain it. The implication of this research (exemplified by Edwards 1981) is that the fear that Hispanics will not become Anglified may be no more than nativistic fantasy at its worst. The fear may reflect a one-generation delay (compared to smaller and older minorities in the US) due to ongoing legal and illegal Hispanic immigration. However, as Jonz (1978) and Limón (1982) have shown, even highly mixed Spanglish which represents an interlectal stage in the transition to English when diglossia is absent can become a reflection of the quest for group solidarity and authenticity.

Bilingual education continues to interest sociolinguists, primarily because of widespread media and man-in-the-street suspicions that it not only delays the acquisition of English but leads to political separatism as well. While the latter charge has received almost no empirical attention, perhaps because of its farfetched nature, the former has benefited from empirical evidence and theoretical elaboration that is increasingly more refined. Templin (1980) has provided a fine case study of a very successful bilingual school that clearly accomplishes outstanding results, both in English and in the vernacular of its students. This resulted from adoption of a curricular model in accord with the theory of the Canadian, J. Cummins (1980). His theory predicts superior language learning as a result of bilingual education that initially stresses non-English mother tongues (and that continues a mother-tongue component through the grades) with pupil populations derived from communities with meager literacy. Historical parallels with eighteenth and nineteenth century monolingual vernacular education for just such populations should not be overlooked. However, such parallels cannot argue for the ability of schools per se to attain minority language maintenance. Liebe-Harkort (1980) correctly observes that much more powerful institutions than schools are needed for this purpose.

Black English counterparts to bilingual education have also been argued pro (Schuster-Webb 1980) and con (Templin 1980) on grounds very similar to those advanced in the Hispanic case. Atheoretical though such articles may be, they clearly provide data for theoretical examination. Thus, Fishman, et al (1982) ask how the United States can be so lacking in diglossia settings (most non-English mother-tongue groups failing to reach the three-plus generational criterion of diglossic stability) and yet reveal such across-the-board increases in census-reported claims of a mother tongue other than English, from 1940 or 1960 to 1970. The impact of the ethnic revival is found to be far greater and different in claims to a foreign mother tongue than in actual non-English language use—the former rising and the latter falling.

Language Planning: Corpus

Status planning deals with authoritative efforts to influence the functions of languages in society. Minority languages are in need of status planning on their behalf, particularly since some governments actively engage in status planning to "destablize" minority languages. The literature dealing with this topic is extensive and interesting. However, it may be more instructive to turn our attention in conclusion to corpus planning—problems of planning the lexicon, orthography, writing system—to vary our focus somewhat (status planning, after all, is once more concerned with issues of national integration and language legitimacy, whether in ideology or in practice) and to show that corpus planning too is never free of larger societal issues.

Xenophobia, social conflict, and suspicions of internal divisiveness are often no further beneath the surface in corpus planning than they are in status planning. Indeed, Salzmann's (1980) discussion of Czech pre–World War II attempts to "influence" Slovak in the direction of Czech, and Jackson & T'Sou's (1979) discussions of Chinese governmental sensitivity to the political consequences of simplifying the writing system, clearly reveal that corpus planning may simultaneously be status planning and that the two may be more separable in theory than in practice.

Corpus planning seems often to be engaged with, or in pursuit of, an image of authenticity and unity that may not be prompted by fears of external attack or internal secession. Certainly there are no such fears in Finland's concern for a unified standard to attain a unified society (Koivusalo 1978) or in Iceland's concern for minimizing foreignisms and for preserving the etymological (rather than pursuing the phonetic) principal in its orthography (Jonsson 1978). Even the efforts of Latin American, French, and Russian authorities to counteract English borrowings (see Leon Rey 1981, Bashkin 1980, and Keipert 1978, respectively) are due more to self-images, to culture policy and culture planning, than to fears of American political intervention, manipulation, or influence.

If status considerations are evident even in the cases of the corpus concerns of well-established integrative languages, how much more must this be the case in conjunction with languages whose integrative functions are still somewhat threatened? Accordingly, recent suggestions concerning language planning for Hindi as a pan-Indian language, at least for administrative functions, have suggested compromises that would initially render Hindi less pure and less complex than its official planners have hitherto desired (Krishnamurti 1976, Kumar 1980, Rao 1980). Apparently, their struggles for purity are luxuries that can be afforded only when fundamental issues of functional acceptability have been solved.

Even English in the United States has its corpus issues (Ferguson 1979) with the long-standing stress of English teachers and gatekeepers on "proper English" now having boiled over into elitist concerns that "something is wrong" with the way most Americans use their language and that "something should be done about it before it is too late." American English, the specter that haunts the world, lives in a haunted house itself!

Macrosociology of Language: Conceptually Integrative or Topically Discrete?

To what extent has recent macrosociology of language revealed itself to be integrated by a powerful and parsimonious set of common concepts? It seems that this is so about to the same extent that macrosociology in general is integrated in that fashion. Likewise, conceptual bridges exist between macro-sociology of language and microsociolinguistics about to the same extent, probably, as they do between microsociology and macrosociology more generally (Cicourel 1982). In each case some integration and some bridges exist, but more are obviously needed. Within the macrosociology of language or between it and its micro counterpart, integration exists only in a recognition of the social contexts and concomitants of language use, language attitudes, and, to some extent, language structures per se. There is obviously some parallelism, feedback, and interrelatedness between language characteristics and characteristics of the social contexts in which given languages are employed and evaluated, but causality can rarely be assumed in either direction.

While it is hard to say that macro and micro moved more closely together during the period under review, it does seem to me that a long-term trend along those very lines can be noted, particularly with respect to the training of younger investigators. However, until most major sociology departments begin to participate actively in the training of sociolinguists/sociologists of language, until they assume equal responsibility for the intellectual and methodological preparation, socialization and certification of sociolinguists/sociologists of language, until then the sociological potential of the sociolinguistic enterprise will not yet have been realized and the sociological responsibility, therefore, will not yet have been discharged. Obviously, sociologists must take more initiative in this connection in the future for they not only have the most still to give to, but also the most still to gain from a sociologically stimulated sociolinguistics/sociology of language.

Literature Cited

Alpatov, V. M., Kryuchkova, T. B. 1980. O muzhskom-zhenskom variantakh yaponskogo yazyka. *Voprosy Yazykoznaniya*. 29: 58–68

Anderson, Alan B. 1981. The problem of minority languages: reflections on the Glasgow conference. *Language Problems and Language Planning*. S:291–304

Angle, J., Hesse-Biber, S. 1981. Gender and prestige preference in language. *Sex Roles*. 7:449–61

Bashkin, E. I. 1980. Termin kak obyekt sotsialnogo interesa. *Vestnik Leningradskovo Universiteta: Istoriya-yazyk-literatura*. 35:111–13

Boulding, E. 1979. Ethnic separatism and world development. *Research in Social Movements, Conflicts and Change*. 2:259–81

Chaudenson, R. 1979. Les parlers créoles et l'enseignement du francais. *Le francais dans le Monde*. 19:12–17

Cicourel, V. 1982. Notes on the integration of micro and macro levels of analysis. In *Advances in Social Theory and Methodology: Toward an Integration of Micro and Macro Sociologies*, ed. K. Knorr-Centia, A. V. Cicourel. Boston: Routledge & Kegan Paul

Cooper, R. L. 1982. A framework for the study of language spread. In *Language Spread: Studies in Diffusion and Social Change*, ed. R. L. Cooper, pp. 5–36. Bloomington and Washington, DC: Indiana University Press and Center for Applied Linguistics

Cooper, R. L. 1985. The avoidance of androcentric generics. *Int. J. Sociol. Lang.* 56: In press

Cummins, J. 1980. The construct of language proficiency in bilingual education. *Georgetown Univ. Round Table Lang. Linguist.* 1980:81–103

Dorian, N. C. 1980. Linguistic lag as an ethnic marker. *Language in Society*. 9:33–41

Eastman, C. M., Reese, T. C. 1981. Associated language: how language and ethnic identity are related. *Gen. Linguist*. 21:109–16

Edwards, J. R. 1981. The defense of English in the United States. *English Around the World*. 24:2–3

Ferguson, C. A. 1979. National attitudes toward language planning. *Georgetown Univ. Round Table on Lang. Linguist.* 1979:51–60

Fichtelius, A., Johansson, I., Kerstin, N. 1980. Three investigations of sex-associated speech variation in day schools. *Women's Stud. Int. Q.* 3:219–225

Fishman, J. A. 1980a. Language maintenance and ethnicity. In *Harvard Encyclopedia of American Ethnic Groups*, ed. S. Thernstrom, pp. 629–38. Cambridge: Harvard Univ. Press

Fishman, J. A. 1980b. The Whorfian hypothesis: Varieties of validation, confirmation and disconfirmation. I. *Int. J. Sociol. Lang.* 26:25–40

Fishman, J. A. 1985. "Nothing new under the sun": A case study in alternatives in the language and ethnicity linkage. In *The Rise and Fall of the Ethnic Revival*. ed. J. A. Fishman, M. Gertner, W. Milan and E. Lowy, pp. 77–104. Berlin: Mouton. In press

Fishman, J. A., Gertner, M., Lowy, E., Milan, W. 1982. Maintien des langues, "renouveau ethnique" et diglossie aux Etats Unis. *La Linguistique* 18:45–64

Gardy, Philippe, Lafont, Robert. 1981. La diglossie comme conflit: l'example occitan. *Languages*. 15:75–91

Grandguillaume, G. 1979. Langue, identite et culture nationale au Maghreb. *Peuples Mediterraneens*. 9:3–28

Greif, E. B. 1980. Sex differences in parent-child conversations. *Women's Stud. Int. Q.* 3:253–58

Guiora, Z., ed. 1984. *An Epistemology for the Language Sciences*. Detroit: Wayne State University

Hudson-Edwards, A., Bills, G. D. 1982. Intergenerational language shift in an Albuquerque barrio. In *Spanish in the United States: Sociolinguistic Aspects*, ed. J. Amastre, Lucia Elias-Olivares, pp. 135–153. Cambridge: Cambridge Univ. Press.

Isayev, M. I. 1977. *National Languages in the USSR: Problems and Solutions*. Moscow: Progress Publishers, 432 pp.

Jackson, R., T'Sou, B. K. Y. 1979. Language problems and language reform in the People's Republic of China. *Modern Languages*. 60:78–88

Jacob, N. 1981. Sprachplanung in einer komplexen Diglossie-situation dargestellt am Beispiel Luxemburg. *Lang. Probl. Lang. Plan.* 5:153–74

Jonsson, J. H. 1978. Zur Sprachpolitik und

Sprachpflege in Island. *Muttersprache.* 88:353–62

Jonz, J. G. 1978. Language and La Academia; if English works, por qué se emplea español? *J. of Ethn. Stud.* 5:65–79

Keipert, H. 1978. Puristische tendenzen in der russichen Sprachpflege der Gegenwart. *Osteuropa.* 28:285–309

Koivusalo, E. 1978. Yleiskieli-kielenhuoltoyhteiskunta. *Virittäjä.* 82:316–8

Kremnitz, G. 1981. Du "bilinguisme" au "conflit linguistique." Cheminement de termes et de concepts. *Languages.* 15:63–74

Krishnamurti, B. 1976. Problems of language standardization in India. *Osmania Pap. Linguist.* 2:1–21

Kumar, Suresh 1980. A sociolinguist view of Hindi in administration. *Indian Linguistics.* 41:21–30

Lefevre, A. 1979. Nationalisme linguistique et identification linguistique: le cas de Belgique. *Int. J. Sociol. Lang.* 20:37–58

Leon Rey, J. A. 1981. Augusto Malaret, los americanismos y la Asociación de Academias de la lengua Española. *Bol. Acad. Colomb.* 31:102–9

Liebe-Harkort, M.-L. 1980. Recent developments in Apachean language maintenance. *Int. J. Am. Linguist.* 46:85–91

Limón, J. E. 1982. El meeting: history, folk Spanish, and ethnic nationalism in a Chicano student community. In *Spanish in the United States: Sociolinguistic Aspects,* ed. J. Amastae, Lucia Elias-Olivares, pp. 301–32. Cambridge: Cambridge Univ. Press

Lopez, D. E. 1982. *The Maintenance of Spanish Over Three Generations in the United States.* Los Alamitos: Center for Bilingual Research. Mimeo

Mansour, G. 1980. The dynamics of multilingualism: The case of Senegal. *J. Multiling. Multicult. Devel.* 4:273–93

Maynor, N. 1981. Males, females and language propriety. *J. Eng. Linguist.* 15:17–20

Parasher, S. V. 1980. Mother tongue-English diglossia: a case study of educated Indian

bilinguals' language use. *Anthropol. Linguist.* 22:151–62

Paulston, C. B., Paulston, R. G. 1980. Language and ethnic boundaries. *Lang. Sci.* 2:69–101

Pool, J. 1979. Language planning and identity planning. *Int. J. Sociol. Lang.* 20:5–21

Prudent, L.-F. 1981. Diglossie et interlecte. *Languages.* 61:13–38

Rao, J. 1980. Proposal for pan-Indianization of Hindi structure. *Psycho-Lingua.* 10:47–54

Salzmann, Zdenek. 1980. Language standardization in a bilingual state: the case of Czech and Slovak, two closely cognate languages. *Language Problems and Language Planning.* 4:38–54

Schuster-Webb, Karen 1980. The case for Black English revisited. *Viewpoints Teach. Learn.* 56:88–95

Skrabenek, R. L. 1970. Language maintenance among Mexican-Americans. *Int. J. Compar. Sociol.* 11:272–82

Tabouret-Keller, Andrée, Lucket, F. 1981. Maintien d l'alsacien et adoption du francais. Elements de la situation linguistique en milieu rural en Alsace. *Languages.* 15:39–62

Taylor, Karyn 1978. A Black perspective on the melting pot. *Soc. Pol.* 8:31–7

Templin, Rebecca 1980. Rock Point Community School: A model for bilingual education. *Linguist. Report.* 22:4–11

Thernstrom, S. et al., eds. 1980. *Harvard Encyclopedia of American Ethnic Groups.* Cambridge: Harvard Univ. Press. 1105 pp.

Turcotte, D. 1979. La planification linguistique en Cote d'Ivoire: faire du francais le vehiculaire national par excellence. *Revue canadienne des etudes africaines.* 13:423–39

Weinreich, M. 1946. *Hitler's Professors.* New York: Yiddish Scientific Institute

Zughoul, R. 1980. Diglossia in Arabic: Investigating solutions. *Anthropol. Linguist.* 22, (5):201–17

Ann. Rev. Sociol. 1985. 11:129–49

QUALITY OF LIFE RESEARCH AND SOCIOLOGY

K. F. Schuessler

Department of Sociology, Indiana University, Bloomington, Indiana 47405

G. A. Fisher

Department of Sociology, University of Massachusetts, Amherst, Massachusetts 01003

Abstract

This review examines research literature on the Quality of Life (QOL) published in Canada and the United States since 1975. Of particular interest are the definition and measurement of QOL, theoretical perspectives of QOL, the findings of QOL research, and the impact of this research on public policy. A brief critical assessment accompanies the discussion of each topic, and a forecast is ventured of the future of QOL research in sociology.

INTRODUCTION

Quality of Life (hereafter referred to as QOL) usually designates the desired outcome of social policies and programs. Because of its applied focus, research in this area spans many disciplines, including economics, psychology, political science, and sociology, and is pursued in many nations, particularly those with central or planned economies. By intention, this review is limited largely to Canadian and US publications; to works classifiable as social science, and in particular sociology; and to studies of QOL in North American populations. Not all important studies are discussed in this article, but the list of references covers practically all important studies. Social indicators are excluded, notwithstanding their close ties with QOL, because the literature in this area tends to focus on change rather than outcomes, and because reviews of this literature already exist (see Land 1983). Because the focus of this review is on the current state of QOL research, only works published since 1970 are considered.

The reader will find several references that are especially useful for assembling topical bibliographies on QOL research. Larson (1978) is a review of QOL research in gerontology; Palys & Little (1980) review QOL research in psychology; *Sociological Abstracts,* 1979–1984, indexes a number of European studies; Gilmartin et al (1979) list 40 or so entries on QOL in their annotated bibliography; George (1980) reviews scales designed to measure QOL among older persons. The scope and method of QOL research may be abstracted from the 13 volumes of *Social Indicators Research,* 1974–1984. In view of the exclusion of literature on social indicators from this review, it is pertinent that this journal is subtitled *An International and Interdisciplinary Journal of Quality-of-Life Measurement.*

This review is organized around what appear to be the major issues in the field, expressed here as questions: When did research in QOL begin and where is it headed? How is QOL defined? How is it measured? What are its correlates and/or predictors? Is there a theory of QOL? What is the relationship between QOL research and public policy? What are the problems facing QOL as a research field?

NOTES ON HISTORY

QOL as a research field came into being around 1960. The Report Of The President's Commission On National Goals (1960) and Bauer's work (1966) on the secondary effects of national space programs on American society are regularly mentioned as having given impetus to the emergence of QOL as a separate area of research. Campbell (1981:4) quotes the late President Johnson as saying in 1964:

> The task of the Great Society is to ensure our people the environment, the capacities, and the social structures which will give them a meaningful chance to pursue their individual happiness. Thus the Great Society is concerned not with how much, but with how good—not with the quantity of goods, but with the quality of our lives.

The climate of opinion in the early 1960s was generally favorable to the study of QOL.

Putting the start of QOL research in 1960 is, of course, arbitrary. While the term is recent—it does not appear in the *International Encyclopedia of Social Sciences* (1968), and it appears for the first time in 1979 as an index term in *Sociological Abstracts*—the concept itself has a long history. Concern about the good life is probably as old as civilization. In terms of scientific inquiry, what is being done today under the heading of QOL research was done by earlier generations of American sociologists under various other labels. Burgess & Cottrell's study (1939) of happiness in marriage is a case in point.

The Russell Sage Foundation promoted research on QOL and social indicators throughout the 1960s and into the 1970s. The Institute of Social Research, University of Michigan, has been active in the field since the late 1960s, as has the National Opinion Research Center at the University of Chicago.

The story of QOL as a research movement, at least an important part of it, might be written from the publications of the forenamed organizations.

DEFINING QUALITY OF LIFE

Numerous attempts have been made to provide a definition of QOL (see, for example, US *Environmental Protection Agency* 1973). In formulating a definition most specialists agree that the term *quality* has the same meaning as *grade,* and that grade ranges from high to low, from better to worse. Hence, one reads statements such as "Their QOL is improving" and "Their QOL is worse than ours." There is less agreement about the meaning of the term *life*. The dominant trend is to restrict the term to mean only mental life, but the view that QOL inheres in environmental conditions is encountered now and then (McCall 1975). In empirical studies of QOL one finds a continual shifting back and forth between the objective side of life (food and shelter) and the subjective (attitudes and feelings). Typically, however, environmental conditions are seen as fostering or facilitating QOL, and not as constituting or creating it.

Mental life is usually taken narrowly to mean satisfaction and kindred states, such as a person's sense of well-being, his or her satisfaction or dissatisfaction with life, or happiness or unhappiness (Dalkey & Rourke 1973). Other mental states connoted by QOL include: feelings of love and self-realization arising from interpersonal relationships (Allardt 1976); perceptions of the worth or value or life (Michalos 1980b); and a dynamic blend of satisfactions elicited by freedom from hunger and poverty, opportunity for personal growth, self-fulfillment and self-esteem (Report Of The President's Commission for a National Agenda for the Eighties, 1980).

To distinguish between general satisfaction (or happiness) and satisfaction about something in particular, it is customary to speak of global satisfaction and domain-specific satisfactions. Campbell et al (1976) define QOL as a general sense of well-being, but prefer to study domain-specific satisfactions because of the greater relevance for public policy. The trend is limit quality of life to a particular domain is reflected in such phrases as the quality of urban life, the quality of work life, and the quality of family life.

QOL and well-being are sometimes used interchangeably. The Organization for Economic Cooperation and Development prefers well-being to QOL, but only because it "has fewer roots in any particular scientific discipline" (OECD 1976:12). Extending its attempt to establish a uniform terminology in this area, the OECD recommends that the term "social well-being" refer to the aggregate well-being of a group of individuals, and that the term "societal well-being" be used when evaluating the institutional structures of society.

QOL may mean one thing to the public at large and something else to public officials and their consultants (Harwood 1976). Whether the multidimensional nature of QOL can be given scientific status remains uncertain. The term functions in a metatheoretical way to reference research aimed at policy outcomes. It can also be used rhetorically to create a favorable attitude toward a public official or his cause, as in President Johnson's declaration cited above. But a precise and universally accepted definition of the concept has yet to be framed. Rodgers (1977) suggests that QOL may be a term whose time has passed.

MEASURING QOL

Measures of QOL are often called QOL indicators, because the concept is not susceptible to direct measurement and because QOL research and the social indicators movement have a common origin. A distinction is made between objective and subjective indicators of QOL. The former register observable environmental conditions, such as per capita income or average daily temperature, most of which are presumed causes of QOL. The latter consists of responses to survey items measuring feelings of satisfaction, happiness, or related attitudes. Subjective measures of QOL have come mainly from sociology and social psychology, and within these fields they appear to have received relatively more attention in the last ten years or so than objective measures. This circumstance explains why subjective measures loom larger in this review than objective measures.

The majority of subjective measures pertain to either happiness or satisfaction, and within these categories they pertain to either a general (global) feeling (for example, satisfied with life as a whole) or to a domain-specific feeling (for example, satisfied with my job). In many cases, domain-specific feelings are combined to predict and/or to measure global feeling. For purposes of this review, measurement studies are arranged according to their emphasis on scale construction, scale validity, or on correlations between scales.

Scale Construction

Milbrath & Sahr's (1974) scale to measure how people feel about their environment was one of the first of its kind. It brings out most of the issues that arise in this kind of scaling. For example, what latent trait is being measured? Do the measures measure that trait and no other? Are measures reliable in the sense that repeated application of the instrument gives the same result?

Since social and economic activities may differ in the happiness they bring, Jones & Pierce (1977) find it reasonable to weight activity-specific happiness scores by time spent in activity and to combine these weighted scores into a single index. Juster et al (1981) created a similar index, called process—well being, by weighting activity-specific satisfaction scores by the time spent in each activity. Scales based on time allocations, while attractive in the abstract, have the practical disadvantage of requiring that people maintain records of time spent in each of several activities, as well as arriving at a happiness rating for each activity.

Campbell et al (1976) have devised a questionnaire for measuring general affect. Subjects are instructed to characterize their lives at present using eight semantic differential scales: boring-interesting; miserable-enjoyable; hard-easy; useless-worthwhile; lonely-friendly; empty-full; discouraging-hopeful; tied-down–free; disappointing-rewarding; and doesn't give me a chance–brings out the best in me. Scores based on these items have a fairly high reliability (0.89) and are moderately correlated with a global measure of happiness (0.52) and with a global measure of satisfaction (0.55).

Liu (1976) developed a QOL index using objective indicators drawn from US Census Statistics for 1970. Indicators were chosen to reflect the average QOL—defined as subjective satisfaction, or more precisely, utility—of the residents of each of more than 120 Standard Metropolitan Statistical Areas. The indicators were scored positive or negative on the basis of their theoretically predicted relation to QOL. Subindexes were developed for each of five major domains: economic, political, environmental, health and education, and social. Examples of the indicators within each domain are savings per capita and median value of owner-occupied, single-family dwelling units (economic); Sunday newspaper circulation and local government revenue per capita (political); mean level of sulfur dioxide and motorcycle registrations per 1000 population (environmental); infant mortality rate and median school years completed (health and education); percent of population under 18 living with parents and total crime rate (social). A complex system of weighting was used both in combining individual indicators into domain-specific subindexes and in combining these into an overall QOL index.

Scale Validity

In studying the validity of subjective measures, investigators have relied mainly on three techniques: comparing groups thought to differ in QOL; crossing methods and traits; and allocating the score variance to its components.

Measures taken from individuals at one point in time have been correlated with scores on the same test taken at a later point in time. In one such study Atkinson (1982) found that respondents reporting no change in QOL during the two-year period separating the interviews had slightly higher between-year correlations on both "general QOL" scores and "domain satisfaction" scores (0.55 and 0.60) than did respondents reporting some change in QOL (0.52 and 0.56). This finding and the tendency of QOL and domain-specific satisfaction scores to improve wherever the social circumstances of the respondents improved were taken as evidence favoring the validity of the measures.

Andrews & Crandall (1976) used a multitrait, multimethod design to check the validity of responses to six questions on well-being. In four of six methods (self-ratings using Likert scales anchored in different ways) the variance of single items was on average composed of 64% valid variance, 10% method variance, and 26% measurement error variance. It thus appears, in the authors' words (p. 16), that "perceptions of well-being can be measured with substantial validity . . . using a variety of methods for qualitatively different aspects of life, and under conditions typically encountered in national household-interview type surveys."

When measures of well-being have affect and cognition as their components, the correlation between such measures and such factors as age, income, and education may be attenuated, as McKennell (1978) found in a secondary analysis of Andrews & Withey's (1976) survey data. Pursuing the matter, Andrews & McKennell (1980) estimated the variance attributable to affect, cognition, and method in each of eight measures of sense of well-being. The contribution of affect ranged from a low of 14% to a high of 33% of the total item variance. The contribution of cognition ranged from 12% to 35% and the contribution of method from 0% to 10%. Further exploring the effects of affect and cognition on the perception of QOL, McKennell & Andrews (1980) fitted differently specified structural equation models to global and domain-specific responses on well-being. Their findings suggest that both cognition and affect are components in measures of global well-being.

Campbell et al (1976:489–91) question the practical value of breaking down global indicators of well-being into affect and cognition. They raise what is perhaps a more important question: whether measures of well-being should have happiness or satisfaction as their underlying construct. Since cognition and affect are present in both happiness and satisfaction, neither feeling can claim superiority by reason of being composed of one element or the other but not both. Campbell et al (1976) prefer satisfaction over happiness on the practical grounds that satisfaction is more responsive to policy interventions. Furthermore, satisfaction appears to change slowly but systematically over time, whereas happiness exhibits considerable volatility while maintaining a rather drift-free equilibrium (Campbell et al 1976:24, 48 footnote 11).

Buttel et al (1977) investigated the possibility that responses to questions on satisfaction may be measuring political ideology as well as QOL. They found a small but statistically significant correlation between feelings of satisfaction and political cynicism. The correlation remained after controls for differences among respondents in SES were introduced. Using what he considered to be a more conventional measure of political cynicism, Wasserman (1982) found no relationship, but he replicated Buttel et al's findings when he correlated items indicative of resentment against the rich and powerful with general life satisfaction. These studies, in tandem, are a reminder that scales with the same name, in this case, political cynicism, may not be measuring the same trait, just as scales with different names are not necessarily measures of different traits. (For an elaboration of this point, see Schuessler & Freshnock 1978.)

Correlations Between Scales

Since QOL has many facets, and since each may be represented by a different measure, it is no surprise that different measures are unevenly correlated, and in some cases are relatively independent. Gehrmann (1978) ranked German cities on different measures of QOL and compared the rankings. A city's standing appeared to depend in part on which measure was used. Rodgers (1981) correlated indexes of population density for local areas in Detroit with perceptions of crowding for those same areas. Most of the 30 correlations were significant at the 5% level, but only 4 were greater than 0.20. From these results one may infer that the rank of a local area on the QOL indicator "crowded living conditions" will depend in part on which measure, population density or perceived crowding, the areas are ordered.

Building on an earlier study (1974) and using data from four surveys, Andrews & Withey (1976) found that domain-specific concerns accounted for 61% of the variance in their best single global QOL measure; and that a simple, unweighted sum of these concern scores performed almost as well as any alternative multivariate model, including multiple regression and AID analysis. The strong correlation between both sets of scales argues for their validity, but in most studies the variance in global measures of well-being explained by domain-specific satisfaction is too small to permit substituting a combination of specific measures for a global measure as Bharadwaj & Wilkening (1977) and Kennedy et al (1978) proposed.

The above and related studies on correlations between QOL scales permit one to draw the following inferences: depending on which QOL measure is selected, (a) a person or group may rank high or low on QOL; (b) predictors may explain little or much of the variance in QOL; and (c) trends in QOL over time may be upward or downward.

Critical Assessment

Many of the measurement problems identified above arise because QOL is a latent trait, not subject to direct observation. The literature reviewed shows no clear consensus on what indicators to use, even within the broad groupings of objective versus subjective indicators. Focusing only on the subjective indicators, where the problem of valid and reliable measurement of QOL has been given the most attention, only the line of work initiated by McKennell (1978) has made use of covariance structure modeling introduced by Jöreskog (1978). Alternative methodologies that make explicit provision for dichotomous or ordered categorical indicators of latent traits (Amemiya 1981, Andersen 1980,

Bartholomew 1980, 1983; Bock & Lieberman 1970, Clogg 1979, Goodman 1978, Muthén 1978, 1984; Rasch 1960) have yet to be tried in QOL research.

Nor have QOL studies addressed the issue of reliably measuring change, although methodologies have been developed for this purpose for interval measures (Kessler & Greenberg 1981) and are under development for discrete data (Duncan et al 1982). The somewhat erratic performance of QOL scales currently in use argues cogently for at least experimentation with the more sophisticated scaling methods now being developed.

EMPIRICAL STUDIES OF QOL

A rather wide range of variables has been correlated with QOL to determine the extent to which satisfaction and happiness are affected by policy interventions as compared to those features of the social structure, such as kinship bonds, that are virtually impervious to governmental intervention; and the extent to which measures of QOL reflect adjustments and accommodations to a changing, but on the part of the individual an unchangeable, social and physical environment. In line with this objective QOL is taken as the variable to be explained, the dependent or criterion variable, in most studies, but now and again it is treated as the variable which explains, the independent or regressor variable.

Background Variables

The usual background variables—age, sex, income, e.g.—have been routinely correlated with subjective measures of QOL, both to specify the nature of this variable and to assess the reliability and validity of its measurement. Wilkening & McGranahan (1978) analyzed the respective contributions of socioeconomic status, social participation, and change in interpersonal relations to feelings of satisfaction. Change in interpersonal relations appears to contribute more heavily to satisfaction than does either SES or social participation. Ackerman & Paolucci (1983) related feelings of satisfaction to adequacy of income. They found that as adequacy of income increases, whether measured objectively (in relation to a modest standard of living) or subjectively (as the income perceived as required to live comfortably), QOL also increases, whether QOL is measured globally (as satisfaction with life as a whole) or specifically (as satisfaction with income and satisfaction with one's level of consumption). Interestingly, subjective ratings of income were found to be better predictors of feelings of satisfaction than were objective ratings. Campbell et al (1976) consider in detail their findings on the relation between education and satisfaction. Davis (1981) reported the odd finding that education, the mightiest predictor of social life feelings such as anomie, has no effect on satisfaction in any form, and none on happiness.

Rodgers (1977) found that women who expected to continue working when money was no longer needed showed a higher degree of life satisfaction than women who expected to stop working at that time, suggesting that future studies relating employment status to life satisfaction should include perceived needs as a control variable. Gratton (1980) reported that differences between socioeconomic groupings on QOL were significantly reduced after adjusting for differences in needs.

In a study relating religious commitment to satisfaction with life Hadaway & Roof (1978) found that the importance one assigns to faith was the strongest of the predictors they considered. QOL was measured by a single item indicating the "worthwhileness" of life. Religious commitment then showed a similar relationship to one other QOL indicator, a scale ranging from "hopeful" to "discouraging" but the relationship of religious commitment to other QOL indicators, such as global and domain-specific satisfactions was not tested. The authors recommended that QOL be defined in terms of worthwhileness because "it is less concerned with achieved rewards and has more to do with one's outlook" (Hadaway & Roof 1978:306).

The finding that marital status is associated with lower than average QOL occurs with some regularity. Glenn & Weaver (1979) in a reanalysis of the Campbell et al (1976) data found that marriage contributes to overall happiness, but having very young or teenage children has a stronger offsetting effect. Campbell et al (1976:335) found a similar relationship for domain-specific marital satisfaction. Among the married, the presence of children reduces satisfaction with marriage, especially among those who are less than completely satisfied with their spouses. [Campbell et al (1976) argue that the two domains, marriage and spouse, are distinct, despite the high correlation, $r = 0.57$, between them.] They also found that education reduces marital satisfaction, and that divorce has a chilling effect on satisfaction with family life.

Community Standard of Living

Regions with economic development below the US norm have received attention, because they are presumably responsive to policy intervention. Amos et al (1982) compared the responses of persons living in 22 less economically developed counties in Oklahoma to questions on life satisfaction with the responses of persons living elsewhere in the state. Except for satisfaction with health, no difference between the two groups was found. The authors hypothesized that residents of less developed counties are satisfied with less because they aspire to less. Wilkening & McGranahan (1978) found that residents of northwest Wisconsin, another area below average in economic development, had higher levels of satisfaction than residents in the rest of the state. They also attributed this effect to lower expectations and suggested that the high levels of dissatisfaction among residents of metropolitan areas (e.g. Milwaukee) increased the difference between the two groups. They reported that when industrial development came to the northwest Wisconsin area—a change which the residents themselves had sought—it was accompanied by sharply lowered levels of satisfaction brought about by low wages, job insecurity, higher taxes, and pollution. Fernandez & Kulik (1981) also found that urbanites scored lower on life satisfaction than did residents of rural areas.

Targeted Populations

QOL among the elderly and the ill has been studied intensively, because these groups are the target populations of many large-scale government programs. Studying satisfaction and happiness in a sample of older persons living in rural Canada (Ontario), Michalos (1982) found that satisfaction with housing contributes most to satisfaction with life as a whole, while satisfaction with spouse and friends contributes most to general happiness. Ross & Duff (1982) considered factors affecting the health and psychological well-being of children. Family SES, the principal indicator of these factors, appears to affect physical health directly and psychological well-being indirectly via its effect on physical health.

Strauss (1975) has studied the QOL of patients with chronic (and even lifelong) illnesses such as rheumatoid arthritis, childhood diabetes, and emphysema. Time allocation appears to be a critical variable in the several cases examined. Patients with chronic illnesses must juggle their schedules considerably in order to achieve the semblance of normal living. Simmons et al (1977) found that the QOL of patients on hemodialysis generally improves after a kidney transplant. Irwin et al (1982) compared cancer survivors (persons living three to seven years after radiation therapy) with the general population and found that both were equal on perceived QOL, but survivors were more satisfied with life as a whole, contrary to the authors' initial expectation. Since satisfaction is relative to aspiration, a mental rescaling of aspiration could have produced this unexpected result.

Asian Americans have been the object of at least one study: Nandi (1980) investigated the QOL of Asiatic Americans living in a medium size American city. He found that the QOL of this group was average or above on most indicators, but noted that there remains "an uneasiness in the mind of the Asian American who has neither the inner peace nor the stability so well known in the East" (Nandi 1980: 193). In such emphasis on assimilation, this investigation differs little from work on the adjustment of immigrants done by sociologists at the University of Chicago in the 1920s. To the immigrants themselves it will of course make no difference whether they are asked to report on the quality of their lives or to describe the problems they face in learning the language and in finding good jobs.

International Comparisons

Several international studies assessing the effects of various political systems on QOL appeared in our survey. Closest to home is the massive five-volume study undertaken by Michalos (1980a) comparing Canada to the United States on numerous QOL indicators including population density and health; crime and political activity; science, education and recreation; environment, transportation and economics; and housing, religion, and mortality. The study period is the decade 1964–1974. The comparison is made cumulatively, not unlike the scoring of a ball game. For each indicator on which the United States scores higher than Canada, the United States gains a point, and vice versa. Points are also earned when one country shows a greater improvement than the other over the study period. For the period 1964 to 1974 Canada wins by a comfortable margin, mostly because Canada's QOL tended to improve between 1964 and 1974, whereas that of the United States declined, and also because during that time Canada produced its outputs (e.g. research) at less cost than did the United States, even though the latter produced more. Needless to say, many (including Michalos himself) have questioned the scoring system.

Andrews & Inglehart (1979) analyzed the responses of persons living in 9 different countries to 11 statements on satisfaction with personal and social circumstances. Countries were similar in their scale patterns (as determined by a Multi-Dimensional Scaling procedure), but the 8 (West) European countries were more similar to one another than to the United States. The application of a somewhat different clustering procedure to these data produced a somewhat different result (Borg & Bergermaier 1981).

Ostroot et al (1982) gave a questionnaire on community satisfaction to residents of Springfield, Illinois, and a translation of that same questionnaire to residents of Aix-en-Provence, France. Specific items, such as satisfaction with medical care, the neighborhood, police protection and public schools, were ranked similarly in both samples; however, Springfield residents were generally more satisfied in all respects. The authors speculate that the greater satisfaction in Springfield may be due in part to better community facilities in Springfield; in part to an imperfect translation from English to French; and in part to a cultural difference in verbal styles between the two countries.

Effects of QOL

As noted, QOL now and then appears as an independent variable. One expects, for example, that publics low on QOL will be more inclined toward political protest than contented groups. Using path analysis Citrin (1977) found that QOL had little influence on political protest net of political alienation. That is, QOL makes for political protest only insofar as it first makes for political alienation.

Bharadwaj & Wilkening (1980) investigated the feasibility of predicting social integration (conceptualized as self-to-other belongingness) from satisfaction ratings on a variety of domains. Satisfaction accounted for a modest portion (23 percent) of the variation in integration scores. Satisfaction with family life had the strongest effect on social integration. But since social integration is measured as "a positive evaluation by the individual of affective inputs (such as love and esteem) from valued others" (Bharadwaj & Wilkening 1980:339), one wonders whether the criterion variable and its predictors are sufficiently distinct to support an asymmetrical causal model. Perhaps the better hypothesis to test is that QOL and social integration are mutually reinforcing.

Newman (1975) used both objective and subjective indicators of QOL to predict strength of desire to move. Also included in the prediction equation were nine background factors such as age and sex. The QOL indicators performed as expected, with the subjective indicators producing a larger increment in the explained variance than that produced by the objective indicators.

Comment and Perspective

The use of subjective indicators has yielded a consistent body of replicated findings, but very little that is of direct use to policymakers. QOL appears to be most closely associated with interpersonal relationships at the primary group level. Individuals use various mechanisms, such as lowering aspirations, to bring their perceptions of life quality in line with social reality. On the other hand, changes in the structure of society (e.g. urbanization) do appear to have had some effect on QOL (Wilkening 1982; Campbell et al 1976:30), but research in this area has yet to explain the apparent decline in the QOL of urban residents since 1960. One may anticipate that future studies will focus more on trends in QOL and will attempt to specify linkages between the larger social structure and the interactional processes that engender a sense of QOL.

The foregoing account of empirical studies may have left an impression that QOL research is a Canadian-American specialty; in fact, participation and coverage are worldwide. During the last 10 years or so, studies on QOL have been conducted in Germany (Glatzer & Zapf 1984), Switzerland (Walter-Busch 1983), South Africa (Møller & Schlemmer 1983), Hungary (Andorka & Falussy 1982), and Korea (Shin, Ahn, Kim & Lee 1983), to mention only a few. Hoffman-Nowotny's (1976) symposium volume reflects the international dimension of QOL research, although its main concern is how to construct social indicators and what to do with them after they have been constructed. A dozen or so nationalities are represented in Szalai & Andrew's (1980) collection of comparative studies on life quality; similarly, as many nationalities as papers are represented in a recent issue of *Social Indicators Research* (1984, Vol. 14, No. 3) devoted entirely to social indicators and social well-being.

Comparative studies and the like are pertinent for the light they throw on the social conditions correlated with the emergence of QOL as a public preoccupation and on the programs devised to improve it. Two broad generalizations may be drawn from the literature: First, concern with quality of life intensifies in proportion as less time and energy are required to meet the basic necessities of living. Second, solutions for improving QOL differ from one group to another according to their emphasis on changing the individual or changing the system. Minority groups tend to emphasize changing the system, while the establishment tends to emphasize changing the person.

THEORIZING ABOUT QOL

Theories about QOL attempt to describe the cognitive, affective, and symbolic processes through which individuals assess, determine, and experience the quality of their lives. They differ in the centrality they accord to cognition, affect, and social interaction. For example, psychological theories stress need fulfillment; economic theories stress rational resource allocation. Each theory proceeds from its particular view of the individual and society.

Social Psychological Approaches

By emphasizing psychological man (a phrase apparently from Tolman 1941), the late Professor Campbell (1981) distanced himself from those emphasizing economic man. Psychological man, or the self, experiences a sense of well-being when the needs he feels are appreciably reduced. The details of this process change continually because the self has many needs, and needs may be satisfied in many ways. The feeling of well-being is given a negative valence when needs are not met. QOL inheres in the totality of all such feelings of need satisfaction, whether strong or weak, negative or positive. The mechanisms of need arousal and satisfaction are presumed to be "hard wired", i.e. contained in the genetic endowments of *Homo sapiens,* but social interactions appear to channel the operation of this machinery along culturally predetermined paths called need dispositions (Parsons & Shils 1951). For related views on this topic see Freud (1930), Murray (1951), and Maslow (1954).

Gerson's (1976) analysis of QOL (the only one encountered in the *American Sociological Review*) is an elaboration of Mead's (1934) idea that the minutiae of self and society are aspects of the same social process. QOL inheres in the positive and negative self-feelings engendered as the process unfolds. Although the processes that form such attitudes may be enormously intricate, the attitudes themselves depend largely on four commodities: time, sentiment, skill, and money. In this respect, Gerson's theory is quite similar to Juster's rational behavior theory, summarized below.

The defining characteristic of the phenomenological approach is its insistence on the essential inexpressibility of the affect that characterizes the experience of QOL. Ziller (1974) presents a phenomenological theory of QOL that is in his judgement amenable to scientific research. In his view QOL inheres in self-appraisal, which in turn inheres in the interaction of self with significant others. Self-regard, rather than satisfaction, is the key outcome in such interactions. The alienated personality has low self-regard; the synergic personality has high self-regard. Self-regard is felt, but is not communicated verbally via such categories as happiness or satisfaction (this is the phenomenological part). However, a person's self-regard may be inferred from his or her performance on nonverbal tests (this is the scientific part). Smedley (1979) is an example of a purely phenomenological approach to QOL. She urges that emphasis be placed on the subjectivity, relativity, and complexity of the concept.

Economic Approaches

Economic theory stresses the processes by which individuals rationally allocate resources to meet their needs, thereby "producing" utility or satisfaction. Economists characterize the problem of resource allocation in terms of maximizing utility, given constraints on the availability and substitutibility of resources, and have developed a general method to model the maximization process. Liu (1976) is an attempt to integrate "the quality of life concept into the general framework of production theory in conventional microeconomic analyses" (p. 39). A far more elaborate attempt has been made by Juster et al (1981), who sought "to bridge the gap between the way in which economists have thought about material well-being and the way other social scientists have thought about social indicators" (Juster et al 1981:23). As inputs to the QOL "production" function, Juster et al consider the usual capital goods such as money and time but add also intangible assets and skills, such as knowledge and membership in social networks. A further class of contingencies affecting time allocation covers what Juster et al call contexts, nonmeasurable "states of the world" that provide the environment or setting of the resource allocation process. The economic problem is to maximize QOL given available stocks, contexts, and time.

From these general ideas an entire social accounting system is built in which time, instead of dollars, is the basic unit by which flows are measured. "In principle, the entire market economy as well as the production and use of goods within the household can be understood in terms of the allocations of time across alternative activities" (Juster et al 1981:32). Two outcomes of the system are noted. The first are the satisfactions which result from the allocation of time. These are called "process benefits". The second class of outcomes are evaluations of the state of the world, that is to say, of the levels of stocks and of the contexts that individuals possess or use. The second set of outcomes need not depend on the first. Its inclusion in the model represents a major departure from conventional economic production function theory, because it allows for inputs to QOL that do not arise from an "economizing" process.

Ecological Approach

The ecological perspective is eclectic in that it sees both social and physical worlds as one, or sees one world with physical and social aspects. In this perspective (Bubolz et al 1980) QOL is viewed as an element in a general process in which each element is subject to the influence of every other element. QOL depends on habitat in the broadest sense of that term, but habitat changes in response to the efforts people make to improve their quality of life. Thus, the ecological approach focuses on the interconnectedness of things, both animate and inanimate. Bubolz et al supply a (rather specialized) empirical example to illustrate the approach.

Milbrath (1982) presents QOL not as an aspect of the ecological process, but rather as an element with ecological aspects—perhaps a distinction without a difference. In his view, habitat and QOL alternate as input and output (our terminology). If the sequence is started (arbitrarily) with habitat as input and QOL as output, QOL subsequently becomes an input, changing the environment, and the latter subsequently alters QOL, and so on. In this cyclical manner QOL influences itself over time. Milbrath's system is a reminder that QOL, whether at the level of the person or the group, will change over time, because it is an element of an intrinsically dynamic process.

Comment

Discussing theoretical approaches separately may be misleading, since they overlap considerably. In its concern with the relation of species to habitat in all of its ramifications, the ecological approach is necessarily co-disciplinary, drawing on the biological sciences as well as the social. The economy may be regarded as an institutionalized pattern for meeting human needs, and at least some of the feelings of satisfaction people experience may come from economizing activities. Juster et al (1981) exemplify best the interdisciplinary viewpoint, making room in their theorizing for both psychological man and economic man. Process benefits are credited to economizing activities, while feelings about the state of the world are the product of psychological man. While both benefits are elements of QOL, they need not covary; at least Juster et al report a virtually zero correlation between a measure they developed of process benefits and a conventional measure of life satisfaction.

QOL RESEARCH AND PUBLIC POLICY

No quantitative assessment of the impact of QOL research on public policy was encountered in this survey. That impact is an important issue for QOL specialists, because of the tacit assumption that the expense of doing QOL research is justified by its expected contribution to policy. Therefore, most papers have at least a few paragraphs discussing ethical dilemmas and economic costs implied by their findings.

Finding that QOL generally improves after a kidney transplant, Simmons et al ask whether "the transplantation of kidneys is worth the enormous expenditure of money and effort being applied to it" (1977:421). They give a generally positive answer, at the same time voicing concern over issues such as these: Should treatment be made available to those who have little chance of surviving? Can society afford treatment for all? Where will the money come from? Might the money be spent better on prevention than on therapy? Do healthy kinfolk have a moral obligation to donate a kidney? These questions, the authors note, have no categorical answers.

Findings based on different measures of QOL may imply policies that work against one another. Horowitz (1979) points out by way of example that more air conditioning may improve QOL indoors, while less air conditioning may improve QOL outdoors. It is noted that any given policy entails costs as well as benefits, and these are seldom distributed equitably among all persons.

Differences between schools in educational achievement are relevant to QOL on the assumption of a link between educational achievement and QOL (Mushkin 1973). In a comparison of public and private high schools, Coleman et al (1982) found that private schools had a somewhat better record of academic achievement and were racially less segregated. On the basis of these findings, they recommended increasing the role of private schools in American education through a system of vouchers. (For pros and cons see the three journal issues devoted exclusively to critical reviews of the Coleman et al report: *Sociology of Education,* Spring 1982 and Fall 1983; and *Harvard Educational Review,* Fall 1983.)

In a study addressing the same issues but using a different data set and a different statistical model, Morgan (1983) found no significant differences between private and public schools in academic achievement. But, as in the Coleman et al study, differences were found in favor of private schools on six items asking students to rate the discipline, personal safety, job counselling, instructional quality, peer relations, and freedom of inquiry of their schools. Although Morgan views these items as indicators of quality of school life (Coleman interprets them as indicators of school "climate"), he recommends against expanding participation of the private sector in education, arguing that the public funds needed to sustain a system of vouchers might better be spent on improving the quality of public schools. These fragments, abstracted from an exceedingly complex policy debate, suggest that policy recommendations are influenced more by social and economic philosophy than by the content of QOL-related findings.

CRITICISM

Criticism of QOL research has come mainly from the people doing that research; it is thus self-imposed. Most of the criticisms have been mentioned in passing throughout the review. They are repeated here together with possible rebuttals, also extracted from the literature.

Criticism	Rebuttal
1) QOL has no technical meaning; its meaning and use in everyday speech and social science are the same.	Elements of everyday speech may take on scientific meaning in time. As with *standard of living*, QOL may eventually become standardized in meaning.
2) The concept lacks specificity; it has as many meanings as life has aspects. Life has social and physical aspects, each endlessly divisible.	Most sociological concepts have multiple connotations. Society connotes land and people, associations and networks, statuses and roles.
3) The rhetorical use of QOL by evangelists and politicians lessens its usefulness in scientific work.	It is impossible to restrict the use of words. White-collar crime, technical in its original sense, is now used prejoratively against business and government.
4) Time series that have no well-defined purpose may be justified on grounds that they throw light on QOL.	Most federal statistics in the U.S. are collected for the conduct of domestic and foreign affairs, and by implication for the good of the people, that is, their quality of life.
5) Correlations between objective and subjective measures of QOL are weak, as are correlations between subjective measures and for objective measures among themselves. In consequence, levels of QOL vary from one measure to another.	There is no reason to expect that feelings and behavior will be correlated. Whites and blacks may live side by side and still dislike one another. Similarly, there is no reason to suppose that feelings about different circumstances will coincide. Close friends —almost by definition—are more likely to bring satisfaction than international politics.
6) Some objective measures apply only to populations and not to persons. Results based on one level of aggregation may appear to contradict results based on another.	There is no reason to suppose that findings based on different levels of aggregation will be consistent. The problem is to find the statistical basis of the inconsistency.
7) Scores based on common scaling methods, for example, paired comparisons, are ordinal; they have neither an additive interval, nor a fixed zero; they do not qualify as fundamental measures.	Until better methods are invented, these state-of-the-art methods must do, unless one is willing to do without scales. Item response theory may help to overcome some of the limitations of conventional methods (Duncan, 1984).
8) No standard questionnaires for measuring subjective traits exist. Hence no strict comparisons from time to time at same place or from place to place at same time can be made.	Special-purpose questionnaires which are used only occasionally may play an important part in developing standard scales. From the contents of many such scales it may be possible to derive a few all-purpose scales that could eventually serve as standard measures (Schuessler, 1982).
9) QOL research is atheoretical. What theory there is tends to be a description of life in modern industrial societies. There is no body of propositions that explain differences in QOL regardless of place and time.	Since QOL research is usually undertaken to improve QOL, its emphasis on predictive knowledge is justified. Such knowledge may be a source of theoretical insights.

Criticism	Rebuttal
10) Theory is drawn from correlations instead of the other way around. Interpretation of the best-fitting structural equation model comes to be regarded as a theory.	Theory may be inferred inductively as well as deductively derived. Moreover, there is an interplay between statistical fitting and theorizing. A good fit suggests a theory which may then be tested and revised as required.
11) Models of QOL as a dynamic process are conceptual; these conceptual models are merely a reminder that QOL feeds on itself in time.	It is always a useful first step to depict a dynamic process by a flow chart. Later functional forms may be specified. The debate is academic, since there is presently little data available for testing dynamic models.
12) The content of QOL research reflects concerns of business and government rather than concerns of social science.	Many lines of sociological research reflect practical concerns: family, race, poverty, crime. Research may help to resolve theoretical issues, as well as help to solve social problems.
13) Policymakers draw on QOL findings when it suits their purposes; otherwise they ignore them. QOL findings are disregarded not because they are irrelevant to policy but rather because their implications are philosophically unacceptable.	QOL findings may contribute to sociology even though they are disregarded by policymakers. Moreover, findings disregarded for a while may later be called on. Myrdal's *An American Dilemma* (Myrdal, et al, 1944) is a case in point.
14) Sociologists differ among themselves about their obligations to QOL policy. They are divided on the question of whether it is enough to report findings, or whether in addition they should make recommendations.	This is hardly a criticism of QOL research. Differences of opinion on matters of this sort occur naturally in a free society.

THE FUTURE OF RESEARCH IN SOCIOLOGY

While most sociologists have some interest in programs for improving the nation's well-being, relatively few have done research on QOL as such. Why this is so is a matter of speculation. Some probably see the concept, with its emphasis on inner tranquility, as distracting from institutionalized patterns of unfairness and discrimination in American society. Some are probably indifferent to the bearing of their findings on QOL, and possibly to even the concept itself; their interest is in a strictly scientific sociology. Many probably feel that in their investigations they can get along with standard sociological concepts and see little or no advantage in viewing their dependent variable(s) as just another aspect of QOL.

If pressed to forecast the extent to which sociologists will become involved in this area, we would guess that the steady growth of funding in this area will attract sociologists in ever greater numbers over the next decade. Some will simply elaborate on the research into subjective well-being, but we anticipate that others will address these fundamental issues: To what extent are happiness and satisfaction individual "productions", and to what extent are they merely affective responses to perceived social situations? To what extent can these feelings be manipulated by mental and emotional therapies without a concomitant change in the individual's social situation? How are social life feelings—including happiness, satisfaction, powerlessness and alienation—interrelated, and does a full understanding of the attitudinal complex suggest a more adequate definition of QOL? How does one bridge macro-level social processes and micro-level social feelings? Finally, we expect that sociologists will be experimenting with some of the newer scaling methods, as well as with alternative methods of tracking changes in QOL over time.

ACKNOWLEDGMENTS

We are indebted to Phillip Converse and Albert Reiss who commented on a draft of this paper; also to advisory editors at the Review who made suggestions; Fisher's work on this paper was supported in part by NIMH Grant T32 MH 15789–05.

Literature Cited

Ackerman, N., Paolucci, B. 1983. Objective and subjective income adequacy: Their relationship to perceived life quality measures. *Soc. Indic. Res.* 12:25–48

Allardt, E. 1976. Dimensions of welfare in the comparative Scandinavian study. *Acta Sociol.* 19:227–39

Amemiya, T. 1981. Qualitative response models: A survey. *J. Econ. Lit.* 19:1483–1536

Amos, O. M. Jr., Hitt, M. A., Warner, L. 1982. Life satisfaction and regional development: A case study of Oklahoma. *Soc. Indic. Res.* 11:319–31

Andersen, E. B. 1980. *Discrete Statistical Models with Social Science Applications.* Amsterdam: North Holland

Andorka, R., Falussy, B. 1982. The way of life of the Hungarian society on the basis of the time budget survey of 1976–1977. *Soc. Indic. Res.* 11:31–74

Andrews, F. M., Crandall, R. 1976. The validity of measures of self-reported well-being. *Soc. Indic. Res.* 3:1–19

Andrews, F. M., Inglehart, R. F. 1979. The structure of subjective well-being in nine western societies. *Soc. Indic. Res.* 6:73–90

Andrews, F. M., McKennell, A. C. 1980 Measures of self-reported well-being: Their affective, cognitive, and other components. *Soc. Indic. Res.* 8:127–55

Andrews, F. M., Withey, S. B. 1976. *Social Indicators of Well-Being: Americans' Perceptions of Life Quality.* New York: Plenum

Atkinson, T. 1982. The stability and validity of quality of life measures. *Soc. Indic. Res.* 10:113–32

Bartholomew, D. J. 1983. Latent variable models for ordered categorical data. *J. Economet.* 22:229–43

Bartholomew, D. J. 1980. Factor analysis for categorical data (with discussion). *J. R. Stat. Soc. B* 42:293–321

Bauer, R. A. 1966. *Social Indicators.* Cambridge, Mass: MIT Press

Bharadwaj, L., Wilkening, E. A. 1977. The prediction of perceived well-being. *Soc. Indic. Res.* 4:421–39

Bharadwaj, L., Wilkening, E. A. 1980. Life domain satisfactions and personal social integration. *Soc. Indic. Res.* 7:337–51

Bock, R. D., Lieberman, M. 1970. Fitting a response model for *n* dichotomously scored items. *Psychometrika* 35:179–97

Borg, I., Bergermaier, R. 1981. Some comments on 'The structure of subjective well-being in nine western societies' by Andrews and Inglehart. *Soc. Indic. Res.* 9:265–78

Bubolz, M. M., Eicher, J. B., Evers, J., Sontag, S. 1980. A human ecological approach to quality of life: Conceptual framework and results of a preliminary study. *Soc. Indic. Res.* 7:103–36

Burgess, E. W., Cottrell, L. S. 1939. *Predict-*

ing Success or Failure in Marriage. Engle-wood Cliffs, NJ: Prentice-Hall

Buttel, F. H., Wilkening, E. A., Martinson, O. B. 1977. Ideology and social indicators of the quality of life. *Soc. Indic. Res.* 4:353–69

Campbell, A. 1981. *The Sense of Well-Being in America: Recent Patterns and Trends*. New York: McGraw-Hill

Campbell, A., Converse, P. E., Rodgers, W. L. 1976. *The Quality of American Life*. New York: Russell Sage

Citrin, J. 1977. Political alienation as a social indicator: Attitudes and action. *Soc. Indic. Res.* 4:381–419

Clogg, C. C. 1979. Some latent structure models for the analysis of Likert-type data. *Soc. Sci. Res.* 8:287–301

Coleman, J. S., Hoffer, T., Kilgore, S. 1982. *High School Achievement: Public, Catholic, and Private Schools Compared*. New York: Basic

Dalkey, N. C., Rourke, D. L. 1973. The delphi procedure and rating Quality of Life factors. In *The Quality of Life Concept*, US Environ. Prot. Agency, pp. 209–21. Washington, DC: USGPO

Davis, J. A. 1981. Achievement variables and class cultures: Family, schooling, job, and forty-nine dependent variables in the cumulative GSS. *Am. Sociol. Rev.* 47:569–86

Duncan, O. D. 1984. *Notes on Social Measurement: Historical and Critical*. New York: Russell Sage

Duncan, O. D., Sloane, D. M., Brady, C. 1982. Latent classes inferred from response-consistency effects. In *Systems Under Indirect Observation*, ed. K. G. Joreskog, 1:19–64. Amsterdam: North Holland

Fernandez, R. M., Kulik, J. C. 1981. A multi-level model of life satisfaction: Effects of individual characteristics and neighborhood composition. *Am. Sociol. Rev.* 46:840–50

Freud, S. 1930. *Civilization and Its Discontents*. Transl. J. Cape, H. Smith. London: Hogarth

George, L. K., Bearon, L. B. 1980. *Quality of Life in Older Persons: Meaning and Measurement*. New York: Human Sci.

Gerhmann, R. 1978. 'Valid' empirical measurement of quality of life? *Soc. Indic. Res.* 5:78–109

Gerson, E. M. 1976. On 'Quality of Life.' *Am. Sociol. Rev.* 41:793–806

Gilmartin, K. J., Rossi, R. J., Lutomski, L. S., Reed, D. F. 1979. *Social Indicators: An Annotated Bibliography of Current Literature*. New York: Garland

Glatzer, W., Zapf, W. 1984. *Lebensqualität in der Bundesrepublik*. Frankfurt: Campus Verlag

Glenn, N. D., Weaver, C. N. 1979. A note on family situation and global happiness. *Soc. Forc.* 47:960–67

Goodman, L. A. 1978. *Analyzing Qualitative/*

Categorical Data: Log Linear Models and Latent Structure Analysis. Reading, Mass: Addison-Wesley

Gratton, L. C. 1980. Analysis of Maslow's need hierarchy with three social class groups. *Soc. Indic. Res.* 7:463–76

Hadaway, C. K., Roof, W. C. 1978. Religious commitment and the quality of life in American society. *Rev. Relig. Res.* 19:295–307

Harwood, P. D. L. 1976. Quality of life: Ascriptive and testimonial conceptualizations. *Soc. Indic. Res.* 3:471–96

Hoffman-Nowotny, H. J. 1976. *Soziale Indikatoren*. Fruenfeld: Huber

Horowitz, I. L. 1979. Methods and strategies in evaluating equity research. *Soc. Indic. Res.* 6:1–22

Irwin, P. H., Gottlieb, A., Kramer, S., Danoff, B. 1982. Quality of life after radiation therapy: A study of 309 cancer survivors. *Soc. Indic. Res.* 10:187–210

Jones, M. B., Pierce, J. M. 1977. Time-use auditing: An approach to validating social indicators. *Soc. Indic. Res.* 4:289–315

Jöreskog, K. G. 1978. Structural analysis of covariance and correlation matrices. *Psychometrika*. 43:443–77

Juster, F. T., Courant, P. N., Dow, G. K. 1981. The theory and measurement of well-being: A suggested framework for accounting and analysis. In *Social Accounting Systems: Essays on the State of the Art*, ed. F. T. Juster, K. C. Land, pp. 23–94. New York: Academic

Kennedy, L. W., Northcott, H. C., Kinzel, C. 1978. Subjective evaluation of well-being: Problems and prospects. *Soc. Indic. Res.* 5:457–74

Kessler, R. C., Greenberg, D. F. 1981. *Linear Panel Analysis*. New York: Academic

Land, K. C. 1983. Social Indicators. *Ann. Rev. Sociol.* 9:1–26

Larson, R. 1978. Thirty years of research on the subjective well-being of older Americans. *J. Gerontol.* 33:109–25

Liu, B. C. 1976. *Quality of Life Indicators in U.S. Metropolitan Areas*. New York: Praeger

Maslow, A. H. 1954. *Motivation and Personality*. New York: Harper & Row

McCall, S. 1975. Quality of life. *Soc. Indic. Res.* 2:229–48

McKennell, A. C. 1978. Cognition and affect in perceptions of well-being. *Soc. Indic. Res.* 5:389–426

McKennell, A. C., Andrews, F. M. 1980. Models of cognition and affect in perceptions of well-being. *Soc. Indic. Res.* 8:257–98

Mead, G. H. 1934. *Mind, Self and Society*. Chicago: Univ. Chicago

Michalos, A. C. 1980a. *North American Social Report*. Boston: Reidel

Michalos, A. C. 1980b. Satisfaction and happiness. *Soc. Indic. Res.* 8:385–422

Michalos, A. C. 1982. The satisfaction and happiness of some senior citizens in rural Ontario. *Soc. Indic. Res.* 11:1–30

Milbrath, L. W. 1982. A conceptualization and research strategy for the study of ecological aspects of the quality of life. *Soc. Indic. Res.* 10:133–57

Milbrath, L. W., Sahr, R. C. 1974. Perceptions of environmental quality. *Soc. Indic. Res.* 1:397–438

Møller, V., Schlemmer, L. 1983. Quality of Life in South Africa: Towards An Instrument For the Assessment of Quality of Life and Basic Needs, *Soc. Indic. Res.* 12:225–279

Morgan, W. R. 1983. Learning and student life quality of public and private school youth. *Sociol. Educ.* 56:187–202

Murray, H. A. 1951. Toward a classification of action. In *Toward A General Theory of Action,* ed. T. Parsons, E. A. Shils, pp. 434–65. New York: Harper & Row

Mushkin, S. J. 1973. *National Assessment and Social Indicators.* Washington, DC:USGPO

Muthen, B. 1984. A general structural equation model with dichotomous, ordered categorical and continuous latent variable indicators. *Psychometrika* 49:115–32

Muthen, B. 1978. Contributions to factor analysis of dichotomous variables. *Psychometrika* 43:551–60

Myrdal, G., Steiner, R., Rose, A. 1944. *An American Dilemma.* New York: Harper & Row

Nandi, P. K. 1980. *The Quality of Life of Asian Americans.* Chicago: Pacific/Asian Am. Ment. Health Res. Cent.

Newman, S. 1975. Objective and subjective determinants of prospective residential mobility. *Soc. Indic. Res.* 2:53–63

Organization for Economic Cooperation and Development Indicator Development Programme. 1976. *Measuring Social Well-Being: A Progress Report on the Development of Social Indicators.* Paris: OECD

Ostroot, N., Shin, D., Snyder, W. 1982. Quality of life perceptions in two cultures. *Soc. Indic. Res.* 11:113–38

Palys, T. S., Little, B. R. 1980. Social indicators and the quality of life. *Can. Psychol.* 21:67–74

Parsons, T., Shils, E. A., eds. 1951. *Toward a General Theory of Action.* New York: Harper & Row

Rasch, G. 1960. *Probabilistic Models for Some Intelligence and Attainment Tests.* Copenhagen: Danish Inst. Educ. Res.

Report of the President's Commission on

National Goals. 1960. *Goals for Americans.* Englewood Cliffs, NJ: Prentice-Hall

Report of the President's Commission for a National Agenda for the Eighties. 1980. *The Quality of American Life in the Eighties.* Washington, DC: USGPO

Rodgers, W. L. 1977. Work status and the quality of life. *Soc. Indic. Res.* 4:267–87

Rodgers, W. L. 1981. Density, crowding, and satisfaction with the residential environment. *Soc. Indic. Res.* 10:75–102

Ross, C., Duff, R. S. 1982. Medical care, living conditions, and children's well-being. *Soc. Forc.* 61:456–74

Schuessler, K. F. 1982. *Measuring Social Life Feelings.* San Francisco: Jossey-Bass

Schuessler, K. F., Freshnock, L. 1978. Measuring attitudes toward self and others in society: State of the art. *Soc. Forc.* 56:1228–44

Shin, D. C., Ahn, C. S., Kim, K. D., Lee, H. K. 1983. Environmental effects on perceptions of life quality in Korea, *Soc. Indic. Res.* 12:393–416

Simmons, R. G., Klein, S. D., Simmons, R. L. 1977. *Gift of Life: The Social and Psychological Impact of Organ Transplantation.* New York: Wiley

Smedly, L. 1979. The assessment of QOL. *Humanitas* 5:203–8

Strauss, A. L., ed. 1975. *Chronic Illness and the Quality of Life.* St. Louis: Mosby

Szalai, A., Andrews, F. M. 1980. *The Quality of Life: Comparative Studies.* Beverly Hills, CA: Sage

Tolman, E. C. 1941. Psychological man. *J. Soc. Psychol.* 13:205–18

US Environmental Protection Agency. 1973. *The Quality of Life Concept.* Washington, DC: USGPO

Walter-Busch, E. 1983. Subjective and Objective Indicators of Regional Quality of Life in Switzerland. *Soc. Indic. Res.* 12:337–91

Wasserman, I. M. 1982. Political beliefs and subjective indicators of quality of life. *Soc. Indic. Res.* 11:167–80

Wilkening, E. A. 1982. Subjective indicators and the quality of life. In *Social Structure and Behavior,* ed. R. M. Hauser, D. Mechanic, A. O. Haller, T. S. Hauser, pp. 429–41. New York: Academic

Wilkening, E. A., McGranahan, D. 1978. Correlates of subjective well-being in northern Wisconsin. *Soc. Indic. Res.* 5:211–34

Ziller, R. C. 1974. Self-other orientations and quality of life. *Soc. Indic. Res.* 1:301–27

REFERENCE ADDED IN PROOF

Andrews, F. M., Withey, S. B. 1977. Developing measures of perceived life quality: Results from several national surveys. *Soc. Indic. Res.* 1:1–26

Ann. Rev. Sociol. 1985. 11:151–80
Copyright © 1985 by Annual Reviews Inc. All rights reserved

ETHNICITY

J. Milton Yinger

Department of Sociology and Anthropology, Oberlin College, Oberlin, Ohio 44074

Abstract

The near universality of multiethnicity in contemporary states, the persistence—culturally and structurally—of the ethnic factor, contradicting modernization and Marxist theories, and the strong public interest in ethnic phenomena have stimulated a great deal of research in sociology and other social sciences. This review examines the wide diversity of definitions and interpretations in that research. The demography of ethnic groups, the sources of ethnic survival and revival (primordial attachments, political and economic interests, and estrangement from the larger society), and the major themes in the literature on ethnicity are examined. Three themes are emphasized: 1) the relationship of ethnicity to social stratification and discrimination—in particular with reference to internal colonialism, split labor markets, and resource mobilization; 2) ethnicity as culture, illustrated by reference to studies of family and religion; and 3) the connections between ethnicity and politics in developing states, in developed states, and in the armed forces and police of many societies.

INTRODUCTION

Changes in relationships among major subdivisions of a society are often reflected in the development of an active sociological specialty designed to analyze those changes. Currently important work goes on, for example, in the study of male-female relationships and sex roles, of life course and age, of the simultaneous appearance of "new religions" and old fundamentalism, and—more perennially—of class conflict and social stratification. None of these topics is new, of course, but in recent years they have carried unusual salience.

To this list of significant topics of new or resurgent interest we must now certainly add ethnicity. The flood of material from research centers, new

151

0360-0572/85/0815-0151$02.00

journals, book series, government agencies, and individual scholars is overwhelming; it has been called an academic ethnicity industry (Basham & DeGroot 1977:423). Undoubtedly this flood expresses not only the readily apparent importance of the ethnic factor in most of the societies of the world, but also the varying and often conflicting interests and commitments of the writers.

Although the proportion of contemporary work on ethnicity may be higher in sociology, major research is also being carried out in anthropology, political science, history, economics, and social psychology. In this review I shall pay little attention to disciplinary origins. Since the topics addressed and even the methodologies overlap extensively, it seems more appropriate to focus on the problems being investigated than on the professional identities of authors.[1]

Varying Perspectives on Ethnicity

It is not as easy to disregard the differences in assumptions, premises, and ideologies of those studying ethnicity as it is to disregard their disciplines. Although I shall not undertake an essay in the sociology of knowledge, we need at least to be aware of the range of values here. In his preface to a collection of papers taken from the journal *Ethnicity*, published by the Center for the Study of American Pluralism, McCready (1983:xvii) observes that differentiation is a good in its own right. Novak (1972:60) is concerned that America without strong ethnic identities will become a tasteless homogenized soup.

I believe it is fair to say that a large majority of the students of ethnicity applaud its current resurgence and/or its continuing strength. Ethnic attachments are variously seen as ways to preserve a precious cultural heritage; to soften class lines; to protect or to win economic and political advantages for disadvantaged groups; to furnish a more intimate and flavorful connection with large, impersonal societies; and to retard the shift of overwhelming power to the state.

It would sometimes appear, however, that in social science as in the physical world, for every action there is an equal and opposite reaction. The strong emphasis in the last 20 years on the importance of (and value of) ethnicity has been countered—although by a relatively small number of persons—on both evidential and ideological grounds. It is the "Lebanization of Americans," as a recent headline put it. Or in the words of Czeslaw Milosz (in DeVos & Romanucci-Ross 1975:352): "Perhaps those sardines fighting each other in the mouth of a whale are not untypical of the relations between humans when they search for self-assertion through ethnic values magnified into absolutes."

---

[1]Representative recent theoretical and historical works from a variety of perspectives include Archdeacon 1983; Banton 1983; Cohen 1978; Dinnerstein, Nichols & Reimers 1979; Francis 1976; Glazer 1983; Hall 1979; Heisler 1977; Keyes 1981; Lieberson 1980; Mason 1982; Pettigrew 1978; Rex 1981; Simpson & Yinger 1985; A. Smith 1981; Thernstrom 1980; Williams 1978; Wilson 1980; Wolf 1982; Young 1976.

A tendency to exaggerate the salience of ethnic identities and to overlook the strong pressures toward assimilation—most of this with reference to the United States—has been discussed in several recent works (eg, G. J. Patterson 1979; Stein & Hill 1977; O. Patterson 1977; Gans 1979; Alba 1981; Steinberg 1981). It has been observed that "Anthropologists who have studied truly plural societies would probably feel, for example, that attendance at Polish picnics, membership in a Polish-American voluntary association, and a reluctance to endure Polish jokes does not equate with strong ethnic identity when the individual probably speaks little if any Polish and shows scant evidence of adherence to Polish cultural traditions" (Basham & DeGroot 1977:423).

Sociologically, a more powerful argument is the contention that the current stress on ethnicity is divisive and inegalitarian in its effects (Morgan 1981). Current attention to ethnicity, Steinberg argues (1981), tends to blind us to the structures of discrimination. It leads to cultural rather than to "opportunity" explanations of inequality (see also Lieberson 1980).

> Indeed, black intellectuals and leaders have had good reason to balk at the pluralist doctrine. As a group, blacks have always experienced the bitter side of pluralism, and ideological justifications for maintaining ethnic boundaries carried insidious overtones of racial segregation. . . . Just as ethnic groups have class reasons for tearing down ethnic barriers ahead of them, they also have class reasons for raising ethnic barriers behind them. Thus, it is not uncommon for ethnic groups to invoke democratic principles to combat the ethnic exclusivity of more privileged groups, but to turn around and cite pluralistic principles in defense of their own discriminatory practices (Steinberg 1981:255, 258).

To this argument Juliani replies (1982:370): " . . . the rejection of certain aspects of assimilation may mean for many Americans, for the first time in their history as members of this society, finally understanding themselves and coming to peace with their cultural origins. Such awareness may also enable them to understand others better, across ethnic and racial boundaries, and may promote social justice far better than assimilation ever did."

Orlando Patterson argues that emphasis on ethnicity is inherently conservative, even though its proponents may believe it to be liberal. At its worst, he says, it is "vulgar chauvinistic polemics," and even at its best it is "a sophisticated attack on modern industrial civilization" (1977:152). In their emphasis on ethnicity, black Americans " . . . have found their own weapon used against them. Once lower-middle-class whites realized that it was now fair play to return to the old technique, the field was wide open for the revival of ethnic politics on a statewide scale" (Patterson 1977:158).

As these citations illustrate, what was formerly a rather sharp line between race relations and ethnic-group relations in a gradual transition has been nearly erased, with the recognition that genetic variation is important in human interaction only because it is often correlated with cultural, historical, and status differences.

Although some of these authors, particularly Steinberg, have sought to analyze the sources and consequences of both pluralism and assimilation (see also Yinger 1981), in the main their goal has been to remedy what they see as neglect of the facts of assimilation and of the results of ethnic separatism.

Since a recent chapter in the *Annual Review of Sociology* deals mainly with assimilation (Hirschman 1983), I refer to the concept only briefly. Despite its ambiguity and the controversies surrounding it, assimilation continues to be an important concept for students of ethnicity, particularly those dealing with the United States and Britain, where many group boundaries have historically been more permeable than in most other societies. In this discussion I shall use assimilation as a descriptive and analytic, not an evaluative, term. It is a variable, not an attribute. Assimilation is a multidimensional process, the various aspects of which, although highly interactive, can vary independently at different rates and in different sequences.

Assimilation is a process of boundary reduction that can occur when members of two or more societies, of ethnic groups, or of smaller social groups meet. When the process is carried to completion, "an assimilated ethnic population is defined operationally as a group of persons with similar foreign origins, knowledge of which in no way gives a better prediction or estimation of their relevant social characteristics than does knowledge of the behavior of the total population of the community or nation involved" (Lieberson 1963:10).

Some fear that emphasis on assimilation is factually wrong (Young 1976; Glazer & Moynihan 1975), others that it reinforces oppressive systems (Blauner 1972). Still others fear that failure to recognize cases when some assimilation does occur under various conditions leads to poor social analysis and promotes inequities (Pettigrew 1969; Kuper 1977).

In his well-known discussions of types of assimilation Gordon (1964:71; 1978:169) outlines seven variables. Three of these—absence of prejudice, absence of discrimination, and absence of value and power conflict—can better be seen, in my judgment, as causes and then as consequences of the extent of assimilation, rather than as types of assimilation. The other four, with some modification, can be seen as the separate but interdependent subprocesses of which assimilation is constituted. They are: integration, acculturation, identification, and amalgamation—the structural, cultural, psychological, and biological aspects of assimilation.

These four subprocesses are not usually discussed separately or distinguished in a sharply analytic way, mainly perhaps because they are empirically almost always mixed (see Yinger & Simpson 1978). Special attention may be given to one or another, however, and it will be useful to refer to each one.

"A group is integrated to the degree that its members are distributed across the full range of associations, institutions, and regions of a society in a pattern similar to that of the population as a whole" (Yinger 1985). It is conceivable, but not likely, that an ethnic group could be highly integrated and yet minimally acculturated and amalgamated, with little shift of identification to the larger society. Studies of integration mainly focus on political, occupational, educational, and marital data, often seen against a background of the regional and metropolitan demographic situation (see Murguia 1975; Woodrum 1981; Garcia 1981; Astin 1982; Shavit 1984; Burke 1981; Ogbu 1978; Stryker 1981; Alexander et al 1978; see also references below dealing with politics, stratification, and intermarriage).

Acculturation refers to the degree that values, norms, and usages of a group correspond with those of the society at large. As a process it is almost always two-way, even though smaller, less compact, resource-poor groups are more likely to be affected by it than to affect it strongly (see Padilla 1980; Hurh et al 1979). Dominant ethnic groups, however, are likely to overlook the extent to which they have been culturally influenced by those whom they dominate. They are also likely to exaggerate the persistence of cultural elements among the deprived, as in the conception of a presumed culture of poverty (see O. Lewis 1959, 1966; and for a few recent critiques, M. Lewis 1978; Waxman 1977; Abell & Lyon 1979; Hill & Ponza 1983).

Identification is perhaps the least well conceptualized and measured of the four processes of assimilation, although recent research is beginning to fill the gap (Alba & Chamlin 1983; Melville 1983; DeVos 1978; Horowitz 1975). Most Americans know the ethnic origins of their grandparents, but evidence of the salience of this knowledge and of its behavioral outcomes is scarce. One topic that is closely related to identification has been carefully studied. The work of Clark & Clark on self-esteem among black children (1947), although widely accepted for many years, has recently been seriously challenged, primarily for failing to distinguish clearly between group identification and self-esteem. Nonwhite children may have high self-esteem and still identify with whites, not because they "view white as intrinsically better than brown, black, or red" but because "they understand that certain societal avenues are better open to those who *are* white" (Beuf 1977:102; see Rosenberg & Simmons 1972; Rosenberg 1979; Louden 1981; Della Fave 1980; Taylor & Walsh 1979; Gecas 1982; Porter & Washington 1979).

Despite the valuable research by Rosenberg and others, perhaps the last word has not yet been written on this subject. Were the Clarks wrong because their methodology was inadequate; or were the times different; or has ideology shifted so that evidence of "the mark of oppression" is less likely to be emphasized than the creative responses of the oppressed [note the similar shift in studies of slavery (compare Elkins 1959 with Gutman 1976, for example)]; or is the evidence now available to us much richer? Some worry with Adam (1978) that these recent studies may tend to obscure the great harm done by oppression.

The amalgamation of an ethnic group, seen as a variable, is the degree to which the genetic make up of its members is similar to that of the society as a whole. A more sociologically relevant definition would be: "Groups are amalgamated when no *socially visible* genetic differences separate their members" (Yinger 1985). Genetic lines in the United States population, for example, are significantly blurred (80% of black Americans have European ancestors; 50% or more of Mexican Americans have both Indian and European ancestors; perhaps 20% of "white" Americans have African or Native American ancestors (Stuckert 1976:137). The socially visible genetic differences, however, are not as rapidly reduced in a race conscious society.

The Larger Theoretical Setting

A number of theoretical developments, although not directly concerned with ethnicity, are relevant to its study, to which in some instances they have been applied. I will mention only four such developments, to suggest the importance of the larger circle of theoretical work for the sociology of ethnicity.

The comparative sizes and ratios of groups and the experience of "solo" situations have been shown, in many studies, to have important consequences for individuals and groups (see Blau 1977; Kanter 1977; Spangler, Gordon & Pipkin 1978; Frisbie & Neidert 1977). Sizes and ratios of ethnic groups are clearly important for every aspect of their situation in a society. Token or solo experience is a common event, particularly for minority ethnic group members, under many conditions.

The study of status-organizing processes is revealing significant aspects of interpersonal relations. These are processes "in which evaluations of and beliefs about the characteristics of actors become the basis of observable inequalities in face-to-face interaction" (Berger, Rosenholtz & Zelditch 1980:479). Thus defined, their importance for the study of contacts across ethnic group lines, as for other kinds of contact, is apparent (see also Cohen & Roper 1972; Cohen 1982; Dovidio & Gaertner 1981; Humphreys & Berger 1981).

One of the postulates of network analysis, as developed by Laumann (1973:5), states that "Similarities in status, attitudes, beliefs, and behavior facilitate the formation of intimate (or consensual) relationships among incumbents of social positions." In his study, Laumann shows how the bonds of pluralism are strengthened in urban social networks in a way suggested by the postulate.

As a final illustration of theoretical work not specifically concerned with ethnicity, but important for it, I would call attention to studies of the ways in which individual actions can lead to an outcome that no one, or only a minority wished. Interpretations of outcomes may be faulty, as is well shown by Schelling in *Micromotives and Macrobehavior* (1978), if the process of interaction among individual actions, based on a range of motives or levels of intensity, is disregarded. If 20% of X's do not want non-X children in their school and pull their children out when non-X's become 20%, the percentage of non-X's goes up, motivating some of those who were content with the earlier percentage but opposed to the new distribution to withdraw, motivating those who were content . . . *ad segregatum*. This is not, of course, an inevitable process. The new percentages may prove, on experience, to be acceptable. Nevertheless, the process by which individual actions can lead to results that none or only a few desired or anticipated is not uncommon in human experience. The study of this process is a valuable lead for theories of ethnicity.

THE DEFINITION AND MEASUREMENT OF ETHNICITY

Durkheim encouraged sociologists to "treat social facts as things." This advice is difficult to follow, not only because his own usage was rather ambiguous, but also because the boundaries of the things of interest to sociologists are often drawn in different ways by different observers. Theoretical perspectives, ideologies, and the data being examined—all affect the process of definition. Thus "ethnic groups" range, in various usages, from small, relatively isolated, nearly primordial "kin and culture" groups within which much of life proceeds, all the way to large categories of people defined as alike on the basis of one or two shared characteristics (e.g. Hispanics or Asian Americans). It seems unlikely that the term will be pared down to some small part of this range. We do not yet have even a clear typology marking different points, in terms of salience and identification, along the range (see T. Smith 1980, 1982). It is essential therefore, that students of ethnicity be alert to differences in usage. Current ethnic movements in developed societies are different in many ways from what can be called primary ethnic groups (Stein & Hill 1977).

Ethnicity, nationality, and country of origin are often used as synonyms. In commenting on the coding of answers to the question, "From what countries or part of the world did your ancestors come", NORC, in its *Cumulative Codebook, 1972–1982* combined those who named only one country (54%) with those who named two or more but selected one as the country they felt closer to (24%), identifying both as "the ethnicity of the respondent" (p. 43). This is valuable information for many purposes. It is of questionable value, however, if one is concerned with ethnicity more narrowly defined in reference, for example, to persons whose ancestors came from Mexico, the Philippines, Poland, Puerto Rico, Yugoslavia, or many other countries. If language is used as an important sorting criterion, "an immigrant from Argentina and one from Uruguay may clearly seem to be Hispanic, but what if the first is of Italian birth or descent and the second a German?" (Davis, Haub & Willette 1983:4).[2]

[2]For valuable works on language and ethnicity, see Fishman 1984, 1966; Fishman et al 1968; Heath 1983; Lieberson & Hansen 1974.

Geertz emphasizes the primordial tie, the "longing not to belong to any other group," as the critical defining characteristic of ethnicity (1963:109)—a criterion not easily applied to most persons in modern societies. This is a more stringent definition than Weber's reference to ethnic groups as "groups that entertain a subjective belief in their common descent," although Weber adds that "this belief must be important for the propagation of group formation" (Weber 1968:389). Using NORC data, Greeley (1974) wisely divides state-origin groups by religion, into what he calls religio-ethnic groups, in order to study ethnicity in the United States; but the data do not permit him to study the effect of "the longing not to belong to any other group"—a definition that he applauds.

Most empirical work is based on the single fact of an ethnic (or state-origin) label, with little attention to the salience of the label, to the strength of identification with the ethnic group compared with other identities, or to distinction between country of origin and ethnicity. The United States Census in 1980 sought to use the concept of ethnic group more precisely, but found it too difficult or costly to separate such labels as Belgian, Swiss, Nigerian, and Indonesian (each referring to an ethnically heterogeneous population) from more clearly ethnic labels such as Czech or Welsh. An explanatory footnote in the census report could be used for much of the data in ethnic studies, particularly in the United States: "In this report, the terms 'ancestry' and 'origin' (and ancestry group and ethnic group) are used interchangeably" (US Census 1983:1).

Using 1977, 1978, and 1980 data from the General Social Survey, Alba & Chamlin (1983) observe a rising number of individuals who, although of mixed ethnic (country of origin?) ancestry, identify themselves with only one. "This occurrence appears to corroborate assertions of a 'resurgence of ethnicity' but points as well to a fundamental change in the nature of ethnicity, as ethnic identifiers are increasingly individuals with mixed ethnic ancestry, who are likely to have a muted ethnic identity" (Alba & Chamlin 1983:240).

Race and Ethnicity

Is race one of the defining characteristics of ethnicity? Dozens of books and articles include both race and ethnicity in their titles or discussions in a way that indicates overlapping concepts; this is testimony to a certain ambiguity on the question (see, e.g., Stone 1977; van den Berghe 1983; Eisinger 1980; Steinberg 1981; Williams 1975). Specifically in the United States, the question arises. Are Blacks an ethnic group? Are they distinguished by culture rather than, or more than, or in addition to race? Are Mexican Americans a racial group?

If race is thought of strictly in physical anthropological terms, it has no place in the definition of ethnicity. Its technical biological meaning should not be confused with ethnicity (M. G. Smith 1982). Such a concept, however, is of interest to the geneticist. Its dimensions are measured only by sophisticated instruments, not by a few readily visible morphological traits. [And in this sense, there are dozens of races—34 in Dobzhansky's analysis (1962).] Sociology is interested in races only as socially visible divisions. Although these are based on some genetic component, the changing attention to and interpretation of that component is the critical sociological fact. There is now widespread if not universal agreement among scholars that "racial differences derive social significance from cultural diversity" (Kuper in Kuper & Smith 1971:13, see van den Berghe 1983:222; M. Kilson in Glazer & Moynihan 1975:236–266; A. Smith 1981:160–2; Keyes 1976; Taylor 1979).

In sum, to keep the definition within bounds, I will define an ethnic group . . . as "a segment of a larger society whose members are thought, by themselves and/or others, to have a common origin and to share important segments of a common culture and who, in addition, participate in shared activities in which the common origin and culture are significant ingredients" (Yinger: 1976:200). Some mixture of language, religion, race, and ancestral homeland with its related culture is the defining element. No one of these by itself demarcates an ethnic group.

DEMOGRAPHIC ASPECTS OF ETHNICITY

It is a truism to say that the absolute and proportionate sizes of ethnic groups in a society, their comparative rates of change, and their locations are highly significant aspects of that society's ethnic situation. One can scarcely begin a study of ethnicity without observing, for example, that over 80% of South Africa's population is nonwhite, that the size of the guest worker population has greatly increased Western Europe's diversity, that the dominant Russians in the Soviet Union will soon be a numerical minority, that the black, Native American, Asian, and Hispanic population of the United States increased from 17% of the total to over 23% between 1970 and 1980. In societies all over the world, differential rates of natural increase and incoming streams of migrants and refugees are changing the ethnic mix.

Since at least two *Annual Review of Sociology* articles (Petersen 1978; Massey 1981) have dealt with important aspects of this issue, I will call attention only to some of the recent literature and some of the questions examined therein. One cannot distinguish sharply between refugees (of whom there have been at least ten million in the world continuously during the last several years) and immigrants. Four criteria, however, can help one think of a continuum: (a) the degree to which the migrants are pushed out of their homeland or pulled into a new land by perception of opportunity and safety; (b) the degree to which they are subordinated in an ethnic-racial stratification system or are given opportunities for status improvement; (*c*) the illegality or legality of their migration; and (*d*) the likelihood that the move will be temporary or permanent (Simpson & Yinger 1985: Ch. 3).

Refugees are almost certainly destined for a prolonged period as seriously handicapped ethnic minorities, especially when they make up a high proportion of the population in a country with few economic opportunities, such as Somalia, Pakistan, Jordan, and Sudan.

Western Europe has relatively few refugees in the strict sense. However, the decision in the early 1970s to restrict and if possible reverse the flow of guest workers, sought and welcomed in large numbers over a 20-year period, has created something close to a refugee population. They face an uncertain legal situation, a sometimes hostile public opinion, and sharply diminished job opportunities. Yet many of the refugees see little to be gained by returning to their homelands—Turkey, North Africa, India, Jamaica, for example—and their children have known life only in Europe (see, e.g., Krane 1978; Rist 1978; Amersfoort 1982; Rex & Tomlinson 1979; Freeman 1979; Dignan 1981; Martin 1980).

Changes in the U.S. law in 1965 and in the economic and political situations around the world had a profound effect on the countries of origin of immigrants to the United States. In the 1961–1965 period, the countries with the largest representation (in thousands) were Mexico (223), Canada (175), Germany (136), Great Britain (92) and Italy (83). In the 1976–1980 period these had shifted to Mexico (303), the Philippines (197), Vietnam (162), Cuba (159), and Korea (153). (Data furnished by the Statistical Analysis Branch, Immigration and Naturalization Service, US Department of Justice.) These data do not directly indicate a shift in the ethnic situation. There is strong indication, however, of growth in ethnic awareness among many of these newcomers and of discrimination against them (see, eg, Bryce-Laporte 1980; Reimers 1981; Burawoy 1976; Portes 1984).

America's changing ethnic situation has been influenced not only by the approximately 750,000 immigrants and refugees who have been admitted per year during the last decade, but also by an unknown number of undocumented aliens who have entered. The Bureau of the Census has estimated that number to be between 3.5 million and 6 million. The physical difficulty of reducing this number (half or more of whom have crossed the long border with Mexico) is matched by the political difficulty of arriving at a policy that will simultaneously satisfy two competing interests. Those who want "to regain control over our borders," to reduce labor competition, to slow the rate of population growth, or to lower the alleged drain on welfare budgets conflict with those who welcome the ready supply of low-cost labor, who put a high value on maintaining friendly relations with Mexico, or who believe that a steady flow of new immigrants is of great value to the country (see Bustamante 1977; Ehrlich et al

1979; Crewdson 1983). In 1984 the US Congress was engaged in struggle with a bill that sought to satisfy several of these desires, including some that are, at least to a degree, mutually contradictory.

THE SOURCES OF ETHNIC SURVIVAL AND REVIVAL

Although developmental theory, Marxist theory, and widespread beliefs about the effects of urbanization predicted a sharp decline in the strength of ethnic attachments, the ethnic factor continues to be a significant element in most societies. Is this simply a matter of a theoretical error being corrected, an assumption being effectively challenged?

In my judgment, earlier theories may be no more in error than their critics, who, while making a necessary and valuable correction, tend to exaggerate the ethnic revival, especially with reference to the United States. The nature of ethnicity has changed, in some ways drastically. To think of oneself as an Oglala Sioux or Chippewa is quite different from thinking of oneself as a Native American resident of Chicago or Los Angeles. We lose explanatory power if we equate contemporary urban ethnicity—with its large symbolic, affective qualities—with the more deeply rooted attachments and firmer boundaries of less mobile times and places. The latter may decline in some settings even while the former grows in influence.

Can the several, partly contradictory explanations of the sources and strengths of ethnicity be brought within one system? A number of recent studies have moved significantly in that direction by combining attention to the interest basis of ethnic strength with attention to the symbolic and affective aspects of a primordial attachment (McKay 1982; Lal 1983; A. Smith 1981; Stein & Hill 1977; I. Light in Keyes 1981:54–86; Glazer & Moynihan 1975). One can agree with Epstein's remark (1978:xi): "The one major conviction that emerged [from his study of ethnicity] was the powerful emotional charge that appears to surround or to underlie so much of ethnic behavior." That charge is strong in part, however, not simply because it is connected with primordial sentiments, but also because it is connected with contemporary interests. Daniel Bell argues persuasively (in Glazer & Moynihan 1975:169) that material interests are well served by ethnically based movements precisely because they "combine an interest with an affective tie."

Although less often discussed, a third major source of the continuing influence of ethnicity requires attention. Not only is ethnicity felt as a primordial sentiment, an emotional attachment to "my people," and a valuable tool for the protection or enhancement of status. It is, in addition, a way of trying to deal with the experience of anomie and the feeling of alienation. It can be seen as a "mode of reintegration of population elements into structures which are less anomic and alienative than their members might otherwise be exposed to" (T.

Parsons in Glazer & Moynihan 1975:69; see also Greeley 1971: Ch. 13; DeVos in DeVos & Romanucci-Ross 1975:25–6). In a rapidly changing society, strongly influenced by instrumentalism and rationality, it is difficult to know who one is. We look for a "brand name" (Herberg 1955) or declare with Jesse Jackson that "I am somebody."

When social conflict brings renewed attention to one's ancestry, and it appears that one's interests will be served by affirming that background, these influences may combine with feelings of alienation from the larger society and with the sense of living in an anomic world to strengthen an ethnic identity (Yinger 1976, 1983).

Many current students of ethnicity emphasize that it is situational, emergent, adaptable, durable through flexibility, an instrument in economic and political struggles (Allworth 1977; Yancey, Eriksen, & Juliani 1979; Hannan 1979; Galaty 1982; Okamura 1981; Cohen 1974; Gans 1979). Interpretations of this fact, however, vary. Some see it as a sign of ethnic strength and durability, an indication of the weakness of the assimilationist argument. Others regard this situational, flexible quality as a sign of the fragility of ethnicity as usually understood. To some degree this disagreement is a matter of definition. I recently sat in on a conference of university students that was organized around the theme: "Asian Americans, an Etcetera Minority in Search of a Definition." It was fascinating, and a bit startling, to watch persons of Chinese, Japanese, Korean, Indian, Filipino, and Vietnamese backgrounds begin to define themselves as an ethnic group. This is quite different from seeing oneself, let us say, as a Kaoshan-Chinese from Taiwan or a Hakka from Fukien (Dreyer 1976; L. Pye in Glazer & Moynihan 1975:489–512). It is essential, if the term ethnicity is to be used to cover such a range—from Hakka immigrants to Asian Americans, e.g.—that the differences as well as the similarities be thoroughly examined.

Some scholars, it should be noted, are not comfortable with complex, multivariable explanations of ethnic survival and revival. Such explanations seem to them to be ad hoc descriptions rather than fundamental interpretations. A few have sought one basic reductionist principle to account for ethnic solidarity. Van den Berghe, for example, has developed what he believes to be a parsimonious theory based on sociobiology; according to him, "ethnic and racial sentiments are extensions of kinship sentiments" (van den Berghe 1981:80). They should therefore express the sociobiological principle of inclusive fitness.

This may be a plausible (but scarcely testable) partial explanation of the origins of ethnicity. However, it is of little use, in my judgment, to explain the ethnic solidarity of large, heterogeneous, and changing ethnic groups in modern societies—groups influenced by intermarriage, conversion, adoption, and intergroup alliances, not to speak of the highly diluted effect of the principle of inclusive fitness in very large and mixed populations.

Another reductionist approach to the study of ethnicity is the application of rational choice theory. Behavior is seen as the result of interaction between the structural conditions and individual preferences (Hechter et al 1982; Banton 1983). Based on or similar to classic economic theory, rational choice theory sees little to be gained by introducing unconscious motives or normative influences. I would emphasize that the overwhelming dominance of structural conditions in some circumstances leaves little room for the play of choice, rational or otherwise. It is those conditions—their origins and supports—that are often most in need of analysis in ethnic relations theory. Yet I shall make a rational choice to wait and see. This approach is new and relatively undeveloped. There may be a way to blend it into a more complex theory rather than substituting it for all the others. Its conservative implications may not be intrinsic.

APPROACHES TO THE STUDY OF ETHNICITY

The current strong scholarly interest in ethnicity is the result of the convergence of several different approaches to the study of the dynamic ethnic situation. Three in particular should be noted: (*a*) studies of racial and cultural minorities, of stratification, discrimination, and social conflict; (*b*) major theoretical strands in urban sociology and in ethnology concerned with cultural variation— strands that have become interwoven as formerly somewhat isolated peoples come together in metropolitan areas; and (*c*) studies developing from the interest shared by political sociology and political science in state building, development, and the impact of cultural heterogeneity on the political process.

Ethnicity, Social Stratification, and Discrimination

Most studies combine two or all three of these approaches to some degree. In this section I note recent work, mainly in the well established social stratification tradition, that emphasizes how ethnic and racial systems are involved in patterns of inequality and conflict (Yinger, 1983). Basic general studies include the continuing examination of ethnocentrism and cultural differences (Brewer & Campbell 1976; LeVine & Campbell 1972; Turner & Singleton 1978), of prejudice (Apostle et al 1983; Seeman 1981), and of stereotypy (Hamilton 1981; Miller 1982; Tajfel 1982; Lieberson 1982).

Apostle et al (1983) strengthen our understanding of racial attitudes by distinguishing among perceptions, explanations, and prescriptions—aspects of such attitudes that have somewhat different sets of causes and effects. (They prefer the term "racial attitudes" to "prejudice." In my judgment they are not synonyms. Presumably there can be nonprejudiced perceptions, explanations, and prescriptions.)

Recent studies of stereotypes have been of particular value in strengthening the theoretical base in cognitive social psychology. Stereotypes affect interaction in ways that restrict the flow of disconfirming information and may actually produce confirming experience. In many instances, the old adage has to be reversed: Believing is seeing. In what Pettigrew calls "the ultimate attribution error" (1979), negative acts of members of outgroups are seen as caused by their permanent, even genetic, characteristics. Their positive acts, however, are explained by transitory, situational forces.

A phenomenon closely related to stereotypy is opposition to members of an ethnic minority because of their perceived tendency to violate traditional values, such as self-reliance, the work ethic, and discipline. This has been called "symbolic racism" (see, e.g., McConahay & Hough 1976; Rosenthal 1980; Kinder & Sears 1981). By most measures, older forms of prejudice and stereotyping have declined, but opposition to minorities remains at quite a high level, supposedly because they are seen as threatening central values. The implied causal connection, however, requires careful study. The concept of symbolic racism focuses our attention in a useful way on the shifting bases of interethnic discrimination; but it may cause us to exaggerate the shift. In many ways, symbolic racism is quite old-fashioned, with roots, as Kinder & Sears observe (1981), not only in deep feelings of morality and propriety, but also in early-learned racial fears and stereotypes.

Some of the consequences of those fears and stereotypes are examined in the continuing stream of studies of ethnic and racial discrimination, particularly with reference to the United States, although Great Britain, Israel, the Soviet Union, South Africa, and other societies have been extensively examined. To cite only some of the most recent work, the wartime relocation of Americans of Japanese background continues to be the subject of great interest (Irons 1984; Commission on Wartime Relocation 1982). With the large increase in the number of persons of Chinese background in the American population, they too are receiving increased attention (Cheng & Bonacich 1984; Glick 1980).

Discrimination carried to its ultimate degree—genocide—continues to be a topic of study and commentary (as well as of enormous outrage and grief) because it continues as a fact of human experience and because the consequences of genocide in the past persist (see Kuper 1982; Fein 1978; Dadrian 1976; Horowitz 1976). At least since the United Nations Convention on Genocide, 1951 (the United States is not among the 80 countries that have signed it), the concept of genocide has been stretched beyond its literal meaning to include serious bodily and mental harm and efforts at the cultural destruction of an ethnic group (Dadrian 1975). This usage is found particularly in victimology, which can be defined as the study of violent discrimination.

I will illustrate only some of the additional lines of investigation of the way ethnic differences are involved in stratification systems and in the pursuit of interests by referring to internal colonialism, split labor markets, and resource mobilization. In each instance, the interaction between dominant and minority groups is the focus of attention.

INTERNAL COLONIALISM   This concept is not new, but only in the last two decades has it been used extensively to help account for ethnic differences in economic and political strength. Blauner's influential paper (1969) character-ized the colonization complex as one in which the minority was brought in by force, its culture and social organization weakened, its life "managed and manipulated" by ethnic outsiders—all of this justified by racist doctrines. In the most ambitious development of this theme, Hechter (1977) argued that in Britain, even extensive industrialization and urbanization, social and physical mobility, and the growth of literacy and political participation did not succeed in bringing the Celtic fringe or periphery into the core of British national development.

The concept of internal colonialism has been applied to a number of settings, for example to a Marxist society (Karlovic 1982), and to the Southwest of the United States (Barrera 1979), and has been studied comparatively (Stone 1979; A. Smith 1981: 29–35). Once a group has established its dominance, according to internal colony theory, it is often able to maintain "a cultural division of labor: a system of stratification where objective cultural distinctions are super-imposed upon class lines" (Hechter 1977:30).

This interpretation is not without its weaknesses and its critics. It can make a "colony" appear to be more homogeneous in class and culture than it is, deflect attention from the domination over lower classes within the core, and cause one to overlook offsetting processes of integration of core and periphery (see, e.g., Glazer 1971; Moore 1976).

SPLIT LABOR MARKETS   A substantial body of literature in both economics and sociology develops a segmented, or dual, or split labor market theory of ethnic and racial domination. It builds upon earlier theories of class conflict, particularly Marxist, but with a stronger empirical basis and a more complex picture of the forces at work (for example, see Bonacich 1972, 1975, 1976; Cain 1976; Cummings 1980; Edwards, Reich, & Gordon 1975; Marshall 1974; Mukabe 1981; Szymanski 1976). The basic structure of a split labor market as described by Bonacich (1972, 1975) is one with three classes: capitalist, cheap-labor, and higher-priced labor. The outcome of this situation is not fixed.

> If employers are powerful they can drive out or drastically weaken the position of higher-priced labor, as is the case under slavery. If higher-priced labor is powerful enough they can drive the cheaper labor out of the labor market or block its entrance. Under other conditions, higher-priced labor can get a kind of compromise with employers under which they win a monopoly over the best jobs. Finally, under such conditions as a high demand for labor, political democracy, low ratio of minority workers, and the like, higher- and lower-priced labor may combine in an attempt to reduce the power of employers. In large and complex labor markets all four of these processes may be going on at once, as we believe to be the case in the United States (Simpson & Yinger 1985: Ch. 3).

These observations based on split labor market theories are derived in a general sense from Marxist thought. They clearly demand, however, significant modifications of the belief that ethnic divisions would fade in the modern capitalist world or that "false consciousness" would disappear in light of the recognition by the members of several ethnic groups that they were all being exploited (see Rex 1973).

Identification of the conditions under which the various processes occur and in what mixtures and comparative strengths has not been fully explored. Segmentation is not clear-cut under open market conditions (Greenberg 1980). Employers are sometimes ambivalent, for a mixture of profit, legal, and moral reasons. Some dominant workers are more vulnerable than others to minority competition, increasing the likelihood that they will show prejudice and will try to strengthen barriers to the entrance of lower-priced workers into their markets (Cummings 1980). Even less-skilled workers can mobilize resources to improve their positions (Hodson & Kaufman 1982).

RESOURCE MOBILIZATION   This last point leads to a more general comment on resource mobilization. Since two recent chapters in the *Annual Review of Sociology* have dealt with this topic (Jenkins 1983; Olzak 1983), I will refer to it only briefly. "Ethnic mobilization is the process by which groups organize around some feature of ethnic identity (for example, skin color, language, customs) in pursuit of ethnic ends" (Olzak 1983:355). This is, of course, a strategy of dominant as well as of minority groups (see, e.g., Adam & Giliomee 1979). It is only recently, however, that much attention has been paid to efforts by the less powerful to improve their circumstances, even though minority group strategies have often contained an implicit, if not entirely explicit theory of resource mobilization. Such theories define what are believed to be the best ways to activate members, to aggregate their limited, scattered resources, and to secure outside help. Social policy of dominant groups may stimulate this process by helping the poor and disadvantaged who are entering a segmented labor market to define themselves as an ethnic group with common interests (Herbstein 1983). Although weak in competitive resources, a group may not be weak in pressure resources, to use a distinction developed by Blalock (1979:53–54), including leadership (Leifer 1981; see also Coleman 1971; Lithman 1983).

This issue in the study of ethnic groups has, fortunately, been built upon the general theory of resource mobilization (see, for example, particularly, Zald & McCarthy 1979; Gamson 1975; Gamson, Fireman, & Rytina 1982; Oberschall 1973; Piven & Cloward 1977; Jenkins & Perrow 1977; Tilly 1978).

Ethnicity as Culture

Drawing on the pioneering work of Park, Thomas, and Znaniecki and a kind of second generation in such studies as those of Gans (1962), Keil (1966), Suttles (1968), and Hannerz (1969), students of ethnicity have written scores of books with an emphasis on particular groups more than on intergroup relations. To be sure, virtually all of these studies, including those of Park and Thomas (see Lal 1983), also deal with the stratification aspects of ethnic relations. They approach those aspects, however, most commonly within the framework of cultural analysis.

I will merely list a small sampling of such works, with reference only to the United States and to the last few years, before commenting on some of the themes found in these kinds of studies (see, for example, Horowitz 1983; Saran & Eames 1980; Fallows 1979; Connor 1977; Tomasi 1977; Lopata 1976). Many of the books that focus in particular on a single ethnic group deal, among other things, with family patterns and religion—topics that lead inevitably back to society-wide and interethnic questions.

FAMILIES AND ETHNICITY   This is well illustrated by interpretations of ethnic families. Many would agree, I believe, with the summary of Mindel & Havenstein (1981:431): "Somewhere between these great grindstones that would pulverize traditional family organization a type of family, once consigned to oblivion—being ground or melted down—persists: protean, adaptive, conservatizing, generating meanings, and forming a sense of identity partly from the realities of an earlier time, partly from the exigencies of the present."

Such an analysis is incomplete until it is put alongside the evidence regarding intermarriage, which I will define simply as marriage across a socially significant line of distinction. Rates of intermarriage vary widely, with the United States having among the highest. Because the lines drawn by religion, race, and ethnicity (in the sense of national origin) do not coincide, interpretation is difficult (Benson 1981). I think it is correct to say, however, that rates of intermarriage in the United States are higher than is noted by most students of ethnicity, that they are higher among younger cohorts, and that attitudes have become more favorable toward intermarriage.

Drawing on a number of sources, one can make the following estimates of intermarriage rates in the United States: Catholic, 40%; Jewish, 40%; Protestant, 18%. (Conversion of one or the other partner after marriage reduces these rates by about half.) Asian American rates are 10%–25% (depending upon country of origin); Black, 2%; Native American, 30% (not including Hispanics, many of whom have Indian ancestors). Ethnicity defined as national origin (which is the way most of the data are given) shows rates of intermarriage ranging from 5% to over 80%, depending upon country of origin, the time period, generation in the country, rural or urban residence, status, locality and region of the country, and other variables.[3] (See Alba 1981; Alba & Kessler 1979; Blau et al 1982, 1984; S. Cohen 1977; Gurak & Fitzpatrick 1982; B. Kim 1977; McRae 1983; Murguia 1982; Peach 1980; Porterfield 1978; Schoen & L. Cohen 1980).

RELIGION AND ETHNICITY   It is difficult to doubt that religion today, as in the past, is one of the crucial defining characteristics in ethnic identity and one of the rallying points in ethnic conflict. Whether religion is a major cause of that conflict is much more difficult to determine, since religion often covaries with class, with demographic characteristics, with length of residence in a society, and other factors. Reversing generations of Muslim religious tolerance, Shiite fundamentalism in Iran, for example, directs its attacks not only against other societies but also against minority religious groups within Iran. Many of the Bahais, Zoroastrians, Jews, and Christians differ from the majority in ethnicity as well as religion; but they also differ in occupation and class.

The conflict in Northern Ireland is sometimes seen in religious and ethnic terms, a continuation of the generations-long struggle between the Irish-Irish and the Scotch-Irish. Religious leaders seeking to stop the violence speak of "Protestant fundamentalism and Catholic nationalism" as "equally guilty in supposing that God had sanctified their national and cultural prejudices" (*Irish Times,* July 21, 1983:14). These national and cultural facts, however, rest on a strong base of economic and political issues.

In Latin America, some segments of the Catholic Church, long seen as a bastian of strength for the ruling groups, are now major participants in the struggle to increase the economic and political rights of peasants, most of whom are Indian or mestizo (Lernoux 1982; Levine 1981).

Research on religion and ethnicity in the United States during the last several years has continued along well-established lines. Greeley (1976) has documented the rapid and educational advance of ethnic Catholics. Black-white church segregation has continued to decline (Hadaway et al 1984). The Black church, although sharing leadership positions more widely with politicians, lawyers, and others, continues to be seen as a major source of influence (Childs 1980; Lincoln 1974). The dominant branch of the former Black

---

[3]These are rates of intermarriages, which are not always distinguished from individual rates. If 60 persons from a given group *intra*marry and forty *inter*marry, 57% of the 70 marriages involving a member of that group are intermarriages. Transposition of one rate into the other can be made by use of the following formulas, with x being the group rate and y the individual rate:

$$y = \frac{100x}{200 - x} \qquad x = \frac{200y}{100 + y}$$

Muslims, now the American Muslim Mission, is moving in the direction of Sunni Muslim orthodoxy (see, for example, Mamiya, 1982), but some of the black Americans who feel most alienated continue to support the harshly separatist Black Muslim approach of Louis Farrakhan. And, as a final illustration, the controversial relationships between Native Americans and dominant Christian churches and missions have been the subject of renewed attention (Bowden 1981; Deloria 1973).

Ethnicity and Politics

We need only the headlines to tell us how frequently ethnic borders and state borders fail to coincide. Connor (1972) notes that in 53 of 132 states there were more than five significant ethnic groups. Only 12 (9%) were essentially homogeneous; in 25 others (19%) one ethnic group made up more than 90% of the population. The nation-state is a powerful idea; but the facts and the ideology of ethnic diversity are also powerful. Much of the recent literature on ethnicity deals with the various ways in which the collision between these two conflicting views on how to organize a multiethnic society are dealt with and the consequences of the various choices.

ETHNICITY IN DEVELOPING STATES   With dozens of new states formed since World War II, the process of nation-building (or, more appropriately, state-building, whether around one or more nations) and the related process of modernization have been subjects of a great deal of study (see, for example, C. Young 1976, 1982; Burgess 1981; Smock & Smock 1975; Bell & Freeman 1974; Lee 1983; Horowitz 1975; Schermerhorn 1978; Weiner 1978; Rothschild 1981; Williams 1982; Connor 1972; W. Skinner in Despres 1975:131–57). Young (1982:84–5) skillfully states the prevailing interpretation and, I think it fair to say, the prevailing fact:

> A number of strategies were pursued in executing the nation-building design. The colonial pattern of avid classification largely ceased; indeed, the state frequently sought to replace ethnic categories by those based on territory. . . . Thus the overly exuberant celebration of ethnicity is viewed with suspicion by the state. A number have forbidden the formation of ethnic associations, which were generally tolerated by the colonial state. . . . That politicized ethnicity is a potential—and potent—threat to the nation-building mission has been a prime factor in the widespread adoption of single-party or military formulas of governance, where open political competition is averted.

In some developing states, of course, ethnicity has been accepted as an organizing principle, to some degree because no one ethnic group has had sufficient power to declare itself the core. The results have been mixed, with states such as Yugoslavia (Rusinow 1977; Karlovic 1982; Bertsch 1977) and Malaysia (Hirschman 1975; Nagata 1980; Abraham 1983) having contained, but by no means eliminated, the conflict, while others such as Lebanon (Hewitt

1977; Baaklini 1983) have suffered protracted civil war that belies the fairly optimistic views of a decade ago (Smock & Smock 1975).

ETHNICITY IN DEVELOPED STATES   Ethnicity is an important political fact in most industrialized states also. The sub-nations of Western Europe, as William Petersen calls them (in Glazer & Moynihan 1975:177–208), and those of Canada have not only persisted but in several instances have become more assertive in recent decades. In Belgium, Great Britain, Holland, Spain, and Canada, for example, they have tested the efforts to maintain central state dominance if not absolute hegemony (Ragin 1979; Hall 1979; Dofny & Akiwowo 1980; Thompson 1983; Richmond 1984; Rex & Tomlinson 1979; Hechter 1977; Nielsen 1980; Olzak 1982; Guindon 1978).

Communist societies have not escaped these difficulties (Connor 1984). Ethnic attachments remain strong in China, among the at least 40 million non-Han ethnics, many of them along the USSR border (Dreyer 1976). Such attachments are more clearly a significant political fact in the Soviet Union, especially among residents in the Baltic region, Jews, and the Muslims along the southern border (King 1973; Azrael 1978; Allworth 1977; Rakowska-Harmstone 1977).

The ethnic relations of few countries have been studied with such intensity as those of Israel; over 25% of the population is Arabic, mainly Palestinian. Toward them, government policy and individual attitudes and behavior are powerfully influenced by the stressful international situation. Among the great variety of Jews—North African, Middle Eastern, and European in origin—ethnic lines among those from more similar backgrounds are being drawn less clearly (one may be European, for example, rather than Polish), but the more distinctive cultural groups remain distinct, their separate identities underlined and intensified by class differences and conflict (see, eg, Shokeid & Deshen 1982; Smooha 1978; Lustick 1980; Simon 1980; Rosenstein 1981).

ETHNICITY IN AMERICAN POLITICS   As Rothschild notes (1981: Ch. 7), ethnopolitics is not always or necessarily uncompromising, zero-sum, and strident. Although it can make life much more complicated for the central elites, it can also be a resource and a vivid reminder of problems that, if not resolved, will seriously weaken the state. Many of the studies of ethnicity and politics in the United States are built, in various ways, around that theme. They deal with the degree to which the ethnic factor strengthens the influence of otherwise underrepresented groups or, on the other hand, how it divides and weakens the democratic process.

For some time the political aspects have had a place in the studies of American ethnicity. The many political dimensions of the civil rights movement brought the issue clearly into the public arena. And the influence, or alleged influence, of American ethnic groups on foreign policy continues to attract both scholarly and public attention (as a sample, see Eisinger 1980; Said 1977; Enloe 1981; Lambert 1981; Clark & Ferguson 1983: Chs. 3, 4; M. Kilson in Glazer & Moynihan 1975: Ch. 8).

Enloe observes that states (she is referring primarily to the United States) seeking to expand and solidify their authority may attempt to co-opt ethnic organizations, to block their influence by denying them access to essential activities, and to reenforce a public ideology supporting individual rights while discrediting communal rights. These very activities, however, can contribute to the mobilization of ethnic groups. Even though "the BIA [Bureau of Indian Affairs] has always been viewed by Indian activists as a vehicle by which the American state made Indians poor and dependent" (Enloe 1981:133), it has also been a focus of Indian mobilization. The Immigration and Naturalization Service [INS] makes day-by-day decisions of vital importance to Hispanics but mainly out of their control. "The INS has become a stimulus for Chicano (and other Hispanic groups) mobilization. One result of that ethnic mobilization is that the INS today has its first Hispanic director, just as the BIA has its first Indian director" (Enloe 1981:133).

A final question regarding the impact of ethnicity on politics receives more public than scholarly attention. How do ethnic groups influence a state's international relations? In the United States, ethnic group spokesmen (how representative they are is problematic) and individual activities have been concerned—to cite the most visible cases—with American policies toward and the internal politics of Israel, the Arabic states, the USSR, Ireland, Vietnam, South Africa, Mexico, Cuba, and Central America. Among the nearly half-million refugees from Vietnam in the United States, some (in a way similar to that of some Cuban refugees and immigrants) seek to organize opposition to the current regime in Hanoi. One group claimed "credit" for the murder of a Vietnamese refugee who supported that regime (Talbot 1982).

Do such internally divided ethnic groups and those that are more nearly unified pose a threat to a state? Based on their study of several cases, Suhrke & Noble (1977) believe that the answer is no in most instances. This is also the judgment of most of the authors in *Ethnicity and U.S. Foreign Policy* (Said 1977), although their views tend to be more qualified. In the Preface, Said observes, I think correctly, that in his judgment "the image of national interest has become blurred." Perhaps the strongest effects of ethnic concern and activity on foreign policy issues are not directly on the government, but on interethnic relations, as between Jews and Blacks, for example, or between Mexican Americans and Anglos.

ETHNICITY, THE MILITARY, AND THE POLICE   Despite pioneering work by Stouffer and his associates (1949), Janowitz (1964, 1965), Moskos (1966), and others, it is only since about 1970 that the issue of the ethnic makeup of military and police forces has been a topic of extensive research. The increase in interest reflects, in particular, the fact that the ethnic makeup of new states strongly influenced control over their armed forces and also that the civil rights movement in the United States focused attention on the ethnic and racial membership in the armed forces and the police as well as on their treatment of minorities.

Colonial powers have often used as foot soldiers or junior officers persons from smaller ethnic groups, or those presumed to have a martial tradition, or believed to be more likely to be loyal to the regime (Janowitz 1981; Enloe 1977, 1980; Kirk-Greene 1980). Most of the new states, are made up of diverse ethnic groups, sometimes hostile to each other and almost certainly competitive. One of the most difficult tasks is to shape statewide constabulary and armed forces out of units whose main loyalty has been given to the separate ethnic groups. The dominant ethnic group may soon come to be seen as repressive if, in the name of state-building, it seeks complete control over the military forces. Lacking a relatively homogeneous civic culture, the leaders may seek to forge a kind of military unity.

Industrialized and developed societies have not escaped the problems associated with ethnic imbalance in the military and police forces (W. Young 1982; Binkin & Eitelberg 1982). They may seek to diversify and democratize the selection process by affirmative action programs, civil rights laws, and executive orders, as has happened in the United States. If the society at large, however, contains discriminatory structures, these will affect the outcomes. The least powerful racial and ethnic groups in the United States are still greatly underrepresented in the police forces (Cooper 1980). Although they are not underrepresented in the armed forces (Blacks constitute nearly twice as large a proportion in the military as in the total population), they make up a much lower share of the senior officers, due to lack of seniority, lower average amounts of training, and discrimination (Binkin & Eitelberg 1982). They also face problems of discrimination from the surrounding communities at home and abroad, and are more likely to receive harsh sentences from the criminal justice system (see Hayles & Perry 1981; Moskos 1973; Hope 1979). Among civilians, police brutality and discrimination are often alleged by members of ethnic minorities, not without cause (see, e.g., *The New York Times*, Oct. 19, 1980:1 & Nov. 11, 1982:35; Fernandez, Haug & Wagner 1976:84–98).

Enloe (1977:137) summarizes this issue well: "Militaries and police forces are rarely neutral actors in ethnic conflicts. They are typically ethnically imbalanced as a result both of historical socioeconomic maldistributions of opportunities and of deliberate recruitment strategies pursued by central government elites." She goes on to note that modernization and professionalization of security forces do not guarantee their communal or political neutrality.

CONCLUSION

Slowly research is moving beyond the rather strongly ideological discussions to ask: To what degree, in what ways, under what conditions, and with what consequences do ethnic groups occupy an important place in a social structure? Under what conditions are they relatively less salient? Perhaps the best way to conclude this review is to note a few of the corollary questions that linger in my mind after study of the immense body of literature that has appeared in the last several years.

How does widespread emphasis on and identification with ethnic groups, rather than (or more than) on classes, influence the level and the nature of conflict? When societal strains are organized along ethnic boundaries, are they less negotiable, more intractable, with a higher emotive component? Or does such organization make it possible for the otherwise powerless to mobilize resources that are out of reach when they act as individuals?

Who within an ethnic group, if anyone, profits in terms of status, income, and power, by an emphasis on ethnic divisions? Ethnic movements are typically inspired and led by higher-status persons. Is it they who have the most to gain?

Under what conditions does assimilation begin and persist; what conditions retard it; and what are its long-run effects on various groups? These are intrinsically difficult questions, made more difficult by the varying premises and values that influence researchers. If one assumes that assimilation is inevitable and desirable, important questions are not even asked. If one assumes that it is always one-way, discriminatory, and results in dead-level uniformity, contradictory evidence may be overlooked.

Perhaps we need continuously to emphasize a dilemma faced by multiethnic societies: Under assimilative pressure, cultures may be lost that contain elements needed for adaptation to a changing world—the loss of a kind of cultural gene pool. Under pluralistic and separatist pressures, cultural forms may be preserved that are maladaptive and unjust—sexist, racist, harshly stratified, and militarized.

Ongoing research gives promise that we will be able to examine these questions and issues more powerfully in the years ahead.

Literature Cited

Abell, T., Lyon, L. 1979. Do the differences make a difference? An empirical evaluation of the culture of poverty in the United States. *Am. Ethnol.* 6:602–20

Abraham, C. E. R. 1983. Racial and ethnic manipulation in colonial Malaya. *Ethn. Racial Stud.* 6:18–32

Adam, B. 1978. Inferiorization and 'self-esteem'. *Soc. Psychol.* 41:47–53

Adam, H., Giliomee, H. 1979. *Ethnic Power Mobilized: Can South Africa Change?* New Haven, Conn: Yale Univ. Press

Alba, R. D. 1981. The twilight of ethnicity among American Catholics of European ancestry. *Ann. Am. Acad. Polit. Soc. Sci.* 454:86–97

Alba, R. D., Chamlin, M. B. 1983. A preliminary examination of ethnic identification among whites. *Am. Sociol. Rev.* 48(2):240–47

Alba, R. D., Kessler, R. C. 1979. Patterns of interethnic marriage among American Catholics. *Soc. Forc.* 57(4):1124–40

Alexander, K. L., Cook, M., McDill, E. L. 1978. Curriculum tracking and educational stratification: some further evidence. *Am. Sociol. Rev.* 43:47–66

Allworth, E., ed. 1977. *Nationality Group Survival in Multi-Ethnic States: Shifting Support Patterns in the Soviet Baltic Region.* New York: Praeger

Amersfoort, H. van. 1982. *Immigration and the Formation of Minority Groups: The Dutch Experience 1945–1975.* Cambridge: Cambridge Univ. Press

Apostle, R. A., Glock, C. Y., Piazza, T., Suelzle, M. 1983. *The Anatomy of Racial Attitudes.* Berkeley: Univ. Calif. Press

Archdeacon, T. J. 1983. *Becoming American: An Ethnic History.* New York: Free

Astin, A. W. 1982. *Minorities in Higher Education: Recent Trends, Current Prospects, and Recommendations.* San Francisco: Jossey-Bass

Azrael, J. R., ed. 1978. *Soviet Nationality Policies and Practices.* New York: Praeger

Baaklini, A. I. 1983. Ethnicity and politics in contemporary Lebanon. In *Culture, Ethnicity, and Identity: Current Issues in Research,* ed. W. C. McCready, pp. 17–56. New York: Academic

Banton, M. 1983. *Racial and Ethnic Competition.* New York: Cambridge Univ. Press

Barrera, M. 1979. *Race and Class in the Southwest.* South Bend, Ind: Univ. Notre Dame Press

Basham, R., DeGroot, D. 1977. Current approaches to the anthropology of urban and complex societies. *Am. Anthropol.* 79(2):414–40

Bell, W., Freeman, W. E., eds. 1974. *Ethnicity and Nation-Building: Comparative International and Historical Perspectives.* Beverly Hills, Calif: Sage

Benson, S. 1981. *Ambiguous Ethnicity: Interracial Families in London.* New York: Cambridge Univ. Press

Berger, J., Rosenholtz, S. J., Zelditch, M. Jr. 1980. Status organizing processes. *Ann. Rev. Sociol.* 6:479–508

Bertsch, G. K. 1977. Ethnicity and politics in socialist Yugoslavia. *Am. Acad. Polit. Soc. Sci.* 433:88–99

Beuf, A. H. 1977. *Red Children in White America.* Philadelphia: Univ. Penn. Press

Binkin, M., Eitelberg, M. J., with Schexnider, A. J., Smith, M. M. 1982. *Blacks and the Military.* Washington, DC: The Brookings Inst.

Blalock, H. M. Jr. 1979. *Black-White Relations in the 1980s: Toward a Long-Term Policy.* New York: Praeger

Blau, P. M. 1977. A macrosociological theory of social structure. *Am. J. Sociol.* 83:26–54

Blau, P. M., Beeker, C., Fitzpatrick, K. M. 1984. Intersecting social affiliations and intermarriage. *Soc. Forc.* 62(3):585–606

Blau, P. M., Blum, T. C., Schwartz, J. E. 1982. Heterogeneity and intermarriage. *Am. Sociol. Rev.* 47:45–62

Blauner, R. 1972. *Racial Oppression in America.* New York: Harper & Row

Blauner, R. 1969. Internal colonialism and ghetto revolt. *Soc. Probl.* 16:393–408

Bonacich, E. 1976. Advanced capitalism and black/white relations in the United States: a split labor market interpretation. *Am. Sociol. Rev.* 41:34–51

Bonacich, E. 1975. Abolition, the extension of slavery, and the position of free blacks: a study of split labor markets in the United States, 1830–1863. *Am. Sociol. Rev.* 81(3):601–28

Bonacich, E. 1972. A theory of ethnic antagonism: the split labor market. *Am. Sociol. Rev.* 37:547–59

Bowden, H. W. 1981. *American Indians and Christian Missions: Studies in Cultural Conflict.* Chicago: Univ. Chicago Press

Brewer, M. B., Campbell, D. T. 1976. *Ethnocentrism and Intergroup Attitudes: East African Evidence.* Beverly Hills, Calif: Sage

Bryce-Laporte, R. S., ed. 1980. *Sourcebook on the New Immigration: Implications for the United States and the International Community.* New Brunswick, NJ: Transaction

Burgess, M. E. 1981. Ethnic scale and intensity: the Zimbabwean experience. *Soc. Forc.* 59:601–26

Burke, F. G. 1981. Bilingualism/Biculturalism

in American education: An adventure in wonderland. *Ann. Am. Acad. Polit. Soc. Sci.* 454:164–77

Burawoy, M. 1976. The function and reproduction of migrant labor: comparative material from southern Africa and the United States. *Am. J. Sociol.* 81(5):1050–87

Bustamente, J. A. 1977. Undocumented immigration from Mexico: research report. *Int. Migration Rev.* 11:149–77

Cain, G. G. 1976. The challenges of segmented labor market theories to orthodox theory: a survey. *J. Econ. Lit.* 14(4):1215–57

Cheng, L., Bonacich, E., eds. 1984. *Labor Immigration Under Capitalism: Asian Workers in the United States before World War II.* Berkeley: Univ. Calif. Press

Childs, J. B. 1980. *The Political Black Minister: A Study in Afro-American Politics and Religion.* Boston: Hall

Clark, K. B., Clark, M. P. 1947. Racial identification and preference in negro children. In *Readings in Social Psychology,* ed. T. M. Newcomb, E. L. Hartley, pp. 169–78. New York: Holt

Clark, T. N., Ferguson, L. C. 1983. *City Money: Political Processes, Fiscal Strain, and Retrenchment.* New York: Columbia Univ. Press

Cohen, A. 1974. *Two-Dimensional Man.* Berkeley: Univ. Calif. Press

Cohen, E. G. 1982. Expectations states and interracial interaction in school settings. *Ann. Rev. Sociol.* 8:209–35

Cohen, E. G., Roper, S. S. 1972. Modification of interracial interaction disability: an application of status characteristic theory. *Am. Sociol. Rev.* 37:643–57

Cohen, R. 1978. Ethnicity: problem and focus in anthropology. *Ann. Rev. Anthropol.* 7:379–403

Cohen, S. M. 1977. Socioeconomic determinants of intraethnic marriage and friendship. *Soc. Forc.* 55(4):997–1010

Coleman, J. S. 1971. *Resources for Social Change: Race in the United States.* New York: Wiley

Commission on Wartime Relocation and Internment of Civilians. 1982. *Personal Justice Denied.* Washington, DC: USGPO

Connor, J. W. 1977. *Tradition and Change in Three Generations of Japanese Americans.* Chicago: Nelson-Hall

Connor, W. 1984. *The National Question in Marxist-Leninist Theory and Strategy.* Princeton, NJ: Princeton Univ. Press

Connor, W. 1972. Nation building or nation destroying. *World Politics* 24:319–50

Cooper, J. L. 1980. *The Police and the Ghetto.* Port Washington, NY: Kennikat

Crewdson, J. 1983. *The Tarnished Door: The New Immigrants and the Transformation of America.* New York: Times Books

Cummings, S. 1980. White ethnics, racial prejudice, and labor market segmentation. *Am. J. Sociol.* 85:938–50

Dadrian, V. N. 1976. The Victimization of the American Indian. *Victimology* 1:517–37

Dadrian, V. N. 1975. The common features of the Armenian and Jewish cases of genocide: a comparative victimological perspective. In *Victimology: A New Focus,* Vol. IV, *Violence and Its Victims,* ed. I. Drapkin, E. Viano, pp. 99–120. Lexington, Mass: Heath

Davis, C., Haub, C., Willette, J. 1983. U.S. Hispanics: changing the face of America. *Pop. Bull.* 38(3):whole issue

Della Fave, L. R. 1980. The meek shall not inherit the earth: self-evaluation and the legitimacy of stratification. *Am. Sociol. Rev.* 45:955–71

Deloria, V. Jr. 1973. *God Is Red.* New York: Dell

Despres, L. A., ed. 1975. *Ethnicity and Resource Competition in Plural Societies.* The Hague: Mouton

DeVos, G. A. 1978. Selective permeability and reference group sanctioning: psychocultural continuities in role degradation. In *Major Social Issues,* ed. J. M. Yinger, S. J. Cutler, pp. 7–24. New York: Free

DeVos, G., Romanucci-Ross, L., eds. 1975. *Ethnic Identity.* Palo Alto, Calif: Mayfield

Dignan, D. 1981. Europe's melting pot: a century of large-scale immigration into France. *Ethn. Racial Stud.* 4(2):137–52

Dinnerstein, L., Nichols, R. L., Reimers, D. M. 1979. *Natives and Strangers: Ethnic Groups and the Building of America.* New York: Oxford Univ. Press

Dobzhansky, T. 1962. *Mankind Evolving.* New Haven, Conn: Yale Univ. Press

Dofny, J., Akiwowo, A., eds. 1980. *National and Ethnic Movements.* Beverly Hills, Calif: Sage

Dovidio, J. F., Gaertner, S. L. 1981. The effects of race, status, and ability on helping behavior. *Soc. Psychol. Q.* 44(3):192–203

Dreyer, J. T. 1976. *China's Forty Millions: Minority Nationalities and National Integration in the People's Republic of China.* Cambridge, Mass: Harvard Univ. Press

Edwards, R. C., Reich, M., Gordon, D. M. 1975. *Labor Market Segmentation.* Lexington, Mass: Heath

Ehrlich, P. R., Bilderback, L., Ehrlich, A. H. 1979. *The Golden Door: International Migration, Mexico and the United States.* New York: Ballantine

Eisinger, P. K. 1980. *The Politics of Displacement: Racial and Ethnic Transition in Three American Cities.* New York: Academic

Elkins, S. M. 1959. *Slavery: A Problem in American Institutional and Intellectual Life.* Chicago: Univ. Chicago Press

Enloe, C. H. 1981. The growth of the state and ethnic mobilization: the American experience. *Ethn. Racial Stud.* 4(2):123–36

Enloe, C. H. 1980. *Ethnic Soldiers: State Security in Divided Societies.* Athens: Univ. Georgia Press

Enloe, C. H. 1977. Police and military in the resolution of ethnic conflict. *Ann. Am. Acad. Polit. Soc. Sci.* 433:137–49

Epstein, A. L. 1978. *Ethos and Identity: Three Studies in Ethnicity.* London: Tavistock

Fallows, M. R. 1979. *Irish Americans: Identity and Assimilation.* Englewood Cliffs, NJ: Prentice-Hall

Fein, H. 1978. *Accounting for Genocide: National Response and Jewish Victimization During the Holocaust.* New York: Free

Fernandez, C. A., Haug, J. M., Wagner, N. N. 1976. *Chicanos.* St. Louis, Mo: Mosby

Fishman, J. A. 1984. *The Rise and Fall of the Ethnic Revival: Language and Ethnicity in Sociolinguistic Perspective.* Berlin: Mouton

Fishman, J. A., ed. 1966. *Language Loyalty in the United States.* The Hague: Mouton

Fishman, J. A., Ferguson, C. A., Das Gupta, J., eds. 1968. *Language Problems of Developing Nations.* New York: Wiley

Francis, E. K. 1976. *Interethnic Relations: An Essay in Sociological Theory.* New York: Elsevier

Freeman, G. P. 1979. *Immigrant Labor and Racial Conflict in Industrial Societies: The French and British Experience 1945–1975.* Princeton, NJ: Princeton Univ. Press

Frisbie, W. P., Neidert, L. 1977. Inequality and the relative size of minority populations: a comparative analysis. *Am. J. Sociol.* 82(5):1007–30

Galaty, J. G. 1982. Being 'Massai'; being 'people-of-cattle': ethnic shifters in East Africa. *Am. Ethnol.* 9:1–20

Gamson, W. A. 1975. *The Strategy of Social Protest.* Homewood, Ill: Dorsey

Gamson, W. A., Fireman, B., Rytina, S. 1982. *Encounters with Unjust Authority.* Homewood, Ill: Dorsey

Gans, H. J. 1979. Symbolic ethnicity: the future of ethnic groups and cultures in America. *Ethn. Racial Stud.* 2:1–20

Gans, H. J. 1962. *The Urban Villagers: Group and Class in the Life of Italian-Americans.* New York: Free

Garcia, J. A. 1981. Political integration of Mexican immigrants: explorations into the naturalization process. *Int. Migration Rev.* 15:608–25

Gecas, V. 1982. The self-concept. *Ann. Rev. Sociol.* 8:1–33

Geertz, C. 1963. *Old Societies and New States.* New York: Free Press

Glazer, N. 1983. *Ethnic Dilemmas 1964–1982.* Cambridge, Mass: Harvard Univ. Press

Glazer, N. 1971. Blacks and ethnic groups: the difference, and the political difference it makes. *Soc. Probl.* 18:444–61

Glazer, N., Moynihan, D. P., eds. 1975. *Ethnicity: Theory and Experience.* Cambridge: Harvard Univ. Press

Glick, C. E. 1980. *Sojourners and Settlers: Chinese Migrants in Hawaii.* Honolulu: Univ. Hawaii Press

Gordon, M. M. 1978. *Human Nature, Class, and Ethnicity.* New York: Oxford Univ. Press

Gordon, M. M. 1964. *Assimilation in American Life.* New York: Oxford Univ. Press

Greeley, A. M. 1976. *Ethnicity, Denomination, and Inequality.* Beverly Hills, Calif: Sage

Greeley, A. M. 1974. *Ethnicity in the United States: A Preliminary Reconnaissance.* New York: Wiley

Greeley, A. M. 1971. *Why Can't They Be Like Us.* New York: Dutton

Greenberg, S. B. 1980. *Race and State in Capitalist Development: Comparative Perspectives.* New Haven, Conn: Yale Univ. Press

Guindon, H. 1978. The modernization of Quebec and legitimacy of the Canadian state. *Can. Rev. Sociol. Anthropol.* 15:227–45

Gurak, D. T., Fitzpatrick, J. P. 1982. Intermarriage among Hispanic ethnic groups in New York City. *Am. J. Sociol.* 87:921–34

Gutman, H. G. 1976. *The Black Family in Slavery and Freedom 1725–1925.* New York: Pantheon

Hadaway, C. K., Hackett, D. G., Miller, J. F. 1984. The most segregated institution: correlates of interracial church participation. *Rev. Relig. Res.* 25(3):204–19

Hall, R. L., ed. 1979. *Ethnic Autonomy—Comparative Dynamics: The Americas, Europe and the Developing World.* New York: Pergamon

Hamilton, D. L., ed. 1981. *Cognitive Processes in Stereotyping and Intergroup Behavior.* Hillsdale, NJ: Erlbaum

Hannan, M. 1979. The dynamics of ethnic boundaries in modern states. In *National Development and the World System,* ed. J. Meyer, M. Hannan, pp. 253–75. Chicago: Univ. Chicago Press

Hannerz, U. 1969. *Soulside: Inquiries into Ghetto Culture and Community.* New York: Columbia Univ. Press

Hayles, R., Perry, R. W. 1981. Racial equality in the American naval justice system: An analysis of incarceration differentials. *Ethn. Racial Stud.* 4:44–55

Heath, S. B. 1983. *Ways with Words: Language, Life, and Work in Communities and Classrooms.* London: Cambridge Univ. Press

Hechter, M. 1977. *Internal Colonialism: The Celtic Fringe in British National Develop-*

ment, 1536–1966. Berkeley: Univ. Calif. Press

Hechter, M., Friedman, D., Appelbaum, M. 1982. A theory of ethnic collective action. *Int. Migration Rev.* 16(2):412–34

Heisler, M. O., issue ed. 1977. Ethnic conflict in the world today. *Ann. Am. Acad. Polit. Soc. Sci.* 433:whole issue

Herberg, W. 1955. *Protestant-Catholic-Jew.* Garden City, NY: Doubleday

Herbstein, J. 1983. The politicization of Puerto Rican ethnicity in New York: 1955–1975. *Ethn. Groups* 5:31–54

Hewitt, C. 1977. Majorities and minorities: a comparative study of ethnic violence. *Ann. Am. Acad. Polit. Soc. Sci.* 433:150–60

Hill, M. S., Ponza, M. 1983. Poverty and welfare dependence across generations. *Econ. Outlook USA* Summer:61–64

Hirschman, C. 1983. America's melting pot reconsidered. *Ann. Rev. Sociol.* 9:397–423

Hirschman, C. 1975. *Ethnic and Social Stratification in Peninsular Malaysia.* Washington, DC: Am. Sociol. Assoc.

Hodson, R., Kaufman, R. L. 1982. Economic dualism: a critical review. *Am. Sociol. Rev.* 47:727–39

Hope, R. Θ. 1979. *Racial Strife in the U.S. Military.* New York: Praeger

Horowitz, D. L. 1975. Ethnic identity. In *Ethnicity: Theory and Experience,* ed. N. Glazer, D. P. Moynihan, pp. 111–40. Cambridge: Harvard Univ. Press

Horowitz, I. L. 1976. *Genocide: State Power and Mass Murder.* New Brunswick, NJ: Transaction

Horowitz, R. 1983. *Honor and the American Dream: Culture and Identity in a Chicano Community.* New Brunswick, NJ: Rutgers Univ. Press

Humphreys, P., Berger, J. 1981. Theoretical consequences of the status characteristic formulation. *Am. J. Sociol.* 86:953–83

Hurh, W. M., Kim, H. C., Kim, K. C. 1979. *Assimilation Patterns of Immigrants in the United States: A Case Study of Korean Immigrants in the Chicago Area.* Washington, DC: Univ. Press America

Irons, P. 1984. *Justice at War: The Story of the Japanese Internment Cases.* New York: Oxford Univ. Press

Janowitz, M., ed. 1981. *Civil-Military Relations: Regional Perspectives.* Beverly Hills, Calif: Sage

Janowitz, M., in coll. with Little, R. 1965. *Sociology and the Military Establishment.* New York: Russell Sage. Rev. ed.

Janowitz, M. 1964. *The Military in the Political Development of New Nations.* Chicago: Univ. Chicago Press

Jenkins, J. C. 1983. Resource mobilization theory and the study of social movements. *Ann. Rev. Sociol.* 9:527–53

Jenkins, J. C., Perrow, C. 1977. Insurgency of the powerless. *Am. Sociol. Rev.* 42(2):249–68

Juliani, R. N. 1982. Ethnicity: myth, social reality, and ideology. *Contemp. Soc.* 11(4):368–70

Kanter, R. M. 1977. Some effects of proportions on group life: skewed sex ratios and responses to token women. *Am. J. Sociol.* 82:965–90

Karlovic, N. L. 1982. Internal colonialism in a Marxist society: the case of Croatia. *Ethn. Racial Stud.* 5:276–99

Keil, C. 1966. *Urban Blues.* Chicago: Univ. Chicago Press

Keyes, C. F., ed. 1981. *Ethnic Change.* Seattle: Univ. Wash. Press

Keyes, C. F. 1976. Towards a new formulation of the concept of ethnic group. *Ethnicity* 3(3):202–13

Kim, B. C. 1977. Asian wives of U.S. servicemen: women in shadows. *Amerasia* 4:91–115

Kinder, D. R., Sears, D. O. 1981. Prejudice and politics: symbolic racism versus racial threats to the good life. *J. Pers. Soc. Psychol.* 40(3):414–31

King, R. R. 1973. *Minorities Under Communism: Nationalities as a Source of Tension among Balkan Communist States.* Cambridge, Mass: Harvard Univ. Press

Kirk-Greene, A. H. M. 1980. 'Damnosa Herditas': ethnic ranking and the martial races imperative in Africa. *Ethn. Racial Stud.* 3:393–414

Kuper, L. 1982. *Genocide: Its Political Use in the Twentieth Century.* New Haven, Conn: Yale Univ. Press

Kuper, L. 1977. *The Pity of it All.* Minneapolis: Univ. Minn. Press

Kuper, L., Smith, M. G., eds. 1971. *Pluralism in Africa.* Berkeley: Univ. Calif. Press

Lal, B. B. 1983. Perspectives on ethnicity: old wine in new bottles. *Ethn. Racial Stud.* 6:154–73

Lambert, R. D. 1981. Ethnic/racial relations in the United States in comparative perspective. *Ann. Am. Acad. Polit. Soc. Sci.* 454:189–205

Laumann, E. O. 1973. *Bonds of Pluralism: The Forms and Substance of Urban Social Networks.* New York: Wiley

Leifer, E. M. 1981. Competing models of political mobilization: the role of ethnic ties. *Am. J. Sociol.* 87(1):23–47

Lernoux, P. 1982. *Cry of the People: The Struggle for Human Rights in Latin-America—The Catholic Church in Conflict with U.S. Policy.* New York: Penguin

Levine, D. H. 1981. *Religion and Politics in Latin America.* Princeton, NJ: Princeton Univ. Press

LeVine, R. A., Campbell, D. T. 1972. *Ethno-*

centrism: Theories of Conflict, Ethnic Attitudes and Group Behavior. New York: Wiley

Lewis, M. 1978. The Culture of Inequality. Amherst: Univ. Mass. Press

Lewis, O. 1966. The culture of poverty. Sci. Am. 215:19–25

Lewis, O. 1959. Five Families: Mexican Case Studies in the Culture of Poverty. New York: Basic

Lieberson, S. 1982. Stereotypes: their consequences for race and ethnic interaction. In Social Structure and Behavior: Essays in Honor of William Hamilton Sewell, ed. R. Hauser et al, pp. 47–68. New York: Academic

Lieberson, S. 1980. A Piece of the Pie: Blacks and White Immigrants Since 1880. Berkeley: Univ. Calif. Press

Lieberson, S. 1963. Ethnic Patterns in American Cities. New York: Free

Lieberson, S., Hansen, L. K. 1974. National development, mother tongue diversity, and the comparative study of nations. Am. Sociol. Rev. 39(4):523–41

Lincoln, C. E. 1974. The Black Experience in Religion. Garden City, NY: Anchor

Lithman, Y. G. 1983. The Practice of Underdevelopment and the Theory of Development—The Canadian Indian Case. Stockholm: Univ. Stockholm

Lopata, H. Z. 1976. Polish Americans: Status Competition in an Ethnic Community. Englewood Cliffs, NJ: Prentice-Hall

Louden, D. 1981. A comparative study of self-concepts among minority and majority group adolescents in English multi-racial schools. Ethn. Racial Stud. 4:153–74

Lustick, I. 1980. Arabs in the Jewish State. Austin: Univ. Texas Press

Mamiya, L. H. 1982. From Black Muslim to Bilalian: the evolution of a movement. J. Sci. Study Relig. 21:138–52

Marshall, R. 1974. The economics of racial discrimination: a survey. J. Econ. Lit. 12(3):849–71

Martin, P. L. 1980. Guestworker Programs: Lessons from Europe. Washington, DC: USGPO

Mason, D. 1982. Race relations, group formation and power: a framework for analysis. Ethn. Racial Stud. 5:421–39

Massey, D. S. 1981. Dimensions of the new immigration to the United States and the prospects of assimilation. Ann. Rev. Sociol. 7:57–85

Massey, D. S., Mullan, B. P. 1984. Processes of Hispanic and Black spatial assimilation. Am. J. Sociol. 84(4):836–73

McConahay, J. B., Hough, J. C. Jr. 1976. Symbolic racism. J. Soc. Iss. 32(2):23–45

McCready, W. C., ed. 1983. Culture, Ethnicity, and Identity. New York: Academic

McKay, J. 1982. An exploratory synthesis of primordial and mobilizationist approaches to ethnic phenomena. Ethn. Racial Stud. 5:395–420

McRae, J. A. 1983. Changes in religious communalism desired by Protestants and Catholics. Soc. Forc. 61:708–30

Melville, M. B. 1983. Ethnicity: an analysis of its dynamism and variability focusing on the Mexican/Anglo/Mexican interface. Am. Ethnol. 10(2):272–89

Miller, A. G., ed. 1982. In the Eye of the Beholder: Contemporary Issues in Stereotyping. New York: Praeger

Mindel, C. H., Havenstein, R. W., eds. 1981. Ethnic Families in America: Patterns and Variations. New York: Elsevier. 2nd ed.

Moore, J. W. 1976. American minorities and 'new nation' perspectives. Pac. Sociol. Rev. 19:447–67

Morgan, G. D. 1981. America without Ethnicity. Port Washington, NY: Kennikat (Nat'l. Univ. Publ.)

Moskos, C. C. Jr. 1973. The American dilemma in uniform. Ann. Am. Acad. Polit. Soc. Sci. 406:98–106

Moskos, C. C. Jr. 1966. Racial integration in the armed forces. Am. J. Sociol. 72(2):132–48

Mukabe, T. 1981. The theory of the split labor market: a comparison of the Japanese experience in Brazil and Canada. Soc. Forc. 59:786–809

Murguia, E. 1975. Assimilation, Colonialism, and the Mexican American People. Austin: Univ. Texas Press

Murguia, E. 1982. Chicano Intermarriage: A Theoretical and Empirical Study. San Antonio, Tex: Trinity Univ. Press

Nagata, J. A. 1980. Malasian Mosaic: Perspectives from a Polyethnic Society. Vancouver: Univ. British Columbia Press

Nielsen, F. 1980. The Flemish movement in Belgium after World War II: a dynamic analysis. Am. Sociol. Rev. 45(1):76–94

Novak, M. 1972. The Rise of the Unmeltable Ethnics. New York: Macmillan

Oberschall, A. 1973. Social Conflict and Social Movements. Englewood Cliffs, NJ: Prentice-Hall

Ogbu, J. 1978. Minority Education and Caste. New York: Academic

Okamura, J. Y. 1981. Situational ethnicity. Ethn. Racial Stud. 4:452–65

Olzak, S. 1983. Contemporary ethnic mobilization. Ann. Rev. Sociol. 9:355–74

Olzak, S. 1982. Ethnic mobilization in Quebec. Ethn. Racial Stud. 5:253–75

Padilla, A. M., ed. 1980. Acculturation: Theory, Models and Some New Findings. Boulder, Colo: Westview

Patterson, G. J. 1979. A critique of 'the new ethnicity'. Am. Anthropol. 81:103–5

Patterson, O. 1977. *Ethnic Chauvinism: The Reactionary Impulse.* New York: Stein & Day

Peach, C. 1980. Which triple melting pot? A re-examination of ethnic intermarriage in New Haven. *Ethn. Racial Stud.* 3:1–16

Peach, C., Robinson, V., Smith, S., eds. 1981. *Ethnic Segregation in Cities.* London: Croom Helm

Petersen, W. 1978. International migration. *Ann. Rev. Sociol.* 4:533–75

Pettigrew, T. F. 1979. The ultimate attribution error: extending Allport's cognitive analysis of prejudice. *Pers. Soc. Psychol. Bull.* 5:461–76

Pettigrew, T. F. 1978. Three issues in ethnicity: boundaries, deprivations, and perceptions. In *Major Social Issues: A Multidisciplinary View,* ed. J. M. Yinger, S. J. Cutler, pp. 25–49. New York: Free

Pettigrew, T. F. 1969. Racially separate or together? *J. Soc. Iss.* 25:43–69

Piven, F. F., Cloward, R. A. 1977. *Poor People's Movements.* New York: Pantheon

Porter, J. R., Washington, R. E. 1979. Black identity and self-esteem: a review of studies of Black self-concept, 1968–1978. *Ann. Rev. Sociol.* 5:53–74

Porterfield, E. 1978. *Black and White Mixed Marriages.* Chicago: Nelson-Hall

Portes, A. 1984. The rise of ethnicity: determinants of ethnic perceptions among Cuban exiles in Miami. *Am. Soc. Rev.* 49:383–97

Ragin, C. C. 1979. Ethnic mobilization: the Welsh case. *Am. Sociol. Rev.* 44:619–35

Rakowska-Harmstone, T. 1977. Ethnicity in the Soviet Union. *Ann. Am. Acad. Polit. Soc. Sci.* 433:73–87

Reimers, D. M. 1981. Post-World War II immigration to the United States: America's latest newcomers. *Ann. Am. Acad. Polit. Soc. Sci.* 454:1–12

Rex, J. 1981. A working paradigm for race relations research. *Ethn. Racial Stud.* 4(1):1–25

Rex, J. 1973. *Race, Colonialism and the City.* London: Routledge & Kegan Paul

Rex, J., Tomlinson, S. 1979. *Colonial Immigrants in a British City: A Class Analysis.* London: Routledge & Kegan Paul

Richmond, A. H., issue ed. 1984. Ethnic nationalism and postindustrialism. *Ethn. Racial Stud.* 7(1):whole issue

Rist, R. C. 1978. *Guestworkers in Germany: The Prospects for Pluralism.* New York: Praeger

Rosenberg, M. 1979. *Conceiving the Self.* New York: Basic

Rosenberg, M., Simmons, R. G. 1972. *Black and White Self-Esteem: The Urban School Child.* Washington, DC: Am. Sociol. Assoc.

Rosenstein, C. 1981. The liability of ethnicity in Israel. *Soc. Forc.* 59:667–86

Rosenthal, S. J. 1980. Symbolic racism and desegregation: divergent attitudes and perspectives of Black and White university students. *Phylon* 41:257–66

Rothschild, J. 1981. *Ethnopolitics: A Conceptual Framework.* New York: Columbia Univ. Press

Rusinow, D. 1977. *The Yugoslavian Experiment: 1948–1974.* Berkeley: Univ. Calif. Press

Said, A. A., ed. 1977. *Ethnicity and U.S. Foreign Policy.* New York: Praeger

Saran, P., Eames, E. 1980. *The New Ethnics: Asian Indians in the United States.* New York: Praeger

Schelling, T. C. 1978. *Micromotives and Macrobehavior.* New York: Norton

Schermerhorn, R. A. 1978. *Ethnic Plurality in India.* Tucson: Univ. Ariz. Press

Schoen, R., Cohen, L. E. 1980. Ethnic endogamy among Mexican American grooms: a reanalysis of generational and occupational effect. *Am. J. Sociol.* 86:359–66

Seeman, M. 1981. Intergroup relations. In *Social Psychology: Sociological Perspectives,* ed. M. Rosenberg, R. H. Turner, pp. 378–410. New York: Basic

Shavit, Y. 1984. Tracking and ethnicity in Israeli secondary education. *Am. Sociol. Rev.* 49(2):210–20

Shokeid, M., Deshen, S. 1982. *Distant Relations: Ethnicity and Politics among Arabs and North African Jews in Israel.* New York: Praeger

Simon, R. J. 1980. *Continuity and Change: A Study of Two Ethnic Communities in Israel.* New York: Cambridge Univ. Press

Simpson, G. E., Yinger, J. M. 1985. *Racial and Cultural Minorities.* New York: Plenum. 5th ed.

Smith, A. D. 1981. *The Ethnic Revival.* Cambridge: Cambridge Univ. Press

Smith, M. G. 1982. Ethnicity and ethnic groups in America: the view from Harvard. *Ethn. Racial Stud.* 5:1–22

Smith, T. W. 1980. Ethnic measurement and identification. *Ethnicity* 7:78–95

Smith, T. W. Feb. 1982. *Problems in Ethnic Measurement: Over-, Under-, and Misidentification.* Chicago: GSS Tech. Rep. No. 29

Smock, D. R., Smock, A. C. 1975. *The Politics of Pluralism: A Comparative Study of Lebanon and Ghana.* New York: Elsevier

Smooha, S. 1978. *Israel: Pluralism and Conflict.* Berkeley: Univ. Calif. Press

Spangler, E., Gordon, M. A., Pipkin, R. M. 1978. Token women: an empirical test of Kanter's hypothesis. *Am. J. Sociol.* 84:160–70

Stein, H. F., Hill, R. F. 1977. *The Ethnic Imperative: Examining the New White Ethnic Movement.* University Park: Pa. State Univ. Press

Steinberg, S. 1981. *The Ethnic Myth: Race Ethnicity, and Class in America*. New York: Atheneum

Stone, J., issue ed. 1979. Internal colonialism. *Ethn. & Racial Stud.* 2(3):whole issue

Stone, J., ed. 1977. *Race, Ethnicity, and Social Change*. North Scituate, Mass: Duxbury

Stouffer, S. A., et al. 1949. *The American Soldier*. 2 vols. Princeton, NJ: Princeton Univ. Press

Stryker, R. 1981. Religio-ethnic effects on attainments in the early career. *Am. Sociol. Rev.* 46:212–31

Stuckert, R. P. 1976. 'Race' mixture: the Black ancestry of White Americans. In *Physical Anthropology and Archaeology*, ed. P. B. Hammond, pp. 135–39. New York: Macmillan

Suhrke, A., Noble, L. G., eds. 1977. *Ethnic Conflict in International Relations*. New York: Praeger

Suttles, G. D. 1968. *The Social Order of the Slum: Ethnicity and Territory in the Inner City*. Chicago: Univ. Chicago Press

Szymanski, A. 1976. Racial discrimination and White gain. *Am. Sociol. Rev.* 41(3):403–14

Tajfel, H. 1982. Social psychology of intergroup relations. *Ann. Rev. Psychol.* 33:1–39

Talbot, S. 1982. The Vietnamese front—in America. *The Nation* (Dec. 11):618–20

Taylor, M. C., Walsh, E. J. 1979. Explanations of Black self-esteem: some empirical tests. *Soc. Psychol. Q.* 42(3):242–53

Taylor, R. L. 1979. Black ethnicity and the persistence of ethnogenesis. *Am. J. Sociol.* 84(6):1401–23

Thernstrom, S., ed. 1980. *Harvard Encyclopedia of American Ethnic Groups*. Cambridge: Harvard Univ. Press

Thompson, J. L. P. 1983. The plural society approach to class and ethnic political mobilization. *Ethn. Racial Stud.* 6:127–53

Tilly, C. 1978. *From Mobilization to Revolution*. Reading, Mass: Addison-Wesley

Tomasi, S. M., ed. 1977. *Perspectives in Italian Immigration and Ethnicity*. New York: Cent. Migration Stud.

Turner, J. H., Singleton, R. Jr. 1978. A theory of ethnic oppression: toward a reintegration of cultural and structural concepts in ethnic relations theory. *Soc. Forc.* 56(4):1001–18

US Department of Commerce, Bureau of the Census. April 1983. *1980 Census of Population: Ancestry of the Population by State: 1980*. Suppl. Rep. PC80-S1-10. Washington, DC: USGPO

van den Berghe, P. L. 1983. Class, race and ethnicity in Africa. *Ethn. Racial Stud.* 6:221–36

van den Berghe, P. L. 1981. *The Ethnic Phenomenon*. New York: Elsevier

Waxman, C. I. 1977. *The Stigma of Poverty: A*

Critique of Poverty Theories and Policies. New York: Pergamon

Weber, M. 1968. *Economy and Society*, Vol. 1, ed. G. Roth, C. Wittich. New York: Bedminister

Weiner, M. 1978. *Sons of the Soil: Migration and Ethnic Conflict in India*. Princeton, NJ: Princeton Univ. Press

Williams, C. 1982. Social mobilization and nationalism in multicultural societies. *Ethn. Racial Stud.* 5:349–65

Williams, R. M. Jr. 1978. Competing models of multiethnic and multiracial societies: an appraisal of possibilities. In *Major Social Issues: A Multidisciplinary View*, ed. J. M. Yinger, S. J. Cutler, pp. 50–65. New York: Free

Williams, R. M. Jr. 1975. Race and ethnic relations. *Ann. Rev. Sociol.* 1:125–64

Wilson, W. J. 1980. *The Declining Significance of Race*. Chicago: Univ. Chicago Press. 2nd ed.

Wolf, E. R. 1982. *Europe and the People without History*. Berkeley: Univ. Calif. Press

Woodrum, E. 1981. An assessment of Japanese American assimilation, pluralism and subordination. *Am. J. Sociol.* 87:157–69

Yancey, W. L., Ericksen, E. P., Juliani, R. N. 1979. Emergent ethnicity: a review and reformulation. *Am. Sociol. Rev.* 41:391–402

Yinger, J. M. 1985. Assimilation in the United States: with particular reference to Mexican Americans. In *Mexican Americans in Comparative Perspective*, ed. W. Connor. Washington, DC: Urban Inst. In press

Yinger, J. M. 1983. Ethnicity and social change: the interaction of structural, cultural, and personality factors. *Ethn. Racial Stud.* 6:395–409

Yinger, J. M. 1981. Toward a theory of assimilation and dissimilation. *Ethn. Racial Stud.* 4:249–64

Yinger, J. M. 1976. Ethnicity in complex societies. In *The Uses of Controversy in Sociology*, ed. L. A. Coser, O. N. Larsen, pp. 197–216. New York: Free

Yinger, J. M., Simpson, G. E. 1978. The integration of Americans of Indian descent. *Ann. Am. Acad. Polit. Soc. Sci.* 436:137–51

Young, C. 1982. Patterns of social conflict: state, class, and ethnicity. *Daedalus* 111(2):71–98

Young, C. 1976. *The Politics of Cultural Pluralism*. Madison: Univ. Wis. Press

Young, W. L. 1982. *Minorities and the Military: A Cross-National Study in World Perspective*. Westport, Conn: Greenwood

Zald, M. N., McCarthy, J. D., eds. 1979. *The Dynamics of Social Movements: Resource Mobilization, Social Control, and Tactics*. Cambridge, Mass: Winthrop

Ann. Rev. Sociol. 1985. 11:181–207
Copyright © 1985 by Annual Reviews Inc. All rights reserved

THE PETITE BOURGEOISIE IN LATE CAPITALISM

F. Bechhofer and B. Elliott

Department of Sociology, 18 Buccleuch Place, University of Edinburgh, Edinburgh
EH8 9LN, United Kingdom

Abstract

Over the past decade or so social scientists and policy makers have grown
increasingly interested in the role of the petite bourgeoisie in capitalist
societies. The paper begins by sketching the major sociological approaches to
the study of this stratum and the diverse characteristics of and propositions put
forth about the fortunes of the petite bourgeoisie.

The second section draws together evidence from several western societies in
an attempt to appraise arguments about the alleged archaism, the long run
decline, or the possible regeneration of the small business sector of western
economies.

The economic significance of the petite bourgeoisie is assessed with respect
to information about the capacity of the stratum to provide employment, to
generate new jobs, and to stimulate innovation. The small business sector also
has considerable political significance. Though its role in the political life of
particular societies shows considerable variation it is everywhere an important
repository of ideas and sentiments supportive of capitalism and the institutions
of liberal democracy. This is a fact which contemporary right wing governments have been quick to recognize. The petite bourgeoisie is a socially
distinctive and persistent element in capitalist societies. Factors that do much to
account for its reproduction include the effects of recession, processes of
technical change, and government policies that support and encourage small-
scale entrepreneurial activity. The paper concludes by arguing that even in
economies dominated by large corporations, petits bourgeois businesses continue to provide jobs for a substantial proportion of the population and the most
personal and direct experience of capitalism for many citizens.

0360-0572/85/0815-0181$02.00

INTRODUCTION

Over the past decade or so a section of the population hitherto given little attention by academics or policy makers has suddenly attracted a good deal of interest. In various scholarly disciplines—economics, history, sociology (and to a lesser degree politics and anthropology)—articles and books have appeared concerned with the part played by the petite bourgeoisie in the development of modern capitalist societies and with the role of this group in present day economic, political, and social life. Many of the pieces begin with statements about the general neglect of those who make a living by using small amounts of personal capital together with their own and their family's labor. Many also conclude by suggesting that this form of business enterprise with its associated social life and conceptions of the world has a substantial—and some would say, growing—significance.

That kind of conclusion, of course, sits happily with an increasing volume of political discussion and policy-making in western nations focused on what is loosely referred to as small business. Legislators, opinion-makers, and those who implement public policy have, mainly since the mid-1970s, sought to arrest the commonly observed decline of the small, independent business elements and often pinned quite extravagant hopes on a renaissance of small business activity. A flourishing small business sector is frequently held by politicians and others to be vital to the general health of the modern economy: It will play a major role in the creation of new employment in a period when the dole queues have lengthened frighteningly; it will stimulate innovation because small enterprises are better able or more willing to spot new needs and take the risks that large corporations eschew. Those, at least, are two of the most common claims, and there is more than rhetoric here. In most of the advanced capitalist societies, governments have taken steps to increase the flow of new business entrants and to nurture those already in evidence. Public agencies have been set up to give loans and advice, to develop appropriate infrastructures, and to promote (usually in collaboration with colleges and universities) new and, it is hoped, relevant forms of education.

Academically and publicly the petite bourgeoisie is being reassessed, and the coincidence of these two streams of interest is not difficult to explain. Both the social scientists and the politicians are concerned with social change: the one to understand and interpret it and maybe to influence it in the long run, the other to manipulate its trajectory more immediately. Both are responding to the fact that since the early seventies the economic foundations of the capitalist economies have been seriously shaken, and the discernible shifts in economic and social structures have already been attended by quite profound changes at the levels of ideology and political practice. The common assumption is that the part played by the petite bourgeoisie ought to be looked at more closely, not only in terms of how it has been affected by changes in the wider economic and political environments but also in terms of the effects it has had and may in future have upon these environments.

Our central concern in this paper is with the treatment of the petite bourgeoisie in recent, specifically sociological writing. The literature now is very much richer than it was when we first began our researches fifteen or more years ago. Certainly it is large enough for a recent commentator (Scase 1982) to discuss a small number of reasonably distinct theoretical positions and several lines of interest upon which attention appears to be converging.

TRADITIONS AND THEMES

Studies of class and stratification have long been central to British sociology, and in the 1970s a series of projects examining the place of hitherto rather poorly researched groups emerged. These studies shared a broadly similar theoretical orientation deriving more from Weber than from Marx. Among these, our own work on shopkeepers (Bechhofer et al 1971; Bechhofer & Elliott 1974a,b, 1978; Bland et al 1978); that of Newby & Bell (Bell & Newby 1974; Newby 1977; Newby et al 1978; Newby 1979) on farmers, including small farmers; Elliott & McCrone (1975a,b, 1980) on urban landlords; and Stanworth & Curran (1973) on small businessmen began to provide descriptions and analyses of the position of petits bourgeois groups in the class structure of the period. Towards the end of the decade investigations by other writers (Scase & Goffee 1980, 1982, Curran & Stanworth 1979a,b) extended this work.

Central to all of the early studies in this tradition was the interest in the relationships between the petits bourgeois elements and those who lay above and below them in the class structure: the capitalists who exercised profound influence upon their economic fortunes through the control of credit, supplies, marketing, and the availability of diverse resources; and the working class from whom the petits bourgeois derived profits and rents and over whom they could exert a generally limited authority. Initially, a good deal was made of the idea of marginality. Petits bourgeois elements were depicted as somewhat detached from the interests and concerns of workers on the one hand and 'real' capitalists on the other. There was even some attempt to give the idea of studying marginal groups some methodological cachet in arguments claiming that the nature of class relations and class ideologies might best be revealed by looking at those in somewhat interstitial positions. (It is interesting to note how a similar idea lies behind Wright's (1979, 1982) focus on contradictory class locations and Clement's (1983) recent analysis of the rights of property.) The empirical materials from these studies certainly highlighted the fact that in terms of objective conditions and normative commitments the petite bourgeoisie was indeed distinct and somewhat estranged socially and ideologically from both capital and labor. However, the notion of marginality became less and less salient as the studies developed. It became increasingly clear that the petite bourgeoisie should be seen as a live force *within* rather than *marginal to* the class structure. Thus, the authors concerned were able to argue and to show that the petite bourgeoisie was a persistent element in modern economies and to trace its economic and political significance within capitalism (Bechhofer & Elliott 1976, Crossick 1979).

A second feature of these kinds of researches was the growth within them of a specific concern with the historical development of the small business and self-employed groups, and the part they had played in the political as well as the economic life of western countries. By the mid-1970s it was plain that historically informed sociologists and sociologically sensitive historians had begun to converge on this as on a number of other topics. Studies by Neale (1972) and Nossiter (1972) had examined the part played by radical artisans and retailers in early nineteenth century Britain. Hennock (1973) and Fraser (1976) were writing urban history in a way that allowed us to see just how petits bourgeois elements clashed with the bigger capitalists. Mayer (1975) underlined the importance of looking at the diversity of social types for whom petits bourgeois occupations were refuges or steps on a ladder of upward mobility. Gray (1976) and Crossick (1976) explored social relations between sections of the labor aristocracy and the petite bourgeoisie, and Gellately (1974) showed how an organized petite bourgeoisie in Germany became, in the years just prior to the First World War, a force to be reckoned with.

In our own work we came more and more to recognize the need to gain some cross-national appreciation of the role of the petite bourgeoisie. Though there have been (and to be sure there still are) important differences in the size, composition, and political role of the small entrepreneurs in different countries, nonetheless there are some very obvious common structural elements in their fortunes. Our volume of essays (Bechhofer & Elliott 1981) illustrated a number of these and also served to raise a third general issue which has emerged from much of this writing.

That issue is the 'reproduction' of the petite bourgeoisie. How is it that a sector of the population that looks in many ways so vulnerable manages to reproduce itself from generation to generation often (as in socialist regimes) in political and economic climates that are far from warm? Some limited insight may be gained from social mobility studies (Mayer 1977; Goldthorpe et al 1980), and writers like Bertaux and Bertaux-Wiame (1981) provide excellent ethnographic materials for a particular trade, but the matter awaits proper exploration. It is a matter to which, however, we shall return later in this paper.

A second school, quite varied in character, derives directly from Marx. The key feature of most Marxian studies of the petite bourgeoisie is the representation of this class as a legacy of an earlier mode of production. Although some writers who draw on Marx avoid this representation, most Marxists argue that while the petite bourgeoisie may persist within a capitalist system it is essentially to be seen as an anachronism, a vestige of the simple commodity form of production which attended the transition from feudalism to capitalism. That is the first step in the argument at least. Not surprisingly then, most authors in this tradition emphasize the shrinkage of the petite bourgeoisie, and while they hold back from predictions of its imminent demise, nonetheless, they retain something of Marx's and Engels's original prophecy of doom for the small business element.

Among recent Marxist writers who have most directly addressed themselves to the condition of this group Poulantzas (1975) introduced a distinction whose effect is to accentuate the vestigial character of what is usually taken to be the traditional petite bourgeoisie. His analysis of the changing class structures of modern western economies separates the 'traditional' from the 'new' petite bourgeoisie (usually rendered as *petty* rather than *petite* which, of course, carries a somewhat pejorative implication in English). The new petite bourgeoisie in Poulantzas' terms is a large class consisting of all those who, while they do not own capital, nonetheless discharge the functions of capital—helping to control labor, helping to extract surplus value, and aiding the necessary circulation of goods and capital. Thus, many of the so-called middle class, people involved in supervisory, technical, and professional and semiprofessional occupations may be lumped together in this formulation and distinguished not only from the old petite bourgeoisie but obviously from capitalists and proletarians. The 'new petty bourgeoisie' is made up of those who do unproductive labour. They are not directly exploited and thus lie outside the basic relationship of capitalism. The rapid growth and size of this new class serves further to accentuate the rather peripheral and anachronistic character of the traditional petite bourgeoisie.

The weaknesses in Poulantzas' account—not least the fact that his 'new petty bourgeoisie' seems to account for something like 70% of the economically active population—and his failure adequately to distinguish the old petite bourgeoisie from the minor capitalists have been discussed by several authors, for example, Wright (1976), Mackenzie (1982), Scase (1982). In his studies Wright (1979, 1982) has gone to some lengths to try to draw the line between the last two. The petits bourgeois in his scheme are those who do not employ labor (other than their own). Therefore they are not involved in the exploitative processes whereby they extract from others surplus value. But small capitalists by contrast are so involved, albeit on a comparatively modest scale. Small businesses, each employing a handful of workers, exist and are constantly reproduced within capitalism because it suits the interests of the dominant economic blocs—the big corporations and financial institutions. Small enterprises are to be found in those economic niches not colonized by large capital, and that generally means those where the profits are typically low and the risks higher. Small capital survives as dependent capital, its fortunes intimately and immediately affected by the decisions of big business.

Wright's analysis then leads him to argue that small employers occupy 'contradictory class locations' wedged, as it were, between the simple commodity mode of production with its traditional petite bourgeoisie on one side and the capitalist mode with its real bourgeoisie on the other. While descriptively attractive, however, it is difficult to get much analytic leverage from this formulation.

Behind the various efforts to tease out the distinctiveness of the petite bourgeoisie in the Marxist work lies the wish to explore just how the various rights of property are constructed and exercised. Clement's (1983) work, drawing on Macpherson (1973, 1978) as well as Poulantzas, reveals this most clearly. He argues that formal ownership—i.e. a bundle of legal rights to something—should be distinguished from real or active ownership. According to Poulantzas (1975), this latter has two aspects: first, economic ownership or 'the power to assign the means of production to given uses and so to dispose of the products obtained,' and secondly, possession of 'the capacity to put the means of production into operation'. In the view of most Marxian writers many petits bourgeois retain formal ownership and possession but they have progressively lost effective economic ownership as big capital has come to control more and more immediately the circumstances of production and distribution. This, of course, is well illustrated in the cases of, say, small farmers and fishermen whose dependency on large corporations for credit and for the purchase and distribution of their products has become increasingly evident, but it is also true of many other forms of small business enterprise—retailing and franchising, for example. In Clement's view, and it would surely be shared by most writers in this camp, Marx's general assumption that the petite bourgeoisie would become progressively subordinated to capital and proletarianized has proved correct. To be sure, the petite bourgeoisie survives, but the appearance of independence and the distinctiveness of their property relations are often deceiving, for beneath the surface we find a substantial erosion of the traditional rights, a progressive dependency upon major forms of capital.

The recent Marxist contribution then to this area of study has been substantial, but in Scase's view (Scase 1982) there are a number of weaknesses. Chief among them is a failure to explore adequately in a detailed and empirical way the relationships between the petite bourgeoisie and big capital; secondly, there is a tendency, at least among those who lean heavily on the Althusserian formulations, to devote little attention to the active agency of those who struggle as petits bourgeois against the forces of corporate capitalism; and finally there is remarkably little by way of explanation of just how this dependent class manages to reproduce itself.

A third group of writers associated with the growing interest in the petite bourgeoisie in western societies focuses upon the allegedly post-industrial or post-capitalist characteristics that have developed. Here the main argument is that, contrary to the Marxists' belief, the petite bourgeoisie is by no means doomed. Rather, it is claimed that 'after years of decline, the number of entrepreneurs and small enterprises in Europe appears to be increasing' (Boissevain 1981:4). Boissevain goes on to present no fewer than five reasons for this. The increasing burden of taxation induces some people to take up forms of independent business from the profits of which they will be able to retain a larger fraction of their earnings than they could do in employment. Support for that idea is found in a recent article by Clark (1982). Looking at reasons for the growth of self-employment in Britain, he observes 'the self-employed individual may pay considerably less tax on a given level of income than an employee' (1982:286).

The growth of the service sector opens up a host of new opportunities for small-scale entrepreneurial activity as does the tendency for corporations, public as well as private, to decentralize many of their activities, putting out to contract tasks hitherto handled 'in house' or creating new firms which have varying degrees of autonomy. Two further factors add impetus to the growth of small businesses, according to Boissevain. Increased immigration, over the past thirty years, mainly of workers from former colonial and other less developed economies, has created a new pool from which recruits to self-employment are drawn. Finally there is a concern for improvements in the quality of life, ranging from workers' desire to escape the alienation of the large enterprises to environmentalist enthusiasm for simple, natural products and a general wish for a more human scale in the provision of urban services.

Many other writers, of course, have contributed to the individual arguments here. Some of the writing on the informal economy (Burns 1979; Gershuny & Pahl 1980; Pahl 1980) touches on Boissevain's ideas both about the wish to escape taxation and also about quality of life considerations. Work on the service economy (Kumar 1978, Gershuny 1978) has provided evidence of some of the ways in which technical change, the growth of leisure, and other factors have been altering the range of economic niches available to those with a little capital and a desire for independence. On each of the other aspects of his argument, Boissevain is also able to point to research that gives some plausibility to his general hypothesis. The reasons for 'excluded, non-assimilated minorities' (Light 1979) engaging successfully in small-scale entrepreneurial activity have been well explored both in the United States (Bonacich 1972, 1973; Bonacich et al 1976; Light 1972) and in the United Kingdom (Aldrich et al 1979; Aldrich 1980; Watson 1977).

Support for ideas about how concern with the quality of life contributes to the formation of new small enterprises is less satisfactory, but the growth of specialist shops and services geared to particular lifestyle demands (e.g. whole food, sporting and leisure interests) offers some rough evidence. And the comments of many writers about widespread disillusionment with the cult of bigness (symbolized by the development of very large and complex organizations in the postwar years) undoubtedly have some foundation. In a very recent article Granovetter (1984) has tried to show that sociologists working in the areas of social stratification and organizational studies have rather exaggerated the significance of large enterprises and tended to identify modernity with complexity and complexity with size. In so doing, they have neglected not only the detailed study of social relations within small enterprises but have failed to notice that there is now some evidence that the long-run tendency for workers to be increasingly concentrated in large establishments has ceased and in some instances been reversed.

The sociological literature on the petite bourgeoisie seems then to contain a number of general propositions, propositions that are not all compatible. First there is the claim made by many Marxian writers that the petite bourgeoisie represents the survival of an archaic mode of production. Secondly, there is the judgment, most commonly expressed by Marxists but shared by many others, that the stratum has declined markedly in the course of capitalist development and will continue to do so. Thirdly, there is the suggestion that though it may have declined, the petite bourgeoisie is not set for any imminent collapse, that it seems to be a persistent and integral element of late capitalist economies. Finally, there are some who claim to find evidence of recent revival and growth of the petite bourgeoisie. In what follows we can try to evaluate these claims.

APPRAISING THE ARGUMENTS

Assessing the fortunes of this group is by no means an easy task. We need to begin with as clear a definition of the petite bourgeoisie as we can manage. The elements upon which writers of almost all persuasions would agree are these: the petite bourgeoisie comprises all those men and women who use their own (typically modest) capital to take over or establish an enterprise, who invest in it their own labor, supplementing that with the efforts of family or kin. The goods or services they produce are disposed of in diverse markets with the object of making profits. We would want to allow that petits bourgeois enterprises may also employ small numbers of other employees (though strict Marxian definitions would preclude this), and to argue that the small scale of employment offered to nonkin leads to the extraction of surplus value or involvement in the free market for labor only in the most trivial way. There is no precise boundary between the petits bourgeois and those more properly termed 'small capitalists' (Aldrich & Weiss 1981). We can recognize that fact while insisting that for those we would term petits bourgeois, *personal* capital and *personal* labour remain central.

Let us address then the general propositions noted in the previous section. The first need not detain us long. Petits bourgeois enterprises are far too varied to be characterized simply as archaic. To be sure, there are some in this group involved in petty commodity production but they are a small minority. Many others are engaged in forms of production, distribution, and the provision of services in ways that attach them to the most modern aspects of capitalist manufacture, trade, and circulation of finance. Representing the petite bourgeoisie as the carriers of an outdated mode of production will not do.

The second proposition about the long-run decline of the stratum is much more important and very difficult to assess simply. To begin with, we need to recognize that claims about decline involve judgments about both the relative and the absolute numbers of petits bourgeois in modern economies. In both cases we encounter serious deficiencies in the data when we try to chart the shifts in size and composition of our group. In official statistics on economic sectors, labor markets, and contributions to gross national product we find that the time-series materials are patchy and the categories used frequently spread beyond the boundaries we would wish to impose. Most commonly, we are constrained to use material which, at best, enables us to identify 'small business'. Small business thus becomes a surrogate for petite bourgeoisie and that is not satisfactory. For not only do most definitions of the former catch up many enterprises that are larger than those we would like to know about, but when we attempt to make international comparisons the methods used in the analysis vary a good deal. Some data relate to numbers of employees in individual establishments, others to workers in firms (some of which have several establishments). Other sources like the Department of Industry, Trade, and Commerce in Canada (Government of Canada 1979a,b) set boundaries between different sizes of businesses not on the basis of employees but of turnover. Some produce extensive statistics on manufacturing but much less on services and other sectors. However, provided that the materials are treated cautiously, there are data that take us some way to satisfying our curiosity about the changing size, composition, and significance of the group we are interested in. These do give some support to the argument that the petite bourgeoisie has experienced relative decline. There is no doubt that our economies have become more concentrated, and little enterprises now make a smaller contribution to employment or output in all major sectors.

In his recent article on labor markets and the contribution of small establishments to these, Granovetter (1984) provides material that gives some indication of changes over time. He traces the patterns for US manufacturing showing that in 1904 some 13.6% of all employees were in establishments of less than 20 and that 39.2% were in those with fewer than 100 employees. Comparable figures for 1923 were 9.4% and 28.8%; in 1939, 9.5% were in the 'less than 20' category and 26.7% in establishments with fewer than 100 workers. By 1967 the relevant figures were 5.6% and 23.2%. His data suggest that the sharpest decline of small manufacturing business in the United States took place in the early years of the century and that between 1923 and 1967 the proportion of workers in smaller establishments changed less substantially.

British data assembled for the Bolton Report (1971) show a rather similar pattern. The contribution of small firms to employment and output in manufacturing fell substantially from the mid-1920s to the mid-1960s. Scase & Goffee (1982:34) observe that "between 1935 and 1963 employment in small manufacturing enterprises fell from 38% to 20% of the total and output from 35% to 16%". Using more limited time-series data, Oakey (1984) traces the decline of small firms in manufacturing employment in other western economies—Germany, Sweden, Norway, France, Switzerland, and Canada. And the relative decline of small business can be observed in other sectors of these economies. Granovetter (1984) provides data on the substantial reductions in contribution to employment in the retail and services areas of the US economy on the part of small establishments. The Bolton Report also concluded that such decline was evident in sectors other than manufacturing in the United Kingdom. It should, however, be observed that the really sharp declines in these sectors—retailing, for instance—have taken place much more recently than in manufacturing; our own work on retailing (Bechhofer et al 1971) shows a pattern for the United Kingdom that is similar to that given by Granovetter.

At first glance, then, the data may appear to substantiate the general observations about the decline of the petite bourgeoisie, but before we accept that too wholeheartedly, there are some important reservations to be entered. First, the data define small business too broadly to allow accurate assessment of the fortunes of the petite bourgeoisie. Most analyses use 'less than 200 employees' when referring to small business—occasionally they are broken down to 'less than 100' or 'less than 20', but even at the lowest figure, they capture many enterprises that are larger than and different from those we want to know about. Looking at the contribution of such businesses to overall patterns of employment offers a very general picture from which we can make only rough guesses at the trends for our stratum. Secondly, these materials do not suggest that there has been a steady and general decline in the relative contribution of small business, but rather they highlight the fact that periods of sharpest change have occurred at different points—the 1920s for manufacturing, the 1960s for retailing in both the United States and the United Kingdom, for instance. Thirdly, they reveal that among the capitalist economies there remain substantial differences in the importance of the small business sector. In all areas of the Japanese economy small business remains very important (see Bannock 1981; Storey 1982; Rothwell & Zegveld 1982; Granovetter 1984).

Oakey's figures in Table 1 give some indication of the range of differences among the major western nations. In terms of the small business contribution to manufacturing employment, the United Kingdom is at one end of the distribu-

Table 1 Contribution of smaller enterprises to employment in manufacturing

Country	Year of data	% of total manufacturing employment in small firms with 1–99 employees	100–199 employees
United Kingdom	1976	17.1	22.6
Denmark[ab]	1973	36.3	52.1
Ireland[b]	1968	33.0	49.8
Italy[a]	1971	n.a.	47.3
Netherlands	1973	36.0	47.8
Belgium	1970	33.2	43.4
Germany	1970	28.8	37.0
France	1976	25.2	34.2
Luxembourg	1973	19.1	28.2
Japan	1970	51.6	na
United States	1972	24.8	na

[a]Includes energy and water industries.
[b]Figures exclude employment in very small enterprises and understate the contribution of small enterprises.
Source: Oakey (1984)

tion, Japan at the other, and the range is very large. Enterprises with less than 100 employees provided only 17.1% of employment in manufacturing in the United Kingdom in 1976, 25.2% in France in the same year, and 51.6% in Japan in 1970. Figures like these require us at least to qualify general statements concerning the decline of the petite bourgeoisie.

And in all of this we are still dealing with the relative size of the stratum. Michael Mann, in a chapter of his forthcoming book, invites us to think about the absolute numbers of this stratum. Drawing on materials from several western countries, he tries to show that in absolute terms the group has not declined. Belgian figures that he cites covering the period 1846 to 1961 show that while there was a relative decline of the petite bourgeoisie among the nonagricultural working population, the absolute numbers tell a different story. Between 1846 and 1910, he argues, the nonagricultural working population increased by two and a half times, and the actual numbers of petits bourgeois rose by 50% and thereafter remained relatively stable. Figures for Germany indicate slight increases in absolute numbers from 1882 to 1936 and again from 1946 to 1961; those for France show increases in absolute numbers through the first three decades of this century and then some sectorally specific declines.

Over the past hundred years or so the actual composition of the petite bourgeoisie altered a good deal. Artisan production was replaced by factory production, industries like engineering or textiles offered fewer opportunities for small entrepreneurs—retailing, consumer goods, and diverse services offered more. There has been much internal change; there has been relative decline. But, Mann argues, if we look at the absolute figures we can see that the commonly accepted notion of petit bourgeois decline is a myth. His is the most robust rejection of this idea that we have encountered.

Our own conclusions are less bold. They are that the most recent data serve to qualify the impressions of general decline and to bolster the interpretation that petits bourgeois enterprises have, all things considered, shown remarkable resilience in the face of major changes–not only those of general booms and slumps, but of major shifts in the technical bases of our economies and substantial alterations in political and social environments. It is the adaptability of the stratum and its role as a dependent but integral part of modern capitalist economies that most impresses us.

Statistical data for the most recent period allow us to go beyond that and give some credence to the view that not only has the decline of the stratum been arrested but that some revival of its fortunes is under way. Oakey (1984) points out that some evidence of increases in the small firm's share of manufacturing employment are to be found for the United Kingdom, Switzerland, Canada and the United States. Granovetter's analysis of manufacturing employment in small enterprises in the United States adds weight to this. However, increases in their contribution to levels of employment do not tell us that the actual numbers of small businesses have increased, they merely indicate that proportionately more people are finding jobs in little enterprises. Marginal increases in the average number of employees in the small firms may be all that we are looking at. Boissevain (1981), however, who makes the most confident claims about entrepreneurial revival, uses different and rather better data sources, ones that enable us to get closer to the stratum in which we are interested. Statistics gathered by the European Economic Community (Eurostat figures as they are known), enabled him to show how, over the last decade or so, the shape of the employment structures in the countries making up the EEC changed. Our own reworking of the most recent data from this source arrayed in Tables 2, 3, and 4, provides a more detailed picture.

The grouping of employers, self-employed, and family workers is once again a wider category than we would like: some of the employers are certainly more than petits bourgeois but in absolute numbers the petits bourgeois are likely to predominate. The figures for industry indicate that in the EEC as a whole there has been a small increase in the proportion of those listed as employers, self-employed, or family workers in the late 1970s and early 1980s. Denmark and Luxembourg are exceptions to this, the former experiencing decline in the last three years for which there are data—from 11.0% in 1980 to 8.6% in 1982—and the latter showing stability at a very low 4.0% over the last four years of the series. For all the other countries, though, there are increases. For the most part, to be sure, the shifts are very modest, but for France, Italy, the Netherlands, Belgium, the United Kingdom, and Ireland, the recent in-

Table 2 Employers, self-employed, and family workers in Industry as percentage of nonagricultural working population 1970–1982

Year	Germany	France	Italy	Netherlands	Belgium	Luxembourg	UK	Ireland	Denmark	European 9
1970	6.0	7.8	15.4	5.5	7.4	5.2	4.0	6.4	11.1	7.6
1971	5.6	7.5	14.5	5.6	7.3	4.9	4.5	6.8	11.3	7.4
1972	5.7	7.3	14.1	5.4	7.2	4.8	5.1	6.6	10.4	7.5
1973	5.6	7.2	13.7	5.5	7.1	3.3	5.6	6.8	11.2	7.5
1974	5.7	7.1	13.4	5.5	7.0	4.2	5.5	6.9	11.3	7.4
1975	5.7	7.1	13.6	5.3	7.3	4.0	5.3	7.4	12.4	7.5
1976	5.6	7.1	13.6	5.4	7.4	4.2	5.1	7.7	11.5	7.5
1977	5.6	7.2	13.9	5.2	7.6	4.1	4.8	7.4	11.8	7.5
1978	5.4	7.4	14.4	5.2	7.9	4.1	5.1	7.7	11.5	7.6
1979	5.4	7.6	14.2	5.4	7.9	4.0	5.4	7.7	10.9	7.7
1980	5.4	7.7	15.1	5.1	8.1	4.0	6.0	7.8	11.0	8.0
1981	5.4	8.0	15.4	5.3	8.6	4.0	6.9	9.4	9.7	8.4
1982	5.5	8.1	16.0	5.7	8.9	4.0	7.3	10.5	8.6	8.7

Source: *Eurostat* (1984) Table II/6

Table 3 Employers, self-employed, and family workers in Services as percentage of nonagricultural working population 1970–1982

Year	Germany	France	Italy	Netherlands	Belgium	Luxembourg	UK	Ireland	Denmark	European 9
1970	14.6	15.9	31.3	12.9	20.7	18.6	8.8	13.5	14.6	16.3
1971	13.7	15.4	30.2	12.9	19.7	18.0	9.3	12.9	14.2	15.8
1972	13.5	14.9	30.2	12.4	19.2	17.0	8.8	12.9	12.4	15.4
1973	13.2	14.3	29.6	12.0	18.6	16.8	8.3	12.5	12.2	15.0
1974	13.0	13.9	29.7	11.6	18.2	16.2	8.2	12.1	11.6	14.8
1975	12.7	13.7	28.8	11.1	18.1	15.3	8.3	13.7	11.9	14.6
1976	12.3	13.3	28.3	10.5	18.0	14.8	8.2	13.4	11.8	14.3
1977	12.0	13.0	27.7	10.2	17.7	14.2	8.0	13.3	11.4	14.0
1978	11.8	12.7	27.8	10.3	17.5	13.7	7.7	12.9	11.1	13.8
1979	11.5	12.6	27.4	10.2	17.3	13.3	7.3	12.9	10.7	13.6
1980	11.2	12.5	27.5	10.7	17.2	12.7	7.7	12.6	10.4	13.7
1981	11.0	12.3	28.0	11.0	17.5	12.4	8.3	12.4	9.2	13.9
1982	10.9	12.0	28.2	11.3	17.3	12.0	8.4	12.2	8.6	13.9

Source: *Eurostat* (1984) Table II/6

Table 4 Employers, self-employed, and family workers in Industry and Services as percentage of nonagricultural working population 1970–1982

Year	Germany	France	Italy	Netherlands	Belgium	Luxembourg	UK	Ireland	Denmark	European 9
1970	10.1	12.3	23.7	9.9	14.9	12.2	6.6	10.6	13.1	12.2
1971	9.6	11.9	22.7	10.0	14.3	11.6	7.2	10.4	13.0	11.9
1972	9.5	11.6	22.6	9.7	14.1	11.2	7.2	10.3	11.7	11.8
1973	9.4	11.3	22.2	9.6	13.8	10.4	7.2	10.2	11.8	11.6
1974	9.4	11.0	22.2	9.3	13.5	10.5	7.0	9.9	11.5	11.5
1975	9.4	10.9	21.9	9.0	13.7	10.1	7.1	11.1	12.1	11.5
1976	9.2	10.8	21.8	8.7	13.8	10.1	6.9	11.2	11.7	11.4
1977	9.0	10.7	21.6	8.5	13.8	9.9	6.7	11.0	11.5	11.3
1978	8.8	10.6	22.0	8.5	14.0	9.7	6.7	10.9	11.2	11.3
1979	8.7	10.6	21.7	8.5	13.9	9.5	6.6	10.8	10.7	11.2
1980	8.5	10.6	22.2	8.9	14.0	9.2	7.0	10.7	10.6	11.4
1981	8.4	10.7	22.7	9.2	14.5	9.1	7.8	11.3	9.4	11.7
1982	8.5	10.5	23.2	9.6	14.6	8.9	8.0	11.6	8.6	11.9

Source: *Eurostat* (1984) Table II/6

creases put the employers, self-employed, and family workers in a stronger position than they enjoyed in 1970. The data for Ireland and the United Kingdom are probably the most striking. At the beginning of the series—in 1970—a mere 4% of all the industrial workers in the United Kingdom fell into this category, but by 1980 7.3% did. In Industry, at least, the United Kingdom was no longer bottom of the league.

The tabulations for the service sector again show very slight increases in the proportions involved as employers, self-employed, and family workers between 1979 and 1982, though the 1982 figure still represents a decline over that for the beginning of the period. All the European countries except Italy and the United Kingdom actually experienced a drop in the proportion of 'own-account' workers in the last three or four years, and the recent gains made in the United Kingdom—from 7.3% in 1979 to 8.4% in 1982—still leave that country with the lowest proportion of self-employed service workers (though Denmark looks set to steal that distinction).

Statistics that combine the data for industry and for services give us the broadest picture, and the array of figures makes it quite obvious that although there has been very little change from 1970 to 1982 for the EEC as a whole, the small shifts in the past four years may suggest that the self-employed have been making something of a comeback. In Germany, France, Luxembourg, and Denmark this was not the case. In those countries the decline of the petite bourgeoisie continued, but in the remaining five countries there is evidence of some resurgence. When the data are aggregated the gains outweigh the losses. It looks as though, in a very modest way, the small business elements are increasing in strength or at least are now holding their own.

That the proportion of employment in small enterprises, having decreased through the 1960s and much of the 1970s, has been increasing in the last few years is suggested by evidence from Japan and the United States as well as from Europe (Granovetter, 1984). We really do seem to be looking at a remarkably widespread tendency.

This brief review of the fortunes of the petite bourgeoisie does not provide a satisfactory account of how the stratum has fared over the past one hundred years or so; the data are simply inadequate for that. However, it does suggest that we need to refine and qualify our statements about its general, historical decline. There are substantial differences in the size of the stratum in the various capitalist economies. How should we explain that? And what significance does this have for the workings of the economic and political systems? Plainly, much more information is needed about changes in the internal composition of the petite bourgeoisie—the migration of small business activity across sectors—and about differences in composition from country to country. Those hints of some revival of petits bourgeois activity also deserve our attention. Can they be accommodated by our existing theories?

One thing that the present data do suggest is that in all western economies, the petite bourgeoisie still matters. It matters in terms of its contribution to employment and output; it matters politically and socially. So what can we say about the significance of this group?

SIGNIFICANCE OF THE PETITE BOURGEOISIE

We can begin by considering the economic significance of the petite bourgeoisie. Discussions of this commonly revolve around three basic ideas. The first concerns the importance of small business as a source of employment in western economies. Granovetter (1984) addresses this issue directly. His general argument is that in sociology and in economics, researchers have tended to focus most attention on the large firms, on the supposition that these were somehow indicative of the most important features and tendencies of modern industrial nations. This has led to a distortion of our images of the labor markets and patterns of employment in capitalist systems. Small firms are numerous and only a minority of workers actually find employment and make careers in very large establishments with more than 1000 employees.

For a great many people the experience of work is the experience of quite small concerns. For instance, in 1977 40% of the service workers in the United States were employed in establishments with no more than 20 employees, and 42.7% of those in the retail sector were working in establishments of this size. In manufacturing, of course, the size of the enterprises was typically much larger, and only 6.5% of that industry's workforce were found in establishments with 20 or fewer workers (Granovetter 1984:326). Still it should be pointed out that if one took a 'small' establishment in manufacturing to be less than 100 employees, then more than a quarter of all US industrial workers were involved in this size of enterprise.

Using different data sources, Granovetter also shows that in 1981 49% of all US employees were to be found in establishments with fewer than 100 workers. That, he suggests, is rather surprising. It is a finding that does not fit with the general idea of very large, impersonal workplaces as the modal ones in a modern economy. Data from other countries tend to reinforce Granovetter's view that 'small is bountiful'. He shows that in Sweden, for instance, 27.5% of all wage earners in mining and manufacturing were in establishments with less than 100, while in Japan no less than 58.4% of manufacturing employees were in businesses of that size. So, in terms of its significance for employment, small business certainly cannot be dismissed as trivial.

A second way of looking at the economic significance of small enterprises is to ask about their capacity to create new job opportunities. Birch's study (1979) suggested that firms with 20 or fewer employees accounted for more than two thirds of all new jobs generated in the United States between 1969 and 1976.

Not surprisingly, Birch's findings were quickly seized on by the small business associations and incorporated in their lobbying activity. A paper by the Canadian Federation of Independent Business appearing only a few months after Birch's report made much of his findings that small, independent, and recently established firms were the ones doing most to provide new jobs. Data from the Canadian Census appeared to support Birch's results. Between 1971 and 1977 the small firm sector (less than 20 employees) accounted for 59% of overall employment growth (Bulloch 1979). In the United Kingdom Fothergill & Gudgin (1982) added further support to this with their analysis of the cumulative growth of employment in a sample of firms in Leicestershire. With high unemployment and a rapid reduction in manufacturing jobs, especially in the United Kingdom, it was hardly surprising to observe among politicians a newfound enthusiasm for small enterprises.

The third line of argument about the economic significance of the petite bourgeoisie concerns their innovative potential. Ever since Schumpeter's (1939) refinement of Kondratiev's (1935) thesis about long waves in the world economy, a refinement which introduced the notion of technological revolutions as key explanatory factors, there has been curiosity about where technical innovation occurs. In recent years, much has been made of the role of small enterprises in this, and a number of studies have suggested that, as Rothwell & Zegveld (1982:61) put it, "small firms and entrepreneurship play a particularly important role when the technology is new and fluid, and when markets are expanding rapidly". It might well be argued that this describes the present state of the so-called electronic revolution currently affecting all western economies. Thus, small business is often seen by politicians and some economists as vital to a country's or a region's capacity for technological development. Some sectors of the petite bourgeoisie, far from being survivors from an earlier mode of production, are depicted as being in the vanguard of technical and economic change.

A quite different strand of writing stresses the political significance of this hitherto neglected group. Mann's as yet unpublished work depicts the petite bourgeoisie as part of a subaltern middle class, one whose loyalty to capitalism and to the nation has been an important factor in the maintenance of the superiority of a capitalist class. If we trace its development since the early nineteenth century, we can see it losing its attachment to a sector of the working class—the artisans—and to those radical ideas and programs it once shared with them (Neale 1972), losing too its connections to small-scale rural property holders and the populist dissent that once lodged with them (Lipset 1950; Conway 1981, 1984). The processes whereby an urban petite bourgeoisie became detached from the artisans and from the small farmers have unfolded gradually and at different points in the histories of the various western countries.

The very early destruction of the peasantry in Britain and the proletarianization of the artisans in the first industrial nation have meant that certainly for
more than a century the petite bourgeoisie in that country has developed no
effective, organized resistance to capitalism. It has, of course, articulated some
discontents, criticizing the monopoly powers of big business and the coercive
role of the modern state, but it has been at best a muted protest, one whose edge
is blunted by the basic acceptance of the institutions of the liberal democracy,
which after all were in part shaped deliberately to include men of small
property, and of the capitalist market (albeit they claim they would like it to be
'freer').

But in other countries the petite bourgeoisie or elements of it retain a
somewhat more distinctive voice. In the United States and Canada, the rural
petite bourgeoisie was politically important and did dissent in the interwar
years. In Germany at the turn of the century the exclusion of this group from the
polity and the impositions of rapidly developing big businesses did produce the
politics of the Mittelstand. In France and in Belgium the linking of agrarian and
urban petits bourgeois produced in the 1950s and 1960s substantial political
movements which, while they did not challenge the essential elements of
capitalism, did have coherence and specificity (as well as contradictions). Even
more recently, in Denmark, the overthrow of the Social Democrats by the
Progressive Party in 1973 owed much to Glistrop's articulation of specifically
petits bourgeois discontents. In a country where they were numerically so
important, the agrarian and urban petits bourgeois made a political response to
the economic pressures that had led first to the decline of the rural fraction, later
to that of the urban elements. Esping-Andersen's data (1980) show that the
Progressive Party became increasingly dominated by the petite bourgeoisie.

So it is important to remind ourselves that this group, particularly in those
countries where it has remained relatively numerous, has considerable potential
for independent political organization and action. However, when we look
closely at the content of the political programs, it is hard to see much of it as
radical. It is certainly not radicalism of the left; nor is it radicalism of the far
right. It generally boils down to a plea for a laissez-faire market system, for a
curbing of the rights and powers of labor, for a bridling of the big corporations,
for less interventionist government. But it retains at its heart support for the
rights of private property, for the rights of family inheritance and transmission,
for the rights of owners over workers. In terms of its attachment to the key
structures and symbols of capitalist liberal democracy it remains loyal.

Finally in this section, we should say something about the specifically social
significance of the petite bourgeoisie. A number of the most recent studies have
begun to capture and to describe the true character of the relationships engendered by petit bourgeois activity and to reveal just why these are not simply
those of capital and labor. In France the work on petits bourgeois bakers

(Bertaux & Bertaux-Wiame 1981) provides a vivid picture of the ways in which the character of the job imposes itself upon the whole life experience of the bakers and their wives and families. In the United Kingdom, studies of small builders (Scase & Goffee 1980; Goffee & Scase 1982) and small farmers (Newby et al 1978) enable us to see how relationships between petits bourgeois owners and those who work with them and for them are invested with a host of particularistic and affective ties. For many petits bourgeois, work dominates their lives. In the struggle to keep the business afloat, husbands, wives, children, and often a wider network of kin and friends are drawn into the routines of the workplace. The insulation of work from home, family from job—so familiar to most people in a modern capitalist society—is neither possible nor, in many instances, desired. Their work is their life. The sense of self-hood, the day-to-day domestic relationships take their character from the rhythms and routines of the shop, the bakery, or the small farm. The relationships between the owners of the productive resources and those who work alongside them are seldom simply those of boss and worker. Commonly the worker is also a spouse, or a son or daughter, for the greatest number of petits bourgeois businesses are family businesses. Marsden (1984) points, in his study of family farms, to the truth of Harrison's statement (Harrison 1975) that such enterprises are not simply run by families, they are run for families.

Even where nonkin are employed, they are not treated, as a rule, as mere workers. Newby and his colleagues (1978:29) in their analysis of the 'deferential dialectic' show us how a host of particularistic noneconomic obligations bind together the small farmer and his workers, how the farmer's interest is on the one hand to maintain a degree of hierarchical differentiation but on the other to encourage a real identification of the worker with what is depicted as an organic and cooperative enterprise. In the building industry Goffee & Scase (1982) argue that the bond between employers and workers is frequently constructed as a fraternal one. In many small concerns the boss and the worker work alongside each other, and in the building trades particularly they may both be time-served men, sharing a common artisan identity. In these circumstances, the one who runs the business claims not the mechanical authority of the capitalist owner but the obligations of fraternity in the day-to-day organization of the enterprise.

All of this helps to convey the distinctiveness of petit bourgeois activity. Sociologists have so far failed to explore this adequately. Small businesses are frequently family affairs, a fact that sits uncomfortably with some of the most widely held assumptions about the nature of modern society.

Traditionally sociologists have seen family and industrial society as opposed. This characterisation stems from a view of industrial society which sees its autonomy as economic and therefore 'rational'; this rationality being contrasted with the 'traditional' character of early social forms of which the family is a survival. Kin relations and market relations are seen as two incompatible structural principles. (Harris 1977)

Harris points to the inadequacy of that, and studies of the petite bourgeoisie do much to support his observation. This heterogeneous stratum is an integral part of the modern industrial world. Within its ranks are numbered not only the hole in the wall shops but also small family-based enterprises using, even developing, sophisticated modern technologies.

The specificity of the petite bourgeoisie in modern society resides in its ability to interweave the structures of kin and family relations with those of the market and to operate as a dependent partner with capital and all its institutions. This is the secret of its capacity to regenerate itself.

THE PROCESSES OF REPRODUCTION

Three factors seem most important in explaining the reproduction of the petite bourgeoisie. The first points to the somewhat paradoxical fact that in periods of economic recession a great many new businesses, mostly small ones, are set up. Economic downturns affect the little enterprises in contradictory ways. On the one hand, a good many do go to the wall. Bankruptcies are but the tip of the iceberg here, for most of those who cease trading do so without that formality. Certainly there are observable processes of capital concentration as more successful or robust companies swallow up their competitors, but there is a good deal of evidence to suggest that in this, as in other recessions, small concerns have on average weathered the storm better than a good many larger ones. Most importantly, as men and women are made redundant by the contraction or closure of companies, a new pool of potential recruits is created. A good many workers, from all sectors and at all levels, turn to forms of self-employment, using whatever stocks of capital and expertise they possess to do what some of them have certainly considered before—to branch out on their own, to become their own bosses, to find a way to enjoy 'independence'. It is virtually impossible to assess accurately the scale of this activity, but it is certain that the fragmentary evidence grossly underestimates its extent.

What we know with some certainty is that entering small business is for many people an event precipitated less by careful calculation than by luck, chance, or force of circumstances. Economic recessions often provide the impetus for would-be new recruits to venture into the precarious world of independent business.

It is also becoming clear that in order to explain the reproduction of the petite bourgeoisie, we need to explore the links between the formal economy, the household economy, and the hidden or 'black' economy. The evidence is scarce, but we can safely say that a good many small businesses start outside the formal economy. Little sidelines are run from home; moonlighting activities may involve the setting up of small informal enterprises; and we find businesses within businesses, where work is carried out for private gain using the premises, tools, information services and even the clients of the employer.

Often such activities do not turn into regular businesses but remain informal, sometimes with the collusion of the employer, who knows that only by operating in this subsidized way are such enterprises viable; but some undoubtedly do provide a route into self-employment. Recent and ongoing studies of the 'black' and the household economies (Krohn et al 1977; Henry 1978; Mars 1982; Gershuny & Pahl 1979; Pahl 1980) are beginning to give us some information on these processes which almost certainly become more extensive in periods of recession.

A second factor that encourages a flow of newcomers to the ranks of the petite bourgeoisie appears at those moments when major technological changes occur. The impact of new technologies serves both to shake out workers from enterprises committed to obsolete techniques and processes and at the same time to open up a number of new opportunities for those with appropriate skills and entrepreneurial ambition. As we observed earlier, some forms of innovative activity appear to be easier to carry out in small companies, and historical evidence suggests that in periods of rapid technological change, change of a kind that has a broad impact upon the economy, a host of new businesses appear. The early phase of Britain's industrial development was accompanied by such a growth of small-scale capitalism. So too was Japan's post World War II industrial take-off, and the early indications are that the so-called electronic revolution through which we are living is having a similar effect.

It is important not to exaggerate the effects of this, for it is most unlikely that the scale of new business formation will be adequate to absorb the large numbers thrown on to the dole queues as a consequence of the collapse of traditional forms of manufacturing. It is necessary too to stress that a good many of the new opportunities will have only an indirect relationship to the new technology. Many new enterprises will be servicing not the new forms of production, but the new kinds of life-style that emerge out of the technologically driven shifts in patterns of work and recreation.

A third factor that bears on the reproduction of the petite bourgeoisie is government policy. The capacity of modern governments to manipulate the size of this group has been commented on by Berger (1981), and there is little doubt that over the past few years, governments in most capitalist societies have taken steps to boost the prospects for petit bourgeois activity. Many forms of subsidy are now available to aspiring small-scale entrepreneurs. There are special grants, loans, tax concessions, and even short-run supplies of income offered to those who wish to set up their own businesses. Banks as well as public institutions have been persuaded to increase the availability of capital and to provide sources of counselling specifically for small business. In some countries, government ministers have been appointed with special responsibility for encouraging the development of that form of enterprise that is believed to hold the promise of rapid job creation and accelerated technical innovation.

And if we are considering the political support for the petite bourgeoisie, we should recognize that it involves more than narrow economic considerations. Governments of a right wing character have been looking to the petite bourgeoisie for possible support in their efforts to engineer change of a much broader—essentially 'moral' kind—(Bechhofer et al 1978, King 1979). The petite bourgeoisie is seen by conservative elements as the repository of certain key values whose maintenance is held to be vital to modern capitalism and its liberal democratic institutions. The petits bourgeois are looked upon by capitalist ruling classes as valuable allies. They have good reason to be confident of support not only in their project to defend existing institutions and practices but also in their campaigns to undermine socialistic and collectivistic ideologies and practices.

It is easy then to see how and why the petite bourgeoisie may be propped up by right wing regimes but it is probably more instructive to reflect on how they fare under left wing governments. In socialist societies, the petite bourgeoisie has been viewed with great suspicion, looked upon as the seedbed of counterrevolutionary tendencies. Efforts have been made then to reduce or, in a few instances, to destroy the petite bourgeoisie. These efforts, we should observe, have rarely led to the total demise of the group. Though the size of the small business sector may have been drastically cut, even in socialist economies it seems to have a capacity for survival and subsequent resurgence. In parts of Eastern Europe and in China, we are witnessing the reappearance of forms of petty property and family-based enterprises. In the histories of socialist countries there is much evidence of the durability and distinctiveness of this form of social organization.

All of this portrays the petite bourgeoisie as acted upon, its size and character molded by broad societal processes—economic, technological, and political. That is deliberate, for central to our understanding of the stratum is a recognition of its dependent or subordinate place. Its loyalties lie with the dominant economic interest, now even more certainly than in the days when its lower boundaries merged into a substantial artisan element. It is a dependent and manipulable stratum.

But that should not blind us to the fact that individually and collectively the members of the petite bourgeoisie struggle to defend their interests. They may not have formed separate political parties to do this in many countries, but there are other ways of exerting influence. Since the mid-1970s, in almost all capitalist systems, small business associations have flourished, and though they have often begun with a handful of very specific grievances and sought simply to protest in various noisy ways, many of them have survived to become effective and persistent pressure groups (McHugh 1979; Elliott et al 1982). International congresses bring together members of these associations, and all the indications are that they have learned very quickly the techniques of successful lobbying. Just as governments and parties have had to take seriously other sectoral interests—like farmers for instance—so too in recent years they have had to respond to an increasingly well organized and sophisticated small business lobby. Their policies in support of small business then owe something to pressure from below. In this sense the independent businessmen have sought to take charge of their own destiny. To depict the stratum as dependent is not to portray it or its members as totally impotent.

CONCLUSION

The petite bourgeoisie then is in no danger of disappearing. It may be dependent on the interests of big capital and of governments, but its capacity for adapting material and familial resources to the shifts in its wider environment is well proven. The secret of its survival is that it adjusts to its habitat—to capitalism in all its phases.

In the period of late capitalism, when the economies and polities of western nations are so powerfully shaped by monopoly capital and by state intervention, it is easy to dismiss the petite bourgeoisie as a small and rather unimportant stratum. To do so would be wrong. Petits bourgeois concerns are numerous. The work environments they offer shape the employment experience of a great many people. For thousands, if not millions of youngsters, the first casual jobs they hold are in local stores, garages, restaurants, many of them petits bourgeois enterprises. In the course of their adult working lives, untold millions spend some time in small businesses of one kind or another, and many of course never experience anything other than the routines and relations of these enterprises. For many citizens the most immediate, personal, and direct experience of capitalism is of petty capitalism. It is here that they encounter the spirit of the system—seldom Max Weber's quest for profit and ever renewed profit, but more often the search for a reasonable living, the chance to be your own boss, and the prospect of a little social mobility. The pervasiveness and sheer familiarity of these small enterprises not only makes understandable the reproduction of the stratum but spreads hopes, ideals, and commitments that sustain the system. That is not a petty matter.

Literature Cited

Aldrich, H., Cater, J., McEvoy, D. 1979. Retail and service businesses and the immigrant community: a test of the ecological and middleman minority models in three English cities. Report submitted to the Social Sciences Research Council, Grant HR 5520, London

Aldrich, H. 1980. Asian shopkeepers as a middleman minority. In *The Inner City: Employment and Industry*, ed. A. Evans, D. Eversley, pp. 389–407. London: Heinemann

Aldrich, H., Weiss, J. 1981. Differentiation within the U.S. capitalist class. *Am. Sociol. Rev.* 57:59–72

Bannock, G. 1981. *The Economics of Small Firms: Return from the Wilderness*. Oxford: Blackwell

Bechhofer, F., Elliott, B., Rushforth, M. 1971. The market situation of small shopkeepers. *Scot. J. Pol. Econ.* xvii:161–80

Bechhofer, F., Elliott, B. 1974a. The petite bourgeoisie in the class structure: the case of small shopkeepers. In *The Social Analysis of Class Structure*, ed. F. Parkin, pp. 103–28. London: Tavistock

Bechhofer, F., Elliott, B. 1974b. Small shopkeepers: matters of money and meaning. *Soc. Rev.* 22:465–82

Bechhofer, F., Elliott, B. 1976. Persistence and change: the petite bourgeoisie in industrial society. *Arch. Eur. Sociol.* xvii:74–99

Bechhofer, F., Elliott, B., McCrone, D. 1978. Structure, consciousness and action: a sociological profile of the British middle class. *Brit. J. Sociol.* xxix:410–36

Bechhofer, F., Elliott, B. 1978. The voice of small business and the politics of survival. *Soc. Rev.* 26:57–88

Bechhofer, F., Elliott, B. 1981. *The Petite Bourgeoisie: Comparative Studies of the Uneasy Stratum*. London: Macmillan

Bell, C., Newby, H. 1974. Capitalist farmers in the British class structure. *Sociol. Ruralis* 14:86–107

Berger, S. 1981. The uses of the traditional sector in Italy: why declining classes survive. In *The Petite Bourgeoisie: Comparative Studies of the Uneasy Stratum*, eds. F. Bechhofer, B. Elliott, pp. 71–89. London: Macmillan

Bertaux, D., Bertaux-Wiame, I. 1981. Artisanal bakery in France: how it lives and why it survives. In *The Petite Bourgeoisie: Comparative Studies of the Uneasy Stratum*, ed. F. Bechhofer, B. Elliott, pp. 155–181. London: Macmillan

Birch, D. L. 1979. *The job generation process*. Working Paper, *M.I.T.* Program on Neighbourhood and Regional Change. Cambridge, Mass.

Bland, R., Elliott, B., Bechhofer, F. 1978. Social mobility among small shopkeepers. *Acta Sociol.* 3:229–48

Boissevain, J. 1981. *Small entrepreneurs in changing Europe: towards a research agenda*. 61pp. Presented to Eur. Cent. Work Soc., Utrecht

Bolton, J. E. 1971. *Small Firms: Report of the Commission of Enquiry on Small Firms*. Cmnd. 4811. London: HMSO

Bonacich, E. 1972. A theory of ethnic antagonism: the split labour market. *Am. Sociol. Rev.* 37:547–59

Bonacich, E. 1973. A theory of middleman minorities. *Am. Sociol. Rev.* 38:583–94

Bonacich, E., Light, I., Wong, C. 1976. Small business among Koreans in Los Angeles. In *Counterpoint: Perspectives on Asian America*, ed. E. Gae, pp. 437–49. Los Angeles: Asian Am. Stud. Cent. Univ. Calif. Press

Bulloch, J. 1979. *The vital role of small scale enterprise in job creation and business development*. Presented at 6th Int. Symp. Small Business, Berlin

Burns, S. 1979. *The Household Economy*. Boston: Beacon

Clark, G. 1982. Recent developments in working patterns. *Empl. Gaz.* July:284–88

Clement, W. 1983. *Class, Power and Property*. Toronto: Methuen

Conway, J. 1981. Agrarian petits bourgeois responses to capitalist industrialisation: the case of Canada. In *The Petite Bourgeoisie: Comparative Studies of the Uneasy Stratum*, ed. F. Bechhofer, B. Elliott, pp. 1–37. London: Macmillan

Conway, J. 1984. *The West: the History of a Region in Confederation*. Toronto: Lorimer

Crossick, G. 1976. *The Lower Middle Class in Britain, 1870–1914*. London: Croom Helm

Crossick, G. 1979. La petite bourgeoisie Britannique en xix^e siecle. *Mouvement Soc.* 108:21–61

Curran, J., Stanworth, J. 1979a. Worker involvement and social relations in the small firm. *Hum. Relat.* 34:343–66

Curran, J., Stanworth, J. 1979b. Self-selection and the small firm worker: a critique and an alternative view. *Sociology* 13:427–44

Elliott, B., McCrone, D. 1975a. Landlords in Edinburgh: some preliminary findings. *Soc. Rev.* 23:539–562

Elliott, B., McCrone, D. 1975b. Property relations in the city: the fortunes of landlordism. In *Proc. Conf. Urban Change and Conflict*, ed. M. Harloe, pp. 31–61. London: Cent. Environ. Stud.

Elliott, B., McCrone, D. 1980. Urban development in Edinburgh: a contribution to the political economy of place. *Scot. J. Sociol.* 4:1–26

Elliott, B., Bechhofer, F., McCrone, D., Black, S. 1982. Bourgeois social movements in Britain: repertoires and responses. *Soc. Rev.* 30:71–96

Esping-Andersen, G. 1980. *Social Class, Social Democracy and State Policy*. Copenhagen: Inst. Organ. Ind. Sociol.

Eurostat. 1983. *Employment and Unemployment 1970–1982*. Luxembourg: Stat. Off. Eur. Communities

Fothergill, S., Gudgin, G. 1982. *Unequal Growth*. London: Heinemann

Fraser, D. 1976. *Urban Politics in Victorian England: the Structure of Politics in Victorian Cities*. Leicester: Leicester Univ. Press

Gellately, R. 1974. *The Politics of Economic*

Despair: Shopkeepers and German Politics 1890–1914. London: Sage

Gershuny, J. 1978. *After Industrial Society: The Emerging Self-Service Economy.* London: Macmillan

Gershuny, J., Pahl, R. E. 1979. Work outside employment: some preliminary speculations. *New Univ. Q.* 34:120–35

Gershuny, J., Pahl, R. E. 1980. Britain in the decade of the three economies. *New Soc.* 900:7–9

Goffee, R., Scase, R. 1982. 'Fraternalism' and 'Paternalism' as employer strategies in small firms. In *Diversity and Decomposition in the Labour Market*, ed. G. Day, et al, pp. 107–24. Aldershot: Gower

Goldthorpe, J. H., Llewellyn, C., Payne, C. 1980. *Social Mobility and Class Structure in Modern Britain.* Oxford: Oxford Univ. Press

Government of Canada. 1979a. *New Statistics on Small Business in Canada.* Ottawa: Dep. Industry, Trade and Commerce

Government of Canada. 1979b. *Small Business in Canada: A Statistical Profile,* Ottawa: Dep. Industry, Trade and Commerce

Granovetter, M. 1984. Small is bountiful: labour markets and establishment size. *Am. Sociol. Rev.* 49:323–34

Gray, R. Q. 1976. *The Labour Aristocracy in Victorian Edinburgh.* Oxford: Oxford Univ. Press

Harris, C. C. 1977. Changing conceptions of the relationship between the family and societal forms in western society. In *Industrial Society: Class, Cleavage and Control,* ed. R. Scase, pp. 74–89. London: Allen & Unwin

Hennock, E. P. 1973. *Fit and Proper Persons. Ideal and Reality in Nineteenth-Century Urban Local Government.* London: Edward Arnold

Henry, S. 1978. *The Hidden Economy.* London: Martin Robertson

King, R. 1979. The middle class revolt and the established parties. In *Respectable Rebels: Middle Class Campaigns in Britain in the 1970s,* ed. R. King, N. Nugent, pp. 153–182. London: Hodder Stoughton

Kondratiev, N. D. 1935. The long waves in economic life. *Rev. Econ. Stat.* 17:105–15

Krohn, R. G., Fleming, B., Manzer, M. 1977. *The Other Economy.* Toronto: Peter Martin

Kumar, K. 1978. *Prophesy and Progress: The Sociology of Industrial and Post-Industrial Society.* Harmondsworth: Penguin

Light, I. 1972. *Ethnic Enterprise in America.* Berkeley: Univ. Calif. Press

Light, I. 1979. Disadvantaged minorities in self-employment. *Int. J. Comp. Sociol.* xx:31–45

Lipset, S. M. 1950. *Agrarian Socialism: the Cooperative Commonwealth Federation in Saskatchewan.* Berkeley: Univ. Calif. Press

Mackenzie, G. 1982. Class boundaries and the labour process. In *Social Class and the Division of Labour: Essays in honour of Ilya Neustadt,* ed. A. Giddens, G. Mackenzie, pp. 63–86. Cambridge: Cambridge Univ. Press

Macpherson, C. B. 1973. *Democratic Theory: Essays in Retrieval.* London: Clarendon

Macpherson, C. B. 1978. *Property: Mainstream and Critical Positions.* London: Oxford Univ. Press

Mars, G. 1982. *Cheats at Work.* London: Allen & Unwin

Marsden, T. 1984. Capitalist farming and the farm family: a case study. *Sociology* 18:205–24

Mayer, A. 1975. The lower middle class as a historical problem. *J. Mod. Hist.* 47:409–36

Mayer, N. 1977. Une filiere de mobilite ouvriere: l'access a la petite entreprise artisanale et commerciale. *Rev. Francaise de Sociol.* xviii:25–45

McHugh, J. 1979. The self-employed and the small independent entrepreneur. In *Respectable Rebels: Middle Class Campaigns in Britain in the 1970s,* eds. R. King, N. Nugent. See pp. 46–75. London: Hodder & Stoughton

Neale, R. S. 1972. *Class and Ideology in the Nineteenth Century.* London: Routledge & Kegan Paul

Newby, H. 1977. *The Deferential Worker.* London: Allen Lane

Newby, H. 1979. *Green and Pleasant Land.* London: Hutchinson

Newby, H., Bell, C., Rose, D., Saunders, P. 1978. *Property, Paternalism and Power.* London: Hutchinson

Nossiter, T. J. 1972. Shopkeeper radicalism in the nineteenth century. In *Imagination and Precision in the Social Sciences,* ed. T. J. Nossiter, A. H. Hanson, S. Rokkan, pp. 407–38. London: Faber & Faber

Oakey, R. 1984. *High Technology Small Firms: Regional Development in Britain and the United States.* London: Frances Pinter

Pahl, R. E. 1980. Employment, work and the domestic division of labour. *Int. J. Urban Regional Res.* 4:1–20

Poulantzas, N. 1975. *Classes in Contemporary Capitalism.* London: New Left

Rothwell, R., Zegveld, W. 1982. *Innovation and the Small and Medium Sized Firm.* London: Frances Pinter

Scase, R., Goffee, R. 1980. *The Real World of the Small Business Owner.* London: Croom Helm

Scase, R., Goffee, R. 1982. *The Entrepreneurial Middle Class.* London: Croom Helm

Scase, R. 1982. The petty bourgeoisie and modern capitalism: a consideration of recent theories. In *Social Class and the Division of Labour: Essays in honour of Ilya Neustadt,* ed. A. Giddens, G. Mackenzie, pp. 148–61. Cambridge: Cambridge Univ. Press

Schumpeter, J. A. 1939. *Business Cycles.* New York: McGraw-Hill

Stanworth, J., Curran, J. 1973. *Management Motivation in the Smaller Business.* Epping: Gower

Storey, D. 1982. *Entrepreneurship and the Small Firm.* London: Croom Helm

REFERENCE ADDED IN PROOF

Harrison, A. 1975. *Farmers and Farm Business in England.* Reading: Univ. Reading, Dept. Agric. Econ. Mgmt. Misc. Study No. 62

Watson, J. L. 1977. *Between Two Cultures: Migrants and Minorities in Britain.* Oxford: Blackwell

Wright, E. O. 1976. Class boundaries in advanced capitalist societies. *New Left Rev.* 98:3–41

Wright, E. O. 1979. *Class Structure and Income Determination.* New York: Academic

Wright, E. O., Costello, C., Hacken, D., Sprague, J. 1982. The American class structure. *Am. Soc. Rev.* 47:709–26

Ann. Rev. Sociol. 1985. 11:209–29
Copyright © 1985 by Annual Reviews Inc. All rights reserved

SOCIAL PROBLEMS THEORY: THE CONSTRUCTIONIST VIEW

Joseph W. Schneider

Department of Sociology, Drake University, Des Moines, Iowa 50311

Abstract

This paper reviews and critiques the origin and development of a new specialty in sociology, the sociology of social problems. While social problems long has been a topic of sociological attention, it is only since the work of Blumer and, most especially, Spector & Kitsuse in the early 1970s, that a theoretically integrated and empirically viable tradition of writing and research has developed. The central proposition of this tradition is that social problems are the definitional activities of people around conditions and conduct they find troublesome, including others' definitional activities. In short, social problems are socially constructed, both in terms of the particular acts and interactions problem participants pursue, and in terms of the process of such activities through time. The founding theoretical statements are reviewed and the research is discussed in terms of the following categories: containing trouble and avoiding problems; the creation, ownership, and processing of problems; public regulatory bureaucracies and legal institutions; medicalizing problems and troubles; and social problems and the media. The paper closes with an overview of problems and insights of the perspective. There is a bibliography of 105 items.

INTRODUCTION

The social constructionist perspective offers a way to define, understand, and study social problems that is decidedly distinct from previous perspectives. The past decade has witnessed considerable research that, in varying degree, uses or is relevant to the social constructionist or definitional view. In this essay, I review the core statements of this perspective, describe selected research relevant to it, and discuss some of the problems with and insights from using the perspective in research.

209

0360-0572/85/0815-0209$02.00

PROGRAMMATIC STATEMENTS: MAJOR THEMES

The possibility of a research-based sociology of social problems integrated around a distinct theoretical perspective is not new. More than forty years ago, Waller (1936), Fuller & Myers (1941a, 1941b), and others pursued this goal under the banner of value-conflict theory. A renewed interest in this goal has developed in the past fifteen years (see Tallman & McGee 1971) along with a detailed critique of previous theory and a sharpened conceptualization of what such a sociology of social problems might look like.

While constructionist research and writing has not been the only sociological work on social problems, it arguably constitutes the only serious and sustained recent discussion of social problems theory—a theory *of* social problems distinct from sociological theory used *in* research on undesirable conditions. This latter accurately describes most previous sociological writing and research on social problems, whether it was guided by functionalist, Marxist, conflict theory, or other perspectives. While these latter constitute legitimate sociological work, none informs the question of whether a distinct theory of social problems is possible, what its subject matter might be, or how it might be developed in empirical research. These are precisely the questions Blumer (1971) and particularly Spector & Kitsuse (1973, 1977; Kitsuse & Spector 1973) address.

The question of just what "social problems" means as a sociological concept and how we might study such phenomena has been at the center of the dilemma surrounding this topic since its emergence in the last century. Given this long-lived confusion, Blumer (1971:298) called for a fundamental change in conceptualization to reflect a definition of social problems as "products of a process of collective definition" rather than "objective conditions and social arrangements." Traditional work, he says, reflects a "gross misunderstanding of the nature of social problems" and is virtually useless as a basis for policy since it defines social problems as objective conditions harmful to society. Moreover, sociologists have identified such conditions based on public concern. This is problematic, Blumer says, since many ostensibly "harmful conditions" are not recognized as such by the public, and thus are ignored by sociologists.

Concepts such as "deviance," "dysfunction," and "structural strain" have been "impotent" as guides for research to identify social problems. They can not account for why some conditions fail to become social problems while others do. Sociologists instead "ought to study the process by which a society comes to recognize its social problems" (Blumer 1971:300).

Spector & Kitsuse have called for a similar change, claiming: "There is no adequate definition of social problems within sociology, and there is not and never has been a sociology of social problems" (1977:1). They, like Blumer, critique the familiar functionalist perspective (e.g. Merton & Nisbet 1971) that concentrates on dysfunctional conditions and turns on abstractions such as "latent problems," "collective purposes," society as an "integrated social system," and so on. The sociologist here is a technical expert whose moral vision supersedes that of the people studied. Kitsuse & Spector say this view is empirically problematic, morally infused, and grossly presumptuous. It provides no distinctive subject matter for the sociology of social problems and no effective direction for research.

Kitsuse & Spector endorse the early value-conflict emphasis on the "subjective component" of social problems, but argue that these authors compromised a distinct theory of social problems by their continued attention to objective conditions as a necessary part of the conceptualization. This dualism and confusion as to what social problems are is also found in Blumer's essay, when he speaks of social problems as "products" of collective definitional process, as outcomes, and of objective conditions as a "corrective for ignorance and misinformation" about the "objective makeup of social problems" (Blumer 1971:305). Even Becker's (1966) view of social problems endorses this dualism. This is precisely what Spector & Kitsuse reject. Blumer also cites policy relevance as a criterion to evaluate theory, and implies that public definitions of social problems are somehow inadequate bases for sociological theory (cf. Manis 1984, on "public" definitions). Spector & Kitsuse say that these differences confound the value-conflict approach and thus make it a poor guide for empirical research.

Conventional usage of the term social problems makes it difficult to distinguish what Spector & Kitsuse see as crucial, namely, that it refers to a social process of definition and to the activities that move this process along. For Kitsuse & Spector, participants' definitional activities *constitute* the social problem (Rains 1975, Woolgar 1983), rather than leading to social problems as a product or outcome (cf. Mauss 1975).

Social problems are "*the activities of groups making assertions of grievances and claims with respect to some putative conditions*" (Kitsuse & Spector 1973:415, emphasis in original). Social problems sociology, so defined, should "account for the *emergence and maintenance of claim-making and responding activities*" (Kitsuse & Spector, 1973:415, emphasis in original). Claims making includes: "demanding services, filling out forms, lodging complaints, filing lawsuits, calling press conferences, writing letters of protest, passing resolutions, publishing exposes, placing ads in newspapers, supporting or opposing some governmental practice or policy, setting up picket lines or boycotts. . . ." (Spector & Kitsuse 1977:79). To study the causes of social problems is to examine how such activities come about and how they have been sustained. Toward this end, Spector & Kitsuse, like Fuller & Myers, Blumer, and others, suggest an heuristic, four-stage natural history model.

Stage one comprises "collective attempts to remedy a condition that some group perceives and judges offensive and undesirable. . . . Initial social problems activities consist of attempts to transform private troubles into public issues . . . and . . . the contingencies of this transformation process" (Spector & Kitsuse 1973:148). How claims and grievances are formed and presented, the varieties and nature of the claims and grievances, strategies to press these claims and gain wider attention and support, the power of the group(s) making claims, and the creation of a public controversy are important issues.

Stage two begins with recognition of these claims by "governmental agencies or other official and influential institutions." To continue beyond stage two a social problem must involve "an institution . . . to deal with the claims and complaints concerning the condition in question" (Spector & Kitsuse 1973:154). Social problems thus become routinized in an organization charged with doing something about the putative conditions.

Spector & Kitsuse say that whereas past natural history models end with legitimation and implementation, theirs is open-ended and takes official acceptance as possible grounds for a "new generation" of definitional activities around this official response. When participants claim such response is problematic, *stage three* begins. *Stage four* is marked by claimants' "contention that it is no longer possible to 'work within the system' . . ." and their attempts to develop alternative institutions (Spector & Kitsuse 1973:156).

In their view, sociologists who act as experts on problematic conditions are social problems participants. They become part of the problem rather than analysts of it. Whether he or she "will be treated as a scientist by other participants in the process and accorded the special status of a disinterested and unbiased expert is a problematic empirical question" (Spector & Kitsuse 1977:70). This means sociologists of social problems should not concern themselves with the validity of participants' (their colleagues included) claims about conditions, but with how such claims and definitions are created, documented, pressed, and kept alive. Documenting claims or definitions about conditions constitutes participation. The point is to account for the viability of these claims, not to judge whether they are true. And while social problems participants attribute values to their own and others' activities, sociologists of social problems should not. Gusfield (1984) has characterized this stance as being "on the side" or neutral, rather than choosing "whose side" we are on (Becker 1967).

Besides crediting Fuller & Myers, Becker, and Blumer as important resources in developing their constructionist view, Spector & Kitsuse cite Mauss (1975) and his attention to definitions in his analysis of social problems as social movements. They endorse Ross & Staines's (1971) emphasis on the politics of the definitional process, and they cite as particularly relevant the Hewitt & Hall (1973) analysis of how participants use "quasi-theories" to order problematic situations.

RELEVANT RESEARCH

Containing Trouble and Avoiding Problems

Logically prior to but thus far relatively ignored in research are those diverse definitional activities that occur before professional, bureaucratic, and media categories and personnel become involved. Emerson & Messinger (1977) see such informal reactions as "trouble" and as forerunners of official labeling.

Most research on this informal activity examines how normal others use vernacular categories of mental illness to define troublesome persons. Before Emerson & Messinger (1977) are the well-known studies by Yarrow et al (1955), Sampson et al (1962), Lemert (1962), and Goffman (1959,1969). Goldner (1982) continues this tradition in a study of how others react to "pronoids" in various bureaucratic settings, and Lynch (1983) studied how normals respond to and manage "crazies" in everyday settings.

Research on the origins and development of trouble is not limited to craziness and mental illness. Shearing & Stenning's (1983) study of private security in Canada and the United States shows how owners of mass private property (e.g. shopping malls, apartment complexes, college campuses) define threats to security in precisely such a prebureaucratic, prepublic (in this case precrime) way. Public labeling and processing is something owners usually want to avoid. Private security agents are hired to control anything the owners do not like. This can include behaviors not in violation of the law (e.g. absenteeism, breaches of confidentiality), as well as those that are in violation but not troublesome to owners (e.g. victimless crimes are ignored). By making prevention more important than retribution or restitution, owners and their security forces create a new kind of offender—the employee who allows the theft, damage, or breach to occur. The ultimate wrong is to be nonvigilant in loyalty to owners' interests (see also, Ghezzi 1983, on private control of insurance fraud).

Ball & Lilly (1984) analyze data from a study of a motel used for clandestine sexual encounters to see how motel owners and their staff work to deflect problem-defining activities by three relevant publics: the morally concerned citizenry, the police, and the patrons. The authors show how motel staff attempt to take the role of these three others toward their operations so as to prevent or modify conditions that might become grounds for claims making. They demonstrate that just as conditions are not inherently problematic, neither are they inherently normal. The staff worked hard to create and sustain definitions of the motel as a tolerated and even desirable part of what they saw as a potentially critical environment.

Schneider (1984) studied moral vocabularies used by antismoking and smoking respondents to see how they defined and dealt with trouble around smoking in various public and private settings. He details how antismoke people made claims (or did not) against smokers. While respondents used many negative words to describe smoking and smokers in the interviews, they found confronting bothersome smokers considerably more difficult. The best values to ground their claims were their own health interests and their rights. These claimants and responders were sensitive to the importance of the words they used. Personal dislike alone was considered insufficient grounds for claims.

The language of claims is also important in a study by Cohn & Gallagher (1984) of a social problem involving a gay student group at the University of Maine, a proposed gay conference, a local newspaper, and a group of fundamentalist ministers. Initial claims by the ministers against the University and the gay student group were couched in Biblical terms of sin and immorality. They claimed that the University was condoning such conduct. The University defended itself with a Constitutional and civil rights vocabulary, without mentioning homosexuality or gays. This was strategic. The University thus assured that the issue would not be joined, that they and their critics would not communicate in the ministers' more perilous moral rhetoric. Various sympathetic yet conventional audiences could then support the University while leaving their private opinions about homosexuality unspoken. The case demonstrates how responses are contingent upon, but not determined by initial claims. It also shows that respondents may want not to debate the issue as framed by those initiating claims, particularly if these claims are in unfriendly or difficult vocabularies. Smokers, for instance, felt there was virtually no effective defense against others' health claims.

The Creation, Ownership, and Processing of Problems

The most popular topic for constructionist research has been the creation of bureaucratic and professional categories for problematic conditions, conduct, and persons. Coincidental to Spector & Kitsuse's work, Gusfield (1975,1976,1981), pursuing past interests in the nature of symbolic action (Gusfield 1963,1967), has raised these questions in research on public definitions and policy toward drinking, driving, and accidents in the United States.

Gusfield begins by noting the dominance of one view of this problem: accidents are caused by a category of drivers, "the drunk driver," and their careless and dangerous conduct. Much official data that detail characteristics of the driver, the presence of alcohol, and degree of intoxication have been produced to support this view (cf Kitsuse & Cicourel 1963). Policy has followed accordingly: make drunk drivers control themselves and/or keep them from driving. The laws and public programs that reflect this dominant view, Gusfield argues, contribute to our sense of social order.

To underscore the selective quality of this construction, he details some of what the dominant view omits. Where are such systematic data on vehicle design, the roadway, age and condition of the car, weather, and available emergency assistance as related to "accidents involving alcohol"? How different would definitions and solutions of the problem be were they built on these data?

Gusfield emphasizes connections between the organizational ownership of the problem—a concept he aligns with Becker's (1963) concept, "moral entrepreneur," the construction of supportive scientific facts and causal explanations—and the attribution of political responsibility to "do something about" the problematic condition. This affirms the sociology of knowledge theme in the constructionist approach (see also Aronson 1984) and shows how scientists and experts participate in social problems they purport to analyze. Champions and owners of this favored view of drinking and driving have been The National Safety Council, major auto and life insurance companies, the legal system, the alcoholism industry, and the National Institute on Alcohol Abuse and Alcoholism (NIAAA). Only recently have they been challenged by other groups offering alternate definitions, explanations, and interventions.

Gusfield shows how social context—an important element in constructionist analysis (Woolgar & Pawluch 1985)—facilitates these drunk driver–centered definitions and claims. These favored definitions and explanations allow social drinkers to continue to drive unperturbed and are resources for the alcohol and alcoholism industries to portray the problem of drinking as due to certain sick drinkers rather than the drink. Wiener (1981) examines this social world of alcoholism treatment, policy, and research, and the connections between its participants and their diverse, shifting definitions and claims.

The study of organizational ownership and management of social problems directs attention to how people do this work, to how they handle various kinds of problems and troubles. This parallels earlier work on the organizational processing of deviants and deviance. Recent studies examine how various workers, clients, and others negotiate these definitions. Schwartz & Kahne (1983, Kahne & Schwartz 1978) studied how professionals and clients in a college psychiatric unit negotiated the nature and treatment of students' troubles. Maynard (1982) studied plea bargaining sessions to uncover how court officials use defendants' personal attributes to make sentencing decisions. Miller (1983) examined how workers in a work incentive program used conciliation sessions to reaffirm program morality about responsibility and encourage conformity among troublesome clients. Spencer (1983) examined the familiar probation officer–client relationship and how probation officers negotiate a moral character for their clients to fit the sentencing recommendations they make.

Some studies have focused on how workers, clients, and others use official categories or rules so work can proceed. Joffe (1978) studied how lay abortion counselors balance their ideological support of abortion services with their revulsion at clients who refuse to acknowledge the moral aspects of abortion. McCleary et al (1982) examined how workers in police departments code officers' observations using Uniform Crime Report codes. Pontell et al (1982) studied how California State government reviewed possible fraud and abuse by physicians who used the public medical insurance program. Lynxwiler et al (1983) show how mine inspectors, working for the Office of Surface Mining Reclamation and Enforcement, use discretion in making and processing claims against mining companies. Peyrot (1982) analyzed how community mental health workers used discretion to categorize clients so as to make the best use of scarce resources.

Routinizing and managing people's problems is the essence of the "public interest state"—that complex of federal and state administrative rules, regulations, and personnel that define eligibility for various public endorsements and support (Reich 1964). Spector (1981) says that personnel in these public bureaucracies and programs define troublesome people as "ineligible" to receive benefits (rather than criminal, deviant, or sick) and manage them accordingly.

Public Regulatory Bureaucracies and Legal Institutions

Public regulatory bureaucracies both initiate and receive social problems claims (Chauncey 1980, Randall & Short 1983). Several studies show government agencies as social problems entrepreneurs. Becker's (1963) analysis of how the Treasury Department's Bureau of Narcotics defined the "marijuana problem" is well known (see also Galliher & Walker 1977). Gusfield (1981) and Wiener (1981) point to the NIAAA as a central participant in the world of alcoholism. Nuehring & Markle (1974) and Troyer & Markle (1983, Markle & Troyer 1979) identify the Public Health Service, the Federal Trade Commission, the Civil Aeronautics Board, the Surgeon General, and former Health Education and Welfare Secretary Joseph Califano as important entrepreneurs against smoking.

Chauncey (1980) studied how NIAAA officials tried to convince the nation of the seriousness of teenage drinking. These attempts largely failed because NIAAA was unable to secure endorsement from various private and nonofficial public groups. Public reception ranged from minimal to confused. Specific local teenage drinking programs were few, parents did not buy the definition, doctors did not support it, it had to compete with the drug problem, school officials did not see the problem, and it was rarely reported to police, who, in any case, had little access to special programs. Troyer & Markle (1983) show that antismoking claims made by government agencies have fared considerably better in terms of such grass roots and organization support (see also Ball & Lilly 1982, on the shifting fate of margarine).

When bureaucracies receive citizens' complaints, these claims are transformed by a language that is created and controlled by experts or bureaucrats (cf Latour 1983). Citizens' complaints become part of a system of proper procedures. Murray's (1982) study of the abolition of the short-handled hoe in California farm work makes this clear. While workers and their attorney won the case against managers and the hoe, Murray asks what they did not and could not win, namely, attention to the hazards of all corporate production and to power differences between workers and management. Where claims are made, that is, to whom, can constrain subsequent definitional activities in loosely predictable ways—if one has detailed and current knowledge of the bureaucracy (see also Randall & Short 1983). Without the counsel of legal experts, claimants usually do not possess this knowledge. Murray describes how these experts can control and even change the problem.

Randall & Short (1983) studied a controversy over an Idaho mining company's policy requiring women workers to be sterilized to continue work in an area declared a risk for genetic damage. OSHA initiated claims against the company's policy on behalf of these women. OSHA ultimately lost this case because it could not marshall the necessary external power resources. A court rejected its claims to jurisdiction in such cases, and the Ford Administration was explicitly hostile to all OSHA actions (see also Calavita 1983, and Murray 1982 for similar views of the larger political context and such agencies' claims). The company's claims, definitions, and policy remained intact.

Calavita's (1983) study of the dismantling of OSHA, especially by the Reagan Administration, uncovers the paradox of one part of government making claims against another. By replacing the heads of OSHA (and the FTC) with antiregulators, the Administration was able not only to undermine these agencies and their claims, but to discredit the agency's past work publicly through media stories. Randall & Short say such public agencies are able to make claims, propose general remedies, and gain legitimacy all in one set of activities, effectively collapsing Spector & Kitsuse's first and second stages.

Kitsuse et al (1984) studied the *kikokushijo mondai*—returning student problem—in Japan. In contrast to the Randall & Short case, their study shows how a receptive context—the highly stratified educational system that is considered an essential prerequisite to career success in Japan as a Japanese— can be used to enhance the viability of claims made to a government bureaucracy. This problem consisted of definitional activities by diplomatic, academic, and corporate parents about the educational deficiencies they felt their school-age children experienced upon returning to Japan from foreign residence and education. The authors detail the many and varied ways this problem has become institutionalized, both in the Japanese educational system and in the larger society, while alternative, positive definitions of the returning students' situation (they are "broadened" and "internationalized") have foundered.

Filing a law suit is a common form of claims making today. People, groups, and institutions, including the state, attempt to transform various troubles into legal issues. Such claims making allows us to observe how social problems participants use social structure as a resource.

One topic of study is how various devalued people and their lawyers have challenged owners by invoking the Constitution. Kitsuse (1980) describes how these people have "come out" to demand their civil rights and integrity. Spector (1981) describes these claims as demands to government for "entitlements." These deviants have gone beyond deviance to create new social problems, sometimes with radical social and political implications (see Weitz 1984).

Civil rights, public interest, and consumer law have grown apace. The law here becomes a set of official symbolic categories for making claims to effect social change (cf Gusfield 1981). Using this law, attorneys for black people, the poor, consumers, juveniles, mental patients, prisoners, and others, have attacked a variety of traditional definitions and practices in our public life.

Feminists have been one such challenging group, and rape a particularly important object of their attention. Rose (1977) calls the social problem of rape "a by-product of the feminist movement" and details how women's groups have attacked traditional rape laws and police and court treatment of rape victims. These feminist criticisms offer new definitions of rape (e.g. Brownmiller 1975) and an analysis of its source in traditional gender roles. Alternate institutions run for women by women, some who are themselves rape victims, have grown. As with gay activists and reformed alcoholics, these claimants have taken ownership of the problem away from traditional experts and bureaucrats and made it the object of their and others' routine work (see also Tierney 1982, on the battered women problem).

Spector (1981) and Spector & Batt (1983) compare criminal and civil court procedures concerning rape. These two legal institutions offer victims distinct experiences and opportunities. To define rape as a crime makes the conflict one between the state and the accused. Rape victims sometimes do not even participate in the state's case, which is controlled by lawyers and the judge. If they do, they act as witnesses for the state rather than in their own interests. Spector & Batt use Christie's (1977) idea of conflicts as property to argue that criminal categories, procedures, and professionals steal this conflict from rape victims and transform it into a legal case that seems little related to the victim's experience. By contrast, civil law defines rape as a wrong done to an individual. The state provides the formal setting, judge, and rules to guide the claims-making process. Lawyers (ideally) advise rather than manipulate clients. Rape victims can own their conflicts and express moral outrage against offenders. Spector & Batt examined 31 civil rape cases since the turn of the century and found evidence that rape victims' experiences, compared with those of victims in criminal proceedings, support their analysis.

In another study of legal change, Frank (1983) shows how civil law has replaced criminal law in problems of health and safety in the workplace and the environment since the turn of the century. Through detailed attention to major participants, definitions, and contests in this history, Frank effectively challenges " 'knee-jerk' applications of conflict theory" that portray this change as a simple function of corporate capitalist power (see also Donnelly's 1982 study of the origins of the Occupational Safety and Health Act of 1970).

Medicalizing Problems and Troubles

Much recent research on the medicalization of deviance draws on the constructionist perspective. This work examines the implications of these new medical meanings and personnel for participants and the society, and the ownership struggles between professional and lay claims makers. In an early paper, Conrad (1975) draws on Becker (1963), Freidson (1970), and Zola (1972) to describe the origins, rise, and legitimacy of the medical diagnosis hyperkinesis at the hands of a small number of medical researchers, two drug companies, a Congressional Subcommittee on Privacy, and the Association for Children with Learning Disabilities. Conrad contrasts the implications of these medical definitions and interventions around children's troublesome behavior with those contained in the deviant labels "bad" or "problem" child. These new definitions solve problems for teachers and parents responsible for children's difficult behavior, and displace social contextual explanations potentially critical of the educational status quo.

Pfohl's (1977) analysis of child abuse also identifies professional moral entrepreneurs: a few pediatric radiologists who created the new diagnosis, "Battered Child Syndrome." Context is again important in that these radiologists saw this "discovery," says Pfohl, as a welcome opportunity to do significant, career-enhancing work.

The Conrad and Pfohl studies highlight an important kind of professional claims making: scientific publication in a respected professional journal. Such publication is usually not seen as relevant social problems data. These studies also show that those outside medicine can use medical definitions to their own ends, which experts may see as contrary to their own. When professionals become social problems participants, they often must share definitional prerogatives with diverse individuals and groups (see Wiener 1981). Ownership does not always ensure complete control.

Schneider (1978) studied the viability of the "humanitarian" disease concept of alcoholism and found that medical experts in fact were not the primary entrepreneuers. Alcoholics Anonymous, a few scientists and "recovered alcoholics," research centers at Yale and Rutgers Universities, the National Council on Alcoholism, and the NIAAA were the most active political champions of this disease definition (cf Wiener 1981). Similarly, Johnson & Hufbauer (1982) found parents of Sudden Infant Death Syndrome (SIDS) victims were the most active claimants behind new scientific and Congressional awareness and research support for SIDS. These lay champions used scientific research, official medical statements, and public sympathy as important contextual resources to establish the viability of their claims. Troyer & Markle (1983, 1984) reiterate this kind of lay participation around problems of smoking and coffee drinking.

Conrad & Schneider (1980; Schneider & Conrad 1980) studied mental illness, alcoholism, opiate addiction, children's deviant behavior, and homosexuality as prime cases where medical definitions and technology have been championed over sin and crime designations. They used medical journals, professional speeches, editorials, news stories, popular magazines, autobiographies, historical studies, and court cases as sources of data. They identified the actors behind these historic changes and how this definitional work was done. Those who could establish their prerogatives to define the problem and designate who should be responsible for it were powerful figures in these social dramas (cf Gusfield 1975, Latour 1983, Peyrot 1984).

Lay persons can be critics as well as champions of professional owners' definitions and can even win this ownership. The demedicalization of homosexuality illustrates this. Following Spector (1977), Conrad & Schneider (1980) show how gay liberation advocates, with the support of a few insider psychiatrists, challenged the medical disease diagnosis of homosexuality. Using the psychiatrists' own medical, scientific culture, these lay challengers scored a definitional victory that led ultimately to gays themselves becoming the new owner-experts of homosexuality as a "lifestyle." McCrea (1983) studied how a few doctors championed the "deficiency disease" of menopause and a treatment of estrogen replacement. They were effectively challenged by feminists, who used independent scientific research on the link between cancer and estrogen therapy, who defined menopause as a natural part of women's lives, and who claimed that the disease view was sexist. Troyer & Markle's (1984) study of the definition of coffee reiterates the importance of sympathetic professionals and/or supportive research for such challenge. This research enlightens us about how stage three claims are made and successfully pursued.

Studies of the medicalization of deviance also illustrate how professionals create the problems they own and treat (see Hughes 1971, Freidson 1970). In doing this, they make moral judgments both in the technical language of the profession and in the popular moral meanings so far as this language often incorporates popular moral meanings. This second kind of morality seems to be a useful resource for critics, as McCrea's (1983) study demonstrates. Billings & Urban's (1982) analysis of the medical construction of transsexualism and the transsexual shows how doctors became dupes of well-schooled patients who effected key diagnostic criteria to gain treatment, which they later criticized. Loseke & Cahill (1984) describe and criticize—that is, participate in the social problem of—the way experts on battered women label the women who remain in such relationships as unable to control their lives and in need of experts' counsel.

Pawluch's (1983) analysis of the history of pediatrics shifts attention from problematic individuals to how some pediatricians responded to a declining professional market. As childhood diseases and problems of baby feeding were controlled, pediatricians had both less work and less medically worthwhile work to do. Some began to champion new definitions of the baby doctor's role to include, as one advocate said, "shades of difference between health and disease, conditions whereby the child is not invalided, but his social and individual efficacy is decreased" (Pawluch 1983:457; see also Riessman 1983, on women as vulnerable to such medical definitions).

Such professional claims making about problematic conditions in the society is found in science more generally. Aronson's (1982) study of the origins and institutionalization of nutrition research shows how conditions outside science that were seen to threaten powerful interests provided an opportunity for scientist-entrepreneurs to gain financial support and legitimacy by defining themselves and their science as a solution to those "problems." Nutrition's leading late nineteenth-century advocate, Wilbur Atwater, argued he could solve the problem of labor unrest over wages by teaching workers to buy and prepare food in a more economical and healthy way. Such claims appealed to capitalist owners, who sought a productive and cooperative workforce without raising wages. Nutrition advocates finally won official endorsement from Congress, with an appropriation to support their research in US Agricultural Experiment Stations.

Aronson says this case shows some of the conditions under which scientists will make such activist, "social problems interpretive claims" (Aronson 1984) to groups and organizations outside science. When resources to support research are scarce and the opportunity for public funding exists, such enterprising activities might be expected. Johnson & Hufbauer's (1982) study of SIDS shows a contrasting situation in which demands from parents for more research were important as both a direct and indirect impetus to a new medical research community (see also Wiener 1981, on alcoholism research). Latour (1983) makes the most bold argument here, citing the history of Pasteur's capture of the anthrax problem in late nineteenth century France to show how distinctions between science and society, upon close scrutiny, virtually disappeared in the face of compelling scientific facts. Clearly, problems in the larger society and problems in science are often linked, with significant consequences for social organization.

Social Problems and the News Media

Social problems participants usually hope the news media will help them publicize claims and thus enhance their legitimacy. Research shows, however, that the media do not function simply as mirrors claimants can use to reflect "what is really going on." Rather, they decidedly shape the images they convey. Newsworkers are, in short, the true "newsmakers" (Glasgow University Media Group 1980, Fishman 1980), and relevant questions include the following: What happens to claims and definitions that go to media organizations? How do they emerge? What is the place of the media in the social problems process? Do media communicate claims and definitions of their own, quite aside from what other claims makers say?

Fishman (1978) shows that a crime wave against the elderly reported by three New York City media organizations was, in fact, a growing, overlapping media coverage. He details how editors created this news theme to solve routine problems of news work. The theme became a media wave when it was reiterated in other news reports. Fishman calls crime news ideological because it reports crime as the police see it (e.g. street crimes and violent crimes) and because routine newswork produces stories that convey meanings all their own. For instance, news workers recognize good and newsworthy stories by using criteria that systematically filter out things that are not (see also Wiener, 1981:207–211, discussion of media coverage of the Rand Report).

News reporters' routine dependence for information on official owners of problems effectively discourages interpretations foreign to or in conflict with those interpretations on which owner organizations rest. This is what Randall & Short (1983) suggest about the link between OSHA and other official bureaucracies and the media. These agencies are a news beat; they regularly provide the information reporters use to do their work.

Gitlin's (1980) study of how the media covered the New Left and the antiwar movement of the 1960s describes how claims makers who challenge dominant institutions fare in encounters with the media. He studied coverage of antiwar activity by the *New York Times* and CBS News in 1965. When movement spokespersons sought to use the media to convey their views of American society and the war, they found to their dismay that what came out usually gave short shrift to important ideas, but gave full play to conflict, the dramatic, and the bizarre. Individuals in action were important to reporters, who are taught that objectivity and balance are produced by quoting spokespersons for various sides. Gitlin shows how the media created these spokespersons, how they made them "movement leaders" and then celebrities who, overwhelmed by the spotlight, became less concerned with conveying movement claims. The agendas that shape rudimentary news work, then, augur poorly for seriously conveying protest arguments.

Tierney's (1982) research on wife beating reiterates Gitlin's point about what media cover. Wife beating was a topic that was new and controversial, contained violence, was timely and serious, and touched on the familiar themes of feminism, equality, and family life; all of these could still be handled in an entertaining way. Tierney argues that as definitions of wife beating were publicized, social service agencies responded to the conditions described.

Cohn & Gallagher (1984), in the study noted above, detail an incident in which a "conservative" Maine newspaper was involved in a social problem concerning a homosexual group and a planned gay conference at the University of Maine. Fundamentalist ministers attacked the University for allowing the student group on campus and for hosting the conference, after they read about it in the paper (one wonders if a Regents' board meeting was a news beat). The newspaper became a forum for and reporter of the controversy. The editors pursued a delicate balance between their sense of the paper's responsibility to the community, good journalism, and local definitions of the kind of paper theirs was (it did not cause news or stir up trouble). Once the problem developed, it had to be covered, but in a way that would not harm the University and its elite trustees—important figures in the community. By reporting the University's Constitutional defense and the ministers' demands that the University be punished by a legislative budget cut, the paper helped channel the problem. The ministers became the threat against whom the University and community had to be protected.

It is particularly revealing, Cohn & Gallagher say, that, coincidental to this controversy, a major revision of the Maine Criminal Code that decriminalized homosexual intercourse was being voted into law. A second gay conference was planned at the University for a year later. There was no coverage of and virtually no public attention directed to either. Asked about this lack of coverage, editors said that good news stories were about conflict and controversy. There were none around either event; they were not newsworthy. By using these journalistic criteria and their sense of being a responsible paper, editors precluded more social problems concerning homosexuality.

PROBLEMS WITH AND INSIGHTS OF THE PERSPECTIVE

Problems

CONDITIONS AND SOCIAL PROBLEMS   An important source of both confusion and disagreement among those using the constructionist perspective is the question of how conditions should figure in social problems analysis. As Rains (1975) focused attention on the "deviant behavior" that societal reaction theory keeps in the background, there has been much comment on Spector & Kitsuse's argument that conditions, as regarded by the sociologist, are irrelevant to a definitional analysis. That these difficulties beset both the labeling and constructionist perspectives suggests that the confusion is perhaps in part a product of the perspective's requirements.

Woolgar (1983), and Woolgar & Pawluch (1985) appropriately note the tension in some constructionist research between a view that sees the natural world, especially in the form of social context, giving rise to various or alternative accounts of what *is* (the "mediative" position), and the view that these accounts, definitions, and claims are "constitutive" of reality (cf Berger & Luckmann 1966). This is the same tension Rains (1975) identifies in labeling work. The criticism is justified for many of the studies identified as constructionist and discussed here.

Sociologists are members of the society they study. The perspective requires them as analysts to suspend both commonsense commitments about what social problems are—e.g. undesirable conditions—and their own scientific judgments about which claims and definitions about these putative conditions are true. The latter proves to be especially difficult (see Gusfield 1984; Aronson 1984). Moreover, as Gusfield (1984) notes, being on the side (that is, standing aside) in the study of social controversies (especially involving differentially powerful participants) has become professionally unpopular as well as personally unsatisfying.

Social problems participants, however, typically neither treat conditions as putative nor suspend their moral convictions, although the perspective does not preclude this possibility. Instead, they see social problems definitions as reflective of the objective reality (Woolgar 1983) in which the problem resides. The sociologist's problem is to avoid participation and, especially, to avoid defending or challenging claims and definitions about putative conditions. This includes avoiding an ironic stance toward some participants' definitions. Few of the authors considered here maintain this distinction consistently in their research. Some make no attempt to do so, even though they call their work definitional.

CLAIMS, DEFINITIONS, AND VIABILITY   Spector & Kitsuse's emphasis on claims and claims making has been broadened. They encourage this in their examples (how "floods" and "morons" are products of the social problems process) and by use of the word definitional. Clearly, some of the activities studied fit the definition of claim the authors cite (Spector & Kitsuse 1977:78), but much is described more accurately as definitional. Researchers should consider as data all verbal and nonverbal behavior that conveys meaning about the problematic condition or object of attention. The import of language and how it shapes interpretations and conduct is here enormous. Definitional activities should be treated as an inclusive but carefully grounded concept.

The concept *viability,* important to judging social problems development, should be clarified. Spector & Kitsuse say that viable claims and definitions are those that "live" and that claimants can "get away with." A clear definition of viability is necessary for accurate data collection and to compare the development of various problems. Viability is evident when participants give credibility to claims and definitions, when they treat them as valid. Viability is often produced by media coverage. It is produced when officials and professionals warrant definitions, implement them, and accept responsibility for problematic conditions. We need a clearer understanding of precisely how participants' activities affect the viability of claims and definitions.

NATURAL HISTORY   The concept *natural history* is heuristic and directs attention to loose similarities across cases. It leads easily, however, to premature generalization and prediction (R. J. Troyer 1983, unpublished manuscript). Since generalizing is an essential part of scientific work, a cautious strategy would be to examine case studies from similar settings (see Peyrot 1984). One might study problems involving public regulatory bureaucracies. What generalizations might be made about how the news media figure in social problems? What casts of characters emerge at various points in this process? One pitfall to avoid here is the ad hoc, overly topical quality of so much past social problems writing. By using comparative, analytic categories defined by their effects on viability, or examining how the definitional process is moved along by the activities in question (J. I. Kitsuse 1984, personal communication), this might be avoided.

Wiener (1981), in her study of the politics of alcoholism, argues that the sequential aspect of natural history models probably misleads us about the definitional process. She believes a more accurate view is one of "overlapping," simultaneous, "continuously ricocheting interaction" (Wiener 1981:7). A natural history model may encourages us to overstate the extent to which kinds of activities occur only at certain points. This seems likely for Spector & Kitsuse's stage one and stage three activities. Wiener's view reinforces Spector & Kitsuse's argument that the social problems process is open-ended rather than moving to some logical end point (see also Peyrot 1984).

SOCIAL MOVEMENTS SOCIOLOGY VS SOCIAL PROBLEMS SOCIOLOGY?   A recent question is whether or not the definitional perspective on social problems is sufficiently distinct from social movements theory to warrant continued attention. Mauss (1984 and unpublished observations) argues it is not, and that social problems are always outcomes of social movements. To study the latter is to study the former.

R. Troyer (1984, unpublished manuscript) uses both definitional and social movements theory and notes the similarities and differences between the definitional approach, the standard structural social movements view, and the more recent resource mobilization perspective on social movements. A traditional social movements approach (e.g. Smelser 1963), with its emphasis on structural strain (to explain grievances) and on organizational considerations and membership recruitment, is contrasted by Troyer with the constructionist view of social problems. Troyer sees the differences as substantial. He also compares the latter with the resource mobilization view (Oberschall 1973, McCarthy & Zald 1973, 1977). While there are general similarities, resource mobilization's emphasis on structural conditions, social movement organizations, and successful outcomes, and its neglect of meaning lead to research agendas quite distinct from those described here. Rather than argue, as Mauss does, that social problems theory should be subsumed by social movements theory, we might better argue that social movements are an example of the social problems process. Moreover, the topics and data of the research cited here seem to challenge the conclusion that the definitional view simply reproduces social movements research.

Insights

The insights of the constructionist perspective as detailed by Spector & Kitsuse appear intact, criticisms notwithstanding. We can still ask, where is a theoretically integrated, empirically based, original research tradition in social problems sociology prior to the work cited here? Have researchers used the core statements and subsequent research to form new and promising questions, as a sociology of social problems? The work described here seems to support an affirmative reply—quite aside from how this or that study could be improved, or whether elements of the core statements are vague or undeveloped. On the other hand, research based ostensibly on a condition-focused approach, or even on a subjective/objective elements approach to social problems has given us few distinct insights. Like the modest claims made by the founders of labeling theory, the definitional view should be judged more by what it has called for and stimulated than what it ignores. Unlike the labeling tradition, Spector & Kitsuse have proposed bold changes. Rather than offering merely another view of social problems sociology, they and others have launched a new speciality and stimulated a sizeable body of work. Whether or not this work would have been done as social movements, Marxist, or conflict sociology we cannot say.

New questions have been asked about what social problems are and how they should be studied. This approach avoids, moreover, some of the major criticisms of labeling by giving attention to the political and historical quality of collective definitional process, and by rejecting an oversocialized view of deviants as "helpless, hapless" victims (see Conrad & Schneider 1980, Kitsuse 1980; Spector 1981). One who carefully reviews this and similar work can hardly reiterate these familiar criticisms (but see Piven 1981).

The perspective and much of the research reaffirms a major strength of labeling, namely, the independence of meaning from the objects to which it is or may be attached by sentient actors as they create, recreate, and are created by social life (cf Matza, 1969, Giddens 1976). Quite contrary to Piven's critique (1981), actors' agency is the source of social action in the constructionist's world.

Finally, this and future work may breathe new life into deviance sociology, particularly as it breaks down old divisions and creates new, more theoretically coherent ones. What might a sociology of trouble or a sociology of morality look like, distinct from theory and research that concentrate on why people behave in ways that happen to break rules or on the social distribution of this behavior and how to control and punish it? I do not say this pejoratively but rather on the assumption that success in these diverse endeavors might be enhanced if we concentrate on the questions our theories ask and on where these theories are incomplete rather than attacking each other because we pursue different questions.

ACKNOWLEDGMENTS:

This review benefited from conversations with John Kitsuse, Malcolm Spector, and Ronald Troyer. Thanks to them. They of course bear no responsibility for my interpretations.

Literature Cited

Aronson, N. 1982. Nutrition as a social problem: A case study of entrepreneurial strategy in science. *Soc. Probl.* 29:474–86

Aronson, N. 1984. Science as a claims-making activity: Implications for social problems research. In *Studies in the Sociology of Social Problems*, ed. J. W. Schneider, J. I. Kitsuse, pp. 1–30. Norwood, NJ: Ablex

Ball, R. A., Lilly, J. R. 1982. The menace of margarine: The rise and fall of a social problem. *Soc. Probl.* 29:488–98

Ball, R. A., Lilly, J. R. 1984. When is a 'problem' not a problem?: deflection activities in a clandestine motel. See Schneider and Kitsuse 1984, pp. 114–39

Becker, H. S. 1963. *Outsiders*. New York: Free

Becker, H. S., ed. 1966. *Social Problems: A Modern Approach*. New York: Wiley

Becker, H. S. 1967. Whose side are we on? *Soc. Probl.* 14:239–47

Berger, P., Luckmann, T. 1966. *The Social Construction of Reality*. New York: Doubleday

Billings, D. B., Urban, T. 1982. The sociomedical construction of transsexualism: An interpretation and critique. *Soc. Probl.* 29:266–82

Blumer, H. 1971. Social problems as collective behavior. *Soc. Probl.* 18:298–306

Brownmiller, S. 1975. *Against Our Will: Men, Women and Rape*. New York: Simon & Schuster

Calavita, K. 1983. The demise of the Occupational Safety and Health Administration: A case study in symbolic action. *Soc. Probl.* 30:437–48

Chauncey, R. L. 1980. New careers for moral entrepreneurs: Teenage drinking. *J. Drug Issues* 10:45–70

Christie, N. 1977. Conflicts as property. *Br. J. Criminol.* 17:1–15

Cohn, S. F., Gallagher, J. E. 1984. Gay movements and legal change: Some aspects of the dynamics of a social problem. *Soc. Probl.* 32:72–86

Conrad, P. 1975. The discovery of hyperkinesis: Notes on the medicalization of deviant behavior. *Soc. Probl.* 23:12–21

Conrad, P., Schneider, J. W. 1980. *Deviance and Medicalization: From Badness to Sickness*. St. Louis: Mosby

Donnelly, P. G. 1982. The origins of the Occupational Safety and Health Act of 1970. *Soc. Probl.* 30:13–25

Emerson, R. M., Messinger, S. L. 1977. The micro-politics of trouble. *Soc. Probl.* 25:121–35

Fishman, M. 1978. Crime waves as ideology. *Soc. Probl.* 25:531–43

Fishman, M. 1980. *Manufacturing the News*. Austin, Texas: Univ. of Texas Press

Frank, N. 1983. From criminal to civil penalties in the history of health and safety laws. *Soc. Probl.* 30:532–44

Freidson, E. 1970. *Profession of Medicine* New York: Dodd Mead

Fuller, R., Myers, R. 1941a. Some aspects of a theory of social problems. *Am. Sociol. Rev.* 6:24–32

Fuller, R., Myers, R. 1942b. The natural history of a social problem. *Am. Sociol. Rev.* 6:320–28

Galliher, J. F., Walker, A. 1977. The puzzle of the social origins of the Marijuana Tax Act of 1937. *Soc. Probl.* 24:367–76

Ghezzi, S. G. 1983. A private network of social control: Insurance investigation units. *Soc. Probl.* 30:521–31

Giddens, A. 1976. *New Rules of Sociological Method: A Positive Critique of Interpretive Sociologies.* New York: Basic

Gitlin, T. 1980. *The Whole World Is Watching: Mass Media in the Making and Unmaking of the New Left.* Berkeley, Calif: Univ. of Calif. Press

Glasgow University Media Group. 1980. *More Bad News.* London: Routledge & Kegan Paul

Goffman, E. 1959. The moral career of a mental patient. *Psychiatry* 22:123–42

Goffman, E. 1969. The insanity of place. *Psychiatry* 32:357–388

Goldner, F. H. 1982. Pronoia. *Soc. Probl.* 30:82–91

Gusfield, J. 1963. *Symbolic Crusade.* Urbana, Ill: University of Ill. Press

Gusfield, J. 1967. Moral passage: The symbolic process in the public designations of deviance. *Soc. Probl.* 15:175–88

Gusfield, J. 1975. Categories of ownership and responsibility in social issues: Alcohol abuse and automobile use. *J. Drug Issues* 5:285–303

Gusfield, J. 1976. The literary rhetoric of science: Comedy and pathos in drinking driver research. *Am. Sociol. Rev.* 41:16–34

Gusfield, J. 1981. *The Culture of Public Problems: Drinking Driving and the Symbolic Order.* Chicago: Univ. of Chicago Press

Gusfield, J. 1984. On the side: Practical action and social constructivism in social problems theory. See Schneider & Kitsuse pp. 31–51

Hewitt, J. P., Hall, P. M. 1973. Social problems, problematic situations, and quasi-theories. *Am. Sociol. Rev.* 38:367–74

Hughes, E. C. 1971. *The Sociological Eye.* Chicago: Aldine

Joffe, C. 1978. What abortion counselors want from their clients. *Soc. Probl.* 26:112–21

Johnson, M. P., Hufbauer, K. 1982. Sudden infant death syndrome as a medical research problem since 1945. *Soc. Probl.* 30:65–81

Kahne, M. J., Schwartz, C. G. 1978. Negotiating trouble: The social construction and management of trouble in a college psychiatric context. *Soc. Probl.* 25:461–75

Kitsuse, J. I. 1980. Coming out all over: Deviants and the politics of social problems. *Soc. Probl.* 28:1–13

Kitsuse, J. I., Cicourel, A. V. 1963. A note of the uses of official statistics. *Soc. Probl.* 12:131–9

Kitsuse, J. I., Spector, M. 1973. Toward a sociology of social problems: Social conditions, value-judgments, and social problems. *Soc. Probl.* 20:407–19

Kitsuse, J. I., Murase, A. E., Yamamura, Y. 1984. *Kikokushijo:* The emergence and institutionalization of an educational problem in Japan. See Schneider & Kitsuse 1984, pp. 162–79

Latour, B. 1983. Give me a laboratory and I will raise the world. In *Science Observed: Perspectives on the Social Study of Science.* ed. K. D. Knorr-Cetina, M. Mulkay, pp. 141–70. Beverly Hills, Calif.: Sage

Lemert, E. M. 1962. Paranoia and the dynamics of exclusion. *Sociometry* 25:2–20

Loseke, D. L., Cahill, S. E. 1984. The social construction of deviance: Experts on battered women. *Soc. Probl.* 31:296–310

Lynch, M. 1983. Accommodation practices: Vernacular treatments of madness. *Soc. Probl.* 31:152–64

Lynxwiler, J., Shover, N., Clelland, D. A. 1983. The organization and impact of inspector discretion in a regulatory bureaucracy. *Soc. Probl.* 30:425–36

Manis, J. G. 1984. *Serious Social Problems.* Boston: Allyn & Bacon

Markle, G. E., Troyer, R. J. 1979. Smoke gets in your eyes: Cigarette smoking as deviant behavior. *Soc. Probl.* 26:611–25

Matza, D. 1969. *Becoming Deviant.* Englewood Cliffs, NJ: Prentice-Hall

Mauss, A. L. 1975. *Social Problems as Social Movements.* Philadelphia: Lippincott

Mauss, A. L. 1984. The myth of social problems theory. *Social Problems Theory Division Newsletter.* Summer, 1984. Buffalo, NY: Society for the Study of Social Problems

Maynard, D. W. 1982. Defendant attributes in plea bargaining: Notes on the modeling of sentencing decisions. *Soc. Probl.* 29:347–60

McCarthy, J. D. Zald, M. N. 1973. *The Trend of Social Movements in America: Professionalization and Resource Mobilization.* Morristown, NJ: General Learning Press

McCarthy, J. D. Zald, M. N. 1977. Resource mobilization and social movements: A partial theory. *Am. J. Sociol.* 82:1212–41

McCleary, R., Nienstedt, B. C., Erven, J. M. 1982. Uniform crime reports as organizational outcomes: Three time series experiments. *Soc. Probl.* 29:361–72

McCrea, F. B. 1983. The politics of menopause: The "discovery" of a deficiency disease. *Soc. Probl.* 31:111–23

Merton, R. K., Nisbet, eds. 1971. *Contemporary Social Problems.* New York: Harcourt Brace Jovanovich

Miller, G. 1983. Holding clients accountable: The micro-politics of trouble in a work incentive program. *Soc. Probl.* 31:139–51

Murray, G. L. 1982. The abolition of *el cortito,* the short-handled hoe: A case study in social conflict and state policy in California agriculture. *Soc. Probl.* 30:26–39

Nuehring, E., Markle, G. E. 1974. Nicotine and norms: The re-emergence of a deviant behavior. *Soc. Probl.* 21:513–26

Oberschall, A. 1973. *Social Conflicts and Social Movements.* Englewood Cliffs, NJ: Prentice-Hall

Pawluch, D. 1983. Transitions in pediatrics: A segmental analysis. *Soc. Probl.* 30:449–65

Peyrot, M. 1982. Caseload management: Choosing suitable clients in a community mental health agency. *Soc. Probl.* 30:157–67

Peyrot, M. 1984. Cycles of social problem development: The case of drug abuse. *Sociol. Q.* 25:83–96

Pfohl, S. J. 1977. The "discovery" of child abuse. *Soc. Probl.* 24:310–23

Piven, F. F. 1981. Deviant behavior and the remaking of the world. *Soc. Probl.* 28:489–508

Pontell, H. N., Jesilow, P. D., Geis, G. 1982. Policing physicians: Practitioner fraud and abuse in a government medical program. *Soc. Probl.* 30:117–25

Rains, P. 1975. Imputations of deviance: A retrospective essay on the labeling perspective. *Soc. Probl.* 23:1–11

Randall, D. M., Short, J. F. 1983. Women in toxic work environments: A case study of social problem development. *Soc. Probl.* 30:410–24

Reich, C. A. 1964. The new property. *Yale Law J.* 73:733–87

Riessman, C. K. 1983. Women and medicalization: A new perspective. *Soc. Policy* 14:3–18

Rose, V. M. 1977. Rape as a social problem: A byproduct of the feminist movement. *Soc. Probl.* 25:75–89

Ross, R., Staines, G. L. 1971. The politics of analyzing social problems. *Soc. Probl.* 18:18–40

Sampson, H., Messinger, S. L., Towne, R. D. 1962. Family processes and becoming a mental patient. *Am. J. Sociol.* 68:88–96

Schneider, J. W. 1978. Deviant drinking as disease: Alcoholism as a social accomplishment. *Soc. Probl.* 25:361–72

Schneider, J. W. 1984. Morality, social problems, and everyday life. See Schneider & Kitsuse 1984, pp. 180–205

Schneider, J. W., Conrad, P. 1980. The medical control of deviance: Contests and consequences. *Research in the Sociology of Health Care* 1:1–53. Greenwich, Conn: JAI

Schneider, J. W., Kitsuse, J. I., eds. 1984. *Studies in the Sociology of Social Problems.* Norwood, NJ: Ablex

Schwartz, C. G., Kahne, M. J. 1983. Medical help as negotiated achievement. *Psychiatry* 46:333–50

Shearing, C. D., Stenning, P. C. 1983. Private security: Implications for social control. *Soc. Probl.* 30:493–506

Smelser, N. J. 1963. *Theory of Collective Behavior.* New York: Free

Spector, M. 1977. Legitimizing homosexuality. *Society* 14:20–24

Spector, M. 1981. Beyond crime: Seven methods to control troublesome rascals. In *Law and Deviance.* H. L. Ross, ed., pp. 127–157. Beverly Hills, Calif: Sage.

Spector, M., Batt, S. 1983. *Toward a more active victim.* Unpublished manuscript. Department of Sociology, McGill University, Montreal, Quebec, Canada

Spector, M., Kitsuse, J. I. 1973. Social problems: A reformulation. *Soc. Probl.* 20:145–59

Spector, M., Kitsuse, J. I. 1977. *Constructing Social Problems.* Menlo Park, Calif: Cummings

Spencer, J. W. 1983. Accounts, attitudes, and solutions: Probation officer-defendant negotiations of subjective orientations. *Soc. Probl.* 30:570–81

Tallman, I., McGee, R. 1971. Definition of a social problem. In *Handbook of the Study of Social Problems,* E. Smigel, ed., pp. 19–59. Chicago: Rand McNally

Tierney, K. J. 1982. The battered women movement and the creation of the wife beating problem. *Soc. Probl.* 29:207–20

Troyer, R. J., Markle, G. E. 1983. *Cigarettes: The Battle Over Smoking.* New Brunswick, NJ: Rutgers University Press

Troyer, R. J., Markle, G. E. 1984. Coffee drinking: An emerging social problem? *Soc. Probl.* 31:403–16

Waller, W. 1936. Social problems and the mores. *Am. Sociol. Rev.* 1:922–34

Weitz, R. 1984. From accommodation to rebellion: Tertiary deviance and the radical redefinition of lesbianism. See Schneider & Kitsuse 1984, pp. 140–61

Wiener, C. 1981. *The Politics of Alcoholism: Building an Arena Around a Social Problem.* New Brunswick: Transaction

Woolgar, S. 1983. Irony in the social study of science. In *Science Observed: Perspectives on the Social Study of Science.* K. D. Knorr-Cetina, M. Mulkay (eds.), pp. 239–66. Beverly Hills, Calif: Sage

Woolgar, S., Pawluch, D. 1985. Ontological gerrymandering: The anatomy of social problems explanations. *Soc. Probl.* 32: (forthcoming)

Yarrow, M. R., Schwartz, C. G., Murphy, H. S., Deasy, L. C. 1955. The psychological meaning of mental illness in the family. *J. Soc. Issues* 11:12–24

Zola, I. K. 1972. Medicine as an institution of social control. *Sociol. Rev.* 20:487–504

Ann. Rev. Sociol. 1985. 11:231–58

URBAN POVERTY

William Julius Wilson and Robert Aponte

Department of Sociology, University of Chicago, 1126 East 59th Street, Chicago, Illinois 60637

Abstract

This chapter is a state of the art review of the research and theoretical writing on urban poverty. We reveal that there has been an ebb and flow in the study of urban poverty in America. The social reform movement of early twentieth century, responding to the dislocation that accompanied rapid industrialization, prompted a number of descriptive and muckraking studies of poverty in urban areas. At roughly the same time, sociologists at the University of Chicago conducted a prodigious volume of research on urban life, including a number of ethnographic studies on poverty that were far more analytical and systematic than those of the social reformers. However, by the late 1930s scholarly research on urban poverty was on the wane, only to be revived again in the 1960s following the rediscovery of poverty and the emergence of the Great Society program.

We point out that the subject of urban poverty and the structure of the family has drawn considerable attention from researchers since the mid-1960s and has helped to raise the level of national interest in the problems of the inner city and the crystallization of a sizable ghetto underclass. It is emphasized, however, that with the emergence of longitudinal data sets many assumptions about the intergenerational transmission of poverty and persistent poverty in the inner city have been challenged. We furthermore maintain that research on urban poverty and migration has raised questions and generated new insights on the contribution of the urban migrant to the current problems of inner-city poverty and social dislocations; and that several recent studies, possibly representing a trend in urban poverty research, have provided significant insights on the relationship between poverty and welfare dependency. However, we point out that since the results of the public policy research are so mixed, it would be risky to draw policy recommendations from them. On the other hand, the most recent studies of the effects of the Reagan budget cuts (the Omnibus Budget Reconciliation Act of 1981) on the working

0360-0572/85/0815-0231$02.00

poor are clear and consistent: they reveal the nature of the federal government's dramatic retreat from the Great Society programs of the 1960s.

INTRODUCTION

Before the Civil War poverty was not widely recognized as a social problem in the United States. The prevalent attitude was that personal misfortunes were personal affairs, that poverty was an individual problem that neither could nor should be alleviated by society. Thus, people unable to make it in the East were advised to go West; the general feeling was that individuals had only themselves to blame if they were mired in poverty. In a largely rural society provided with an abundance of vacant fertile land, this view could be developed and sustained. However, the dislocations that accompanied industrialization in the post-Civil War period prompted changes in this attitude. In the face of massive unemployment, poor working conditions, inadequate wages, and inferior housing, preindustrial conceptions of poverty eroded and efforts to combat these problems evolved into major social reforms. They included the regulation of working hours, working conditions, and the employment of children. Laws were passed pertaining to public health and housing, as well. By the turn of the century, social reform was a dominant theme in the fight against poverty (Bremner 1956, Miller 1966).

A number of early descriptive studies of urban poverty emanated from this social reform movement. Most notable were Jacob Riis's (1890) vivid description of life in the tenements of New York, and Jane Addams's (1902) and Sophonsiba Breckenridge's (1936) works on poverty and housing in Chicago. Although these studies detailed the deleterious conditions of urban poverty, they provided little in the way of analytical insights on the relationship between poverty and the social organization of an industrializing society. However, appearing at roughly the same time as these fact-finding social reform inquiries were a series of ethnographic studies on urban life conducted by sociologists at the University of Chicago. In 1918, W. I. Thomas collaborated with Florian Znaniecki in publishing the first volume of a classic five-volume work, *The Polish Peasant* (1918–20). This work plus the research of Robert E. Park (1925) on human behavior in an urban environment helped to establish Chicago as the main center of urban sociological research in the earlier twentieth century. A good deal of this research focused on urban poverty and related problems (Anderson 1923, 1940; Thrasher 1927; Wirth 1928; Zorbaugh 1929; Frazier 1932; Sutherland & Locke 1936; Faris & Dunham 1931). Although many of the Chicago studies incorporated data collected by the social reformers, their discussions of urban poverty were informed by sociological insights into the nature and processes of urban life in a changing industrial society (Suttles 1976).

However, the early interest in urban poverty research was not sustained despite the heightened public awareness of poverty generated by the Depression of the 1930s, and the nationwide discussion and debate concerning the New Deal antipoverty programs (e.g. Aid to Dependent Children, unemployment compensation, social security, and old age assistance). By the late 1930s, scholarly research on urban poverty and social dislocation was on the wane. Ironically, "the Depression had the effect of arresting some of the questions that had given urban ethnography its impetus," argued Gerald Suttles. "Contemporary poverty and social disorder, and the reason for them, were so obviously social in origin that there was little mystery that would incline ethnographers to go into our cities as if they were almost foreign lands. Ethnography became mostly something done by anthropologists, and that mostly in genuinely foreign and obscure places" (1976:7). Furthermore, in the 1930s urban ethnographic studies began to compete with, and in the 1940s eventually gave way to, studies that employed more sophisticated techniques of data gathering and analysis. In short, the decline of urban ethnography amounted to a decline in the study of urban poverty. But there were other factors involved in the shift away from poverty studies. The onset of World War II created interest in issues other than poverty; and the generally prosperous decade of the 1950s was hardly a stimulus to social scientists and policymakers to recognize and address the problems of a growing concentration of citizens in our nation's central city slums and ghettos.

REDISCOVERY OF POVERTY

If interest in the fate of the poor declined following World War II, in the late 1950s and early 1960s there was notable political activity in behalf of disadvantaged groups even though the issue of poverty was not explicitly raised. Following the 1954 Supreme Court Decision on school segregation, President Eisenhower sent national guardsmen into Little Rock, Arkansas, in 1957 to force compliance with that decision, and the United States Congress passed the first civic rights law in eighty years. In 1959, the Kerrs-Mills Act increased funds for health care for the aged; in 1961, President John F. Kennedy approved a pilot food stamp program and expanded and liberalized the surplus commodity program; and in 1962 Congress passed the Manpower Development and Training Act and soon broadened its coverage to include the disadvantaged (Plotnick & Skidmore 1975).

By 1963 the issue of poverty began to receive explicit attention in the New Frontier administration of John F. Kennedy with the recognition "that public receptiveness to the issues of poverty amid plenty could provide a rallying point for the coming election of 1964" (Plotnick & Skidmore 1975:2). In May 1963, Walter Heller, Chairman of President Kennedy's Council of Economic Advisors, wrote a memorandum to the President and concluded that certain large segments of the poor population (families headed by women, the aged, and the disabled) would remain poor even if full employment in the economy were reached. In response to this memorandum President Kennedy instructed his executive agency heads to develop a case for a major policy effort to confront poverty. That fall, he requested that antipoverty proposals be included in the legislative program of 1964 (Plotnick and Skidmore 1975).

After the assassination of President Kennedy in late 1963, the interest in poverty at the Federal level was sustained by Lyndon Baines Johnson. His 1964 economic report included a detailed statement on poverty in the United States and a number of proposals for attacking poverty. The report was followed by the creation of an independent agency within the House to draft a bill consistent with the ideas expressed in the economic report. In 1964, the War on Poverty was officially approved by Congress with emphasis on job-training programs, and community participation and development (Plotnick & Skidmore 1975).

This rediscovery of poverty by officials at the federal level and the emergence of the Great Society programs occurred, paradoxically, during an era of general prosperity and economic growth. Following the publication of John Kenneth Galbraith's (1958) classic study, *The Affluent Society,* generally acknowledged as providing the initial impetus to the revival of interest in poverty, came Michael Harrington's (1962) celebrated work, *The Other America.* It was Harrington's passionate portrayal of poverty in America that actually launched the poverty problem prominently into the public consciousness. Stimulated by Galbraith's study, Harrington argued that at least 40 million, or a fifth of the population, was poor; that much of this population was invisible partly because it included large proportions of children and the elderly (groups unlikely to stray far from home) as well as nonwhites (who were being increasingly isolated in urban ghettos); that motivational deficiencies (e.g., fatalistic attitudes) resulting from prolonged poverty were impeding the economic advancement of the poor; and, therefore, that poverty had become a vicious cycle for millions of Americans.

According to Dorothy Buchton James (1972), the studies by Galbraith and Harrington spurred Kennedy's administration to formulate proposals to combat the problems of poverty in America. Sundquist (1969), an administration insider, suggests that these works helped the Kennedy team to see poverty as underlying a number of other social ills (e.g. juvenile delinquency, illiteracy, urban blight) that were being unsuccessfully addressed by government programs at that time. However, it would be a mistake to assume that the emergence of the Great Society was due solely to thoughtful studies of the American poor. Sundquist (1969) is careful to note that during the early 1960s the timing and intellectual climate were right for new ideas and new approaches to the study of poverty and related social problems. The high level of confidence in social science theorizing and empirical research in the 1960s resulted in an unprecedented incorporation of the ideas of social scientists in the federal antipoverty thrust (Moynihan 1970; Friedman 1977; Aaron 1978).

Even more significantly, a budget surplus existed in the early 1960s and economists then predicted, in the face of widespread optimism about economic growth, that it would rise steadily throughout the latter part of the decade. Indeed, federal revenues were increasing so rapidly that many economists (not anticipating the Vietnam War buildup) were fearful that the growing tax surplus would ultimately slow economic growth if new expenditures could not be generated to reduce the surplus (Moynihan 1970). Finally, as Friedman (1977) and Aaron (1978) have argued, the great power of the presidency, at a peak under the early Johnson administration, was also an important element in the federal antipoverty initiatives. According to Aaron (1978:150–151), the combination of the death of Johnson's predecessor and the weakness of his opponent "led to the electoral landslide of 1964. The nature and quantity of legislation dealing with poverty . . . that followed were determined in no small measure by the political adroitness of the new president."

The foregoing arguments collectively represent the "conventional view" on the rediscovery of poverty and the emergence of the Great Society programs. It should be noted that little attention was given to the importance of the civil rights movement and the heightened public awareness of poverty and related problems in the inner city. Moynihan (1968), Sundquist (1969), Yarmolinsky (1969), and Levine (1970) argue that although there was some discussion of the problems of black poverty, the focus of attention shortly before and immediately after the assassination of President John F. Kennedy was disproportionately on white Appalachian poverty.

However, several other writers, representing divergent views and philosophies (Glazer 1965; Raab 1966; Levitan 1969; Levine 1970; Piven & Cloward 1971), attribute greater significance to issues of race in the development of the War on Poverty. Nathan Glazer (1965:20), for example, argues forcefully that "the race problem" was "the chief reason why poverty has become a major issue in this country . . . it is true that the statistics show that only one quarter of the poor . . . are Negroes. But this . . . is in part a statistical artifact. The poorest, as defined by the public assistance rolls, are in much larger proportion Negro, Mexican American, and Puerto Rican. It is the civil rights revolution that makes poverty a great issue in America, not merely poverty." Furthermore, Levitan (1969:15) suggests that "the civil rights movement, which had become a potent power by 1963, could have supplied the political pressure for a program in aid of the poor." Moreover, Raab (1966) notes that even before the antipoverty legislation was passed in 1964 there were discussions with city representatives on the central involvement of racial and ethnic communities. Finally, Piven & Cloward (1971), in their elaborate and controversial thesis, argue that the federal antipoverty program was an attempt to foster the political allegiance of ghetto residents.

The preceding arguments reveal the complexity of the events leading to the rediscovery of poverty and the emergence of the Great Society programs. Until a definitive social history of these developments is established, perhaps the most judicious approach is to consider the merits of all of these arguments as background information for understanding the nature and direction of the proliferation of urban poverty research since the mid-1960s.

THE RESURGENCE OF POVERTY RESEARCH

As we indicated in a previous section, there was virtually no poverty research in the scholarly community during the post–World War II period. Indeed, the dearth of research was so pronounced that in the early months of the Johnson administration a task force assembled to study the problem of poverty in America began "almost from scratch" and had to rely upon a bibliography running "less than two pages" (Yarmolinsky 1969:37). So little research had been conducted that "when the poverty issue arose," states Bell (1968:163), "nobody was really prepared, nobody had any data, nobody knew what to do" (cited in Patterson 1981:78).

Yet, after the issue of poverty reached the public consciousness and especially after the campaign against poverty was launched by the federal government, research mushroomed dramatically. A turning point seems to be 1965. Prior to that year, only a handful of publications on poverty were available, many were government documents (e.g., Lampman 1959, Orshansky 1963, 1965), and most were post-1960 products. But, after 1965, an explosion of research occurred. For example, a study by Kerbo (1981) revealed that the number of articles on poverty published annually in five prestigious sociology journals increased from three in 1965 to an average of ten a year in the early 1970s. In 1966, a journal, *Poverty and Human Resources Abstract,* devoted to studies of poverty was created (the word 'poverty' was dropped from the title in 1975 at a time of declining interest in poverty). Conferences with a poverty theme proliferated throughout the late 1960s and generated numerous publications (Gordon 1965, Fishman 1966, Burns 1968). Issues of intense interest and contention at that time include the controversy over the "culture of poverty" thesis (Lewis 1966, Valentine 1968), and the debate over the disintegration of the black family (Moynihan 1965, Rainwater & Yancey 1967). Research on how poverty related to education, health, housing, the law, and public welfare were also vigorously pursued. Moreover, a substantial number of studies were published on the research, development, and evaluation of federal antipoverty initiatives (Aaron 1978). Indeed, a comprehensive bibliography of poverty studies centered on the 1960s filled well over 500 printed pages, and most of the entries were published toward the latter years of the decade (Tompkins 1970).

DEFINING AND MEASURING POVERTY

The resurgence of scholarly attention to poverty in America is also reflected in the increased attention to problems of definition and adequate measurement of the concept 'poverty.' The official poverty line, formulated in 1964 by the Social Security Administration, was drawn by combining a set of rock-bottom food allowances (i.e. cheapest costs of feeding a given family yearly) with estimated proportions of yearly family income directed to food purchasing. Except for a few modifications, such as pegging changes in the poverty schedules to general inflation, the official poverty line has remained fundamentally as originally formulated. Despite its widespread use, the official poverty statistic has come under heavy criticism in the literature. The most often cited criticism is that in-kind government transfers are not considered as income in computing the poverty line. A recent government publication (US Bureau of the Census 1984a), produced specifically to address this issue, indicates that the inclusion of in-kind income reduces the official 1982 poverty figure, at most, by about one-third (from 34.4 to 22.9 million persons). Yet even this figure could be substantially reduced if adjusted for underreporting of income.

However, other critics suggest that the official poverty statistic understates the problem. Some writers (Huber 1974, Korpi 1980) argue that an "absolute" poverty line (i.e., changing only with inflation) is fundamentally inappropriate because even though the poverty schedules rise with inflation, they remain fixed in constant dollars. In times of economic growth, this neglects the rising real incomes of the nonpoor, thereby allowing for a greater gap between the standard of living of the poor and the nonpoor. Other writers maintain that the poverty schedules are far too stringent to be taken seriously. They remind us that the poverty thresholds were initially based on an "economy" food budget deemed sufficient to maintain individuals only through "temporary" or "emergency" times (Rodgers 1979, Perlman 1976). Rodgers (1978) points out that the 1975 poverty line for a nonfarm family of four was drawn at $5,500. That same year the Bureau of Labor Statistics, which also generates yearly series on the costs of living, found that a "moderate" lifestyle for a nonfarm family of four would require $15,138, whereas an "austere" standard of living called for as much as $8,588. As Schiller (1976:21) succinctly put it: "The line we have drawn separating the poor from the nonpoor does not indicate what is enough—it only asserts with confidence what is too little."

It could be argued that the two most recognized shortcomings of the poverty figures, the omission of in-kind income and the stringency of the income cutoffs, counteract one another. Few analysts take both problems into account when adjusting the poverty figure. Generally, only the omission of in-kind income is adjusted for. However, a recent government study to assess the impact of in-kind transfers on poverty contains statistics for 1979 to 1983 that allow the consideration of both problems simultaneously (US Bureau of the Census 1984a). This study demonstrates that raising the income cutoffs by 25% and adjusting for the impact of in-kind income by the method of estimation most favorable to poverty reduction—the "market value" approach which assigns the highest values to in-kind transfers—would result in only a slight decrease in the poverty figures for 1979 and 1980, and an actual *increase* of 5% and 4.5% in 1981 and 1982 respectively. Thus, on balance, it would appear that the extent of poverty is not exaggerated by the official poverty formula. Furthermore, in spite of its flaws, it yields an accurate account of gross trends over time; retains the strengths of wide recognition, public access, and extensive use; and provides a rich array of detailed series such as poverty trends by race, residence and family type.

THE URBANIZATION OF POVERTY

On the basis of the official definition of poverty, the number of poor persons in the United States decreased from 39.5 million in 1959 to 25.4 million in 1968, a reduction of 36%. During this same period the proportion of persons living in poverty dropped from 22% in 1959 to 12.8% in 1968, that is, by nearly half. Because the total population in the United States steadily increased during these nine years, the absolute decrease in the *number* of those in poverty produced an even greater decline in the *proportion* of poor persons (Downs 1970).

In metropolitan areas the number of poor persons dropped by 24%, from 17 million in 1959 to 12.9 million in 1968. Moreover, the proportion of individuals below the poverty level decreased from 15.3% in 1959 to 10% in 1968 (or by 35%). Record levels of economic prosperity in the 1960s combined with a number of public policies to combat poverty effectively reduced the number of poor persons both in and outside of metropolitan areas.

However, the sharp decline in both the absolute number and the relative proportion of the poor did not extend beyond the 1960s (US Bureau of the Census, 1984b). Indeed the number and proportion of poor people actually increased respectively from 24.1 million (12.1%) in 1969 to 34.4 million (15%) in 1982. Nonetheless, changes in the incidence of poverty have been conspicuously uneven when metropolitan areas are compared with nonmetropolitan areas. The number and proportion of poor people in nonmetropolitan areas continued to decline from 1969 to 1979—from 11 million (17.9%) in 1969 to 9.9 million (13.8%) in 1979—but increased to 13.2 million (17.8%) by 1982. In contrast, the number of poor people in metropolitan areas increased steadily from 13.1 million in 1969 to 21.2 million in 1982 (a 62% increase), and the proportion of persons in poverty rose from 9.5 percent to 13.6 percent (a 43% gain), with a substantial part of this increase occurring between 1979 and 1982.

The central cities accounted for most of the metropolitan increase in poverty. The number of central city poor climbed from 8 million in 1969 to 12.7 million in 1982 (or by 59%), while the proportion in poverty increased from 12.7 to 19.9 (or by 57%). Accordingly, to say that poverty has become increasingly urbanized is to note a *remarkable change in the concentration of poor people in the United States in only slightly more than a decade*. It is significant to note that during this period poverty rose among both urban blacks and whites. Specifically, while the number of poor central-city blacks increased by 74% (from 3.1 million in 1969 to 5.4 million in 1982), the number of poor central-city whites increased by 42% (from 4.8 to 6.8 million). And while the proportion of central-city blacks in poverty increased by 52% (from 24.3 to 36.9), the proportion of poor central-city whites increased by 49% (from 9.7 to 14.5) (US Bureau of the Census, 1984b).

However, these figures do not reveal some fundamental transformations in the makeup and characteristics of the urban poverty population, transformations that have been the subject of a number of research studies including those that detected the beginnings of a qualitative shift in urban poverty in the mid-1960s.

URBAN POVERTY AND THE STRUCTURE OF THE FAMILY

Although the official poverty figures show that whites constitute a majority of the poor population, even in urban areas, many of the social dislocations related to poverty (e.g. crime, out-of-wedlock births, female-headed families, and welfare dependency) reflect a sharply uneven distribution by race (Wilson 1984b). This is most clearly revealed in the studies on the changing relationship between urban poverty and family structure.

The subject of urban poverty and family structure became a topic of widespread discussion and debate following the release of Daniel Patrick Moynihan's (1965) report on the Negro family. Moynihan (1965:5–6) argued that "the Negro community is dividing between a stable middle-class group that is steadily growing stronger and more successful and an increasingly disorganized and disadvantaged lower-class group." He stressed that the disintegration of the black family—as seen in the increasing rates of marital dissolution, female-headed homes, out-of-wedlock births, and welfare dependency among urban blacks—was one of the central problems plaguing the black lower class. And he argued that the problems of the lower-class black family, which seriously impeded the black movement toward equality, stemmed from previous patterns of racial oppression that began with slavery and were sustained by years of discrimination. Moynihan concluded his report by recommending a shift in the focus of civil rights activities to "bring the Negro American to full and equal sharing in the responsibilities and rewards of citizenship" and thereby to increase the "stability and resources of the Negro American family" (1965:48). Although the report integrated familiar themes (cf. Frazier 1939, Clark 1965, Rainwater 1966, Rustin 1965), it nonetheless drew fire from many outraged parties—see Rainwater & Yancey (1967) for a chronology of the controversy. However, aside from some problems in historical accounting (cf. Gutman 1976), Moynihan's analysis proved to be prophetic.

In 1960 22% of all black families were headed by a woman, by 1982 that figure had climbed to 42% (US Bureau of the Census 1983). Furthermore, as Moynihan suggested, the problem is concentrated in urban areas. In 1982, 81% of all black female–headed families with children resided in metropolitan areas, and of these, 77% were inner-city residents. Furthermore, almost half (49.5%) of all metropolitan black families with children were female headed, and in the inner cities of these metropolises, well over half (54%) were (US Bureau of the Census, 1983). Moreover, 57% of all metropolitan black female headed families were officially poor in 1982. Finally, 81% of all central-city poor black children under age 18 and 81% under age six lived in female-headed households in 1982 (US Bureau of the Census, 1984b).

The increase in the number of female-headed families, as Moynihan suggested, partially reflects the increasing incidence of out-of-wedlock births. Despite a decline in the illegitimacy rate (i.e., the number of births per 1,000 unmarried black women) since well before 1960, the proportion of black babies born outside of marriage (the illegitimacy ratio) increased from 15% in 1959 to 56% in 1981 (National Center for Health Statistics 1968, 1983). In 1982 the number of out-of-wedlock black births (328,879) nearly matched the number of illegitimate white births (337,050) (Wilson 1984a). "White or black, the women bearing these children are not always mature adults. Almost half of all illegitimate children born to blacks today will have a teenager for a mother" (Wilson 1984a:92). Research, not surprisingly, reveals a strong connection between out-of-wedlock births and welfare dependency. One study (Moore & Caldwell 1976) estimates that, nationwide, about 60% of the children born out-of-wedlock and not adopted receive welfare.

Although serious scholarship on these sensitive issues was temporally curtailed during the aftermath of the controversy over the Moynihan Report (Wilson 1984b), a number of studies have addressed issues that relate either directly or indirectly to the Report. In the late 1960s and early 1970s the focus of attention was on family life style (Hannerz 1969; Heiss 1972; Liebow 1967; Rainwater 1970; Schulz 1968, 1969; Stack 1974), the question of a matriarchal subculture among blacks (Berger & Simon 1974; Hyman & Reed 1969; Rosen 1969; Yancey 1972), and the effects of absent fathers on the well-being of offspring (Hartnagel 1970; Hunt & Hunt 1975; Ladner 1973; Rosen 1969; Rosenberg & Simmons 1972). A recurrent theme in this literature is that the disorganization of urban black families in poverty is not a function of any inherent matriarchal tendency, but a rational, adaptational response to conditions of deprivation (see especially Liebow 1967; Stack 1974).

The most recent studies on black female-headed families are largely unconcerned with questions about black matriarchy or adaptation. Rather, they give more attention to the strong association between female-headed families and poverty (Auletta 1982; Farley & Bianchi 1982; McLanahan 1983; Pearce 1978, 1983; Wilson 1984a, 1984b; Wilson & Neckerman 1984)); to the effects of family disorganization on children (Earl & Lohmann 1978, Kellam et al 1977, McLanahan, 1983); to demographic and socioeconomic factors that are correlated with different single parent statuses—separated, divorced, and never married (Ross & Sawhill 1975; Bane & Ellwood 1984a, 1984b); to empirical variables (rates of contraception, frequency of premarital sex, indices of deprivation, etc.) that predict different rates of illegitimacy among different groups (Hogan & Kitagawa 1983; Hogan, Astone & Kitagawa 1984), and to the connection between the economic status of black men and the rise in black female headed families (Joe 1984a; Wilson & Neckerman 1984).

In short, this collection of studies has shown that female-headed families are heavily represented in the poverty population, are highly urbanized, and are disproportionately black; that black female heads are much less likely to marry if single, or to remarry if divorced or widowed, and therefore that female headed families among whites tend to be of relatively short duration, whereas among blacks they tend to be prolonged; that teenage pregnancies are strongly associated with being reared in female-headed families, poverty, and ghetto residence; that black children are increasingly growing up in families without fathers not only because more black women are getting divorced, separated, or are becoming widows, but also because more black women are not marrying; and that the increasing joblessness of black men is one of the major reasons black women tend not to be married. This research strongly suggests that the urban core has spawned a sizable and growing black underclass of marginally productive and unattached men, and of women and children in female-headed homes. How well this view is upheld by the recent longitudinal survey research is a subject to which we now turn.

THE UNDERCLASS, INTERGENERATIONAL TRANSMISSION OF POVERTY, AND PERSISTENT POVERTY

Although the subject of poverty and socioeconomic mobility had been discussed in a number of earlier studies (Morgan et al 1962; Blau & Duncan 1967; Galloway 1966; Thernstrom 1968; Schiller 1970), the problems of intergenerational and persistent poverty did not receive detailed empirical and systematic attention until it became possible to track the actual experiences of poor individuals over time with adequate longitudinal data such as that provided by the Michigan Panel Study of Income Dynamics (PSID). Using data from the PSID for the years 1968 to 1976, Levy (1980) examined the poverty status, receipt of welfare, and labor-market characteristics of young adults who had been teenagers living at home at the outset of the survey, but who had formed independent households by the last year of the survey. Levy found only weak support for the arguments that poverty and welfare dependency were transmitted across generations. Only three of every ten young adults reared in poverty homes, compared to one of ten reared in nonpoverty homes, set up poverty households on their own; even using the "worst case" background situation (being black and reared in a low-income, welfare-supported, female-headed household), the probability of a young woman forming her own welfare dependent household was only about one in three.

The issues of intergenerational transmission of poverty and welfare were also explored, using a fourteen-year segment of the Michigan PSID, by Hill & Ponza (1983a, 1983b). Drawing from a sample of offspring who were living with panel families in 1968 but had formed their own households by 1981, these authors found "a great deal of income mobility from one generation to the next, even among the poorest households" (1983a:64). Although there is an association between the economic circumstances of the parents and those of the children, Hill & Ponza report that there is only a very limited form of intergenerational transmission of long-term welfare dependency among whites and none among blacks; and that "parental attitudes and values had little effect on children's later economic outcomes and welfare dependence" (1983a:64).

However, McLanahan (1983), who used ten years of data from the PSID to examine the relationship between family structure and the reproduction of persistent poverty, reinforced the intergenerational transmission of poverty thesis by finding that regardless of parent's race, education, or place of residence, children who lived in female-headed households were significantly more likely to have dropped out of high school than those who lived in husband-wife households. The major reason for this relationship was not the long-term absence of a male role model, but the income differences that exist between female-headed and married-couple families.

Perhaps the most surprising findings from the research based on the PSID data are those involving the issue of persistent poverty (Coe 1978, Hill 1981, Corcoran et al 1983). One essential conclusion of this work is that a considerably smaller proportion of Americans in poverty are persistently poor, year in and year out, than the poverty statistics imply. For example, using the official definition of poverty, Coe (1978) found only 1% and Hill (1981) only 3% of the population to be poor throughout the time span (nine and ten years, respectively) of their studies; and Corcoran et al found only 2.2% of the population to be poor eight of the ten years (1968–78) that covered their PSID Time span. Moreover, the Corcoran et al findings indicate that although 62% of the persistently poor are black and 61% are members of female-headed households, the proportion of the persistently poor residing in large cities is substantially smaller than the proportion of those living is rural areas or small towns.

If students of poverty question whether or not these findings really reflect the depths of the problems of persistent poverty in urban America, they are provided with powerful ammunition from two PSID studies by Bane & Ellwood (1983a, 1983b). These authors point out that other studies using PSID data to determine the length of time that people are in poverty or on welfare normally observe the poor or welfare recipients over a fixed time frame—say, eight or ten years—and then ascertain what proportion was poor or on welfare for a specific period (1, 2, 5, or 10 years) during this time frame. However, they emphasize that this approach fails to take account of the fact that some individuals who appear to have short spells of poverty or welfare dependency are actually *beginning or ending long spells*. Thus, describing them as having short spells of poverty or welfare dependency can lead both to underestimations of the average length of their spells and to inaccurate descriptions of the characteristics of those who are experiencing either short-term or long-term spells.

By estimating the duration of spells from ten years of PSID data with a special methodology (that identifies spells of poverty or of welfare, calculates exit probabilities by year, and uses these probabilities "to generate distributions of spell length for new spells, and for completed and uncompleted spells observed at a point in time" [1983a:10]), Bane & Ellwood found that although most people who become poor at some point in their lives endure poverty for only one or two years, *a substantial subpopulation remains poor for a very long time*. Indeed, their findings indicate that at any given point in time, these long-term poor represent about 60% of the poverty population and are in the midst of a poverty spell that will last at least eight years. These conclusions are similar to those reported in their study of "welfare spells" (1983b). This latter study revealed that even though most AFDC mothers experience brief spells of welfare dependency, "the bulk of person-years of AFDC receipt and the bulk of the AFDC expenditures are accounted for by women who have spells of eight years or more" (1983b:ii). These long-term welfare mothers tend to be non-whites, unwed, and high school dropouts.

Thus, despite the optimistic findings that characterize some of the reports based on the PSID data (Hill & Ponza 1983a, 1983b; Corcoran et al 1983), there is still a firm basis for accepting the notion that a ghetto underclass has emerged and embodies the problems of long-term poverty and welfare dependency (cf. Wilson 1984b; Ball-Rokeach & Short 1985).

URBAN POVERTY AND MIGRATION

The relationship between migration and the emergence of an urban underclass has received a good deal of attention in the sociological literature. One of the major questions discussed is the extent to which joblessness and related problems, such as rising welfare expenditures, are associated with in-migration of the poor (Beale 1971; Piven & Cloward 1971, DeJong & Donnelly 1973). Using 1970 census data to test for migration status, receipt of welfare, and official poverty status by family head in six large cities (Chicago, New York, Philadelphia, Washington DC, Los Angeles, and Detroit), all with at least a half a million blacks, Long (1974:48) provided the first rigorous test of this question. Contrary to conventional wisdom, black families with *nonmigrant* heads had higher welfare participation rates and higher poverty rates than did families with heads originating in the South. On the other hand, the opposite, and expected, relationship was found for white families (i.e. families with heads originating in the South fared less well economically than families with nonmigrant heads).

In a second and more elaborate study on this subject, Long & Heltman (1975) utilized measures of income, rather than receipt of welfare and poverty status, as the main dependent variable, and considered the effects of education, labor force participation, occupation, and extent of unemployment. They found that southern blacks earned more than northern blacks even after controlling for education. Black southern migrants not only had higher labor force participation rates, but, except for the most recent migrants, had lower unemployment rates as well. The gap between the black migrants and nonmigrants was especially noticeable among the least educated. Long & Heltman suggested that since the "cost" of dropping out of the labor force is minimal at the lowest levels of education, northern-born, uneducated blacks may be more easily induced to pursue other alternatives (e.g. welfare) than to work for minimal pay. On the other hand, the southern black may have a different point of reference—southern wages—and thus may be more willing to take the dead-end jobs usually available to the uneducated. White southern migrants at the lowest educational levels also had higher incomes than comparable north-erners. However, overall, white migrants earned slightly less than the nonmi-grants.

Although these two studies have not escaped criticism (Philliber & Seufert 1975, Lieberson 1978, Norton 1979), it is important to emphasize that the criticisms have been mainly technical and methodological in nature and that the main finding—blacks migrating north experience greater economic success in terms of employment rates, earnings, and welfare dependency than northern-born blacks—has withstood the scrutiny of critical reviews. Moreover, a study by Ritchey (1974), that analyzes rural to urban migration and poverty, reached compatible conclusions, namely, that "urban poverty and the plight of the cities are the consequences of broader structural features of our society—the handicap of age, being a female head of household, or . . . the status ascribed to blacks—and not the product of rural to urban migration" (Ritchey 1974:26).

It should be emphasized that these studies refer to the relationship between poverty and relatively recent migration. Many present day problems in the ghetto are partly the result of the heavy black urban migration throughout most of the first half of this century. As Lieberson (1980) has appropriately pointed out, because substantial black migration to the metropolises continued several decades after the early Asian and new European migration ceased, urban blacks, their ranks continually replenished with poor migrants, found it much more difficult to follow the path of both the Asian immigrants and the new Europeans in overcoming the effects of discrimination. Thus, the issue is not whether the migrants have contributed to the growth of the urban ghetto, but whether recent sharp increases in poverty and welfare dependency, associated with the crystallization of a ghetto underclass, can be tied to urban migration. The evidence suggests otherwise. Indeed, recent data amassed by Farley & Allen (1984) suggest that black migration to the largest metropolitan areas has substantially declined. Of the 14 metropolitan areas that have been among the top 10 in black population at one time or another in recent census years (1960, 1970, 1980), only 2 of those in the North (Newark, New Jersey, and Detroit, Michigan) gained blacks through migration between 1970 and 1980, and the gains were proportionately small. The largest gains were experienced by such "boom town" metro areas as Houston, Atlanta, Los Angeles, and Dallas-Fort Worth. Indeed, their tally of the welfare status of black in-migrants to the North and West reveals that only eight percent of the pre-1975 black male migrants aged 25–64 reported any public assistance income for 1979. And as little as three percent of the post-1975 migrants (compared with seven percent among nonmigrant males) listed public assistance income.

On the whole then, this research suggests that the big "urban crisis" cities such as Chicago, New York, Philadelphia, Cleveland, and Detroit are now gaining little or no black population via migration. They appear to be losing more poor through out-migration than they are receiving through in-migration, and this may be true for blacks as well as for whites. Moreover, the arriving blacks appear increasingly less likely to be on public assistance.

If black migration to urban areas is generally on the wane, the "new immigrant" migration is on the upswing. As Massey (1981) has shown, the new immigrants tend to come from Asia and Latin America, with virtually all the illegal immigration from the latter region. The incidence of poverty is well known to be highest among the Mexican "illegals." Whereas the size and distribution of the illegal immigrant population is not exactly known, they are believed to number between three to six million and to follow a pattern of settlement similar to the legal Mexican immigrants. Mostly working-age males, they are generally employed in agricultural production, or when urbanized, in the "secondary labor market" (small scale enterprises with low wages, irregular employment, and little chance for advancement). However, recent research has shown that despite their image as an overly exploited underclass, "illegals" are increasingly gravitating to urban areas and, in the process, escaping the employer-exploitation burdens more prevalent in agricultural production (Cornelius 1978, Portes 1979, Waldinger 1982). The migration process "does not uproot random individuals into totally unfamiliar contexts," states Waldinger (1982:212), "rather migration is a social process that is mediated by long-standing family, friendship and community ties that facilitate moving and ease the migrants integration into the new environment." In short, legal and illegal immigration from Mexico tends to occur by way of a "chain" migration largely insuring a process that "operates swiftly and effectively, often netting the migrants a job shortly after arrival" (Waldinger 1982:213). Nonetheless, exploitation and poverty can accompany migrants even into urban areas (Waldinger 1982). One report, cited by Waldinger (1982), showed that around one third of the 826 employed illegals surveyed in Los Angeles were underpaid. Moreover, illegals tend to find employment in the secondary labor market where their prospects for advancement are slim (Massey 1981, Waldinger 1982).

The question of urban poverty and the new immigration is also relevant to recent changes in the Asian population. As revealed in data released by the US Census Bureau, Asians, who constitute less than 2% of the Nation's population, were the fastest growing American ethnic group in the 1970s. Following the liberalization of United States immigration policies, immigrants from Taiwan, China, and especially, Hong Kong have poured into urban areas and "upset the social organization of 'Chinatowns' " (Wilson 1984b:97). Most of these newcomers speak little English and are at a competitive disadvantage in their quest for jobs, housing, and other resources in the broader society. As a result, poverty and overcrowding, problems even before the new immigration, have substantially increased (Light & Wong 1975).

That poverty is a severe problem in "Chinatowns" is seen in figures revealing, for example, that in San Francisco 27% of Chinatown housing was cited as substandard, recently, compared to 10% in the city at large; in Boston the infant mortality rate in Chinatown is two and one-half times higher than the rate for the city as whole; in New York 43% of Chinatown families reported incomes of under $4,000 annually in 1969, compared with only 21% reported for the city as a whole (Light & Wong 1975). Gang activity has also sharply increased in the Chinatowns of the large metropolises (Bernstein 1982). Indeed, "once homogeneous and stable, Chinatowns are now suffering from problems that have plagued inner-city black neighborhoods, such as joblessness, violent street crimes, gang warfare, school dropouts, and overcrowding" (Wilson 1984b:97). Although there is no systematic research to show the extent to which the new immigration contributes to these problems, it would appear to be a substantial factor (Light & Wong 1975). The core area of San Francisco's Chinatown, for example, consisted mainly of immigrants by the late 1970s and was the most densely populated area in Chinatown (Loo & Mar 1982).

URBAN POVERTY AND STRUCTURAL CHANGES IN THE ECONOMY

The relationship between migration and urban poverty is ultimately shaped by the state of the economy. The United States has entered a postindustrial revolution characterized by a capital-intensive restructuring of the industrial and manufacturing sector and a phenomenal growth of the service sector. Neither the emerging technical fields nor the traditional heavy industries are likely to be a major source for new jobs. Instead, the expansion of the labor market will take place mainly in the service sector—government, food services, sales, and maintenance (Joe 1984b). The implications of these changes for urban poverty have not been the subject of a heavy research agenda. However, there are a few important studies that relate these changes to the life chances of economically disadvantaged groups in urban areas.

John Kasarda (1980, 1983), in particular, has shown that poor inner-city minorities have been especially vulnerable to the structural transformation occurring in urban metropolises—from centers of production and distribution of physical goods to centers of administration, information exchange, trade, finance, and government services. This process has wiped out millions of wholesale, retail, and manufacturing jobs in the nation's central cities since 1948, a process which has accelerated since 1967. Simultaneously, in urban areas "postindustrial society" occupational positions that usually require levels of education and training beyond the reach of poor inner-city residents have significantly increased. Shifts in the urban job structure have accompanied changes in the demographic composition of large central cities from predominantly European white to predominantly black and Hispanic, resulting in a decrease both in the total population of central cities and in aggregate personal income levels (Kasarda 1983).

The accumulative effect of these economic and population changes, as Kasarda (1983) carefully outlines, has been deeper "ghettoization," solidification of high levels of poverty, mounting institutional problems in the inner city (e.g. poorer municipal services and the declining quality of public schools), and an increase in social dislocations (joblessness, crime, female-headed families, teenage pregnancies, and welfare dependency).

The ascendancy of service occupations apparently presents only limited opportunities for the inner-city poor. A recent study by Stanback & Noyelle (1982:1), identifying "some of the critical dimensions of the change undergone by metropolitan labor markets during the 1970s," reveals that despite the growth of jobs in the service sector, the urban labor market has actually become more polarized—with the poorly paid service workers, laborers, and clericals facing increasingly restricted opportunities for advancement in the face of "the relative dearth of 'middle-layer' " service jobs (1982:128), and the training and education required for well-paying professional, managerial, and technical positions.

Relating the problems of poverty in the inner city to the broader issues of American economic organization, a recent government publication (Sheingold 1982) complements several of the points raised by Kasarda. More specifically, this study indicates that many of the newly "dislocated workers" (victims of plant shutdowns, technological displacements, etc), especially those in the North East and North Central industrial regions, will not be reabsorbed in the industrial sector because of the modernization of production, import competition, and changes in consumer demand. For example, it is estimated that the spread of microtechnology alone will result in the loss of three million manufacturing jobs by 1990 (Sheingold 1982); and increased automation and import-competition is expected to decrease automobile manufacturing by 200,000 between 1982 and 1985 (Barth 1982). It takes little imagination to recognize the relevance of these projections for current and future problems of urban joblessness and poverty.

THEORETICAL ISSUES IN STUDIES OF URBAN POVERTY

During the past two decades social scientists have debated the relative importance of culture versus environment (or social situation) in accounting for the experiences and behavior of impoverished urban Americans. The debate was generated in large measure by the work of the anthropologist Oscar Lewis, who coined the concept "culture of poverty." Relying on participant observation and life-history collections, Lewis described the culture of poverty as "both an adaptation and a reaction of the poor to their marginal position in a class-stratified, highly individuated, capitalistic society" (1968:188). It represents, in other words, efforts to cope with feelings of despair and hopelessness that invariably accompany poor people's realization of the overwhelming odds against their achieving success in terms of the values and goals of mainstream society. The net result is a series of special adaptations to existential circumstances, including a sense of resignation and passivity because of enduring poverty; a present-time orientation because of the pressures of day-to-day survival; feelings of fatalism and powerlessness because of separation from the political process; low aspirations because of lack of opportunity; feelings of inferiority because of the larger society's contempt and aversion for the poor; and creation of female-headed families because of the inability of poor men to be adequate breadwinners (Lewis 1968; Steinberg 1981). Lewis maintained that basic structural changes in society may alter some of the cultural characteristics of the poor and that if the poor become involved in an active trade-union movement or become class conscious, "they are no longer part of the culture of poverty although they still may be desparately poor" (1968:193). Lewis's conceptions were expanded by a number of social scientists (Harrington 1962, Miller 1965, Matza 1966, Banfield 1970), and some have used them to suggest that the poor have to be rehabilitated culturally before they can advance in society (cf. Banfield 1970).

Critics of the culture of poverty thesis, especially the later versions proffered by conservative theorists, argued that it places blame on the victim and therefore conceals the social causes of poverty and leads to social policies that focus on changing the attitudes and behavior of the poor rather than on reforming the society (Valentine 1968, Steinberg 1981). These critics tend to believe that the poor share the aspirations and values of the larger society and that the so-called pathological consequences of poverty will disappear when they are provided with decent jobs and other resources that facilitate social mobility. As Herbert Gans has observed (1968:205) "the arguments between those who think that poverty can best be eliminated by providing jobs and other resources and those who feel that cultural obstacles and psychological deficiencies must be overcome as well is ultimately an argument about social change, about the psychological readiness of people to respond to change, and about the role of culture in change." In other words, the advocates of resources, those who advance a situational view of social change (and of personality), feel that people's behavior and attitudes change when opportunities and situations available to them change (Kriesberg 1963, Rainwater 1966, 1968, 1970). The proponents of the centrality of culture, those who advance a cultural view of social change, maintain that prior values and patterns of behavior determine how people will react to change and therefore only changes that are congruent with one's culture will be adopted (Miller 1965, Lewis 1966). The acrimonious debate (see Valentine et al 1969) over these issues during the past several years has often resulted in rigid either/or positions; but the truth, as Herbert Gans suggests, probably "lies somewhere in between" (1968:206). Unfortunately, there is as yet no definitive research to determine precisely the relative significance of the situational versus the cultural views of poverty and social change.

Clearly, the poor are not monolithic. Considerable variations among them suggest that responses to situational changes will vary. The poor range from those who have only periodic experiences with poverty to those who have been poor for several generations; from those who are upwardly mobile to those who are downwardly mobile; from those who embrace middle-class values to those who share working-class values (Gans 1968). We are beginning to gather data on these variations (see the discussion of the Michigan PSID research above), and sufficient data exist to demonstrate divergence between behavioral norms and aspirations among the poor (c.f. Rodman 1963, Hannerz 1969, Anderson 1978). More research is needed on both micro- and macro-processes to help explain variations and similarities in responses to changing situations not only among the poor, but also between segments of the poor and others in the larger society.

A reasonable hypothesis developed by Gans (1968) is that the gap between behavior norms and aspirations among affluent people is narrower than that among poor people. Even if the affluent fail to fulfill occupational aspirations, he argues, they are often able to satisfy other aspirations, such as those for their families. Because the poor have fewer options, and because they lack the economic resources to fulfill their aspirations, they are forced to develop behavioral norms that diverge from mainstream areas of life, even though they still retain many of the aspirations and values of the affluent society. For all these reasons, research on the cultural patterns of the poor should focus both on behavioral norms and on aspirations and other values. "The norms must be studied because they indicate how people react to their present existence," states Gans (1968:209), "but limiting the analysis to them can lead to the assumption that behavior would remain the same under different conditions when there is no reliable evidence, pro or con, to justify such an assumption."

In short, the theoretical position that integrates arguments from both the cultural and situational perspectives, following Gans (1968), focuses on responses to recurrent situations in the form of behavior patterns, norms, and aspirations. As economic and social opportunities change, new behavioral solutions originate and develop into patterns, later to be upheld and complemented by norms. If new situations emerge, both the behavior patterns and the norms eventually undergo change. "Some behavioral norms are more persistent than others, but over the long run, all of the norms and aspirations by which people live are nonpersistent; they rise and fall with changes in situations" (Gans 1968:211).

URBAN POVERTY, DEPENDENCY, AND PUBLIC POLICY RESEARCH

There is a growing suspicion in many quarters that liberal welfare policies—especially those associated with the Great Society program (which extended eligibility for income transfer programs, increased benefit levels, and created new programs such as food stamps and Medicaid)—have had adverse effects on the norms and aspirations of large segments of the urban poor in the sense that they now have little incentive either to work or to create or maintain stable families and are therefore increasingly dependent on welfare (Murray 1984).

These concerns have helped to provide the impetus and direction for a good deal of public policy research on the extent to which public assistance creates work and family disincentives. A number of studies have attempted to measure the effects of Aid for Families with Dependent Children (AFDC) on the supply of labor (Garfinkle & Orr 1974; Saks 1975; Williams 1975; Barr & Hall 1981; Masters & Garfinkel 1977; Levy 1979) and, with the exception of the study by Masters & Garfinkel, all found that AFDC payments had small but significant negative effects on labor-force participation. However, Danziger et al (1981) uncovered a variety of methodological problems that plague this body of research. These included ". . . reliance on statutory instead of effective tax rates (Garfinkle & Orr, Levy), poor or missing measures of unearned non-AFDC income (Garfinkle & Orr, Saks, Williams, Master and Garfinkel), neglect of administrative and/or local labor market variables (all but Garfinkel & Orr), and poor measures of the dependent variable (Barr & Hall)" (1981:995).

There are also difficulties with the research on welfare and family disincentives. Before the Seattle-Denver Income Maintenance Experiment (SIME-DIME), most researchers and policymakers believed that a program of welfare that would support both intact and split families would result in fewer marital dissolutions than a program that only supported split families (Garfinkle & Haveman 1982). However, when early reports (Hannon et al 1977, 1978) on the SIME-DIME revealed that marital splits were greater in the experimental group (i.e. the group receiving negative income tax payments) than in the control group, support for extending welfare to intact families decreased among policymakers (Lynn & Whitman 1981). As revealed in the final report (Groeneveld et al 1983:344) of the SIME-DIME "the NIT increased the proportion of families headed by single females. For blacks and whites, the increase was due to the increase in dissolution; for Chicanos, the increase was due to the decrease in the marital formation rate. For all three race-ethnic groups, the net effect is increased welfare costs because the proportion of the population most likely to depend upon welfare rises." Nonetheless, a careful review of the original SIME-DIME analysis by Cain (1981) questions the validity of the findings because the effects of experimental training programs were confounded with those of the experimental Negative Income Tax program; the effects on childless couples (who are ineligible for AFDC) were not distinguished from those of couples with children; the possibility that the results were biased by the differential attrition between experimentals and controls was incorrectly ruled out; and the experiment focused arbitrarily on couples enrolled for five years and thereby excluded two thirds of the sample enrolled for only three years.

Additional research examining the effect of income transfers on intact families in natural urban settings or combined urban/rural settings offers mixed results. Honig (1974) found a significant positive association between the level of AFDC payments and rates of female family headship for both blacks and whites in 44 metropolitan areas in 1960, but by 1970 the relationship had diminished and was significant only for blacks. Ross & Sawhill (1975), using cross-sectional 1970 census data for 41 cities, found small but significant effects of AFDC payment levels (including average food stamp benefits) on the rate of female family headship for nonwhites, but not for whites. In research based on both urban and rural samples, Minarik & Goldfarb (1976) found nonsignificant effects of AFDC payment levels on marital instability. However, Hoffman & Holmes (1976) found a significant positive effect of AFDC level payments on marital instability.

Thus, despite popular opinion and theoretical assumptions on the negative impact of public assistance, the studies described above not only fail to provide definitive conclusions on the general association between the level of AFDC payments and the rate of female-headed households, they also yield virtually no information on the extent to which levels of benefits stimulate marital dissolution, discourage remarriage, or deter marriage.

These problems were addressed, however, in a recently completed landmark study (Ellwood & Bane 1984) on the effects of AFDC on family structure and living arrangements. The authors of this study correctly pointed out that previous nonexperimental studies "included a variety of measured variables to control for state differences. But generally they did little to erase any problems caused by unmeasured differences across states that might be correlated with benefit levels" (Ellwood & Bane 1984:9). Using three different methods based on different data sets (Survey of Income and Education, aggregate national data from the Census and Vital Statistics Reports, aggregate Census data by state) to control these unmeasured differences and to provide a "check for consistency across method," Ellwood & Bane found that AFDC has virtually no effect on the fertility of unmarried black and white women, only a modest effect on separation and divorce among young married mothers, and a substantial impact on the living arrangements in the sense that it increases the movement of single mothers from subfamilies to their own independent households. In short, "welfare simply does not appear to be the underlying cause in the dramatic changes in family structure of the past few decades" (Ellwood & Bane 1984:4).

The results of Ellwood & Bane's (1984) research and the inconsistent findings of other studies on the relationship between welfare and family structure and on welfare and illegitimate births seriously undermine claims that changes in welfare policies are at the root of the decreased proportion of intact families and increased proportion of out-of-wedlock births (Wilson & Neckerman 1984).

Finally, the effects of the Reagan budget cuts (the Omnibus Budget Reconciliation Act of 1981 [OBRA]) on the poor, particularly the working poor, have been the subject of recent research by Joe (1982), Joe et al (1984), and Moscovice & Craig (1983). These studies placed special emphasis on the effects of the AFDC regulatory changes on working women and their children. These changes affected the "tax" on earned income and imposed lower ceilings on the income criteria for AFDC eligibility. One immediate consequence was a punitive effect for working. But the more important consequences were the millions of partially dependent families either completely removed from the welfare rolls or made to sustain severe declines in living standards. For example, Joe (1982) estimated that under the OBRA average disposable income of working AFDC families (including net earnings, benefits, and food stamps) for the nation declined from 101% of the poverty line to 81%. And average AFDC benefits were reduced from $186 to only $20 monthly. Thus, as Bawden & Palmer (1984) appropriately argue, the rise in official poverty between 1979 and 1982 is not simply due to macroeconomic conditions (mild recession of 1980, high inflation, then deep recession), but is a function also of fundamental changes in the federal government's response to conditions of poverty.

CONCLUSION

There has been an ebb and flow in the study of urban poverty in America. The social reform movement of the early twentieth century, responding to the dislocations that accompanied rapid industrialization, prompted a number of descriptive and muckraking studies on poverty in urban areas. At roughly the same time, sociologists at the University of Chicago conducted a prodigious volume of research on urban life, including a number of ethnographic studies on poverty that were far more analytical and systematic than those of the social reformers. By the late 1930s, scholarly research on urban poverty was on the wane, only to be revived again in the 1960s following the rediscovery of poverty and the emergence of the Great Society program.

The subject of urban poverty and the structure of the family has drawn considerable attention from researchers since the mid-1960s and has helped to raise the level of national interest in the problems of the inner city and the crystallization of a sizable ghetto underclass. However, with the emergence of longitudinal data sets many assumptions about the intergenerational transmis-

254 WILSON & APONTE

sion of poverty and persistent poverty in the inner city have been challenged. Likewise, research on urban poverty and migration has raised questions and generated new insights on the contribution of the urban migrant to the current problems of inner-city poverty and social dislocations. And several recent studies, possibly representing a trend in urban poverty research, have provided significant insights on the relationship between poverty in the inner city and the broader problems of American economic organization.

The study of urban poverty is not blessed with elaborate and definitive theoretical schemes. Nonetheless, a synthesis of the cultural and situational perspectives reveals a coherent theoretical framework that relates to a good deal of the substantive research, including recent public policy research, on the relationship between poverty and welfare dependency. The results of the public policy research are so mixed, however, that it would be risky to draw policy recommendations from them. On the other hand, the most recent studies on the effects of the OBRA on the working poor are clear and consistent: they reveal the nature of the federal government's dramatic retreat from the Great Society programs of the 1960s.

ACKNOWLEDGMENTS

Research for this paper was supported by grants from the Ford and Spencer Foundations. We would like to thank Lee Rainwater for helpful comments on an earlier draft of this paper.

Literature Cited

Aaron, H. J. 1978. *Politics and the Professors: The Great Society in Perspective.* Washington, DC: Brookings Inst.

Addams, J. 1902. The housing problem in Chicago. *Ann. Am. Acad. Polit. Soc. Sci.* 20:97–107

Anderson, E. 1978. *A Place On The Corner.* Chicago: Univ. Chicago Press

Anderson, N. 1923. *The Hobo.* Chicago: Univ. Chicago Press

Anderson, N. 1940. *Men On the Move.* Chicago: Univ. Chicago Press

Auletta, K. 1982. *The Underclass.* New York: Random House

Ball-Rokeach, S. J., Short, J. F. Jr. 1985. Collective violence: the redress of grievance. In *American Violence and Public Policy,* ed. L. A. Curtis. New Haven, Conn: Yale Univ. Press

Bane, M. J., Ellwood, D. 1983a. *Slipping into and out of poverty: the dynamics of spells,* Work. Pap. 1199. Cambridge, Mass. Natl. Bur. Econ. Res.

Bane, M. J., Ellwood, D. 1983b. *The dynamics of dependence: the routes to self-sufficiency.* Washington, DC: Dept. Health Hum. Serv. Rep.

Bane, M. J., Ellwood, D. 1984a. *The dynamics of children's living arrangements,* Work. Pap. (HHS-100-82-0038). Washington, DC: Dept. Health Hum. Serv.

Bane, M. J., Ellwood, D. 1984b. *Single mothers and their living arrangements,* Work. Pap. (HHS-100-82-0038). Washington, DC: Dept. Health Hum. Serv.

Banfield, E. 1970. *The Unheavenly City.* Boston: Little, Brown. 2nd ed.

Barr, N., Hall, R. 1981. The probability of dependence on public assistance. *Economica* 48:109–23

Barth, M. C. 1982. Dislocated workers. *J. Inst. Socioecon. Stud.* 7:23–35

Bawden, D. L., Palmer, J. L. 1984. Social policy: challenging the welfare state. In *The Reagan Record: An Assessment of America's Changing Domestic Priorities,* ed. J. L. Palmer, I. V. Sawhill, pp. 177–215. Cambridge, Mass: Ballinger

Beale, C. L. 1971. Rural-urban migration of blacks: past and future. *Am. J. Agric. Econ.* 53:302–7

Bell, D. 1968. Relevant aspects of the social scene and social policy. See Burns 1968, pp. 163–71

Berger, A. S., Simon, W. 1974. Black families and the Moynihan Report: a research evaluation. *Soc. Probl.* 22:145–61

Bernstein, R. 1982. Tension and gangs mar the Chinatown image. *New York Times* (Dec. 24):13

Blau, P. M., Duncan, O. D. 1967. *The American Occupational Structure.* New York: Wiley

Breckenridge, S. 1936. *The Tenements of Chicago: 1908–35.* Chicago: Univ. Chicago Press

Bremner, R. H. 1956. From the Depths: *The Discovery of Poverty in the United States.* New York: Univ. Press

Burns, E. M., ed. 1968. *Childrens Allowances and the Economic Welfare of Children.* New York: Committee For The Children of New York

Cain, G. 1981. *Comments of August 18th version of marital stability findings,* Chap. 3 SIME-DIME Final Rep. Washington, DC: Dept. Health Hum. Serv. Rep.

Clark, K. 1965. *Dark Ghetto.* New York: Harper & Row

Coe, R. 1978. Dependency and poverty in the short and long run. In *Five Thousand American Families-Patterns of Economic Progress,* Vol. 6, ed. G. J. Duncan, J. N. Morgan, pp. 273–96. Ann Arbor, Mich: Inst. Soc. Res., Univ. Michigan

Corcoran, M., Duncan, G. J., Gurin, P. 1983. *Psychological and demographic aspects of the underclass.* Presented at Ann. Meet. Popul. Assoc. Am., Pittsburgh

Cornelius, W. 1978. *Mexican Migration to the United States: Causes, Consequences, and U.S. Responses.* Migration and Development Monogr. c/78–9. Cambridge, Mass: MIT Cent. Int. Stud.

Danziger, S., Haveman, R. H., Plotnick, R. 1981. How income transfer programs affect work, savings, and the income distribution: a critical review. *J. Econ. Lit.* 19:975–1028

DeJong, G. F., Donnelly, W. L. 1973. Public welfare and migration. *Soc. Sci. Q.* 54:329–44

Downs, A. 1970. *Who Are The Urban Poor.* New York: Com. Econ. Devel.

Earl, L., Lohmann, N. 1978. Absent fathers and black male children. *Soc. Work* 23:413–15

Ellwood, D. T., Bane, M. J. 1984. The impact of AFDC on family structure and living arrangements. Washington, DC: Dept. Health Hum. Serv. (Grant No. 92A-82)

Faris, R. E. L., Dunham, W. 1931. *Mental Disorder in Urban America.* Chicago: Univ. Chicago Press

Farley, R., Allen, W. 1984. *Recent trends in black migration in the United States.* Presented at Ann. Meet. Popul. Assoc. Am., Minneapolis, Minn.

Farley, R., Bianchi, S. M. 1982. *Social and economic polarization: is it occurring among blacks.* Presented at Ann. Meet. Am. Sociol. Assoc., San Francisco

Fishman, L., ed. 1966. *Poverty Amid Affluence.* New Haven, Conn: Yale Univ. Press

Frazier, E. F. 1932. *The Negro Family in Chicago.* Chicago: Univ. Chicago Press

Frazier, E. F. 1939. *The Negro Family in the United States.* Chicago: Univ. Chicago Press

Friedman, L. M. 1977. The social and political context of the War on Poverty. In *A Decade of Federal Antipoverty Programs: Achievements, Failures, and Lessons,* ed. R. H. Haveman, pp. 20–40. New York: Academic

Galbraith, J. K. 1958. *The Affluent Society.* Boston: Houghton-Mifflin

Galloway, L. E. 1966. On the importance of picking one's parents. *Q. Rev. Econ. Bus.* 6:7–15

Gans, H. J. 1968. Culture and class in the study of poverty: an approach to anti-poverty research. See Moynihan 1968, pp. 201–28

Garfinkle, I., Haveman, R. H. 1982. *Income transfer policy in the United States: a review and assessment,* Discuss. Pap. 701–82. Inst. Res. Poverty, Madison, Wisc.

Garfinkle, I., Orr, L. L. 1974. Welfare policy and employment rate of AFDC mothers. *Natl. Tax J.* 27:275–84

Glazer, N. 1965. A sociologist's view of poverty. See Gordon 1965, pp. 12–26

Gordon, M. S., ed. 1965. *Poverty in America.* San Francisco: Chandler

Groeneveld, L. P., Hannon, M. T., Tuma, N. B. 1983. *Marital Stability. Final Report of the Seattle-Denver Income Maintenance Experiment,* Vol. 1, *Design and Results* (Pt. V). Menlo Park, Calif: SRI Int.

Gutman, H. G. 1976. *The Black Family in Slavery and Freedom.* New York: Pantheon

Hannon, M. T., Tuma, N. B., Groeneveld, L. P. 1977. Income and marital events: evidence from an income-maintenance experiment. *Am. J. Sociol.* 82:1186–1121

Hannon, M. T., Tuma, N. B., Groeneveld, L. P. 1978. Income and independence effects on marital dissolution: results from the Seattle and Denver income maintenance experiments. *Am. J. Sociol* 84:611–33

Hannerz, U. 1969. *Soulside: Inquiries Into Ghetto Culture and Community.* New York: Columbia Univ. Press

Harrington, M. 1962. *The Other America: Poverty In The United States.* New York: Macmillan

Hartnagel, T. F. 1970. Father absence and self conception among lower class white and Negro boys. *Soc. Probl.* 18:152–63

Heiss, J. 1972. On the transmission of marital instability in black families. *Am. Sociol. Rev.* 37:82–92

Hill, M. S. 1981. Some dynamic aspects of

poverty. In *Five Thousand American Families-Patterns of Economic Progress*, ed. M. S. Hill, D. H. Hill, J. N. Morgan, 9:93–120. Ann Arbor, Mich: Inst. Soc. Res., Univ. Mich.

Hill, M. S., Ponza, M. 1983a. Poverty and welfare dependence across generations. *Econ. Outlook U.S.A.* 10:61–4

Hill, M. S., Ponza, M. 1983b. *Intergenerational transmission of poverty: does welfare dependency beget dependency?* Presented at Ann. Meet. South Econ. Assoc. (Revised) Washington, DC

Hoffman, S., Holmes, J. 1976. Husbands, wives, and divorce. In *Five Thousand American Families-Patterns of Economic Progress*, Vol. 4, ed. J. N. Morgan. Ann Arbor, Mich: Inst. Soc. Res., Univ. Mich.

Hogan, D. P., Astone, N. M., Kitagawa, E. M. 1984. *The impact of social status, family structure, and neighborhood on contraceptive use among black adolescents.* Chicago: Popul. Res. Cent., Univ. Chicago

Hogan, D. P., Kitagawa, E. M. 1983. *The impact of social status, family structure, and neighborhood on the fertility of black adolescents.* Chicago: Popul. Res. Cent., Univ. Chicago

Honig, M. 1974. AFDC income, recipient rates, and family dissolution. *J. Hum. Resour.* 9:303–22

Huber, J. 1974. Political implications of poverty definitions. In *The Sociology of American Poverty*, ed. J. Huber, P. Chalfant, pp. 300–23. Cambridge, Mass: Schenkman

Hyman, H. H., Reed, J. S. 1969. "Black Matriarchy" reconsidered: evidence from secondary analysis of sample surveys. *Publ. Opinion Q* 33:346–54

Hunt, L. L., Hunt, J. G. 1975. Race and the father-son connections: the conditional relevance of father absence for the orientations and identities of adolescent boys. *Soc. Probl.* 23:35–52

James, B. J. 1972. *Poverty, Politics and Change*. New York: Prentice Hall

Joe, T. 1982. *Profiles of families in poverty: effects of the FY 1983 budget proposals on the poor*. Washington, DC: Center Study Soc. Policy

Joe, T. 1984a. *The "flip-side" of black families headed by women: the economic status of men*. Washington, DC: Cent. Study Soc. Policy

Joe, T. 1984b. *The Social Consequences of Economic Neglect*. Washington: The Center for the Study of Social Policy

Joe, T., Sarri, R., Ginsberg, M., Mesnikoff, A., Kulis, S. 1984. *Working female-headed families in poverty: three studies of low-income families affected by the AFDC policy changes of 1981*. Washington, DC: Cent. Study Soc. Policy

Kasarda, J. D. 1980. The implications of contemporary redistribution trends for national urban policy. *Soc. Sci. Q.* 61:373–400

Kasarda, J. D. 1983. Caught in the web of change. *Society* 21:41–47

Kerbo, H. R. 1981. Characteristics of the poor: a continuing focus in social research. *Sociol. Soc. Res.* 65:323–31

Kellam, S. G., Ensminger, M. E., Turner, R. J. 1977. Family structure and the mental health of children. *Arch. Gen. Psychiatry* 34:1012–22

Korpi, W. 1980. Approaches to the study of poverty in the United States: critical notes from a European perspective. In *Poverty and Public Policy: An Evaluation of Social Science Research*, ed. V. T. Covello, pp. 287–314. Cambridge, Mass: Schenkman

Kriesberg, L. 1963. The relationship between socio-economic rank and behavior. *Soc. Probl.* 10:334–53

Ladner, J. 1973. *Tomorrow's Tomorrow*. New York: Doubleday

Lampman, R. J. 1959. *The Low Income Population and Economic Growth*, Study Pap. No. 12. Joint Econ. Com., 86th Congr. 1st Session

Levine, R. A. 1970. *The Poor Ye Need Not Have With You: Lessons From The War On Poverty*. Cambridge, Mass: MIT Press

Levitan, S. A. 1969. *The Great Society's Poor Law: A New Approach to Poverty*. Baltimore: Johns Hopkins Univ. Press

Levy, F. 1979. The labor supply of female household heads, or AFDC work incentives don't work too well. *J. Hum. Resour.* 14:76–97

Levy, F. 1980. *The intergenerational transfer of poverty*, Work. Pap. 1241-02. Washington, DC: Urban Inst. Work.

Lewis, O. 1966. The culture of poverty. *Sci. Am.* 215:19–25

Lewis, O. 1968. The culture of poverty. See Moynihan 1968, pp. 187–200.

Lieberson, S. 1978. A reconsideration of the income differences found between migrants and northern-born blacks. *Am. J. Sociol.* 83:940–66

Lieberson, S. 1980. *A Piece of the Pie: Blacks and White Immigrants Since 1880*. Los Angeles: Univ. Calif. Press

Liebow, E. 1967. *Tally's Corner: A Study of Negro Streetcorner Men*. Boston: Little, Brown

Light, I., Wong, C. C. 1975. Protest or work: dilemmas of the tourist industry in American Chinatowns. *Am. J. Sociol.* 80:1342–68

Long, L. H. 1974. Poverty status and receipt of welfare among migrants and nonmigrants in large cities. *Am. Sociol. Rev.* 39:46–56

Long, L. H., Heltman, L. R. 1975. Migration and income differences between black and white men in the North. *Am. J. Sociol.* 80:1391–1409

Loo, C., Mar, D. 1982. Desired residential mobility in a low income ethnic community: a case study of Chinatown. *J. Soc. Issues* 38:95–106

Lynn, L. E., Whitman, D. F. 1981. *The President As Policymaker: Jimmy Carter and Welfare Reform*. Philadelphia: Temple Univ. Press

Massey, D. S. 1981. Dimensions of the new immigration to the United States and the prospects for assimilation. *Ann. Rev. Sociol.* 7:57–85

Masters, S., Garfinkle, I. 1977. *Estimating the Labor Supply Effects of Income Maintenance Alternatives*. New York: Academic

Matza, D. 1966. The disreputable poor. In *Class, Status, and Power: A Reader in Social Stratification*, ed. R. Bendix, S. M. Lipset. New York: Free

McLanahan, S. 1983. *Family structure and the reproduction of poverty*, Discuss. Pap. 720A-83. Inst. Res. Poverty

Miller, H. P. 1966. *Poverty American Style*. Belmont, Calif: Wadsworth

Miller, W. B. 1965. Focal concerns of lower class culture. In *Poverty in America*, ed. L. A. Ferman, J. L. Kornbluh, A. Haber, pp. 261–70. Ann Arbor, Mich: Univ. Mich. Press

Minarik, J. J., Goldfarb, R. S. 1976. AFDC income, recipient rates, and family dissolution: a comment. *J. Hum. Resour.* 11:243–50

Moore, K. A., Caldwell, S. B. 1976. *Out-of-wedlock pregnancy and childbearing*, Work. Pap. 992–02. Washington, DC: Urban Inst.

Morgan, J. N., David, M. H., Cohen, W. J., Brazer, H. E. 1962. *Income And Welfare In The United States*. New York: McGraw-Hill

Moscovice, I., Craig, W. J. 1983. *The impact of federal cutbacks on working AFDC recipients in Minnesota*. Cent. Health Serv. Res., Univ. of Minn.

Moynihan, D. P. 1965. *The Negro Family: The Case For National Action*. Washington, DC: US Dept. Labor

Moynihan, D. P. 1968. The professors and the poor. In *On Understanding Poverty: Perspectives From The Social Sciences*, ed. D. P. Moynihan, pp. 3–35. New York: Basic

Moynihan, D. P. 1970. *Maximum Feasible Misunderstanding*. New York: Free

Murray, C. A. 1984. *Losing Ground: American Social Policy 1950–1980*. New York: Basic

National Center for Health Statistics. 1968. Trends in illegitimacy: United States, 1940–1965. *Vital and Health Statistics* 21, No. 15

National Center for Health Statistics. 1983. Advanced report of final natality statistics,

1981. *Monthly Vital Statistics Report* 32: 9

Norton, C. B. 1979. Comment on Long. *Am. Sociol. Rev.* 44:177–78

Orshansky, M. 1963. Children of the poor. *Soc. Secur. Bull.* 26 (July): 3–13

Orshansky, M. 1965. Counting the poor: another look at the poverty profile. *Soc. Secur. Bull.* 28:3–29

Park, R. E. 1925. *The City*. Chicago: Univ. Chicago Press

Patterson, J. T. 1981. *America's Struggle Against Poverty, 1900–1980*. Cambridge, Mass: Harvard Univ. Press

Pearce, D. M. 1978. The feminization of poverty: women, work and welfare. *Urban Soc. Change Rev.* 11:28–36

Pearce, D. M. 1983. The feminization of ghetto poverty. *Society* 21:70–74

Perlman, R. 1976. *The Economics of Poverty*. New York: McGraw-Hill

Philliber, W. W., Seufert, R. 1975. An untested hypothesis: the effect of size of public assistance benefits on migration. *Am. Socio. Rev.* 40:845–47

Piven, F. F., Cloward, R. A. 1971. *Regulating The Poor: The Functions of Public Welfare*. New York: Academic

Plotnick, R. D., Skidmore, F. 1975. *Progress Against Poverty: A Review of the 1964–1974 Decade*. New York: Academic

Portes, A. 1979. Illegal immigration and the international system, lessons from recent legal Mexican immigrants to the United States. *Soc. Probl.* 26:425–37

Raab, E. 1966. A tale of three wars: what war and which poverty. *Publ Inter.* 3:45–56

Rainwater, L. 1966. Crucible of identity: the Negro lower-class family. *Daedalus* 95: 172–216

Rainwater, L. 1968. The problem of lower-class culture and poverty-war strategy. See Moynihan 1968, pp. 229–59

Rainwater, L. 1970. *Behind Ghetto Walls: Black Families in a Federal Slum*. New York: Aldine

Rainwater, L., Yancey, W. L., ed. 1967. *The Moynihan Report and the Politics of Controversy*. Cambridge, Mass: MIT Press

Riis, J. 1890. *How The Other Half Lives: Studies Among The Tenements Of New York*. New York: Scribner's

Ritchey, P. N. 1974. Urban poverty and rural to urban migration. *Rur. Sociol.* 39:12–27

Rodgers, H. R. 1978. Hiding versus ending poverty. *Polit. Soc.* 8:253–66

Rodgers, H. R. 1979. *Poverty Amid Plenty*. Reading, Mass: Addison-Wesley

Rodman, H. 1963. The lower-class value stretch. *Soc. Forc.* 42:206–15

Rosen, L. 1969. Matriarchy and lower class Negro male delinquency. *Soc. Probl.* 17:175–89

Rosenberg, M., Simmons, R. G. 1972. *Black and White Esteem: The Urban School Child.* Washington, DC: Am. Sociol. Assoc.

Ross, H. L., Sawhill, I. V. 1975. *Time of Transition: The Growth of Families Headed By Women.* Washington, DC: Urban Inst.

Rustin, B. 1965. From protest to politics: the future of the Civil Rights Movement. *Commentary* 39:25–31

Saks, D. H. 1975. *Public Assistance for Mothers in an Urban Labor Market.* Princeton, NJ: Indust. Rel. Sect., Princeton Univ.

Schiller, B. R. 1970. Stratified opportunities: the essence of the "vicious circle". *Am. J. Sociol.* 76:426–42

Schiller, B. R. 1976. *The Economics of Poverty and Discrimination.* Englewood Cliffs, NJ: Prentice Hall

Schulz, D. A. 1968. Variations in the father role in complete families of the Negro lower class. *Soc. Sci. Q.* 49:651–59

Schulz, D. A. 1969. *Coming Up Black: Patterns of Ghetto Socialization.* Englewood Cliffs, NJ: Prentice Hall

Sheingold, S. 1982. *Dislocated Workers: Issues and Federal Options.* Washington, DC: Congress. Budget Off.

Stack, C. 1974. *All Our Kin: Strategies For Survival in a Black Community.* New York: Harper & Row

Stanback, T. M., Noyelle, T. J. 1982. *Cities in Transition.* Totowa, NJ: Allanheld, Osmun

Steinberg, S. 1981. *The Ethnic Myth: Race, Ethnicity, and Class in America.* New York: Atheneum

Sundquist, J. L. 1969. The origins of the war on poverty. In *On Fighting Poverty: Perspectives From Experience,* ed. J. L. Sundquist, pp. 6–33. New York: Basic

Sutherland, E. H., Locke, H. 1936. *20,000 Homeless Men.* Philadelphia: Lippincott

Suttles, G. R. 1976. Urban ethnography: situational and normative accounts. *Ann. Rev. Sociol.* 2:1–18

Thernstrom, S. 1968. Poverty in historical perspective. See Moynihan 1968, pp. 160–86

Thomas, W. I., Znaniecki, F. 1918–1920. *The Polish Peasant in Europe and America.* 5 Vols. Boston: Brager

Thrasher, F. M. 1927. *The Gang.* Chicago: Univ. Chicago Press

Tompkins, D. C. 1970. *Poverty in the United States During the Sixties: A Bibliography.* Berkeley, Calif: Inst. Gov. Stud., Univ. Calif.

US Bureau of the Census. 1983. Marital status and living arrangements: March 1982. *Current Population Reports.* Ser. P-20 No. 380, Washington, DC: USGPO

US Bureau of the Census. 1984a. *Estimates of Poverty Including The Value of Non-Cash Benefits,* Tech. Pap. 51. Washington, DC: USGPO

US Bureau of the Census. 1984b. Characteristics of the population below the poverty level: 1982. *Current Population Reports.* Ser. P-60 No. 144. Washington, DC: USGPO

Valentine, C. A. 1968. *Culture and Poverty: Critique and Counter Proposals.* Chicago: Univ. Chicago Press

Valentine, C. A., Berndt, C. H., Boissevain, E., Bushnell, J. H., Carstens, P., et al. 1969. *Culture and Poverty: Critique and Counter Proposals* (Book Review and Author's Precis/Reply). *Curr. Anthropol.* 10:181–200

Waldinger, R. 1982. The occupational and economic integration of the new immigrants. *Law Contemp. Probl.* 45:197–222

Williams, R. 1975. *Public Assistance and Work Effort.* Princeton, NJ: Indust. Rel. Sect., Princeton Univ.

Wilson, W. J. 1984a. The black underclass. *Wilson Q.* 8:88–99

Wilson, W. J. 1984b. The urban underclass. In *Minority Report,* ed. L. W. Dunbar. New York: Pantheon

Wilson, W. J., Neckerman, K. M. 1984. *Poverty and family structure: the widening gap between evidence and public policy issues.* Presented at Conf. Inst. Res. Pov./Dept. Health Hum. Serv., Williamsburg, Va.

Wirth, L. 1928. *The Ghetto.* Chicago: Univ. Chicago Press

Yancey, W. L. 1972. Going down home: family structure and the urban trap. *Soc. Sci. Q.* 52:893–906

Yarmolinsky, A. 1969. The beginnings of OEO. See Sundquist 1969, pp. 34–51

Zorbaugh, H. W. 1929. *The Gold Coast and The Slum.* Chicago: Univ. Chicago Press

Ann. Rev. Sociol. 1985 11:259–80

THE NONMETROPOLITAN POPULATION TURNAROUND

Glenn V. Fuguitt

Department of Rural Sociology, University of Wisconsin-Madison, Madison, Wisconsin 53706

Abstract

Over the 1970–1980 period, US nonmetropolitan areas grew more rapidly than previously, achieving overall a faster growth rate than metropolitan areas, with more migrants going from metropolitan to nonmetropolitan areas than in the opposite direction. This paper reviews the literature that has emerged in seeking to understand this new trend, which was contrary to expectations and became known as the nonmetropolitan turnaround. Work includes macroanalyses of changes in nonmetropolitan settlement structure, changes in the distribution of employment, migration streams and differentials, as well as research on residential preferences and migration decision making. This is a new trend in terms of population distribution processes, although evidence that it reflects a greater importance of noneconomic factors in migration is mixed. Nonmetropolitan growth slowed in the latter part of the 1970s and overall the turnaround reversed in the early 1980s, but a return to a generally concentrating settlement pattern appears unlikely. The amount of research accomplished over a short span of time as a consequence of the turnaround is noteworthy, and the findings have contributed to increased understanding of US population change.

INTRODUCTION

In 1973 analyses of post-1970 data revealed that nonmetropolitan areas of the United States were growing more rapidly than metropolitan areas and that there were more people moving from metropolitan to nonmetropolitan areas than in the opposite direction (US Bureau of the Census 1973, Beale 1974). This trend was in striking contrast with previous decades and appeared to run counter to generally accepted interpretations of population redistribution processes and

259

0360-0572/85/0815-0259$02.00

assumptions about trends for the immediate future. Although after the fact one can find predictions of such a deconcentration (for example, Berry 1970, Lampard 1968), and empirical evidence of the developing trend was discussed earlier by Beale (1969), evidently no one can claim to have anticipated a shift of this magnitude for the 1970s. Prevailing wisdom had been that concentration in and around large cities would continue, along with decentralization within the commuting vicinity of these centers.

In the decade following this discovery, the nonmetropolitan turnaround, as it came to be called, generated a great deal of popular interest and speculation. It also inspired a considerable amount of research by sociologists, geographers, and economists, on the empirical basis of this trend, along with speculations and practical and theoretical explanations of why and how it was taking place. Much of the completed work to date has addressed theoretical concerns. To be sure, the turnaround was a surprise because a long-standing empirical trend was reversed, but also it was a surprise because many theoretical statements justified an expectation that the older trends would continue with minor modification. This made the empirical fact of the turnaround controversial from the beginning and understandably gave rise to efforts to explain these facts in the context of older paradigms.

Human ecologists, economists, and geographers have emphasized the advantages of proximity, or population agglomeration, in the location of economic activities and complex organizational structures. Is the turnaround really consistent with this? Do methodological or measurement problems underlie apparent contradictions? In the first section of this paper I will consider research on the patterns of differential population change that contributes to this issue. Does the population turnaround reflect changes in the structure of activities? In particular, does the new phenomenon somehow reflect a diminishing relation between population redistribution and the location of economic opportunities? This will be considered at the macro level in the second section.

Differential population growth within the United States is today largely due to migration streams, since fertility is low and differentials among areas not very pronounced (Long & Frey 1982, Wardwell & Brown 1980, Beale 1975). Possible changes in migration streams and differentials are considered in the third section. Is the shift to nonmetropolitan areas indicative of a change in residential preferences and migration decisions that may favor more remote areas and reflect a greater concern for noneconomic factors? This is assumed or implied in many general statements about the turnaround, and I will note some research that pertains to this issue. Finally, the recent dampening of the turnaround trend will be noted and some conclusions drawn about this area of study.

A great deal of research relates to this new trend and so the present review must be highly selective. Although there is considerable evidence of a parallel trend taking place in other advanced countries (Vining & Kontuly 1978; Wardwell 1980; Vining 1982) attention must be restricted to the United States. Basic concern here is with determinants of the nonmetropolitan side of the US turnaround.

A NEW SETTLEMENT STRUCTURE?

Many writers have viewed the spatial organization of society as dominated by a system of metropolises differentiated by size and economic function (Hawley 1950, Duncan et al 1960, Berry 1977). Attention has been given to the increasingly diffuse nature of this metropolitan-oriented settlement and to some deconcentration of industry (particularly low-wage, labor-intensive manufacturing) extending into nonmetropolitan areas. However, researchers generally assumed prior to 1970 that the growth forces should lead to continued slow growth or decline outside the commuting fields of larger cities, with an emptying out of the remote rural areas due to decreasing employment in agriculture and other extractive industries.

So when it was announced in 1973 that nonmetropolitan areas were growing more rapidly than metropolitan areas, an immediate assumption was that the pattern must be consistent with the above perspective. If the more rapid nonmetropolitan growth was primarily in counties peripheral to metropolitan areas, or in other counties having larger cities that might soon achieve metropolitan status, then the old trend would be continuing as metropolitanization, albeit in a somewhat more diffuse form. On the contrary, using county population estimates that were available prior to 1980, along with previous census data, several researchers reported that instead the new nonmetropolitan growth trend was widespread throughout the country even in counties not adjacent to metropolitan areas. As well, the trend was no longer associated with level of local urbanization (Beale 1975, Beale & Fuguitt 1978, Lamb 1978, McCarthy & Morrison 1979). Patterns for 1950–1960 and 1960–1970 are quite consistent with established theory: more rapid growth and net migration gain in adjacent counties, very slow growth or decline in nonadjacent counties, and a positive association of growth and migration for counties classed by the size of their largest city. In the post-1970 period, all nonmetropolitan rates were considerably higher than previously. Although growth continued to be greatest near metropolitan centers, where two thirds of the absolute increment was found, within more remote locations the most rapid growth was in completely rural counties.

Consistent with the more rapid growth in adjacent counties, a continued positive association of both population change and net migration for counties grouped by percent of employed who were commuting to metropolitan areas emerged (Long 1981:22). The importance of commuting to metropolitan areas, however, is evidently less than this relationship implies. Using the 1975 Annual Housing Survey, Bowles & Beale (1980) found that only 9% of employed nonmetropolitan household heads commuted to metropolitan jobs, and among recent metro to nonmetro migrants, only 17% worked in metropolitan locations.

Another possible relationship that would be consistent with earlier concepts of urbanization is the association of growth with presence of an interstate highway. Recent national level studies, however, give only limited support to the view that the decentralization of population and economic activities are channelled along interstate highways (Lichter & Fuguitt 1980, Briggs 1980, Miller 1979).

Taaffe et al (1980) combine the two preceding issues by examining commuting in a specific intermetropolitan area connected by an interstate highway. They conclude there is little evidence for the metropolitan absorption of the periphery due to the expansion of commuting into nonmetropolitan areas.

An important aspect of the change in nonmetropolitan population distribution is seen by comparing growth in and outside of urban places (Long 1978, 1981; Fuguitt et al 1981; Lichter & Fuguitt 1982; Long & DeAre 1982a). Prior to 1970, nonmetropolitan cities as a whole were growing almost as rapidly as metropolitan cities, with decline or negligible growth in the remainder of the population. During the 1970s, although place growth increased somewhat in nonmetropolitan areas, the major increase was in the population outside cities. This shows that the turnaround was almost entirely due to increased growth in nonurban locations, even in areas remote from nonmetropolitan centers.

Vining & Strauss (1977) used another approach in measuring change in population distribution in their much-cited "clean break" article. In updating the work of Duncan et al (1961) the authors calculated a time series of Hoover indices of population concentration for different sized geographic units. (Each of these is an index of dissimilarity comparing the distributions of population and land area among a set of units.) They showed population deconcentration at the regional and state level, but concentration at the Economic Subregion, State Economic Area, and county levels, indicating differential growth in and around large cities from 1900 through 1970. ("Economic Subregions" and "State Economic Areas" are groupings of counties formerly used by the US Census Bureau.) After 1970, however, all the geographic units showed deconcentration. Gordon (1979) criticizes the conclusion of this article, contending that the change can still be explained by a "wave"—i.e. metropolitan—influence theory. This he does by giving more weight to the fact that adjacent counties continue to have higher growth and inmigration rates than nonadjacent counties than he does to the fact that the increase in growth level over the past two decades was greater in nonadjacent counties.

Overall, the "clean break" issue has generated more heat than light. In answer to the question posed at the beginning of this section, it is clear that growth patterns have changed, particularly as they affect more remote parts of the country and differential rural-urban growth most everywhere. But numerically most of the nonmetropolitan growth continues to be at the peripheries of metropolitan areas. Work comparing more than two time periods, however, (for example Beale & Fuguitt 1978) also has shown the trend was not really a drastic post-1970 shift, as there was evidence of increasing nonmetropolitan growth in the 1960–1970 period, with the 1960–1970 migration differential partially masked by higher fertility levels. "Clean break" or "new settlement structure" may even suggest to some people that we are somehow dismantling the metropolitan system; yet, using constant 1974 metropolitan areas, we find instead a continuation of the growth levels of the early 1970s with a higher proportion of population metropolitan in the year 2000 than prevailed in 1950 (Fuguitt & Beale 1977).

This brings us to a paradox. Metropolitan areas, like cities, grow in two ways: by adding more people to existing territory, and by adding more territory either to existing areas or in the formation of new metropolitan areas. Using constant areas, whether defined according to 1980 or an earlier time, results in a declining proportion that is metropolitan over the 1970–1980 decade. Allowing for the addition of new metropolitan counties, however, results in a continuation of the increase in the proportion that is metropolitan to a high in 1980 of 75%. This is further complicated by the fact that the definition of metropolitan has become more liberal in recent years (Forstall 1981, Fuguitt et al 1983). The extent to which we are bound to our definitions is troublesome (see discussion in Bourne 1980). Zelinsky (1977) argues that metropolitan-nonmetropolitan is simply too gross a distinction, and indeed as we have seen, research routinely disaggregates these two sectors. Hawley & Mazie (1981a) suggest that just as the Metropolitan District and SMSA definitions partially displaced the urban distinction in response to metropolitan deconcentration, so we may soon need new categories to understand settlement and its changes. Just what these categories should be is not clear, however.

A NEW STRUCTURE OF ACTIVITIES?

In seeking to understand the turnaround as a possible aspect of societal change, it is necessary to consider the relations between population and the structure of activities in nonmetropolitan areas. Here three research strands may be identified.

The first strand is a comparative areas approach, in which various social and economic characteristics of geographic units (primarily counties) were associated with population change and net migration, contrasting the post-1970 period with earlier decades. Several generalizations emerged about the bases of nonmetropolitan growth (Beale 1974, 1975, 1976, 1977; Beale & Fuguitt 1978, McCarthy & Morrison 1979). For example, the association of net migration or population change with median family income for counties changed from clearly positive before 1970 to essentially no association after 1970. (Under the traditional view that population growth is associated with economic opportunities, one would expect a continued positive association.) Over the 1950 to post-1970 period, the level of manufacturing activity and government variables (state capitals, presence of a 4-year state college, military bases) generally declined in their association with population change or migration, whereas recreation and/or retirement and mining typically became more highly associated with growth. Other variables considered were percent employed in agriculture, and for the South, percent Black, both of which generally retained negative associations with change for each time period. Results using multiple regression, though including varying sets of variables, generally supported these findings except that the importance of mining usually was diminished.

Instead of growth, or net migration, some included a turnaround variable comparing change in post-1970 levels of growth with that for 1960–70 (McCarthy & Morrison 1979, Krout 1977). In a similar vein, Hansen (1973), Brown & Beale (1981), Poston (1983), and Johansen & Fuguitt (1984) contrasted the characteristics of areas differentiated by two-decade growth patterns.

Several of the works cited above also considered the geographic clustering of counties characterized by recent growth or decline and associated with various economic activities (see also Hart 1984). Although manufacturing was more dispersed, recreation and retirement were particularly notable as a resource-related activity important in certain rapidly growing areas such as the Ozarks and the Upper Great Lakes regions. Similarly a contiguous area of slow growth and decline remains in the Great Plains after 1970. Yet for no large area could growth be attributed primarily to a single factor.

The second strand concerned changes in nonmetropolitan employment. During the 1970s the farm population continued its decline (Banks & Kalbacher 1980). But perhaps the significant point here is that the new population change came at a time when the agricultural population had become a very small proportion of the total, clearly no longer dominant in affecting population change.

During the 1960s a marked increase in nonmetropolitan manufacturing and related industries became evident. Haren (1970) reported that although three quarters of the manufacturing jobs were in metropolitan areas, more than one third of the new manufacturing jobs in 1962–1969 were in nonmetropolitan areas, and manufacturing provided one half of the new job additions in rural and semi-rural counties. The growth of nonmetropolitan manufacturing employment slowed down in the 1970s, although its share of total manufacturing employment rose because of manufacturing decline in metropolitan areas. Only about a fifth of the nonmetropolitan job growth in the 1962–1978 period came from manufacturing, however (Haren & Holling 1979).

Till (1973) compared southern county locational patterns of change in manufacturing and in total nonfarm employment (based on County Business Patterns data) with change in total population. (Unlike population census data, County Business Patterns data are by job location, rather than by residence of the employed.) With counties classed according to adjacency and size of largest place in the county, he set up hypotheses based on the centralization and metropolitan deconcentration literature, which generally were confirmed for the 1960–1970 population trends. Contrary to the hypotheses, he found that a large amount of 1960–1970 industrialization occurred in distant rural counties. Till explained the discrepancy between the pattern for jobs and for population as due to the fact that new jobs were taken up by the labor pool made available by the decline in farm employment.

Till's work was updated and extended to the entire United States by Long & DeAre (1982b). Using more recent County Business Patterns data and county population estimates, they compared the change in numbers of jobs with population change by residence groups for 1975–1979. Employment growth across most industries followed population in this more recent period, higher in nonmetropolitan counties but not consistently higher in adjacent or more urban counties.

Research on possible reasons behind these trends in deconcentration of employment must remain beyond the scope of this review. More attention seems to have been given to the consequences of rural industrialization than to its possible determinants (Summers et al 1976; but see Smith et al 1978 and Lonsdale & Browning 1971 for examples of research on determinants). A very influential interpretation, however, was that of Thompson (1969) in which he argued that low-wage, labor-intensive industries could decentralize economically, with more innovative and higher wage activity remaining in or near the centers of the metropolis. Subsequent work confirmed the importance of low-wage labor-intensive industries in nonmetropolitan locations, but the proportion of other industrial activities has increased over time in remote locations (Till 1973, Petrulis 1979, Long & DeAre 1982b). Menchik (1981) argues that the service sector similarly is deconcentrating due to the routinization and segregation of service functions.

A third related strand of research on the deconcentration of activities relates to work force migration by place of work, as indicated through the Continuous Work History file of the Social Security Administration. Results show patterns of employment deconcentration in the 1970s among types of counties and subregions consistent with those for the total population discussed previously. This data set allows examination of migration streams (though between workplaces rather than residences), and findings include the fact that nonmetropolitan areas had both an increase of inmovement and a decline in outmovement of job locations as a part of the new trend, with most of the inmovement from the larger metropolitan areas (Wardwell & Gilchrist 1980, Brown 1981). For

Michigan, a large decrease after 1975 in the nonmetropolitan ratio of worker to population net migration was interpreted as indicating that a major component of population deconcentration is independent of changes in the workforce (Zuiches & Price 1980). From the Continuous Work History McCarthy & Morrison (1979) obtained county average 1971 earnings for all workers and 1971–1973 earnings changes for all working inmigrants. This they introduced into a regression of US nonmetropolitan counties using change in 1960–1970 and 1970–1974 net migration from Census sources as the dependent variable. Level of earnings had a negative coefficient, and change in migrant's earnings was not significant, not supporting an economic opportunity explanation of the net migration change. Carpenter (1980) considered the retention of persons who changed employment from a metropolitan to a nonmetropolitan county between 1961 and 1972 and found that the percentage of those remaining longer than three years increased substantially between 1967 and 1969.

Overall, the results in this section have led to somewhat divergent conclusions. The finding, for example, that areas with an initial concentration in manufacturing were not growing as rapidly as amenity areas after 1970, and the finding that the previous positive association between county family median income and migration or population change no longer holds, have led some to assert that noneconomic factors are more important in explaining the new trend than the old. Yet some other work comparing counties showed that increased employment in most nonagriculture industries ran parallel with increased population in the turnaround period. This discrepancy is in part due to the fact that the first approach—largely because of lack of available post-1970 data—associated migration and population change with the initial level of socioeconomic variables and could not pick up shifts in the location of economicactivity.

Of course the emphasis on economic and noneconomic factors is a matter of degree. Even writers who stress residential preferences as a basis for the turnaround recognize that most migrants need to be employed at their new location (for example, Wardwell 1980). Chalmers & Greenwood (1980) are among those positing a cumulative causation, with employment attracting migrants and new migrants leading to increases in employment. Hirschl & Summers (1982) show that nonmetropolitan areas with retirement transfer payments at a high level have experienced increased service employment.

Two macro-level studies have addressed the question of economic and noneconomic factors by comparing elderly and nonelderly migration. Heaton et al (1981) contrasted locational and traditional economic variables (percent in agriculture, mining, manufacturing, median family income) with amenity variables (presence of a lake, river, or ocean; temperature; recreational development) as of the beginning of each period. Although amenities may indicate economic opportunities as well as a pleasant environment, they nevertheless show a striking shift in patterns of net migration for the nonelderly population with 40 percent of the variance explained by traditional economic variables in the 1950s, but only 2 percent in the 1970s; at that point recreational development and mild temperature emerged as the important determinants of growth. For the elderly, amenity variables were twice as important as economic and locational variables in the 1950s, and the importance of the economic variables declined by the 1970s.

Fitzsimmons et al (1980) used change in employment, based on County Business Patterns data, for their economic variable. They argued that elderly migration is a direct measure of amenity-based migration and concluded, through a correlation analysis with nonmetropolitan counties, that amenities and economic opportunities each have substantial and largely independent influences on nonelderly net migration, with the amenity factor possibly more important. A similar analysis for metropolitan counties gave a slight edge to economic influences. The use of elderly migration as a proxy for amenities here is imprecise, as many elderly surely must move toward their place of origin, children, or care facilities, rather than toward amenities.

In the most elaborate analysis on the economic-noneconomic question to date, Williams (1981) examined age-adjusted 1955–1960 and 1965–1970 inmigration and outmigration streams for State Economic Areas of the North Central region. (Many parts of the Midwest were already undergoing renewed growth in the 1960s.) The migration data were related to census employment change data for 1950–1960 and 1960–1970 along with amenity and other variables in a three-stage least squares model. Williams showed that the most important change between the 1950s and the 1960s was in the determinants of employment growth rather than the determinants of migration. Instead of a decline of employment-related factors as determinants of migration, there was an increase in the association of employment growth with amenity areas.

In sum, work reviewed in this section appears unequivocal in showing a changed structure of activities in nonmetropolitan areas. With the decline in farming there has been a decentralization of manufacturing that was particularly important in the decade preceding the turnaround, whereas the most recent decade has seen the expansion of a wider range of industrial and service activities, and the emergence of growth areas where retirement and recreation are important. Research to date has not settled (if indeed this is possible) the question of the importance of any increase in a noneconomic basis for migration, though clearly economic considerations are very important. More formal causal modeling, following the lead of Williams, is needed. Yet this has been difficult because of the lack of data. Post-1970 data of any kind are only now becoming available, whereas an accurate determination of the interrelation of economic change and population growth using small areas would require gross flows (births, deaths, and migration) of both people and jobs on a short-term basis, repeated over an extended period. The two sections that follow also include consideration of this issue from different perspectives.

NEW MIGRATION STREAMS AND DIFFERENTIALS?

Stream analysis reveals the structure of population movement between areas and types of areas, going behind net patterns of growth that are the consequences of this structure. Has this structure of movement changed with the nonmetropolitan turnaround? The analysis of differential population characteristics of movers and stayers at areas of origin and destination can tell us something about both the determinants of movement and the consequences in terms of human resources. Have recent quantitative shifts in population been associated with shifts in the population characteristics of the sending and receiving areas?

A theoretical perspective on the turnaround to which possible changes in streams and differentials relate is the equilibrium hypothesis set forth by Wardwell (1977, 1980). In brief, he argues that the turnaround is a culmination of the metropolitanization process in which there is a convergence of metropolitan and nonmetropolitan differences, including migration differentials. From this one would predict that the migration streams going in opposite directions should have become more similar over time.

The fact that the distributional patterns of the turnaround were already well underway in many areas by 1970 has led some analysts (including Williams [1981] already discussed) to use the State Economic Area stream data of the 1970 and the 1960 censuses. Roseman & McHugh (1982) and Roseman (1983) examined metropolitan and nonmetropolitan SEAs by size. They found, consistent with Wardwell & Gilchrist (1980) and Brown (1981) cited above, that the largest metropolitan areas were most important as sources of the migration gain of nonmetropolitan areas. Comparing 1955–1960 with 1965–1970 they found that the migration efficiency (net migrants divided by the sum of inmigrants and outmigrants) was less in the later period. On the assumption that movement to nonmetropolitan areas rests on a more diverse set of both economic and noneconomic reasons than the countermovement, they showed further that outmigration fields for metropolitan areas were more varied than inmigration fields over both time periods.

Tucker (1976) compared age data by migration status for the 1965–1970 period from the 1970 census, and the 1970–1975 period from the 1975 Current Population Survey. There was an increase in inmigration and a decrease in outmigration for nonmetropolitan areas for all but two young-adult age groups, but the nonmetropolitan outmigration rate remained considerably above that for the metropolitan outmigration. Consistent with the equilibrium idea, Tucker showed that part of the increase in the relative importance of the metropolitan to nonmetropolitan stream, compared with the one in the opposite direction, is due to the increasing proportion of the population residing in metropolitan areas. Even if rates in both directions should remain constant, as the proportion that is metropolitan increases a level will be reached such that the number moving to nonmetropolitan areas will exceed the number in the other direction.

The feedback between metropolitan-nonmetropolitan, age-specific migration streams and changes in composition and future population growth are explored by Rogerson (1984). Projecting 1970s fertility, mortality, and migration to 2000 would lead to an older population in nonmetropolitan areas and in turn lower rates of natural increase there.

Further work with these data sources has considered variables such as education, occupation, industry, and income status in addition to age and sex (Wardwell 1977, Bowles 1978, Zuiches & Brown 1978; and for two states, DeJong & Humphrey 1976 and Davis & Fuguitt 1976). These showed clearly that the new trend is not due simply to increased movement of people outside the work force, or of those representing any particular economic or occupational group. Generally, this research revealed that the characteristics of the migrant streams in both directions are similar, with younger age structures and higher education and occupational status than for nonmovers in either metropolitan or nonmetropolitan areas, although the nonmetropolitan to metropolitan migrants usually had a disproportionate share of all three, when compared with those moving from metropolitan to nonmetropolitan areas.

Using log-linear analysis, Lichter et al (1979) extended the work reported above by examining changes in migration selectivity and migrant interchange between metropolitan and nonmetropolitan areas for 1955–1960, 1965–1970 and 1970–1975. Compared to earlier times, the post-1970 increase in the rate of outmigration from metropolitan areas can be partially attributed to the oldest, least educated, and lowest occupational status groups, but this has been partially offset by differential retention in nonmetropolitan areas of the young and highest socioeconomic status sectors. These findings have been controlled across the time periods for changes in migration flow and need to be interpreted very carefully, particularly in terms of the suggestion that the turnaround may be making nonmetropolitan areas worse off.

White (1982) examined family size differentials in central city-suburban and metropolitan-nonmetropolitan migration streams. He found results for the two interchanges to be similar and reported that part of the greater growth in nonmetropolitan and suburban areas occurs because families moving there are larger than those that go in the opposite direction.

In sum, research on streams and differentials has shown the new trend to be due both to increased inmigration from and decreased outmigration to metropolitan areas. Large metropolitan areas play a dominant role in originating turnaround migrants. The new trend is not due primarily to people outside the labor force, nor does it consist primarily of any particular educational or occupational groups. Evidence is mixed that the trend may be making nonmetropolitan areas worse off in terms of population, and social and economic characteristics; more definitive answers require analyses of data using characteristics of respondents both at the beginning and the end of the migration period. Similarly, support for the equilibrium hypothesis of Wardwell appears to be mixed. Support comes from Tucker's point about the relation of the metropolitan-nonmetropolitan migration interchange and the proportion that is metropolitan, and a finding by Roseman and McHugh (1982) of declining migration efficiency, but on the other hand Lichter et al (1979) showed the streams in the two directions becoming more dissimilar in composition over time.

NEW MIGRATION DECISIONS?

The nonmetropolitan turnaround was unanticipated in large part because it was assumed that major economic activities would continue to be concentrated in and around big cities, and that most migration would continue to be related to available job opportunities. Thus the macro level shifts ultimately rest on some assumptions about migration decisions (Shaw 1975:105). Many discussions of the turnaround have pointed to the quality of rural living as a basis of the trend, working through individual residential preferences and migration motivations (see Dillman 1979). Research reviewed here to this point has shown clearly that the macro pattern of population growth is new but that similar patterns have developed for the distribution of jobs; the characteristics of migrants to and from metropolitan areas have not undergone drastic change. All this suggests that no necessary shift has taken place in the bases of migration decisions; the turnaround is largely explainable by job-related migration. Yet this considerably oversimplifies thinking by economists, sociologists, and geographers concerning individual migration decisions; factors such as climate and amenities have long been considered along with economic opportunities (Greenwood 1975; Ritchey 1976; Svart 1976; Shaw 1975). Moreover, economists continue to argue the "chicken-egg" question of whether people follow jobs or jobs follow people (Muth 1971; Olvey 1972; Greenwood 1975; Steinnes 1978). The conclusion of Williams (1981) notwithstanding, this research has provided evidence that both processes are at work and so opens the door to suggestions that amenity-based, or noneconomically motivated, migration may result in increased economic opportunities.

Two major research lines relating to individual migration decisions and the population turnaround will be considered here: First, residential preferences, that is, where people say they would prefer to live; and second, reasons for migration, or why people say they move in the process of migration decision-making. Needless to say, neither exhausts the subject and neither has extended very far into the social psychological aspects of motivation. The turnaround, however, has helped to give impetus to the study of migration decision-making, most of which must remain beyond the scope of this brief review. Zuiches (1980, 1981) and Dillman (1979) have presented excellent reviews of work relating to residential preferences whereas decision-making has been included in migration reviews already cited and is the subject of a recent collection (DeJong & Gardner 1981).

Residential Preferences and the Turnaround

Under the old pattern of population change, an inconsistent finding was the high proportion of people who said they prefer to live in small towns and rural areas despite the fact that growth was most rapid in and around big cities. This was found to be true in a series of opinion polls and surveys going back to 1946, as reviewed in Fuguitt & Zuiches (1975), and led some policy-makers to argue that growth in rural areas should be encouraged, since that is where most people want to live. Work by Zuiches & Fuguitt (1972) and Fuguitt & Zuiches (1975) showed that this anomaly could be explained by adding the option of preference for residence within 30 miles of a big city. Surveys in Wisconsin and the United States as a whole showed that most people preferred living in small towns or rural areas but near large cities. Similar conclusions came from work by Dillman for Washington State, later replicated in several other states by coworkers (Dillman 1973). Zuiches (1981), however, argues that the 30-mile range from large cities would actually include considerable nonmetropolitan area, and so achieving this preference pattern would require nonmetropolitan growth. Similarly Dillman & Dobash (1972) found more than 80% of respondents in Washington State survey said they would least like to live in those large metropolitan areas that include a city of more than 500,000 people.

Do preferences lead to migration? There have been a few macro-level studies showing an association of preferences and migration patterns, including McCrae & Carlson (1980) and Lloyd (1976). At the individual level the evidence is scarce, in large part because an answer to this question requires a panel design of data collection. DeJong (1977) reported that after one year among the movers in Pennsylvania, only 14% moved to a location that achieved their preferences. Fredrickson et al (1980), however, reanalyzed these data excluding those not changing size of place, so as to remove most of the local movers among the respondents; they found that 79% moved in the direction of their preferences.

Heaton et al (1979) found persons preferring a type of residence different from their present one were five times more likely to intend to move than those who had attained their type of residence, controlling for satisfaction with present community.

Zuiches & Rieger (1978) and Howell & Frese (1983) report studies with several follow-ups over more than 10 years involving rural or nonmetropolitan high school students in a county in northern Michigan and in portions of the South respectively. Both studies showed an association between initial preference and subsequent residence, but over the study periods there were substantial changes in preferences. Howell & Frese demonstrated a dynamic relationship between preferences and residence through the adult years with initial preferences associated with later residence, but with residence in turn leading to a reformulation of preferences. Thus a change in both residence and preferences led to an increasing association between preference and residence over the time period of the study.

If we can assume there is or can be some association between preference and migration, then preferences could help to explain the turnaround in the following ways: (1) Preferences could change to favor remote rural areas, (2) Preferences could become more salient in the migration decision process and (3) The means to achieve preferences could have changed due to structural shifts in the society. Dillman (1979) reviews evidence from Gallup polls and from the work of Zuiches & Rieger (1978) and Cosby & Howard (1976) to show a definite shift in preferences toward living in rural areas. The greater salience of preferences in decision-making has only been inferred, although some supporting evidence does come from research on stated reasons for moving, covered in the next section. That the means to achieve preferences has changed has been noted by a number of writers (Carpenter 1977). Plausible arguments such as greater affluence, larger number of elderly people of independent means, and improved transportation have been given, but research directly relating to this issue seems to be lacking.

Reasons For Moving

In an effort to understand migration decisions, a fair amount of attention has been given to stated reasons for moving. As already indicated, interest in the turnaround literature has centered on the relative importance of economic and noneconomic reasons, given the presumed importance of the latter in explaining the new trend. Rossi (1955), Williams (1982), and many others have noted the difficulties in obtaining appropriate reasons from respondents, usually after the fact. The difficulty respondents may have in articulating reasons, and multiple interrelated reasons may make it very difficult to untangle economic and noneconomic components, for example.

Nevertheless, a number of national and local studies have asked recent migrants to give one or more reasons for moving. Early US level studies were Current Population Surveys in 1946 and 1963 (US Bureau of the Census 1947, 1966). These were compared with results from the 1973 through 1976 Annual Housing Survey by Long & Hansen (1979) with job-related reasons most often given by long distance (intercounty or interstate) movers over the preceding year in each study.

Long & DeAre (1980) did a similar analysis for movers between metropolitan and nonmetropolitan areas based on the 1975 Annual Housing Survey. People moving to metropolitan areas for economic reasons outnumber those moving in the other direction, so according to this source we would not have a migration turnaround if people moved only for economic reasons. Retirement, however, is a reason given by less than six percent, and change of climate by two percent of the metropolitan to nonmetropolitan migrants, whereas each of these reasons are reported by less than two percent of the nonmetropolitan to metropolitan migrants. Nevertheless, a retirement residence may be the ultimate objective for many middle-aged migrants who continue to work.

In a further analysis with the 1973–1977 Annual Housing Surveys, Sell (1983) classified reasons as forced (as, building demolished, natural disaster), imposed (as, job transfers, armed forces, or to attend college) or preference-dominated. Overall, 72% of the interstate nonmetropolitan-metropolitan moves were employment related, including 32% classed as imposed due to job transfers. Corresponding figures for interstate metropolitan-nonmetropolitan moves were lower, at 55% and 27% respectively. An important conclusion from this work is the need to recognize forces external to the individual or family in studying migration decision-making.

During the 1970s a number of surveys were done in selected nonmetropolitan areas throughout the country, several of which included questions on reasons for moving. Generally these studies, located in areas of high inmigration, showed a greater importance for noneconomic reasons, with a significant minority being return migrants. In an Ozark study, Campbell et al (1977) found that more than one half of the interstate (and not return) inmigrants gave an economic reason, but this was true of less than one third of the return migrants, for whom family ties and amenities were of almost equal importance. Of all migrants, 43% had lived in the area previously.

Thomas & Bachtel (1978) surveyed a five-county turnaround area in southern Ohio and found one third of those who moved in since 1970 were return migrants. In all, only 23% listed a job-related reason in an open-ended response, and almost 50% gave "to live in the country," and "to get out of the city" as very important.

Bradshaw & Blakely (1980) interviewed fifty migrants (moved in within five years) in each of five nonmetropolitan communities (resort, retirement, counterculture, regional trade, and commerce-industrial) in California, with responses indicating rural atmosphere or nearness to family or friends were more important as reasons than job prospects.

A major advance was made by Sofranko and associates (Williams & Sofranko 1979, Voss & Fuguitt 1979, Roseman & Williams 1980, Sofranko &

Williams 1980, Sofranko & Fliegel 1983) in dividing the reason analysis into two parts—why respondents left their place of origin, and why they chose their particular destinations (Brown & Moore 1970; Ritchey 1976). This telephone survey of respondents in rapidly growing nonmetropolitan counties of the North Central states compared 1970–1975 migrants from metropolitan, and from other nonmetropolitan counties with nonmigrants. About one fourth of the metropolitan origin migrants left their place of origin, and the same proportion chose their nonmetropolitan place of destination for employment reasons, but this was true of almost one half of the nonmetropolitan origin migrants. Environmental factors, such as dissatisfaction with urban living, were given by about two fifths of the metropolitan migrants and one fifth of the nonmetropolitan migrants as reasons for leaving their place of origin. Ties to the community were important in choosing a destination for both types of migrants. In resort areas it was typical to have visited regularly for recreation, or to already own a second home in the area.

To sum up, there is evidence that the move to nonmetropolitan areas does have a different motivational basis than the more traditional move in the other direction, or the move between different nonmetropolitan areas. Residential preferences are associated with migration intentions and appear also to be associated with migration behavior. There is some indication of an increase over time in the preference for rural and nonmetropolitan living. Persons moving from metropolitan to nonmetropolitan areas are less likely to give economic reasons than those in the other streams, with antiurban sentiments expressed as reasons for leaving metropolitan areas, and previous ties important as a reason for going to a particular nonmetropolitan area.

THE END OF THE TURNAROUND?

Is the nonmetropolitan population turnaround coming to an end? Richter (1983) obtained a file of county population estimates for single years between 1970 and 1980, adjusted for the results of both censuses. She compared three time periods, 1970–1974, 1974–1977, and 1977–1980 in analyses similar to those done for earlier periods by Beale & Fuguitt (1978) and Heaton et al (1981). Growth differences favoring nonmetropolitan areas peaked in the middle period and were least for 1977–1980. Reduced growth was particularly noteworthy in more remote areas, including some specialized amenity areas such as the Upper Great Lakes. Although the turnaround continued between 1977 and 1980, nonmetropolitan growth by that time can almost be explained as extended deconcentration adjacent to metropolitan areas.

In a follow-up of his earlier work, Tucker (1983) compared age-specific inmigration and outmigration for 1970–1975 with 1975–1980 between US metropolitan and nonmetropolitan areas. He found a continued but diminished net migration to nonmetropolitan areas for the later period, with a slight decrease in metropolitan outmigration and a somewhat greater increase in nonmetropolitan outmigration, compared with 1970–1975.

Similarly a recent decline in the nonmetropolitan advantage in job growth has been noted by Bluestone (1982) and by Garnick (1983). Recently the Census Bureau announced, on the basis of 1982 preliminary county population estimates, that since 1980 once again nonmetropolitan areas have been growing more slowly than metropolitan areas. Undoubtedly there will be considerable activity monitoring and interpreting these population and employment trends as post-1980 data become available.

Whether or not the trends of the early 1970s return, we should continue to have a rather diffuse settlement pattern and, in any event, work inspired by the turnaround has made a significant contribution to our understanding of the changing population distribution in the United States. We know more about changes in employment as well, and how migration and employment trends are interrelated, though the latter needs much more attention. Applying new methodology and employing new data sets has yielded insights in the study of migration streams and differentials. The study of residential preferences as related to rural-urban location was considered something of a curiosity by many a decade ago, but now has been incorporated into micro-migration models, and progress in this work should continue. Similarly, research on reasons for moving engendered by the turnaround has contributed to the growing interest and development of theory and research in migration decision-making.

The turnaround was a new trend in population distribution. There was a parallel shift in the location of jobs, and a minimal shift overall in the importance of various migration streams and differentials between metropolitan and nonmetropolitan areas. Some limited evidence suggests an increase in preference for living in rural areas, and we know that for many movers from metropolitan areas—and not just the elderly—there is the push of anti-urban sentiment. We need to know more about the movement away from metropolitan areas from the perspective of these areas of origin (for a recent macro level study, see Swanson 1983). The importance of ties to the area of destination as an attractive force has been brought out by a number of field studies. The effect of ties at both origin and destination needs to be better understood and may help in better predicting future trends. More generally, we must get a better handle on what "amenities" are, what they mean to people, how they affect migration and the location of economic activities, and how tastes in amenities can change. The importance of economic vs quality of life factors in the move to more rural locations continues to be debated (Ploch & Cook 1982, Williams 1982), and this issue should motivate further research at both macro- and micro-levels of analysis to extend our knowledge of migration.

Finally, the fact that disciplines of the social sciences have together had the capacity to marshall as much effort over a relatively short period of time to study this phenomenon should be mentioned. The contrast with the massive post-World War II outmigration from rural areas is striking. Most of the interest in this earlier movement by researchers and policymakers came in the 1960s after it was almost over. Not only do we have more workers and better facilities for analysis today, we are not tied nearly so much to the decennial censuses, having available intercensal county estimates and other national and local survey data. Whether this capacity and interest will be used to monitor and better explain a continuing "Rural Renaissance," or to examine anticipated or unanticipated shifts in other directions, there should be steady progress in the study of migration and population redistribution.

ACKNOWLEDGMENTS

This work has been supported by the College of Agricultural and Life Sciences, University of Wisconsin-Madison, and the Economic Development Division, US Department of Agriculture, through a cooperative agreement, and by the Center for Demography and Ecology, University of Wisconsin-Madison, through a grant from the Center for Population Research of the National Institute of Child Health and Human Development. The comments of Calvin Beale, David Brown, Tim Heaton, Dan Lichter, Curtis Roseman, and the anonymous reviewers for *Annual Review of Sociology* are gratefully acknowledged, along with the bibliographic and clerical assistance of Karen Weed, Ward Patton, and Kris Zehner.

Literature Cited

Banks, V. J., Kalbacher, J. Z. 1980. *U.S. Farm Populations*. *ESCS-96*, USDA Econ., Stat. Coop. Serv., Washington, DC

Beale, C. L. 1969. Demographic and social considerations for U.S. rural economic policy. *Am. J. Agric. Econ.* 51:411–27

Beale, C. L. 1974. Rural development: population and settlement prospects. *J. Soil. Water Conserv.* 29:23–7

Beale, C. L. 1975. *The Revival of Population Growth in Nonmetropolitan America*. *ERS-605*, USDA, Econ. Res. Serv., Washington, DC

Beale, C. L. 1976. A further look at nonmetropolitan population growth since 1970. *Am. J. Agric. Econ.* 58:953–8

Beale, C. L. 1977. The recent shift of United States population to nonmetropolitan areas, 1970–1975. *Int. Reg. Sci. Rev.* 2:113–22

Beale, C. L., Fuguitt, G. V. 1978. The new pattern of nonmetropolitan population change. In *Social Demography*, ed. K. Taeuber, L. Bumpass, J. Sweet, pp. 157–77. New York: Academic. 336 pp.

Berry, B. J. L. 1970. The geography of the United States in the year 2000. *Trans. of the Inst. of Brit. Geog.* 51:21–53

Berry, B. J. L. 1977. Transformation of the nation's urban system: small city growth as a zero-sum game. See Bryce 1977, pp. 283–300

Bluestone, H. 1982. *Employment growth in metro and nonmetro America: a change in the pattern?* *Ag. Econ. Rep. 492*, USDA Econ. Res. Serv., Washington, DC

Bourne, L. S. 1980. Alternative perspectives on urban decline and population deconcentration. *Urban Geogr.* 1:39–52

Bowles, G. K. 1978. Contributions of recent metro/nonmetro migrants to the nonmetro population and labor force. *Agric. Econ. Res.* 30:15–22

Bowles, G. K., Beale, C. L. 1980. *Commuting Patterns of Nonmetro Household Heads*. Athens, Georgia: Univ. of Georgia Printing Dept.

Bradshaw, T. K., E. J. Blakely. 1980. Migrants to growing small towns. *Proc. of Small*

Cities and Reg. Comm., 3rd, Stevens Point 1980, ed. R. P. Wolensky, E. J. Miller, pp. 45–58. Stevens Point: UWSP Foundation

Briggs, R. 1980. *The impact of the interstate highway system on nonmetropolitan growth.* U.S. Dept. Trans., Res. and Special Prog., Washington, DC

Brown, D. L., Beale, C. L. 1981. Diversity in post-1970 population trends. See Hawley & Mazie 1981b, pp. 27–71

Brown, D. L. 1981. Spatial aspects of the post-1970 work force migration in the US. *Growth and Change* 12:9–20

Brown, D. R., Wardwell, J. M., eds. 1980. *New Directions in Urban-Rural Migration: The Population Turnaround in Rural America.* New York: Academic. 412 pp.

Brown, L. A., Moore, E. C. 1970. The intraurban migration process: a perspective. *Gen. Sys.* 15:109–22

Brunet, Y., ed. 1983. *Urban Exodus, Its Causes, Significance and Future. 83–01.* Dept. of Geog., Univ. of Montreal, Montreal. 208 pp.

Bryce, H., ed. 1977. *Small Cities in Transition: the Dynamics of Growth and Decline.* Cambridge, Mass.: Ballinger. 418 pp.

Campbell, R. R., Stangler, G. J., Dailey, G. H., McNamara, R. L. 1977. *Population change, migration, and displacement along the McClellan-Kerr River Navigation System. Contract Report 77–5,* Inst. for Water Res., Univ. of Mo., Columbia

Carpenter, E. H. 1977. Potential for population dispersal: a closer look at residential location preferences. *Rural Sociol.* 42:357–70

Carpenter, E. H. 1980. Retention of metropolitan-to-nonmetropolitan labor-force migrants. See Brown & Wardwell 1980, pp. 213–32

Chalmers, J. A., Greenwood, M. J. 1980. The economics of the rural to urban population turnaround. *Soc. Sci. Q.* 61:524–44

Cosby, A. G., Howard, W. G. 1976. *Residential preferences in America: the growing desire for rural life.* USDA Ext. Serv., Rur. Dev. Ser., Washington, DC

Davis, N. J., Fuguitt, G. V. 1976. *Metropolitan and nonmetropolitan migration streams in Wisconsin 1965–1970. Pop. Series 70–6,* Appl. Pop. Lab, Univ. of Wisc., Madison

DeJong, G. F. 1977. Residential preferences and migration. *Demography* 14:169–78

DeJong, G. F., Gardner, R. W. 1981. *Migration Decision Making: Multidisciplinary Approaches to Microlevel Studies in Developed and Developing Countries.* New York: Pergamon. 394 pp.

DeJong, G. F., Humphrey, C. R. 1976. Selected characteristics of metropolitan-to-nonmetropolitan area migrants: A study of population redistribution in Pennsylvania. *Rural Sociol.* 41:526–38

Dillman, D. A. 1973. *Population distribution policy and people's attitudes: current knowledge and needed research.* Prepared for Urban Land Inst. aided by U.S. Dep. of Housing and Urban Dev.

Dillman, D. A. 1979. Residential preferences, quality of life, and the population turnaround. *Am. J. Agric. Econ.* 61:960–66

Dillman, D. A., Dobash, R. P. 1972. *Preferences for community living and their implications for population redistribution. Wash. Agric. Exp. Sta. Bul. 764,* Pullman

Duncan, O. D., Cuzzart, R. P., Duncan, B. 1961. *Statistical Geography: Problems in Analyzing Areal Data.* Glencoe, Ill.: Free. 191 pp.

Duncan, O. D., Scott, R. S., Lieberson, S., Duncan, B. D., Winsborough, H. H. 1960. *Metropolis and Region.* Baltimore: The Johns Hopkins Press. 587 pp.

Fitzsimmons, J. D., Borchert, D. G., Adams, J. S. 1980. Recent U.S. population redistribution: a geographical framework for change in the 1980's. *Soc. Sci. Q.* 61:485–507

Forstall, Richard L. 1981. Is America becoming more metropolitan? *Am. Demogr.* 3(11):18–22

Fredrickson, C., Heaton, T. B., Fuguitt, G. V., Zuiches, J. J. 1980. Residential preferences in a model of migration intentions. *Pop. Environ.* 3:280–97

Fuguitt, G. V., Beale, C. L. 1977. Recent trends in city population growth and distribution. See Bryce 1977, pp. 13–27

Fuguitt, G. V., Zuiches, J. J. 1975. Residential preferences and population distribution. *Demography* 12:491–504

Fuguitt, G. V., Lichter, D. T., Beale, C. L. 1981. *Population deconcentration in metropolitan and nonmetropolitan areas of the United States, 1950–1975. Pop. Series 70–15,* Appl. Pop. Lab., Univ. of Wisc., Madison

Fuguitt, G. V., Lichter, D. T., Heaton, T. B. 1983. *Metropolitanization and the Nonmetropolitan Turnaround.* Presented at Ann. Meet. South. Reg. Demog. Group, Chattanooga

Garnick, D. H. 1983. Shifting patterns of the growth of metropolitan and nonmetropolitan areas. *Surv. Curr. Bus.* 63(5):39–52

Gordon, P. 1979. Deconcentration without a 'clean break'. *Environ. Plann.* 11:281–90

Greenwood, M. J. 1975. Research on internal migration in the United States: a survey. *J. Econ. Lit.* 13:397–433

Hansen, N. M. 1973. *The Future of Nonmetropolitan America: Studies in the Reversal of Rural and Small Town Population Decline.* Lexington, Mass.: Lexington. 187 pp.

Haren, C. C. 1970. Rural industrial growth in the 1960's. *Am. J. Ag. Econ.* 52:431–37

Haren, C. C., Holling, R. W. 1979. Industrial development in nonmetropolitan America: a locational perspective. In *Nonmetropolitan Industrialization*, ed. R. E. Lonsdale, H. L. Seyler, pp. 13–46. New York: Wiley

Hart, J. F. 1984. Population change in the Upper Lake States. *Ann. Assoc. Am. Geogr.* 74:221–243

Hawley, A. H. 1950. *Human Ecology: a theory of community structure.* New York: Ronald. 456 pp.

Hawley, A. H., Mazie, S. M. 1981a. An overview. See Hawley & Mazie 1981b, pp. 116–46

Hawley, A. H., Mazie, S. M., eds. 1981b. *Nonmetropolitan America in Transition.* Chapel Hill: Univ. of N. C. Press. 833 pp.

Heaton, T. B., Clifford, W. B., Fuguitt, G. V. 1981. Temporal shifts in the determinants of young and elderly migration in nonmetropolitan areas. *Soc. Forc.* 60:41–60

Heaton, T. B., Fredrickson, C., Fuguitt, G. V., Zuiches, J. J. 1979. Residential preferences, community satisfaction, and the intention to move. *Demography* 16:565–73

Hirschl, T. A., Summers, G. F. 1982. Cash transfers and the export base of small communities. *Rural Sociol.* 47:295–316

Howell, F. M., Frese, W. 1983. Size of place, residential preferences and the life cycle. *Am. Sociol. Rev.* 48:569–80

Johansen, H. E., Fuguitt, G. V. 1984. *The Changing Rural Village in America: Demographic and Economic Trends Since 1950.* Cambridge, Mass.: Ballinger. 259 pp.

Krout, J. A. 1977. *Net migration change in U.S. nonmetropolitan counties between the 1960's and 1970's: an examination of three alternative hypotheses.* Ph.D. thesis. Penn. State Univ. 114 pp.

Lamb, R. F. 1978. Intra-regional migration patterns in rural United States, 1950–1975. *Can. Stud. Pop.* 5:131–39

Lampard, E. E. 1968. The evolving system of cities in the United States: urbanization and economic development. In *Issues in Urban Economics*, ed. H. S. Perloff, L. Wingo, Jr., pp. 81–139. Baltimore: The Johns Hopkins Press. 668 pp.

Lichter, D. T., Fuguitt, G. V. 1980. Demographic response to transportation innovation: the case of the interstate highway. *Soc. Forc.* 59:492–512

Lichter, D. T., Fuguitt, G. V. 1982. The transition to nonmetropolitan population deconcentration. *Demography* 19:211–21

Lichter, D. T., Heaton, T. B., Fuguitt, G. V. 1979. Trends in the selectivity of migration between metropolitan and nonmetropolitan areas: 1955–1975. *Rural Sociol.* 44:645–66

Lloyd, R. E. 1976. Cognition, preference, and behavior in space: an examination of the structural linkages. *Econ. Geogr.* 52:241–53

Long, J. F. 1978. *The deconcentration of non-metropolitan population.* Presented at Ann. Meet. Pop. Assoc. Am., Atlanta

Long, J. F. 1981. *Population deconcentration in the United States. Spec. Demogr. Anal. CDS-81-S,* US Bur. of the Census, Washington, DC

Long, L. H., DeAre, D. 1980. *Migration to nonmetropolitan areas: appraising the trend and reasons for moving. Spec. Demogr. Anal. CDS-80-S,* US Bur. of the Census, Washington, DC

Long, L. H., DeAre, D. 1982a. Repopulating the countryside: a 1980 census trend. *Science* 217:1111–6

Long, L. H., DeAre, D. 1982b. *The economic base of recent population growth in nonmetropolitan settings.* Presented at Ann. Meet. Assoc. Am. Geogr., San Antonio

Long, L. H., Frey, W. H. 1982. *Migration and settlement: 14. United States. RR-82-15.* Int. Instit. for Applied Sys. Anal., Laxenburg, Austria

Long, L. H., Hansen, K. A. 1979. *Reasons for interstate migration jobs, retirement, climate and other influences. Curr. Pop. Rept. Ser. P-23, No. 81,* US Bureau of the Census, Washington, DC

Lonsdale, R. E., Browning, C. E. 1971. Rural-urban locational preferences of southern manufacturers. *Ann. Assoc. Am. Geogr.* 61:255–68

McCarthy, K. F., Morrison, P. A. 1979. *The changing demographic and economic structure of nonmetropolitan areas in the 1970's. Rand Pap. Ser. P-6062,* Rand Corp., Santa Monica, Calif.

McCrae, D., Carlson, J. R. 1980. Collective preferences as predictors of interstate migration. *Soc. Indic. Res.* 8:15–32

Menchik, M. D. 1981. The service sector. See Hawley and Mazie 1981b, pp. 231–54

Miller, J. P. 1979. Interstate highways and job growth in nonmetropolitan areas: a reassessment. *Transp. J.* 19:78–81

Muth, R. F. 1971. Migration: chicken or egg. *South. Econ. J.* 37:295–306

Olvey, L. D. 1972. Regional growth and interregional migration—their pattern of interaction. *Rev. Reg. Stud.* 2:139–63

Petrulis, M. F. 1979. *Growth patterns in non-metro-metro manufacturing employment. Rural Dev. Res. Report 7,* USDA, Washington, DC

Ploch, L. A., Cook, C. M. 1982. Turnaround migration and theoretical perspectives. *The Rur. Sociol.* 2:36–44

Poston, D. L. 1983. Demographic change in nonmetropolitan America in the 1960s and 1970s: population change vs. net migration change. *The Rur. Sociol.* 3:28–33

Richter, K. 1983. Nonmetropolitan growth in

the late 1970's: the end of the turnaround? *Demography* 22: In press

Ritchey, P. N. 1976. Explanations of migration. *Ann. Rev. Sociol.* 2:363–404

Rogerson, P. A. 1984. The demographic consequences of metropolitan population deconcentration in the U.S. *Prof. Geogr.* 36:307–14

Roseman, C. C. 1983. Changes in the spatial patterns of metropolitan to nonmetropolitan migration streams in the United States, 1955 to 1976. See Brunet 1983, pp. 63–75

Roseman, C. C., McHugh, K. E. 1982. Metropolitan areas as redistributors of population. *Urban Geogr.* 3:22–33

Roseman, C. C., Williams, J. D. 1980. Metropolitan to nonmetropolitan migration: a decision-making perspective. *Urban Geogr.* 1:283–294

Rossi, P. 1955. *Why Families Move.* Glencoe, Ill.: Free. 220 pp.

Sell, R. R. 1983. Analyzing migration decisions: the first step—whose decisions? *Demography* 20:299–311

Shaw, R. P. 1975. *Migration theory and fact. Bibliogr. Ser. No. 5.* Reg. Sci. Res. Inst., Philadelphia

Smith, E. D., Deaton, B. J., Kelch, D. R. 1978. Location determinants of manufacturing industry in rural areas. *South. J. Agric. Econ.* 10:23–32

Sofranko, A. J., Fliegel, F. C. 1983. Rural to rural migrants: the neglected component of rural population growth. *Growth and Change* 14:42–49

Sofranko, A. J., Williams, J. D., eds. 1980. *Rebirth of Rural America: Rural Migration in the Midwest.* Ames, Iowa: North Central Regional Center for Rural Development. 215 pp.

Steinnes, D. N. 1978. Causality and migration: a statistical resolution of the 'chicken and egg fowl-up'. *South. Econ. J.* 45:218–226

Summers, G. F., Evans, S. D., Clemente, F., Beck, E. M., Minkoff, J. 1976. *Industrial Invasion of Nonmetropolitan America: A Quarter Century of Experience.* New York: Praeger. 231 pp.

Svart, L. M. 1976. Environmental preference migration: a review. *Geog. Rev.* 66:314–30

Swanson, L. L. 1983. *SMSA characteristics and nonmetro-destined outmigration.* Presented at Ann. Meet. Pop. Assoc. Am., Pittsburgh

Taaffe, E. J., Gauthier, H. L., Maraffa, T. A. 1980. Extended commuting the intermetropolitan periphery. *Ann. Assoc. Am. Geogr.* 70:313–329

Thomas, D. W., Bachtel, D. C. 1978. *The rural turnaround in southern Ohio: A five county study.* Presented at Ann. Meet. Pop. Assoc. Am., Atlanta, Ga.

Thompson, W. R. 1969. The economic base of urban problems. In *Contemporary Economic Issues,* ed. N. W. Chamberlain, pp. 1–50. Homewood, Ill.: Irwin

Till, Thomas. 1973. The extent of industrialization in southern nonmetro labor markets in the 1960's. *J. Reg. Sci.* 13:456

Tucker, C. J. 1976. Changing patterns of migration between metropolitan and nonmetropolitan areas in the United States: recent evidence. *Demography* 13:435–443

Tucker, C. J. 1983. Metropolitan decentralization: United States in the 1970s. See Brunet 1983, pp. 47–62

US Bureau of the Census. 1947. *Postwar migration and its causes in the United States. Curr. Pop. Rept. Ser. P-20, No. 4,* US Bureau of the Census, Washington, DC

US Bureau of the Census. 1966. *Reasons for Moving: March 1962 to March 1963. Curr. Pop. Rept. Ser. P-20, No. 154,* US Bureau of the Census, Washington, DC

US Bureau of the Census. 1973. *Mobility of the population of the United States: March 1970 to March 1973. Curr. Pop. Rept. Pop. Char. Ser. P-20, No. 256,* US Bureau of the Census, Washington, DC

Vining, D. R. 1982. Migration between the core and the periphery. *Sci. Amer.* 247(6):45–53

Vining, D. R., Kontuly, T. 1978. Population dispersal from major metropolitan regions: an international comparison. *Int. Reg. Sci. Rev.* 3:49–73

Vining, D. R., Strauss, A. 1977. A demonstration that the current deconcentration of population in the United States is a clean break with the past. *Environ. Plann.* 9:751–58

Voss, P. R., Fuguitt, G. V. 1979. *Turnaround migration in the upper great lakes region. Pop. Series 70–12,* Appl. Pop. Lab., Univ. of Wisc., Madison

Wardwell, J. M. 1977. Equilibrium and Change in Nonmetropolitan Growth. *Rural Sociol.* 42:156–79

Wardwell, J. M. 1980. Toward a theory of urban-rural migration in the developed world. See Brown & Wardwell 1980, pp. 71–114

Wardwell, J. M., Brown, D. L. 1980. Population redistribution in the United States during the 1970s. See Brown & Wardwell 1980, pp. 5–32

Wardwell, J. M., Gilchrist, C. J. 1980. Employment deconcentration in the nonmetropolitan turnaround. *Demography* 17:145–58

White, R. 1982. Family size composition differentials between central city-surburb and metropolitan-nonmetropolitan migration streams. *Demography* 19:29–36

Williams, J. D. 1981. The nonchanging determinants of nonmetropolitan migration. *Rural Sociol.* 46:183–202

Williams, J. D. 1982. Turnaround migrants: grubby economics or delightful indulgence in ruralism? *The Rur. Sociol.* 2:104–8

Williams, J. D., Sofranko, A. J. 1979. Motivations for the immigration component of population turnaround in nonmetropolitan areas. *Demography* 16:239–56

Zelinsky, W. 1977. Coping with the migration turnaround: the theoretical challenge. *Int. Reg. Sci. Rev.* 2:175–78

Zuiches, J. J. 1980. Residential preferences in migration theory. See Brown & Wardwell 1980, pp. 163–88

Zuiches, J. J. 1981. Residential preferences in the Unites States. See Hawley & Mazie 1981, 72–115

Zuiches, J. J., Brown, D. L. 1978. The changing character of the nonmetropolitan population, 1950–75. In *Rural U.S.A. Persistence and Change,* ed. T. R. Ford, pp. 55–72. Ames: Iowa State Univ. Press. 255 pp.

Zuiches, J. J., Fuguitt, G. V. 1972. Residential preferences: implications for population redistribution in nonmetropolitan areas. In *Population Distribution and Policy,* ed. S. M. Mazie, vol. 5 of *Comm. Res. Rep.* Washington, DC: USGPO

Zuiches, J. J., Price, M. L. 1980. Industrial dispersal and labor-force migration: employment dimensions of the population turnaround in Michigan. See Brown & Wardwell 1980, pp. 333–64

Zuiches, J. J., Rieger, J. H. 1978. Size of place preferences and life cycle migration: A cohort comparison. *Rural Sociol.* 43:618–33

Ann. Rev. Sociol. 1985. 11:281–304

INTERORGANIZATIONAL RELATIONS

Joseph Galaskiewicz

Department of Sociology, University of Minnesota, Minneapolis, Minnesota 55455

Abstract

The article is an extensive review of the literature on interorganizational relations. Three arenas of interorganizational relations (IOR) are identified: arenas of resource procurement and allocation, political advocacy, and organizational legitimation. In studying IOR within arenas of resource procurement and allocation, analysts have focused on power dependency and the problems of overcoming environmental uncertainty. In studying IOR within arenas of political advocacy, students have paid special attention to coalition formation and efforts at collective action. In studying IOR within arenas of organizational legitimation, analysts have examined organizational efforts at identifying with highly legitimate community and/or societal symbols. In this review both the theory and research to date are discussed.

INTRODUCTION

This paper reviews the literature on interorganizational relations and summarizes the main theories and research findings. As we shall see, the body of accumulated knowledge is highly fragmented, and the scholarship uneven. Few studies have been replicated; thus we have a host of "tentative findings" to sort through and synthesize. Our effort at organizing the literature draws heavily on reviews by Guetzkow (1966), Van de Ven (1976), Pfeffer & Salancik (1978), Aldrich (1979), Van de Ven & Ferry (1980), Aldrich & Whetten (1981), Whetten (1981), Rogers & Whetten (1982), and Mulford (1984). The interested reader is strongly encouraged to examine these references; each provides an excellent overview of the literature that is somewhat different from the view presented here.

0360-0572/85/0815-0281$02.00

Interorganizational relations take place in three different arenas: resource procurement and allocation, political advocacy, and organizational legitimation. Research within each of these has been done at the level of the dyad (e.g. Reid 1964, Hall et al 1977, Galaskiewicz & Marsden 1978), action set (e.g. Stern 1979, Hirsch 1972, Alford 1975), and network (Van de Ven et al 1979, Galaskiewicz 1979a, Knoke & Rogers 1979, Burt 1983). This paper reviews the theories and research results that give meaning to interorganizational relations in each of these arenas.

ARENAS OF RESOURCE PROCUREMENT AND ALLOCATION

The direct procurement of facilities, materials, products, or revenues to ensure organizational survival has been an overriding reason for establishing interorganizational relations (Aldrich 1979, Hall 1982, Whetten 1981, Laumann et al 1978). Yuchtman & Seashore (1967) wrote the definitive theoretical treatise outlining the resource procurement position, reflecting an open systems perspective (Katz & Kahn 1966). At the same time, it is assumed that organizations strive for autonomy (Guetzkow 1966, Gouldner 1959, Burt 1982). If given the option, organizations would prefer *not* to establish interorganizational relations inasmuch as these relations can constrain their subsequent actions (Zeitz 1980). This gives rise to an interesting caricature of the reluctant organization striving to maintain its independence from others, while knowing that it must engage in interorganizational relations in order to procure the resources it needs.

Sociologists and organizational theorists have found a wide variety of ways that organizations have gone about solving problems of resource procurement and allocation. At one extreme we have the open competitive market of neoclassical microeconomic theory. Organizations are seen as competitive actors, each striving to achieve its own goals (Laumann et al 1978), with the final allocation of resources the product of a large number of small decisions negotiated at the level of the interorganizational dyad. Alternatively, we have centralized redistributive structures that coordinate the allocation of resources to member organizations (Rogers & Whetten 1982). These interorganizational organizations are often created by members themselves.

Whether they look at market-like or hierarchy-like solutions to the problems of resource allocation, sociologists have been especially sensitive to issues of power dependence and uncertainty in interorganizational transactions. While economists may dismiss these factors as "market imperfections" and thus aberrations, sociologists and organizational theorists see them as central to the resource procurement/allocation process.

Managing Power Dependencies

In the literature on interorganizational relations, power has always been conceived in relational terms and, more specifically, within a social exchange framework. The early work of Levine & White (1961) sensitized the field to the dynamics of barter and exchange in interorganizational relations. However, their conceptualization of exchange among organizations was much too broad. For Levine & White exchange was simply any voluntary activity between two organizations that helped them to realize their goals (see Cook 1977:64; Aldrich 1979:267). It encompassed both cooperative and coordinative behavior under the rubric of exchange. This was unfortunate, since cooperative and coordinative behavior assume common goals and some level of joint decision-making (Mulford & Rogers 1982:12). Obviously these are not prerequisites for an exchange transaction.

A new level of sophistication was reached in articles by Jacobs (1974) and Cook (1977). These authors began to draw a parallel between the exchange processes described by Emerson (1962) and developments in the literature on interorganizational relations.[1] They limited the use of exchange to "voluntary

---

[1]Given the impact power dependency or resource dependency theory has had on the field, it might be well to summarize briefly its basic tenets. Quoting Aldrich (1979:268):

> [Emerson's (1962)] general point was that one's *power* resides implicitly in another's dependency: The parties in a power relationship are tied to each other by the dependency of one on the other, or perhaps by mutual dependence. Emerson (1962:32) defined dependence of an actor A (an individual, group, or organization) on another actor B as "directly proportional to A's *motivational investment* in goals mediated by B, and inversely proportional to the *availability* of those goals to A outside of the A-B relation." The dependence of A on B provides the basis for B's power over A, as B is in control or otherwise has influence over goods and services A desires. To the extent that A cannot do without the resources and is unable to obtain them elsewhere, A is dependent on B. The power to control or influence others thus resides in control over things they value . . .

Cook (1977) notes that the strategy of more dependent actors is to reduce the degree of imbalance in an exchange relation. Designating Y as the resource which A is dependent upon B for, she suggests the following strategies:

1. A decrease in the value of resource Y for A ("Withdrawal"); 2. An increase in the number of alternatives open to A for obtaining Y ("Network Extension"); 3. An increase in the value of some resource X for B which A controls ("Status-Giving" from A to B); 4. A reduction in alternatives open to B ("Coalition Formation") (Cook 1977:73).

A successful pursuit of these strategies should lessen the dependency of A upon B and thus reduce the power differential between the two actors.

transactions involving the transfer of resources between two or more actors for mutual benefit" (Cook 1977:64). Also, the focus was on individual goal attainment rather than joint or collective action. As noted by Aldrich (1979), once exchange relations among organizations were defined in terms of resource dependence, researchers could address the power differentials that exist among exchange partners. Also, following Blau (1964), research could consider the conditions under which actors would be able to maintain their independence in a situation of potential dependence (Aldrich 1979:269).

Resource dependency theory has received a great deal of attention in the interorganization literature and has prompted a number of studies that test propositions derived from it. For example, as predicted by Cook (1977:72), a number of studies have found a strong positive association between organizations' network centrality and their reputed influence in community affairs (Galaskiewicz 1979b, Boje & Whetten 1981, Rogers 1974, Laumann & Pappi 1976). The more that other organizations are dependent upon the focal organization for the resources they need, the more likely that organizations are going to view the focal organization as being influential. Furthermore, because central actors are perceived as more powerful, they are likely candidates for other powerful actors to become aligned with. This, in turn, makes central actors appear even more powerful.

A second set of studies have looked at focal organizations and tried to explain their behavior in terms of their dependencies upon other organizations. Levine & White (1961) showed that those health-related organizations less dependent upon the local health system for resources tended to interact less with local agencies and had more disagreements with locals than organizations more dependent upon local systems. Studying a wider range of organizations Galaskiewicz (1979a:82) found that organizations receiving a greater proportion of their income from extra-local sources were more aloof and peripheral to local resource exchange networks of money, information, and moral support. Both Pfeffer & Leong (1977) and Provan et al (1980) found that United Way agencies tended to get more funds from the United Way if they had funds coming in from outside sources. Using data from Aharoni (1971), Pfeffer & Salancik (1978:56–59) found that firms selling a larger proportion of their output to the government were willing to give up larger yields on investments in order to comply with government requests to channel monies into certain development areas. Using data from Salancik (1976) on affirmative action compliance in the United States, Pfeffer & Salancik (1978:56–58) found that when enforcement pressures were assumed to be the greatest, responses evidencing concern for affirmative action were strongly related to the degree of the organization's dependence on the government for revenues. Finally, Pfeffer & Salancik (1978:126) also showed that industries doing more business with the government tended to diversify more and to have less of their activity concentrated in one industry group. They concluded that "diversification represents an explicit attempt to avoid . . . the control by others who control critical resource exchanges" (Pfeffer & Salancik 1978:131).

Power dependence propositions have also been tested on leadership and control patterns within marketing channels, shifting attention from a channel member's formal authority or power resources (El-Ansary & Robicheaux 1974) to dependencies among actors in the network. The dependency approach was thought to be especially relevant to franchise networks. The theory, though, has not lived up to expectations. In their review of the market channel literature, Reve & Stern (1979) concluded that those studies which looked at the impact of dependency patterns upon the power of channel members found little or no association between the two (El-Ansary & Stern 1972, Wilkinson 1973, Etgar 1976, Hunt & Nevin 1974). The authors suggested that this poor showing could be due to insufficient data and unreliable measures as well as to situational factors (see also El-Ansary 1975, El-Ansary & Stern 1972, Lusch & Brown 1982).

Other resource dependency studies have been more descriptive and methodological in flavor. The purpose has been to describe the pattern of dependency or exchange relations among structural positions within a field of organizations rather than to test for the effects of dependency/dominance on organizations' strategy, structure, or reputation. No doubt many researchers have been seduced by the new methods available to study large social networks. The most popular methods to date have been block modelling (White et al 1976) and hierarchical cluster analysis (Burt 1976). The appeal of these methods is that they enable the analyst to identify structurally equivalent sets of actors in the organizational field and, with the aid of an image matrix, to describe the resource flows between them. Some studies have been able to make substantive sense of the clusters or the dependencies they found (e.g. Van de Ven et al 1979, Knoke & Rogers 1979, Knoke 1983, Knoke & Wood 1981, Galaskiewicz & Krohn 1984, DiMaggio & Romo 1984), but there appears to be no pattern as one compares the results of one study to another.

Critique

One problem with the resource dependency literature is that researchers have underutilized the theory available to them. Resource dependency theory contains several powerful hypotheses predicting how more or less dependent actors will act in different situations (see Cook 1977 and Footnote 1). For example, researchers have paid only scant attention to either the creation of groups among horizontally interdependent organizations or the effects of these groups on resource procurement/allocative processes (see Phillips 1960). That is, there has been little done on the creation and impact of cartels, trade associations, oligopolies, coalitions of consumer organizations, etc, within the resource dependency framework. This is surprising given that resource dependency theory predicts some type of collective response among those in structurally equivalent, dependent positions. Sociologists interested in these issues might look to the economists who have done a considerable amount of research on the effects of cartels and oligopolies on industry profits. (See Khandwalla 1981 for a review of this literature.)

Another problem is that researchers have not paid enough attention to the environmental constraints on strategic choice. For one thing, variation in the resource environment could affect the options open to decisionmakers. As the resource environment becomes richer or leaner, more or less stable, more homogeneous or heterogeneous, or more concentrated or dispersed, the options available to organizations change accordingly (see Aldrich 1979; Emery & Trist 1965). Yet we could not find any empirical research which has looked at such changes in the broader resource environment, their effect on decision-making, and subsequent changes in power dependency relations.

In a similar vein the material environment can delimit the options of organizations (Zeitz 1980:78). Agglomerative economies are still a consideration in the location of manufacturing activity. Human service organizations and consumer product organizations are constrained by the settlement patterns of clients and customers. Once large-scale investments in plants, offices, stores, and transportation have been made, they have a strong tendency to persist, based in part on the physical inertia of their physical constitution. Thus geographical propinquity must weigh as a factor in the option matrix of decisionmakers and must constrain interorganizational strategies to reduce dependencies (see Reid 1964, Schermerhorn 1975).

Another set of environmental constraints is embedded in the institutional environment. Aldrich (1976), Hall et al (1977), and Schmidt & Kochan (1977) have argued and shown that a considerable number of interorganizational relations are mandated by law and that cooperation among human service organizations is often explained primarily by these mandates. Obviously the options of organizations, whose subordinate status is fixed by legal mandate, will be quite limited (Hall 1982:254, Aldrich & Whetten 1981:389). Another example of an institutional constraint on interorganizational behavior is the legal prescription specified in the 1914 Clayton Act against interlocking directorates among competing firms (Fennema & Schijf 1979).

Organizational domains or product lines are another set of constraints on strategic action. Pennings (1981) makes the simple but pointed observation that not every organization in an interorganizational field is a potential source of resources for every other organization. The range of potential transactional partners is delimited by the inputs needed and the outputs produced by organizations. He distinguishes among three types of interdependence: horizontal interdependence, symbiotic interdependence, and vertical interdependence (Pennings 1981:434). Firms horizontally interdependent compete with each other in obtaining similar resources and disposing of similar goods and services. One could argue that these organizations are structurally equivalent (see White et al 1976, Burt 1982). While such actors are clearly problematic to an organization as competitors, they neither have power over it (in resource dependency terms) nor are they potential sources of needed inputs. Symbiotically related organizations complement each other in that they render services to one another, but clearly they do not control resources the other needs. Only vertically interdependent firms are viable transactional partners to which organizations could turn to alleviate their dependency problems. To put it in simpler terms, there are only so many suppliers, donors, or investors to turn to and only so many customers or clients for one's services.

Managing Uncertainty

The interorganizational literature has been continually sensitive to the uncertainties that often plague resource procurement. In our discussion thus far, we have assumed complete information. Yet Simon (1957) and March & Simon (1958) have led sociologists and organizational theorists to realize that reducing uncertainty for organizational decisionmakers can have as much to do with explaining interorganizational relations as power dependency. Faced with a situation—possibly as abhorent as being dependent upon some other organization for resources—organizational decisionmakers often have to either make decisions with insufficient information or pursue strategies to improve their information flow and knowledge of the environment. Here we will argue that environmental uncertainty can motivate organizations to develop interorganizational relations—both vertically and horizontally—to cope with uncertainty.

Pennings (1981:441) distinguishes three general interorganizational strategies to manage vertical and horizontal interdependencies and thus reduce uncertainty: forestalling, forecasting, and absorption. Forestalling is coping behavior that prevents or controls the emergence of unpredictable behavior of other organizations. Examples include horizontal merger, vertical merger, joint venture, innovation, product differentiation, regulation, and overlapping membership. Forecasting is coping behavior that predicts or forecasts the behavior of interdependent organizations. Examples include regulation, overlapping membership, organizational intelligence, and flows of personnel. Finally, absorption is coping behavior that mitigates the negative consequences of other organizations. Examples here include regulation, overlapping membership, organizational intelligence, flows of personnel, licenses and imitations, antitrust suits, and horizontal merger. A summary of the research on these strategies can be found in Pennings (1981).

Furthermore, research by Leblebici & Salancik (1982) found that uncertainty prompts greater formalization and control in interorganizational relations. Studying the social organization of futures markets and the Chicago Board of Trade (CBT), they found that as market prices became more volatile, working rules that regulated transactions among trading partners became more formalized and the CBT was more likely to apply sanctions to deviant traders. In essence, they argued that formalization and tighter controls helped actors in the network offset the uncertainty being experienced in the marketplace.

Galaskiewicz & Shatin (1981) found that greater environmental uncertainty prompted organizational administrators to seek out interorganizational partners whose executives had similar backgrounds to theirs. In more turbulent community environments, cooperation was more likely to take place between organizations whose leaders had similar racial and educational backgrounds. In more placid environments, the race and education of organizational leaders had no effect on cooperation. Evidently organizational decision-makers were willing to forfeit the opportunity of getting the "best deal" on the resources they needed in exchange for the greater security derived from working with organizational leaders who were like themselves and thus more trustworthy.[2]

There has also been research on how uncertainty will give rise to boundary-spanning activities (Aldrich 1979). These activities can be carried out either through boundary-spanning roles (Guetzkow 1966, Thompson 1967, Aldrich & Herker 1977, Adams 1976), interlocking directorates, or interorganizational brokers (Aldrich 1982, Galaskiewicz 1982). As an organization's external environment becomes more turbulent and unstable, the information-processing function of the broker, boundary-spanning role, or interlocking directorate should become central to an organization's ability to effectively gather, analyze, and act on relevant information (see also Aldrich 1979:256–57).

The empirical results on the relation between environmental uncertainty and the activities and power of boundary-spanning roles are mixed. In his study of labor relations between firefighter locals and city governments, Kochan (1975) concluded that environmental complexity and change had no significant effect on the power of boundary personnel; in their study of twelve work groups in a health and welfare organization, Leifer & Huber (1977) concluded that the perceptions of environmental uncertainty by decision-makers might actually be the result of boundary-spanning activities rather than the cause. Only Spekman (1979) found that under conditions of environmental uncertainty did organiza-

---

[2]Hall et al (1977), Benson (1973), and Galaskiewicz (1979a) found that cooperative relations among organizations were more likely if the agencies or administrators had similar operating philosophies or values. Unfortunately, none of these looked at the texture of the environments in which the different actors operated to see if cooperation based on similar values was more likely under more uncertain conditions. We would expect this to be the case, although this is now an empirical question begging investigation.

tional members attribute to the boundary-spanning person greater power in decision-making situations.

The studies examining the relation between environmental uncertainty and board interlocking have been more fruitful. Building on Selznick's (1949) pioneering work on cooptation, the board is viewed as a strategy to coopt problematic elements in the organization's environment and thus reduce uncertainty (Pfeffer 1972, 1973; Aldrich 1979; Schoorman et al 1981). In his study of corporations, Pfeffer (1972) found that "the size of the board was related to the organization's need for linkage to the environment determined both by its capital structure and by its size and visibility" (Pfeffer & Salancik 1978:168). In other words, the more exposed an organization was to an environment, the more board members it included to establish ties to that environment. These findings were replicated in a study by Allen (1974), and Pfeffer (1973) had comparable findings in his study of nonprofit hospitals.

The most impressive studies to date have been conducted by Ronald Burt and his associates (Burt 1980, 1982, 1983; Burt et al 1980). Building on the idea that board interlocks are strategies to coopt problematic elements in the environment, Burt and his associates argued that interlocking directorates should be observed where they can eliminate constraint for corporate actors and should not be observed where there is no constraint to eliminate. In his framework, firms in one industry are constrained by firms in another to the extent that firms in the first industry are highly dependent upon those in the second for resources and those in the second industry are highly centralized so as to collectively pursue their own interests (Burt 1983, Burt et al 1980). Using the input-output table of the 1967 American economy and corresponding concentration ratios, Burt showed that interlocking was greatest where one industrial sector was highly dependent upon another sector for sales and purchasing and where the latter was highly concentrated.[3]

Another approach to the interlock-as-cooptation thesis was provided by Koenig et al (1979), Palmer (1983), and Ornstein (1984). These researchers

---

[3]Other studies have tried to see if interlocking has any effect on performance or organizational well-being. The rationale is that interlocking with strategic sectors of the environment will reduce uncertainty and facilitate the flow of resources to the organization. Studies of nonprofit organizations have found that strategic interlocks with those who control financial resources result in more contributions and growth. Zald (1967) found that the larger the percentage of businessmen on YMCA boards, the more external funding the YMCA received. Galaskiewicz and Rauschenbach (forthcoming) found that if a corporation was represented on the board of a nonprofit cultural organization, it was much more likely to make a cash contribution to the nonprofit than if it did not. Pfeffer (1973) found that hospitals grew larger to the extent that their boards had political connections, ties to financial institutions, and a board composition that was reflective of the agricultural or manufacturing character of the area. In contrast, studies of for-profit firms by Pennings (1980) and Burt (1983) found no association between strategic interlocking and profitability.

argued that interlock ties established to coopt problematic elements in a firm's environment will be continued by the creation of new, or the maintainance of already existing, interlocks between the same firms when ties are accidentally broken. However, Koenig et al (1979) found that only about 6% of the 78 single-interlock ties they examined were continued after the break, and Palmer (1983) found that only about 8.9% of the same sorts of ties in his sample were continued after being broken. Using a somewhat different methodology, Ornstein (1984) found approximately 40% of the broken interlocks in his sample reconstituted. All three researchers concluded that there was little support for the cooptation thesis in their data. If ties were not soon reconstituted after they had been accidentally broken, they must not be that critical in coopting problematic elements and reducing uncertainty.

In contrast, there has been little or no empirical work on the relation between environmental uncertainty and the creation of brokerages. Although the logic of the argument is clear (see Pfeffer & Salancik 1978:285–86; Rose-Ackerman 1980; Aldrich & Whetten 1981), Mitnick's (1984) and Provan's (1983) recent reviews of the literature on the creation of interorganizational organizations and federations listed very few references to environmental uncertainty or the reductions in transaction costs which these brokerages supposedly helped members to realize (see also Rogers & Whetten 1982, Chapter 4). However, in all fairness many of these studies did not even consider environmental uncertainty as a variable (e.g. Stern 1979, Warren et al 1974, Litwak & Hylton 1962).

Critique

The literature relating interorganizational strategies to environmental uncertainty has many shortcomings as well. The most glaring problem is its heavy reliance on an implicit theory of executive anxiety reduction. Organizational decisionmakers are often portrayed as insecure bureaucrats who pursue conservative strategies when the environment becomes too complex to understand completely. Not only does this make the theory reductionist, but it attributes much too much importance to the personalities and input of executive decisionmakers.

An important contribution of Williamson (1975, 1981) and Ouchi (1980a, 1980b) is that they focus on how uncertain environments and the bounded rationality of decisionmakers increase transaction costs for the organization, and that organizational strategies—including interorganizational strategies— are focused on reducing these costs rather than reducing the anxiety level of executives (see Aldrich 1982). Assuming that such costs can be calculated, they become a clear set of efficiency criteria upon which to make organizational decisions (Ouchi 1980a). A central thesis of the transaction cost approach is that as uncertainty in transactions increases, there will be a shift from markets to firms. If transactions are highly problematic for organizations, then they must spend considerably more time and effort harmonizing relationships. In the long run it may simply be more efficient to integrate that function into one's own operations (Williamson 1981:559). Initially, the transactions cost approach has been applied to understanding merger activity and vertical integration (e.g. Walker and Weber 1984). However, Williamson & Ouchi (1981:366) admit that the model may not be of much use outside the for-profit arena and for other types of interorganizational activity. They argue that in the public and nonprofit sectors takeovers are almost nonexistent, and criteria for success are often unclear. Still, we believe that the transaction cost approach has considerable potential and should be given more careful attention.

This literature also suffers serious methodological shortcomings. Measuring environmental uncertainty still remains a problem (Aldrich 1979, Lawrence 1981, and Morrissey et al 1981). Early efforts at measuring uncertainty devised instruments to measure decisionmakers' perceptions of uncertainty (see Lawrence & Lorsch 1967, and Duncan 1975). However, research by Tosi et al (1973) and Downey et al (1975) noted the unreliability of these indicators. Subsequently, we are not surprised to find that most of the studies cited in this article utilized so-called objective indicators of turbulence and complexity while ignoring perceptions of decisionmakers. Yet this bothers us as well. As Aldrich (1979:132) argues, there is really a two-step flow of information: environmental elements filter into the organization and then this filtered information is brought to bear on decision-making (see also Starbuck, 1976). Future research must recognize that perceptions of decisionmakers are a very important element in their theory and must measure them as well as objective environmental conditions. Furthermore, sometimes researchers tend to equate conditions in the resource domain with conditions in the information domain. As Lawrence (1981) points out, they are two separate dimensions of the environment and should be operationalized separately.

Another problem in this literature is that organizational actors are assumed to have complete information on all the options available to reduce their uncertainty. This may seem like a trivial point, but ignorance of options can seriously hinder an organization in its efforts to overcome uncertainty. To illustrate, in studying the interorganizational strategies described above, analysts typically assumed that organizations knew about all the organizations with which they could interlock or coordinate their activities (Hall 1982:249). Yet numerous studies have shown that organizations do not know about all their prospective partners, will interact with those they are aware of, and will avoid the rest. These were essentially the conclusions of Boje & Whetten (1981), Klonglan et al (1976), Galaskiewicz & Shatin (1981), and Van de Ven & Ferry (1980). From these studies we learn that by "awareness" we mean a general knowledge of the goals, services, and resources of other organizations, or personal knowledge of those individuals who are associated with other organizations. Regardless, unless the awareness of other organizations is somehow taken into account, the analyst may find organizations pursuing what the analyst believes are less than optimal strategies in response to environmental uncertainty, when indeed organizations are simply responding the best way they know how.

Discussion

While we have discussed power dependency and uncertainty separately, they are not necessarily independent phenomena. For example, we could assume that environmental uncertainty is just one more constraint organizations face and that, when it was eliminated, organizations would behave as resource dependency theory would have them behave. To illustrate: an organization could be unclear or uncertain of its true position in a resource arena, i.e. the degree of its powerlessness, and so inadvertly pursue a strategy to reduce uncertainties with its prime customer, e.g., creating a board interlock, which however would only help to institutionalize its dependency upon that actor. If an organization had complete information it might instead diversify its product line or set up a cartel with producers in the same structural position instead. In other words, both theories are quite good at explaining patterns of interorganizational behavior. However, the impact of power dependency relations and uncertainty upon organizational strategies are not mutually exclusive, and the researcher has to be constantly aware of the possible interaction between the two. (See Lawrence 1981 for a further discussion of these issues.)

ARENAS OF POLITICAL ADVOCACY

The ultimate authorities governing organizations' actions are the legal norms of the larger social system in which organizations function (Parsons 1956, 1960). Obviously the degree to which the laws of a society affect any one organization will vary depending on the organization's goals or purpose (Pfeffer & Salancik 1978:214). If the legislative environment affects the organization in a significant way, the organization will attempt to use the power of the larger social system and its government to pass legislation more favorable to itself. Palamountain (1955) called this the "politics of distribution". In Pfeffer & Salancik's (1978:190) terms: "the political context is a place for formally institutionalizing the survival of the organization, guaranteeing it access to the resources it needs." Zald (1970) and Benson (1975) referred to an organization's "political economy." Miles (1982:23) argues that "organizations and elements of society may be found constantly engaged in efforts to insert their interests into the mainstream of societal values and, hence, to create or safeguard the legitimacy of their definition of the 'right' social order." In this section we will look at how interorganizational relations affect the mobilization and success of organizations and coalitions of organizations as political interest groups.

Clearly professional organizations and so-called interorganizational organizations have come to replace voluntary associations as the principal actors in interest group politics. Mills (1956), Epstein (1969), Domhoff (1970), Jacoby (1973), Berg & Zald (1978), Miles (1982), and Salisbury (1984) focused on the political activism of corporations, trade associations, and business peak associations. Berry (1977) and Knoke & Wood (1981) examined the activities of public interest organizations. Wood (1982) examined the organizations within the environmental movement. Henig (1982) looked at the political activism of community organizations in Chicago and Minneapolis. Furthermore, there have been studies of the political behavior of organizations representing women (Freeman 1973), farm workers (Jenkins & Perrow 1977), and welfare recipients (Bailis 1974) (see references in Jenkins 1983, and Berg & Zald 1978). The objectives of these political organizations and these coalitions are to gain special monetary favors from government, to manage environmental turbulence created by governmental threats to the legitimacy of organizational goals, or to resist efforts by government to intrude into the traditional private domains of managerial authority (Baysinger 1984). The methods usually include lobbying legislators and administrators of executive agencies, advertising, educational programs, and disseminating information (Berg & Zald 1978).

In explaining the mobilization of organizations and coalitions the classicists in political science focused on shared values and a sense of "we-ness" among the members of the organizations and members of the coalition. As Henig (1982) points out, there was an assumption that the transformation of a latent interest group into a full-blown organized interest group would be frictionless. Natural or corporate actors in structurally equivalent positions, facing comparable political threats, would all come to recognize and act upon their common interest in the threat. Salisbury (1984) contends that not until the classic work of Mancur Olson (1965) did scholars fully realize the special obstacles organizers of public interest organizations faced. Even if a recognized common interest existed among prospective members, the free rider problem would keep many from participating.

The interorganizational literature shed some light on the problem of mobilization when it found that (a) organizations within political coalitions tended to have interorganizational relations among themselves prior to coalition formation and (b) the mobilization of individual organizations was often a function of their centrality in resource networks. For example, Herman Turk (1973, 1977) argued that coalition formation is dependent upon the availability of internal linkages in the community. His indicators of internal linkage availability were the relative scale and diversification of municipal government and the extent to which local voluntary associations were uncontested and citywide. In his analysis he found that where linkage availability was greater, a higher correlation existed between demand for different services and the activation of interorganizational networks or coalitions to petition government authorities to respond to the need (Turk 1977:199). He concluded that existing interorganizational networks provided a latent structure that could be used for coalition building and could provide points of articulation or at least serve as role models for new interorganizational coalitions.

Studying political mobilization in six neighborhoods in Chicago and Minneapolis, Henig (1982) found that where there were cohesive, federated preexisting, interorganizational organizations, neighborhood response to outside development threats was sizable and extremely speedy. He argued that such federative structures enabled actors in the community to learn about their situation more quickly; they coordinate and distribute selective incentives in order to overcome the free-rider impasse to collective response (Henig, 1982:171).

The importance of preexisting networks for coalition mobilization has been highlighted in several community case studies as well. Laumann & Pappi (1976) looked at overlapping memberships among a wide range of organizations in a medium-size German city and were successfully able to predict organizations' positions on different community issues simply by looking at cleavage patterns within this interorganizational network.

Studies have also found that mobilization of individual organizations is a function of being in central positions in interorganizational networks. Perrucci & Pilisuk (1970), examining an interorganizational network of overlapping memberships in West Lafayette, Indiana, found a dense network of ten organizations whose leaders exhibited a high degree of value homophily and were involved in more community issues than leaders of organizations more peripheral to this network. The inference was that these leaders were "selected" to participate because of their key position in the interorganizational network. Galaskiewicz (1979a) found that in four out of the five issues he examined in Towertown, organizational centrality in either the money, information, or support networks had a strong positive effect on activation. Finally, Laumann et al (1984) looked at the effects of centrality on activation for a population of organizations involved in national health policy. They found that centrality in communication exchange networks and resource transaction networks had a significant impact on the scope of active intervention in policy domains both directly and as a mediating mechanism whereby an organization converted its purposive orientations and its resources into action (see also Miller 1980).

Interorganizational relations have also been shown to have some bearing on the success rate of organizations and interorganizational coalitions as they engage in political action. One promising line of inquiry traces the effects of sponsorship on an organization's political success. For example, Jenkins

(1983:535) cites several social movement organizations whose success depended upon interorganizational ties to institutions which controlled needed resources, e.g. the welfare rights movement (Bailis 1974; West 1981), the farm worker movement (Jenkins & Perrow 1977), and the women's movement (Freeman 1973). In his study of 70 social influence organizations in Indianapolis, Knoke (1983) found that the more numerous a social influence association's connections were with powerful community organization actors, the more likely it was to be perceived as influential by key community informants (see also Knoke & Wood 1981). This verified the results of Galaskiewicz (1979a) who found that the greater the amount of money that an organization's interorganizational contacts controlled, the more others in the community viewed it as influential in community affairs and the more successful it was in different community decisionmaking situations. Knoke (1983:1069) pointed out that numerous other studies found similar sponsorship effects, e.g. Steedly & Foley's (1979) reanalysis of Gamson's (1975) data on social protest groups, Salisbury's (1969) study of nineteenth century agrarian movement organizations, and Lipsky's (1970) analysis of the New York City tenants' rights movement. We would also add Aveni's (1978) study of the NAACP.

Critique

A central argument in Olson's thesis is that participants will join in a collective action if there are selective incentives made available to them. Yet, at the interorganizational level very little rigorous work exists on the importance of such incentives in bringing coalitions or action sets together in confronting the institutional environment. Useem (1984) and Galaskiewicz (1985) have shown that peer pressure and the threat of being excluded from business subcultures were very effective stimuli in motivating greater company contributions to charity—a type of collective action. Evidently prestige and good fellowship are selective incentives that business people value greatly. Unfortunately, though, we have seen no evidence to date showing that prestige or good fellowship play any role in organizations joining political coalitions or peak associations.

Alternatively, organizations may be lured into collective action because the collective actor controls resources they value and cannot get elsewhere. At the same time they are bringing about changes in the institutional environment, collective actors may have to monopolize control over some divisible resource in order to provide selective incentives to their membership. At this point, resource dependency theory once again becomes important. Instead of power dependence relations serving the interests of some individual actor who finds itself in an advantaged position, they serve the collective interest. Stern's (1979) discussion of how the NCAA developed as an interorganizational organization is an illustration of how this can happen.

We might also want to go back and reconsider the role of common values in putting together and keeping together these coalitions. Olson's model assumes that organizations as participants in the political arena are as atomistic as they are in competitive resource arenas. Yet there is no reason why organizations, especially if they face similar environment contingencies, could not build a consensus among themselves, even to the point that they would contribute time and resources to the collective effort without being overly concerned about the return they should expect in the short run (e.g. see Warren et al 1974). In this respect we are on the same wave length as DiMaggio and Powell (1983), who focus on the spread of cultural norms in an interorganizational field, Ouchi (1984), who has an interest in so-called M-form superorganizations, and Chatou (1981:491), who discusses the importance of building consensus among organizations and emphasizes what he calls the "consensus network" (see also Meyer & Scott 1983:Chapter 7).

ARENAS OF ORGANIZATIONAL LEGITIMATION

Participation in legitimacy arenas is much different from participation in political arenas. In the former there is no concrete issue around which to mobilize a coalition, there is no decisionmaker or decision-making body on which to target one's energies, and an organization is never sure when it has achieved its purpose. In the legitimacy arena the issue is the adequacy of the organizations' goals or operating procedures as theory. The targets of the effort are licensing boards, funding agents, intellectuals, and public opinion (see Pfeffer & Salancik 1978:193; Meyer & Scott 1983:201–2; and Dowling & Pfeffer 1975). A concern about organizational legitimacy can also be traced directly to Parsons (1956, 1960).

There has been considerable attention to strategies aimed at legitimating the organization or at least improving its image or public relations. Kamens (1977) and Meyer & Rowen (1977) looked at legitimating myths which organizations create about themselves; Lee (1971) and Perrow (1961) examined how organizational elites manipulate external referents of prestige; Lentz & Tschirgi (1963) described how business firms publicize their commitment to an ethic of corporate social responsibility; and DiMaggio & Powell (1983) argue that organizations will often try to imitate other organizations in their environment in an effort to enhance legitimacy.

One interorganizational strategy to enhance legitimacy is to have the organization identified with cultural symbols and/or legitimate power figures in the environment. One way of achieving this end is to recruit prestigious people to the organization's board of directors or to have one's own executives recruited to prestigious boards. In a study of board interlocks between corporations and cultural organizations in Minneapolis-St. Paul, J. Galaskiewicz and B. Rauschenbach (Forthcoming) found that personnel from more influential companies tended to be recruited to more cultural boards and that companies tended to sit on the boards of more prestigious cultural organizations. One interpretation of these findings is that cultural organizations were striving to enhance their own reputations by aligning with the more influential companies in the area; and corporations were striving to enhance their legitimacy by aligning themselves with the more prestigious cultural organizations.

Another way to be identified with cultural symbols and/or legitimate power figures is to obtain endorsements. This strategy was illustrated in Pfeffer & Salancik's (1978:197–202) case study of the American Institute for Foreign Study (AIFS). In an effort to align themselves with powerful political figures the AISF funded scholarships for their overseas educational programs and asked prominent political figures to hand them out. The politicians benefited, because they were giving something gratis to needy students; and the AIFS, of course, was closely associating itself with prominent figures. An interesting aspect of this case is that these efforts at legitimation paid off politically as well resulting in favorable public relations for AIFS programs.

The interorganizational legitimating strategy to receive the most attention is the cash contribution to charitable organizations. Most of the literature agrees that charitable contributions are a very effective way to demonstrate the good will of the donor and thus "win over" problematic or hostile elements in the environment (see Useem 1985). For example, Miles (1982) showed how the tobacco industry, when challenged by the Sloan-Kettering Commission and the Surgeon General's Report on smoking's health hazards, immediately responded by funneling millions of dollars to universities and research institutes that did work on cancer-related topics. Ermann (1978) argued that contributions to the Public Broadcasting System (PBS) between 1972 and 1976 were efforts by upwardly mobile companies to produce good will for themselves among the national elite and the general public. Fry et al (1982) presented further evidence that contributions are motivated by public relations and the need to "sell the firm." Using industry-level data Burt (1983:197–221) found that the amount of industry-wide contributions measured in absolute dollars, per capita dollars, or as a proportion of profits was directly associated with the percentage of sales to households. This association held while controlling for both income and the price of a contribution. Essentially, Burt viewed contributions as just another marketing strategy that companies used to gain a competitive edge in consumer markets. Indeed, one of his most interesting findings was a parallel set of associations between expenditures on advertising and market positions (see also Levy & Shatto 1978, 1980, and Nelson 1970).

Critique

Empirical work on organizations and their attempts to legitimate themselves is clearly in its infancy. The problems of measurement are formidable. Since the goal of the organization is to enhance its legitimacy, research must somehow be able to operationalize organizational legitimacy. This would require that researchers survey various publics and elites on their attitudes towards specific organizations (see, for example, White 1980). Reputational measures of organizational power and influence are commonplace (Laumann & Pappi 1976), and sociologists should have little difficulty operationalizing reputational measures of an organization's "generosity," "social responsibility," "success," "visibility," "necessity," "worthiness," or "worthlessness" (see Galaskiewicz 1985). Unless researchers can operationalize indicators of legitimacy, it will be impossible to evaluate the effectiveness of any legitimating strategy. This problem is reflected in the way that inferences are now made. Researchers are finding correlations, e.g. between advertising revenues and cash contributions, and then interpreting these results as evidence of the legitimacy theory. Without measuring the "legitimacy/illegitimacy" of organizations both before and after they engage in an alleged legitimating strategy, it is impossible to draw firm conclusions.

More critically, this literature lacks an overarching theory of legitimation to guide inquiry. We suspect that an inventory of propositions will gradually accrue that notes the empirical associations between different environmental conditions, organizational strategies, and states of "illegitimacy/legitimacy." For example, Meyer & Scott (1983:202) have speculated that the number of authorities with jurisdiction over an organization and the congruence in the expectations of these authorities may be critical in explaining organizational legitimacy. However, the shape that this theory will ultimately take is not yet clear.

CONCLUDING REMARKS

The purpose of this paper was to present an overview of the theory and research on interorganizational relations. If the review has taught us anything, we have learned that there is no *one* theory of interorganizational relations. The review has been presented in three parts focusing on interorganizational relations in three different arenas of action: the arena of resource procurement/allocation, the political arena, and legitimacy arena. We have tried to make the argument that different theories are appropriate for explaining interorganizational relations in different arenas. Power dependency theory and theories of uncertainty reduction seemed most appropriate in explaining patterns of interorganizational relations in arenas of resource procurement/allocation. Theories of collective action were most useful in explaining interorganizational relations in political arenas.

While these analytical distinctions should prove useful to researchers, interorganizational analysis is most intriguing (and analytically messy) when these arenas intersect or overlap with one another. For example, one way in which these systems do overlap is the phenomenon of *residuals* or *traces*. Residuals or traces are relational structures created in the context of one arena that impinge upon strategic behavior in another. From our discussion above it is clear that organizations play in more than one arena of action at a time. They often pursue resources and legitimacy and participate in efforts at collective action simultaneously. It should then not be surprising that interorganizational structures created in one arena will either be useful or a hindrance to strategic action in another.

To illustrate, we might recall our discussion of how existing networks of interorganizational relations influenced coalition formation. The networks of resource exchange that already existed among corporate actors were the infrastructure upon which political coalitions were built. In all likelihood, however, these resource networks were created out of the competitive struggle for organizational survival by self-seeking and self-centered corporate actors who were seeking to minimize their dependencies upon one another. Now these networks are the infrastructure upon which coalitions to achieve collective goals are built. In turn, as political coalitional structures become institutionalized, we suspect that they impinge on the struggle for dominance in the resource procurement/allocation arena. Residual collectivist sentiments linger on, but more importantly actors now must think twice before pursuing a competitive advantage if it would lead to destroying the coalition which provides collective goods for coalitional members.

A second way in which these systems overlap is the phenomenon of *multiplicity*. This is the situation where the action in one arena is dependent upon the incorporation of strategies more typically found in another arena. For instance, resource dependency theory hypothesizes that those in a structurally equivalent, dependent position will come together to form a group so as to equalize their situation vis à vis dominant actors. The theory hypothesizes collective action. For this group to come together and be successful, it then must solve the problems which all collective actors face. It must provide selective incentives, it must build consensus, and it must coordinate the actions of member organizations. In other words, to lessen their resource dependency on others, individual actors must now strategically behave as a collective actor.

Another example of multiplicity is the collective actor who is short on selective incentives and needs some way to ensure member participation; it solves its problem by borrowing strategies found more typically in resource procurement/allocation arenas. If the collective actor can gain monopoly control over some selective incentive which member organizations have a keen interest in, it could exploit its new power advantage over members to ensure their continued support. The collective actor effectively assumes a dual role. At the same time that it is pursuing the collective interests of member organizations, it finds itself becoming a monopoly supplier of private goods to individual members. In both examples success in one arena is predicated on actors being able to use strategies borrowed from other arenas.

Obviously it is difficult to model organizational and interorganizational behavior when arenas intersect and overlap. Yet this is obviously on the agenda. All that we can suggest is that the analyst learn as much as possible about the context of the transaction, the motives of the actors, and the rules that they are operating under. To look just at content or at networks of relations will not be enough. Researchers must know the system they are studying in all these ways before they can develop some credible theories of residuals or multiplicity, let alone add to the existing body of knowledge on power dependency relations, information reduction strategies, collective action, and organizational legitimation.

ACKNOWLEDGMENTS

Funding for this paper was provided by a grant from the National Science Foundation (SES-831-9364). I would like to thank Andrew Van de Ven, Richard Hall, David Knoke, Howard Aldrich, David Whetten, Gerald Salancik, and an anonymous reviewer for their comments on an earlier draft of the paper. I followed most although not all of their suggestions. Thus any shortcomings are solely the responsibility of the author. I would also like to thank Gloria DeWolfe for typing the manuscript.

Literature Cited

Adams, J. S. 1976. The structure and dynamics of behavior in organizational boundary roles. In *Handbook of Industrial and Organizational Psychology*, ed. M. D. Dunnette, 1175–99. Chicago: Rand-McNally, Inc. 1,740 pp.

Aharoni, Y. 1971. *The Israeli Manager*. Tel Aviv: Israeli Institute of Business Research, Tel Aviv Univ.

Aldrich, H. 1976. Resource dependence and interorganizational relations. Relations between local employment service offices and social services sector organizations. *Admin. Soc.* 7:419–454

Aldrich, H. 1979. *Organizations and Environments*. Englewood Cliffs, N.J.: Prentice-Hall. 384 pp.

Aldrich, H. 1982. The origins and persistence of social networks. In *Social Structure and Network Analysis*, ed. P. V. Marsden, N. Lin, pp. 281–293. Beverly Hills, Calif: Sage. 319 pp.

Aldrich, H., Herker, D. 1977. Boundary spanning roles and organization structure. *Acad. Manage. Rev.* 2:217–230

Aldrich, H., Whetten, D. A. 1981. Organizational sets, action sets, and networks: Making the most of simplicity. See Nystrom & Starbuck 1981, pp. 385–408

Alford, R. 1975. *Health Care Politics*. Chicago: Univ. Calif. Press, 294 pp.

Allen, M. 1974. The structure of interorganizational elite cooptation: Interlocking corporate directorates. *Am. Sociol. Rev.* 39:393–406

Aveni, A. F. 1978. Organizational linkages and resource mobilization: the significance of linkage strength and breadth. *Sociol. Q.* 19:185–202

Bailis, L. 1974. *Bread or Justice*. Lexington, Mass: Heath. 254 pp.

Baysinger, B. D. 1984. Domain maintenance as an objective of business political activity: An expanded typology. *Acad. Manage. Rev.* 9:248–58

Benson, J. K. 1973. *Coordinating Human Services: A Sociological Study of an Interorganizational Network*. Columbia, Mo: Regional Rehab. Res. Inst, Univ. Missouri, Columbia. 151 pp.

Benson, J. K. 1975. The interorganizational network as a political economy. *Admin. Sci. Q.* 20:229–49

Berg, I., Zald, M. 1978. Business and society. *Ann. Rev. Sociol.* 4:115-43

Berry, J. M. 1977. *Lobbying for the People: The Political Behavior of Public Interest*

Groups. Princeton, NJ: Princeton Univ. Press, 331 pp.

Blau, P. 1964. *Exchange and Power in Social Life*. New York: Wiley. 352 pp.

Boje, D. M., Whetten, D. A. 1981. Effects of organizational strategies and constraints on centrality and attributions of influence in interorganizational networks. *Admin. Sci. Q.* 26:378–395

Burt, R. S. 1976. Positions in networks. *Soc. Forc.* 55:93–122

Burt, R. S. 1980. Cooptive corporate actor networks: A reconsideration of interlocking directorates involving American manufacturing. *Admin. Sci. Q.* 25:557–582

Burt, R. S. 1982. *Toward a Structural Theory of Action: Network Models of Social Structure, Perception, and Action*. New York: Academic. 381 pp.

Burt, R. S. 1983. *Corporate Profits and Cooptation: Networks of Market Constraints and Directorate Ties in the American Economy*. New York: Academic. 331 pp.

Burt, R. S., Christman, K. P., Kilburn, H. C. Jr. 1980. Testing a structural theory of corporate cooptation: Interorganizational directorate ties as a strategy for avoiding market constraints on profits. *Am. Sociol. Rev.* 45:821–41

Chatou, R. 1981. Cooperation between government and business. See Nystrom & Starbuck 1981, pp. 487–502

Cook, K. 1977. Exchange and power in networks of interorganizational relations. *Sociol. Q.* 18:62–82

DiMaggio, P. J., Romo, F. 1984. Domination and stratification in organizational fields. Presented at *Ann. Meet. Am. Sociol. Assoc,* San Antonio, Tex.

DiMaggio, P. J., Powell, W. W. 1983. The iron cage revisited: Institutional isomorphism and collective rationality in organizational fields. *Am. Sociol. Rev.* 48:147–60

Domhoff, G. W. 1970. *The Higher Circles: The Governing Class in America*. New York: Random. 367 pp.

Dowling, J., Pfeffer, J. 1975. Organizational legitimacy: Social values and organizational behavior. *Pacific Sociol. Rev.* 18:122–136

Downey, H. K., Hellriegel, D., Slocum, J. 1975. Environmental uncertainty: The construct and its applications. *Admin. Sci. Q.* 20:613–29

Duncan, R. E. 1975. Characteristics of organizational environments and perceived environmental uncertainty. *Admin. Sci. Q.* 17:313–327

El-Ansary, A. I. 1975. Determinants of power-dependence in the distribution channel. *J. Retailing* 51:59–74

El-Ansary, A. I., Robicheaux, R. A. 1974. A theory of channel control: Revisited. *J. Marketing* 38:2–7

El-Ansary, A. I., Stern, L. W. 1972. Power measurement in the distribution channel. *J. Marketing Res.* 9:47–52

Emerson, R. 1962. Power-dependence relations. *Am. Sociol. Rev.* 27:31–41

Emery, F. E., Trist, E. L. 1965. The causal texture of organizational environments. *Hum. Relat.* 18:21–31

Epstein, E. M. 1969. *The Corporation in American Politics*. Englewood Cliffs, NJ: Prentice Hall. 365 pp.

Ermann, M. D. 1978. The operative goals of corporate philanthropy: Contributions to the Public Broadcasting Service, 1972–1976. *Soc. Probl.* 25:504–14

Etgar, M. 1976. Channel domination and countervailing power in distributive channels. *J. Marketing Res.* 13:254–62

Fennema, M., Schijf, H. 1979. Analyzing interlocking directorates: Theory and methods. *Soc. Networks* 1:297–332

Freeman, J. 1973. The origins of the women's liberation movement. *Am. J. Sociol.* 78: 792–811

Fry, L. W., Keim, G., Meiners, R. E. 1982. Corporate contributions: Altruistic or for profit. *Acad. Manage. J.* 25:94–106

Galaskiewicz, J. 1979a. *Exchange Networks and Community Politics*. Beverly Hills, Calif: Sage. 205 pp.

Galaskiewicz, J. 1979b. The structure of community organizational networks. *Soc. Forc.* 57:1346–64

Galaskiewicz, J. 1982. Networks of control and resource allocation: Corporate contributions to nonprofit organizations. In *Social Structure and Network Analysis,* ed. P. V. Marsden, N. Lin, pp. 235–53. Beverly Hills, Calif: Sage. 319 pp.

Galaskiewicz, J. 1985. *Social Organization of an Urban Grants Economy: A Study of Corporate Contributions to Nonprofit Organizations*. New York: Academic

Galaskiewicz, J., Krohn, Karl. 1984. Positions, roles, and dependencies in a community interorganization system. *Sociol. Q.* 25: 527–50

Galaskiewicz, J., Marsden, P. 1978. Interorganizational resource networks: Formal patterns of overlap. *Soc. Sci. Res.* 7:89–107

Galaskiewicz, J., Rauschenbach, B. The corporate-cultural connection: A test of interorganizational theories. In *Resource Dependency and Community Organization,* ed. C. Milofsky. Forthcoming

Galaskiewicz, J., Shatin, D. 1981. Leadership and networking among neighborhood human service organizations. *Admin. Sci. Q.* 26: 434–48

Gamson, W. A. 1975. *The Strategy of Social Protest*. Homewood, Ill: Dorsey. 217 pp.

Gouldner, A. 1959. Organizational analysis. In *Sociology Today,* ed. R. Merton, L. Broom, L. Cottrell, pp. 400–28. New York: Basic. 623 pp.

Guetzkow, H. 1966. Relations among organizations. In *Studies on Behavior in Organizations,* ed. R. Bowers, pp. 13–44. Athens, Ga: Univ. Georgia Press. 364 pp.

Hall, R. H. 1982. *Organizations: Structure and Process,* Englewood Cliffs, NJ: Prentice-Hall. 356 pp. 3rd ed.

Hall, R. H., Clark, J., Giordano, P., Johnson, P. Van roekel, M. 1977. Patterns of interorganizational relationships. *Admin. Sci. Q.* 22:457–74

Henig, J. R. 1982. *Neighborhood Mobilization: Redevelopment and Response.* New Brunswick, NJ: Rutgers Univ. Press. 283 pp.

Hirsch, P. 1972. Processing fads and fashions: An organization-set analysis of cultural industry systems. *Am. J. Sociol.* 77:639–59

Hunt, S. D., Nevin, J. R. 1974. Power in a channel distribution: Sources and consequences. *J. Marketing Res.* 11:186–93

Jacobs, D. 1974. Dependency and vulnerability: An exchange approach to the control of organizations. *Admin. Sci. Q.* 19:45–59

Jacoby, N. H. 1973. *Corporate Power and Social Responsibility.* New York: Macmillan. 282 pp.

Jenkins, J. C. 1983. Resource mobilization theory and the study of social movements. *Ann. Rev. Sociol.* 9:527–53

Jenkins, J. C., Perrow, C. 1977. Insurgency of the powerless. *Am. Sociol. Rev.* 42:249–68

Kamens, D. 1977. Legitimating myths and educational organization: The relationship between organizational ideology and formal structure. *Am. Sociol. Rev.* 42:208–19

Katz, D., Kahn, R. 1966. *Social Psychology of Organizations.* New York: Wiley. 498 pp.

Khandwalla, P. N. 1981. Properties of competing organizations. See Nystrom & Starbuck 1981, pp. 409–32

Klonglan, G., Warren, R., Winkelpleck, J., Paulson, S. 1976. Interorganizational measurement in the social service sector: Differences by hierarchical level. *Admin. Sci. Q.* 21:675–87

Knoke, D. 1983. Organization sponsorship and influence reputation of social influence associations. *Soc. Forc.* 61:1065–87

Knoke, D., Rogers, D. L. 1979. A blockmodel analysis of interorganizational networks. *Sociol. Soc. Res.* 64:28–52

Knoke, D., Wood, J. R. 1981. *Organized for Action: Commitment in Voluntary Associations.* New Brunswick, NJ: Rutgers Univ. Press. 263 pp.

Kochan, T. A. 1975. Determinants of the power of boundary units in an interorganizational bargaining relation. *Admin. Sci. Q.* 20:434–52

Koenig, T., Gogel, R., Sonquist, J. 1979. Models of the significance of interlocking corporate directorates. *Am. J. Econ. Sociol.* 38:173–86

Laumann, E. O., Knoke, D., Kim, Y. 1984. The effects of interorganizational networks and resource mobilization on organizational participation in the national health policy domain. Presented at *Ann. Meet. Midwest Sociol. Soc,* 48th. Chicago, Ill.

Laumann, E. O., Galaskiewicz, J., Marsden, P. 1978. Community structure as Interorganizational linkages. *Ann. Rev. Sociol.* 4:455–84

Laumann, E. O., Pappi, F. 1976. *Networks of Collective Action: A Perspective on Community Influence Systems.* New York: Academic. 329 pp.

Lawrence, P. 1981. The Harvard organization and environment research program. In *Perspectives on Organization Design and Behavior,* ed. A. H. Van de Ven, W. F. Joyce, pp. 311–337. New York: Wiley. 486 pp.

Lawrence, P., Lorsch, J. 1967. *Organization and Environment: Managing Differentiation and Integration.* Boston: Division of Research, Grad. School Bus. Admin. Harvard Univ. 279 pp.

Leblebici, H., Salancik, G. R. 1982. Stability in interorganizational exchanges: Rulemaking processes of the Chicago Board of Trade. *Admin. Sci. Q.* 27:227–42

Lee, M. L. 1971. A conspicuous production theory of hospital behavior. *S. Econ. J.* 38:48–59

Leifer, R., Huber, G. P. 1977. Relations among perceived environmental uncertainty, organizational structure, and boundary-spanning behavior. *Admin. Sci. Q.* 22:235–47

Lentz, A., Tschirgi, H. 1963. The ethical content of annual reports. *J. Bus.* 36:387–93

Levine, S., White, P. 1961. Exchange as a conceptual framework for the study of interorganizational relationships. *Admin. Sci. Q.* 5:583–601

Levy, F. K., Shatto, G. M. 1978. The evaluation of corporate contributions. *Public Choice* 33:19–28

Levy, F. K., Shatto, G. M. 1980. Social responsibility in large electric utility firms: The case for philanthropy. In *Research in Corporate Social Performance and Policy,* ed. L. E. Preston, 2:237–49. Greenwich, Conn: JAI

Lipsky, M. 1970. *Protest in City Politics: Rent Strikes, Housing, and the Power of the Poor.* Chicago: Rand McNally. 214 pp.

Litwak, E., Hylton, L. 1962. Interorganizational analysis: A hypothesis of coordinating agencies. *Admin. Sci. Q.* 6:395–421

Lusch, R. F., Brown, J. R. 1982. A modified model of power in the marketing channel. *J. Marketing Res.* 19:312–23

March, J., Simon, H. 1958. *Organizations*. New York: Wiley. 262 pp.

McCarthy, J. D., Zald, M. N. 1977. Resource mobilization and social movements. *Am. J. Sociol.* 82:1212–41

Meyer, J., Rowen, B. 1977. Institutionalized organizations: Formal structure as myth and ceremony. *Am. J. Sociol.* 83:340–63

Meyer, J., Scott, W. R. 1983. *Organizational Environments: Ritual and Rationality*. Beverly Hills, Calif: Sage. 302 pp.

Miles, R. H. 1982. *Coffin Nails and Corporate Strategies*. Englewood Cliffs, NJ: Prentice-Hall. 298 pp.

Miller, J. 1980. Access to Interorganizational Networks as a Professional Resource. *Am. Sociol. Rev.* 45:479–96

Mills, C. W. 1956. *The Power Elite*. New York: Oxford Univ. Press. 423 pp.

Mitnick, B. M. 1984. *Agents in the environment: Managing in boundary-spanning roles*. Graduate School of Business Work. pap. 490, Univ. Pittsburgh, Pittsburgh, Pa.

Morrissey, J. P., Hall, R. H., Lindsey, M. L. 1981. *Interorganizational Relations: A Sourcebook of Measures for Mental Health Programs*. Albany, NY: NY State Of. Mental Health. 199 pp.

Mulford, C. L. 1984. *Interorganizational Relations: Implications for Community Development*. New York: Human Sciences. 227 pp.

Mulford, C. L., Rogers, D. L. 1982. Definitions and models. In *Interorganizational Coordination: Theory, Research, and Implementation*, ed. D. L. Rogers, D. A. Whetten, pp. 9–31. Ames, Ia: Univ. Ia Press. 206 pp.

Nelson, R. L. 1970. *Economic Factors in the Growth of Corporation Giving*. New York: Russell Sage Foundation. 116 pp.

Nystrom, P., Starbuck, W. H. 1981. *Handbook of Organizational Design*. Vol. 1. London: Oxford Univ. Press, 560 pp.

Olson, M. 1965. *The Logic of Collective Action: Public Goods and the Theory of Groups*. Cambridge, Mass.: Harvard Univ. Press. 186 pp.

Ornstein, M. 1984. Interlocking directorates in Canada: Intercorporate or class alliance? *Admin. Sci. Q.* 29:210–31

Ouchi, W. G. 1980a. A framework for understanding organizational failure. In *The Organizational Life Cycle*, J. R. Kimberly, R. H. Miles, et al, pp. 395–429. San Francisco: Jossey-Bass. 492 pp.

Ouchi, W. G. 1980b. Markets, bureaucracies, and clans. *Admin. Sci. Q.* 25:129–41

Ouchi, W. G. 1984. *The M-Form Society: How American Teamwork Can Recapture the Competitive Edge*. Reading, Mass: Addison-Wesley. 315 pp.

Palamountain, J. C. 1955. *The Politics of Distribution*. Cambridge, Mass: Harvard Univ. Press. 270 pp.

Palmer, D. 1983. Broken ties: Interlocking directorates and intercorporate coordination. *Admin. Sci. Q.* 28:40–55

Parsons, T. 1956. Suggestions for a sociological approach to the theory of organizations. *Admin. Sci. Q.* 1:63–69, 74–80

Parsons, T. 1960. *Structure and Process in Modern Societies*. New York: Free. 344 pp.

Pennings, J. M. 1980. *Interlocking Directorates: Origins and Consequences of Connections Among Organizations' Boards of Directors*. San Francisco: Jossey-Bass. 220 pp.

Pennings, J. M. 1981. Strategically interdependent organizations. See Nystrom & Starbuck 1981, pp. 433–55

Perrow, C. 1961. Organizational prestige: Some functions and dysfunctions. *Am. J. Sociol.* 66:335–41

Perrucci, R., Pilisuk, M. 1970. Leaders and ruling elites: The interorganizational bases of community power. *Am. Sociol. Rev.* 35:1040–57

Pfeffer, J. 1972. Size and composition of corporate boards of directors: The organization and its environment. *Admin. Sci. Q.* 17:218–228

Pfeffer, J. 1973. Size, composition, and function of hospital boards of directors: A study of organization-environment linkages. *Admin. Sci. Q.* 18:349–364

Pfeffer, J., Leong, A. 1977. Resource allocations in United Funds: Examination of power and dependence. *Soc. Forc.* 55:775–90

Pfeffer, J., Salancik, G. 1978. *The External Control of Organizations: A. Resource Dependence Perspective*. New York: Harper & Row. 300 pp.

Phillips, A. 1960. A theory of interfirm organizations. *Q. J. Econ.* 74:602–13

Provan, K. G. 1983. The federation as an interorganizational linkage network. *Acad. Manage. Rev.* 8:79–89

Provan, K., Beyer, J. M., Kruytbosch, C. 1980. Environmental linkages and power in resource-dependence relations between organizations. *Admin. Sci. Q.* 25:200–25

Reid, W. 1964. Interagency coordination in delinquency prevention and control. *Soc. Serv. Rev.* 38:418–28

Reve, T., Stern, L. W. 1979. Interorganizational relations in marketing channels. *Acad. Manage. Rev.* 4:405–16

Rogers, D. L., Whetten, D. A. 1982. *Interorganizational Coordination: Theory, Research, and Implementation*. Ames, Ia: Univ. Ia Press. 206 pp.

Rogers, D. L. 1974. Sociometric analysis of interorganizational relations: Application of theory and measurement. *Rural Sociol.* 39:487–503

Rose-Ackerman, S. 1980. United charities: An economic analysis. *Public Policy* 28:323–350

Salancik, G. R. 1976. *The role of interdependencies in organizational responsiveness to demands from the environment: The case of women versus power.* Unpublished manuscript, University of Illinois

Salisbury, R. H. 1969. An exchange theory of interest groups. *Midwest J. Polit. Sci.* 13:1–32

Salisbury, R. H. 1984. Interest representation: The dominance of institutions. *Am. Polit. Sci. Rev.* 78:64–76

Schermerhorn, Jr., J. R. 1975. Determinants of interorganizational cooperation. *Acad. of Manage. J.* 18:846–56

Schmidt, S. M., Kochan, T. A. 1977. Interorganizational relationships: Patterns and motivations. *Admin. Sci. Q.* 22:220–34

Schoorman, F. D., Bazerman, M. H., Atkin, R. S. 1981. Interlocking directorates: A strategy for reducing environmental uncertainty. *Acad. Manage. Rev.* 24:243–51

Selznick, P. 1949. *TVA and the Grass Roots: A Study in the Sociology of Formal Organization.* New York: Harper & Row. 274 pp.

Simon, H. 1957. *Administrative Behavior,* New York: Macmillan. 259 pp. 2nd ed.

Spekman, R. E. 1979. Influence and information: An exploratory investigation of the boundary-role person's basis of power. *Acad. Manage. J.* 22:104–117

Starbuck, W. H. 1976. Organizations and their environments. In *Handbook of Industrial and Organizational Psychology,* ed. M. D. Dunnette, pp. 1089–1123. Chicago: Rand McNally. 1,740 pp.

Steedly, Jr., H. R., Foley, J. W. 1979. The success of protest groups: Multivariate analyses. *Soc. Sci. Res.* 8:1–15

Stern, R. 1979. The development of an interorganizational control network. *Admin. Sci. Q.* 24:242–66

Thompson, J. 1967. *Organizations in Action.* New York: McGraw Hill. 192 pp.

Tosi, H., Aldag, R., Storey, R. 1973. On the measurement of the environment: An assessment of the Lawrence and Lorsch environmental subscale. *Admin. Sci. Q.* 18:27–36

Turk, H. 1973. *Interorganizational Activation in Urban Communities: Deductions from the Concept of Systems.* Washington, DC: The Arnold and Caroline Rose Monograph Series, *Am. Sociol. Assoc.* 67 pp.

Turk, H. 1977. *Organizations in Modern Life: Cities and Other Large Networks.* San Francisco: Jossey-Bass. 283 pp.

Useem, M. 1984. *The Inner Circle: Large Corporations and the Rise of Business Political Activity in the U.S. and U.K.* New York: Oxford Univ. Press. 246 pp.

Useem, M. 1985. Corporate philanthropy. In *The Handbook of Non-Profit Organizations,* ed. W. W. Powell. New Haven: Yale Univ. Press

Van de Ven, A. H., Ferry, D. L. 1980. *Measuring and Assessing Organizations.* New York: Wiley. 552 pp.

Van de Ven, A. H., Walker, G., Liston, J. 1979. Coordination patterns within an interorganizational network. *Human Relat.* 32:19–36

Van de Ven, A. H. 1976. On the nature, formation, and maintenance of relations among organizations. *Acad. Manage. Rev.* 4:24–36

Walker, G., Weber, D. 1984. A transaction cost approach to make-or-buy decisions. *Admin. Sci. Q.* 29:373–91

Warren, R., Rose, S., Bergunder, A. 1974. *The Structure of Urban Reform.* Lexington, Mass: Lexington Books. 220 pp.

West, G. 1981. *The National Welfare Rights Movement.* New York: Praeger. 451 pp.

Whetten, D. A. 1981. Interorganizational relations: A review of the field. *J. Higher Education* 52:1–28

White, A. H. 1980. Corporate philanthropy: Impact on public attitudes. In *Corporate Philanthropy in the Eighties,* pp. 17–19. Washington, DC: National Chamber Foun.

White, H., Boorman, S., Breiger, R. 1976. Social structure from multiple networks. I. blockmodels of roles and positions. *Am. J. Sociol.* 81:730–80

Wilkinson, I. F. 1973. Power and influence structures in distribution channels. *Eur. J. Marketing* 7:119–29

Williamson, O. E., Ouchi, W. G. 1981. The markets and hierarchies program of research: Origins, implications, prospects. In *Perspectives on Organization Design and Behavior,* ed. A. H. Van de Ven, W. F. Joyce, pp. 347–370. New York: John Wiley. 486 pp.

Williamson, O. E. 1981. The economics of organization: The transaction cost approach. *Am. J. Sociol.* 87:548–77

Williamson, O. E. 1975. *Markets and Hierarchies: Analysis and Antitrust Implications.* New York: Free. 286 pp.

Wood, P. 1982. The environmental movement. In *Social Movements: Development, Participation, and Dynamics,* ed. J. L. Wood, M. Jackson, pp. 201–20. Belmont, Calif: Wadsworth. 287 pp.

Yuchtman, E., Seashore, S. 1967. A systems resource approach to organizational effectiveness. *Am. Sociol. Rev.* 32:891–903

Zald, M. 1970. *Organizational Change: The Political Economy of the YMCA.* Chicago: Univ. Chicago Press. 260 pp.

Zald, M. 1967. Urban differentiation characteristics of boards of directors, and organizational effectiveness. *Am. J. Sociol.* 73:261–72

Zeitz, G. 1980. Interorganizational dialectics. *Admin. Sci. Q.* 25:72–88

Ann. Rev. Sociol. 1985. 11:305–28

SOCIAL MOBILITY AND FERTILITY

John D. Kasarda

Department of Sociology, University of North Carolina at Chapel Hill, Chapel Hill, North Carolina, 27514

John O. G. Billy

Battelle Human Affairs Research Center, 4000 NE 41 St., Seattle, Washington, 98105

Abstract

This review examines four possible causal links between social mobility and fertility: (1) fertility affects social mobility; (2) social mobility affects fertility; (3) fertility and social mobility simultaneously affect each other; and (4) social mobility and fertility are unrelated. Because of the lack of systematic theory guiding the research, conceptualizations and measures of social mobility and fertility vary markedly from study to study, leading to inconsistent findings. Research also differs regarding what constitutes a "true" mobility effect, particularly whether one must distinguish the process of mobility from the additive effects of origin and destination variables used to define mobility. The review focuses on theoretical perspectives underpinning the research, causal operators proposed to interpret observed associations, and analytical methods used. We highlight the multifaceted, complex, and incompletely understood nature of the social mobility–fertility relationship and suggest some fruitful avenues future research might pursue.

INTRODUCTION

Our consideration of the extensive literature on the relationship of social mobility and fertility may be summarized in terms of four propositions:

305

0360-0572/85/0815-0305$02.00

1. Fertility affects social mobility;
2. Social mobility affects fertility;
3. Social mobility and fertility affect each other; and
4. Social mobility and fertility are causally unrelated.

The sections that follow will be organized around these propositions.

Before we embark on this effort, we believe the reader should be alerted to some general characteristics of the literature in this area. Simply put, the literature on the relationship between social mobility and fertility represents a research quagmire. Often it is difficult to ascertain exactly what investigators have tested, and sometimes it is not even possible to tell whether a particular study supports or refutes the existence of a relationship.

The basic problem has been the paucity of systematic theory guiding the research. As a result, specific hypotheses about the nature of the relationship, along with conceptualizations and measures of social mobility and fertility, vary markedly from study to study without reference to the theoretical reasons for such variability. For example, some investigators place emphasis on the subjective dimension of mobility, i.e. aspirations and motivations to be socially mobile. Others examine the effect of an objective dimension of social mobility, e.g. intragenerational, intergenerational, or nuptial mobility. All too often the multidimensionality of the concept goes unrecognized, and researchers treat their particular measurement as evidence of the existence or nonexistence of an association between social mobility and fertility in general. Similarly, reproductive behavior (fertility) is variously measured in terms of completed family size, children ever born, spacing of births, early and later childbearing, and intended or unintended births.

Further contributing to the complexity and confusion is the lack of clear guidelines as to the direction of causality or the expected nature of the relationship. Hence, at least four theoretical perspectives to account for an effect of mobility on reproductive behavior can be identified in the literature. There is even substantial debate as to whether a relationship should be expected to obtain.

Methods of analysis also diverge without contributing to our further insight. Of particular importance is the question of what is to be accepted as an indication of a social mobility–fertility relationship. That is, what constitutes a "true" mobility effect? Researchers differ according to whether or not they distinguish between the effect of *process* of mobility and the *additive* effects of the status origin and destination variables used to define mobility.

These multifaceted approaches with respect to operationalizations of the concepts of mobility and fertility, theoretical development, and methodology often go undetected by investigators who proceed to compare their findings with those of previous works. Consequently, they are prone to conclude that the findings to date are inconclusive, if not negative. Indeed, we detect a sense of exasperation on the part of Blau & Duncan when they comment:

> It is the plausibility of the hypothesis rather than the quality of any supporting evidence that seems to account for its continuing appeal. Although no set of negative results can be definitive—because a different outcome might follow from studies in different populations or with alternative measures of mobility—it appears that at some point the burden of proof may fairly be shifted to the proponents of the hypothesis (1967:371).

Rather than reviewing the plethora of inconsistent findings studies have generated, however, we shall focus on theoretical perspectives underpinning the research, causal operators proposed to interpret observed associations, and analytical methods used.[1] In so doing, we hope to highlight the multifaceted, complex, and incompletely understood nature of the relationship as well as to suggest fruitful avenues future research might pursue.

FERTILITY AFFECTS SOCIAL MOBILITY

Despite the inconclusive findings to date, there are a number of reasons to suspect that fertility affects social mobility. One such reason is contained in the "selectivity" perspective (Bean & Swicegood 1979). This perspective has its roots in Dumont's (1890) contention that a family must be small in order to rise on the social scale. Early commentators stressed the biological aspects of the relationship, the social promotion of the relatively infertile (Galton 1900, Fisher 1930, Wagner-Manslau 1932). There is self-selection of subfecund and involuntarily sterile individuals or couples into the upwardly mobile stream. Why this is so, and how fecundity or infecundity affects downward as well as upward mobility is left unanswered.

More recently, the strictly biological component of the relationship has been deemphasized and the effect of family size, whether involuntarily or voluntarily induced, on social mobility has been stressed. For example, Berent (1952) simply states that persons are able to rise in status because of smallness of families and others are constrained to move down under the burden of large families. Children require the expenditure of resources (time, money, effort), and couples with high fertility may therefore find it difficult to maintain their social position; couples with low fertility may find it easier to achieve social gains because they have excess resources that can be used to improve their chances for status achievement.

This explanation, either explicitly or implicitly, has guided the work of Bean & Swicegood (1979), Featherman (1970), Deming (1974), and Hargens et al (1978). However, little support for the "selectivity" hypothesis has been found. Bean & Swicegood find no support for it, and Deming finds that early child-

---

[1]A thorough review of social mobility–fertility findings is presented in Kasarda et al (forthcoming).

bearing has debilitating consequences for subsequent occupational achievement only for migrants. Hargens et al find support for the hypothesis, but their
sample is limited to one very specific occupational group (male and female
Ph.D. chemists). Indeed, the purpose of their research was to "discover" an
occupational group where the hypothesis may be applicable. Featherman finds
that cumulative fertility between 1957 and 1963–67 has a small, insignificant,
but positive effect on occupational and economic status achieved by 1963–67.
Thus, children induce slightly higher levels of status achievement. This accords
well with Riemer & Kiser's (1954) suggestion that family responsibilities may
stimulate the energy and ambition of some so that they achieve more than those
without the burdens of a family.

SOCIAL MOBILITY AFFECTS FERTILITY

The vast majority of studies have been concerned with this hypothesis. To
account for why one would expect social mobility to affect fertility, four
theoretical perspectives have been used: status enhancement; relative economic
status; social isolation; and stress and disorientation (Bean & Swicegood 1979,
Stevens 1981). Each posits that social mobility accounts for variance in fertility
above that which is associated with the independent effects of origin and status
destination. Each, however, makes a different prediction with regard to the
upwardly and/or downwardly mobile compared to the fertility of the nonmobile.

Status Enhancement

This perspective, which finds greatest expression in the now classic Indianapolis (Kantner & Kiser 1954, Riemer & Kiser 1954) and Princeton (Westoff et al
1961; 1963) fertility studies, contends that childbearing and social mobility are
inimical to one another. Westoff (1953) states that the disposition to be mobile
leads to a voluntary limitation of childbearing because of a high degree of
rationality on the part of the upwardly mobile, a success-orientation, and all
that is implied by it. The desire to improve one's status is an important motive
for restricting family size because, as noted, rearing children absorbs energy
and capital that parents could otherwise use to rise on the social scale (Espenshade 1980, Mincer & Ofek 1982, Hofferth 1984).

The status enhancement perspective is framed more in terms of the subjective dimension of mobility than the objective dimension. That is, the argument
is that undergoing the process of upward mobility is a less important cause of
lower fertility than the aspiration, perceived opportunity, and motivation to be
upwardly mobile. Note, for example, the phrases "disposition to be mobile"
and "desire to improve one's status" in the preceding paragraph.

That the status enhancement perspective stresses the subjective rather than objective dimension of mobility has important implications for the predicted effect of downward mobility on fertility. Boyd (1971), Bean & Swicegood (1979), and Stevens (1981) maintain that given this perspective one would predict that the downwardly mobile have lower fertility than the nonmobile because the former try to regain their lost social position or halt their social decline. This reasoning, however, is not consistent with the perspective's emphasis on mobility aspirations. No one aspires to be downwardly mobile, but those who are downwardly mobile are likely to be persons who did not aspire or were not motivated to increase their status or maintain their former status. Not caring if they lose status, the downwardly mobile are likely to have higher fertility than the nonmobile; they choose to invest their resources in children rather than in activities that will serve to enhance or maintain their prior social status. Thus, we argue that the status enhancement perspective is more in line with a prediction that the downwardly mobile will have higher fertility than the nonmobile, rather than lower fertility. It is worth noting as well that the impediments to status enhancement discussed by these researchers presuppose a society in which the family and consanguinity are not a means to status enhancement.

Relative Economic Status

This perspective is drawn primarily from the work of Easterlin (1969, 1973, 1975, 1978), wherein he attempts to explain fluctuations in period fertility rates in the U.S. He does so by formulating a hypothesis at the "macro" decision-making level that employs the concept of relative economic status, perceived permanent income relative to tastes. Tastes are defined as consumption preferences formed while the individual was in the parental household. He hypothesizes that the baby boom was caused by increases in relative economic status for couples in the reproductive ages, while the subsequent decline in US fertility was caused by decreases in relative economic status.

The hypothesis can be directly applied to data of a micro nature such that high relative economic status is predicted to cause an increase in a couple's fertility and low relative economic status causes a decrease in fertility. That is, if perceived permanent income is high relative to tastes for consumer goods formed in the parental household, fertility is expected to be high. If permanent income is low relative to tastes, fertility is expected to be low. Easterlin argues that relative economic status will have its greatest effect on age at marriage and the pace of early marital fertility. When the comparison between income and tastes is unfavorable, marriage and family building will be delayed; when it is favorable, marriage and family building will occur relatively early. To the extent that relative economic status affects age at marriage and the pace of childbearing, it indirectly affects completed fertility (MacDonald & Rindfuss 1981).

Assuming that the upwardly and downwardly mobile have respectively higher and lower relative economic status than the nonmobile, this perspective predicts that the upwardly and downwardly mobile will have respectively higher and lower fertility (Bean & Swicegood 1979). The Easterlin hypothesis is one of a family of relative income hypotheses that differ with respect to the reference point for tastes. Thus, there seems to be little problem in treating intergenerational mobility as current status relative to tastes formed in the parental household, and treating career mobility as current status relative to tastes existing at marriage or first job.

We should note that the formulation of this perspective is relatively new in the mobility-fertility literature. Bean & Swicegood (1979) are the first researchers to offer it as an alternative hypothesis. However, the relative economic status perspective, which has its roots in the general concept of relative deprivation, appeared earlier in Riemer & Kiser's (1954) work. These researchers attempted to tap the subjective dimension of mobility by introducing the concept of "economic tension," the difference between the actual and desired standard of living. Boyd's (1973) comment that upward mobility may increase family size because couples may choose to invest their social gains in more children also indicates the potential applicability of the concept of relative economic status to mobility-fertility research.

Social Isolation

This perspective is mainly derived from Blau & Duncan (1967) and predicts that both the upwardly mobile and downwardly mobile will have higher fertility than the nonmobile. The process of mobility is viewed as having socially disintegrative aspects; it disrupts established social relationships and forces people into new and potentially alienating environments. The mobile individual or couple is poorly integrated into the new social class and does not receive much social support from the former social class. Lack of firm social support creates feelings of insecurity, and this causes the mobile couple to assume an extreme position with regard to its behavior.

One form of extreme behavior is increased fertility. Mobile couples compensate for previously lost social ties with unusually large families. How large families compensate for lost social ties is not made clear in the literature. We, however, suggest two ways. Stuckert (1963) finds that socially mobile couples are less likely to be oriented toward their extended families and less likely to participate in voluntary associations than nonmobile couples. Perhaps, then, having a large number of children is viewed by a couple as a means to gain additional persons with whom they may interact. Second, having many children may be regarded as a way for the couple to increase interaction with the community or social class into which they have entered. The more children there are, the greater the opportunity for couples to be involved in school activities, scouting, communication with neighbors, etc. Presumably, this is what Boyd (1973) has in mind when she comments that social insecurity might augment fertility as a means for couples to gain reintegration.

Stress and Disorientation

Decreased fertility is the other extreme position that mobile couples may assume because of lost social support and subsequent feelings of insecurity. The stress-and-disorientation perspective predicts that both upwardly and downwardly mobile couples will have lower fertility than the nonmobile. According to Blau (1956) feelings of insecurity inhibit fertility because of physical and emotional stress. While not adequately discussed in the literature, physical and emotional stress may inhibit fertility in several ways. It may cause an impairment in the biological capacity to reproduce, that is, it may affect a couple's fecundity. Alternatively, it may affect a couple's desire for children. Physical and emotional stress may precipitate a feeling of anomie; a couple may not desire to bring children into a world which they perceive to be normless or chaotic.

Lost social ties, such as the lack of extended family relations, might also lead to lower fertility of mobile couples because of the reduced availability of child-care possibilities. The couple may feel that they have no one to rely on when the burden of a large number of children becomes too heavy to bear. Hence, they may elect to use contraception or use it more effectively. We should qualify this remark, however, by noting that Bean & Aiken (1976) find support for the hypothesis that strain and disorientation contribute to greater contraceptive failure.

Conflicting Predictions of Theoretical Perspectives

Each of the four perspectives makes a different prediction with regard to the fertility of the upwardly and downwardly mobile compared to the fertility of the nonmobile. These predictions are diagrammed below:

	Upmobile	Nonmobile	Downmobile
Social Isolation	+	0	+
Stress and Disorientation	−	0	−
Status Enhancement	−	0	+
Relative Economic Status	+	0	−

Note, the social isolation perspective predicts that both the upwardly and downwardly mobile will have higher fertility than the nonmobile, while the stress and disorientation perspective predicts that both mobile categories will exhibit lower fertility than the nonmobile. For these two perspectives no prediction is made with regard to differences in fertility between the upwardly mobile and downwardly mobile themselves. Status enhancement predicts that the upwardly mobile and downwardly mobile will have respectively lower and higher fertility than the nonmobile, while relative economic status predicts the reverse.

Our assessment of the four perspectives leads us to suggest that there may be a hierarchy of mobility models: a difference in fertility between the mobile and nonmobile and a difference in fertility according to direction moved. The social isolation and stress-and-disorientation perspectives suggest that a simple mobile/nonmobile contrast is sufficient to describe the effect of mobility on fertility. The status enhancement and relative economic status perspectives suggest that direction moved must be considered to describe the effect adequately. Implicit in our diagram is the possibility that distance moved needs to be considered. Each + (or −) may be interpreted to mean that the greater the amount of social mobility, the higher (or lower) the couple's fertility.

BOTH FERTILITY AND SOCIAL MOBILITY AFFECT EACH OTHER

Many investigators of the social mobility–fertility relationship (e.g. Berent 1952, Riemer & Kiser 1954, Boyd 1971, 1973) have recognized that there is some degree of mutual causation between the two variables. Indeed, rather than argue which causal direction is correct, it seems more reasonable to acknowledge that both variables act on each other over time. For example, there is considerable evidence to suggest that attitudes and decisions about childbearing change during a couple's reproductive life cycle and that these decisions depend on the couple's particular economic and noneconomic circumstances at the time they are made (Freedman et al 1965, Bumpass & Westoff 1970, Namboodiri 1974, Simon 1975, and Hout 1976). With respect to the present topic, at any given time a couple may aspire or be preparing for a change in status, and their childbearing decision may reflect this aspiration or preparation. Alternatively, a couple's decision to have a child may reflect recently changed status and the social isolation or perceived gains or losses resulting from the change (Riemer & Kiser 1954).

It also seems reasonable to assume that attitudes, perceived opportunities, and decisions regarding a change in status may be altered over time and that these decisions depend on the particular family size circumstances at the moment they are made. Thus, Namboodiri suggests that the mobility-fertility relationship be viewed as a sequential process. "The probability of a change in parity is influenced by the family's current situational circumstances and the sequence of changes therein up to the point of time in question, and a change, in turn, is considered as affecting the family's chances of changing its situational characteristics" (Namboodiri 1972: 470). Even this view, however, is a simplification of the complex relationship, for it fails to take into account the aspirations or decisions with regard to either childbearing or mobility which may occur before, during, or after either type of event.

The point we wish to stress is that at any time in a couple's reproductive life cycle the decision or actual experience of either social mobility or fertility may influence the decision or actual experience of the other variable. At one moment, mobility may affect fertility, while at another, fertility may affect mobility. Moreover, both past mobility aspirations and decisions and past fertility preferences and decisions can affect subsequent mobility and subsequent timing and number of children. These subsequent aspirations and preferences may also be reciprocally related. In short, both mobility and fertility are cumulative processes which are constantly and perpetually acting and reacting on one another.

The Direction of Causality Problem

Recognizing reciprocal causation and being able to deal with it are two different matters. Many mobility-fertility researchers have concluded their studies with suggestions for future research. Most of these suggestions have involved a call for a causal analysis of the relationship using longitudinal data. Among the earliest advocates, Riemer & Kiser state:

> Consideration of the time sequence—the time at which shifts in socio-economic status occur, the stage of career at which marriage takes place, the timing of births within marriage in relation to status changes—is necessary in order to assess the significance of fertility as a selective factor in upward and downward mobility, and conversely, to assess the degree to which fertility reflects the socio-economic status of childhood and youth, acculturation to a new status, or the severity of the struggle to improve or maintain status at various stages of marital life (Riemer & Kiser 1954:212).

Similarly, Boyd's "ideal" study entails "a temporal study which utilizes birth intervals as indicative of reproductive behavior and which assesses the aspirations and occupational status at the time of each pregnancy and decisions concerning family size made prior to or after each pregnancy" (Boyd 1973:14–15). In effect, Boyd calls for a data set which to our knowledge has never been and perhaps never can be collected. Not only should complete information with regard to the objective dimensions of fertility and mobility be gathered, but reliable data on the subjective dimensions of reproductive behavior and mobility should be obtained for each important moment of a couple's life-course.

In the absence of highly detailed longitudinal data or cross-sectional data containing complete histories of two variables of interest, researchers have resorted to using various methodological techniques designed to evaluate direction of causality. Empirical testing of the reciprocity of a relationship is most pronounced in female labor force participation–fertility research. Waite &

Stolzenberg (1976) and Smith-Lovin & Tickamyer (1978) use two-stage least squares analysis to demonstrate the simultaneous effects of labor force participation on fertility and vice versa and to gain insight into which is the dominant causal path. This technique has yet to be applied to the mobility-fertility association, and there is growing evidence that it would not be the solution to the question of causality if it were. Cramer (1980), for example, provides a cogent discussion of the problem of two-stage least squares analysis to support his assertion that the technique may not be the answer to demographers' prayers to help them untangle nonrecursive causal complexities.

THE CONCEPT AND DIMENSIONS OF SOCIAL MOBILITY

We have yet to discuss a formal definition of the term *social mobility*. Barber's conceptualization is among the most straightforward:

> We have been using the term social mobility to mean movement, either upward or downward, between higher and lower social classes; or more precisely, movement between one relatively full-time, functionally significant social role and another that is evaluated as either higher or lower (1957:356).

There is concensus among demographers and sociologists that this is an adequate representation of the most general meaning of the term. More problematic, however, are the meanings or operational definitions of two concepts used in the above definition—*social class* and *movement*.

How one best measures a person's social class is an issue that has long been debated by scholars. Both theoretical and empirical reasoning have been applied in an effort to resolve this debate.[2] We will not dwell on this issue. Instead, we merely point out that mobility-fertility research has defined an individual's or couple's position in terms of income, education, or occupation with occupation used most often as a single index of social class and indexes of social mobility developed by comparing persons' changes in occupational position. Use of occupation as the single best measure of social position has been justified on the grounds of both practicality (Kahl 1957) and theory (Hauser 1972).

---

[2]For a sample of the literature relevant to the question of how one operationalizes the concept of social class and social mobility, and particularly whether occupation is an adequate measure, the interested reader is referred to Hatt (1950); McGuire (1950); Kahl & Davis (1955); Kahl (1957); Inkeles & Rossi (1956); Lipset & Zetterberg (1956); Haer (1957); Tumin & Feldman (1957); Morris & Murphy (1959); Lawson & Boek (1960); Schnore (1961); Mitra (1966); Duncan (1968); Goodman (1969); Treiman (1970, 1975, 1977); Hope (1971); Hauser (1972); Featherman & Hauser (1973); Featherman et al (1974); Hazelrigg (1974); Bibby (1975); Featherman et al (1975); Pullum (1975); Hazelrigg & Garnier (1976); Hodge & Siegel (1968); Hodge (1981); Vanneman (1977); Breiger (1981); Yamaguchi (1983); and Hout (1983, 1984).

Even if the term *social mobility* is narrowed and redefined as occupational mobility, the concept remains multidimensional. Westoff et al (1960) discuss five fundamental problems in the conceptualization of "movement": (1) the unit of analysis (individual, family, society); (2) the direction of movement (vertical, horizontal); (3) the reference points of movement (intergenerational, intragenerational); (4) the unit of measurement in movement (amount, distance); and (5) the visibility of movement (subjective, objective). Given this degree of multidimensionality, it is important to clarify how previous investigators have treated each of the five problems.

The unit of analysis has typically been the female respondent, but in most cases social position or the change therein has been regarded as pertaining to the couple, and occupational mobility has been measured in terms of the husband's change in status. Mobility has most often been defined in terms of the male's position—either wife's father's, husband's father's, or husband's occupation. This is based on the premise that the status of the wife depends largely on the status of her husband, while the reverse is rarely the case. "The fact that a woman works is certainly relevant to her reproductive behavior, but it is usually her husband's status that is of major importance in defining her social position" (Kantner & Kiser 1954:70). This is less likely to be true in modern, industrialized societies when greater numbers of women enter the labor force and do so for more reasons than simply providing supplemental family income (Rosenfeld 1978). However, in many less developed countries where relatively few women are gainfully employed, it may be reasonable to accept the validity of the premise.

The issues of direction of movement and unit of measurement in movement require little discussion. While not denying that horizontal social mobility, the transition from one social group to another situated on the same level, may affect a couple's reproductive behavior, most studies have focused exclusively on the effects of vertical social mobility, the transition from one social stratum to another.[3] Less interest has also been expressed in the amount of social mobility, the proportion of individuals who are upwardly or downwardly mobile within a given population, than in the distance of mobility, the number of steps an individual or couple moves upward or downward. Usually, however, the amount of mobility in a given sample has been examined in order to get an idea of how "fluid" or "open" the stratification system is.

The issue of the visibility of movement has received much attention in mobility-fertility research. Indeed, the status enhancement perspective is large-

---

[3]For a good discussion of the "situs" (horizontal) dimension of mobility and its utility for the further understanding of individual behavior, see Morris & Murphy (1959).

ly predicated on the assumption that the subjective dimension of mobility (aspirations, perceived opportunity, and motivation to be mobile) is more important for accounting for fertility behavior than the objective dimension (the actual process of moving). As previously noted, researchers involved in the Indianapolis Study (Kantner & Kiser 1954, Riemer & Kiser 1954) and Princeton Fertility Study (Westoff et al 1961, 1963, Featherman 1970) argue that fertility and actual achievement depend on the operation of a motivational complex; the disposition to be mobile is a determining condition of family size and actual socioeconomic achievement.

Westoff (1953) contends that the subjective dimension cannot be entirely deduced from the objective dimension since some aspire but are not mobile and some who are mobile have not had any great aspirations to be so. Westoff et al (1960) later test this hypothesis using data from the Princeton Fertility Study. They factor anaiyze 22 measures of mobility and find nine orthogonal factors: five account for the objective dimensions of mobility and four are concerned with the subjective dimensions. Hence, they conclude that it is erroneous to treat the objective and subjective dimensions of mobility as interchangeable.

Therefore, while empirical evidence exists to suggest that measures of subjective mobility need to be included in mobility-fertility analysis, we note that previous research has been less than successful in finding a relationship between this more elusive dimension and reproductive behavior. Riemer & Kiser's (1954) use of "economic tension" failed because of its particular susceptibility to causality problems. Westoff et al's (1961; 1963) measures of the importance attached to mobility values, perception of opportunity for getting ahead, drive to get ahead, and aspirations for sending children to college had little effect on couples' desired or actual family size. Similarly, Featherman (1970) found no relationship between fertility and a couple's primary work orientation, materialistic orientation, and subjective achievement evaluation.

Researchers have blamed their failure to find a relationship between mobility aspirations and reproductive behavior on measurement problems. For example, Westoff et al (1961:250) comment that measuring the subjective dimension of mobility is at a primitive stage in social research. Unfortunately, whether failure is due to inadequate measurement or simply that aspirations and motivations to be mobile are not as important as has been claimed still remains unanswered. Most previous research has concentrated primarily on the effects of objective occupational movement. With respect to the evaluation of the status enhancement perspective, it has therefore been assumed that those who are actually upwardly or downwardly mobile accurately represent those who aspired to improve their status or those who were not motivated to maintain their social position.

One aspect of subjective mobility that can be measured rather easily but which has not received a great deal of attention in mobility-fertility research per se is the respondent's occupational aspirations for her offspring. Thus, Westoff et al (1961) point out that many persons conceive of mobility in terms of the future status of their children and view their own role as that of maximizing the opportunities for their children. A couple may perceive that in order for their children to reach a higher social position than their own, they must take specific steps to provide the necessary finances and education. One such step may be to restrict family size; by doing so, a couple can minimize resource expenditures and maximize the resources available to one or a few children. Hence, we might expect that couples who reveal high mobility aspirations for their children will have lower fertility than those who have more modest aspirations for their offspring.

While previous investigators have been somewhat limited in the extent to which they could analyze the subjective dimension of mobility, this is not the case with respect to the objective dimension of the concept. Measures of the occupational position of the wife's father, husband's father, husband at marriage, and husband at interview have been extensively used in prior research. These permit the construction of a number of indexes of mobility that differ according to the reference point of movement. Westoff et al's (1960) factor analysis of 22 measures of mobility reveals that it may be a mistake to posit interchangeabilities between husband and wife variables and intergenerational and intragenerational mobility. Orthogonal factors representing different objective dimensions emerge. The researchers suggest that each objective measure should be regarded as a unique, independent component of the general concept of social mobility. Unfortunately, most previous researchers have used only one or two objective dimensions to examine the effect of social mobility on fertility. Many, after finding or failing to find a significant relationship, have concluded that social mobility either has or does not have an effect on reproductive behavior. We emphasize that this need not be the case. It seems reasonable to allow for the possibility that one type of mobility will have an effect while another does not. Given the presumed orthogonal nature of the dimensions, it also seems reasonable to expect that one of the four noted theoretical perspectives might account for the effect of one type of mobility while another perspective may account for the effect of a different dimension of mobility. The four theoretical perspectives are not mobility dimension specific; each may be applied to any type of social mobility.

Stevens's (1981) work comes closest to avoiding the tenuous assumption that the examination of one or two dimensions is sufficient for testing the relationship between social mobility and reproductive behavior. Not only does Stevens examine three objective dimensions, but she also divides each dimension into its relative (individual) and mean (structural) components. She recognizes that for some mobility is a result of their own effort while for others it is a result of changing labor market conditions. This is a variation of Westoff et al's contention that social mobility is a multifaceted phenomenon. Moreover,

Stevens discusses how each of the four theoretical perspectives may be applied to each of the relative and mean components.

In sum, social mobility is a multidimensional concept. Despite the large number of studies that have dealt exclusively with an examination of the mobility-fertility relationship, it is our opinion that this literature has barely scratched the surface in measuring and then relating to reproductive behavior all that is implied by the term, social mobility.

THE INTERMEDIATE VARIABLES

Reproductive behavior is also a multidimensional concept. Related to this issue is exactly *how* social mobility affects fertility. In their classic article, Davis & Blake (1956) posit 11 "intermediate" variables affecting intercourse, conception, gestation, and birth. Davis & Blake contend that any cultural factor must affect fertility via one or more of these intermediate variables; there can be no direct effect of any social or cultural factor on fertility (see also Bongaarts 1978).

Mobility-fertility researchers have not been totally unmindful of Davis & Blake's argument. The reader will recall that the central theme of the studies conducted prior to 1940 was "the social promotion of the relatively infertile." Also, the stress and disorientation perspective suggests that mobility may cause an impairment in a couple's biological capacity to reproduce. Hence, some theoretical attempts have been made to relate social mobility to involuntary subfecundity. Aside from the literature on delayed childbearing (see Baldwin & Nord 1984), no empirical research has been conducted that directly examines subfecundity as a cause or consequence of mobility.

A few attempts have also been made to examine mobility's effect on age at entry into sexual unions. Hollingsworth (1957), Perrucci (1967), and Zimmer (1979) include an age at marriage variable explicitly in their mobility-fertility models. Several researchers have also examined either directly or indirectly the differential use of contraception between mobile and nonmobile couples. In the Indianapolis Study (Kantner & Kiser 1954, Riemer & Kiser 1954), a distinction is made between planned and unplanned births and social mobility as it affects family planning effectiveness. In the Princeton Study (Westoff et al, 1961, 1963), percentage of successful family planners is used as a dependent variable. Bean & Swicegood (1979) divide fertility into intended and unintended births and therefore obtain some evidence of contraceptive failure. Boyd (1971) assesses the effect of mobility on Latin American women's knowledge and use of contraception. Finally, Zimmer (1979) examines whether the prevalence of voluntary sterilization differs by mobility status.

In general, however, these attempts to take Davis & Blake's analytical framework into account have been modest. A great deal more empirical research could and should be conducted to assess directly the impact of social mobility on the "intermediate" variables. Such investigations would be helpful in further clarifying whether and exactly how mobility and reproductive behavior are related.

CONDITIONING FACTORS

A common theme throughout much of the research literature is that the existence (or nature) of an effect of social mobility on fertility depends on the societal conditions of a given population. Boyd (1973) provides a detailed discussion of this argument. Developed countries are characterized by "fluid" or "open" stratification systems. In these societies mobility may not have disruptive effects because mobility rates are high and it becomes institutionalized through participation in the educational system. Mobility is no longer the exception, nor as costly, and hence is not associated with extreme behavioral modifications of individuals. Developed countries are also characterized by widespread use of contraceptives and limited variation in fertility by socioeconomic status. Treiman (1970:226) suggests that this may reflect the nature of the stratification system. He contends that one of the outcomes of high rates of mobility is increasing behavioral heterogeneity within classes and increasing homogeneity between classes.

In contrast, less developed countries display higher levels of fertility, differential access to and use of contraceptives, and differential fertility by socioeconomic status. This may reflect the stratification system in these societies, where there are high degrees of discontinuity and large behavioral differences between classes. The stratification system is less "fluid." Individual mobility is more the exception than the rule, and mobility mechanisms are not institutionalized by education. Mobile persons are likely to receive little social support, experience much stress, and incur substantial "costs" in moving. Consequently, mobility is more likely to have disruptive effects on behavior in more traditional, static, and class-homogeneous societies.

Most mobility-fertility research has been based on data collected in more developed countries, and many investigators have used the above argument to explain their failure to find a relationship. Boggs (1957) maintains that restriction of fertility is a consequence of social mobility under conditions that demand greater sacrifices in return for higher status. With the urban occupational system came prosperity, higher education, and successful experience in adapting to social mobility. All of these features minimize the impact of social mobility; it becomes an accepted and expected part of urban life and therefore does not elicit such responses as modifications in fertility behavior. Similarly, Westoff et al (1961) talk about middle-class suburbia with its emphasis on the family as the basic social unit. The family, and presumably a standard family size, becomes fashionable in the urban environment. Also related to this line of reasoning is Riemer & Kiser's (1954) and Tien's (1961) suggestion that in some countries it might be necessary to perform separate analyses for two or more marriage cohorts. The effect of mobility on fertility might be especially pronounced for those couples who experienced an economic setback early in marriage.

Freedman (1962) cogently argues that the mobility-fertility hypothesis is limited to transitional urban societies that are developing indigenous institutions and drawing large masses of migrants from rural areas. He suggests that it may be the migrant component of a population that causes an effect of social mobility on fertility to obtain. Rural to urban migrants are most likely to experience the disruptive effect of social mobility and therefore most likely to modify their behavior severely. Hence, we might hypothesize that the effect of social mobility on fertility differs for different subgroups of a population—migrants versus nonmigrants. This is consistent with the findings of Goldberg (1959), Blau & Duncan (1967), and Deming (1974). At the very least, Freedman's comments suggest that migration should be introduced as a control variable when examining the effect of social mobility on fertility.[4]

Finally, we should note the important role that education plays in the mobility-fertility relationship. In explaining their failure to find an effect of mobility on family size in a developed country, both Scott (1958) and Tien (1965) stress that education, rather than social mobility, will have the dominant effect on fertility. In developing countries, however, this may not be the case. In these societies, social mobility may be expected to have an impact on reproductive behavior, independent of the effect of education (Boyd 1973).

MEASURING MOBILITY EFFECTS

Regardless of findings, most studies through the mid-1960s used a common measurement method to assess whether a mobility effect existed. This method compared the reproductive behavior of the upwardly and/or downwardly mobile with that of the nonmobile at origin and/or destination (cf Berent 1952, Baltzell 1953, Kantner & Kiser 1954, Kirk 1957, Scott 1958, Westoff et al 1961, 1963, Tien 1961, 1965, Tomasson 1966, Perucci 1967). The criterion for determining if social mobility affects reproductive behavior is whether there are sizeable differences in mean levels of fertility between or among mobile and

---

[4]The relationship between geographic and social mobility is as complex and multi-faceted as the social mobility–fertility association. In some studies migration is regarded as a form or dimension of social mobility. In others, migration is treated as either a cause or effect of occupational mobility. For a discussion of the relationship between these two variables, the interested reader is referred to Freedman & Hawley 1949; Goldstein 1955; Hutchinson 1958, 1961; Pihlblad & Aas 1960; Richmond 1964; Macisco et al 1969; Prehn 1967; Zelinsky 1971; Martine 1972; Ramu 1972; Guzman 1975; Byrne 1975; Freeman et al 1976; Hiday 1978; and Berry 1983.

nonmobile groups. Those using this approach have disregarded the independent effects that status of origin and of destination may have in determining fertility levels of the mobile. The question, then, is whether a researcher should take the effects of origin and destination into account *before* assessing whether mobility affects fertility. Most authors of more recent empirical works have argued that one should (Duncan 1966, Blau & Duncan 1967, Boyd 1973, Bean & Swicegood 1979; Stevens 1981; Hope 1971, 1975, 1981; Sobel 1981, 1984).

Zimmer (1979, 1981), to the contrary, contends that it is precisely origin and destination statuses that researchers should focus upon. In particular, he critiques the Princeton fertility studies (Westoff et al 1961, 1963), arguing that their inability to find support for a mobility-fertility relationship resulted from their failure to disaggregate the nonmobile by status and the upwardly and downwardly mobile by both status of origin and destination. Zimmer asserts that one must devise a table of mean levels of fertility by cross-classifying past and current status and compare each cell mean of the mobile with that of the nonmobile at origin and destination.

Westoff (1981) in his rebuttal to Zimmer's allegations points out that he and his investigators did exactly what Zimmer said should be done. In fact, reexamining the Princeton Fertility Study data, Westoff conducts an analysis which conforms as closely as possible to the mobility matrix which Zimmer proposed. Based on this reanalysis, Westoff reaffirms his earlier findings of no relationship between social mobility and fertility.

The Zimmer-Westoff exchange raises important conceptual as well as methodological issues. Again, these issues boil down to whether one should distinguish between the effect of the process of social mobility on fertility and that of the additive combination effects of classes of origin and destination on reproductive behavior. Let us elaborate this critical point in terms of its epistomological evolution.

Duncan's Approach

In an epoch-making work, Duncan reanalyzed Berent's data to see if they reveal a "true" mobility effect: "The gist of the argument is that one is not entitled to discuss "effects" of mobility . . . until after he has established that the apparent effect cannot be due merely to a simple combination of effects of the variables used to define mobility" (Duncan 1966:91). According to Duncan, if one finds fertility of the upwardly mobile intermediate between the nonmobile at origin and destination, he may argue that these persons have changed status levels and that their reproductive behavior differs from that of people in either former or current status. One may be tempted to conclude that mobility has affected fertility. Yet, the term, mobility, as used by Duncan and in common parlance, connotes a process. If the additive model fits the data, the process of moving has not altered fertility behavior; the family size of the upwardly mobile can be correctly predicted simply with a knowledge of the fertility levels of their classes of origin and destination. If, however, the expected values of average family size calculated on the basis of the additive model differ significantly from the observed values, the deviations indicate a mobility effect, and an interactive model is regarded as better fitting the data. The process of mobility exerts an effect on fertility above and beyond that explained by past and present social class.

Reanalyzing Berent's data by calculating effects based on an additive model, Duncan found that the model reproduced the data reasonably well. Since mobile couples thereby combined the fertility patterns of their status origins and destinations (i.e. their fertility fell in between), he concluded that the mobility process has no consequence.

Other Methods for Assessing Mobility Effects

Hope (1971, 1975, 1981) has published a series of articles in which he demonstrates that his technique reveals mobility effects on individual behavior that are undiscoverable using Duncan's approach. The key to Hope's objection to Duncan's approach is that the definition of mobility as "interaction" is too restrictive; instead, Hope argues, mobility should be defined more broadly as deviation from the linear additive model.

Duncan's model for examining mobility effects is commonly referred to as the "square-additive" model, where rows and columns represent class of origin and class of destination, respectively. Hope takes the square table and rotates it 135° to create a "diamond-additive" model. In the diamond model the rows represent mobility ($A-B$, where A is class of origin and B is class of destination) and the columns represent a mean of origin and destination class ($A+B$).

In Hope's model tests of mobility effects are derived from the following equations:

$$\hat{Y} = a + b_1 (A+B); \hspace{3cm} 1.$$

$$\hat{Y} = a + b_1 (A+B) + b_2 (A-B). \hspace{2cm} 2.$$

If Equation 2 explains more variance in the dependent variable than Equation 1, a mobility effect is said to exist. In other words, in Hope's model, mobility is defined as discrepancy rather than interaction.

Hope's objection to Duncan's approach is therefore more theoretical than methodological. Whether Hope's definition of mobility (or status inconsistency) and the model derived from this definition accord better with the sociologist's notion of what should constitute a mobility effect is essentially a theoretical argument of how mobility is best conceptualized. House (1978) argues in favor of Duncan's approach and criticizes the "diamond-additive" model: "Hope's diamond model yields evidence of an inconsistency effect whenever the status variables involved have unequal effects on a dependent variable.. . .

Obviously, Hope has a very different conception than previous analysts of what constitutes status inconsistency and an effect thereof" (House 1978:441). We will not attempt to resolve this debate. We merely advise the reader interested in conducting mobility-fertility research to consider carefully Namboodiri's (1972) caution that the model one chooses to fit to the data will affect substantive interpretations.

Finally, we briefly note one other technique that has been developed to examine mobility effects on individual behavior. Sobel (1981) argues that neither Duncan's "square-additive" model nor Hope's "diamond-additive" model delimits the main effects of class of origin and class of destination correctly. He therefore proposes a new class of models, the "diagonal mobility" model, for the analysis of mobility effects on fertility and other types of behavior. Sobel claims that his model correctly establishes a correspondence between sociological theory and statistical method.

Sobel's models are statistically rigorous, and we will not present this methodology here. Instead, we invite the reader to review the technique critically. We should note, however, that Sobel's model more closely resembles Duncan's "square-additive" model than Hope's "diamond-additive" model. It tests against the null hypothesis of the additive effects of class of origin and class of destination and provides for a systematic search for the most appropriate and succinct way to describe the mobility effect. That is, the technique consists of a class of models, each member of which is designed to test whether the existence, direction, or magnitude of mobility is the most parsimonious way to capture its effect on a particular behavior.

In a more recent manuscript, Sobel (1984) expands his methodology and demonstrates how predictor variables other than class of origin, class of destination, and mobility may be incorporated into diagonal mobility models as controls. To illustrate the technique, Sobel reanalyzes Blau & Duncan's (1967) data. He finds support for the additive model (typically called the acculturation hypothesis)—the fertility of mobile couples lies intermediate between the nonmobile at origin and the nonmobile at destination. He also finds that the relative effects of origin and destination statuses depend on origin status.

Thus, whereas there is little statistical evidence to date suggesting that fertility is affected by mobility per se (i.e. by the unsettling process of the move itself) we should be careful not to throw the baby out with the bath water. Support for the acculturation hypothesis does indicate differential fertility by mobility status. Moreover, without mobility, origin and destination status will not differ. This is particularly pertinent to macrolevel outcomes. Although low status of origin will continue to affect fertility, provided there is an inverse relationship between socioeconomic status and fertility, those who rise in status will partially adopt the lower fertility patterns of their higher status destination groups. And if more upward than downward mobility occurs, the fertility of the population will decrease.

A final conceptual and measurement issue we must note is the problematic retention of a male-oriented focus in most research. That is, analysis of social mobility and its relationship to reproductive behavior remains largely geared to married women and their status measured by that of their fathers and/or husbands.

The structure under which both mobility and childbearing take place has substantially changed in recent decades. Increasingly, women are attaining status independent of that of their fathers or husbands (Safilios-Rothschild 1982; Stycos 1982; Mason 1984; Kasarda et al forthcoming). Concurrently, newer conceptualizations of female role behavior are emerging such as egalitarian marriage relations, increased participation of women in the mainstream economy, feminization of poverty, family dissolution-reformation, out-of-wedlock childbearing, single parenting, and female involvement in all aspects of reproductive decision-making. A shift from a predominantly male-dependent status orientation to a more female-oriented focus in social mobility–fertility research is long overdue.

SUMMARY AND CONCLUSIONS

In this review we have examined the multifaceted and complex relationship between social mobility and fertility. We have discussed four possible causal links between the variables: (1) fertility affects social mobility; (2) social mobility affects fertility; (3) fertility and social mobility simultaneously affect each other; and (4) social mobility and fertility are unrelated. While the bulk of previous research has treated social mobility as the independent variable and fertility as the dependent variable, there is undoubtedly some degree of mutual reciprocity between the two variables. Researchers have been hampered in their efforts to deal with the direction of causality problem because of the limitations of their data that permit only a static analysis of two dynamic processes. The causality problem will only be resolved through temporal analysis of longitudinal data.

We also reiterate that mobility is a multidimensional concept. Researchers have only scratched the surface in attempting to relate all that is implied by the term, *social mobility,* to reproductive behavior. Another neglected area in mobility-fertility research is a specification of exactly how social mobility affects fertility. Far too little consideration has been given to an examination of social mobility's effect on the intermediate variables. Moreover, numerous researchers have stressed that the effect of social mobility on fertility depends on the societal conditions of a given population. Yet, there has been little empirical testing of these conditional effects. Clearly, an analysis using a comparative framework is needed to investigate this hypothesis further.

Finally, although it seems reasonable to define a mobility effect as that which is independent of class of origin and class of destination effects, there is no standard, agreed-upon method to do so. It is our feeling that the various methodological techniques that have been proposed or used in mobility-fertility research add to this topic's reputation as a quagmire of social research. It would be most helpful if someone were to demonstrate systematically the extent to which inferences drawn about the effects of mobility on fertility would differ in a given data set by application of these various techniques. In the meantime, anyone interested in investigating the mobility-fertility relationship must be mindful of the alternative methodologies available and must decide what to accept as evidence of a mobility effect.

ACKNOWLEDGMENTS

Preparation of this manuscript was supported, in part, by a grant from USAID and by the Carolina Population Center. We are grateful for comments on an earlier draft by Ronald Rindfuss, Rachel Rosenfeld, and two anonymous reviewers of the *Annual Review of Sociology*.

Literature Cited

Baldwin, W. H., Nord, W. W. 1984. Delayed childbearing in the U.S.: Facts and fictions. *Pop. Bull.* 39(4)

Baltzell, E. D. 1953. Social mobility and fertility within an elite group. *Milbank Mem. Fund Q. Health Soc.* 31:411–20

Barber, B. 1957. *Social Stratification. A Comparative Analysis of Structure and Process*. New York: Harcourt, Brace & World

Bean, F. D., Aiken, L. H. 1976. Intermarriage and unwanted fertility in the United States. *J. Marriage Fam.* 38:61–72

Bean, F. D., Swicegood, C. G. 1979. Intergenerational occupational mobility and fertility: A reassessment. *Am. Sociol. Rev.* 44:608–19

Berent, J. 1952. Fertility and social mobility. *Pop. Stud.* 5:244–60

Berry, E. H. 1983. *Migration, fertility and social mobility: An analysis of the fertility of Ecuadorian women*. Presented at Ann. Meet. Pop. Assoc. Am., 52nd, Pittsburgh, Penn.

Bibby, J. 1975. Methods of measuring mobility. *Qual. Quant.* 9:107–36

Blau, P. M. 1956. Social mobility and interpersonal relations. *Am. Sociol. Rev.* 21:290–95

Blau, P. M., Duncan, O. D. with Tyree, A. 1967. *The American Occupational Structure*. New York: Wiley

Boggs, S. T. 1957. Family size and social mobility in a California suburb. *Eugen. Q.* 4:208–13

Bongaarts, J. 1978. A framework for analyzing the proximate determinants of fertility. *Pop. Dev. Rev.* 14:105–32

Boyd, M. 1971. *Occupational mobility and fertility in urban Latin America*. PhD thesis. Duke Univ., Durham, NC

Boyd, M. 1973. Occupational mobility and fertility in metropolitan Latin America. *Demography* 10:1–17

Breiger, R. L. 1981. The social class structure of occupational mobility. *Am. J. Sociol.* 87:578–607

Bumpass, L. L., Westoff, C. F. 1970. *The Later Years of Childbearing*. Princeton: Princeton Univ. Press

Byrne, J. J. 1975. *Occupational mobility, geographic mobility, and secondary migrants*. Presented at Ann. Meet. Pop. Assoc. Am., Seattle

Cramer, J. C. 1980. Fertility and female employment: Problems of Causal direction. *Am. Sociol. Rev.* 45:167–90

Davis, K., Blake, J. 1956. Social structure and fertility: An analytic framework. *Econ. Dev. Cult. Change* 4:211–35

Deming, M. B. 1974. *The influence of marriage and childbearing on occupational mobility in the Philippines*. Presented at Ann. Meet. Pop. Assoc. Am., 43rd, New York

Dumont, A. 1890. *Dépopulation et civilisation. Étude démographique*. Bibliothèque Anthropologique. Paris: Lecrosnier & Babé

Duncan, O. D. 1966. Methodological issues in the analysis of social mobility. In *Social Structure and Mobility in Economic Development*, ed. N. J. Smelser, S. M. Lipset, pp. 51–97. Chicago: Aldine.

Duncan, O. D. 1968. Social stratification and

mobility: Problems in the measurement of trend. In *Indicators of Social Change; Concepts and Measurements*, ed. E. B. Sheldon, W. E. Moore, pp. 675–719. New York: Russell Sage Found.

Easterlin, R. A. 1969. Towards a socioeconomic theory of fertility: A survey of recent research on economic factors in American fertility. In *Fertility and Family Planning: A World View*, ed. S. J. Behrman, L. Corsa, Jr., R. C. Freedman, pp. 127–56. Ann Arbor: Univ. of Mich. Press

Easterlin, R. A. 1973. Relative economic status and the American fertility swing. In *Family Economic Behavior: Problems and Prospects*, ed. E. B. Sheldon, pp. 170–223. Philadelphia: Lippincott

Easterlin, R. A. 1975. An economic framework for fertility analysis. *Stud. Fam. Plann.* 6:54–64

Easterlin, R. A. 1978. What will 1984 be like? Socioeconomic implications of recent twists in age structure. *Demography* 15:397–432

Espenshade, T. J. 1980. Raising a child can now cost $85,000. *Intercom* 8(9):10–12

Featherman, D. L. 1970. Marital fertility and the process of socioeconomic achievement: An examination of the mobility hypothesis. See Bumpass & Westoff 1970, pp. 104–31

Featherman, D. L., Hauser, R. M. 1973. On the measurement of occupation in social surveys. *Sociol. Methods Res.* 2:239–51

Featherman, D. L., Hauser, R. M., Sewell, W. H. 1974. Toward comparable data on inequality and stratification: Perspectives on the second generation of national mobility studies. *Am. Sociol.* 9:18–25

Featherman, D. L., Jones, F. L., Hauser, R. M. 1975. Assumptions of social mobility research in the U.S.: The case of occupational status. *Soc. Sci. Res.* 4:329–60

Fisher, R. A. 1930. *The Genetical Theory of Natural Selections.* Oxford: Clarendon

Freedman, R. C. 1962. American studies of family planning and fertility: A review of major trends and issues. In *Conference on Research in Family Planning, Carnegie International Center, New York, Oct. 13–19, 1960*, ed. C. V. Kiser, pp. 211–27. Princeton: Princeton Univ. Press

Freedman, R. C., Coombs, L. C. 1966. Child-spacing and family economic position. *Am. Sociol. Rev.* 31:631–48

Freedman, R. C., Coombs, L. C., Bumpass, L. L. 1965. Stability and change in expectations about family size: A longitudinal study. *Demography* 2:250–75

Freedman, R. C., Hawley, A. Y. 1949. Migration and occupational mobility in the depression. *Am. J. Sociol.* 55:171–77

Freeman, D. H., Jr., Freeman, J. L., Koch, G. G. 1976. *An application of log-linear models to the study of occupational mobility and*

migration. Presented at Ann. Meet. Pop. Assoc. Am., 45th, Montreal

Galton, F. 1900. *Hereditary Genius: An Inquiry into Its Laws and Consequences.* New York: Appleton. 2nd ed.

Goldberg, D. 1959. The fertility of two-generation urbanities. *Pop. Stud.* 12:214–22

Goldstein, S. 1955. Migration and occupational mobility in Norristown, Pennsylvania. *Am. Sociol. Rev.* 20:402–08

Goodman, L. A. 1969. On the measurement of social mobility: An index of status persistence. *Am. Sociol. Rev.* 34:831–50

Guzman, E. A. de. 1975. *Occupational mobility in the Philippines: 1973 data.* Research Note no. 38. Manila: Population Institute, Univ. Philippines System

Haer, J. L. 1957. Predictive utility of five indices of social stratification. *Am. Sociol. Rev.* 22:541–46

Hargens, L. L., McCann, J. C., Reskin, B. F. 1978. Productivity and Reproductivity: Fertility and professional achievement among research scientists. *Soc. Forc.* 57:154–63

Hatt, P. K. 1950. Occupation and social stratification. *Am. J. Sociol.* 55:533–43

Hauser, R. M. 1972. *The mobility table as an incomplete multiway array: An analysis of mobility to first jobs among American men.* Presented at Ann. Meet. Pop. Assoc. Am., 41st, St. Louis

Hazelrigg, L. E. 1974. Cross-national comparisons of father-to-son occupational mobility. In *Social Stratification: A Reader*, ed. J. O. Lopreato, L. S. Lewis, pp. 469–93. New York: Harper & Row

Hazelrigg, L. E., Garnier, M. A. 1976. Occupational mobility in industrial societies: A comparative analysis of differential access to rank in seventeen countries. *Am. Sociol. Rev.* 41:498–511

Hiday, V. A. 1978. Migration, urbanization, and fertility in the Philippines. *Intern. Migration Rev.* 12:379–85

Hodge, R. W. 1981. The measurement of occupational status. *Soc. Sci. Res.* 10:396–415

Hodge, R. W., Siegel, P. M. 1968. The measurement of social class. In *International Encyclopedia of the Social Sciences*, ed. D. L. Sills, 15:316–25. [New York]: Macmillan & the Free Press

Hofferth, S. L. 1984. Long-term economic consequences for women of delayed childbearing and reduced family size. *Demography* 21:141–55

Hollingsworth, T. H. 1957. A demographic study of British ducal families. *Pop. Stud.* 11:4–26

Hope, K. 1971. Social mobility and fertility. *Am. Sociol. Rev.* 36:1019–32

Hope, K. 1975. Models of status inconsistency and social mobility effects. *Am. Sociol. Rev.* 40:322–43

Hope, K. 1981. Vertical mobility in Britain: A structural analysis. *Sociology* 15:19–55

House, J. S. 1978. Facets and flaws of Hope's diamond model. *Am. Sociol. Rev.* 43:439–42

Hout, M. 1976. *The determinants of marital fertility in the United States, 1960–1970*. PhD thesis, Indiana Univ., Bloomington

Hout, M. *Mobility Tables*. 1983. Beverly Hills, CA: Sage

Hout, M. 1984. Status, autonomy, and training in occupational mobility. *Am. J. Sociol.* 89:1379–1409

Hutchinson, B. 1958. Structural and exchange mobility in the assimilation of immigrants to Brazil. *Pop. Stud.* 12:111–20

Hutchinson, B. 1961. Fertility, social mobility and urban migration in Brazil. *Pop. Stud.* 14:182–89

Inkeles, A., Rossi, P. H. 1956. National comparisons of occupational prestige. *Am. J. Sociol.* 61:329–39

Kahl, J. A. 1957. *The American Class Structure*. New York: Rinehart

Kahl, J. A., Davis, J. A. 1955. A comparison of indexes of socioeconomic status. *Am. Sociol. Rev.* 20:317–25

Kantner, J. F., Kiser, C. V. 1954. The interrelation of fertility, fertility planning, and intergenerational mobility. *Milbank Mem. Fund Q. Health Soc.* 32:69–103

Kasarda, J. D., Billy, J. O. G., West, K. B. *Status Enhancement and Fertility: Reproductive Response to Social Mobility and Educational Opportunity*. Petaluma, Calif: Academic. Forthcoming

Kirk, D. 1957. The fertility of a gifted group: A study of the number of children of men in "Who's Who." In *The Nature and Transmission of the Genetic and Cultural Characteristics of Human Populations; Papers Presented at the 1956 Annual Conference of the Milbank Memorial Fund*, pp. 78–98. New York: Milbank Memorial Fund

Lawson, E. D., Boek, W. E. 1960. Correlations of indexes of families' socio-economic status. *Soc. Forc.* 39:149–52

Lipset, S. M., Zetterberg, H. L. 1956. A theory of social mobility. In *Transactions of the Third World Congress of Sociology. Koninklijk Instituut voor de Tropen, Amsterdam, 22–29 August, 1956. Problems of Social Change in the 20th Century*, Vol. 3. *Changes in Class Structure*, pp. 155–77. London: International Sociol. Assoc.

MacDonald, M. M., Rindfuss, R. R. 1981. Earnings, relative income, and family formation. *Demography* 18:123–36

Macisco, J. J., Bouvier, L. F., Qenzi, M. J. R. 1969. Migration status, education and fertility in Puerto Rico, 1960. *Milbank Mem. Fund Q. Health Soc.* 47:167–87

Mason, K. O. 1984. The status of women,

fertility, and mortality: A review of interrelationships. *Research Report no. 84-58*. New York: Population Sci. Div., Rockefeller Found.

Martine, G. R. 1972. Migrant fertility adjustment and urban growth in Latin America. In *International Population Conference, Liege, Belgium, Aug. 27–Sept. 1, 1973; Proceedings*, pp. 293–304. Liege: Int. Union Sci. Study Pop.

McGuire, C. 1950. Social stratification and mobility patterns. *Am. Sociol. Rev.* 15:195–204

Mincer, J., Ofek, H. 1982. Interrupted work careers: Depreciation and restoration of human capital. *J. Hum. Resour.* 17:3–24

Mitra, S. 1966. Occupation and fertility in the United States. *Eugen. Q.* 13:141–46

Morris, R. T., Murphy, R. J. 1959. The situs dimension in occupational structure. *Am. Sociol. Rev.* 24:231–39

Namboodiri, N. K. 1972. The integrative potential of a fertility model: An analytical test. *Pop. Stud.* 26:465–85

Namboodiri, N. K. 1974. White couples at given parities expect to have additional births? An exercise in discriminant analysis. *Demography* 11:45–56

Perrucci, C. C. 1967. Social origins, mobility patterns and fertility. *Am. Sociol. Rev.* 32:615–25

Philblad, C. T., Aas, D. 1960. Residential and occupational mobility in an area of rapid industrialization in Norway. *Am. Sociol. Rev.* 25:369–75

Prehn, J. W. 1967. Vertical mobility and community type as factors in the migration of college graduates. *Demography* 4:283–92

Pullum, T. W. 1975. *Measuring Occupational Inheritance*. Progress in Mathematical Social Sciences, Vol. 5. Amsterdam: Elsevier

Ramu, G. H. 1972. Geographic mobility, kinship and the family in South India. *J. Marriage Fam.* 34:147–52

Richmond, A. H. 1964. Social mobility of immigrants in Canada. *Pop. Stud.* 18:53–69

Riemer, R., Kiser, C. V. 1954. Economic tension and social mobility in relation to fertility planning and size of planned family. *Milbank Mem. Fund Q. Health Soc.* 32:167–231

Rosenfeld, R. A. 1975. Women's intergenerational occupational mobility. *Am. Sociol. Rev.* 43:36–46. Madison: Cent. Demog. Ecol. Univ. of Wis.

Safilios-Rothschild, C. 1982. Female power, autonomy and demographic change in the Third World. In *Women's Roles and Population Trends in the Third World*, ed. R. Anker, M. Buvinić, N. H. Youssef, pp. 117–32. London: Croom Helm

Schnore, Leo F. 1961. Social mobility in demographic perspective. *Am. Sociol. Rev.* 26:407–23

Scott, W. 1958. Fertility and social mobility among teachers. *Pop. Stud.* 11:251–61

Simon, J. L. 1975. The welfare effect of an additional child cannot be stated simply and unequivocally. *Demography* 12:89–105

Smith-Lovin, L., Tickamyer, A. R. 1978. Nonrecursive models of labor force participation, fertility behavior and sex role attitudes. *Am. Sociol. Rev.* 43:541–57

Sobel, M. E. 1981. Diagonal mobility models: A substantively motivated class of designs for the analysis of mobility effects. *Am. Sociol. Rev.* 46:893–906

Sobel, M. E. 1984. *Social mobility and fertility revisited: Some new models for the analysis of the mobility effects hypothesis.* Presented at Ann. Meet. Am. Sociol. Assoc., 79th, San Antonio, Tex.

Stevens, G. 1981. Social mobility and fertility: Two effects in one. *Am. Sociol. Rev.* 46:573–85

Stuckert, R. P. 1963. Occupational mobility and family relationships. *Soc. Forc.* 41:301–07

Stycos, M. J. 1982. Status of women. In *International Encyclopedia of Population,* ed. J. A. Ross, 2:620–22. New York: Free

Tien, H. H. 1961. The social mobility/fertility hypothesis reconsidered: An empirical study. *Am. Sociol. Rev.* 26:247–57

Tien, H. Y. 1965. *Social Mobility and Controlled Fertility, Family Origins and Structure of the Australian Academic Elite.* New Haven, Conn: College & Univ. Press

Tomasson, R. R. 1966. Social mobility and family size in two high-status populations. *Eugen. Q.* 13:113–21

Treiman, D. J. 1970. Industrialization and social stratification. In *Social Stratification: Research and Theory for the 1970s,* ed. E. O. Laumann, pp. 207–34. Indianapolis: Bobbs-Merrill

Treiman, D. J. 1975. Problems of concept and measurement in the comparative study of occupational mobility. *Soc. Sci. Res.* 4:183–230

Treiman, D. J. 1977. *Occupational Prestige in Comparative Perspective. Quantitative Studies in Social Relations.* New York: Academic

Tumin, M. M., Feldman, A. S. 1957. Theory and measurement of occupational mobility. *Am. Sociol. Rev.* 22:281–88

Vanneman, R. 1977. The occupational composition of American classes: Results from cluster analysis. *Am. J. Sociol.* 82:783–807

Wagner-Manslau, W. 1932. Human fertility. A demonstration of its genetic base. Trans., E. O. Lorimer. *Eugen. Rev.* 24:195–210 (From German)

Waite, L. J., Stolzenberg, R. M. 1976. Intended childbearing and labor force participation of young women: Insights fron nonrecursive models. *Am. Sociol. Rev.* 41:235–51

Westoff, C. F. 1953. The changing focus of differential fertility research: The social mobility hypothesis. *Milbank Mem. Fund Q. Health Soc.* 31:24–38

Westoff, C. F. 1981. Another look at fertility and social mobility. *Pop. Stud.* 35:132–35

Westoff, C. F., Bressler, M., Sagi, P. C. 1960. The concept of social mobility. *Am. Sociol. Rev.* 25:375–85

Westoff, C. F., Potter, R. G., Sagi, P. C. 1963. *The Third Child: A Study in the Prediction of Fertility.* Princeton: Princeton Univ. Press

Westoff, C. F., Potter, R. G., Sagi, P. C., Mishler, E. G. 1961. *Family Growth in Metropolitan America.* Princeton: Princeton Univ. Press

Yamaguchi, K. 1983. The structure of intergenerational occupational mobility: Generality and specificity in resources, channels, and barriers. *Am. J. Sociol.* 88:718–45

Zelinsky, W. 1971. The hypothesis of the mobility transition. *Geogr. Rev.* 61:219–49

Zimmer, B. G. 1979. *Urban Family Building Patterns: The Social Mobility-Fertility Hypothesis Re-Examined.* Springfield, VA: National Technical Information Service

Zimmer, B. G. 1981. The impact of social mobility on fertility: A reconsideration. *Pop. Stud.* 35:120–31

Ann. Rev. Sociol. 1985. 11:329–46

NEW BLACK-WHITE PATTERNS:
How Best to Conceptualize Them?

Thomas F. Pettigrew

Stevenson College, University of California, Santa Cruz, California 95064, and Netherlands Institute for Advanced Studies, 2242 PR Wassenaar, The Netherlands

Abstract

Black-white relations have changed sharply in recent years. But no overarching sociological perspective has emerged to explain these changes. Many ideas with contrasting conceptualizations have been advanced, however. This chapter uncovers empirical agreements across these rival theoretical positions. At the structural level, race and class studies appear to converge on an interactional position—one that emphasizes the importance of both race and class factors as well as their interactions. A parallel convergence is emerging at the social psychological level. Though increasingly ambivalent and indirect, racist attitudes remain important; but racism must now be placed in a wider context of subjective self-interest, stratification beliefs, and cognitive bias. Hence, the causal complexity and indirectness of modern race relations are repeatedly shown in current research at both the macro- and microlevels. Closer attention to this emerging empirical convergence would further the needed theoretical convergence. The chapter closes with calls for more attention to black American responses and to the links between the macro- and microlevels of analysis.

THE PROBLEM

Black-white patterns in the United States have changed sharply over the past two decades. But, while there is consensus on this general point, there is little agreement about precisely how these patterns have changed. Within American sociology, there is even pointed debate on how best to conceptualize modern

329

0360-0572/85/0815-0329$02.00

race relations. This review addresses this conceptualization issue by discussing the complexities of the problem that have constrained progress and the initial attempts at conceptualization at both the macro- and microlevels of analysis.

THE COMPLEXITY OF THE PROBLEM

Current black-white relations in the United States are more subtle, indirect, and ostensibly nonracial than earlier forms. Modern racial discrimination varies widely in its degree of embeddedness in large-scale organizations (Feagin & Eckberg 1980). Indirect forms of discrimination, embedded deep in organizational structures, can even be unintentional. Yet the American racist past remains a prominent part of the scene as well. Given this confusing melange, it is not surprising that observers of diverse bents have abstracted conflicting conceptualizations of the present racial scene.

Four interrelated factors make the understanding of modern race relations more difficult. (*a*) The past 20 years have witnessed sharply conflicting trends across institutions, regions, and social classes. (*b*) The problem is multilevel, but most analysts work at either the micro- or macrolevel without concern for links between them. (*c*) The greater subtlety of newer forms of discrimination and prejudice makes research and theory more complex and inferential. Indirect effects of racial discrimination have become more important and invoke causal models further removed from the actual observations. (*d*) The question is highly politicized. In an ideological era in American politics, work on the nation's historically most divisive issue is often both aimed and judged with an eye to its immediate political implications.

Conflicting Trends

One can easily sketch a glowing picture of racial progress across a broad canvas. To be sure, the effort requires a judicious selection of the evidence; but the result is persuasive for many. Consider some of the indicators of improved black-white relations:

1. The Voting Rights Act of 1965 secured black American political participation—even in the South. For the 1982 Congressional elections, 10.4 million blacks were registered to vote, and 73% of the black registrants reported voting compared to 76% of the white population (US Bureau of the Census 1983:23). In the 11 ex-Confederate states, black registration rose dramatically from 29% in 1960 to 59% by 1980; and this increase made possible an elevenfold expansion in black southern elected officials, from only 177 in 1968 to 2009 in 1980 (Thompson 1982).

2. The educational attainment of young blacks has far surpassed that of previous black generations and begun closing racial disparities in schooling for

both sexes. For secondary school completion, young blacks have almost "caught up" with whites (Farley 1984).

3. Occupational upgrading of black workers has been substantial, with black growth in nonmanual and craft jobs more rapid than that of whites during the 1960s and 1970s (Farley 1977, 1984).

4. Black married couples gained 6.9% in real median family income from 1971 to 1981 compared with a 2.6% for white married couples (US Bureau of the Census 1983:4, 6).

5. Black business has expanded. The total receipts of minority firms tripled in just eight years—from 10.6 to 32.8 billion dollars between 1969 and 1977—compared to a doubling of the receipts of white firms (Collins 1983).

6. These macrolevel changes are matched by comparable microlevel changes in interracial interaction and attitudes. Both black and white Americans report more contact under favorable, equal-status conditions (Campbell & Hatchett 1975). White racial attitudes had by the 1970s overwhelmingly rejected blatant forms of racial discrimination. For example, only 42% of surveyed whites in 1942 thought blacks "should have as good a chance as white people to get any kind of job," but 95% did so by 1972. Some of this improvement is a result of generational replacement; but most of it reflects shifting white positions (Pettigrew 1979a).

With equal ease, one can present a dismal view of American race relations. The rule of thumb is that black data look best when compared to earlier black data but pale when compared to current white data. Thus, each item above can be placed in a selectively gloomy context:

1. Despite electoral gains, blacks still represent less than 3% of the nation's elected officials and typically can gain office only in predominantly black districts. Structural means to dilute black votes operate in many areas—typified by at-large races where blacks as a minority could only win smaller district races (Thompson 1982, Wasby 1982).

2. Though most young blacks now finish high school, college has become the critical employment threshold. And only 13% of blacks, compared with 25% of whites, had completed four years of college by 1982 (US Bureau of the Census 1983:16).

3. Black occupational upgrading is concentrated among younger members of the labor force. Convergence with the white occupational distribution has tended to occur in occupations where the share of the white labor force was already stable or declining. Moreover, black shifts out of such low-status occupations as domestic servants and laborers were achieved partly by higher rates of black absence from the labor force (Hauser & Featherman 1974). A closer look at the 1980 Census's detailed occupational categories reveals that blacks are still less than 3% of the nation's lawyers and engineers, but 33% of

all garbage collectors and 40% of the remaining private household servants. Even in white collar positions, blacks are concentrated in government jobs (e.g. 25% of all postal clerks), serving black populations (e.g. 20% of all social workers) (US Bureau of the Census 1983:12–14). Black unemployment and underemployment rates remain devastatingly high—over twice those of whites—throughout the 1970s and 1980s; and among those discouraged workers who have withdrawn from the labor force, black rates continue over three times those for whites (US Commission on Civil Rights 1982; US Department of Labor 1983).

4. Only black married couples showed real income gains, and they are a declining proportion of black families—from 64% in 1972 to 55% in 1982. In real terms, the median income for all black families fell 8.3% from 1971 to 1981. In one year alone, 1980–1981, it dropped 5.2%, compared to a 2.7% decline for white families. Consequently, the ratio of the median incomes of black to white families has been steadily falling back—61% in 1970, 58% in 1974, and 56% in 1981. This decline is due partly to the poverty of female-headed households, a category that rose in 1970–1982 from 28.0% to 40.6% of all black families. Moreover, compared to 10% of whites, 34% of blacks were below the federal poverty income level in both 1970 and 1981—with an absolute increase from 8 to 9 million black people (US Bureau of the Census 1983).

5. Black business remains a miniscule component of the nation's economy. All minority firms accounted for only 2% of the total receipts of U.S. firms in 1977, and that includes more than black firms. Moreover, the growth of this tiny sector is heavily dependent on the federal government. While total federal procurement doubled in nonconstant dollars between 1969 and 1980, minority procurement rose from just 13 million to over 3 billion dollars (Collins 1983).

6. Microlevel changes have been far less sweeping than suggested by the attitude changes of whites against racial injustice in principle. Large white majorities remain opposed to measures necessary to eliminate discrimination, such as affirmative action, and busing children for school desegregation. Social psychological experiments on current racial interaction reveal considerable ambivalence (Crosby, Bromley, & Saxe 1980; Gaertner 1976).

Multilevel Changes

The contradictions between genuine progress in American race relations and continued racism, and even retrogression, operate at both the macro- and microlevels. Indeed, proposed structural explanations parallel proposed social psychological explanations. But attempts to combine levels in the same theoretical or empirical effort are rare. The necessary new conceptualization, however, must explain the diverse patterns of modern race relations at both levels.

Causal Subtlety and Indirection

Older discriminatory forms of total exclusion or color-line thresholds were anything but subtle. It was precisely their direct operation that made them easily discernible to the media, judges, the public, and social scientists themselves. New forms, however, are more subtle, indirect, and ostensibly nonracial.

The cumulative nature of modern discrimination creates part of this subtlety. A developed research literature demonstrates how this process operates (Braddock, 1980; Braddock & McPartland, 1982, 1983; Crain, 1970; Crain & Mahard, 1978; Crain & Weisman, 1972; McPartland & Braddock, 1981; McPartland & Crain, 1980). Early school segregation makes high school segregation more likely; then high school segregation makes college entry and attainment less likely—especially at mostly white colleges. This process follows through to the job market. Segregated school products are more likely to work at lower-paying traditional jobs, less likely to gain white-collar employment. In the North, the lack of educational experience with whites makes it likely that these blacks will be located in segregated occupational work groups. Some dispute that such findings reflect racial discrimination; this is characteristic of indicators of indirect discrimination. Plausible rival explanations abound. To wit: it is individual talent and social class that make the difference; these results reflect the operation of a self-selection bias whereby less talented, lower-class black children tend to go to all-black schools and obtain manual jobs. Such rival accounts of indirect discrimination often take the form of dispositional attributions: assumed characteristics of blacks are said to be the causal agents. In this case, however, the research limits this possibility by demonstrating these segregation effects after controlling for the influences of region, sex, age, family background, and academic qualifications. But the ready availability of nondiscriminatory explanations contributes to the obscurity of indirect discrimination and the newer forms of racial prejudice.

This research also suggests some of the means by which this Chinese-box quality of modern discrimination operates. First, cross-racial friendship networks are important. Whites have held a near-monopoly on critical information about higher educational and job opportunities. Segregated black children are restricted from such vital information; desegregation allows informal flows of information across racial lines. Second, credentialism, an increasingly critical aspect of modern opportunity structures, is involved. In the simplest case, grades and reference letters from interracial institutions are granted greater weight than equivalent records from segregated institutions. Third, integrated education provides its products with the interpersonal skills necessary for successful interracial interaction, while segregated education cannot.

Hence, northern black workers from segregated schools in comparison with comparable products of desegregated schools find interracial work groups less friendly and make more racial distinctions about the friendliness of their co-workers and the competence of their supervisors (Braddock & McPartland 1983). These processes show how direct discrimination in one institution at one time can generalize to different institutional settings and stages of the life cycle.

Thus, the nature of indirect discrimination places its detection and causal pattern beyond public view and increases its difficulty as an object for sociological research. Increasingly complex causal models are used, especially at the macrolevel; such models are necessarily more abstract and removed from actual observations. As they become more technical, these models also become less accessible and convincing to nonspecialists, all the more so when their methods and assumptions specify conflicting definitions of "discrimination" and yield divergent results.

Two examples demonstrate this critical point. Taylor (1984) contrasts two ways of estimating discrimination-produced inequity. Both ways define discrimination as residual inequality after controlling for a range of background variables. The first problem is that indirect discrimination may well be operating in these background variables, thereby causing an underestimation of the total discrimination effect. But the key point is that this same procedure yields contrasting estimates depending on whether the white mean is substituted into the black regression equation (Farley 1977) or the black mean into the white equation (Featherman & Hauser 1978).

The Farley method tends to yield higher estimates of discrimination, since it asks what does blackness cost for a black with an average white background. Closer to common conceptions of discrimination, the Featherman-Hauser method tends to yield lower estimates by asking what does blackness cost for a black with an average black background. Taylor (1984) estimates that income discrimination for 1970 and for 1977 by the Farley method was $3,804 and $1,838, by the Featherman-Hauser method $1,749 and $1,271. Both show improvement in the 1970s but quite different magnitudes of gain. Both are correct for the different questions they address and the different implicit definitions of discrimination they employ. The Farley method shows substantial gains for the black elite; the Featherman-Hauser method shows less impressive gains for the average black male. Reverse regression provides another instructive illustration. Instead of the direct regression approach that asks if blacks are more qualified than equally paid whites, reverse regression inverts the question to ask if whites are less qualified than equally paid blacks (Goldberger 1984). A judge is likely to see these two questions as equivalent. But this reasoning holds only if it is a determinate relationship, and in practice this is seldom the case. In fact, studies using reverse regression to determine racial or gender discrimination often reveal either no discrimination or even "discrimination" in favor of females or blacks, while the direct procedure yields the usual discrepancies in favor of males or whites. Advocates of reverse regression argue that it is more appropriate when relevant control qualifications are not fully measured—a common situation. Goldberger (1984) refutes this reasoning and provides an argument against the use of the reverse regression procedure save in a single limited case. Technical as it is, this debate between advocates of the two methods has already spilled over into the courtroom in discrimination suits.

Highly Charged Political Issue

The Reagan Administration reversed federal policy of previous decades by opposing racial change initiatives. This abrupt shift has made race relations work even more politically sensitive than it was already. Especially is this true when the work is thought to have relevance for the altered federal policies. Consider the reaction to W. J. Wilson's *The Declining Significance of Race* (1978). Supporters of Reagan policies cited the volume as "scientific" support for their political preferences; those opposed generally condemned the volume. Ironically, the fervor was irrelevant to the class argument of the book. In the spirit of the times, the volume had been misnamed. It contained no evidence for the claim of its title; but the title alone was enough to set off sparks (Pettigrew 1980).

INITIAL ATTEMPTS AT CONCEPTUALIZATION

Macro Conceptions

Three models of race relations have long dominated American sociological thought: race, class, and "caste-and-class" (Pettigrew 1981). Not surprisingly, then, the search for new conceptualizations to fit the modern racial scene have followed these well-worn paths.

RACE MODEL CONCEPTIONS   This perspective holds that US black-white relations are essentially unique. America's special racial history, from slavery to current racism, has shaped these relations into persistent patterns that do not allow easy comparisons with class conflict, white ethnic conflict, or even racial situations elsewhere in the world. Such comparisons are thought to obscure the problem's uniquely racist core.

The scholarly underpinnings of the race model are extensive. Myrdal's *An American Dilemma* (1944) and Jordan's *White Over Black* (1968) are squarely within this dominant tradition of American thought. The strongest current evidence for this model involves housing patterns. Urban blacks are residentially segregated from their fellow Americans far more intensively than any other urban ethnic or racial group. Puerto Ricans, for example, in one generation dispersed more in Chicago than blacks managed throughout the century. Little of this imposed housing segregation can be attributed to economic factors.

Until recently the black middle class has been almost as victimized by this massive discriminatory pattern as the black working class (Taeuber & Taeuber 1965). From such data, race theorists argue that three centuries of slavery and legalized racial segregation created unique structural, cultural, and psychological barriers to democratic relations between black Americans and white Americans (Jones 1972).

CLASS MODEL CONCEPTIONS   Recent Marxist influence in sociology has brought renewed attention to class accounts of black-white relations. Two Marxist subtheories have often been applied: super-exploitation, and split labor markets (Bonacich 1980). Marxists see an exploited group as serving five functions for the capitalist class. They say black Americans: (*a*) act as a reserve labor force, permitting flexibility to deal with business cycles; (*b*) allow employers to fill diverse needs—such as the dual requirements of whites as skilled labor in the monoply sectors and blacks as unskilled, low-wage labor in the competitive sectors; (*c*) do the "dirty-work" out of desperation; (*d*) accumulate capital for capitalists by having their wealth shifted to the white bourgeoisie; and (*e*) stabilize the system by fragmenting the working class.

Split labor markets arguments focus on labor competition and challenge the idea that racial conflict is the sole creation of the dominant bourgeoisie. They emphasize that white labor seeks to prevent capitalists from using blacks to undercut them. Thus, white labor contributes to the exclusion of blacks from advanced sectors of the economy and even from employment altogether. Split labor markets theory, then, asserts that there are two contrasting types of antiblack discrimination—one derived from capitalist exploitation, the other from labor exclusion (Bonacich 1980).

Different authors in this tradition stress different contentions. Blauner (1972) is an exponent of the exploitation thesis; Bonacich (1980) of the split labor markets thesis; and Wilson (1978) employs both for earlier periods in American history. Wilson rejects both theories as insufficiently focused on the polity to shed light on current race relations. But he fails to offer an alternative. His provocative note is his insistence that "class has become more important than race in determining black life-chances in the modern industrial period" (Wilson 1978:150). No supportive evidence for this statement is provided. What is provided is evidence for growing stratification within black America—long a widely noted feature of modern race relations (Brimmer 1966; Pettigrew 1965). The break with previous writing is the misconception that increasing black stratification necessarily signals "the declining significance of race." The fallacy lies in the belief that an increase in the predictive power of one set of variables (class) requires a decrease in the predictive power of another set (race).

By contrast, other class theorists avoid a direct confrontation with the race model save for the insistence that racial conflict and discrimination " . . . are, at root, the product of class forces" (Bonacich 1980:21). Though rooted in class conflict, American race relations are typically seen as involving a distinctively racist dimension that crosscuts class concerns. Exponents of race theory might quibble with the insistence on the class origins of American racism, but they too typically grant the operation of a class dimension that crosscuts racial concerns. Hence, there is some consensus for versions of the third, interactional position.

CONCEPTIONS OF RACE AND CLASS INTERACTION   The caste-and-class model was the first formal statement of this third perspective (Warner 1937). In its new form, the race-and-class-interaction perspective represents a rapprochement between the race and class models (Pettigrew 1981). For a wide range of dependent variables, this perspective holds that both race and class are important. Sociologists with this view further maintain that the main effects of race and class together do not adequately account for the growing complexity of modern race relations. Thus, beyond their main effects it is the statistical interaction between race and class that is of increasing importance. This model agrees, then, with central contentions of the other models, but it holds that racial phenomena generally operate differently across class lines just as class phenomena generally operate differently across racial lines. Developers of this model agree that class factors are gaining in significance, but insist that race-and-class interactions are also increasing in significance.

The relative importance of race, class, and their interaction will vary, of course, across different realms. But a study by Wright (1978) neatly illustrates the perspective. It reveals the importance of class position in mediating racial differences in income returns to education. Wright employed manager, supervisor, and worker class categories in analyzing national survey data on male income. He showed that sizable racial differentials in educational returns are severely narrowed when regressions are run within class positions. He also uncovered an interesting statistical interaction: Black supervisors and workers have returns similar to those of comparably situated whites, but black managers have significantly smaller returns than white managers. Note that these results do not choose between race and class. Rather, in the spirit of the interactional model, they specify the phenomenon more precisely: Gross racial differentials in income return to education are due in part to return differences between the races at higher class positions and even more to differences in the racial distribution of class positions. Wright makes the point succinctly:

> [These results do] . . . not imply that race is an insignificant dimension of inequality in American life. The empirical and theoretical problem is to sort out the complex interplay of racism and class relations, not to absorb the former into the latter (Wright 1978:1389).

Micro Conceptions

Recent social psychological theories parallel but do not link directly with the macrotheories. To explain modern racial attitudes and interaction, social psychological theories of symbolic racism, of self-interest and group conflict, and of stratification beliefs mirror the race, class, and race-and-class contentions of sociology. In addition, a psychoanalytically inspired theory of racial ambivalence has received experimental attention together with a psychologically inspired theory of cognitive bias.

SYMBOLIC RACISM   One major social psychological formulation to account for the modern racial attitudes and behavior of whites toward blacks is that proposed by Sears and his colleagues (Kinder & Sears 1981; McConahay 1982, 1983; McConahay, Hardee, & Bates 1981; Sears & Allen 1984; Sears & Kinder 1971; Sears, Hensler, & Speer 1979; Sears, Lau, Tyler, & Allen 1980). Their symbolic racism formulation centers on three contentions.

1. In a way similar to earlier forms of racial bigotry, symbolic racism is rooted among whites in an attitudinal predisposition toward blacks that derives from early childhood socialization. Often this socialization includes political conservatism as well. Symbolic racism is also highly charged emotionally, made more so by "moral feelings that blacks violate such traditional American values as individualism and self-reliance . . ." (Kinder & Sears 1981:416).

2. But, unlike earlier forms, symbolic racism rejects gross black stereotypes and blatant discrimination. Instead, it finds more sophisticated expression in opposing racial change by attaching negative affect to ostensibly nonracial objects—"busing," "quotas." These views are then rationalized after the fact by unfounded beliefs about the object ("busing is dangerous"). Some degree of indirection has long been part of American racism—e.g. Myrdal's "convenient ignorance." But the pervasiveness of this phenomenon is held to be greater than ever before.

3. Consequently, symbolic racism—and not direct personal self-interest— is the driving force that underlies white opposition to contemporary remedies that address indirect or past-in-present discrimination. This formulation is, then, a dispositional trait theory: Symbolic racism is a characteristic of individual white Americans that causes the modern expression of racism when triggered by symbols often attached to racial change efforts perceived to be violations of the moral order.

Numerous surveys have been reanalyzed to demonstrate the predictive value of the various symbolic racism measures. Both voting against a black mayoralty candidate in Los Angeles (Kinder & Sears 1981, Sears & Kinder 1971) and opposing busing for school desegregation (McConahay 1982, Sears et al 1979; Sears et al 1980) are related positively to various measures of symbolic racism and political conservatism. These relationships are consistently higher than those generated by self-interest measures of direct racial threats to the jobs, neighborhoods, or schools of individual respondents.

Three interrelated criticisms of the symbolic racism formulation concern its conceptualization, the way it is measured, and the view of self-interest it assumes. The term "symbolic" is slippery. The Sears group uses it loosely as an adjective to refer to affect-laden objects related to racial reform. As a codeword routinely used in the mass media, an emotional term such as "reverse discrimination" becomes "symbolic" for whites of generalized racial feelings. This conceptual vagueness leads to empirical confusion. Though a unitary dimension is claimed, a diversity of attitude items have been employed in various cross-sectional analyses. The use of secondary analyses of surveys led to this item variety and to the limited research design. But this empirical translation of the theory causes difficulties. The cross-sectional designs cannot test the contention that policy beliefs are largely after-the-fact rationalizations rather than causes of policy choices. More importantly, many of the indicators used for symbolic racism are items long used to tap traditional antiblack prejudice: one on black intelligence, others on attitudes towards racial segregation and blacks in general (Sears et al 1979; Sears et al 1980). Indeed, similar items have been employed as measures of "old-fashioned racism" to contrast with symbolic racism (McConahay et al 1981). Both conceptually and empirically, then, a close reading reveals considerable overlap between symbolic racism and both traditional racism and political conservatism.

The symbolic racism scales also fail to yield a unitary dimension. Bobo (1983) reanalyzed the same national survey items used by Sears in two key papers (Sears et al 1979; Sears et al 1980). Unlike Sears who used unrotated orthogonal factor analysis (Sears et al 1979), Bobo employed oblique rotations and obtained the best fits for multifactor solutions. The first factor taps the traditional racism dimension: support of segregation, all-white neighborhoods, and racial intelligence differences. The remaining factors included items closer to modern prejudice forms, such as dislike of "black militants," plus beliefs that black protests have been violent, and that "the civil rights people have been trying to push too fast." Further, Bobo shows that these items—especially those that reveal perceived threat from racial protest—predict white opposition to school busing as well as all the scales used by Sears.

This raises a final criticism of the symbolic racism thesis: its narrow definition of "self-interest." Many studies have replicated Sears's finding that direct personal involvement of a white in racial change—e.g. having a child riding a school bus for desegregation—does not strongly predict white opposition (Bobo 1983, Caditz 1975, Kelley 1974, Kinder & Rhodebeck 1982, Jacobson 1978, McConahay 1982, McClendon & Pestello 1982, Weidman 1975). This persistent result counters popular opinion as well as numerous formal rational models. But these objective threats of direct involvement do not exhaust the possibilities of self-interest, for they omit subjectively perceived threat. Indeed, the emotional nature of prejudice should make subjective threat the more important measure. When Bobo (1983) found that survey items that measure perceived threat of the civil rights movement are strong predictors of anti-busing attitudes, he interpreted this as support for his thesis that subjective threat, together with racism, contributes to white opposition to racial change. Yet, as suggested by Bobo's use of oblique factor structure, the two classes of variables are so intercorrelated that a broader perspective is clearly required.

SELF-INTEREST AND GROUP CONFLICT   Without denying the involvement of racial prejudice, those who emphasize the importance of group conflict stress that prejudice is a sufficient but not necessary cause of white resistance to racial change. Such opposition can be easily justified to themselves and others as simply a defense of status and privilege they feel they have earned (Bobo 1983, Rothbart 1976, Wellman 1979). Symbolism is not involved, goes this argument, save that busing serves as a publicized instance "of how the demands and political activities of blacks can produce real changes in aspects of their lives. . . . Busing is a controversial and divisive issue because it portends substantial changes in relationships between blacks and whites. . . . It is in this sense that white opposition to busing should be understood as a reflection of the actual features of group relations and conflicts between blacks and whites in America today" (Bobo 1983:1209).

Note how this argument serves as a microlevel reflection of the class contentions at the macrolevel. By placing race relations in a larger context of group competition, this theory conflicts with the argument of uniqueness that is central to the racial contentions at both the macro- and microlevels. We have seen that the survey evidence rejects the importance of objectively measured variables of individual involvement in racial change. But this same evidence can be read as supporting the significance of expanded versions of subjective self-interest and group conflict. Thus, the perception of fraternal deprivation—the sense that one's own group is being unfairly surpassed and ignored—is a consistent predictor of white opposition to black mayoralty candidates (Vanneman & Pettigrew 1972).

STRATIFICATION BELIEFS   A possible resolution to the problem is advanced by Kluegel & Smith (1983) who stress the importance of stratification beliefs. They offer a comprehensive test of the correlates of affirmative action attitudes using a 1980 national survey. Their four affirmative action items range from the programs most acceptable to whites (helping blacks "get ahead"—with 76% agreement), through middle-range programs (colleges and employers setting aside for "qualified blacks . . . a certain number of positions"—with 51–60% agreement), to the least acceptable to whites ("preferential treatment"—with 65% rating it "unfair").

As predictor variables, Kluegel & Smith used measures of economic self-interest, symbolic racism, and stratification beliefs as well as demographic and class identification indicators. They employed measures of self-interest that were both objective (percentages of blacks in respondent's job category, using detailed occupation and industry codes) and subjective (perceived likelihood of being laid off). The results of this analysis are clarifying. All three classes of explanatory variables contributed independently to the prediction of the affirmative action attitudes of whites. Self-interest measures, however, were the weakest predictors—though subjective indicators performed markedly better than objective ones. Thus, a fraternal-deprivation scale, tapping the sense of belonging to a group overlooked politically, related significantly to all four of the affirmative action items.

Symbolic racism proved to be a consistent negative predictor. In addition to the self-interest, racism, and demographic effects, stratification beliefs were also independently important. Both egalitarianism and the greater use of structural explanations of poverty significantly predicted pro-affirmative action attitudes. There is also a link between these stratification beliefs and the racism scores. Racist respondents were more likely to hold individualistic explanations for poverty and to believe in the benefits of societal inequality—findings reminiscent of the authoritarian personality syndrome (Adorno, Frenkel-Brunswik, Levinson, & Sanford 1950). The consistency of these results with those of earlier work lends credence to this broad, if still crude, overview of the predictors of the modern racial positions of white Americans. Racism is still important; particular forms of subjective threat are also important; and so are widely shared conceptions and misconceptions of the American stratification system.

RACIAL AMBIVALENCE   Experimental research in social psychology extends this microanalysis by testing modern forms of black-white interaction. This work assumes that the denial of one's own prejudice is indeed the essence of modern white racism. So, in contrast to surveys, it attempts to be unobtrusive by using hidden manipulations and measures often in natural settings.

Three types of experiments typify this literature: studies that measure differential behavior toward members of an opposite race (*a*) in giving help, (*b*) in aggression, and (*c*) in such nonverbal behaviors as tone of voice. According to Crosby, Bromley, & Saxe (1980), the 43 helping studies reveal varying degrees of discrimination. Nineteen (44%) noted that subjects gave more aid to their own race than to the opposite race. Black subjects were as likely to demonstrate this tendency as white subjects. Interestingly, whites were less likely to discriminate in face-to-face than in noncontact situations (e.g. over the phone).

This indication of the inhibition of prejudice when negative sanctions are possible has also emerged in aggression research. Donnerstein & Donnerstein (1973, 1976) employed an experimental procedure that socially sanctions aggression. The subject applies bogus shocks to "a learner"—a confederate of the experimenter—each time an error is made in a learning task. The intensity of the shock applied is considered an index of direct aggression, the less obvious duration of the shock an index of indirect aggression. The later possibility of retaliation, of censure, or of anonymity all affected the behavior of white subjects toward black, but not white, targets. The possibility of negative consequences led white subjects to employ less direct aggression but more indirect aggression against blacks. One study found complex but similar effects for black subjects (Wilson & Rogers 1975).

Nonverbal research focuses on behaviors that lie largely beyond awareness. These studies have noted how white college students often sit further away, use a less friendly voice tone, make less eye contact and more speech errors, and terminate the interview faster when interacting with a black interviewer than with a white (Hendricks & Bootlin 1976; Weitz 1972; Word, Zanna, & Cooper 1974). Poskocil (1977) questions whether such results betray covert racism and discrimination. From a symbolic interactionist perspective, he suggests a "situational self" model that argues the whites in these situations were simply anxious and unskilled because of inexperience with blacks. This explanation fits some nonverbal findings; but it runs counter to the principal result that whites discriminate more in noncontact situations.

Other models are more promising. Kelman's (1961) three processes of social influence provide a generic account. The Civil Rights Movement of the 1960s established new norms of nondiscrimination that are followed when there is surveillance or obvious costs for discrimination in the situation. Hence, whites tend to comply with these new norms in face-to-face situations. But many whites have not as yet internalized these norms, so discrimination emerges in situations without surveillance and apparent costs. Yet this inconsistency often generates ambivalence, perhaps even guilt on occasion. Following Kovel's (1970) psychoanalytic argument, this describes "the aversive racist" as opposed to the traditional, unabashed "dominative racist." Aversive racism, Gaertner (1976) maintains, is the pattern being uncovered in these unobtrusive studies. The white subjects comply with and even accept the new norms, but their failure to internalize them fully reflects their earlier socialization.

Katz, Glass, & Cohen (1973) provide a pointed demonstration of this ambivalence. Using the Donnerstein procedure, these investigators had white subjects administer either "mild" or "strong" shocks to either black or white "learners." As expected, denigration of the victim—presumably to reduce guilt—was greatest in the "strong shock to the black learner" condition. Further, this denigration was expressed most by the most ambivalent subjects—those who scored high on scales both of antiblack attitudes and of "sympathy with the racial underdog."

Note how this description of "ambivalent, aversive racism," emerging from psychoanalytic and experimental sources, resembles the "symbolic racism" conception emerging from survey data.

COGNITIVE BIAS   Social psychologists have also examined modern racial prejudice from the perspective of cognitive functioning (Hamilton 1981). They find that group stereotyping is a special case of regular cognitive processes, not a result of "aberrant thinking." Yet they note significant shifts in American stereotypes of blacks and women. The older, global stereotypes (lazy blacks) have faded. But they have been replaced with an array of sub-stereotypes that are often role related and situationally triggered—"the street black," "the angry militant." These newer images may be less confining than the traditional global ones, but they are more difficult to refute. If one does not fit, another can be applied.

Biased causal attributions also contribute to belief perseverance. With "the ultimate attribution error" (Pettigrew 1979b), we confirm our beliefs by not granting disliked outgroups "the benefit of the attributional doubt." Antiblack beliefs can be reinforced by attributing negative acts dispositionally ("That's the way they are!") and explaining away positive acts as luck, unfair advantage, unrealistically high motivation, "the exception that proves the rule," or situational attributions ("What else could she do in that situation?"). Working with survey data, Apostle, Glock, Piazza, & Suelzle (1983) agree on the importance of causal attributions. They note that dispositional attributions (innate and free will causes) for minority behavior characterize more traditional, conservative white Americans, while situational attributions (social and cultural causes) characterize "liberal" and "radical" thinking.

The cognitive model has been linked to situational contexts. Kantor (1977) and Taylor, Fiske, Close, Anderson, & Ruderman (1975) isolated in the field and the laboratory the cognitive consequences of "the solo role"—being the only X in a group of Y's. Solos, whether male, black, or female, are more prominent than nonsolos. Evaluations of their performance are exaggerated— either extremely low or extremely high—so feedback on their performance is not reliable. Contemporary racial situations, such as those involving affirmative action hiring, often reflect these effects (Word, Zanna, & Cooper, 1974).

CONCLUSIONS AND RECOMMENDATIONS

There is no dearth of ideas for explaining the present racial scene in the United States. But there is no consensus on an overarching perspective that makes use of these ideas and shares a common conceptualization. Consequently, sociology may be as unprepared to interpret future events and trends in black-white relations as it was on the eve of the Civil Rights Movement in the 1950s.

In spite of the clash of frameworks, this review has uncovered empirical agreements across theoretical positions. At the structural level, race and class research appears to be converging on an interactional perspective—one that recognizes the importance of both race and class factors as well as their statistical interactions. A comparable convergence is occurring at the social psychological level. Racist attitudes—though in an increasingly ambivalent and indirect form—remain important; but racism must be placed in a wider context of subjective self-interest, stratification beliefs, and cognitive bias. In fact, the causal complexity and indirectness of modern racial patterns are documented repeatedly in research at both the micro- and macrolevels. Closer attention to this emerging empirical convergence would further the needed theoretical convergence.

Four directions for future work are suggested. 1. Greater attention should be given to black American responses. Especially in social psychological research, there is a gross imbalance of studying race relations by looking only at white reactions to blacks. 2. More microlevel work needs to be conducted in institutional settings outside of the laboratory. In addition, social psychological research needs to consider in its research direct measures of class and status in order to articulate with macrotheories and concerns. 3. More "clearing of the structural underbrush" is required to understand modern race patterns. That is, we need more detailed "causal maps" to grasp the new and subtle race patterns. Mare & Winship (1984) supply a cogent example. They help to resolve the paradox of higher unemployment among young blacks with improving status on other dimensions. They show that the unemployment of young blacks is enhanced by: the substitution of schooling and military service for employment; reduced and disrupted work experience resulting from more years in school and the military; and the increased "creaming" of talented young blacks by schools and the military. 4. Finally, the review's principal plea is an urgent call for integrative work across "theories" and across the micro- and macrolevels. Such work is easier to call for than to conduct, of course, for it requires innovative approaches and data collection strategies. Without them, however, little progress will be made toward understanding the newly emerging racial patterns.

Literature Cited

Adorno, T. W., Frenkel-Brunswik, E., Levinson, D., Sanford, R. N. 1950. *The Authoritarian Personality*. New York: Harper & Row

Apostle, R. A., Glock, C. Y., Piazza, T., Suelzle, M. 1983. *The Anatomy of Racial Attitudes*. Berkeley: Univ. Calif. Press. 342 pp.

Blauner, R. 1972. *Racial Oppression in America*. New York: Harper & Row. 309 pp.

Bobo, L. 1983. Whites' opposition to busing: Symbolic racism or realistic group conflict? *J. Pers. Soc. Psychol.* 45:1196–1210

Bonacich, E. 1980. Class approaches to ethnicity and race. *Insurgent Sociologist* 10:9–23

Braddock, J. H. 1980. The perpetuation of segregation across levels of education: A behavioral assessment of the contact-hypothesis. *J. Educ.* 53:178–86

Braddock, J. H., McPartland, J. M. 1982. Assessing school desegregation effects: New directions in research. In *Research in Sociology of Education and Socialization*, ed. A. C. Kerkhoff, 3:259–82. Greenwich, Conn: JAI

Braddock, J. H., McPartland, J. M. 1983. More evidence on social-psychological processes that perpetuate minority segregation: The relationship of school desegregation and employment desegregation. Unpublished paper presented at Am. Sociol. Assoc. Meet., Johns Hopkins Univ., Cent. Organ. Schools

Brimmer, A. 1966. The Negro in the national

economy. In *The American Negro Reference Book*, ed. J. P. Davis, pp. 266–71. Englewood Cliffs, NJ: Prentice-Hall

Caditz, J. 1975. Dilemmas over racial integration: Status consciousness vs. direct threat. *Sociol. Inquiry* 45:51–8

Campbell, A., Hatchett, S. 1975. Cross-racial contact increases in seventies; Attitude gap narrows for blacks and whites. *Inst. Soc. Res. Newsl.* 3:4–5, 7

Collins, S. M. 1983. The making of the black middle class. *Soc. Probl.* 30:369–82

Crain, R. L. 1970. School integration and occupational achievement of Negroes. *Am. J. Sociol.* 75:593–606

Crain, R. L., Mahard, R. E. 1978. School racial composition and black college attendance and achievement test performance. *Sociol. Educ.* 51:81–101

Crain, R. L., Weisman, C. S. 1972. *Discrimination, Personality and Achievement*. New York: Seminar. 225 pp.

Crosby, F., Bromley, S., Saxe, L. 1980. Recent unobtrusive studies of black and white discrimination and prejudice: A literature review. *Psychol. Bull.* 87:546–63

Donnerstein, E., Donnerstein, M. 1973. Variables in interracial aggression: Potential ingroup censure. *J. Pers. Soc. Psychol.* 27:143–50

Donnerstein, M., Donnerstein, E. 1976. Variables in interracial aggression. *J. Soc. Psychol.* 100:111–21

Farley, R. 1977. Trends in racial inequalities: Have the gains of the 1960s disappeared in the 1970s? *Am. Sociol. Rev.* 42:189–208

Farley, R. 1984. *Blacks and Whites: Narrowing the Gap?* Cambridge, Mass.: Harvard Univ. Press

Featherman, D. L., Hauser, R. M. 1978. *Opportunity and Change*. New York: Academic. 572 pp.

Feagin, J. R., Eckberg, D. L. 1980. Discrimination: Motivation, action, effects, and context. *Ann. Rev. Sociol.* 6:1–20

Gaertner, S. 1976. Nonreactive measures in racial attitude research: A focus on "liberals." In *Towards the Elimination of Racism*, ed. P. A. Katz, pp. 183–211. New York: Pergamon. 444 pp.

Goldberger, A. 1984. Reverse regression and salary discrimination. *J. Hum. Resour.* 19: 293–318

Hamilton, D. L. 1981. *Cognitive Processes in Stereotyping and Intergroup Behavior*. Hillsdale, NJ: Erlbaum

Hauser, R. M., Featherman, D. L. 1974. White-nonwhite differentials in occupational mobility among men in the United States, 1962–1972. *Demography* 11:247–65

Hendricks, M., Bootzin, R. 1976. Race and sex as stimuli for negative affect and physical avoidance. *J. Soc. Psychol.* 98:111–20

Jacobson, C. K. 1978. Desegregation rulings and public attitude changes: White resistance or resignation? *Am. J. Sociol.* 84:698–705

Jones, J. M. 1972. *Prejudice and Racism*. Reading, Mass.: Addison-Wesley. 196 pp.

Jordan, W. D. 1968. *White Over Black: American Attitudes Toward the Negro, 1550–1812*. Chapel Hill: Univ. NC Press

Kantor, R. M. 1977. Some effects of proportions on group life: Skewed sex ratios and responses to token women. *Am. J. Sociol.* 82:965–91

Katz, I., Glass, D. C., Cohen, S. 1973. Ambivalence, guilt, and the scapegoating of minority group victims. *J. Exp. Soc. Psychol.* 9:423–36

Kelley, J. 1974. The politics of school busing. *Public Opinion Q.* 38:23–39

Kelman, H. C. 1961. Processes of opinion change. *Public Opinion Q.* 25:57–78

Kinder, D. R., Rhodebeck, L. A. 1982. Continuities in support for racial equality, 1972 to 1976. *Public Opinion Q.* 46:195–215

Kinder, D. R., Sears, D. O. 1981. Symbolic racism versus racial threats to the good life. *J. Pers. Soc. Psychol.* 40:414–31

Kluegel, J. R., Smith, E. R. 1983. Affirmative action attitudes: Effects of self-interest, racial affect, and stratification beliefs on whites' views. *Soc. Forc.* 61:797–824

Kovel, J. 1970. *White Racism: A Psychohistory*. New York: Pantheon

Mare, R. D., Winship, C. 1984. The paradox of lessening racial inequality and joblessness among black youth: Enrollment, enlistment, and employment, 1964–1981. *Am. Sociol. Rev.* 49:39–55

McClendon, M. J., Pestello, F. P. 1982. White opposition: To busing or to desegregation? *Soc. Sci. Q.* 63:70–81

McConahay, J. B. 1982. Self-interest versus racial attitudes as correlates of anti-busing attitudes in Louisville: Is it the busses or the blacks? *J. Polit.* 44:692–720

McConahay, J. B. 1983. Modern racism and modern discrimination: The effects of race, racial attitudes and context on simulated hiring decisions. *Pers. Soc. Psych. Bull.* 9: 551–58

McConahay, J. B., Hardee, B. B., Bates, V. 1981. Has racism declined in America? *J. Confl. Resol.* 25:563–80

McPartland, J. M., Braddock, J. H. 1981. The impact of desegregation on going to college and getting a good job. In *Effective School Desegregation*, ed. W. D. Hawley, pp. 141–54. Beverly Hills, Calif.: Sage

McPartland, J. M., Crain, R. L. 1980. Racial discrimination, segregation, and processes of social mobility. In *Poverty and Public Policy: An Evaluation of Social Science Research*. Boston, Mass: Hall

Myrdal, G. 1944. *An American Dilemma*. New York: Harper & Row. 1330 pp.

Pettigrew, T. F. 1965. Complexity and change in American racial patterns: A social psychological view. *Daedalus* 94:974–1008

Pettigrew, T. F. 1979a. Racial change and social policy. *Ann. Am. Assoc. Polit. Soc. Sci.* 441:114–31

Pettigrew, T. F. 1979b. The ultimate attribution error: Extending Allport's cognitive analysis of prejudice. *Pers. Soc. Psychol. Bull.* 5:461–76

Pettigrew, T. F. 1980. The changing—not declining—significance of race. *Contemp. Sociol.* 9:19–21

Pettigrew, T. F. 1981. Race and class in the 1980s: An interactive view. *Daedalus* 110: 233–55

Poskocil, A. 1977. Encounters between blacks and white liberals: The collision of stereotypes. *Soc. Forc.* 55:715–27

Rothbart, M. 1976. Achieving racial equality: An analysis of resistance to social reform. In *Towards the Elimination of Racism*, ed. P. A. Katz, pp. 341–75. New York: Pergamon. 444 pp.

Sears, D. O., Kinder, D. R. 1971. Racial tensions and voting in Los Angeles. In *Los Angeles: Viability and Prospects for Metropolitan Leadership*, ed. W. Z. Hirsch, pp. 51–88. New York: Praeger

Sears, D. O., Hensler, C. P., Speer, L. 1979. Whites' opposition to busing: Self-interest or symbolic politics? *Am. Polit. Sci. Rev.* 73:369–84

Sears, D. O., Lau, R. R., Tyler, T. R., Allen, H. M. 1980. Self-interest or symbolic politics in policy attitudes and presidential voting. *Am. Polit. Sci. Rev.* 74:670–84

Sears, D. O., Allen, H. M. 1984. The trajectory of local desegregation controversies and whites' opposition to busing. In *Groups in Contact: The Psychology of Desegregation*, ed. M. Brewer, N. Miller. Orlando, Fla: Academic. pp. 123–5

Taeuber, K. E., Taeuber, A. F. 1965. *Negroes in Cities*. Chicago, Ill: Aldine

Taylor, M. 1984. Different estimates of discrimination-produced inequity. Pa. State Univ., Dept. of Sociol. Unpublished paper

Taylor, S. E., Fiske, S. T., Close, M., Anderson, C., Ruderman, A. 1975. Solo status as a psychological variable: The power of being distinctive. Harvard Univ., Dept. of Psychol. & Soc. Rel. Unpublished paper

Thompson, K. H. 1982. *The Voting Rights Act and Black Electoral Participation*. Washington, DC: Joint Center for Political Studies. 45 pp.

US Bureau of the Census. 1983. *America's Black Population: 1970 to 1982*. Washington, DC: USGPO 27 pp.

US Commission on Civil Rights. 1982. *Unemployment and Underemployment Among Blacks, Hispanics, and Women*. Washington, DC: USGPO. 98 pp.

US Dept. of Labor. 1983. *Employment in Perspective: Minority Workers*. Washington, DC: USGPO 4 pp.

Vanneman, R. D., Pettigrew, T. F. 1972. Race and relative deprivation in the urban United States. *Race* 13:461–86

Warner, W. L. 1937. American caste and class. *Am. J. Sociol.* 42:234–7

Wasby, S. L. 1982. *Vote Dilution, Minority Voting Rights, and the Courts*. Washington, DC: Joint Center for Political Studies. 52 pp.

Weidman, J. C. 1975. Resistance of white adults to the busing of school children. *J. Res. Devel. Educ.* 9:123–9

Weitz, S. 1972. Attitude, voice and behavior: A repressed affect model of interracial interaction. *J. Pers. Soc. Psychol.* 24:14–21

Wellman, D. 1979. *Portraits of White Racism*. New York: Cambridge Univ. Press. 254 pp.

Wilson, L., Rogers, R. W. 1975. The fire this time: Effects of race of target, insult, and potential retaliation of black aggression. *J. Pers. Soc. Psychol.* 32:857–64

Wilson, W. J. 1978. *The Declining Significance of Race: Blacks and Changing American Institutions*. Chicago: Univ. Chicago Press. 204 pp.

Word, C. O., Zanna, M. P., Cooper, J. 1974. The nonverbal mediation of self-fulfilling prophecies in interracial interaction. *J. Exp. Soc. Psychol.* 10:109–20

Wright, E. O. 1978. Race, class, and income inequality. *Am. J. Sociol.* 83:1368–97

Ann. Rev. Sociol. 1985. 11:347–67

FAMILY VIOLENCE

Richard J. Gelles

College of Arts and Sciences, University of Rhode Island, Kingston, Rhode Island
02881

Abstract

This chapter reviews research on family violence. Once viewed as rare and confined to a few mentally ill offenders, family violence has rapidly captured public and social scientific attention. The review examines the "discovery" of family violence as a social and sociological problem. Among the major problems that confront students of family violence are defining, both nominally and operationally, child abuse, wife abuse, and violence. Access to cases, sampling, and measurement of violence are additional issues that are reviewed. Research on family violence is described with a specific focus on the extent of the various forms of family violence and the factors associated with violence in the home. Seven theoretical models that have been developed to analyze the specific issue of family violence are briefly reviewed. The chapter concludes by covering new issues in the field of family violence, including research on the responses of victims of wife abuse, studies of the consequences of child abuse, and evaluation studies of prevention and treatment programs.

THE DISCOVERY OF A LATENT FAMILY AND SOCIAL PROBLEM

Sociologists came late to the study of family violence. Social workers recognized but did not write about child abuse and child maltreatment in the nineteenth century. Pediatric radiologists in 1946 identified the pattern of broken bones and healed fractures that were thought to be caused by children's caretakers (Caffey 1946, 1957; Silverman 1953). Physician C. Henry Kempe and his colleagues published their seminal article, "The Battered-Child Syndrome," in the July, 1962, issue of the *Journal of the American Medical*

0360-0572/85/0815-0347$02.00

Association. This article and an accompanying editorial served to focus medical and public attention on the problem of child abuse and shaped the way scientists and the lay public thought about child abuse in the ensuing years (Nelson 1984). By the mid-1960s there was a growing literature on child abuse; yet, in the complete bibliography on child abuse published by the then US Department of Health, Education, and Welfare in 1969, not a single entry was authored by a sociologist.

Violence towards women, or wife abuse, received little public or scientific attention until the 1970s. Yet here too the earliest writings were not by sociologists. Wife abuse was initially approached from a psychiatric point of view (Schultz 1960; Snell, Rosenwald & Robey 1964).

What sociological work there was on family violence prior to 1970 was embedded in criminological studies of homicide (see for example Gillen 1946, Palmer 1962, Pokorny 1965, Wolfgang 1958).

In spite of the historical and crosscultural evidence that the family has been the scene of interpersonal violence for as long as we have had written records of humankind and family life (Bakan 1971, DeMause 1974, 1975; Korbin 1981, Radbill 1980, Taylor & Newberger 1979, Shorter 1975), and despite the fact that other disciplines had begun to study abuse and violence in families, sociological research and recognition of these topics did not begin in earnest until the 1970s. Why were sociologists late in identifying family violence as a topic for investigation? What forces resulted in the discipline's change from selective inattention and the assumption that family violence was a latent social problem? How did family violence finally capture attention as a manifest social problem?

Star (1980) claims that the silence that traditionally surrounded the issue of family violence was attributable to three factors: (*a*) lack of awareness, (*b*) general acceptance, and (*c*) denial. Straus (1974) notes that three factors influenced the emergence of family violence as a social and sociological problem: (*a*) the sensitization to violence that occurred in the late 1960s and early 1970s due to the Vietnam war, political assassinations, violent social protest, and the rise in the homicide and assault rates; (*b*) the reemergence of the women's movement; and, (*c*) theoretical challenges to the consensus model of society by proponents of the conflict and social action models of society.

There are additional factors that may help explain why and how sociologists first overlooked and then discovered family violence. First, violence in the home is a family issue, a violence issue, and a criminological issue. While it touches all these specialties in sociology, family violence finds no "home" in any one specialty. For the criminologist, family violence is but one form of criminal violent behavior. Students of family relations frequently group family violence into a residual "deviance in the family" category. A second problem is that family violence is a private matter. Unlike assassination, riots, rebellion, and street violence, most family violence is hidden behind the symbolic and literal closed doors of the home (Gelles 1974). The private nature of family violence not only hides the problem from public and scientific view, it also makes the victims and offenders nearly inaccessible to many social researchers. While social workers, psychiatrists, and physicians have access to participants in family violence, sociologists' access to cases and subjects is frequently limited to public instances of violence—homicides, assaults, or officially reported cases of child abuse. Social service personnel and hospital personnel frequently have denied sociologists access to subjects on the grounds of confidentiality.

The early 1970s saw a number of changes. First, all states instituted official reporting of child abuse and neglect cases, and aggregate statistics on child abuse became available for sociological analysis. Second, safe houses, or battered wife shelters, were established to serve the needs of battered women. Many of these shelters were established by feminist organizations, who granted female sociologists access to the shelters for purposes of sociological research. The vast majority of published research on wife battering has been based on samples drawn from such shelters (see for example Dobash & Dobash 1979, Pagelow 1981). Third, exploratory studies of family violence (O'Brien 1971, Levinger 1966, Steinmetz 1971, Straus 1971) demonstrated that research could be conducted (using nonclinical samples) on family violence. These early studies paved the way by outlining appropriate methods and research strategies for uncovering and examining instances of family violence.

A final constraint on sociological research was that the earliest writings on child abuse and wife abuse shaped the scientific and public perception of the problem. Thus, because the medical/psychiatric model was the first applied to studying abuse and violence in the family, there has been a tendency to see abuse as a psychiatric problem. The first reports on child abuse not only profiled the suspected psychopathology that led to abuse, but also claimed that social factors were essentially irrelevant as a generative cause (Galdston 1965, Steele & Pollock 1974).

The Sociological Perspective

When sociologists did become involved in studying family violence, they found that they had a twofold mandate. First, they were debunkers, critiquing the early, medical-model dominated research. Sociologists critiqued research on child and wife abuse on methodological grounds—small, nonrepresentative samples, lack of comparison groups, and improper data analysis (see Gelles 1973 for a critique of the early child abuse research); and on theoretical grounds—unicausal models and post-hoc theorizing (Dobash & Dobash 1979, Gelles 1974). Sociologists attacked the myths that family violence was rare and was confined to mentally disturbed people (Steinmetz & Straus 1974), that only poor people abused their wives and children; and that battered women liked being abused. Sociologists also helped discover hidden forms of family violence, such as sibling violence (Steinmetz 1977), violence towards parents (Steinmetz 1978c; Cornell & Gelles 1982a), and violence towards the elderly (Cornell & Gelles 1982b; Steinmetz 1984).

A second mandate was the use of the sociological perspective and research tools to help establish the nature, extent, and dynamics of family violence as a social problem. Sociologists were consulted for research on incidence and prevalence, for studies of the factors correlated with abuse and violence, and for causal models and theories. In addition, social service and medical personnel, starving for information to help deal with the emotionally trying cases of violence they encountered, sought advice about how best to treat and prevent violence and abuse.

The first decade of research on family violence focused on four major issues: (*a*) defining (nominally and operationally) abuse and violence; (*b*) attempting to measure the incidence and prevalence of family violence; (*c*) assessing the factors correlated with violence in the home; and (*d*) developing causal models to explain family violence. The last four years have seen sociologists go beyond these initial concerns and begin to assess the consequences of violence, the dynamics of violence, and the impact of interventions on the occurrence of violence in the home.

DEFINITIONAL ISSUES

One of the major problems confronting researchers who attempt to study violence in the family has been the quagmire of definitional dilemmas encountered. The concepts "violence" and "abuse" have frequently been used interchangeably by those who study domestic violence. These concepts, however, are not conceptually equivalent. Moreover, there are considerable variations in how each concept is nominally defined.

Defining Abuse

The first form of family violence that was uncovered and recognized as a problem was child abuse, or the battered child syndrome. The first widely disseminated article defined the battered child syndrome as a clinical condition (with diagnosable physical and medical symptoms) having to do with those who have been deliberately injured by physical assault by a parent or caretaker (Kempe et al 1962). The term "battered child syndrome" quickly gave way to the terms child abuse, child abuse and neglect, and child maltreatment. Abuse was not only physical assault, but also malnutrition, failure to thrive, sexual abuse, educational neglect, medical neglect, and mental abuse. The official federal definition of child abuse, stated in the Federal Child Abuse Prevention and Treatment Act of 1974 (PL 93–237) was:

". . . the physical or mental injury, sexual abuse, negligent treatment, or maltreatment of a child under the age of eighteen by a person who is responsible for the child's welfare under circumstances which would indicate that the child's health or welfare is harmed or threatened thereby."

This definition is consequential because it became the model for state definitions, which are in turn the basis for state laws that require reporting of suspected cases of child abuse and neglect. Also, the federally funded national incidence survey of officially reported child abuse and neglect (Burgdorf 1980) employed this nominal definition of child abuse. Thus, most official report data on child abuse are influenced, to one degree or another, by the federal definition.

It would be a mistake, however, to assume that since there is a federal definition of abuse, there is uniformity in how child abuse is nominally defined by researchers. In point of fact, most studies of child abuse and violence towards children cannot be compared to one another because of the wide variation of nominal definitions employed by scholars. While some investigators study only violence towards children (see for example Gelles 1978), others examine the full range of acts of commission and omission (see for example Newberger et al 1977). Thus, reports of incidence, correlations, cause, and effect vary from study to study for many reasons, one being that researchers infrequently define child abuse the same way.

The new interest in cross-cultural research on child abuse further illustrates the definitional problem (Gelles and Cornell 1983, Korbin 1981). Korbin (1981) points out that since there is no universal standard for optimal child rearing, there is no universal standard for what is child abuse and neglect. Thus, those who seek to develop cross-cultural definitions of abuse face the dilemma of choosing between a culturally relative standard in which any behavior can be abusive or nonabusive depending on the cultural context, or an idiosyncratic standard whereby abusive acts are those behaviors at variance with the normal cultural standards for raising children. Korbin and others have tended towards using the latter standard as they develop and carry out cross-cultural research (Korbin 1984).

To a lesser extent, the same definitional problems that have plagued the study of violence towards children have been part of the development of research on violence towards women. Initial definitions of wife abuse focused on acts of damaging physical violence directed toward women by their spouses or partners (Gelles 1974, Martin 1976). As wife abuse became recognized as a social problem, the definition was sometimes broadened to include sexual abuse, marital rape, and even pornography (London 1978).

The major definitional controversy surrounding wife abuse emerged as a result of published research on violence towards husbands (Steinmetz 1978a) and the use of the terms domestic violence, family violence, and spouse abuse when referring to violence between adult partners or married couples.

Sociologists and psychologists, including Dobash & Dobash (1979), Pagelow (1979), and Wardell, Gillespie & Leffler (1983) have argued that to discuss violence and abuse of adults is to miss the point that the preferential victims of violence in the family are women. These authors argue that the true problem is *wife* assault, *wife* abuse, or violence towards *wives,* and that evenhanded attempts to discuss spousal violence misdirect scientific and public attention and are an example of misogyny. This controversy will be reviewed in more detail in the discussion of incidence and prevalence of violence.

Defining Violence

Violence has also proven to be a concept that is not easy to define. First, violence has frequently been used interchangeably with the term "aggression." While violence typically refers to a physical act, aggression frequently refers to any malevolent act that is intended to hurt another person. The hurt may not be only physical but may be emotional injury or material deprivation. Second, because of the negative connotation of the term violence, some investigators have tried to differentiate between hurtful violence and more legitimate acts. Thus, Goode (1971) tried to distinguish between legitimate acts of force and illegitimate acts of violence. Spanking a child who runs into a street might be considered force, while beating the same child would be violence. Research on family violence has demonstrated the difficulty in distinguishing between legitimate and illegitimate acts, since offenders, victims, bystanders, and agents of social control often accept and tolerate many acts that would be considered illegitimate if committed by strangers (Gelles 1974, Steinmetz 1977, Straus et al 1980).

Additional theoretical and ideological concerns influence the ways in which the concept of violence is defined. Violence is frequently a political concept used to attract attention to undesirable behaviors or situations. Thus, some members of the political left will define various federal programs, such as Aid to Families with Dependent Children, as violent. Members of the political right will likewise claim that abortion is a violent act. The entire capitalist system has been derided as violent.

One frequently used nominal definition of violence, proposed by Gelles & Straus (1979), defines violence as "an act carried out with the intention, or perceived intention of physically hurting another person." This definition includes spankings and shovings as well as other forms of behavior; injury and/or death are also included under this broad definition.

By and large, the remainder of this review and the majority of research on family violence focus on the most severe and abusive forms of violence. Injurious violence or violence that has the high potential for causing an injury has captured the attention of scholars who measure the incidence of family violence, identify factors associated with violent behavior, and develop theories to explain family violence.

METHODOLOGICAL APPROACHES: SOURCES OF DATA, OPERATIONAL DEFINITIONS, AND THE SOCIAL CONSTRUCTION OF FAMILY VIOLENCE

Sources of Data

Data on child abuse, wife abuse, and family violence have come from three sources. Each source has certain advantages and specific weaknesses that influence both the nature and generalizability of the findings derived from the research.

CLINICAL SAMPLES   The most frequent source of data on family violence are clinical studies carried out by psychiatrists, psychologists, and counselors. The clinical setting (including battered wife shelters) provides access to extensive, in-depth information about particular cases of violence. The pioneer studies of child abuse and wife abuse were based almost exclusively on such clinical samples (Steele & Pollock 1974, Snell, Rosenwald & Robey 1964, Schultz 1960, Kempe et al 1962, Galdston 1965, Walker 1979). Such studies, while important for breaking new ground and rich in qualitative data, cannot be used to generalize information on the frequency of factors associated with violence or the representativeness of the findings or conclusions.

As stated earlier, studies of wife abuse and violence towards women have relied heavily on samples of women who seek help at battered wife shelters (Dobash & Dobash 1979, Walker 1979, Giles-Sims 1983, Pagelow 1981). Such samples are extremely important because they are the best and sometimes the only way of obtaining detailed data on the most severely battered women. Such data are also necessary to study the impact of intervention programs. However, these data are not generalizable to all women who experience violence; and the study designs (see for example Walker 1979) frequently fail to employ comparison groups.

OFFICIAL STATISTICS   The establishment of mandatory reporting laws for suspected cases of child abuse and neglect made case-level and aggregate-level data on abuse available to researchers. The American Humane Association collects data from each state on officially reported child abuse and neglect (American Humane Association 1982, 1983), and the Federal government sponsored its own national survey of officially reported child maltreatment (Burgdorf, 1980). Official report data provide information on an extremely large number of cases. But these cases are limited only to those known by service providers. Incidence rates from these data are likely to be lower than the true rates, and the data are biased in a number of ways (Finkelhor & Hotaling 1984). As with many other types of official records on deviant behavior, the poor are typically overrepresented in official reports, as are ethnic and racial minorities (Gelles 1975, Newberger et al 1977).

RANDOM SAMPLE SURVEYS   The low base rate of most forms of abuse poses a problem for those who desire to apply standard survey research methods to studying family violence. The low base rate requires investigators to use purposive or nonrepresentative sampling techniques to identify cases (such as drawing samples from social agencies or police reports) or to draw large representative samples. The high costs associated with large samples may, in turn, require that interviews be reduced in length. Some scholars are wary of applying survey research to studying abuse and violence because they assume that subjects will not provide reliable or valid information to interviewers (Pelton 1979). However, a number of random sample survey studies (Harris 1979, Straus et al 1980, US Department of Justice 1980, 1984) have been conducted. While these studies derive data which are generalizable, the amount of information elicited is frequently limited. Moreover, operationalizing violence and abuse in survey instruments frequently results in compromises. Straus and his colleagues (1980), for example, introduced their violence measure, the Conflict Tactics Scale, by setting the stage in the context of family conflicts. Critics of this form of measurement note that such a procedure limits discussions of violence to conflict situations (Pagelow 1981, Dobash & Dobash 1979). Moreover, the Conflict Tactics Scales did not measure the context, consequences, or outcomes of violent acts or whether an injury resulted from the violence.

Operational Definitions

While there is considerable variation in nominal definitions of violence and abuse, the reliance on official statistics and clinical samples has produced surprising similarity in the way that researchers in all disciplines operationally define family violence and especially child abuse. Child abuse, and other forms of family violence (especially abuse of the elderly) are typically defined operationally as those instances in which the victim becomes publically known and labeled by an official agency.

Researchers have criticized this uniformity of operationalization and claimed that it is biased by the process by which cases come to public attention and are labeled (Gelles 1975). Support for such criticism comes from Turbett & O'Toole's (1980) experiment which found that physicians are more likely to label minority children and children from lower-class families abused. Survey research conducted by Giovannoni & Becerra (1979) also found that attitudes and definitions of child abuse vary by professional group and social status.

The Social Construction of Family Violence

The tendency to operationalize child abuse, wife abuse, and family violence as those cases that come to professional and official attention, or those individuals who choose to seek professional help or flee to a shelter, results in confounding the factors leading people to come forward or be publically labeled with the factors causing wife abuse, child abuse and family violence. Because research results are used by clinicians, police, and other labelers to identify suspected cases of family violence, the confounding thus becomes built into the system. Research is based on official reports or cases that come to public attention. Clinicians, agents of social control, and other "gatekeepers" read the literature and use it to diagnose injuries and situations as either instances of abuse or "accidents." Thus, the definition of the situation of violence and abuse is caused and becomes causal. An emergency room physician may treat an injured woman who is reluctant to discuss the nature of her injury. The physician may draw on the literature on wife abuse to see if the woman fits the "profile". If she does, she becomes a case. Later, a researcher may choose to draw cases from the population of the emergency room, and include (or exclude) the woman based on the diagnosis.

The social construction of family violence is consequential for estimating extent, patterns, and causes, and also for studying the impact of intervention and preventions. Researchers may study the impact of interventions and prevention programs on officially known cases and then generalize to the wider population of abuse and violence victims. Obviously, since the wider population is quite distinct from those cases that are publically identified, the interventions and prevention outcomes may not be generalizable to the undetected or hidden instances of domestic abuse.

THE EXTENT AND NATURE OF FAMILY VIOLENCE

Considerable effort has been expended on discussion, debate, and research concerning the extent of family violence. Part of this effort is aimed at exploding the myth that violence in the home is rare. Another goal has been to convince policymakers, opinion leaders, and the public that child abuse, wife abuse, and other forms of domestic violence are extensive enough to be considered legitimate social problems—especially since one part of the definition of a social problem is that a behavior is found harmful to a *significant* number of people (Merton & Nisbet 1976). Lastly, social scientists need data on incidence when they plan social survey research.

Numerous methods have been used to assess the extent of the various forms of family violence. First, scientists employ educated guesses. The majority of estimates that were made about the extent of child abuse were little more than guesstimates (see for example Fontana 1973, US Senate 1973, *Pediatric News* 1975). Others who have tried to base estimates on actual data have used survey data on physical punishment (Erlanger 1974, Stark & McEvoy 1970), homicide data (Curtis 1974, Steinmetz & Straus 1974), assault (Pittman & Handy 1964, Boudouris 1971), and applicants for divorce (Levinger 1966, O'Brien 1971), or reports by subjects who know of a case of abuse in their community (Block & Sinnott 1979, Gil 1970).

Three national surveys have been conducted with the purpose of assessing the national incidence of domestic violence. Straus, Gelles & Steinmetz (1980) surveyed a representative sample of 2143 couples. Data were collected on violence towards children, violence between spouses, violence between siblings, and violence towards parents. Data on the extent of domestic violence have also been abstracted from the National Crime Survey (US Justice Department 1980, 1984). These estimates are based on a sample of subjects 12 years of age and older who report crimes against persons or households, whether reported or unreported to the police. The sample includes some 60,000 housing units, and data are available from 1973 to 1981. Lastly, the National Center on Child Abuse and Neglect conducted a national incidence survey of child maltreatment (Burgdorf 1980), and these data include acts of physical maltreatment of children.

ESTIMATES OF INCIDENCE AND PREVALENCE

Estimates of incidence range from thousands to millions. Some authors claim that family violence is an epidemic and that perhaps half of all wives are abused.

The survey by Straus and his colleagues found that the yearly incidence of acts that they defined as abusive violence (all acts that had the high probability of causing an injury—whether or not an injury occurred) was about 3.8 to 4.0 instances per 100 individuals (Straus et al 1980). About 3.8% of children 3–17 years of age were victims of severe or abusive violence. The same percentage of wives were victims of abusive spousal violence. The percentage of husbands victimized was found to be higher than that of wives (Straus et al 1980, Steinmetz 1978a), and this stirred up a storm of professional and public controversy. The data on husband abuse were attacked as invalid because the survey did not measure the consequences of the violence (women are thought to be the most likely to be injured) and because the survey did not assess the context of the violence (women are thought to use violence to protect themselves from violence initiated by their husbands; Pleck et al 1978, Jones 1980).[1] One of the main points of contention arising out of the incidence data on violence towards husbands is that the national incidence study indicating large numbers of male victims did not square with findings from clinical research that found few if any battered men. Obviously, the clinical studies employed differing definitions and sampling techniques than the national survey. Studying only women who seek aid from battered wife shelters produces different

---

[1]In addition to the methodological criticisms was the concern by those who feared that the issue of husband abuse would take both attention and resources away from the problem of wife abuse.

samples and different results than national surveys. Few men are actually interviewed in clinical studies, and data about male victimization is based on their wives' or partners' reports.

The national incidence survey (Straus et al 1980) found that in one fourth of the homes where there was couple violence, men were victims but not offenders. In one fourth of the homes, women were victims but not offenders, and in one half of the violent homes, both men and women were violent—although the survey could not detect whether the wives' violence was retaliatory or in self-defense.

Despite the clamor about husband abuse data, nominal and operational definitions of violence, and plausible interpretations of the data, it does seem clear that while women are the most likely victims of spousal violence, there are indeed men who are victimized. Little additional research has been conducted on violence towards husbands.

Sibling violence and abuse were found to be the most common forms of domestic violence in Straus and his colleagues' survey (1980). Finally, the investigators reported that child-to-parent violence was comparable to other forms of family violence—3.5% of teenagers (15–17 years of age) used severe violence towards a parent during the survey year.

Data from the National Crime Survey (US Department of Justice 1984) indicate that the yearly incidence rate of domestic violence (among those 12 years of age and older) was 1.5 per 1000 people in the population.

The incidence survey by the National Center on Child Abuse and Neglect yielded a figure of 10.5 children per 1000 who are known by agencies to be maltreated (Burgdorf 1980). More than 200,000 children were victims of physical assault.

There are few data on other forms of family violence. There have been some preliminary attempts to assess the extent of the abuse of the elderly (see for example Block & Sinnott 1979; and Cornell & Gelles 1982b for a review of major studies). Additionally, a number of states have instituted mandatory reporting laws for elder abuse; thus, some official report data on elder abuse are available.

One unintended outcome of the various attempts to measure the incidence of family violence is that the effort has been partially counter-productive. While the use of incidence estimates is partly designed to promote and maintain interest in the problem of family violence, the wide range of estimates has frequently led opinion and policymakers to conclude that the real magnitude of family violence remains unknown (Nelson 1984).

Factors Associated With Family Violence

Other reviews have carefully analyzed the factors associated with various forms of family violence (for child abuse, see Maden & Wrench 1977, Parke &

Collmer 1975; for spouse abuse, see Byrd 1979. For family violence in general
see Gelles 1980; Gelles 1982; Steinmetz 1978b).

The last two decades of research on the various aspects of family violence are
in agreement on one major point—there are a multitude of factors associated
with violence in the home. Nevertheless, the unusual, emotional, and bizarre
nature of some instances of family violence has led some researchers, popular
writers, and the public alike to grasp at single factor explanations. Mental
illness, character disorders, psychopathology, alcohol and drugs, stress, poverty, growing up in a violent home, and diet have all been pointed to as *the* cause
of domestic strife. Social scientists are obviously aware of the drawbacks of
single factor explanations, but they too sometimes select explanations that are
single factor in nature. Dobash & Dobash argue that patriarchy and male
domination are the primary causes of violence towards wives (1979).

Among the factors that researchers have consistently found related to various
aspects of domestic violence are:

1. The cycle of violence—the intergenerational transmission of violence.
2. Low socioeconomic status.
3. Social and structural stress.
4. Social isolation and low community embeddedness.
5. Low self-concept.
6. Personality problems and psychopathology.

It is important to point out that the research that supports the claim for these
associations is far from definitive and is often based on empirical research
suffering from methodological problems. These include the fact that most
studies are based on "caught cases," that is, only cases that come to official
attention; studies frequently either do not include comparison groups or have
comparison groups that are not equivalent; and studies frequently have small
samples and lack generalizability (Gelles 1982).

In addition to the methodological limitations, there are other problems.
Associations found tend to be quite modest (perhaps as a result of the low base
rate of family violence and the multidimensional nature of the behavior).
Frequently, the publicly perceived strength of an association is based on how
often the finding is cited, not how strong the statistical association is or how
well the research meets the standards of scientific evidence. Houghton (1979)
calls this the "Woozle Effect" (based on the Winnie the Pooh story—Milne
1926). In the Woozle Effect, findings are initially stated with a qualification,
then repeated in the literature without the qualification. Reviews of the literature cite other reviews, and the strength of a finding grows without the original
qualifications or evidence being confirmed through replication. Fortunately,
the majority of the factors cited in this section have been found to be associated
with family violence by investigators who have used various methods of
research and have drawn their data from all three sources of data.

CAUSAL MODELS

As noted previously, the field of family violence abounds with simplistic theoretical models. In the earliest research reports the model advanced was psychopathology—mental illness caused people to abuse their children, wives, and parents (Steele & Pollock 1974). Other intraindividual models proposed that family violence is caused by alcohol and drugs.

The major theoretical approaches to family violence have been reviewed extensively elsewhere (Gelles 1980, Gelles 1982, Gelles 1983, Gelles & Straus 1979). Of interest here is the fact that students of family violence have chosen to view family violence as a *special case* of violence that requires its own body of theory to explain it (Gelles & Straus 1979). Thus, existing theories of violence and aggression, such as frustration-aggression theory (Berkowitz 1962, Dollard et al 1939, Miller 1941), self-attitude theory (Kaplan 1962), functional theory (Coser 1967), and culture of violence theory (Wolfgang & Ferracuti 1967) have typically not been directly applied to the study of violence in the home. The only existing theoretical model from the general study of violence to be frequently applied to violence in the home has been social learning theory (Bandura et al 1961, Singer 1971).

Students of family violence have justified the development of a special body of theory to explain family violence on the basis of the high incidence of violence in the home, because of the unique nature of the family as a small group, and because of the distinctive nature of the family as a social institution (Gelles & Straus 1979).

While special theories of family have been developed, the development has gone in three different directions. Theories have been developed to explain the abuse of children; there are theories that attempt to explain spouse abuse; and there are those theories that are designed to explain family violence in general.

Theories of Family Violence

Among the special approaches developed to explain family violence are: resource theory (Goode 1971), general systems theory (Straus 1973), an ecological model (Garbarino 1977), an exchange model (Gelles 1983), a patriarchy explanation (Dobash & Dobash 1979), a sociobiological perspective; an economic model; and a sociocultural explanation.

RESOURCE THEORY   A resource theory, the first theoretical approach applied to family violence, proposes that all social systems rest to some degree on force or its threat (Goode 1971). The use of violence depends on the resources a participant in a system or family member can command. The more resources, the more force can be used, but the less it actually is employed. Those with the fewest resources tend to employ force and violence the most. For instance, husbands tend to resort to violence when they lack the traditional resources associated with the culturally assumed dominant role of the male in the family (Gelles 1974, O'Brien 1971).

GENERAL SYSTEMS THEORY   Straus (1973) and Giles-Sims (1983) use a social system approach to explain family violence. Here, violence is viewed as a system product rather than the result of individual pathology. System operations can maintain, escalate, or reduce levels of violence.

AN ECOLOGICAL PERSPECTIVE   Garbarino has proposed an ecological model of child maltreatment. The model rests on three levels of analysis: the relationship between organism and environment; the interacting and overlapping systems in which human development occurs; and environmental quality (Garbarino 1977). Garbarino proposes that maltreatment arises out of a mismatch of parent, child, and family to neighborhood and community.

EXCHANGE THEORY   Exchange theory (Gelles 1983) proposes that family violence is governed by the principles of costs and rewards. Violence is used when rewards are higher than costs. The private nature of the family, the reluctance of social institutions and agencies to intervene in violence, and the low risk of other interventions reduce the costs of violence. The cultural approval of violence as both expressive and instrumental behavior raises the potential rewards for violence.

PATRIARCHY   Dobash & Dobash (1979) see abuse of women as a unique phenomenon that is caused by the social and economic processes that directly and indirectly support a patriarchal social order and family structure. Patriarchy leads to the domination of women by men and explains the historical pattern of systematic violence directed at women.

SOCIOBIOLOGY   One of the newest theoretical models, a sociobiological perspective (or evolutionary perspective) suggests that violence towards human or nonhuman primate offspring is the result of the reproductive success potential of children and parental investment. The theory proposes that parents will not invest in children with low reproductive potential. Thus, children not genetically related to the parent (e.g. stepchildren, adopted or foster children), or children with low reproductive potential (e.g. handicapped or retarded) are at the highest risk for abuse and infanticide (Hrdy 1979, Burgess & Garbarino 1983). It logically follows the risk is greatest that adoptive parents, foster parents, and caretakers not genetically related to the child (e.g. a boyfriend) will become abusers. Risk of abuse is high where there is lack of bonding between parent and child and where paternity is highly uncertain (Burgess

1979). Large families can dilute parental energy and lower attachment to children (Burgess 1979).

AN ECONOMIC MODEL   The economic or social-structural model explains that violence and abuse arise out of socially structured stress. Stress, such as low income, unemployment, and illness, is unevenly distributed in the social structure. When violence is the accepted response or adaptation to stress, stress can lead to violence and abuse (Coser 1967, Gelles 1974).

A SOCIOCULTURAL EXPLANATION   Finally, students of family violence have explained the occurrence of violence by drawing on sociocultural attitudes and norms concerning violent behavior. Societies, cultures, and subcultures that approve of the use of violence are thought to have the highest rates of domestic violence (Straus et al 1980).

SUMMARY   The recency of family violence as an area of study for sociologists is best exemplified by the limited level of theoretical development of the field. The field has not developed to the point where theories have actually been subjected to rigorous empirical testing. Individual theories have been tested in limited ways (typically with small, nonrepresentative data sets), and there has yet to be a critical test that pits one theory against another to see which best fits the data. Various criticisms have been leveled against each of the theories. A major limitation of ecological theory is the argument that the theory commits the ecological fallacy by attributing aggregate level demographics to individual level behavior. The patriarchy explanation suffers from being a "single factor" explanation. Moreover, the variability of the independent variable (patriarchy) has not been adequately specified by the theorists. In its present form, a patriarchy theory is not amenable to an empirical test. This is also the case with sociobiological explanations. Additionally, while sociobiological explanations seem empirically to fit the data on infanticide, the theory does not logically seem to explain nonlethal instances of child maltreatment; nonlethal violence and neglect do not remove the child or increase the inclusive fitness of the other children. Abuse and neglect may actually require a greater parental investment of time and energy in the victimized child. The available data do fit the propositions of resource, exchange, economic, and sociocultural explanations. The next decade of research is likely to be devoted to testing theories and to theoretical integration of the supported theories and propositions.

OTHER RESEARCH ISSUES

The most recent research on domestic violence has moved beyond the study of incidence and correlations and the proposing of causal models. Researchers have begun to test theories, to study the consequences of family violence, and to examine the impact of interventions on violence in the family. While a full examination of all the developing research issues and questions is beyond the scope of this paper, this review highlights some of the work that has addressed key questions in the study of domestic violence.

The Responses of Victims of Wife Abuse

One question that is frequently raised concerning wife abuse is why the victims choose to stay or to leave battering husbands. Common sense would argue that a victim of a beating would flee to protect herself. Yet common sense overlooks both the structural and interpersonal nature of family relations. One reason the issue of staying or leaving has captured and continues to hold public and scholarly attention is that some of the wives who have killed their husbands have claimed self-defense and have drawn upon scholarly research on the "battered wife syndrome" to justify their choice to kill rather than flee their husbands. Walker's theory of "learned helplessness" (1979) is the frequent explanation offered by those defending battered women. Walker claims that battered women develop an inability to protect themselves from future assaults. The beatings leave them with a diminished capacity to control events that go on around them (Walker 1979).

Gelles (1976) found three factors influenced whether a woman stays or leaves a violent relationship: frequency and severity of violence is directly related to leaving; limited education and poor occupational skills are indirectly related to leaving; and women who experience violence in their childhoods are more likely to remain in a violent relationship.

Pagelow's research (1981) did not support the hypothesis concerning frequency and severity of violence or the hypothesis relating experience of violence to staying or leaving. Pagelow (1981) did find that diminished educational and occupational resources and skills inhibit women from leaving violent relationships. Strube & Barbour's (1983) study of 98 women also found that economically dependent women are more likely to remain with their abusive husbands. They also found evidence that *commitment* to the marital relationship was an important and independent factor related to the decision to leave a violent relationship.

The results of research on women's decisions to stay or leave violent relationships must be interpreted with caution, since these studies rely exclusively on small, nonrepresentative samples. Differing results from study to study may be partially due to differing sampling procedures.

Bowker analyzed the situation of battered women from a different perspective (1983). Bowker interviewed 136 women who reported that they had been beaten and that their husbands had stopped being violent. Bowker attempted to identify what the battered women had done to get their husbands to cease the violent behavior. Passive defense (defending oneself by covering the body with one's hands, arms, and feet) was the most common personal strategy used by women; calling friends was the most commonly used informal strategy; and social services were the most widely used formal source of help. Bowker, however, found no single technique worked best. What mattered was that women showed their determination that the violence must stop (Bowker 1983).

The Consequences of Child Maltreatment

Students of child abuse and child maltreatment have begun to turn their attention to the question of the consequences of being an abused child. The clinical literature strongly suggests that abused children have higher rates of developmental delays and difficulties and as adults they have higher rates of drug abuse, alcohol abuse, criminal behavior, and psychiatric disturbances (Smith, Hansen & Nobel 1973, Galdston 1975, Martin 1972).

Survey data also suggest that abused children have higher rates of juvenile delinquency (Alfaro 1977, Carr 1977).

Research on the consequences of abuse and violence typically suffers from numerous methodological flaws (differing definitions, small clinical samples, no comparison groups, and retrospective data—Garbarino & Plantz 1984). Preliminary data from a prospective study do point to deficits suffered by abused children (Egeland & Jacobvitz 1984).

Preventing and Treating Family Violence

The study of family violence has always had an implicit applied mandate. The search for knowledge has been carried out with the assumption that such knowledge could be useful in designing and implementing prevention and treatment programs. As yet, there are few empirical studies that assess the impact of existing prevention and treatment efforts in the fields of child abuse and domestic violence. An evaluation of child abuse treatment programs was carried out in the late 1970s. The study found that while one-on-one therapy conducted by professional therapists was the most costly treatment, it was the least effective (in terms of recidivism data collected over a very limited time period). The most effective intervention was group counseling provided by lay therapists. This program of intervention was also the least expensive intervention (Berkeley Planning Associates 1978).

Sherman & Berk (1984) conducted a natural experiment to assess the impact of police interventions in cases of wife abuse. Of three randomly applied interventions—arrest, removing the husband from the home, and trying to cool down the situation—arrest resulted in fewer calls for help and fewer instances of repeated violent behavior.

CONCLUSION: FUTURE RESEARCH

The study of family violence is still relatively new. The psychologist Edward Zigler once claimed that the current knowledge base on child abuse is about equal to what we knew about mental illness in the late 1940s (1976). Zigler could be either too pessimistic about family violence or too optimistic in his assessment of our understanding of mental illness. Nevertheless, it is clear that those who study domestic violence are still struggling with definitional issues, methodological constraints and problems, and have yet to actually test the major theoretical assumptions and models that have been developed.

The study of family violence continues to be an interdisciplinary effort. Psychologists, sociologists, anthropologists, physicians, and social workers frequently share interests, questions, models, and authorship of research reports. In the future, we should expect to see continued efforts to study family violence cross-culturally. Korbin (1981) has already contributed to that effort and her work, and the work of others, is useful in challenging and informing some of the sociocultural assumptions that developed out of research on violence in the United States (Straus et al 1980). Research on family violence is examining violence in alternative families (e.g. stepfamilies). Research continues to be conducted by those interested in how professionals label and approach cases of domestic violence (e.g. Hampton & Newberger 1984). There is considerable interest in the topic of sexual abuse, and marital rape, but space limitations and definitional issues precluded reviewing that literature in this article. Researchers have recently begun to try to collect data directly from men who batter, rather than relying only on reports from the victims (e.g. Rouse 1984). There has also been an expansion of the study of violence between partners by those interested in courtship violence (e.g. Makepiece 1981, 1983; Cate et al 1982). Sociologists are contributing as well to study of the consequences of child maltreatment and are using survey data to complement clinical data on this topic.

The literature on family violence has expanded at a rapid pace over the last few years. Sociologists can be expected to continue to be part of this interdisciplinary effort, as theoreticians, methodologists, and as debunkers of conventional wisdom.

Literature Cited

Alfaro, J. 1977. *Report on the relationship between child abuse and neglect and later socially deviant behavior*. Presented at Exploring the Relationship Between Child Abuse and Delinquency Symposium, Seattle, Univ. Wash.

American Humane Association. 1982. *National Analysis of Official Child Neglect and Abuse Reporting*. Englewood, Colo: Am. Humane Assoc.

American Humane Association 1983. *Highlights of Official Child Neglect and Abuse Reporting*. Denver, Colo: Am. Humane Assoc.

Bakan, D. 1971. *Slaughter of the Innocents: A Study of the Battered Child Phenomenon*. Boston, Mass: Beacon

Bandura, A., Ross, D., Ross, S. 1961. Transmission of aggression through imitation of aggressive models. *J. Abnorm. Soc. Psychol.* 63:575–582

Berkeley Planning Associates. 1978. *Executive*

summary: Evaluation of the joint OCD/SRS national demonstration program in child abuse and neglect. Mimeographed

Berkowitz, L. 1962. Aggression: A Social Psychological Analysis. New York: McGraw-Hill

Block, M., Sinnott, J. 1979. The Battered Elder Syndrome: An Exploratory Study. Unpublished manuscript, Univ. Md.

Boudouris, J. 1971. Homicide and the family. J. Marriage Fam. 33:667–682

Bowker, L. H. 1983. Beating Wife-Beating. Lexington, Mass.: Lexington

Burgdorf, K. 1980. Recognition and Reporting of Child Maltreatment. Rockville, Md: Westat

Burgess, R. L. 1979. Family violence: Some implications from evolutionary biology. Presented at Ann. Meet. Amer. Soc. Criminology, Philadelphia, Penn.

Burgess, R. L., Garbarino, J. 1983. Doing what comes naturally? An evolutionary perspective on child abuse. In The Dark Side of the Family: Current Family Violence Research, ed. D. Finkelhor, R. Gelles, M. Straus, G. Hotaling, pp. 88–101. Beverly Hills, Calif: Sage

Byrd, D. E. 1979. Intersexual assault: A review of empirical findings. Ann. Meet. Eastern Sociological Society, New York.

Caffey, J. 1946. Multiple fractures in the long bones of infants suffering from chronic subdural hematoma. Am. J. Roentgenology, Radium Therapy, Nucl. Med. 58: 163–173

Caffey, J. 1957. Some traumatic lesions in growing bones other than fractures and dislocations. Br. J. Radiol. 23:225–238

Carr, A. 1977. Some preliminary findings on the association between child maltreatment and juvenile misconduct in eight New York counties. Report to Admin. for Children, Youth and Families, National Center on Child Abuse and Neglect. Kingston, RI

Cate, R. M., Henton, J. M., Christopher, F. S., Lloyd, S. 1982. Premarital abuse: A social psychological perspective. J. Fam. Iss. 3:79–90

Cornell, C. P., Gelles, R. J. 1982a. Adolescent to parent violence. Urban Soc. Change Rev. 15:8–14

Cornell, C. P., Gelles, R. J. 1982b. Elder abuse: The status of current knowledge. Fam. Rel. 31:457–465

Coser, L. A. 1967. Continuities in the Study of Social Conflict. New York: Free Press

Curtis, L. 1974. Criminal Violence: National Patterns and Behavior. Lexington, Mass: Lexington

De Mause, L. 1974. The History of Childhood. New York: Psychohistory Press

De Mause, L. 1975. Our forebearers made childhood a nightmare. Psychol. Today 8:85–87

Dobash, R. E., Dobash, R. 1979. Violence Against Wives. New York: Free

Dollard, J. C., Doob, L., Miller, N., Mowrer, O., Sears, R. 1939. Frustration and Aggression. New Haven, Conn: Yale Univ. Press

Egeland, B., Jacobvitz, L. 1984. Intergenerational continuity of parental abuse: Cause and consequence. Presented at Social Science Research Council Con. on Biosocial Perspectives on Child Abuse and Neglect, York, Me.

Erlanger, H. B. 1974. Social class and corporal punishment in childrearing: a reassessment. Am. Sociol. Rev. 39:68–85

Finkelhor, D., Hotaling, G. 1984. Sexual abuse in the national incidence study of child abuse and neglect: An appraisal. Child Abuse Neglect: Int. J. 8:23–33

Fontana, V. 1973. Somewhere a Child Is Crying: Maltreatment—Causes and Prevention. New York: MacMillan

Galdston, R. 1965. Observations of children who have been physically abused by their parents. Am. J. Psychiatry 122:440–443

Galdston, R. 1975. Preventing abuse of little children: the parent's center project for the study and prevention of child abuse. Am. J. Orthopsychiatry 45:372–381

Garbarino, J. 1977. The human ecology of child maltreatment. J. Marriage Fam. 39:721–735

Garbarino, J., Plantz, M. C. 1984. An ecological perspective on the outcomes of child maltreatment: What difference will the differences make? Presented at Social Science Research Council Conference on Biosocial Perspectives on Child Abuse and Neglect. York, Me.

Gelles, R. J. 1973. Child abuse as psychopathology: A sociological critique and reformulation. Am. J. Orthopsychiatry. 43:611–621

Gelles, R. J. 1974. The Violent Home: A Study of Physical Aggression Between Husbands and Wives. Beverly Hills, Calif: Sage

Gelles, R. J. 1975. The social construction of child abuse. Am. J. Orthopsychiatry 45:363–371

Gelles, R. J. 1976. Abused wives: Why do they stay? J. Marriage Fam. 38:659–668

Gelles, R. J. 1978. Violence towards children in the United States. Am. J. Orthopsychiatry 48:580–592

Gelles, R. J. 1980. Violence in the family: A review of research in the seventies. J. Marriage Fam. 42:873–885

Gelles, R. J. 1982. Applying research on family violence to clinical practice. J. Marriage Fam. 44:9–20

Gelles, R. J. 1983. An exchange/social control theory. In The Dark Side of the Family: Current Family Violence Research. ed. D. Finkelhor, R. Gelles, M. Straus, G. Hotaling, pp. 151–165. Beverly Hills, Calif: Sage

Gelles, R. J., Cornell, C. P. 1983. *International Perspectives on Family Violence*. Lexington, Mass: Lexington

Gelles, R. J., Straus, M. A. 1979. Determinants of violence in the family: Toward a theoretical integration. In *Contemporary Theories About the Family (Vol. 1)*. ed. W. R. Burr, R. Hill, F. I. Nye, I. L. Reiss, pp. 549–581. New York: Free

Gil, D. 1970. *Violence Against Children: Physical Child Abuse in the United States*. Cambridge, Mass: Harvard Univ. Press

Giles-Sims, J. 1983. *Wife-Beating: A Systems Theory Approach*. New York: Guilford

Gillen, J. 1946. *The Wisconsin Prisoner: Studies in Crimogenesis*. Madison, Wis: Univ. Wis. Press

Giovannoni, J. M., Becerra, R. M. 1979. *Defining Child Abuse*. New York: Free

Goode, W. 1971. Force and violence in the family. *J. Marriage Fam.* 33:624–636

Hampton, R., Newberger, E. 1984. *Child abuse incidence and reporting by hospitals: Significance of severity, class and race*. Presented at Second National Conference for Family Violence Researchers. Durham, NH

Harris, L., and associates. 1979. *A Survey of Spousal Abuse Against Women in Kentucky*. New York: Harris & Assoc.

Houghton, B. 1979. *Research of research on women abuse*. Presented at Ann. Meet. Am. Society of Criminology, Philadelphia, Penn.

Hrdy, S. B. 1979. Infanticide among animals: A review classification, and examination of the implications for reproductive strategies of females. *Ethol. Sociobiol.* 1:13–40

Jones, A. 1980. *Women Who Kill*. New York: Holt, Rinehart, & Winston

Kaplan, H. 1982. Toward a general theory of psychosocial deviance: The case of aggressive behavior. *Soc. Sci. Med.* 6:593–617

Kempe, C. H., Silverman, F. N., Steele, B. F., Droegemueller, W., Silver, H. K. 1962. The battered child syndrome. *J. Am. Med. Assoc.* 181:107–112

Korbin, J. 1981. *Child Abuse and Neglect: Cross-Cultural Perspectives*. Berkeley, Calif: Univ. Calif. Press

Korbin, J. 1984. *Child maltreatment and the cultural context: Current knowledge and future directions*. Presented to Social Science Research Council Conference on Child Abuse and Neglect. York, Me.

Levinger, G. 1966. Sources of marital dissatisfaction among applicants for divorce. *Am. J. Orthopsychiatry* 26:803–897

London, J. 1978. Images of violence against women. *Victimology* 2:510–524

Maden, Marc F., Wrench, D. F. 1977. Significant findings in child abuse research. *Victimology*. 2:196–224

Makepiece, J. M. 1981. Courtship violence among college students. *Fam. Rel.* 30:97–102

Makepiece, J. M. 1983. Life events stress and courtship violence. *Fam. Rel.* 32:101–109

Martin, D. 1976. *Battered Wives*. San Francisco, Calif: Glide

Martin, H. P. 1972. The child and his development. In *Helping the Battered Child and His Family*, ed. C. H. Kempe, R. E. Helfer, pp. 93–114. Philadelphia: Lippincott

Merton, R. K., Nisbet, R. 1976. *Contemporary Social Problems*. New York: Harcourt Brace Jovanovich

Miller, N. 1941. The frustration-aggression hypothesis. *Psychol. Rev.* 48:337–342

Milne, A. A. 1926. *Winnie-the-Pooh*. New York: Dell

Nelson, B. J. 1984. *Making an Issue of Child Abuse: Political Agenda Setting for Social Problems*. Chicago: Univ. Chicago Press

Newberger, E. et. al. 1977. Pediatric social illness: Toward an etiologic classification. *Pediatrics* 60:178–185

O'Brien, J. 1971. Violence in divorce prone families. *J. Marriage Fam.* 33:692–698

Pagelow, M. 1979. Research on woman battering. In *Stopping Wife Abuse*, ed. J. B. Fleming, pp. 334–349. New York: Anchor

Pagelow, M. 1981. *Woman-Battering: Victims and Their Experiences*. Beverly Hills, Calif: Sage

Palmer, S. 1962. *The Psychology of Murder*. New York: Crowell

Parke, R. D., Collmer, C. W. 1975. Child abuse: An interdisciplinary analysis. In *Review of Child Development Research*, Vol. 5, ed. M. Hetherington, pp. 1–102. Chicago: Univ. Chicago Press

Pediatric News. 1975. One child dies daily from abuse: Parent probably was abuser. *Pediatric News*, vol. 9:3

Pelton, L. G. 1979. Interpreting family violence data. *Am. J. Orthopsychiatry* 49:194

Pittman, D., Handy, W. 1964. Patterns in criminal aggravated assault. *J. Criminal Law Criminol.* 55:462–470

Pleck, E. J., Pleck, M., Grossman, M., Bart, P. 1978. The battered data syndrome: A comment on Steinmetz's article. *Victimology* 2:680–683

Pokorny, A. D. 1965. Human violence: A comparison of homicide, aggravated assault, suicide, and attempted suicide. *J. Crim. Law, Criminol.* 56:488–497

Radbill, S. 1980. A history of child abuse and infanticide. *The Battered Child*, ed. R. Helfer, C. Kempe, pp. 3–20. Chicago: Univ. Chicago Press

Rouse, L. 1984. *Conflict tactics used by men in marital disputes*. Presented at Second National Conference for Family Violence Researchers, Durham, NH

Schultz, L. G., 1960. The wife assaulter. *J. Soc. Therapy*. 6:103–111

Sherman, L. W., Berk, R. A. 1984. Deterrent

effects of arrest for domestic violence. *Am. Sociol. Rev.* 49:261–272

Shorter, E. 1975. *The Making of the Modern Family*. New York: Basic

Silverman, F. 1953. The roentgen manifestations of unrecognized skeletal trauma in infants. *Am. J Roentgenology, Radium Therapy, Nucl. Med.* 69:413–427

Singer, J. 1971. *The Control of Aggression and Violence*. New York: Academic

Smith, S., Hanson, R., Noble, S. 1973. Parents of battered babies: A controlled study. *Br. Med. J* 4:388–391

Snell, J. E., Rosenwald, R. J., Robey, A. 1964. The wifebeater's wife: A study of family interaction. *Archives Gen. Psychiatry* 11:107–113

Star, B. 1980. Patterns of family violence. *Soc. Casework* 61:339–346

Stark, R., McEvoy, J. 1970. Middle class violence. *Psychol. Today* 4:52–65

Steele, B. F., Pollock, C. 1974. A psychiatric study of parents who abuse infants and small children. In *The Battered Child* (2nd edition). ed. R. Helfer, C. Kempe, pp. 89–134. Chicago: Univ. Chicago Press

Steinmetz, S. K. 1971. Occupation and physical punishment: A response to Straus. *J. Marriage Fam.* 33:664–666

Steinmetz, S. K. 1977. *The Cycle of Violence: Assertive, Aggressive, and Abusive Family Interaction*. New York: Praeger

Steinmetz, S. K. 1978a. The battered husband syndrome. *Victimology* 2:499–509

Steinmetz, S. K. 1978b. Violence between family members. *Marriage Fam. Rev.* 1:1–16

Steinmetz, S. K. 1978c. Battered parents. *Society* 15:54–55

Steinmetz, S. K. 1984. Family violence towards elders. In *Violence Individuals and Families: A Handbook for Practitioners*, ed. S. Saunders, A. Anderson, C. Hart, G. Rubenstein, pp. 137–163. Springfield, Ill: Thomas.

Steinmetz, S. K., Straus, M. A. 1974. *Violence in the Family*. New York: Harper, Row.

Straus, M. A. 1971. Some social antecedents of physical punishment: A linkage theory interpretation. *J. Marriage Fam.* 33:658–663

Straus, M. A. 1973. A general systems theory approach to a theory of violence between family members. *Soc. Sci. Inf.* 12:105–125

Straus, M. A. 1974. Forward. In *The Violent Home: A Study of Physical Aggression Between Husbands and Wives*. R. J. Gelles, pp. 13–17. Beverly Hills, Calif: Sage

Straus, M. A., Gelles, R. J., Steinmetz, S. K. 1980. *Behind Closed Doors: Violence in the American Family*. Garden City, NY: Anchor/Doubleday

Strube, M. J., Barbour, L. S. 1983. The decision to leave an abusive relationship: Economic dependence and psychological commitment. *J. Marriage Fam.* 45:785–793

Taylor, L., Newberger, E. H., 1979. Child abuse in the International Year of the Child. *N. Engl. J. Med.* 301:1205–1212

Turbett, J. P., O'Toole, R. 1980. *Physician's recognition of child abuse*. Presented at Ann. Meet. of American Sociological Association, New York

US Department of Justice 1980. *Intimate Victims: A Study of Violence Among Friends and Relatives*. Washington, DC: USGPO

US Department of Justice 1984. *Family Violence*. Washington, DC: Bureau of Justice Statistics

United States Senate 1973. Hearing before the Subcommittee on Children and Youth of the Committee on Labor and Public Welfare. United States Senate, 93rd Congress First Session, on S.1191 Child Abuse Prevention Act. Washington, DC: USGPO

Walker, L. 1979. *The Battered Woman*. New York: Harper Row.

Wardell, L., Gillespie, D. L., Leffler, A. 1983. Science and violence against wives. In *The Dark Side of the Family: Current Family Violence Research*. ed. D. Finkelhor, R. Gelles, G. Hotaling, M. Straus, pp. 69–84. Beverly Hills, Calif: Sage

Wolfgang, M. 1958. *Patterns in Criminal Homicide*. New York: Wiley

Wolfgang, M., Ferracuti, F. 1967. *The Subculture of Violence*. London: Tavistock

Zigler, E. 1976. *Controlling child abuse in America: An effort doomed to failure*. Presented at First National Conference on Child Abuse and Neglect, Atlanta

Ann. Rev. Sociol. 1985. 11:369–87

SOCIAL THEORY AND TALCOTT PARSONS IN THE 1980s

David Sciulli

School of Government and Public Administration, American University, Washington, DC 20016

Dean Gerstein

Committee on Basic Research in the Behavioral and Social Sciences, National Research Council, Washington, DC 20418

Abstract

In recent years a revival has occurred in analytical and empirical studies related to the social theory of Talcott Parsons. The newer analytical work addresses the whole of Parsons' effort in the context of general questions that bear on all social theory. Especially important works by Bershady, Habermas, Münch, and Alexander establish a new baseline for future analytical assessments of the theory. Much of the empirical work focuses on specification and assessment of theoretical propositions, particularly concerning the more normative components of social systems, and on "general action complexes" that synthesize social, cultural, personality, and behavioral aspects of major phenomena in modern societies.

INTRODUCTION

For a number of years, the mark of sophistication on the subject of action theory has been to ask: "Who now reads Parsons?" (Bryant 1983). The old structure-functional schema with its cargo of concepts finally disappeared over the horizon, it seems, its sails filled by the critical blasts of many theorists such as Gouldner (1970) and Giddens (1968, 1976). Booklists and journals harbor vital discussion of hermeneutics, networks, rational expectations, and structuralism, while the abandoned theory of action glides unread toward its wreckage in the rocky straits between Introduction to Theory and The History of Social Thought.

369

0360-0572/85/0815-0369$02.00

In this idyll, the appearance of a Parsonian revival in the 1980s must rank as a major surprise to many in the discipline, catching unaware even one as accomplished at sounding theoretical tides as Mullins (1983). The year 1980 was a significant turning point. Shortly after Parsons' death in 1979, new critical readings of Parsons began to appear with increasing prominence, led by Münch (1981b, 1982a) and Alexander (1982a, b, 1983a, b). The distinctive mark of this new commentary and debate is an attempt to account for and derive theoretical insights from Parsons' entire fifty-year project rather than to focus narrowly on single works or isolated dimensions of Parsonian thought.

The decline of structure-functionalism was to a substantial degree self-inflicted. As initiated by Parsons and associates in *Toward a General Theory of Action* (Parsons & Shils 1951) and *The Social System* (Parsons 1951), structure-functionalism degraded much too readily from the supple framework of analytical concepts in *The Structure of Social Action* (Parsons 1937) into an "ideal type" approach that Parsons himself had attacked and laid the basis for transcending in that earlier work. This defect manifested itself in hardening of the categories: a tendency to convert sound theoretical insights into elaborate typologies and to treat ongoing empirical research mostly as a question of properly assigning events or structures to the "correct" categories.

In large part because Parsons strove toward logical completeness, his major works of the early 1950s were long on formal distinctions and short on interesting research findings. Parsons was unable to let these conceptual schemes rest, so that the immense effort of concentration and study demanded by the 1951 volumes was repaid by Parsons revising their most complex conceptual machinery following new theoretical "breakthroughs", e.g. Parsons' (1960) response to Dubin's (1960) analysis of the pattern-variable scheme. The potential for accumulation, parsimony, and clarity tended to vanish in these formal complexities; and with it vanished the possibility that most readers of *The Social System* (such as Mills 1959) might ever again willingly venture to read anything Parsons wrote.

The movement toward a more sophisticated analytical theory began in *Economy and Society* (Parsons & Smelser 1956) and continued over the next quarter of a century.[1] But many of the empirical researchers (e.g. Levy 1952, Apter 1965, Almond & Powell 1966)—and their readers—who took the categories in *The Social System* literally in good faith could credibly claim that Parsons had misled them with many implied propositions about empirical social life that turned out to be unsupportable. Having built his work into a

---

[1]Parsons revised or reversed key formulations of *The Social System* in a variety of later texts; for explicit examples, see Parsons 1961, pp. 331–2; 1969a, p. 395n; 1969b, p. 486n; 1971, pp. 383–5; 1978b, p. 367n. More subtle or less explicitly acknowledged departures from *The Social System* are pervasive (see, e.g., Parsons 1967, pp. 15, 28; 1970, pp. 844ff).

dominant influence on the discipline during the 1940s, Parsons in *The Social System* simply did not deliver the anticipated goods. By the time he recovered from the excesses of the middle period and regained the intellectual momentum of the earlier phase, enough devastating broadsides had landed against *The Social System* that virtually the whole sociological audience had lost any further interest in action theory.

In spite of the defects of the early 1950s, action theory overall—across Parsons' 50 years of publications—has a major strength which becomes clear when Parsons' overall project is compared with other major projects in theory-building: comprehensiveness on an analytical level. The appeal of Parsons in Germany today (exemplified by Münch 1982b and documented by Alexander 1984b) is largely due to his rigorous pursuit of a logically complete and integrated system of concepts that can mediate, accumulate, and transmit knowledge from every branch and sub-branch of the social and behavioral sciences as well as closely allied humanities and natural sciences.

The scope of his project—ranging from biology to theology—was in fact too comprehensive to permit him or any other individual theorist, even in 50 years, to personally invent every component it called for. But the framework was suggestive enough for him to recognize when theoretical work in specialized fields, even by those working completely outside the language of action theory, was moving in close approximation to the outlines of Parsons' thinking. On this basis he openly embraced, for example, the work of Freud, Keynes, Schumpeter, Alfred Emerson, James Olds, Ernst Mayr, Jean Piaget, Lon Fuller, Gunther Stent (as outlined in his autobiographical reflection, Parsons 1970; for some accounts of personal collaboration with Parsons, see Smelser 1981, Platt 1981, and Gerstein 1981a).

Through the 1950s, 1960s, and 1970s, Parsons was repeatedly called upon to defend and interpret his work—inevitably his old work—in the face of criticism. There were rumblings that this situation of dealing with Parsons' work piecemeal could not be expected to last but must give way to assessments based on all of Parsons' texts.[2] With Parsons' death in Munich in 1979, the opportu-

---

[2]See, for example, the treatments by Mitchell (1967), Gouldner (1970), Bershady (1973), Rocher (1975), Adriaansens (1976), Loubser et al (1976), Menzies (1977), Bourricaud (1977), and Alexander (1978).

In addition to the published texts, a large body of unpublished material still awaits analysis (V. M. Lidz, private communication); some of this unpublished corpus may be expected to appear over the next several years, particularly (*a*) a long essay written in 1940–41 entitled "Actor, situation, and normative pattern," which is intermediate between the theoretical formulations in Parsons (1937) and Parsons (1951); (*b*) a long empirical and theoretical analysis of social science as a national resource, written by Parsons in 1947 to influence the formation of the National Science Foundation (Klausner & Lidz, 1985); (*c*) the key chapters on American values from a book manuscript written with Winston White between 1958 to 1962, entitled *American Society;* and (*d*) Parsons' last book, in nearly final draft (800 ms pp) at his death, called *The American Societal Community.*

nity to evaluate action theory in terms of its texts alone, and independently of the direct influence of its principal architect, moved from possibility to necessity.

THE TURNING POINT: ACTION THEORY IN THE 1980s

Two events best symbolize the recent revival of interest in Parsons' theories: The *American Journal of Sociology*'s translation and publication of Münch's "Talcott Parsons and the Theory of Action," (1981b, 1982a; these are chapters one and two of Münch 1982b); and the publication of Alexander's four-volume *Theoretical Logic in Sociology* (1982a, 1982b, 1983a, 1983b). In retrospect, however, three important contributions helped to prepare the ground for these events: (*a*) Habermas's (1981a) critical commentary on Parsons at the 1980 meeting of the German Sociological Association, flanked by his discussion of Parsons in the second volume of *The Theory of Communicative Action* (Habermas 1981b), his comparison of Weber, Parsons, and Luhmann in *Legitimation Crisis* (1973) and his (1977) comparison of Parsons and Arendt; (*b*) Alexander's 1978 essay on formal and substantive voluntarism in the *American Sociological Review;* and especially (*c*) Bershady's (1973) masterful criticism, a clear advance beyond the preceding 25 years of debate on Parsons' work.

Bershady, Münch, and Alexander express sharp dissatisfaction with the quality of earlier commentaries. In fact, they find little of worth in the critiques of Parsons still most frequently cited in sociological journals, monographs, and especially textbooks. All four—Habermas included—attempt to account for Parsons' social theory overall, rather than limiting their critique to a particular phase or a particular set of concepts. Each of the four commentators, whatever his opinion on the ultimate merits of Parsons' social theory, raises penetrating questions that go beyond Parsons to address the enterprise of social theory as such. Alternative theories, such as those offered by Habermas, Luhmann, Gouldner, and Giddens, must face the same issues and questions, and the breadth of this new debate is precisely what is elevating the status of Parsons' work in the 1980s.

The contemporary revived interest in Parsons therefore represents a watershed, differing substantially from the debates surrounding his work from the 1950s to the mid-1970s. Nevertheless, the earlier, piecemeal debates form a considerable literature, and we expect that sociologists unfamiliar with Alexander, Münch, Bershady, and Habermas, or unwilling to address Parsons' work in methodical fashion, will fall back on these older arguments out of convenience: conflict vs consensus theory (Lockwood 1956, Dahrendorf 1959, Giddens 1968); distortion of the classics (Cohen, Hazelrigg & Pope 1975, Giddens 1976); conservative or status quo ideological bias (Hacker 1961, Gouldner 1970); functionalism as an oversocialized or collectivized conception of man (Wrong 1961, Homans 1964); functionalism's unacceptable teleology (e.g. Black 1961; but see the counter arguments of Piccone 1968 and Wright

1983); or the reductionist sociology of knowledge focusing on Parsons' family background, position at Harvard during the Depression, and American or WASP ethnocentrism (e.g. Gouldner 1970). This literature defines the conventional wisdom of the discipline and has unfortunately been repeated endlessly in sociology survey texts.

Against this received wisdom, the Münch translation was eventful because it dramatically illustrated to American sociologists that regardless of the waning influence of Parsons in the US (and the conventional American attacks are well known in Germany), action theory, when subjected to close reading, is being found to suffer from fewer manifest self-contradictions or unsupportable assumptions than do Parsons' classical or contemporary alternatives. For all the legitimate questions that can be raised about Parsons' works—and we see no reason why these should be dismissed or ignored—Parsons' social theory has attracted commentary because it offers the possibility of standing up better in the face of rigorous questioning than Marx's, Weber's, or Durkheim's social theories, or the alternatives offered by neo-Marxism, the first generation of the Frankfurt school, or contemporaries like Giddens and Collins.

Alexander's four volumes were significant because they recast fundamental questions of social theory construction that Parsons had posed and then turned those same questions to Parsons' works themselves. Initial critical reviews of Alexander have not stopped to consider that any work in social theory is as important for the avenues of theory construction that it closes off, or prevents from being unreflectively pursued, as for the new avenues it immediately establishes. Alexander successfully forecloses both the casual adoption of ideal-type approaches and the possibility that Parsons' future critics, exegetes, or followers can legitimately return to the earlier literature or earlier ways of bringing Parsons' theories to empirical research. Any commentator attempting to return cannot escape dealing first and systematically with Alexander's *Theoretical Logic* (1982a, 1982b, 1983a, 1983b). In our view, Alexander's conclusion, that Parsons' social theory succumbs ultimately to idealistic determinism, is somewhat over-stated. Nevertheless, we consider *Theoretical Logic in Sociology* the most challenging single contribution to the enterprise of social theory by an American author since Parsons' *The Structure of Social Action* (1937) and Merton's *Social Theory and Structure* (1957).

The frameworks for reading Parsons that have been proposed by Alexander, Münch, Habermas, and Bershady differ markedly from each other, as will become clear below. This suggests that the interpretation of Parsons' work as a whole has only begun to be established. It also suggests a major reason why fruitful uses of Parsons' social theory in detailed empirical research have to date been greatly delayed. This needs to be put bluntly: The discipline of American sociology is only today beginning to understand the project of the most methodical and comprehensive American theorist. The pointed critiques of Parsons made by Bershady (1973) and Habermas (1973, 1977, 1981a) moved the debate beyond its earlier limits by explicating specific standards against which any social theory must be evaluated and applying these standards to Parsons.

Bershady (1973) persistently raised the charge against Parsons of overgenerality: Parsons' analytical framework of concepts may well overarch all individual societies and therefore escape the empirical relativism of ideal-type approaches to social theory, but Parsons' framework "cannot reproduce the features of any single society." Given this problem of separation between theory and empirical specificity, Bershady moved to a more fundamental issue: By what standard should we, or can we, evaluate the merits of Parsons' social theory relative to competing concepts and categories? Bershady insisted that it is meaningless to criticize Parsons' social theory for being "inherently conservative" or incorporating a narrow vision of human creativity or freedom. Bershady notes that Parsons' intention was to distinguish human social action from nonhuman behavior as such, just as Chomsky's (1965) syntactics was intended to distinguish grammatical sentence construction. Each theorist provides a fundamental intersubjective framework that allows and requires human creativity, providing both participants and observers with the possibility of recognizing and understanding in common what human creativity is. Bershady sees Parsons and Chomsky as employing the Kantian approach of basing their theories on the irreducible components of social interaction. This is why Bershady says that Parsons' social theory is "an epistemology of intersubjectivity" and not an epistemology of causality. Bershady's thesis is that we can therefore only criticize Parsons' social theory by showing *either* that his analytical framework is not generalizable and comprehensive (but, rather, succumbs to the relativism of time and place, and/or fails to present methodically all possible analytical components of any possible social action), *or* that Parsons' analytical framework cannot overcome its over-generality so as to inform empirical research or normative debate, i.e. "that Parsons' rules are too meager or faulty to comprehend historical diversity and possible future social worlds, adequately specified."

Turning to Parsons' functionalism to illustrate this problem of overgenerality, Bershady says that Parsons' AGIL schema, the four functional subsystems of adaptation, goal-attainment, integration, and latent pattern maintenance, can only inform empirical research if all four sets of symbolic media of social interchange (in order: money, power, influence, and value commitments) "are perfectly understood." However, the media of influence and value commitments in particular "are conceptually unclear at the macroscopic range, and this vagueness is not merely an imperfect fit between system problems and institutions." For Bershady, Parsons' definitions of the media are ambiguous, the definitions of the boundaries of the functional subsystems are not sharp enough to precisely differentiate functions from dysfunctions, and the interchanges between subsystems are too vague to account in any specific empirical instance for the proposition that I and L are "higher" than A and G rather than vice versa.

Bershady's critique still poses the most fundamental and important challenge to the revitalization of Parsons' social theory. Bershady views the challenge as unanswered by Parsons, though not, in principle, unanswerable by those using Parsons' theoretical framework.

Although not referring directly to Bershady, Habermas (1981b) in essence brings out the implications of the charge of overgenerality. Unlike Bershady, however, he insists that overgenerality is an inherent and irremediable characteristic of Parsons' theory, so that it cannot inform either empirical research or social practice, no matter how it is employed or reworked. Habermas argues that Parsons' early concept of voluntarism is based on "isolated individuals," so that social order for Parsons is a matter of the pure contingency of individual decisionmaking within some larger framework of social values and norms. According to Habermas, as Parsons' theory construction evolved into the 1960s and 1970s, this autonomous individual-based contingency was smothered by "systems theory": extra-individual functional imperatives not only overcome the resistance of recalcitrant individuals but undermine the integrity of any and all resistant cultural patterns. Habermas refers to Menzies (1977) and uses Lockwood's (1956) early distinction between "system integration" and "social integration" to document his reading of Parsons as a systems theorist.

Having read Parsons in this way, Habermas raises three very specific, interrelated challenges to any analyst of advanced societies, but especially to "Parsons' students." Neither Münch nor Alexander nor any other Parsons commentator has directly responded to Habermas' three challenges. In our view, any theorist, Parsonian or otherwise, seeking to demonstrate the potential empirical richness and specificity of a theoretical framework must respond.

First, the challenge of grounding reasoned protection of cultural integrity against the corrosive effects of money and power: Habermas asks whether a theory can identify any barriers strictly within the realm of social values and norms that can resist changes induced by the instrumental adaptation of social systems that characterizes late capitalism. Habermas' thesis is that Parsons' theoretical framework lacks the concepts to explain why any distinctive cultural patterns might be resilient in the face of functional systemic imperatives of "capitalistically rationalized" modernization.

Second, the challenge of a grounded criticism of modernity: Habermas says that "Parsons cannot discern the costs or pathologies of modernization" (e.g. urban decay, the overbureaucratization and thus intellectual impoverishment of higher education) as could Marx, Weber, and Durkheim. For Habermas, misdirected systemic complexity (or misdirected functional differentiation) can be detected only through its pathological effects at the *Lebenswelt* or life-world level, the interpersonal and everyday meanings and experiences of actors. Because Habermas sees Parsons analyzing systemic and functional change with the same categories he uses to analyze instrumental rationalization in the actors' life-worlds, Habermas says that Parsons has no conceptual basis for criticizing modern social change. For Habermas this explains why Parsons' work conveys a sense of harmony rather than a sense of pathos about modern social life.

Third, the challenge of a grounded basis for reasoned, practical reforms: Habermas acknowledges that some of Parsons' students—particularly Rainer Baum (1976b)—attempt to respond to the difficulties in Parsons' work by treating manifest pathologies of modernization as the underdevelopment of the "higher" symbolic media of social interchange, that is, influence and value-commitments. This underdevelopment leads to the "misuse" of the lower-level media of money and power by participants in decisionmaking. However, Habermas counters that the theory of symbolic media of interchange can only be used critically, to locate or reform such pathologies, if "one can assign direct normative significance to well-defined equilibria." He adds: "Whoever starts on this road should not hesitate to take up the task of constructing a theory of value implementation or value realization that can be normatively understood from the perspective of the participants." (Habermas 1981a). It is the participants, after all, who must implement or realize values by acting in concert, and the social theory must account for how they can come to a common recognition and understanding of the problem and then agree on, initiate, and maintain reform. Habermas is "highly doubtful that the normative implications of such an endeavor could be compatible with the character of Parsons' theory" (Habermas: 1981a:195).

Münch (1981b, 1982a) is less interested in the practical ends or empirical uses of action theory than in the integrity or rigor of Parsons' philosophical foundations, a task presented by the German debate in sociology; he therefore does Bershady's or Habermas's challenges. Münch, like Habermas, was trained as a philosopher, and again like Habermas, came to a reading of Parsons through a reading of Luhmann's (1976, 1981) structural or systems theory. Münch's thesis is that "a Kantian core" informs all of Parsons' works as a deep structure, regardless of Parsons' own surface- or self-understanding of his social theory. Thus, Münch does not see Parsons' theory becoming skewed into a one-sided systems theory but, rather, sees it as recapitulating the logical form of Kant's *Critique of Pure Reason* and Kant's epistemological and substantive dualisms, e.g. fact/value, objective/subjective, theory/practical experience. For Münch, Parsons' general action theory and theory of the social system are "exactly parallel, in structure and method, to Kant's critical philosophy," and *"The Structure of Social Action* must be read as the sociological equivalent of Kant's moral philosophy."

Parsons' Kantian dualism is best illustrated, according to Münch, by the relationship between institutionalization of norms at the societal level and internalization of norms at the personality level. For Münch, each process for Parsons transcends the dichotomy of external coercion vs individual calculation of utility; it represents the "interpenetration" of the conditional and the normative. Münch sees Parsons employing the Kantian dualisms and transcending them through "the theorem of interpenetration" by posing and answering the following question: "Given that social order exists, what conditions constitute the framework within which social action necessarily takes place"? Münch says that Parsons' answer is that there must be "a limit on [actors'] arbitrariness of action *determined solely by subjective considerations*" (emphasis in original).

For Kant, subjective choices can only be limited either by moral standards or by calculation of self-interest (in Kantian terms, categorical vs hypothetical principles). Only the first kind of principle "can produce a consistency of choice of actions and, therefore, can account for social order." What Parsons calls a norm, Münch tells us, is a categorical rule in Kant's sense, which must be held valid for all actors rather than merely being based on expectations of (hypothetical) profit or loss. Thus, Münch says, "the paramount question for [any] sociological theory is how is this categorical obligation possible?" For Münch, the key is "interpenetration" which "replaces the old doctrine of differentiation." The interpenetration of each side of the dualism by the other side "elevates the tension" inherent in the dualism "so that unity [social order] can be maintained."

This emphasis on the interpenetration of rational calculation and subjectively acceptable moral limits on self-interestedness provides Münch with the basis to make several assertions regarding Parsons' project: First, not only Parsons but all the classic sociologists came eventually to the theorem of interpenetration to overcome dualism, but "nowhere else in sociology has this basic idea been elaborated as lucidly as in the writings of Parsons." Second, Parsons' Kantian approach has more in common methodologically with common law adjudication, which applies precedents but holds out the possibility of reversals or challenges by local level action, than with "the scientific method" of deduction and causality. Third, Parsons (1937) defined voluntarism as the irreducible free will or freedom of the individual in a two-term framework (goal-rational or instrumental action vs categorical-normative obligation), but beginning in 1951 this "was replaced" by the three-term schema (cultural, social, personality systems, subsequently adding the behavioral system) and "the analysis explicitly revolves around their interpenetration" to explain both social action and social order. Finally, because Münch emphasizes the interpenetration of internalization and institutionalization, he contends that the integrative or societal community subsystem in Parsons' later writings was really "the highest level of control", standing above the latent pattern-maintenance subsystem rather than below it, as Parsons maintained. For Münch, the latter provides too little control over the options of calculating, self-interested actors, whereas the integrative subsystem is the locus of obligations that are both "self-evident" (i.e. internalized and institutionalized) and "imposed" (by the same processes). These subjectively accepted duties control actors' options and thus establish and maintain social order.

Alexander's treatment of Parsons is the longest and most detailed yet to appear. Following a generalized introduction to "theoretical logic" (Alexander 1982a), he discusses four major social theorists—Marx and Durkheim in volume two (Alexander 1982b), Weber in volume three (Alexander 1983a), and Parsons in volume four (1983b)—within an overall exploration of *conflation* (or *conflationary error*) and *multidimensionality* in social theory. Conflationary error involves the collapse of essential analytical distinctions between theoretical levels, particularly the levels of general presuppositions, ideological orientations, empirical propositions, and methodological assumptions. Multidimensionality means the consistently wellbalanced treatment, mainly at the general presuppositional level, of ideal and empirical factors in social life.

For each author, Alexander first presents the strands of multidimensionality in the relevant works. Then he locates where and why each theorist succumbed to a specific type of conflationary error, reifying or overrelying on one or another level of theory construction, and as a result tilted the balance of his theory irretrievably toward either ideal or material factors. In short, Alexander offers the following standard against which any theorist's works may be evaluated: The work must escape conflation and must maintain a multidimensional approach to the study of society, particularly in regard to the two "decisive questions" at the presuppositional level: how are social *action* and social *order* possible? Alexander adopts Parsons' early criterion for the ultimate success of analytical or methodical social theory: ecumenicism, or success in providing a framework of concepts that can render social science knowledge cumulative by making research findings mutually understandable across disciplines, research interests, and levels of analysis.

In the first half of volume four, Alexander argues that Parsons' analytical AGIL interchange model and social change theory marked a clear advance beyond the three classical sociologists in the development of multidimensional social theory. Parsons did not give "epistemological priority" to social norms and values, did not in this sense overemphasize cultural or ideal factors, but rather exposed their interrelationships with material factors and utilitarian calculations of cost and benefit. Nevertheless, the second half of Alexander's volume four builds the case that "Parsons overlays his multidimensional analysis with a reductionistic and highly damaging form of sociological idealism" (Alexander 1983b, p. 152).

In Alexander's view, Parsons' theory, like those of Marx, Weber, and Durkheim, suffers fundamentally from "central equivocations in the theory itself." As a result, Parsons, like his predecessors, was ultimately unable to "resist any presuppositional bias, to maintain an objective, multidimensional orientation . . ." (Alexander 1983b, p. 151). Parsons increasingly attempted to generate action theory strictly by deduction from first principles, thereby reifying his theory and turning it into an arid formalism. Even though Parsons' analytical framework of concepts is epistemologically sophisticated, anticipating the work of Thomas Kuhn and contemporary postpositivist philosophy of science, Alexander sees Parsons as having a commitment to empiricist principles regarding the status of "facts", a commitment he never consistently reconciled with his analytical sophistication. "He believes that his analytic discoveries are, in fact, concrete" (Alexander 1983b, p. 153). Thus Parsons could never overcome his "ambivalence about the relationship between theory and fact" (p. 153). Parsons ultimately held "a positivist faith in the conjunction of theory and fact," not a Kantian view that facts are inherently formed and given pattern by categories. Parsons' "neopositivist formalism" can be found "in every piece of his later work, in every book, every essay, every discussion that utilizes interchange to engage in more specific empirical argumentation" (p. 162). By the 1960s, "each of the interchange model's key terms [. . . is . . .] presented as if it were derived from some inherent logic of systems rather than from Parsons's efforts to model his analytic synthesis of instrumental and normative order" (p. 171).

Alexander's second charge is that Parsons conflates the problems of action and order. According to Alexander, Parsons treats rational action as inherently individualistic, that is, based on actors' narrow calculation of material self-interest. Therefore, collective order is necessarily the product of "supra-individual external force" that is normative rather than instrumental. "Parsons repeatedly defines normative order as the preferable—if not the only—reference point for collectivist theorizing" (Alexander 1983b, p. 218). The possibility that collective order may be based on instrumental calculation is eliminated as a collective or an empirical possibility. "Collective instrumental order becomes a residual category: it is no longer among the central axioms of Parsons' theoretical logic" (Alexander 1983b, p. 214).

NEW DEVELOPMENTS IN ACTION THEORY

Bershady and Habermas concur that the major targets of opportunity for empirical research and theoretical specification in action theory are the "higher order" social media, influence, and value-commitments, and their bases in the societal community and fiduciary subsystems. Probably the most exciting recent efforts by action theorists have focused precisely on these areas. Alongside this process of empirical and analytical specification, the effort to establish a broadly accepted understanding of Parsons' project can be expected to continue because the readings of Parsons offered by Alexander, Münch, Habermas, and Bershady differ in fundamental respects.

Luhmann (1976, 1981) has played a major role in these efforts, as recently outlined by Alexander (1984b). Each of the German social theorists, including Habermas and Münch (and one may add Rainer Baum), who reads Parsons does so through the eyes or under the influence of the theories of Luhmann, who has emphasized the problem of action in terms of contingency, uncertainty, risk, and complexity. He identifies structures, rather than functions, as being primary in accounting for order in social systems. The generalized media, in his view, are specialized mechanisms or ways of managing the expansion and reduction of complexity and contingency. Luhmann also replaces the Parsonian media of influence and commitment with rather differently conceived media of love and trust, opening here as elsewhere rich veins of theoretical discussion that have stimulated many action theorists (e.g. Loubser 1976, Baum 1976a, 1976b, Münch 1981a, 1982b).

Research being undertaken by many action theorists now reflects the need to specify empirically the most important analytical components of the societal community and fiduciary system as these interact with other social structures. Alexander (1980) theorizes that multiethnic societies (whether in the West or the Third World) revolve around a "core group" bearing ascriptive qualities and common internalized substantive beliefs, and that this core presents an insuperable barrier even to successfully assimilated "outside" groups, who can not feel subjectively as comfortable with their place in society as the core group does. Alexander (1984a) is also carrying out a study of the symbolic and affective implications of the Watergate crisis. Münch (private communication) has just completed a two-volume study on the substantive belief systems of four advanced Western societies: Germany, France, Britain and the United States. Lidz (1979a, 1985) has begun publishing works from a study of cultural secularization and socio-political change in the United States in the twentieth century. Colomy (1985) analyzes the uneven rates at which mass-based political parties developed (differentiated) from older patterns of deference and class relations in antebellum American states. Gould (private communication) has applied macroanalytic methods that he earlier (Gould 1976) adapted from Keynesian theory to the English revolution. Wallace (1985) explores the differences between Parsons' and Luhman's approach to religion and pattern-maintenance, focusing on Parsons' greater openness to the implications of religious pluralism.

Baum (1976b, 1981), Baum & Lechner (1981), and Lechner (1985) grapple with the most radical and pathological vehicle of the discontents of modernity: fascism, and particularly German National Socialism. Their approach is to undertake detailed historical studies of the Nazi period with a strong theory on the "loss of societal steering mechanisms" mediated especially by elites; their aim is to elaborate a general theory of fascist movements that will have predictive and explanatory utility and be able to address normative questions of a sort that are highly pertinent in the aftermath of National Socialism and the Holocaust in modern Germany (Baum 1978). Moral authority and influence based on various solidarities, cultural value-patterns, and legal norms may restrain the modern state from its enormous potential for external and internal barbarism. But historically observable conditions that foster fundamentalist attempts to revitalize a dedifferentiated "core" value-pattern and a national ethnic identity clearly permit alignments of state power and bureaucratic efficiency that override commitments to moral decency.

Another line of work here involves value implementation in science. Loubser (1976) used evolutionary AGIL concepts to study the history of American social sciences and the alternations between emphasis on external (general societal) and internal (scientific-cognitive) value-commitments—a dimensional variation sometimes reified in the ideal types of value-relevance vs "value-freedom." Mayhew (1976) locates this dimension as an enduring functional tension within a broader set of such tensions that are inherent in the methodology of social science precisely because congruent tensions are "inherent in the nature of social life itself." Lidz (1981) provides a cogent framework for identifying the methodological and substantive significance of the approaches to the problem of value-relevance taken by Parsons, Weber, Simmel, and Dilthey.

One of the present authors, Sciulli (1984, 1985, 1986), proposes that Parsons increasingly accounted for both action and order in modern societies by turning to procedural norms, collegial forms of organization, and symbolic media of interchange, which orient collective action in the face of the great pluralism of actors' beliefs and motivations. Parsons, in short, purposely and consistently separated "normative motivations," that are internalized substantive beliefs, from "normative orientations," that at least in part involve what Parsons called procedural institutions. Sciulli (1985, 1986) sees Parsons' (1978a) appropriation of Lon Fuller's (1964, 1969) principles of "procedural legality" as central to understanding Parsons' social theory. On the basis of this procedural turn, Sciulli specifies the institutions that must be present in modern society if arbitrary political and/or socioeconomic power is to be restrained, a complex he calls "societal constitutionalism." Sciulli (1985) thereby poses a challenge to Habermas's students, contending that Habermas cannot possibly bring his own procedural communication theory to political practice, above the level of serial interpersonal relations, unless he links his theory to societal constitutionalism or an equivalent.

A second broad line of Parsonian action theory is at the general action level, which treats the social system on an analytical par with personality, culture, and behavioral systems. The accusations that the individual in action theory tends to be "oversocialized" and a "cultural dope" derived in large part from Parsons' difficulties in separating cognitive processes from biological ones and thereby in creating a firm theoretical foundation for individual cognitive autonomy (Warner 1978). Parsons' original concept of the "behavioral organism" (Parsons & Shils 1951) was the least well bounded or defined of the four general action systems, covering an extensive range of biological organizing processes. The organic part of the connection, the heritage of genetic endowment, could not be effectively integrated with the symbolic character of personality, social systems, and cultural systems, and left insufficient room for a concept of individual schemes and/or processes of independent thought or rationality. The problem of finding a nonreductionist accommodation between society and biology is by no means restricted to action theory but is a very broad issue.

This problem came under forceful assault by Lidz & Lidz (1976), leading to a complete reformulation that Parsons accepted (1978b). Instead of a behavioral organism, they present a fully developed "behavioral system" whose content is as symbolic as the personality, but in a fundamentally cognitive vein. The rechristened "behavioral system" operates much in the mold of Piaget's concepts of cognitive structures and operations, though without commitment to Piaget's rigid developmental states. Behavioral processes generate intelligence as a broad resource for social, cultural, and personal action, while structures of perceptual, interpretive, expectational, and formal-categorical knowledge— the AGIL of the behavioral system—constitute intelligent action.

A second innovation in general action theory was to develop relatively middle-range theories of general action "complexes" in empirical case analysis, as suggested by the "cognitive complex" developed in the analysis of the American university by Parsons & Platt (1973). Lidz (1979b) has suggested a "moral matrix" in the analysis of law. An example that has had extended empirical investigation is the "addiction complex", a construct that involves all four general action systems, and builds especially on the Durkheimian aspects of action theory. Walker & Lidz (Gould et al 1974, Lidz & Walker 1978, 1980, Walker & Lidz 1983) develop a comprehensive description and explanation of the manner in which the ideology and politics of the "drug abuse crisis" at the national, state, and local levels, including the microdynamic action of clinical and street life, arose as a systematic working through of a fundamental conflict of moral schemas: instrumental activism vs expressive passivism, in the sharpest formulation. This problem has also been addressed by one of the present authors: Attewell & Gerstein (1979) analyze the effects of ideological and moral conflict on the formation and implementation of methadone maintenance policies; Parsons & Gerstein (1977) explore the theoretical congruence between addiction to heroin and addiction to power; and Gerstein specifies the major social (1976) and cultural (1981b) components of the heroin complex and integrates these within a broader Durkheimian reinterpretation of the general action scheme (1983, 1986).

A final general action reformulation that has come about in the recent period is to emphasize the centrality of language and linguistic processes for meaningful action. Lidz (1976) outlined the idea that the elementary structure of social action was fundamentally congruent to the elementary structure of syntax, and that the composition of complex social structure was continuous with the problem of composing and decoding meaningful sentences. Edelson (1976) and Turner (1976) carried out the most elaborate expressions of the "linguistic drift" in action theory. Edelson applied a notion derived from generative-transformational linguistics to the personality system, relying especially on the notion that the relations between deep structure and surface structure in the analysis of speech can be applied to the relation between wishes and dreams in psychoanalysis. Turner developed a case that familial units express in socialization the deep structure of intergenerational kinship. Hayes (1981) has criticized both these efforts for insufficient rigor in using linguistic concepts, though he calls for continued exploration of the semiotics of specialized media languages, a perspective that seems increasingly appropriate to the nature of analytical action systems.

CONCLUSION

The book on Talcott Parsons has been reopened in the 1980s, and it is not possible to predict where this may lead. The major characteristic of the new work is its explicit attention to the full range of Parsons' published works in contrast to the piecemeal analyses that characterized earlier criticism. Bershady, Habermas, Münch, and Alexander provide an interpretive opening to explore the longer term merits of Parsons' social theory—but only an opening.

Bershady and Habermas concur that Parsons' theory has been overgeneral, and they elaborate specific problems that must be faced in any effort to bring theory—whether Parsonian, neo-Marxian, or any other kind—to bear on empirical problems. Habermas and Bershady disagree about whether Parsons' framework is inherently insufficient to examine the restraints and possibilities of modern societies. In our view, analyses framed entirely within Parsons' theory can be addressed with great specificity to each of Habermas's three questions—questions which strike us as fair, judicious, and central in importance. We concede, with Habermas, that neither Parsons nor his students—nor the students of any theoretical tradition—have as yet given satisfactory responses to these questions.

Münch's elaboration and development of Bershady's insights into the neo-Kantian foundations of Parsons' theory is an important contribution. But a caution must be observed in reading Parsons through the lens of Luhmann and continental, especially German, traditions of social philosophy. As important as the German tradition is for Parsons, his work has also absorbed and been shaped throughout by traditional Anglo-American concerns with pragmatic and procedural restraints on arbitrary power. These concerns are not easily grasped within a strictly Kantian—or, for that matter, Hegelian—interpretation.

Alexander has made a thorough, long overdue, assessment of Parsons' distinctive combination of analytic strength, methodological complexity, and rejection of materialist reduction. At the same time, we are not persuaded that Alexander's case for the presence of strongly neopositivistic and idealistic strands is substantiated by Parsons' work. Alexander's logic is strongly propelled by assertions that Parsons conflated analytic distinctions with concrete observations. We think that Parsons' concepts must, as a rule, be read as analytic except when he explicitly said otherwise. Alexander departs often from this rule, and these departures are the main base on which his case for Parsons' methodological neopositivism and presuppositional idealism are constructed.

The significance of the interpretive analysis of Parsons' work is twofold. In Europe, and particularly in Germany, the rigor and breadth of Parsons' analytical framework, and consequently its value for considering the existential and philosophical problems of modernity, are sufficient to sustain interest in Parsonian theory. But the major indicator for the future acceptance of Parsons' theory in American sociology will be the quality and quantity of empirical work inspired by it. The citations here represent a reopening in this empirical direction following a period of quiescence—but only an opening.

Literature Cited

Adriaansens, H. P. M. 1976. Transl. 1980. *Talcott Parsons and the Conceptual Dilemma*. London: Routledge, 1980

Alexander, J. C. 1978. Formal and substantive voluntarism. *Am. Sociol. Rev.* 43:177–98

Alexander, J. C. 1980. Core solidarity, ethnic outgroup, and social differentiation: A multidimensional model of inclusion in modern societies. In *National and Ethnic Movements*, ed. J. Dofny, A. Akiwowo, pp. 5–28. Beverly Hills: Sage

Alexander, J. C. 1981. The mass news media in systemic, historical, and comparative perspective. In *Mass Media and Social Change*, ed. E. Katz and T. Szecsko, pp. 17–52. Beverly Hills: Sage

Alexander, J. C. 1982a. *Theoretical Logic in Sociology, Volume 1, Positivism, Presuppositions, And Current Controversies*. Berkeley: Univ. of Calif. 234 pp.

Alexander, J. C. 1982b. *Theoretical Logic in Sociology, Volume 2, The Antinomies Of Classical Thought: Marx and Durkheim*. Berkeley: Univ. of Calif. 564 pp.

Alexander, J. C. 1983a. *Theoretical Logic in Sociology, Volume 3, The Classical Attempt At Theoretical Synthesis: Max Weber*. Berkeley: Univ. of Calif. 240 pp.

Alexander, J. C. 1983b. *Theoretical Logic in Sociology, Volume 4, The Modern Reconstruction of Classical Thought: Talcott Parsons*. Berkeley: Univ. of Calif. 544 pp.

Alexander, J. C. 1984a. Watergate and the crisis of civil society. In *Sociological Theory 1984*, ed. R. Collins, pp. 290–314. San Francisco: Jossey-Bass

Alexander, J. C. 1984b. The Parsons revival in Germany. In *Sociological Theory 1984*, ed. R. Collins, pp. 394–412. San Francisco: Jossey-Bass

Almond, G. A., Powell, G. B. 1966. *Comparative Politics: A Developmental Approach*. Boston: Little, Brown

Apter, D. E. 1965. *The Politics of Modernization*. Chicago: Univ. of Chicago. 481 pp.

Attewell, P., Gerstein, D. 1979. Government policy and local practice: the case of methodone maintenance. *Am. Sociol. Rev.* 44: 311–327

Baum, R. C. 1976a. Communication and media. See Loubser et al 1976, pp. 533–556

Baum, R. C. 1976b. On societal media dynamics. See Loubser et al 1976, pp. 579–608

Baum, R. C. 1978. The Holocaust—anomic Hobbesian "state of nature". *Zeitschrift für Soziologie* 7:303–26

Baum, R. C. 1981. *The Holocaust and the German Elite: Genocide and National Suicide in Germany, 1871–1945.* Totowa, NJ: Rowman & Littlefield. 374 pp.

Baum, R. C., Lechner, F. J. 1981. National Socialism: Towards an actional-theoretical interpretation. *Sociol. Inq.* 51:281–308

Bershady, H. J. 1973. *Ideology and Social Knowledge.* New York: Wiley

Bourricaud, F. 1977. (tr. 1981) *The Sociology of Talcott Parsons.* Chicago: Univ. of Chicago. 326 pp.

Black, M. 1961. Some questions about Parsons' theories. In *The Social Theories of Talcott Parsons,* ed. M. Black, pp. 268–88. Carbondale: Southern Ill. Univ. Press

Bryant, C. G. A. 1983. Review article: Who now reads Parsons? *Sociol. Rev.* 31:337–49

Chomsky, N. 1965. *Aspects of the Theory of Syntax.* Cambridge: M.I.T. Press

Cohen J., Hazelrigg L. D., Pope W. 1975. De-Parsonizing Weber: A critique of Parsons' interpretation of Weber's sociology. *Am. Sociol. Rev.* 40:229–41

Colomy, P. 1985. Uneven differentiation: Towards comparative theory. In *NeoFunctionalism,* ed. J. Alexander. Beverly Hills: Sage. In press

Dahrendorf, R. 1959. *Class and Class Conflict in Industrial Society* Stanford: Stanford Univ. Press. 336 pp.

Dubin, R. 1960. Parsons' actors: Continuities on social theory. *Am. Sociol. Rev.* 25:457–66

Edelson, M. 1976. Toward a study of interpretation in psychoanalysis. See Loubser et al 1976, pp. 151–181

Fuller, L. L. 1964. *The Morality of Law.* New Haven: Yale Univ. Press

Fuller, L. L. 1969. *Anatomy of the Law.* New York: Praeger

Gerstein, D. R. 1975. A note on the continuity of Parsonian action theory. *Sociol. Inq.* 45(4):11–15

Gerstein, D. R. 1976. The structure of heroin communities (in relation to methodone maintenance). *Am. J. Drug Alcohol Abuse* 3:571–87

Gerstein, D. R. 1981a. A reminiscence of Talcott Parsons, September 1970 to April 1979. *Sociol. Inq.* 51:166–70

Gerstein, D. R. 1981b. Cultural action and heroin addiction. *Sociol. Inq.* 51:355–70

Gerstein, D. R. 1983. Durkheim's paradigm: Reconstructing a social theory. In *Sociological Theory 1983,* ed. R. Collins, pp. 234–258. San Francisco: Jossey-Bass

Gerstein, D. R. 1986. A theory of the addiction complex. In *Micro and Macro Levels in Sociological Theory,* ed. J. C. Alexander, H. Haferkamp, R. Münch, N. J. Smelser. Berkeley: Univ. of Calif. Press. In press

Giddens, A. 1968. "Power" in the recent writings of Talcott Parsons. *Sociology* 2:257–272

Giddens, A. 1976. Classical social theory and the origins of modern sociology. *Am. J. Sociol.* 81:703–729

Gould, C. C., Walker, A. L., Crane, L. E., Lidz, C. W. 1974. *Connections: Notes from the heroin world.* New Haven: Yale Univ. Press. 236 pp.

Gould, M. 1976. System analysis, macrosociology, and the generalized media of social action. See Loubser et al. 1976, pp. 470–506

Gouldner, A. W. 1970. *The Coming Crisis of Western Sociology.* New York: Basic

Habermas, J. 1973. *Legitimation Crisis.* Boston: Beacon

Habermas, J. 1977. Hannah Arendt's communications concept of power. *Soc. Res.* 44:3–24

Habermas, J. 1981a. Talcott Parsons: Problems of theory construction. *Sociol. Inq.* 51(3/4):173–96

Habermas, J. 1981b. *Theorie des Kommunikativen Handelns.* Frankfurt: Suhrkamp

Hacker, A. 1961. Sociology and ideology. In *The Social Theories of Talcott Parsons,* ed. M. Black, pp. 289–310. Carbondale: Southern Ill. Univ.

Hayes, A. C. 1981. Structure and creativity: The use of transformational-generative models in action theory. *Sociol. Inq.* 51(3/4):219–39

Homans, G. 1964. Bringing men back in. *Am. Sociol. Rev.* 29:808–18

Klausner, S., Lidz, V. W. 1985. *Social Science: A Basic National Resource.* Philadelphia: Univ. Penn. Press. In press

Lechner, 1985. Modernity and its discontents: Revitalization syndromes in action-theoretical perspectives. In *NeoFunctionalism,* ed. J. Alexander. Beverly Hills: Sage

Levy, M. 1952. *The Structure of Society.* Princeton: Princeton Univ. Press

Lidz, C. W., Lidz, V. M. 1976. Piaget's psychology of intelligence and the theory of action. See Loubser et al 1976, pp. 195–239

Lidz, C. W., Walker, A. L. 1978. Therapeutic control of heroin: Dedifferentiating legal and psychiatric controls. *Social System And Legal Process,* ed. H. M. Johnson, pp. 294–321. San Francisco: Jossey-Bass

Lidz, C. W., Walker, A. L. 1980. *Heroin, Deviance, and Morality.* Beverly Hills: Sage. 269 pp.

Lidz, V. M. 1976. Introduction to part II:

General action analysis. See Loubser et al 1976, pp. 124–150

Lidz, V. M. 1979a. Secularization, ethical life, and religion in modern societies. In *Religious Change and Continuity—Sociological Perspectives*, ed. H. M. Johnson, pp. 191–217. San Francisco: Jossey-Bass

Lidz, V. M. 1979b. The law as index, phenomenon, and element—conceptual steps toward a general sc ciology of law. *Sociol. Inq.* 49(1):5–26

Lidz, V. 1981. Conceptions of value-relevance and the theory of action. *Sociol. Inq.* 51:371–408

Lidz, V. M. 1985. Television and the moral order in a secular age. In *Interpreting Television*, ed. W. D. Rowland, Jr., B. Watkins. Beverly Hills: Sage Deleted in proof.

Lockwood, D. 1956. Some remarks on *The Social System. Br. J. Sociol.* 7:134–46

Loubser, J. J., Baum, R. C., Effrat, A., Lidz, V. M. 1976. *Explorations in General Theory in Social Science: Volumes 1 and 2*. New York: Free. 909 pp.

Loubser, J. J. 1976. The values problem in social science in developmental perspective. See Loubser et al 1976, pp. 75–89

Luhmann, N. 1976. Generalized media and the problem of contingency. See Loubser et al 1976:507–32

Luhmann, N. 1981. *The Differentiation of Society*. New York: Columbia Univ. Press

Mayhew, L. 1976. Methodological dilemmas in social science. See Loubser et al 1976, pp. 59–74

Menzies, K. 1977. *Talcott Parsons and the Social Image of Man*. London: Routledge. 197 pp.

Merton, R. K. 1957. *Social Theory and Social Structure*. Revised and enlarged edition. New York: Free Press

Mills, C. W. 1959. In *The Sociological Imagination*. London/New York: Oxford Univ. Press

Mitchell, W. C. 1967. *Sociological Analysis and Politics: The Theories of Talcott Parsons*. Englewood Cliffs, N.J.: Prentice-Hall. 222 pp.

Mullins, N. C. 1983. Theories and theory groups revisited. In *Sociological Theory 1983*. ed. R. Collins, pp. 319–38. San Francisco: Jossey Bass

Münch, R. 1981a. Socialization and personality development from the point of view of action theory, the legacy of Emile Durkheim. *Sociol. Inq.* 51(3/4):331–54

Münch, R. 1981b. Talcott Parsons and the theory of action. I. The structure of the Kantian core. *Am. J. Sociol.* 86:709–39

Münch, R. 1982a. Talcott Parsons and the theory of action. II. The continuity of the development. *Am. J. Sociol.* 87:771–826

Münch, R. 1982b. *Theorie des Handelns—Zur Rekonstruktion der Beitrage, von Talcott Parsons, Emile Durkheim, und Max Weber*. Frankfurt: Suhrkamp. 693 pp.

Parsons, T. 1937. *The Structure of Social Action: A Study in Social Theory with Special Reference to a Group of Recent European Writers*. New York: MacMillan, 817 pp.

Parsons, T. 1951. *The Social System*. Glencoe, Ill.: Free Press

Parsons, T. 1960. Pattern variables revisited: A response to Robert Dubin. *Am. Social. Rev.* 25:466–84

Parsons, T. 1961. The point of view of the author. In *The Social Theories of Talcott Parsons: A Critical Examination*, ed. M. Black, pp. 311–363. Carbondale: Southern Ill. Univ. Press

Parsons, T. 1967. Durkheim's contribution to the theory of integration of social systems. In *Sociological Theory and Modern Society*, pp. 3–34. New York: Free Press.

Parsons, T. 1969a. On the concept of political power. In *Politics and Social Structure*, pp. 352–404. New York: Free Press

Parsons, T. 1969b. Polity and society: Some general considerations. In *Politics and Social Structure*, pp. 473–522. New York: Free Press

Parsons, T. 1970. On building social systems theory: A personal history. *Daedalus* 99:826–81

Parsons, T. 1971. Commentary. In *Institutions and Social Exchange: The Sociologies of Talcott Parsons and George C. Homans*, ed. H. Turk, R. L. Simpson. Indianapolis: Bobbs-Merrill

Parsons, T. 1978a. Law as an intellectual stepchild. In *Social System and Legal Process*, ed. H. M. Johnson, pp. 11–58. San Francisco: Jossey-Bass

Parsons, T. 1978b. A paradigm of the human condition. In *Action Theory and the Human Condition*, ed. T. Parsons. pp. 352–433. New York: Free

Parsons, T., Gerstein, D. R. 1977. Two case of social deviance: Addiction to heroin, addiction to power. In *Deviance and Social Change*, ed. E. Sagarin, pp. 19–57. Beverly Hills: Sage

Parsons, T., Platt, P. 1973. *The American University*. Cambridge: Harvard Univ. Press

Parsons, T., Shils, E. A. 1951. *Toward a General Theory of Action: Theoretical Foundations for the Social Sciences*. Cambridge: Harvard Univ. Press. 506 pp.

Parsons, T., Smelser, N. J. 1956. *Economy and Society*. New York: Free. 322 pp.

Piccone, P. 1968. Functionalism, teleology, and objectivity, *Monist* 52:408–23

Platt, G. M. 1981. The American University: Collaboration with Talcott Parsons. *Sociol. Inq.* 51:155–65

Rocher, G. 1975. *Talcott Parsons and American Sociology.* New York: Harper & Row

Sciulli, D. 1984. Parsons' analytical critique of Marxism's concept of alienation. *Am. J. Sociol.* 90:514–40

Sciulli, D. 1985. The practical groundwork for critical theory: Bringing Habermas to Parsons (and vice versa). In *NeoFunctionalism,* ed. J. C. Alexander. Beverly Hills: Sage. In press

Sciulli, D. 1986. Political Differentiation and Collegiality. In *Differentiation Theory: Problems and Prospects,* ed. J. C. Alexander, P. Colomy. Berkeley: U. of Calif. In press

Smelser, N. J. 1959. *Social Change in the Industrial Revolution.* Chicago: Univ. of Chicago Press

Smelser, N. J. 1981. On collaborating with Talcott Parsons: Some intellectual and personal notes. *Sociol. Inq.* 51:143–54

Turner, T. S. 1976. Family structure and socialization. See Loubser et al 1976, pp. 415–46

Walker, C. W., Lidz, A. L. 1983. Commonalities in troublesome habitual behaviors: A cultural approach. *In Commonalities in Substance Abuse and Habitual Behavior,* ed. P. K. Levison, D. R. Gerstein, D. R. Maloff., pp. 29–44. Lexington: Heath

Wallace, R. A. 1985. Religion, privatization, and maladaptation. *Sociol. Anal.* In press

Warner, R. S. 1978. Toward a redefinition of action theory: Paying the cognitive element its due. *Am. J. Sociol.* 83(6):1317–49

Wright, E. O. 1983. Is marxism really functionalist, class reductionist, and teleological. *Am. J. Sociol.* 89:452–59

Wrong, D. 1961. The oversocialized conception of man in modern sociology. *Am. Sociol. Rev.* 26:183–93

Ann. Rev. Sociol. 1985. 11:389–414

THE POLITICAL ATTITUDES OF PROFESSIONALS

Steven Brint

Department of Sociology, Yale University, New Haven, Connecticut 06520

Abstract

In the 1960s and 1970s, political events and polling data indicated a significant rise in liberal and dissenting political attitudes among American professionals. These data seem to run counter to the historically typical connection between social privilege and conservative politics. The major purpose of this paper is to provide a descriptive portrait of the politics of professionals since 1960, through a review of American survey research. Business executives and nonprofessional workers are used as the principal comparison categories. Professionals are conservative on most economic policy issues and on commitments to American "core values." Like business executives, they are comparatively liberal on civil rights and civil liberties issues. Like nonprofessional workers, they are comparatively liberal on welfare state and business support issues. They are more liberal than either business executives or nonprofessional workers on personal morality and military force issues. Within the professional stratum, important lines of political cleavage exist by occupational category, cohort, and type of employing organization. The anomaly of relatively high levels of liberalism in this high status group is explained with reference to two factors: (1) The rise and fall of issue-based political coalitions; and (2) cumulative changes in the occupational and class structure.

INTRODUCTION

The connection between social privilege and conservative politics is one of the oldest in the history of social thought. In the West, the observation goes back at

389

0360-0572/85/0815-0389$02.00

least to Plato, who remarked on the desire for greater equality among the less advantaged citizens of the ancient world, and to Aristotle, who lamented equally the inflexibility and oligarchical predisposition of the privileged few. It has been captured for contemporary students of political sociology by Anderson & Davidson's (1943) phrase "the democratic class struggle," describing the persistent history of electoral contention in Western democracies between conservative parties representing the upper and middle classes and challenging parties representing the "have nots" (see also Lipset 1981:230–78).

The subject of this paper is American professionals, a high status group that has in recent years confounded such observations. The major purpose of the paper is to provide a descriptive portrait of the politics of professionals since 1960. Since no comprehensive work exists on the patterns of political belief among professionals, the paper attempts to provide such a profile by comparing the political attitudes of professionals to other significant strata, by showing how these attitudes have changed over time, and by identifying the primary locations of liberal and conservative attitudes among professionals. Some theorists have attempted to relate the changing political views of professionals to changes in the class structure. These theorists treat the liberalism of professionals as reflecting the rise of a "new class" of intellectual workers, who are in important respects antagonistic to the ideals and interests of traditional elites, especially business owners and executives. In the conclusion of the paper I use a substantially reformulated version of this "new class" analysis to help account for the political attitudes of American professionals.

Political Change?

In the 1960s and 1970s, political events and polling data indicated a significant rise in liberal and dissenting political attitudes among the privileged, specifically among college students and members of the educated middle class of salaried professionals and managers. One of the first signs of change was the active support of many intellectuals, professionals, and college students for the Civil Rights movement of the early 1960s. The subsequent protest movements of the 1960s were largely middle class in their core constituency, as was the university-based "New Left," and much of the support for reform activity in Congress during the period (Hodgson 1976:263–398, Kirkpatrick 1976:239–57, Westby 1976:236–50, Mitchell 1979, Lipset 1981:503–23). At least since 1968, the Democratic Party, traditionally the party of the "have nots" in the United States, has been split at the presidential level into two major factions—one representing labor liberals and one representing middle-class liberals (Lipset 1981:512–15). Similar developments have occurred in other Western democracies with the middle-class "left" dominating the Social Democratic parties of Britain, Denmark and Sweden, the Green Party of West Germany, the small "New Left" parties in Denmark, and also sharing power, sometimes uneasily, with the labor left in Socialist parties of France, Greece, and Spain (Lipset 1981:515–21).

Attitude surveys further suggest the rise of a politically active middle-class liberal-left. Ladd's (Ladd & Lipset 1975:212–31; Ladd 1978, 1979) extensive analyses of American polling data from 1936 through the mid-1970s showed that college graduates (and those with higher level degrees) reversed their previous conservative preferences in the 1960s and 1970s to become one of the most liberal strata on issues involving government activism, spending on social programs, regulation of business, extending opportunities to minorities and women, and relaxation of restrictions on sexual morality. Researchers also noted changes in the relationship between class and party affiliation, both through the attenuation of the historically strong correlation between status variables and Republican Party preference (Glenn 1973, Knoke 1976, Weiner & Eckland 1979) and through the growth of numbers of independent voters in the higher status categories (Burnham 1975, Nie, Verba & Petrocik 1979: 223–42). By the mid-1970s, both Democratic identifiers and independents had eclipsed Republican identifiers among high status groups (Ladd 1978). Since the mid-1970s, professionals have shifted with the rest of the American population toward more conservative views. Nevertheless, they remain among the most liberal strata on a wide range of political issues (Davis 1980).

Some degree of upper- and middle-class liberalism is certainly not new. The liberal and dissenting tendencies of intellectuals, academics and artists in the United States were widely discussed in the 1930s (Leuba 1934, Lasswell 1936). They were an object of considerable scholarly attention in the 1950s as well (Cunliffe 1955, Lazarsfeld & Thielens 1958, Lipset 1981:318–22, 332–71). Moreover, it has been clear for some time that upward social mobility does not always lead to political conversion in the direction of views favored by stable high status groups. Against the expectations of early writers on suburbanization (Whyte 1956, Greenstein & Wolfinger 1958), researchers in the 1960s and early 1970s found evidence that traditional family political identifications were often carried along into the suburbs and through the ranks of the salariat by those who had experienced upward mobility (C. Bell 1968, Abramson 1974).[1]

What was new in the years after 1960 was the apparent breadth of liberal and left-liberal beliefs among the college-educated professional strata.

---

[1] Some of these "new professionals" from immigrant backgrounds joined older stock inheritors of the Progessive tradition to form local Democratic reform clubs in the 1950s and early 1960s (Wilson 1962). They also formed much of the core constituency for the unsuccessful presidential campaigns of Adlai Stevenson in the 1950s (Lipset 1981:512–3).

Interpretations

Among sociologists and political scientists, these changes found a great many interpreters.[2] Drawing on the work of the psychologist Abraham Maslow (1962), one set of theorists saw a rise in alternative (sometimes termed "post-materialist") values among the educated middle class, and particularly among the middle-class young, whose desires for community and self-fulfillment were built on the satisfaction of more basic needs for security and comfort, and conditioned as well by their great distance from actual centers of power (Reich 1970, Inglehart 1971, 1977, Yankelovich 1974). Other writers emphasized the correspondence between the concerns of middle class liberalism and the secure life conditions, "disinterestedness," and workplace autonomy enjoyed by professionals (Ladd 1978, 1979, Lipset 1981:503–23). Others, as noted, depicted the rise of a "new class" of "knowledge workers" engaged in a struggle for power and status with the still dominant "business class" (Kristol 1972, 1975, Ehrenreich & Ehrenreich 1977, Gouldner 1979). Several of these latter theorists suggested that large sections of the once conservative, business-oriented professional class had been transformed by the early 1970s into an "oppositional intelligentsia."

Even during the period of greatest change, all researchers were convinced that such far-reaching theories and interpretations were warranted. A number of social scientists argued that the old class divisions—those between the conservative "haves" and the change-oriented "have-nots"—remained central on the most politically consequential issues of the day, especially those involving economic policy preferences (Hamilton 1975:120–24, Knoke 1979, van Fossen 1979:302–5, Burris 1981). Others argued that the extent of "new class" liberalism was often exaggerated even on noneconomic issues (Vogel 1980, Brint 1984). Others raised a methodological warning by arguing that mere affirmation of liberal views may reflect little about actual behavior, especially where liberal behavior comes at some personal cost (Jackman 1978).

Many of the disagreements can be resolved through careful examination of the existing empirical research.

BETWEEN-CLASS DIVISIONS

The first step is to show precisely how professionals compare in their political attitudes to other key strata: business executives on one hand and non-professional workers on the other. In making these comparisons, I will concen-

[2]Some of the first interpretations came from political activists rather than social scientists. From critical perspectives on opposite ends of the political spectrum, writers associated with the student left (Students for a Democratic Society 1962, Miles 1973) and the conservative right (Phillips 1969) argued that a new "liberal establishment," the institutionalized product of the Roosevelt-Truman and Kennedy-Johnson reform eras, had displaced more conservative business-oriented elites at the center of American political and social life. They argued that the views of the "liberal establishment" had been assimilated as the conventional wisdom of the educated middle classes.

trate only on issues for which at least reasonably good data are available. By this I mean data that can be broken into categories approximating the business, professional, and nonprofessional strata. In all comparisons, the business category is composed of high income business owners and executives. The income criterion varies somewhat between studies. In all cases, however, the category includes only the top 15% (or fewer) of business owners and managers in the company. The professional category is composed of salaried professionals (as defined by the US Census Bureau) with baccalaureate or higher level degrees. Some of the studies do not separate college graduate professionals from middle-income college graduate managers. When this broader professional-managerial stratum is used as a point of comparison, the term "professional-managerial" is used to reference the category. In all comparisons, high income managers are considered part of the business strata, whether or not they have college degrees. Except as noted, the nonprofessional category is limited to manual workers.[3]

The comparisons will be drawn exclusively from American survery research. Cross-national comparisons would be highly desirable, but, for the time being, good cross-national data are not available across the full range of relevant issues.

A Typology of Issues

Political analysts have long distinguished between political attitudes on "economic" and "social" issues, noting the tendency of the working classes to be liberal on the former and conservative on the latter. Economic issues are usually defined as those separating partisans of governmental intervention and planning and control of business power from those who defend laissez-faire and free enterprise. Social issues, on the other hand, are defined as issues separating those who espouse relaxed restrictions on morals and cultural styles from those who defend "traditional" restrictive values on these matters (Bell 1979:185).

A new typology, however, is necessary to encompass the more complicated cleavages of recent years. "Economic issues" must now be divided between (1) equality-related issues and basic system commitments, on which the divisions between "haves" and "have nots" remain most consequential, and (2) welfare state issues, on which workers and professionals tend to diverge from the still comparatively conservative business strata. "Social issues" too must now be divided into two types: (1) civil liberties and civil rights issues, on which the upper strata remain more liberal than the lower strata and (2) morality and

---

[3]The political attitudes of professional white-collar workers tend to fall between those of blue-collar and professional worker, with college educated white-collar workers resembling professionals to a greater degree and high school educated white-collar workers more closely resembling blue-collar workers.

military force issues, on which workers and businessmen tend to be allied against the comparatively liberal professionals.

Pattern One: Equality-Related Issues and Basic System Commitments

The first pattern involves issues on which members of the business and professional strata tend to be more conservative than nonprofessional workers. These include equality-related economic policy issues involving income redistribution and attitudes toward business and labor leaders. They also include what I will call "basic system commitments" on such matters as private ownership, the role of science and technology, and the justice or rewards in American society. On all of these issues, the idea of an "oppositional" professional class is far off the mark.

EQUALITY-RELATED ISSUES   The closer an issue strikes at notions of economic equality, the more likely traditional divisions between the "haves" and "have nots" will emerge. Researchers have found that both business elites and professionals are less likely than lower status groups to favor governmental actions to reduce income inequalities between rich and poor (Brint 1984) or to guarantee everyone "a job and a good standard of living" (Miller et al 1980:189–91, Research & Forecasts, Inc. 1981:113). Similar patterns have been found on more global questions concerning equality. Upper status groups, in general, favor neither the concept of equality of economic condition, nor policies designed to limit economic inequalities (Huber & Form 1973:107–16, Hamilton 1975:120–24, Robinson & Bell 1978, van Fossen 1979:304–5).

One of the cornerstones of theorizing about the rise of an oppositional "new class" has been the alleged "anti-business animus" found among highly educated professionals. The truth, according to opinion data, is that members of the professional and managerial strata hardly ever indicate antagonistic attitudes toward corporate business or business executives. Brint (1984) found that just 12% of college graduate professionals and managers indicated "hardly any" confidence in business leaders between the years 1972 and 1980, compared to 6% of high income business owners and executives and 17% of blue-collar workers (see also Storer 1982:83–6). Evaluations of the honesty, dependability, and integrity of business and business executives show similar patterns (Marketing Concepts 1978a, 1978b). Moreover, only blue-collar workers showed any appreciable interest in putting a cap on corporate profits. Less than one quarter of college graduates thought this was a good idea compared to 40% of blue-collar workers (Marketing Concepts 1978a, 1978b).

Professionals also resemble business executives in their attitudes toward labor. Compared to blue-collar workers, both groups tend to feel cool toward labor unions (Converse et al 1980:40, Storer 1982:68–70, 99–103), to lack confidence in labor unions and labor leaders (Brint 1981, Lipset & Schneider 1983:310–14), to evaluate labor leaders as "low" in "honesty, integrity and dependability" (Marketing Concepts 1978a, 1978b), and to feel that labor unions have "too much" influence in American political affairs (Lipset & Schneider 1981). According to Gallup and *Los Angeles Times* polls conducted in the late 1970s and early 1980s, over 40% of business and professional people disapproved of labor unions compared to just one quarter of nonprofessional workers (Lipset & Schneider 1981).

BASIC SYSTEM COMMITMENTS   Sociologists have proposed a number of different formulations of the "core values" or "dominant ideology" of American society (see Williams 1960:415–79, Huber & Form 1973:1–12). Most, however, agree that belief in the values of private ownership, scientific and technological progress, equality of opportunity, and monetary success are among the defining elements. Good data exist on these values, and all of it indicates that educated professionals and managers are among the most devout believers in American "core values."

In all studies, very large majorities of all groups endorse private ownership and reject ideas about collective ownership. During the last decade at least eight out of ten have felt that the private business system works better for industrial countries than any other system yet devised, and seven out of ten have said they strongly believe that Americans should be ready to make sacrifices if necessary to preserve the private enterprise system (Lipset & Schneider 1978:41–2, Opinion Roundup 1980b, 1982b; Lipset & Schneider 1983:257–90). Some of these studies indicate that blacks and lower income people are somewhat less likely to agree with these propositions (Opinion Roundup 1982b), but none has found significant differences by education or occupation (Lipset & Schneider 1978).

Large proportions of all Americans think of science and technology as primary forces related to productivity, standard of living and national progress (Martin 1981). Nevertheless, people with high incomes and advanced educations are most likely to feel positively about science (Martin 1981), and to express high levels of confidence in science and scientific leaders (Etzioni & Nunn 1977, Brint 1981).

Business and professional groups are united also in their views about the justice of rewards in American society. Upper status groups are more likely than lower status groups to believe that anyone has the opportunity to move ahead in American society (Hyman 1966, Huber & Form 1973:90–7); that opportunities for achievement are essentially equal for all (Huber & Form 1973:90–9, van Fossen 1979:304, Jackman & Jackman 1983:208–10); and that mobility is the product of hard work and ability rather than luck or having been born to well-to-do parents (Hyman 1966:495, Huber & Form 1973:100–7,

Feagin 1975, van Fossen 1979:238–9). Though all groups tend to feel that personal incomes should not have an upper boundary, those with higher incomes and educations have been especially likely to feel this way (Opinion Roundup 1981b).

Pattern Two: Civil Liberties and Civil Rights Issues

A second pattern emerges on most civil liberties and civil rights issues. Business executives and educated professionals and managers are once again similar in outlook, but on these issues they are more liberal than nonprofessional workers rather than more conservertive. These issues represent a very traditional form of middle and upper class liberalism based on the greater tolerance and cosmopolitanism of the upper classes (Lipset 1981:97–100, 318–24). Liberalism on these issues is most closely related to high levels of education, a characteristic of a majority of high income business people, as well as of the professional and managerial middle class.

CIVIL LIBERTIES ISSUES   Stouffer's (1955:107) major conclusions about the bases of tolerance for nonconformists remain valid today: the better educated are more tolerant, and so are the young. Tolerance scores have risen appreciably since Stouffer's time, but the major bases of differentiation have remained unchanged (Nunn et al 1978, Hyman & Wright 1979:32–44, Davis 1979, Weil 1982). The findings are similar on other first amendment issues, including attitudes on the dissemination of birth control and political information, the sale of pornography, due process guarantees for unpopular groups, and protection of rights to assembly and demonstration (Hyman & Wright 1979:41–6).[4]

CIVIL RIGHTS ISSUES   Attitudes toward extending opportunities for women and minorities are another major area of convergence between business people and professionals. Since 1960, liberal attitudes on civil rights issues have increased dramatically throughout the population, but have always been closely associated with high levels of education (and also with younger age groups) (Taylor et al 1978, Opinion Roundup 1978c, 1980a, 1980d; Converse et al 1980:59–93.) A general index of integration sentiment reported by Brint (1984) showed that professional, managerial, and business executive groups were all at least twice as likely as blue-collar workers to fully support racial integration. The relatively small differences between the business and professional-managerial strata were principally due to the greater age of the businessmen and their somewhat lower levels of education. The same patterns have been found

---

[4]The educated, however, are no more likely than the less educated to favor political nonconformists as teachers or to disapprove the use of wiretapping (Hyman & Wright 1979:33, 42, Opinion Roundup 1982b), and they are even more likely to oppose certain acts of civil disobedience, such as blocking the doors of government buildings (Hyman & Wright 1979:42).

on specific issues. Over the last 20 years, the college educated (and the young) have been the major proponents of school desegration and open housing (Converse et al 1980:67). Similar patterns have been reported for attitudes toward intermarriage, interracial friendships, and voting for a black for President (Davis 1979, Hyman & Wright 1979:48–54, Miller et al 1980:205–12, 223–6). Not surprisingly, given the other evidence, negative stereotypes about blacks are found most frequently among older people with low educational levels (Opinion Roundup 1981a).

Growth of support for extending equal opportunities to women occurred at a somewhat later date (1970–1975) than changes in racial attitudes, but the social bases of liberal attitudes were similar (Hyman & Wright 1979:48–54, Converse et al 1980:123–4, Miller et al 1980:227–32, Fox & Hesse-Biber 1984:32).

Pattern Three: Welfare State and Business Support Issues

A third pattern involves welfare state and business support issues on which high income business executives alone tend to be relatively conservative. Like the issues covered under pattern one, these are economic issues, but they are economic issues on which the equation between the high status and conservative politics no longer fully applies. Instead, they may be described as issues on which relatively liberal attitudes have become the norm for the population at large, though business executives generally remain outside this new mainstream.

WELFARE STATE ISSUES   College graduate professionals and managers were slow to support federal spending on some medical and housing-related programs (Converse et al 1980:392–3), but by the early 1970s they were the strongest supporters of virtually all federal social programs. Using a composite index based on General Social Survey data, Brint (1984) found both college graduate professionals and managers and blue-collar workers to be significantly more likely than high income business owners and executives to favor federal spending on social programs. Some two fifths of professional-managerial and blue-collar respondents were supporters of increased spending on social programs compared to just one quarter of business respondents. The same pattern held on specific issues. In the 1970s college graduates (and those with higher level degrees) were the most likely to support spending to improve and protect the nation's health and education, to solve the problems of the cities, and to improve the conditions of minorities. Blue-collar workers and the poor were also likely to support these programs (Ladd 1979).

Support for social programs declined sharply in the late 1970s and early 1980s (Davis 1980, Opinion Roundup 1982b), but intergroup differences in support of social spending appear to have persisted in much the same form as in the early and mid-1970s (Davis 1980, Opinion Roundup 1980d, 1982b).

In recent years, environmental and consumer protection have become widely accepted as welfare state concerns. Since the 1970s, all strata have wanted more spent on protecting the environment and on preserving national parks (Marketing Concepts 1978a, 1978b; Opinion Roundup 1982a, Brint 1984). When environmental questions have been phrased as a choice between economic development and environmental concerns, the major lines of cleavage have separated businessmen from other strata. In 1978, for example, business elites were significantly less likely than other groups to feel that clean air and water were worth higher prices and taxes. They were also significantly less likely to oppose strip mining or to find environmentalists a credible source of information (Marketing Concepts 1978a, 1978b).

The alliance between blue-collar and professional-managerial workers has been more consistent still on consumer issues. Widespread support for the consumer movement and consumer activists has been reported from the beginning of the organized movement in the 1960s (Lipset & Schneider 1983:245–55). High levels of support have been characteristic of all strata except high-earning business executives. In 1978, for example, blue-collar workers indicated somewhat stronger support for the idea of a "federal agency to be the voice of the consumer movement" and for the proposition that the "government should require the ultimate in product safety regardless of costs," but professional and managerial respondents were significantly closer to blue-collar workers than to business executives on these issues (Marketing Concepts 1978a, 1978b).

BUSINESS SUPPORT ISSUES   Though neither professionals nor workers have adopted an adversary stance toward business, neither have they expressed full support. In 1978, both professional and blue-collar respondents were about three times less likely than business executives to rank "large business" and business executives high on "honesty, dependability and integrity." They were also much less likely than business executives to feel that business "provides high value" to consumers for the money spent, or to feel "great confidence" in the leaders of business corporations (Marketing Concepts 1978a, 1978b; Brint 1984). They were also much more likely to feel that business exercised "too much" influence on political affairs (Storer 1982:85–7). On the basis of similar evidence on business support, Lipset & Schneider (1983:314–5) concluded that "[b]usiness was favored least by highly unionized semi-skilled workers" and that "[s]upport for business is [also] conspicuously weak among . . . professionals for whom business values show no noticeable appeal."

These attitudes translate into support for many specific regulatory activities. In one recent survey, both blue-collar and professional-managerial populations were significantly more likely than business elites to feel that regulation is necessary to assure safe products and safe working conditions. Both were also nearly three times as likely to feel that the cost of regulating business was justified (Marketing Concepts 1978a, 1978b).

Pattern Four: Morality and Military Force Issues

The final pattern involves issues on which professionals are more liberal than either nonprofessional workers or high income business executives. For the most part, these are issues associated either with preferences for freedom of choice and self-expression in personal life or with skepticism about the use of force in public life. "Quality of life" issues, such as certain types of environmental concern, sometimes also reflect this pattern.

PERSONAL MORALITY ISSUES   Personal morality issues include attitudes on such issues as sexual morality, divorce, and abortion. Trend lines for the entire population have moved in a more liberal direction on these issues, with major changes occurring between 1965 and 1975 (Taylor & Smith 1978). These trends, however, have not affected all strata equally. Brint (1984) found that nearly two fifths of college graduate professionals and managers scored in the liberal range of an index measuring moral nonrestrictiveness compared to one fifth of high income business owners and executives and one eighth of manual workers. Clearly, none of the three strata were libertarian, but the professional-managerial middle class was significantly more liberal. (See also Yankelovich 1974, Taylor & Smith 1978, Opinion Roundup 1978c, Research & Forecasts, Inc. 1981:84–98, Davis 1979, Ladd 1979.)

MILITARY FORCE ISSUES   The reputation of professionals for liberalism on law and order issues is exaggerated, but it is not entirely misconceived. Much of this reputation comes from the alleged support of the professional strata for student and black protest in the 1960s. Though professionals were significantly more likely than other strata to feel warmly toward protestors in the 1960s, levels of support were never high in an absolute sense; less than one quarter felt at all warmly toward protestors (Converse et al 1969). They were, however, significantly more likely to criticize the police for using too much force on demonstrators (Robinson 1970). Since the early 1970s, liberal views on law and order issues have declined in all strata (Opinion Roundup 1980c, 1980d; Miller et al 1980:193–6). Along with nonwhites and the young, the highly educated have been the least conservative on these issues, though differences between the three key strata have not typically been statistically significant.

Through 1967, the public showed constant, strong support for the military. The Vietnam protest era (1967–1975) was marked by rapidly declining levels of support for the military. Support increased sharply between 1976 and 1981, before declining again after 1981 (Nathan & Oliver 1975, Watts & Free 1976, Yankelovich & Kaagen 1981, Opinion Roundup 1983a). All social strata have followed these trends in public opinion, but at any given time college graduate professionals and managers have typically been somewhat less supportive of the military than business executives, and much less supportive than blue-collar workers.[5]

The best data exist on support for military spending. Brint (1981) found that during the 1970s half of college graduate professionals and managers felt the federal government was spending "too much" on the military, compared to less than two fifths of high income business owners and managers and less than one quarter of blue-collar workers. These data are consistent with Ladd's (1979) and Ferree's (1980:38) findings using the same data. They are also consistent with Russett & Hanson's (1975:244) conclusion that in the early 1970s business executives were more supportive of military expenditures and military preparedness than other civilian elites. Similarly, professionals expressed least confidence in military leaders throughout the 1970s (Lipset & Schneider 1983:123). By 1980, differences had lessened among the three strata (Opinion Roundup 1980d). Scattered evidence suggests that when questions on military intervention call forth images of military adventurism and precipitate use of force, college graduate professionals and managers are most strongly opposed to intervention. When such questions suggest living up to treaty obligations, however, highly educated professionals and managers do not oppose intervention more often than other groups (Watts & Free 1976, Yankelovich & Kaagan 1981).

"QUALITY OF LIFE" ISSUES   When energy and environment issues are framed as a trade-off between conservation and either employment or standard of living, nonprofessional workers are inclined to sacrifice environmental concerns. College educated professionals, on the other hand, remain in favor of regulations even at the cost of unemployment and inflation (Ladd 1979, Inglehart 1981, Research & Forecasts, Inc. 1981:117). Other "quality of life" issues—such as concern for the "creation of beautiful cities," a more participative and less impersonal society, and a society where "ideas count"—also tend to reveal this pattern of cleavage, though generational differences are at least equally important (Inglehart 1981).

Summary of Between-Class Divisions

Overall, professionals are the most consistently liberal of the major occupational strata in the United States, but they are not at all liberal on economic and equality-related issues.

[5]There are two noteworthy exceptions to this generalization. First, after 1968, no significant differences existed between the three strata on support for withdrawal from Vietnam (Converse et al 1969, Nie, Verba & Petrocik 1979:246–64, Miller et al 1980:239–42). Secondly, the nuclear arms race has been widely perceived as a threat by all strata (Gallup 1983:278).

The question, of course, is what to make of these patterns? With good reason, many scholars consider attitudes on economic issues and basic system commitments to be the true measure of political opposition (see, for example, Weinstein 1968, Hamilton 1975, Gitlin 1982). By this measure, very few highly educated professionals (or managers) could be described as members of an "oppositional intelligentsia." Indeed, the economic conservatism of the stratum is very deep-seated and on several issues, such as income redistribution and many labor issues, extends to otherwise liberal segments of the stratum. Nevertheless, some important political divisions now exist between business executives and the highly educated specialists located at lower levels of American organizational pyramids. One way of describing these differences would be to say that business people tend to prefer traditional restriction in private life but a large degree of laissez-faire in economic life, while "knowledge workers" prefer laissez-faire in private life and some degree of regulation in economic life.

It should also be noted that while much of the liberalism of professionals is new (that is, recorded only since the mid 1960s), these significant continuities are sometimes overlooked. The relative liberalism of professionals on civil rights and civil liberties issues reflects, as it always has, the greater tolerance and cosmopolitanism of the highly educated, and also their greater insulation from potentially threatening strangers.

WITHIN-CLASS DIVISIONS

Important divisions within the educated middle class can be found on welfare state and business support issues (issues discussed under pattern three) and on morality and military force issues (issues discussed under pattern four).[6] In virtually every instance, segments of the class that are liberal on one of these types of issues are liberal on all of them, and segments that are conservative on one are conservative on all. The most important bases of internal division are occupation, cohort, and type of employing organization. Except as noted, the effects of these divisions are significant net of one another.

Occupational Divisions

Artists, writers, journalists, academics, and social scientists stand out for their liberalism. Members of this relatively small category of "social and cultural specialists" (Brint 1984) (under 10% of the professional-managerial total) are by some measures the most liberal occupational wing of the professional-

---

[6]Education and age differences alone tend to account for most of the variation in the civil liberties and civil rights issues discussed under pattern two. The equality and system commitment issues discussed under pattern one tend to engender little internal variation of any sort.

managerial middle class. In a multivariate study, Brint (1984) found that occupation was the most important net predictor of political attitudes among professionals and managers, and that members of the social and cultural category were by far the most liberal. Net of other significant variables, they were far more likely than other occupational segments to support full integration, nonrestrictive attitudes on moral issues, and increased spending on social programs, and they were less likely to indicate full confidence in business leaders. They also scored highest of all occupational groups on Ladd's (1979) "New Liberalism" index (composed mainly of morality and military force issues). They were more than twice as likely as either business executives or blue-collar workers to score in the top quintile, and they were 1.5 times as likely to do so as professionals at large. In his analysis of an earlier period (1968–1972), Storer (1982:79–90) found the social and cultural specialists to be significantly more skeptical in their attitudes toward businessmen than were other professionals and managers and also significantly more liberal in their views on government efforts to guarantee incomes and to assure the rights of accused criminals.

Studies of specific occupations composing the social-and-cultural-professions category have found high levels of liberalism among academics (Ladd & Lipset 1975, Lipset 1979), journalists (Tunstall 1971, Johnstone et al 1973, Rothman 1979), and artists and writers (Lipset 1983:338–40). Clergymen, according to one comparative study of a relatively elite sample, tend to be restrictive on personal freedoms and law and order issues, but liberal on welfare state, civil rights and foreign policy issues (Research & Forecasts, Inc. 1981:218–45).

Several explanations have been put forward for these findings. It seems clear that the social and cultural specialties provide an occupational home for many academically able persons whose values diverge from the core values of a market society (Davis 1965:109–32, Parkin 1968:187, Westby 1976:236–50). The critical skills required for intellectual work may also contribute to the disaffection of these cultural workers from beliefs and values supportive of the political status quo (Schumpeter 1942:142–55, Lipset & Dobson 1972). In addition, the feeling of being in a minority may intensify disaffection from dominant elites, if those elites are identified as the sources of one's feelings of status deprivation (Seeman 1958, Lipset 1981:346–7).

LESS LIBERAL PROFESSIONAL OCCUPATIONS   The "human services" professions of teaching, social work, and nursing are often thought to be a second bastion of liberal politics due to their close connection to the public sector and social welfare activities. The evidence, however, is mixed at best. In his multivariate study of professionals and managers, Brint (1984) found that the human services occupations were the most conservative of all occupational categories on personal morality issues, but were comparatively liberal on welfare state and confidence-in-business issues (see also Storer 1982:61–78). Studies of specific occupations suggest that social workers tend to be politically liberal (Lipset 1981:338, Lipset & Schwartz 1966, Meyer et al 1968), while teachers are relatively conservative (Meyer et al 1968, Barry 1977, Ladd 1979, National Education Association 1982).

The political attitudes of persons in the traditionally elite professions of medicine and law, on the other hand, are more liberal than is often assumed. Doctors, in particular, tend to be less conservative than would be expected given their very high income and status levels (Lipset & Schwartz 1966, Derber & Boren 1983). Lipset & Schwartz (1966) suggest this has to do with their occupational obligation to heal those in need. Lawyers tend to be more conservative politically than doctors, but urban lawyers, at least, remain comparatively liberal on most domestic policy issues (Heinz & Laumann 1982:137–66, Derber & Boren 1983). Members of the two traditionally elite professions scored next to social and cultural specialists in Ladd's (1979) study of the social bases of the "new liberalism."

The conservative wing of the professional-managerial stratum is composed of private sector managers, "technical professionals" (such as industrial scientists and engineers), and "business professionals" (such as accountants, business consultants and public relations specialists). Private sector scientists and engineers are the most consistently conservative of all professional groups (Greenwald 1978, Bailyn 1980, Brint 1984). Middle managers, especially those earning relatively high incomes, also tend to be conservative (Brint 1984). The conservatism of managers and technical professionals may be attributed largely to their centrality in profit-making enterprise and their consequent adherence to the culture of the conservative elites within these organizations. Both self-selection and socialization processes are no doubt at work here, as they would be in the liberal professional occupations (for a further discussion of this issue, see Brint 1982:336–8).

SPECIALTY DIVISIONS   Specialty divisions within occupations are of some consequence. The research suggests at least two important bases of cleavage. The first is a division between those specialties that are in close association with business and those either having little business contact or close association with subordinate groups. Thus, in academe scholars in applied fields like engineering, agriculture, and business management are most conservative, while scholars in fields with little or no business contact are the most liberal (Ladd & Lipset 1975:55–92). Similar findings have been reported for lawyers. Heinz & Laumann (1982:149–51) found that general corporate, tax, patents, and personal business specialists were the most conservative attorneys in their sample of the Chicago bar, while labor, criminal defense, civil rights, and personnel litigation attorneys were the most liberal. Both Erlanger (1977) and Weisbrod (1980) reported very high levels of liberal and left-liberal politics among "public interest" and poverty lawyers. The second important basis of division is between specialties whose practice encourages aggressive, command-oriented activity and those that are more intellectual, detached, and/or consultative. Thus, surgeons are the most conservative of all physicians, while psychologists and general practitioners are more liberal (Erdmann et al 1979). Similarly, line managers are very often political conservatives, while management personnel in the more intellectually-oriented and consultative staff jobs tend more often to have somewhat divergent values (Bailyn 1980:22–31).

Generational Divisions

Next to occupation, generation is the key influence on the political attitudes of professionals. Brint (1984) reported strong net associations between younger cohorts and liberal political views on business-related attitudes, support for increased spending on social programs, support for full racial integration, and support for nonrestrictive attitudes on issues of sexual morality. Generational differences were most pronounced on personal morality issues, where college youth were leaders on changing sexual norms (Yankelovich 1974), and youth has continued to be very strongly associated with liberal views even after educational and occupational differences are controlled (Taylor & Smith 1978, Davis 1979). Other researchers have found particularly high levels of support for environmental protection, civil liberties, and civil rights among younger college educated populations and also a greater sympathy for protest (Robinson 1970, Hoge 1971, Opinion Roundup 1980a, Inglehart 1977, Hoge et al 1981). Throughout the population, youth has been associated with liberalism on most of these issues (Opinion Roundup 1978c, Davis 1979, Opinion Roundup 1980d, Converse et al 1980:38–9, Lipset & Schneider 1983:123). Thus, younger professionals and managers conform to the general pattern of intercohort political differences. However, the joint effects of age, occupation, and education make many young professionals much more liberal than their nonprofessional age-mates on these issues.

Sociologists have pointed to two major causes of cohort effects. Since the turn of the century, all cohorts have experienced the liberalizing effects of urbanization, improved transportation, a more cosmopolitan communications system, and, especially, successive improvements in physical and economic security. The greater part of the differences found between cohorts may be attributed to underlying conditions and trends like these (Lipset & Ladd 1971). At the same time, particular cohorts may be marked, to some degree, by the decisive events of their early adulthood experience. Lipset & Ladd (1971), for example, found that those who were in college during Herbert Hoover's term following the stock market collapse of 1929 were markedly less Republican than the immediately preceding and the immediately following college cohorts.

Similarly, in the case of the Vietnam era college cohorts, decisive experiences such as Civil Rights and antiwar protest, apparently had at least a modest long-term effect (Ferree 1980, Opinion Roundup 1981c).

Differences by Type of Employer

Because experts employed outside the private sector would seem more often to have a material interest in reform, many theorists have concluded that the public and non-profit sectors represent the core institutional locations of "new class" liberalism and dissent (Moynihan 1972, Kristol 1972, Ehrenreich & Ehrenreich 1977, Szelenyi 1980, Derber 1983). The evidence, however, is mixed. When researchers have looked at noneconomic and social spending issues, they have typically failed to find significant net effects of employment sector and sometimes have not even found significant zero-order correlations (Ladd 1979, Wuthnow & Shrum 1983, Brint 1984). However, when economic issues are examined, type of employing organization often does have important net effects. Thus, Brint (1984) found significant net effects of sectoral location on two measures of confidence in business leaders, and Derber & Boren (1983) found major net sectoral differences on an index of economic liberalism, though not on a measure of social liberalism for a sample of Boston area professionals. Research on college graduates in the late 1960s found significant net sectoral effects on support for protest activity (Barry 1977). On the basis of this evidence, it appears that employment sector is an inconsistent predictor of liberal political attitudes, but that it is a relatively strong predictor on some of the more consequential forms of liberalism and dissent.

Other Probable Bases of Within-Class Divisions

The research evidence suggests that four additional variables—religion, city size, income and college quality—may be significantly related to the political attitudes of professionals net of occupation, cohort, and sector. As in the population at large, Jews appear to be particularly liberal and Protestants somewhat conservative (Johnstone et al 1973, Ladd & Lipset 1975:149–68, Barry 1977, Derber & Boren 1983). Research by Greeley (1977:90–111) suggests that Catholic professionals may be relatively conservative on social issues, but relatively liberal on welfare state and business support issues. Professionals located in the largest metropolitan areas appear to be most liberal, while those located in small towns and rural areas are most conservative (Johnstone et al 1973, Handler et al 1978, Ladd 1979). High income professionals are somewhat more liberal than low income professionals on personal morality issues (Brint 1984). However, on welfare state and business support issues, income interacts with occupation. Higher income social and cultural specialists are most liberal, while higher income managers and technical professionals are most conservative (Ladd & Lipset 1975:132–48, Lipset 1979,

1981:332–67, 1982; Brint 1984). Professionals who have attended the most selective colleges appear to be more liberal than those who have attended less selective colleges (Knoke & Isaac 1976, Barry 1977).

The effects of religion, city size, income, and college quality are not as well established as the effects of occupation, cohort, and sector. In the absence of well-controlled studies, conclusions about these variables must remain tentative.

The Historical Dimension

In the population at large political attitudes have shifted in a conservative direction since the mid-1970s (Davis 1980, Yankelovich & Kaagan 1981, Watts 1981). According to Davis (1980:1153), the "conservative shift in the weather" of the mid-1970s struck "in all age and education categories at about the same time and with about the same impacts." Shifts in a conservative direction were especially evident on issues involving federal spending for social programs (Davis 1980, Miller et al 1980:171–7), environmental issues (Davis 1980, van Liere & Dunlap 1980), law and order issues (Opinion Roundup 1978b), and foreign policy issues (Davis 1980, Yankelovich & Kaagan 1981).[7] Between the early and late 1970s, Davis (1980), for example, found shifts of between 8% and 19% in the ratio of General Social Survey respondents who felt "too little" as opposed to those who felt "too much" was being spent by the federal government in five social welfare and environmental areas. Using the same ratio, he also found a 33% increase in support of greater spending on military armaments and defense. Changes in ideological self-identification reflect these conservative trends. The proportion of people calling themselves liberals declined by more than 5% between the early 1970s and the early 1980s—from over one quarter to under one fifth—(National Opinion Research Center 1982), and the proportion of college freshmen who identified themselves as "radicals" declined from 11% to 1% between 1970 and 1980 (American Council on Education 1970, American Council on Education 1980). In the 1980 and 1984 presidential elections, professionals voted three to two for Ronald Reagan, a conservative Republican. In both cases, the professional vote for Reagan was slightly higher than the total vote he received. The 1980 vote, in particular, attests more to the poor economic performance of the previous Democratic administration than to ideological conversion (Burnham 1981), but both votes are consistent with the clear conservative trend among professionals (and the population at large) since the mid-1970s.

---

[7]At the same time, trends toward increasing liberalism have largely continued in the late 1970s and early 1980s on most civil rights and civil liberties issues (Opinion Roundup 1978c, Hoge et al 1981), and trends in attitudes on personal morality issues have been far from consistently conservative (Opinion Roundup 1978c).

Similar shifts are not unprecedented historically. In the 1920s, the middle and upper middle class were, by all accounts, overwhelmingly conservative. Yet, by 1937, at the height of New Deal reform sentiment, two out of five upper white-collar workers said they favored governmental efforts to redistribute income (Kornhauser 1939). One year before, in 1936, 24% of college students told the Roper Organization that they identified most closely with socialists, another 6% said they were most sympathetic to communists, and another 45% called themselves liberals (Lipset & Ladd 1971). By the 1950s, most college students had returned to conservative political outlooks.

Thus, the study of the historical record alone prevents any easy identification of reform attitude with the interests of a rising class of professional experts. It is clear that period effects, not the crystallization of class antagonisms, are responsible for much of the rise in liberalism and dissent among professionals in the 1960s and 1970s. In this vein, it is worth noting that "new class" theories were popular also in the 1930s and early 1940s (Soule 1934, Lasswell 1936, Burnham 1941).

CONCLUSION

Those who have emphasized the inversion of traditional relationships between class and political ideology have made some important errors. They have failed to appreciate the continued conservatism of professionals on economic and equality-related issues. They have often overlooked continuities in the liberalism of professionals on civil liberties and civil rights issues, suggesting a recent inversion where none exists. They have sometimes exaggerated the liberalism of professionals on these issues where professionals have in fact become the most liberal stratum. And they have been too inclined to treat short-term responses to the rise of new issues as evidence of underlying transformations in the social bases of political belief. Those who have been more skeptical about the significance of middle-class liberalism have also made some errors. They have been overly inclined to dismiss some of the real changes that have occurred, particularly on welfare state, business support, personal freedoms, and military force issues. In this way, they have been overwilling to discount the clear evidence that, apart from the very poor, professionals are now the most consistently liberal stratum in American society.

Though the survey evidence helps to clear up many disagreements in the literature about the political attitudes of professionals, it does not in itself lead to much clarification of the central point of interest: how to explain the apparent anomaly of relatively high levels of liberalism and dissent in this high status category. I will argue that this anomaly is best explained by looking simultaneously at the patterns created by two developments: (1) The rise and fall of political issues and the coalitions that form around them; and (2) gradual changes in the occupational and class structure.

The political divisions characteristic of the late 1960s and early 1970s, the high point of liberalism and dissent among professionals, most clearly involve the rise of new political issues rather than the crystallization of new types of class antagonisms. The most divisive of these issues involved minority rights and opportunities, support and opposition to traditional moral and family values, and styles of patriotic expression. For a time, these issues supplanted the New Deal issues of welfare, labor rights, and redistribution that had created substantial lines of division between the economically conservative upper classes and the economically liberal lower classes (Phillips 1969:461–74, Hodgson 1976:412–28, Sundquist 1973:308–31, Nie, Verba & Petrocik 1979:96–109, 194–269). With the rise of these new issues, new patterns of alliance and cleavage formed. Highly educated professionals were often allied with blacks and other "challenging groups," while businessmen and non-professional workers were often allied as defenders of law and order, tradition-al values, and aggressive nationalism (Phillips 1969:461–74, Hodgson 1976:412–28). The effects of this reshuffling are still apparent. When econom-ic concerns regained centrality in the early and mid-1970s, a significant number of nonprofessional workers, in their distaste for the coalition of minorities and worker professionals who remained influential in the Democratic Party, began to espouse the virtues of "free enterprise" and unrestricted competition—a striking departure encouraged by the imaginative policies of populist, "pro-growth" Republican politicians of the 1970s. Following a more predictable cause, many professionals also shifted over time toward views consistent with their traditional conservatism on economic issues.

Yet the fact remains that professionals continue to be comparatively liberal. Though radical attitudes are extremely rare in the United States, professionals are also disproportionately likely to be among the relatively few dissenters on the political left. These facts suggest that, while the rise and fall of issue-based coalitions are of central importance, something more fundamental may also be at work. "New class" theories, stripped of their ideological biases, can provide some help here. Changes in the occupational and class structure have not created an "oppositional intelligentsia," but they have augmented the ties of professionals to the liberal culture of the universities, and they have also encouraged some loosening of the bonds between professionals and business elites.

The social character of the salaried professional class must be defined both in terms of what remains constant and what has changed. Professionals continue to enjoy superior labor market opportunities by virtue of their skills, culture, and training. They also, very frequently, continue to have responsibilities for organizational enhancement and/or profit-making. These characteristics con-tinue to encourage a sympathy for the values of individualism and relatively unrestricted market competition. At the same time, most professionals engage in expressly intellectual functions at work and have increasingly close ties to higher education (Bell 1973:212–42, 371–8, Rodriguez 1978, Gouldner 1979:18–27, 43–7; Derber & Boren 1983). Of all the institutions in American society, the universities provide perhaps the most consequential base for value systems that depart from the materialist, profit-seeking culture of the business corporations. Inside the university, the value strains of humanism, romanticism, socialism, progressivism and populism, to name just a few, compete with the individualism, materialism, and economism of the larger society. To a greater degree, a "culture of critical discourse" prevails in the universities; skepticism is, to some degree, institutionalized (Gouldner 1979:28–37). Culturally, then, professionals are truly in a "contradictory" position. The changing character of ties to intellectual and business elites leads to a greater liberalism, if one takes a long historical view. It follows that younger professionals are affected to a greater degree than those who were shaped by a different configuration of social influences.

One can identify a politically relevant social class by looking for distinctive commonalities in experience, social location and consciousness of kind (Bell 1979:180–1). It seems to me that the middle stratum of credentialed professionals and managers increasingly fits these criteria. So far, theories of the "new class" have not been very helpful to political sociologists, however. The "new class" is not "oppositional" or even consistently "liberal," and its politics reflect period effects as much as stable interests and ideals. Indeed, the culturally contradictory situation of professionals renders the old categories— "conservative" and "liberal"—of limited value for classifying what is distinctive about the professionals' political consciousness. Instead, the central tendency is clearly toward a synthesis of "conservative," market-oriented preferences and "liberal," communally-oriented preferences. Thus, intellectual spokesmen for the class as a whole typically seek a synthesis of "pragmatic" and "idealistic" concerns. Reich (1983:1–12), for example, seeks to unite what he sees as useful principles in both "business" and "civic" cultures. (For another example, see Thurow 1980:191–214.)

Though these synthetic ideals represent the central tendency in the professionals' political consciousness, a spread of political views inevitably exists within the class. The distribution tends to reflect the sources of influence that together form the complex of common experiences defining the class as a whole. Thus, "conservative" views will tend to predominate to a greater degree where market opportunities and profit-making responsibilities are greatest, while "liberal" views will be most in evidence where these opportunities and responsibilities are restricted and where ties between higher education and occupational status are most pronounced.

An understanding of the class situation of professionals contributes to the earlier discussion of the rise and fall of issue-based coalitions. As that earlier discussion suggests, professionals will tend to ally with different coalition partners depending on the type of political issues that are paramount during a particular period./ The dilemma of the "new class" is that its characteristic political outlook gives it little chance for independence where it might be popular, and little chance for popularity where it might be independent. When economic issues are central, most members will ally as junior partners to the higher bourgeoisie. When social and foreign policy issues are in the foreground, much of the class will stake out an independent position, but one which has thus far enjoyed relatively little popularity among less educated and lower status groups and has even stimulated considerable antagonism.[8]

In this sense, it is safe to say that national leaders attuned to the political aspirations of the "new class" have so far failed to discover a means of popularizing the modal class ideology. Nor, in the absence of such a synthesis, have they effectively pursued a strategy that combines independence from the higher bourgeoisie with the possibility of sustained popularity among large numbers of less educated workers. Whether they will discover such a course (and how ably they will pursue it) is one of the significant questions bearing on the future of American politics.

ACKNOWLEDGMENTS

I wish to thank Professors Paul DiMaggio, Eliot Freidson, Seymour Martin Lipset, and James Short for their helpful comments on an earlier draft of this paper. I also wish to thank two anonymous reviewers for *The Annual Review of Sociology,* whose comments substantially improved the paper. Many thanks also go to Patricia Hartman, Marilyn Davis, Nancy Sullivan, and Rita Gold for typing the manuscript drafts.

[8]There is one exception to this generalization—professionals do provide the natural leadership during periods of what Hodgson (1976:73) calls "liberal-conservative consensus." These periods, however, have been both relatively rare and short-lived. The Progressive Era (1900–1917), the "New Frontier" years (1960–1963), and the first years of the Johnson Administration (1964–1965) are the clearest examples of such periods in twentieth century America.

Literature Cited

Abramson, P. R. 1974. Generational change in American electoral behavior. *Am. Polit. Sci. Rev.* 68:93–105

American Council on Education. 1970. *The American freshman: National norms for 1970.* Washington, DC: Am. Coun. Ed.

American Council on Education. 1980. *The American freshman: National norms for 1980.* Washington, DC: Am. Coun. Ed.

Anderson, H. D., Davidson, P. E. 1943. *Ballots and the Democratic Class Struggle.* Stanford, Calif: Stanford

Bailyn, L. 1980. *Living with Technology.* Cambridge: MIT

Barry, J. T. 1977. *Social origins and values of knowledge-based elites in contemporary society.* Ph.D. thesis. State University of New York at Buffalo

Bell, C. G. 1968. A new suburban politics. *Soc. Forc.* 47:280–88

Bell, D. 1973. *The Coming of Post-Industrial Society.* New York: Basic

Bell, D. 1979. The new class: A muddled concept. In *The New Class?,* ed. B. Bruce-Briggs, pp. 169–190. New Brunswick, NJ: Transaction

Brint, S. G. 1981. *Is there a new class ideology?: An empirical assessment of political and cultural outlooks.* Presented at Ann. Meet. East. Sociol. Soc., New York

Brint, S. G. 1982. *Stirrings of an oppositional elite?: The social location and historical trajectory of upper white collar dissent in the United States, 1960–1980.* Ph.D. thesis. Harvard University, Boston, Mass

Brint, S. G. 1984. "New class" and cumulative trend explanations of the liberal political attitudes of professionals. *Am. J. Sociol.* 90:30–71

Burnham, J. 1941. *The Managerial Revolution.* New York: Day

Burnham, W. D. 1975. American politics in the 1970s: Beyond party. In *The American Party Systems,* eds. W. N. Chambers, W. D. Burnham, pp. 308–57. New York: Oxford

Burnham, W. D. 1981. The 1980 Earthquake: Realignment, reaction, or what? In *The Hidden Election,* ed. T. Ferguson, J. Rogers, pp. 98–140. New York: Pantheon

Burris, V. 1981. *Class structure and political attitudes.* Presented at Ann. Meet. Pac. Sociol. Assoc. Portland, Oregon

Converse, P. E., Miller, W. E., Rusk, J. G., Wolfe, A. C. 1969. Continuity and change in American politics: Parties and issues in the 1968 election. *Am. Polit. Sci. Rev.* 63:1083–1105

Converse, P. E., Dotson, J. D., Hoag, W. J., McGee, W. H. III. 1980. *American Social Attitudes Data Source Book, 1947–1978.* Cambridge: Harvard

Cunliffe, M. 1955. The intellectuals: The United States. *Encounter* 4:23–33

Davis, J. A. 1965. *Undergraduate Career Decisions: Correlates of Occupational Choice.* Chicago: Aldine

Davis, J. A. 1979. *Background variables and opinions in the 1972–1977 NORC General Social Surveys: Ten generalizations about age, education, occupational prestige, race, religion and sex, and forty-nine opinion items.* Chicago, Natl. Opinion Res. Cent. General Social Survey Tech. Rep. No. 18

Davis, J. A. 1980. Conservative weather in a liberalizing climate: Change in selected NORC General Social Survey items, 1972–1978. *Soc. Forc.* 58:1129–56

Derber, C. K. 1983. Sponsorship and the control of physicians. *Theory Soc.* 12:561–601

Derber, C. K., Boren, J. 1983. *Professionals as Workers.* Chestnut Hill, Mass., Boston College. Report to the National Institute of Mental Health

Ehrenreich, J., Ehrenreich, B. 1977. The professional-managerial class. *Radic. Am.,* pp. 7–31

Erdmann, J. B., Jones, R. F., Tonesk, X. 1979. *AAMC longitudinal study of medical school graduates of 1960.* Washington, DC: Natl. Center Health Serv. Res. Research Digest Series

Erlanger, H. S. 1977. Social reform organizations and subsequent careers of participants: A follow-up study of early participants in the OEO legal series program. *Am. Sociol. Rev.* 42:233–48

Etzioni, A., Nunn, C. Z. 1977. Public views of scientists. *Science* 181:1123

Feagin, J. R. 1975. *Subordinating the Poor: Welfare and American Beliefs.* Englewood Cliffs: Prentice-Hall

Ferree, G. D. 1980. The generation gap. *Public Opin.* 3 (Feb./March):38–9

Fox, M., Hesse-Biber, S. 1984. *Women at Work.* Palo Alto: Mayfield

Gallup, G. 1983. *The Gallup Poll: Public Opinion 1982.* Wilmington: Scholarly Resources

Gitlin, T. 1982. Television screens: Hegemony in transition. In *Cultural and Economic Reproduction in Education,* ed. M. W. Apple, pp. 202–46. London: Routledge, Kegan Paul

Glenn, N. D. 1973. Class and party support in the United States: recent and emerging trends. *Public Opin. Q.* 37:1–20

Greeley, A. M. 1977. *The American Catholic.* New York: Basic

Greenstein, F. I., Wolfinger, R. E. 1958. The suburbs and shifting party loyalties. *Public Opin. Q.* 22:473–82

Greenwald, H. P. 1978. Politics and the new insecurity: Ideological changes of professionals in a recession. *Soc. Forc.* 57:103–18

Gouldner, A. 1979. *The Future of Intellectuals and the Rise of the New Class.* New York: Seabury

Hamilton, R. 1975. *Restraining Myths.* New York: Wiley

Handler, J. F., Hollingsworth, E. J., Erlanger, H. S. 1978. *Lawyers and the Pursuit of Legal Rights.* New York: Academic

Heinz, J. P., Laumann, E. O. 1982. *Chicago Lawyers: The Social Structure of the Bar.* New York/Chicago: Russell Sage Foun. and Am. Bar Foun.

Hodgson, G. 1976. *America in Our Time.* Garden City, NJ: Doubleday

Hoge, D. R. 1971. College students' value patterns in the 1950s and 1960s. *Sociol. Educ.* 44:170–97

Hoge, D. R., Luna, C. L., Miller, D. K. 1981. Trends in college students' values between 1952 and 1979: A return to the fifties? *Sociol. Educ.* 54:263–74

Huber, J., Form, W. H. 1973. *Income and Ideology: An Analysis of the American Political Formula.* New York: Free

Hyman, H. 1966. The value system of the different classes. In *Class, Status and Power,* eds. R. Bendix, S. M. Lipset, pp. 488–99. New York: Free

Hyman, H. H., Wright, C. R. 1979. *Education's Lasting Influence on Values.* Chicago: Univ. Chicago

Inglehart, R. 1971. The silent revolution in Europe: Intergenerational change in post-industrial societies. *Am. Polit. Sci. Rev.* 65:991–1017

Inglehart, R. 1977. *The Silent Revolution: Changing Values and Political Styles Among Western Publics.* Princeton, NJ: Princeton

Inglehart, R. 1981. Post-Materialism in an Environment of Insecurity? *Am. Polit. Sci. Rev.* 75:880–900

Jackman, M. R. 1978. General and applied tolerance: Does education increase commitment to racial integration? *Am. J. Polit. Sci.* 22:302–24

Jackman, M. R., Jackman, R. W. 1983. *Class Awareness in the United States.* Berkeley: Univ. Calif.

Johnstone, J. W. C., Slawski, E. J., Bowman, W. W. 1973. The professional values of American newsmen. *Public Opin. Q.* 36:522–40

Kirkpatrick, J. J. 1976. *The New Presidential Elite.* New York: Russell Sage

Knoke, D. 1976. *Change and Continuity in American Politics.* Baltimore: Johns Hopkins

Knoke, D. 1979. Stratification and the dimensions of American political orientations. *Am. J. Polit. Sci.* 23:772–91

Knoke, D., Isaac, L. 1976. Quality of higher education and sociopolitical attitudes. *Soc. Forc.* 54:524–9

Kornhauser, A. W. 1939. Analysis of the class structure of contemporary American society—psychological bases of class divisions. In *Industrial Conflict: A Psychological Interpretation,* eds. G. W. Hartmann, T. Newcomb, pp. 199–264. New York: Cordan

Kristol, I. 1972. About equality. *Commentary* 54:41–7

Kristol, I. 1975. Corporate capitalism in America. *Public Inter.* 37:124–43

Ladd, E. C., Jr. 1978. The new lines are drawn: Class and ideology, I. *Public Opin.* 1 (Sept./Oct.):14–20

Ladd, E. C., Jr. 1979. Pursuing the new class: Social theory and survey data. In *The New Class?,* ed. B. Bruce-Briggs, pp. 101–22. New Brunswick: Transaction

Ladd, E. C., Jr., Lipset, S. M. 1975. *The Divided Academy.* New York: Norton

Ladd, E. C., Jr., Hadley, C. D. 1975. *Transformation of the American Party System.* New York: Norton

Lasswell, H. D. 1936. *Politics: Who Gets What, When, How?* New York: Whittlesey

Lazarsfeld, P., Thielens, W. J. 1958. *The Academic Mind.* Glencoe: Free

Leuba, J. H. 1934. Religious beliefs of American scientists. *Harper's* 169:291–300

Lipset, S. M. 1979. The new class and the professoriate. In *The New Class?,* ed. B. Bruce-Briggs, pp. 67–88. New Brunswick: Transaction

Lipset, S. M. 1981. *Political Man: The Social Bases of Politics.* Baltimore: Johns Hopkins. 2nd ed.

Lipset, S. M. 1982. The academic mind at the top: The political behavior and values of faculty elites. *Public Opin. Q.* 46:143–68

Lipset, S. M., Dobson, R. B. 1972. The intellectual as critic and rebel. *Daedalus* 101:137–98

Lipset, S. M., Ladd, E. C., Jr. 1971. College generations from the 1930s to the 1960s. *Public Inter.* 25:99–113

Lipset, S. M., Schneider, W. 1978. How's business? What the public thinks. *Public Opin.* 1 (July/Aug.):41–7

Lipset, S. M., Schneider, W. 1981. Organized labor and the public: A troubled union. *Public Opin.* 3:52–6

Lipset, S. M., Schneider, W. 1983. *The Confidence Gap: Business, Labor and Government in the Public Mind.* New York: Free

Lipset, S. M., Schwartz, M. A. 1966. The politics of professionals. In *Professionalization,* eds. H. M. Vollmer, D. L. Mills, pp. 299–310. Englewood Cliffs: Prentice-Hall

Marketing Concepts, Inc. 1978a. *The Study of American Opinion, 1978 Report, Vol. 1.* New York: US News World Rep.

Marketing Concepts, Inc. 1978b. *The Study of American Opinion, 1978 Report, Vol. 2.* New York: US News World Rep.

Martin, L. J. 1981. Science and the successful society. *Public Opin.* 4 (June/July):16–19, 55–56

Maslow, A. H. 1962. *Toward a Psychology of Being.* Englewood Cliffs, NJ: Van Nostrand

Meyer, H., Litwak, E., Warren, D. 1968. Occupational and class differences in social values: A comparison of teachers and social workers. *Sociol. Educ.* 41:263–81

Miles, M. W. 1973. *The Radical Probe: The Logic of Student Rebellion.* New York: Atheneum

Miller, W. E., Miller, A. H., Schneider, E. J. 1980. *American National Election Survey Data Sourcebook.* Cambridge: Harvard

Mitchell, R. C. 1979. Silent spring/solid majorities. *Public Opin.* 2 (Aug./Sept.):16–19

Moynihan, D. P. 1972. Equalizing education: In whose interest? *Public Inter.* 29:69–89

Nathan, J. A., Oliver, J. K. 1975. Public opinion and U.S. security policy. *Armed Forc. Soc.* 2:46–62

National Education Association. 1982. *Status of the American Public School Teacher, 1980–1981.* Washington: NEA

National Opinion Research Center. 1981. *General Social Surveys, 1972–1980: Cumulative codebook.* Chicago: NORC

Nie, N. H., Verba, S., Petrocik, J. R. 1979. *The Changing American Voter.* Cambridge, Mass: Harvard. 2nd ed.

Nunn, C. Z., Crockett, H. J., Jr., Williams, J.

A., Jr. 1978. *Tolerance for Nonconformity.* San Francisco: Jossey-Bass

O'Conner, J. 1973. *The Fiscal Crisis of the State.* New York: St. Martin's

Opinion Roundup 1978a. The nation's 'most important problem.' *Public Opin.* 1 (May/June):30–2

Opinion Roundup 1978b. The national mood. *Public Opin.* 1 (July/Aug.):21–8

Opinion Roundup 1978c. Left, right, or center: Which way are we going? *Public Opin.* 1 (Sept./Oct.):33–9

Opinion Roundup 1980a. Gaping at the generation gap. *Public Opin.* 3 (Feb./March):38–9

Opinion Roundup 1980b. The balance sheet on business. *Public Opin.* 3 (April/May):21–9

Opinion Roundup 1980c. NORC: portrait of America—part one. *Public Opin.* 3 (Aug./Sept.):28–39

Opinion Roundup 1980d. NORC: portrait of America—part two. *Public Opin.* 3 (Oct./Nov.):22–35

Opinion Roundup 1981a. The state of race relations—1981. *Public Opin.* 4 (April/May): 32–40

Opinion Roundup 1981b. Taking our measure at year 205. *Public Opin.* 4 (June/July):21–40

Opinion Roundup 1981c. Working in America. *Public Opin.* 4 (Aug./Sept.):25–34

Opinion Roundup 1981d. Examining elites. *Public Opin.* 4 (Oct./Nov.):29–33

Opinion Roundup 1982a. Environmental update. *Public Opin.* 5 (Feb./March):32–8

Opinion Roundup 1982b. Enduring patterns in American life: A decade of NORC surveys. *Public Opin.* 5 (Oct./Nov.):25–9

Opinion Roundup 1983a. Five years of public opinion. *Public Opin.* 6:21–31

Opinion Roundup 1983b. The public evaluates government activities. *Public Opin.* 6:32–3

Opinion Roundup 1983c. Foreign affairs: What's past is prologue. *Public Opin.* 6:28–31

Parkin, F. 1968. *Middle Class Radicalism.* New York: Praeger

Phillips, K. P. 1969. *The Emerging Republican Majority.* New Rochelle, NY: Arlington

Reich, C. 1970. *The Greening of America.* New York: Random

Reich, R. B. 1983. *The Next American Frontier.* New York: Times Books

Research and Forecasts, Inc. 1981. *Connecticut Mutual Life Report on American Values in the '80s: The Impact of Belief.* Hartford: Conn. Mutual Life Ins. Co.

Robinson, J. P. 1970. Public reaction to political protest: Chicago 1968. *Public Opin. Q.* 34:1–9

Robinson, R. V., Bell, W. 1978. Equality, success and social justice. *Am. Sociol. Rev.* 43:125–43

Rodriguez, O. 1978. Occupational shifts and educational upgrading in the American labor

force between 1950 and 1970. *Sociol. Educ.* 51:55–67

Rothman, S. 1979. The mass media in post-industrial America. In *The Third Century: America as a Post-Industrial Society,* ed. S. M. Lipset, pp. 345–88. Stanford, CA: Hoover

Russett, B. M., Hanson, E. C. 1975. *Interest and Ideology: The Foreign Policy Beliefs of American Businessmen.* New Haven: Yale

Schumpeter, J. 1942. *Capitalism, Socialism and Democracy.* New York: Harper

Seeman, M. 1958. The intellectual and the language of minorities. *Am. J. Sociol.* 64: 25–35

Soule, G. 1934. *The Coming American Revolution.* New York: Macmillan

Storer, J. F. 1982. *Liberal professions and the 'new class': 1968–1972.* Senior Honors Thesis. Harvard College, Cambridge, Mass.

Stouffer, S. A. 1955. *Communism, Conformity and Civil Liberties: A Cross-Section of the Nation Speaks Its Mind.* New York: Doubleday

Students for a Democratic Society. 1962. *The Port Huron statement.* New York: Students for a Democratic Society

Sundquist, J. 1973. *Dynamics of the Party System.* Washington: Brookings

Szelenyi, I. 1980. *Prospects and limits of power of intellectuals under market capitalism.* Unpublished manuscript. School Soc. Sci., The Flinders Univ. S. Australia

Taylor, D. G., Sheatley, P. B., Greeley, A. M. 1978. Attitudes toward racial integration. *Sci. Am.* 238:42–9

Taylor, D. G., Smith, T. W. 1978. *Public opinion regarding various forms of sexual behavior.* Chicago: National Opin. Res. Cent. GSS Technical Report No. 10

Thurow, L. 1980. *The Zero-Sum Society.* New York: Basic

Tunstall, J. 1971. *Journalists at Work.* Beverly Hills: Sage

van Fossen, B. E. 1979. *The Structure of Social Inequality.* Boston: Little Brown

van Liere, K. D., Dunlap, R. E. 1980. The social bases of environmental concern: A review of hypotheses, explanations and empirical evidence. *Public Opin. Q.* 44: 181–97

Vogel, D. 1980. The inadequacy of contemporary opposition to business. *Daedalus* 109: 47–58

Watts, W., Free, L. A. 1976. Nationalism not isolationism. *Foreign Pol.* 24:3–26

Watts, W. 1981. Americans' hopes and fears: The future can fend for itself. *Psychol. Today* (Sept.):36–48

Weil, F. D. 1982. Tolerance of free speech in the United States and West Germany, 1970–79: An analysis of public opinion survey data. *Soc. Forc.* 60:973–92

Weiner, T. S., Eckland, B. K. 1979. Education and political party: the effects of college or social class. *Am. J. Sociol.* 84:911–27

Weinstein, J. 1968. *The Corporate Ideal in the Liberal State 1900–1918.* Boston: Beacon

Weisbrod, B. A. 1980. *Wage differentials between for-profit and non-profit sectors.* Unpublished paper. Univ. Wisc., Inst. Res. Poverty

Westby, D. L. 1976. *The Clouded Vision: The Student Movement in the United States in the 1960s.* Lewisburg, Penn: Bucknell

Whyte, W. H. 1956. *The Organization Man.* New York: Simon Schuster

Williams, R. M., Jr. 1960. *American Society:*

A Sociological Interpretation. New York: Knopf. 2nd ed.

Wilson, J. Q. 1962. *The Amateur Democrat: Club Politics in Three Cities.* Chicago: Univ. Chicago

Wuthnow, R., Shrum, W., Jr. 1983. Knowledge workers as a 'new class': Structural and ideological convergence among professional-technical workers and managers. *Work Occup.* 10:471–83

Yankelovich, D. 1974. *The New Morality.* New York: McGraw-Hill

Yankelovich, D., Kaagan, L. 1981. Assertive America. *Foreign Aff.* 59:696–713

Ann. Rev. Sociol. 1985. 11:415–36

SOCIAL CONTROL OF OCCUPATIONS AND WORK

Richard L. Simpson

Department of Sociology, University of North Carolina, Chapel Hill, North Carolina 27514

Abstract

Three largely separate literatures—on organizations, on professions, and on manual and clerical work settings—have treated the social control of work. From these writings we identify five modes of control over work: simple, technical, bureaucratic, occupational, and worker self-control. We discuss findings on conditions that underlie the occurrence of different controls. Contingency and resource dependence organization theories help explain the degree of bureaucratic control and the power of work groups within organizations. Literature on occupations and work groups suggests four categories of variables related to modes of control. These pertain to (*a*) the nature of tasks, particularly their degree of uncertainty, (*b*) relations between segments of an occupation, (*c*) how an occupation fits into a division of labor, and (*d*) relations of an occupation to elements of its environment such as clients, markets, or government. Findings on professionals and those on lower-status workers are often similar although stated differently. Some findings of the sociology of work are subsumable under theories about organizations.

INTRODUCTION

Over the past 20 years or so, three main bodies of literature have examined the social control of work: analysis of organizations, particularly of the kinds known as "contingency theory" and "resource dependence theory;" writings on professions; and studies of factories, offices, and other places of manual or low-status white-collar work. These literatures have reached similar conclu-

415

0360-0572/85/0815-0415$02.00

sions, but this fact has been obscured because they have been written by different people, have used different terminologies, and have seldom drawn ideas explicitly from each other.

We begin this essay with a summary of some ideas developed by organization theorists that are pertinent to the social control of occupations and work groups. We then review writings on control and autonomy of professions and of manual and clerical workers and note how some of them relate to organization theory.

CONTINGENCY THEORY

Contingency theory grew up in the 1960s. It asserts that different technologies and environments pose different problems for organizations and hence give rise to characteristic ways of behaving: how an organization works is contingent on its technology and environment.

To oversimplify only slightly, contingency theorists classify organizations or their subunits as being more or less bureaucratic in the Weberian sense. A highly bureaucratic organization emphasizes rules, hierarchical chains of command, and centralized planning of operational details. A relatively unbureaucratic organization is more loosely controlled and less rule-bound, with little stress on routing communication through predetermined hierarchical channels and with discretion granted to lower managers or ordinary workers to make tactical decisions in consultation with whomever they think it expedient to consult.

To explain how bureaucratic an organization will be, contingency theorists invoke two main kinds of variables: the amount of coordination needed, and the uncertainty or variability of technological processes and environmental pressures. The basic idea is that the more coordination is needed, the more bureaucratic the system will be unless technological or environmental factors are too unpredictable or poorly understood to allow much bureaucratic prespecification of work. Writers who have looked at coordination needs as a reason for bureaucratization include Udy (1959) on complexity of technical processes, Thompson (1967) on interdependence of work units, Williamson (1975) on interdependence, and, of course, Weber (1946, 1947). Contingency theorists usually put more stress on technological or environmental uncertainty than on coordination needs, but the chief effect of uncertainty appears to be to limit the bureaucratization that occurs if the need for coordination is high.

Contingency theories argue that technological or environmental uncertainty fosters decentralized decisions and informality in three main ways. First, if the relation between the ends sought and the means to accomplish them is poorly understood, operating decisions are likely to be left to the hunch and wisdom of workers at the front line, unfettered by rules (Burns & Stalker 1961, Thompson

1967, Hickson et al 1969, Perrow 1970, Galbraith 1973, Van de Ven et al 1976, Lawrence 1981). Second, if the problems that require solution are nonroutine and unpredictable, an organization cannot preprogram their solutions and is likely to give workers discretion to use initiative to solve them, consulting and coordinating with whoever seems appropriate (Burns & Stalker 1961, Blau & Scott 1962, Woodward 1965, Perrow 1967, 1970, Hage & Aiken 1969, Child 1972, Scott 1981). Third, if the environment is fast-changing, unpredictable, and uncontrollable, workers or operating subunits are apt to be left free to act on their own initiative; rules cannot cover unexpected situations, and "going through channels" might be too slow for quick adaptation (Burns & Stalker 1961, Chandler 1962, Woodward 1965, Lawrence & Lorsch 1967, Thompson 1967, Dornbusch & Scott 1975, Aldrich 1979, Lawrence 1981).

RESOURCE DEPENDENCE THEORY

The resource dependence perspective on organizations is a special case of human ecology (Hawley 1950). Organizations develop structures and processes that provide for dependable inflows of resources from their environments (Aldrich & Pfeffer 1976, Pfeffer & Salancik 1978, Bidwell & Kasarda 1985). For our purpose, the most important corollary is that if organizational subunits or members are influential in getting scarce or undependable resources, they will have power within the organization (Selznick 1949, Hawley 1950, Woodward 1965, Zald 1970, Bidwell & Kasarda 1985). If we define "resources" broadly to mean anything useful whether externally or internally generated, then by extension a unit that monopolizes knowledge or control over crucial and uncertain parts of an organization's technology (a resource) will have power (Crozier 1964).

TYPES OF CONTROL OF WORK

We can identify five types of control over workers on the job. We take three of them from Edwards's (1979) analysis of industrial control. We add two to cover situations where the source of control is not an employer—chiefly solo proprietor and some professional and craft settings.

Edwards (1979) distinguishes simple vs. technical vs. bureaucratic modes of control. Simple control has two subtypes, direct and hierarchical. Direct control, found in small shops and offices, is that of boss over worker, face to face, untrammelled by rules and wholly arbitrary if the boss so desires. When a firm gets too big for the top boss to control everyone personally, hierarchical control is introduced, with layers of managers each reproducing the simple form of control over subordinates who may themselves be middle or lower managers. Technical control is embedded in the technology of work. An assembly line in which the machines control the workers is an example. Personal surveillance is reduced to a bare minimum if not eliminated. Bureaucratic control reintroduces supervision but rests chiefly on rules, formal incentives and punishments, and other impersonal devices (Weber 1946). Supervisors cannot dominate workers capriciously as in simple control, for they too are bound by bureaucratic control that limits their authority.

The remaining types of work control are not imposed on workers by employing organizations. In occupational control an occupational group controls its own members. Leading professions are its prime contemporary example and guilds its prime historical example. Self-control is a residual category in which individuals control their own work, as is true of self-employed proprietors.

Mixed Controls

These modes of work control are ideal types. They may occur in relatively pure form, but organizations or occupations may also exert more than one kind of control over different workers or even particular workers.

Edwards (1979) describes modern mass production factories as having technical control reinforced by bureaucracy. In addition, occupational or self-control may be mixed with bureaucratic control. Kusterer's (1978) study of paper workers and bank tellers shows how workers devise their own techniques to make the work easy and efficient. Friedman's (1977) examination of small British factories and Burawoy's (1979) study of a machine shop take the analysis of observations similar to Kusterer's farther than he does. According to them, managers whose technologies do not permit technical control deliberately give workers some of what Friedman calls "responsible autonomy" as a means of what Burawoy calls "manufacturing consent" to work toward production goals. They are describing a bureaucratic device to bring about some self- or occupational control in the interest of management.

Government regulations may bring bureaucracy into occupational control systems. Physicians now must submit to the scrutiny of their hospitalized patients' records by Professional Standards Review Organizations (PSROs). Scott (1982a) and Freidson (1983, 1984, 1985) regard this as no real threat to occupational control because the law requires that physicians dominate the PSROs. In support of this view, Anderson & Shields (1982) review literature and find little effect on hospital utilization rates attributable to PSROs. But Westphal et al (1979) report significant declines in length of stay and average charges in one hospital following institution of PSRO admission and length-of-stay review of Medicare and Medicaid patients. Government controls with teeth, such as cost ceilings on Medicaid hospitalization, evidently have more dependable effects than noncoercive peer review.

In group medical practices and hospitals, occupational control appears to be a ritualized facade and self-control a reality (Freidson 1975, Millman 1977,

Bosk 1979). Colleagues supposedly evaluate each other's work, but the real collegial ethic is to live and let live. It is bad form to discipline or even criticize a colleague, though hopeless incompetents may be forced to resign from group practices. Bosk sees the hospital surgeons he studied as having been socialized into a strong ethical sense of self-control that minimized shoddy practice. Freidson (1970a) doubts that medical school socialization has much effect; but even if he is right, a professional's immediate colleagues are a reference group whose behavior and stated values presumably influence the nature of self-control. Carlin (1966) finds that contact with colleagues makes for ethical behavior among lawyers (as lawyers define "ethics"). Zey-Ferrell et al (1979) and Zey-Ferrell & Ferrell (1982) report similar effects of colleague contacts among marketing practitioners and advertising executives.

Segments of an occupation may be subject to different controls. In the building trades, the privileged stratum of unionized workers on big projects has considerable occupational control while nonunion house construction workers are under the simple control of contractors (Riemer 1982). Among lawyers, the elite in large law firms have occupational control (Smigel 1969), while solo practitioners are self-controlled but constrained by client dependence (Carlin 1962, cf. Freidson 1960 on doctors). Industrial scientists are bureaucratically controlled (Marcson 1960, Kornhauser 1962), but academic scientists are in a mixed and far less bureaucratic system that includes elements of self-control and occupational control.

Some Devices of Bureaucratic Control

By "devices" of bureaucratic control we mean features of a work organization that are not parts of the definition of bureaucracy but contribute to its functioning, whether or not that is their intended effect.

INTERNAL LABOR MARKETS   Job ladders with higher positions filled by promotion (internal labor markets) (Doeringer & Piore 1971) have been viewed as a way to individualize workers and forestall a sense of shared fate. Stone's (1974) study of the origins of job structures in the steel industry argues that employers deliberately imposed long ladders of artificial skill distinctions as a means of labor discipline. (For similar analyses, see Dreyfuss 1938, Aronowitz 1973, Acker & Van Houten 1974, Braverman 1974, Marglin 1974, Kanter 1975, Glenn & Feldberg 1977, Goldman & Van Houten 1977, Edwards 1979, Meyer 1981). Elbaum & Wilkinson (1979) point out that workers, not just managers, have fought to establish internal promotion ladders; but Burawoy (1983) maintains that this is precisely the point, since anything that creates a sense of common interest between management and labor is an aid to discipline.

UNIONS   As another bureaucratic control device unions push for internal labor markets, enforce work rules, process grievances, and orient workers to narrowly economistic goals that do not challenge management's essential authority (Edwards 1979, Friedman 1982, Bluestone & Harrison 1982, Gordon et al 1982, Burawoy 1983). To describe unionism as a managerial strategy may seem odd in view of the bloodshed that has accompanied many organizing drives and the current flight of unionized industries to nonunion places. But the point is how unions function in prosperous oligopolistic firms, not whether capitalists like them.

OTHER PRACTICES   Writers have also identified piecework pay as a technique of bureaucratic control. Pieceworkers need no supervision if their products are inspected. Stinchcombe (1983) notes that piecework or sharecropping is likely to be used when simple control would be inefficient, and he analyzes specific conditions that lead to the choice of piecework or supervision. Burawoy (1979) analyzes a machine shop piecework system as a deliberate management device to instill economistic false consciousness and create dissension about who was and was not informally allowed to work at the top rate, given that not all could or the rates would be reset.

Two other practices that have been analyzed as bureaucratic control devices are professionalism (Larson 1977) and worker participation in decisions about production (Krause 1982). Both are thought to motivate workers to strive without supervision to meet management's goals in situations where the work is too variable and its skills too complex for piecework pay schemes.

Some Aspects of Occupational Control

Freidson (1970a, 1970b) distinguishes between the content of work—what an occupation's tasks are and how they are done—and the terms of work, i.e. the social structure in which the work is embedded and which regulates it, including its marketing and compensation. A control system involves, at a minimum, control over the content of work. It may also involve control over the terms of work. An occupational group that controls the terms of work is well situated to control its content.

Monopolistic licensure, with the licensing process in the hands of the professions themselves, is the most obvious way in which professions control the content of their work and, to some extent, its terms (Akers 1968, Shimberg 1982). Some professions, most notably medicine, have gone beyond licensure to establish dominance over an entire division of labor, including control over the work content of subordinate occupations (Freidson 1970b; Kronus 1976). It has been argued that the licensure of numerous allied health occupations has reduced the power of physicians (Armstrong 1976), but Larkin's (1978, 1981) studies of British radiographers and ophthalmic opticians lead him to conclude that medical dominance is unabated. As Larkin explains, the medical profession has exerted political influence to get the licensure laws written in ways that sharply limit the tasks of other health occupations and leave to medicine the tasks it wants. On a smaller scale, dentists dominate lesser dental occupations and lawyers increasingly make use of paralegals who are confined to routine tasks such as monitoring court proceedings, filing documents, computerized legal research, and initial document preparation (Powell 1985).

By translating cultural influence into political power, some professions have gained control over the content of their work and have enlarged their markets. The medical profession, for example, has benefited from society's "medicalization" of deviant behaviors (Zola 1972). Doctors get more business when drunkenness and insanity are redefined as alcoholism and mental illness. In addition, leading professions monopolize what Starr (1982) calls "gatekeeping" functions. Doctors control access to hospitals and prescription drugs. Lawyers control access to criminal justice and, less completely, to such business matters as contracts and torts. Some of the gatekeeping solidifies dominance over other occupations—over pharmacists, for instance.

Types of Variables Affecting the Choice of Work Controls

Neither technology nor environment rigidly foreordains how work will be controlled, at any rate not in detail. Managers choose among possible controls. Nevertheless, there are empirical regularities that relate the technology and environment of work to its most likely types of control. Variables that influence control are of four main kinds which pertain, respectively, to (*a*) the nature of the tasks, mainly their degree of uncertainty vs. routinizability, (*b*) relations between segments of the occupational group, (*c*) the relation of the occupation to other occupations or, more broadly, how it fits into a division of labor, and (*d*) the relations of the occupation to environmental elements such as clients, markets, or government.

In the remainder of this essay we review literature to identify variables of these four kinds that help explain the types of controls and degrees of worker autonomy in different occupations and work settings. Most writings have been about whether control will be bureaucratic or occupational, or which of these will predominate in mixed cases.

SOCIAL CONTROL OF PROFESSIONAL WORK

We focus on control of work on the job. For reasons of space, we say little about macrosocial influences on what the job consists of or the broader aspects of the division of labor.

Task Knowledge, Indeterminacy, and Professional Control

Wilensky (1964) states that an occupation is unlikely to be granted professional autonomy (in our terms, occupational control) if its knowledge is either commonsense or so thoroughly codified as to be easily split into routines. As Wilensky (1964:148) puts it, "If the technical base of an occupation consists of a vocabulary that sounds familiar to everyone . . . or if the base is scientific but so narrow that it can be learned as a set of rules by most people, then the occupation will have difficulty claiming a monopoly of skill or even a roughly exclusive jurisdiction." He develops this idea in analyzing why engineers, whose tasks are scientifically based but partially codifiable as sets of rules, are generally subject to bureaucratic control.

Jamous & Peloille (1970, cf. Nilson 1979) develop this same idea as what they call the indeterminacy/technicality (I/T) ratio. When tasks are so variable, or the relation of means to ends so poorly understood, that the best way to do the job cannot be routinized, then the content of an occupation's work is indeterminate and the worker is likely to be given autonomy, sometimes under the surveillance of occupational colleagues—i.e. there is probably occupational or self-control. The "art" of medicine exemplifies this. An occupation has high technicality and is apt to be bureaucratically controlled if its tasks can be laid out as routines.

Semiprofessions such as schoolteaching, nursing, librarianship, and social work suffer from the first limitation Wilensky mentions. They do not rest on theoretical knowledge that goes beyond what the public knows (or thinks it knows), nor is it theirs alone, rather than taken over from some other profession such as medicine in the case of nursing or psychiatric social work (Etzioni 1969, Simpson & Simpson 1969, Toren 1972, Simpson 1978).

The workings of the I/T ratio can be seen in the case of computer occupations. In the early days of computers the field was considered arcane and indeterminate, and its workers were given autonomy (Danziger 1979). In time, "as the labor process became better understood, occupations which earlier permitted workers substantial self-direction . . . have been subdivided into simpler and more routine jobs which facilitate managerial surveillance and control" (Silver 1982:238, citing Kraft 1979). Computerization has taken away some of the indeterminacy of long-established professions (Child & Fulk 1982). Examples are computerized medical diagnosis, property transfer in law, and some aspects of architectural design. Child & Fulk prophesy that the affected professions will keep their occupational control and will spin off the routinized tasks to subordinate occupations.

Indeterminacy and Occupational Segments

Jamous & Peloille (1970) introduce the I/T ratio to explain dominance within a profession. They analyze how the entrenched clinicians in French hospitals used the prestige of indeterminate clinical diagnosis to defend against an emerging segment of scientific physicians whose knowledge, by virtue of being science-based, was more technical and seemingly routine than the traditional art of clinical medicine. Atkinson et al (1977) use the I/T concept to explain the outcomes of disputes between British Health Service physician segments. They show how the mystique of a claim to indeterminacy of tasks can confer political influence and strengthen occupational control.

Control over areas of uncertainty also brings power within a work organization. Crozier (1964) shows this in analyzing the power of maintenance departments over other subunits in French factories. Blau (1979), looking at architectural firms, reports that the most influential individuals were those whose knowledge enabled them to control areas that were ambiguous for most architects. Albrecht's (1979) study of a juvenile court finds that probation officers resisted computerization of records, which they saw as a tactic to control probation work. Albrecht's analysis is notable for explicitly using a resource dependence perspective, with information about uncertain work conceived as an environmental resource.

Division of Labor and the Monopolization and Proletarianization Theses

Recent writings on professions have featured two main lines of argument pertaining to interoccupational relations in the division of labor. They point in opposite directions. The monopolization thesis seeks to explain how professions have attained occupational control, to which most exponents of the thesis see no immediate end. The proletarianization thesis argues that professionals are increasingly subject to bureaucratic control.

MONOPOLIZATION   The monopolization thesis is an application of Weber's (1947) analysis of group closure. As the term suggests, it is not primarily about how work is controlled but about its markets—both the market for professional services and the professional labor market. The idea, put briefly, is that organized occupational groups have worked successfully in the political arena to obtain legal monopolies of the rights to provide services and, through credentialing, of the rights to decide who is allowed to enter the occupations that provide them (Parkin 1979). The thesis, and ideas resembling it, have informed a number of admirable sociohistorical studies including those of Reader (1966), Freidson (1970a, 1970b), Elliott (1972), Alford (1975), Berlant (1975), Parry & Parry (1976), Larson (1977), Collins (1979), and Starr (1982). To monopolize a service implies at least partially controlling the terms of its work and almost equally implies controlling its content. One cannot satisfactorily monopolize a service if someone else can redefine its content and leave one high and dry with unsalable skills.

The monopolization thesis has been the mainstream view in the sociology of professions since about 1970. The basic historical outline of professional monopolization appears to be beyond dispute, but the sociological analysis of the process has drawn criticism. Saks (1983) observes that neo-Weberian writers on professions have been long on description and short on theoretical explanation of why only some occupations manage to get professional privileges. They may have rejected too completely the earlier functionalist and "trait list" analyses against which the monopolization thesis was a reaction. (See Roth 1974 for a spirited critique of the earlier perspective.) Would we expect a professionalization movement of dishwashers to succeed? If not, why not? The answer takes us back to the traits that set apart professions, perhaps most importantly to an occupationally created body of knowledge pertaining to indeterminate tasks.

PROLETARIANIZATION   One professional trait commonly mentioned in functionalist writings is a systematic theoretical knowledge base. But as we have noted, knowledge may be too systematic for an occupation's own good if it eliminates indeterminacy. An idea akin to this underlies the proletarianization thesis.

Some writers have argued that semiprofessions and professions are becoming so technically rationalized that they are threatened with proletarianization—sinking to the bottom of a bureaucratically controlled division of labor (Oppenheimer 1973, Esland 1980, Larson 1980, McKinlay 1982). Bureaucratization of professions is seen in the elaboration of the division of labor in service organizations and in the growth of salaried employment of professionals. The argument that rationalization of services is substituting routine technique for indeterminacy is a variant of Braverman's (1974) assertion that work is being deskilled. Braverman mentions such occupations as nursing, engineering, and accountancy as victims of the trend. From contingency theory we would expect lowered skills, narrowed tasks, and elaborated divisions of labor to foster bureaucratic control by increasing the need to coordinate tasks and reducing their uncertainty.

The proletarianization thesis is open to criticism. Salaried employment of professionals is nothing new, as is evident when we consider clergymen, military officers, and college professors. Moreover, as Parkin (1979:14) notes, "many of the lower professions were virtually the creation of bureaucracy, having been set up as government agencies for the administration of the welfare state." Freidson (1984) makes this same point and adds that bureaucratization of professional work generally means control by fellow professionals—a form of stratified occupational control—not growth of lay bureaucratic control. Administrative professionals generally do not supervise their junior colleagues closely although they may assign them work and offer nonmandatory suggestions of ways to do it (Scott 1982b, Freidson 1984a). The rationalization of skills into separate occupational specialties need not detract from the autonomy of a profession if the profession itself controls the division of its labor and maintains dominance over ancillary technical occupations (Freidson 1970a, 1970b, Child & Fulk 1982, Starr 1982, Powell 1985).

Time will tell whether professional monopolization gives way to proletarianization. Starr (1982) describes past monopolization in the medical profession but sees for it a possible future of bureaucratic control through government regulation and a takeover of health care by business corporations. His argument may be prophetic but the evidence is not yet in.

Environments and the Control of Professional Work

Johnson (1972) has presented a typology and historical sketch of professional-client relations which requires some qualification of the monopolization thesis. Monopoly brings full occupational control only if the profession has more market power than its clients; otherwise the clients can determine what kinds of services the profession will provide, thus dictating much of its work content.

Johnson (1972:45) classifies professional-client relations on the basis of which party "defines the needs of the consumer and the manner in which these needs are catered for." He distinguishes (a) collegiate (occupational) control, in which an organized profession dominates unorganized clients, (b) patronage, in which an organized clientele or one all-powerful client dominates professionals, and (c) mediation by a third party, such as government or a health insurer, that controls professional-client relations or sets guidelines that affect them. The main variable underlying such distinctions is whether the parties are socially atomized or organized. Organization creates market power and atomization brings weakness. Fully occupational control has arisen when organized professions have dealt with atomized clients. This situation predominated in law and medicine in the midtwentieth century and is the basis for the standard sociological model of collegiate professionalism.

Freidson's (1960) and Carlin's (1962) analyses of client dependence among solo-practice physicians and lawyers predate Johnson's formulation but use similar reasoning. They show that clients who deal with isolated practitioners can exert considerable control over the content of professional work. When clients can shop around, professionals must please them in order to get business. This can lead to such things as physicians' prescribing unnecessary drugs or architects' drawing plans they dislike.

For this reason, some forms of organizational employment, far from proletarianizing professionals, may give them more occupational or self-control than solo practice does. College students, or the unorganized clients of public-interest law firms (Katz 1982), may not have direct access to professionals. They often must accept whatever professor or lawyer the organization assigns them. This arrangement helps the professionals maintain occupational control. Thus Katz (1982) describes poverty lawyers as somewhat distant from their clients and strongly oriented to colleagues as a reference group.

Heinz & Laumann's (1983) study of Chicago lawyers suggests that elite law firms may be more client-dependent than small firms or solo practitioners. The major firms depend heavily on the business they get from a few big corporate clients. (See also Powell 1985.) This suggests movement toward corporate patronage. We might expect patrons of any profession to impose bureaucratic control. But if the work is highly indeterminate, this threat may not materialize. Clients may decide what problems the professionals work on, but observers such as Heinz & Laumann (1983) do not find that clients try to dictate how the work is done.

Third-party mediation potentially threatens occupational control but has not damaged it much—not yet anyway. Third parties such as health insurers and Medicare-Medicaid will pay for only some kinds of treatment. This fact has undoubtedly influenced the kinds of health care tasks that are done, but the third parties have made only slight attempts to dictate how they are done. Starr (1982) describes some government curtailments of occupational control of medical work, but they appear to be nibbling at the fringes rather than attacking the core. Cost containment regulations, such as limits on the length of insurance-paid hospital stays, do intrude on work content, but no more than occurs when clients impose budget ceilings on lawyers.

The government may have influenced the medical profession more through its financial support of medical schools, their research, and their affiliated hospitals than through its mediation of doctor-patient relations. This has not lessened occupational control but has concentrated the control of physical resources and new knowledge in the hands of a medical school oligarchy within the profession (Marsden 1977, Starr 1982).

Another effect that has been attributed to client environments is described in the "deprofessionalization" thesis advanced by Haug and others (Haug & Sussman 1969, Reeder 1972, Haug 1973, 1975, 1977). They argue that consumerism, the rising educational level of the public, and the growing accessibility of knowledge through computerized data banks are destroying the mystique of professionalism. To the extent that this happens, professionals become more nearly equal-status consultants and lose the charismatic authority they have had in the past. Freidson (1984) offers persuasive arguments against this thesis. He observes that polls show continuing public confidence in professionals, that consumerism peaked in about 1970 and has subsided, and that professional knowledge is growing even faster than public knowledge so that the gap may be widening.

Taken as a whole, the evidence suggests that although the environments of professional work have affected the forms taken by occupational control, its essence has scarcely diminished.

SOCIAL CONTROL OF LOWER-STATUS WORK

Managers generally control manual workers closely. As Hill (1981:30) puts it, "Bureaucratic principles of work organization . . . are based on . . . trust, and non-manual workers have normally been allowed far more responsibility and autonomy than the manual labor force." Nevertheless, control of manual work varies in degree and type. We will look at variations based on the nature of the work, its place in the division of labor, and environmental factors.

Technology, Observability, and Control

Meissner (1969) concludes from a secondary analysis of 34 studies of factory work that technologies differ widely in the extent to which they inherently restrict worker autonomy. Technical control is inseparable from some technologies that leave the worker virtually no freedom short of sabotage. Other technologies impose few intrinsic controls and permit management to choose its own.

Research on the effects of automation on work control yields conflicting results. Tracy & Azumi's (1976) data on 44 Japanese factories confirm earlier American and British findings that automation tends to weaken bureaucratic controls and to lodge considerable freedom and responsibility in the individual worker. Blauner's (1964), Susman's (1970), and Gallie's (1978) research on oil refineries in three countries reaches the same conclusion. Susman (1970:570) describes the refinery as operating in an unpredictable environment, and states his conclusion in contingency-theory terms: ". . . under conditions of uncertainty, the efficiency derived from specialization is outweighed by the increased effectiveness of the multi-skilled worker." But Chadwick-Jones's (1969) study of a British tinplate factory that changed from old-fashioned batch technology to an automated technology found that the transition substantially increased bureaucratic and simple control through rules, elaborate scheduling to synchronize work operations, and close supervision. To resolve these apparent contradictions will require research that looks both between and within industries and uses more finely honed concepts of technology than the gross designation of "automated," "continuous process," and the like.

Another of Tracy & Azumi's (1976) findings is that task variability reduces the use of bureaucratic control devices such as formal job descriptions and written work rules. Similarly, Van de Ven et al's (1976) questionnaire study of 197 clerical work units shows that task uncertainty leads to decentralized, informal, lateral and group problem-solving discussions in lieu of impersonal programming and hierarchical coordination. These findings are what we would expect from contingency theories of organization and from the research discussed earlier on control of professional work.

Several excellent studies of police forces show what can happen when the nature of the work makes self-control unavoidable but the occupation lacks the prestige that leads people to trust professionals to control themselves (Banton 1964, Peterson 1971, 1972, Rubinstein 1973, Manning 1977, Black 1980, and several chapters in Punch 1983). The police are so widely dispersed that their work cannot be observed, but there is a desire to monitor their performance. The result is a facade of bureaucratic pseudocontrol that measures things that can be measured and ignores things that cannot be, the latter including the most important things the police do. Thus we have parking ticket quotas and arrest statistics but no attempt to count how many crimes the police have prevented.

Division of Labor, Deskilling, and Control of Work[1]

In many late nineteenth-century US factories, production subprocesses were subcontracted to independent craftsmen who hired and bossed their own crews (Buttrick 1952, Brody 1960, Braverman 1974, Montgomery 1976, Clawson 1980, Gordon et al 1982, Littler 1982). The subcontractors were subject to craft union rules, and the system was thus a mixture of simple and occupational control.

Braverman's (1974) celebrated "deskilling" thesis analyzes the breakdown of this craft system during the twentieth century. Employers, he says, launched a three-pronged attack aimed at the "separation of hand and brain" for the purpose of labor discipline. First they created a hierarchy of managers and experts who monopolized scientific understanding of production. Then they divided the work into narrow, bureaucratically coordinated subtasks. In doing this, they replaced craft tools with modern machinery that controlled the workers more than they controlled it. [This reverses Edwards's (1979) time sequence of technical and bureaucratic control.] A by-product of deskilling not emphasized by Braverman is that it reduces workers' power by making any one of them more easily dispensed with.

Braverman gets (and deserves) credit for systematically analyzing deskilling as a pervasive process linked to bureaucratization and division of labor, but others have also noted it in various industries and occupations. Walker & Guest (1952:85) state that in auto manufacture, "craft skills have been virtually eliminated" (cf. Chinoy 1955). Gross (1958:57) observes that in industry generally, "the whole conception of 'craft' is becoming obsolete" and that a "company advertises not for a tailor but a sewing machine operator, not for a mechanic but for a riveter or a punch press operator." Wallace & Kalleberg (1982) chronicle the sad descent of printers from the occupationally controlled labor aristocrats described by Lipset et al (1956) to the bureaucratically controlled operatives of today.

---

[1]The concept of occupational segments was developed in research on professions. Little if anything has been written about analogous phenomena in manual or clerical occupations, so we present no section here corresponding to the one on relations between segments of professions.

Writers on office clerical work have emphasized a proletarianizing factor little noticed by Braverman: organization size. The combination of big organizations and modern office technology has led to minutely divided labor, the impersonal steno pool in place of the personal tie of secretary to boss, and the replacement of paternalistic simple control by massification and bureaucracy (Mills 1951, Lockwood 1958, Glenn & Feldberg 1977). This picture does not, of course, fit all secretaries. Personal secretaries and others in small offices have the same kinds of social environments as their predecessors and probably are more skilled; they do most of the same things and may additionally operate a great variety of machines, some of them more complicated than a typewriter. In big bureaucratic offices, the main skills that have been lost are the interpersonal and linguistic skills and judgment, that a genuine secretary, as distinct from a clerk or a full-time typist, must have.

Most criticism of Braverman's thesis has come from his fellow Marxists. This may reflect only the fact that most recent shopfloor industrial sociology has been done by Marxists. There are three main criticisms. First, Braverman romanticizes the early industrial era, portraying it as if most of its workers had been skilled artisans—a strange mistake for someone steeped in reading about the dark satanic mills. One critic, Szymanski (1978), estimates that at no time during feudalism or capitalism have more than about 15% of manual workers been skilled enough to become markedly deskilled. Second, Braverman overstates the extent of deskilling. Burawoy (1979) and Sabel (1982) insist that many of the factory workers they studied were highly skilled. Wright & Singelmann (1983) conclude from a survey that while old skills disappear, new skills are created at about the same rate. A third criticism is that Braverman sees workers as passive objects yielding supinely to whatever control tactics managers attempt whereas in reality there is a dialectical struggle between management and labor for control (Friedman 1977, Burawoy 1979, Storey 1983). (On workers' struggles for control, see Montgomery 1979.) Whatever merit these criticisms may have, Braverman's work is invaluable in focusing attention on the process and ramifications of deskilling.

Environmental Variability and Occupational Control in Construction

Research on the construction industry suggests that environmental variability reduces bureaucracy. Historically, unions have flourished earliest and most consistently in the skilled crafts (Commons 1918, Form & Huber 1976). Craft unionism remains particularly strong in the building trades, where well-organized workers often bargain from greater strength than that of the relatively small and atomized employers (Foster & Strauss 1972). Construction unions (along with printers before that trade was mechanized) have won the nearest equivalent in manual work to the occupational control system of the professions.

Construction union rules, embodied in contracts and informal norms, cover such aspects of work control as acceptable tools and methods, safety rules, agreements on what constitutes a fair day's work, and division of labor along craft jurisdictional lines (Caplow 1954, Hall 1975, Riemer 1979, 1982). As Stinchcombe (1959:170) puts it, "craft institutions" in construction "are more than craft trade unions; they are also a method of administering work." They feature informal rather than formal communication and the coordination of much of the work of different crafts through shared understandings (Riemer 1982).

Stinchcombe (1959, 1983) has provided an explanation of the strength of "craft administration," not only in construction but also in other one-at-a time (unit) industries where employers are small and employees are skilled, such as movie making, book publishing, machine tool building, and shipbuilding. His explanation does not hinge on the relative bargaining strength of the parties, but on the extreme variability of the demand for skilled labor in these industries—specifically, he says, seasonal variability in construction, but the essence is variability rather than seasonality *per se*. Subcontracting is a good way to expand and contract a skilled labor force on short notice. Construction subcontractors represent specific crafts and must abide by union rules if they are to keep good workers. Hence the workers at a site bring occupational controls with them, and it would be difficult and is unnecessary to impose extensive bureaucratic controls. As a rough test of the prediction that construction will be less bureaucratic than other industries, Stinchcombe (1959) shows that the percentage of clerical workers is low in construction.

Other writers give the same explanation of the strength of building-trades unionism, though they are focusing more on labor markets than on work control. Lee (1979) shows that craft unionism thrives in unstable industries, where it is economically rational for employers and workers. Piore (1979) states that in job-shop (unit) industries where labor is skilled and demand for it is variable, craft subcontracting is common because it gives workers job security but allows employers to stop paying them in slack times.

Two studies have taken aim at Stinchcombe's analysis. They have not scored direct hits but have grazed it in ways that broaden our view of the matter. Silver (1982) surveyed workers in nine building trades and ten local unions in a northeastern city. He criticizes Caplow (1954), Blauner (1964), Hall (1975), and Riemer (1979) for romanticizing craft work, and reports that union workers sometimes accept substandard conditions in order to get jobs during hard times. He then tests several hypotheses derived, some of them rather loosely, from the craft administration model, and finds no support for most of them; space limits prevent our listing them. Silver's observation of the violation of craft rules is useful, but skepticism is in order regarding his assertion that the craft model is wrong. He hedges: ". . . market conditions may require a certain degree of organizational flexibility which loosens control structures and enhances the opportunities for self-direction and freedom from supervision" (Silver 1982:238). His data analysis compares firms within the building industry, but the craft model contrasts that industry with other industries.

Eccles's (1981) study of construction subcontracting finds that complexity, size, and market extent of general contracting firms explain variance in subcontracting and that seasonality of business does not. Like Silver, he is using within-industry data to attack a between-industry hypothesis. Also like Silver, he says things that seem at odds with his argument: "Subcontracting . . . is a response to uncertainty. . . . A general contractor cannot keep a large number of labor specialties . . . productively occupied because of the great uncertainty about labor requirements . . . by time period . . ." (Eccles 1981:451–52). In other words, craft subcontracting is an adaptation to variable demand for labor, just as Stinchcombe and others say, although seasonality may not be the main reason for variability of demand.

Eccles (1981) does make one point that casts doubt on the craft administration model though not on the craft labor market model. He gives census statistics showing about as high a proportion of administrative personnel in construction as in manufacturing. Stinchcombe (1959) compares only clerical workers and leaves out managers and professionals, whom Eccles includes. While no safe inference of the number of people who "administer" may be possible from census occupational categories, Eccles's measure appears better. But administration is more than controlling workers. Until we know more about what the administrators do, we do not know how the workers are controlled. Eccles did not observe control directly, nor did Stinchcombe. Even if any number of administrators are around the site, if the union rules are observed there is a high degree of occupational control. Silver saw union rules violated. Riemer, who worked as a carpenter, saw them obeyed. We need more studies to learn the conditions under which union requirements of occupational control prevail and the extent of occupational, bureaucratic, and simple control in craft industries.

SOME CONCLUSIONS ON ORGANIZATION THEORY AND CONTROL OF WORK

In general, the same factors are related to types of control of professional and lower-status work. In both, the greater the need to coordinate tasks, the better understood the relations of means to ends, the more routine the problems requiring solution, and the more stable the environment, the more bureaucratic the control of work is likely to be. In professions these variables tend to account for differences between occupations that are bureaucratically controlled and those that are self- or occupationally controlled. In manual work the most frequent distinctions are between degrees of bureaucratic control, but in construction crafts the employers' highly variable demand environments have led to occupational control.

The proposition that control over major environmental resources confers power within a work setting is amply supported in research on professions and receives far less support, but no disconfirmation, in the studies we surveyed on lower-status workers. Among these, the chief support of this hypothesis is evidence favoring Braverman's (1974) deskilling thesis, if we regard craft knowledge as an environmental resource. Manual and clerical employees rarely control significant material resources, so our resource dependence hypothesis applies to them with respect mainly to nonmaterial resources such as knowledge.

All the relationships just mentioned come straight from contingency or resource dependence writings on organizations. Not all findings given earlier on control of work are derivable from extant organization theory, but no finding is inconsistent with any organization theory known to us. This is not surprising since much of what organizations do is to control work. The separate literatures on organizations, professions, and lower-status work often concern the same things, but authors have too seldom taken advantage of this fact to use knowledge about one set of phenomena as a guide to research on the others.

Literature Cited

Acker, J., Van Houten, D. R. 1974. Differential recruitment and control: the sex structuring of organizations. *Admin. Sci. Q.* 19:152–63

Akers, R. L. 1968. The professional association and the legal regulation of practice. *Law Soc. Rev.* 2:463–82

Albrecht, G. L. 1979. Defusing technological change in juvenile courts: the probation officer's struggle for professional autonomy. *Sociol. Work Occup.* 6:259–82

Aldrich, H. E. 1979. *Organizations and Environments.* Englewood Cliffs, NJ: Prentice-Hall

Aldrich, H. E., Pfeffer, J. 1976. Environments of organizations. *Ann. Rev. Sociol.* 2:79–105

Alford, R. R. 1975. *Health Care Politics: Ideological and Interest Group Barriers to Reform.* Chicago: Univ. Chicago Press

Anderson, O. W., Shields, M. C. 1982. Quality measure and control in physician decision making: state of the art. *Health Serv. Res.* 17:125–55

Armstrong, D. 1976. The decline of the medical hegemony: a review of Government reports during the N. H. S. *Soc. Sci. Med.* 10:157–63

Aronowitz, S. 1973. *False Promises: The Shaping of the American Working Class.* New York: McGraw-Hill

Atkinson, P., Reid, M., Sheldrake, P. 1977. Medical mystique. *Sociol. Work Occup.* 4:243–80

Banton, M. 1964. *The Policeman in the Community.* New York: Basic

Berlant, J. L. 1975. *Profession and Monopoly: A Study of Medicine in the United States and Great Britain.* Berkeley: Univ. Calif. Press

Bidwell, C. E., Kasarda, J. D. 1985. *The Organization and Its Ecosystem* (2 vols.). Greenwich, Conn: Jai

Black, D. 1980. *The Manners and Customs of the Police.* New York: Academic

Blau, J. R. 1979. Expertise and power in professional organizations. *Sociol. Work Occup.* 6:103–23

Blau, P. M., Scott, W. R. 1962. *Formal Organizations.* San Francisco: Chandler

Blauner, R. 1964. *Alienation and Freedom: The Factory Worker and His Industry.* Chicago: Univ. Chicago Press

Bluestone, B., Harrison, B. 1982. *The Deindustrialization of America: Plant Closings, Community Abandonment, and the Dismantling of Basic Industry*. New York: Basic

Bosk, C. L. 1979. *Forgive and Remember: Managing Medical Failure*. Chicago: Univ. Chicago Press

Braverman, H. 1974. *Labor and Monopoly Capital: The Degradation of Work in the Twentieth Century*. New York: Monthly Review

Brody, D. 1960. *Steelworkers in America: The Nonunion Era*. Cambridge, MA: Harvard Univ. Press

Burawoy, M. 1979. *Manufacturing Consent: Changes in the Labor Process under Monopoly Capitalism*. Chicago: Univ. Chicago Press

Burawoy, M. 1983. Between the labor force and the state: the face of factory regimes under advanced capitalism. *Am. Sociol. Rev.* 48:587–605

Burns, T., Stalker, G. M. 1961. *The Management of Innovation*. London: Tavistock

Buttrick, J. 1952. The inside contracting system. *J. Econ. Hist.* 12:1205–21

Caplow, T. 1954. *The Sociology of Work*. Minneapolis: Univ. Minn. Press

Carlin, J. E. 1962. *Lawyers on Their Own: A Study of Individual Practitioners in Chicago*. New Brunswick, NJ: Rutgers Univ. Press

Carlin, J. E. 1966. *Lawyers' Ethics: A Survey of the New York City Bar*. New York: Russell Sage

Chadwick-Jones, J. K. 1969. *Automation and Behaviour: A Social Psychological Study*. London: Wiley-Interscience

Chandler, A. D., Jr. 1962. *Strategy and Structure: Chapters in the History of the American Industrial Enterprise*. Cambridge, Mass: MIT Press

Child, J. 1972. Organizational structure, environment and performance: the role of strategic choice. *Sociology* 6:1–22

Child, J., Fulk, J. 1982. Maintenance of occupational control: the case of professions. *Work Occup.* 9:155–92

Chinoy, E. 1955. *Automobile Workers and the American Dream*. New York: Doubleday

Clawson, D. 1980. *Bureaucracy and the Labor Process: The Transformation of U. S. Industry, 1860–1920*. New York: Monthly Review

Collins, R. 1979. *The Credential Society: An Historical Sociology of Education and Stratification*. New York: Academic

Commons, J. R. 1918. *History of Labor in the United States,* Vol 1. New York: Macmillan

Crozier, M. 1964. *The Bureaucratic Phenomenon*. Chicago: Univ. Chicago Press

Danziger, J. N. 1979. The "skill bureaucracy" and intraorganizational control. *Sociol. Work Occup.* 6:204–26

Doeringer, P. B., Piore, M. J. 1971. *Internal Labor Markets and Manpower Analysis*. Lexington, MA: Heath

Dornbusch, S. M., Scott, W. R. 1975. *Evaluation and the Exercise of Authority*. San Francisco: Jossey-Bass

Dreyfuss, C. 1938. *Ideology and Occupation of the Salaried Employees*. Tr. E. E. Warburg. New York: Columbia Univ. Press

Eccles, R. G. 1981. Bureaucratic versus craft administration: the relationship of market structure to the construction firm. *Admin. Sci. Q.* 26:449–69

Edwards, R. 1979. *Contested Terrain: The Transformation of the Workplace in the Twentieth Century*. New York: Basic

Elbaum, B., Wilkinson, F. 1979. Industrial relations and uneven development: a comparative study of the American and British steel industries. *Camb. J. Econ.* 3:275–303

Elliott, P. 1972. *The Sociology of the Professions*. New York: Herder & Herder

Esland, G. 1980. Professions and professionalism. In *The Politics of Work and Occupations*, ed. G. Esland, G. Salaman, pp. 213–50. Toronto: Univ. Toronto Press

Etzioni, A. (ed.). 1969. *The Semi-professions and Their Organization*. New York: Free

Form, W. H., Huber, J. A. 1976. Occupational power. In *Handbook of Work, Organization, and Society*, ed. R. Dubin, pp. 751–806. Chicago: Rand McNally

Foster, H. G., Strauss, G. 1972. Labor problems in construction: a review. *Indust. Rel.* 11:289–313

Freidson, E. 1960. Client control and medical practice. *Am. J. Sociol.* 65:374–82

Freidson, E. 1970a. *Profession of Medicine: A Study of the Sociology of Applied Knowledge*. New York: Dodd, Mead

Freidson, E. 1970b. *Professional Dominance: The Social Structure of Medical Care*. New York: Atherton

Freidson, E. 1975. *Doctoring Together: A Study of Professional Social Control*. New York: Elsevier

Freidson, E. 1983. The reorganization of the professions by regulation. *Law Hum. Behav.* 7:279–90

Freidson, E. 1984. The changing nature of professional control. *Ann. Rev. Sociol.* 10:1–20

Freidson, E. 1985. The reorganization of the medical profession. *Med. Care Rev.* In press

Friedman, A. L. 1977. *Industry and Labour: Class Struggle at Work and Monopoly Capitalism*. London: Macmillan

Friedman, S. R. 1982. *Teamster Rank and File: Bureaucracy and Rebellion at Work in a Union*. New York: Columbia Univ. Press

Galbraith, J. 1973. *Designing Complex Organizations*. Reading, Mass: Addison-Wesley

Gallie, D. 1978. *In Search of the New Working Class: Automation and Social Integration within the Capitalist Enterprise*. Cambridge (UK): Cambridge Univ. Press

Glenn, E. N., Feldberg, R. L. 1977. Degraded and deskilled: the proletarianization of clerical work. *Soc. Probl.* 25:52–64

Goldman, P., Van Houten, D. R. 1977. Managerial strategies and the worker: a Marxist analysis of bureaucracy. *Sociol. Q.* 18:108–25

Gordon, D., Edwards, R. C., Reich, M. 1982. *Segmented Work, Divided Workers: The Historical Transformation of Labor in the United States*. Cambridge (U.K.): Cambridge Univ. Press

Gross, E. 1958. *Work and Society*. New York: Crowell

Hage, J., Aiken, M. 1969. Routine technology, social structure, and organization goals. *Admin. Sci. Q.* 14:366–76

Hall, R. H. 1975. *Occupations and the Social Structure* Englewood Cliffs, NJ: Prentice-Hall. 3rd ed.

Haug, M. R. 1973. Deprofessionalization: an alternative hypothesis for the future. In *Professionalisation and Change* (*Sociol. Rev.* Monograph 20), ed. P. J. Halmos, pp. 195–211. Keele (UK): Univ. Keele

Haug, M. R. 1975. The deprofessionalization of everyone? *Sociol. Focus* 3:197–213

Haug, M. R. 1977. Computer technology and the obsolescence of the concept of profession. In *Work and Technology*, ed. M. R. Haug, J. Dofny, pp. 215–28. Beverly Hills, Calif: Sage

Haug, M., Sussman, M. 1969. Professional autonomy and the revolt of the client. *Soc. Probl.* 17:153–61

Hawley, A. H. 1950. *Human Ecology*. New York: Ronald

Heinz, J. P., Laumann, E. O. 1983. *Chicago Lawyers: The Social Structure of the Bar*. New York: Russell Sage Foun., Am. Bar Foun.

Hickson, D. J., Pugh, D. S., Pheysey, D. C. 1969. Operations technology and organization structure: an empirical appraisal. *Admin. Sci. Q.* 14:378–97

Hill, S. 1981. *Competition and Control at Work: The New Industrial Sociology*. Cambridge, Mass: MIT Press

Jamous, H., Peloille, B. 1970. Changes in the French university-hospital system. In *Professions and Professionalization*, ed. J. A. Jackson, pp. 109–52. Cambridge (U.K.): Cambridge Univ. Press

Johnson, T. J. 1972. *Professions and Power*. London: Macmillan

Kanter, R. M. 1975. Women and the structure of organizations: explorations in theory and behavior. In *Another Voice: Feminist Perspectives on Social Life and Social Structure*, ed. M. Millman, R. M. Kanter, pp. 34–74. Garden City, NY: Doubleday Anchor

Katz, J. 1982. *Poor People's Lawyers in Transition*. New Brunswick, NJ: Rutgers Univ. Press

Kornhauser, W. 1962. *Scientists in Industry*. Berkeley: Univ. Calif. Press

Kraft, P. 1979. The routinization of computer programming. *Sociol. Work Occup.* 6:139–55

Krause, E. A. 1982. *Division of Labor: A Political Perspective*. Westport, Conn: Greenwood

Kronus, C. L. 1976. The evolution of occupational power: an historical study of task boundaries between physicians and pharmacists. *Sociol. Work Occup.* 3:3–37

Kusterer, K. C. 1978. *Know-How on the Job: The Important Working Knowledge of "Unskilled" Workers*. Boulder, Colo: Westview

Larkin, G. V. 1978. Medical dominance and control: radiographers in the division of labour. *Sociol. Rev.* New Series, 26:843–58

Larkin, G. V. 1981. Professional autonomy and the ophthalmic optician. *Sociol. Health Illness* 3:15–30

Larson, M. S. 1977. *The Rise of Professionalism: A Sociological Analysis*. Berkeley: Univ. Calif. Press

Larson, M. S. 1980. Proletarianization and educated labor. *Theory Soc.* 9:131–77

Lawrence, P. R. 1981. The Harvard organization and environment research program. In *Perspectives on Organization Design and Behavior*, ed. A. H. Van de Ven, W. F. Joyce, pp. 311–37. New York: Wiley-Interscience

Lawrence, P. R., Lorsch, J. W. 1967. *Organization and Environment: Managing Differentiation and Integration*. Boston: Grad. School Bus. Admin., Harvard Univ.

Lee, D. J. 1979. Craft unions and the force of tradition: the case of apprenticeship. *Br. J. Indust. Rel.* 17:34–49

Lipset, S. M., Trow, M., Coleman, J. S. 1956. *Union Democracy*. Glencoe, Ill: Free

Littler, C. 1982. *The Development of the Labor Process in Capitalist Societies*. London: Heinemann

Lockwood, D. 1958. *The Blackcoated Worker: A Study in Class Consciousness*. London: Allen & Unwin

Manning, P. K. 1977. *Police Work: The Social Organization of Policing*. Cambridge, Mass: MIT Press

Marcson, S. 1960. *The Scientist in American Industry*. New York: Harper

Marglin, S. A. 1974. What do bosses do? The origins and functions of hierarchy in capitalist production. *Rev. Radical Polit. Econ.* 6:60–112

Marsden, L. R. 1977. Power within a profession: medicine in Ontario. *Sociol. Work Occup.* 4:243–80

McKinlay, J. B. 1982. Toward the proletarianization of physicians. In *Professionals as Workers: Mental Labor in Advanced Capitalism*, ed. C. Derber, pp. 37–62. Boston: Hall

Meissner, M. 1969. *Technology and the Worker*. San Francisco: Chandler

Meyer, S., III. 1981. *The Five Dollar Day: Labor Management and Social Control in the Ford Motor Company, 1908–1921*. Albany: State Univ. NY Press

Millman, M. 1977. *The Unkindest Cut: Life in the Backrooms of Medicine*. New York: Morrow

Mills, C. W. 1951. *White Collar*. New York: Oxford Univ. Press

Montgomery, D. 1976. Workers' control of machine production in the nineteenth century. *Labor Hist*. 17:485–509

Montgomery, D. 1979. *Workers' Control in America: Studies in the History of Work, Technology, and Labor Struggles*. Cambridge (UK): Cambridge Univ. Press

Nilson, L. B. 1979. An application of the occupational "uncertainty principle" to the professions. *Soc. Probl*. 26:570–81

Oppenheimer, M. 1973. The proletarianization of the professional. In *Professionalisation and Social Change (Sociol. Rev.* Monograph 20), ed. P. J. Halmos, pp. 213–27. Keele (UK): Univ. Keele

Parkin, F. 1979. *Marxism and Class Theory: A Bourgeois Critique*. London: Tavistock

Parry, N., Parry, J. 1976. *The Rise of the Medical Profession*. London: Croom Helm

Perrow, C. 1967. A framework for the comparative analysis of organizations. *Am. Sociol. Rev*. 32:194–208

Perrow, C. 1970. *Organizational Analysis: A Sociological View*. Belmont, Calif: Wadsworth

Peterson, D. M. 1971. Informal norms and police practice: the traffic ticket quota system. *Sociol. Soc. Res*. 55:354–62

Peterson, D. M. 1972. Police disposition of the petty offender. *Sociol. Soc. Res*. 56:320–30

Pfeffer, J., Salancik, G. R. 1978. *The External Control of Organizations*. New York: Harper & Row

Piore, M. J. 1979. *Birds of Passage: Migrant Labor and Industrial Societies*. Cambridge (U.K.): Cambridge Univ. Press

Powell, M. J. 1985. Developments in the regulation of lawyers: competing segments and market, client and government controls. *Soc. Forc*. 64. In press

Punch, M. (ed.). 1983. *Control in the Police Organization*. Cambridge, Mass: MIT Press

Reader, W. J. 1966. *Professional Men*. New York: Basic

Reeder, L. J. 1972. The patient-client as a consumer: some observations on the changing professional-client relationship. *J. Health Soc. Behav*. 13:406–12

Riemer, J. R. 1979. *Hard Hats: The Work World of Construction Workers*. Beverly Hills, Calif: Sage

Riemer, J. R. 1982. Worker autonomy in the skilled building trades. In *Varieties of Work*, ed. P. L. Stewart, M. G. Cantor, pp. 225–34. Beverly Hills, Calif: Sage

Roth, J. 1974. Professionalism: the sociologist's decoy. *Sociol. Work Occup*. 1:6–23

Rubinstein, J. 1973. *City Police*. New York: Farrar, Straus & Giroux

Sabel, C. F. 1982. *Work and Politics: The Division of Labor in Industry*. Cambridge (U.K.): Cambridge Univ. Press

Saks, M. 1983. Removing the blinders? a critique of recent contributions to the sociology of professions. *Sociol. Rev*. New Series, 31:1–21

Scott, W. R. 1981. *Organizations: Rational, Natural, and Open Systems*. Englewood Cliffs, NJ: Prentice-Hall

Scott, W. R. 1982a. Health care organization in the 1980s: the convergence of public and professional control systems. In *Contemporary Health Services: Social Science Perspectives*, ed. A. W. Johnson, O. Grusky, B. H. Raven. Boston: Auburn

Scott, W. R. 1982b. Managing professional work: three models of control for health organizations. *Health Serv. Res*. 17:213–40

Selznick, P. 1949. *TVA and the Grass Roots*. Berkeley: Univ. Calif. Press

Shimberg, B. 1982. *Occupational Licensing: A Public Perspective*. Princeton, NJ: Educ. Testing Serv.

Silver, M. L. 1982. The structure of craft work: the construction industry. In *Varieties of Work*, ed. P. L. Stewart, M. G. Cantor, pp. 232–52. Beverly Hills, Calif: Sage

Simpson, R. L. 1978. Is research utilization for social workers? *J. Soc. Serv. Res*. 2:143–57

Simpson, R. L., Simpson, I. H. 1969. Women and bureaucracy in the semi-professions. In *The Semi-professions and Their Organization*, ed. A. Etzioni, pp. 196–265. New York: Free

Smigel, E. O. 1969. *The Wall Street Lawyer: Professional Organization Man?* Bloomington: Ind. Univ. Press

Starr, P. M. 1982. *The Social Transformation of American Medicine*. New York: Basic

Stinchcombe, A. L. 1959. Bureaucratic and craft administration of production: a comparative analysis. *Admin. Sci. Q*. 4:168–87

Stinchcombe, A. L. 1983. *Economic Sociology*. New York: Academic

Stone, K. 1974. The origins of job structures in the steel industry. *Rev. Radical Polit. Econ*. 6:113–73

Storey, J. 1983. *Managerial Prerogatives and the Question of Control*. London: Routledge & Kegan Paul

Susman, G. I. 1970. The impact of automation

on work group autonomy and task specialization. *Hum. Rel.* 23:567–77

Szymanski, A. 1978. Braverman as a neo-Luddite? *Insurgent Sociol.* 8:45–50

Thompson, J. D. 1967. *Organizations in Action.* New York: McGraw-Hill

Toren, N. 1972. *Social Work: The Case Study of a Semi-Profession.* Beverly Hills, Calif: Sage

Tracy, P., Azumi, K. 1976. Determinants of administrative control: a test of a theory with Japanese factories. *Am. Sociol. Rev.* 41:80–94

Udy, S. H., Jr. 1959. *The Organization of Work.* New Haven: Hum. Rel. Area Files

Van de Ven, A. H., Delbecq, A. L., Koenig, R., Jr. 1976. Determinants of coordination modes within organizations. *Am. Sociol. Rev.* 41:322–38

Walker, C. R., Guest, R. 1952. *The Man on the Assembly Line.* Cambridge, Mass: Harvard Univ. Press

Wallace, M., Kalleberg, A. L. 1982. Industrial transformation and the decline of craft: the decomposition of skill in the printing industry, 1931–1978. *Am. Sociol. Rev.* 47:307–24

Weber, M. (Eds. & tr., Gerth, H. H., Mills, C. W.) 1946. *From Max Weber: Essays in Sociology.* New York: Oxford Univ. Press

Weber, M. (Eds. & tr., Henderson, A. M., Parsons, T.) 1947. *The Theory of Social and Economic Organization.* Glencoe, Ill: Free

Westphal, M., Frazier, F., Miller, M. C. 1979.

Changes in average length of stay and average charges generated following institution of PSRO review. *Health Serv. Res.* 14:253–65

Wilensky, H. L. 1964. The professionalization of everyone? *Am. J. Sociol.* 70:137–58

Williamson, O. E. 1975. *Markets and Hierarchies: Analysis and Antitrust Implications.* New York: Free

Woodward, J. 1965. *Industrial Organization: Theory and Practice.* New York: Oxford Univ. Press

Wright, E. O., Singelmann, J. 1983. Proletarianization in the changing American class structure. In *Marxist Inquiries,* ed. M. Burawoy, T. Skocpol, pp. 176–209. Chicago: Univ. Chicago Press

Zald, M. N. 1970. Political economy: a framework for comparative analysis. In *Power in Organizations,* ed. M. N. Zald, pp. 221–61. Nashville: Vanderbilt Univ. Press

Zey-Ferrell, M., Ferrell, O. C. 1982. Role-set configuration and opportunity as predictors of unethical behavior in organizations. *Hum. Rel.* 35:587–604

Zey-Ferrell, M., Weaver, K. M., Ferrell, O. C. 1979. Predicting unethical behavior among marketing practitioners. *Hum. Rel.* 32:557–69

Zola, I. K. 1972. Medicine as an instrument of social control. *Sociol. Rev.,* New Series, 20:487–504

NOTE ADDED IN PROOF   I am grateful to Howard Aldrich and Eliot Freidson for comments on an earlier draft.

Ann. Rev. Sociol. 1985. 11:437–55
Copyright © 1985 by Annual Reviews Inc. All rights reserved

URBAN POLICY ANALYSIS

Terry Nichols Clark

The University of Chicago, Department of Sociology, 1126 East 59 Street, Room 322, Chicago, Illinois 60637

Abstract

Four overlapping subfields of urban policy analysis are reviewed. The political leadership analyses include elite theories, group theory, neo-Marxist work, and network analyses. Consideration of citizen preferences involves populist spatial theories, budget pies, and policy responsiveness. Bureaucratic theories include incrementalism, the dynamic bureau head, and professionalism. Population and economic location analyses increasingly stress small firms, simultaneity of job and residential choice, and impacts of public policy.

These alternative approaches were often advanced as one-factor interpretations. But a contextual relativism approach seeks to reconcile their ostensibly conflicting results. Results differ by context. Current work specifies how rules of the game, identified by distinct political cultures, shift processes across contexts.

INTRODUCTION

This chapter considers four subfields within urban policy analysis: political leaders, citizens, bureaucratic processes and service delivery, and population and economic location. The four are often analyzed in a systems perspective, with political leaders and citizens influencing bureaucratic processes and service delivery, which in turn affect population and employment patterns. Then population and employment patterns feed back to citizens and political leaders. These interrelated processes form the core of urban policy analysis as defined in recent reviews—Clark (1981b), Newton (1981), Katzman (1978), Eberts (1985).

437

0360-0572/85/0815-0437$02.00

The principal variables and interrelations constitute an input-throughput-output-feedback systems model, as shown in Figure 1. The sections below address its separate components and paths.

As have many fields, urban policy analysis has seen shifts from one-factor, deductive theorizing to synthetic consolidation. The 1960s and early 1970s saw new approaches presented with such enthusiasm that other factors seemed ignored. Emphasizing a single factor like citizens or bureau heads was also encouraged by mathematical work on public choice. The early 1980s have seen theories stressing general sociopolitical contexts within which more specific factors operate. This change in emphasis is related to sociopolitical changes in cities, more empirical work with large-scale data sets, and more use of urban policy analysis by policymakers.

Urban policy analysis considers policies of urban governments usually registered in a *fiscal* or *performance policy output* or *policy impact*. Fiscal policy outputs include expenditures for specific items like police, as well as the debt and tax burdens. Fiscal policies themselves assumed more importance as austerity increased over the 1970s in the US (Levine & Rubin 1980; Municipal Finance Officers Association 1982) and elsewhere (Newton 1981, Bouinot 1984). *Performance indicators* measure goods and services produced by the city government. *Policy impacts* are effects of services, like cleaned streets. *Efficiency* or *productivity* (output per unit of input) and *effectiveness* (degree to which the policy achieves its goal) are common criteria for assessing outputs and impacts. *Fiscal strain* is maladaptation of a city government to its resource environment, measured by a ratio of city government expenditure, revenue, or debt to environmental resources like the tax base. Fiscal measures are dependent variables in most political leadership and service delivery studies, but independent variables in population and job location studies. Our knowledge of these issues has grown both from basic science work and from studies seeking to improve urban policies; the distinction is less clear here than in many fields.

A lack of comparable urban data limited past generalizations, but a major

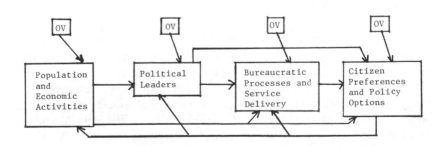

OV = other variables

Figure 1 A basic framework of variables.

effort was launched to change this in 1982: the Fiscal Austerity and Urban Innovation Project is an international survey of cities using a common methodology. Items include 33 strategies (both fiscal and performance policy outputs) for adapting to austerity, such as across-the-board cutbacks or contracting out. The survey also asks about political leaders, organized groups, bureaucratic staff, and citizens. Twenty-six teams are surveying every US city over 25,000, and 25 other teams are surveying cities in 25 other countries; this is the most extensive study of local government ever undertaken (Clark 1985, Walzer 1985). Data will soon be in the public domain. The project is encouraging more systematic analysis of contextual relations, which is discussed below.

POLITICAL LEADERSHIP

Several competing theories stress the importance of alternative mechanisms linking leaders to policy outputs. We first consider the main theories and then place them in a more general framework.

Elite Theories

Mosca, Pareto, and Michels held that whatever the form of government, all societies are ruled by small elites. This perspective substantially influenced subsequent work, encouraging studies of the social and economic composition of political elites. These often used a *positional approach* to calculate, for example, the percentage of businessmen on a city council. Floyd Hunter's (1953) *Community Power Structure* added the *reputational approach* to identify leaders not just by position but their reputed importance according to other elite members. Into the 1960's, dozens of studies followed Hunter's approach. It then met with major criticisms.

Group Theory and Pluralism

The most outspoken critics of the elite tradition were Robert Dahl and his students. Following Bentley, Key, and Truman, they saw competition among interest groups as the primary source of policy outputs. Dahl (1961) also distinguished *resources* and *influence,* measuring influence by participation in actual decisions, using the *decisional approach.* He stressed studying separate *issue areas* since participants may vary by issue area; this illustrates *pluralistic* decision-making. His classic (1961) New Haven study documented these matters. The late 1960s saw two criticisms of pluralism, one leading to Marxism, the other to populism.

Neo-Marxist Work

While criticized for his ambiguity, Hunter claimed to be a "Stalinist Marxist." He stressed that business leaders dominated politics, leading Dahl to spend much time refuting this argument. Dahl's "behavioralism" was criticized in turn; by stressing actual decisions, he ignored "non-decisions" by "vested interests," which affected, for example, the distribution of income or nonparticipation by poor blacks.

Two strains of Marxism developed in the 1970s. A first followed Hunter and others in seeing wealth as driving politics and business leaders as dominating politicians. A second strain, in Althusser and Manuel Castells (1972), stressed not concrete leaders but structural arrangements of capitalism as generating policies. Several writers applied neo-Marxist ideas to urban research in the 1970s, e.g. Friedland et al (1977) and Whitt (1982), who analyzed business influence on public transit decisions in Los Angeles and San Francisco.

Marxist views declined in the late 1970s. In France and Italy, long Marxist centers, leading neo-Marxists declared Marxism dead. Castells (1983) broke with his past work and moved toward an explicitly multicausal approach. Reassessments by American urbanists are clear in *Urban Affairs Quarterly* (1983). The hypothesis that business dominates government has seen too many exceptions to stand unqualified (cf Williams & Zimmermann 1981, Friedland & Bielby 1981, Friedland 1983, Mollenkopf 1983). But Marx's emphasis on the way structural conditions shift the rules of the game remains an enduring contribution.

Network Analysis

This approach emerged vigorously in the 1970s, mainly among younger sociologists, with contributions by Laumann & Pappi (1976), Marsden & Laumann (1977), Burt (1981), Galaskiewicz (1979), and Breiger (1979). The idea that leaders are joined in a network of social contacts is given more rigorous interpretation with statistical tools like multidimensional scaling and block modeling. Several dimensions of networks (nodes, interconnectedness, etc) are similarly analyzed. Still as Burt (1981), Zimmermann (1981), and Eberts & Kelly (1985) point out, networks are usefully considered in a more general framework including citizen preferences, leaders, and community characteristics. The powerful tools of network analysis can be productively joined with ideas from other traditions to explain policy outputs.

Spatial Models of Citizens and Coalitions

While young sociologists turned to Marxism or network analysis in the late 1960s, young political scientists and economists were developing spatial models. Downs (1957) inspired many subsequent efforts. Under perfect market conditions, competition between political leaders should make them "invisible" by forcing them to locate along a policy space at the median voter's position. Many papers in *Public Choice,* the leading journal of such work, elaborated a mathematical deductive perspective. Recent work has grown more empirical and found only modest support for pure citizen preference theory, and this has increased interest in refining the theory, e.g. by considering specific alternative assumptions about preference distributions, issue configurations, and resources. Such developments bring recent work closer to the more inductive efforts of most sociologists. Riker & Ordeshook (1973) and Mueller (1979) are useful overviews.

Coalition theory is another economics-inspired set of ideas. Classic coalition theory stressed the *size* principle: winning coalitions of minimal size are formed to permit minimal division of the spoils of victory (von Neumann & Morgenstern 1944). A next set of propositions considered (ideological) *spatial distance* of policies, suggesting that coalitions were less likely as policy distance among participants increased (Groennings et al 1970). Others stressed coalitions that would minimize the ideological *range* between extreme coalition partners (DeSwann 1973) or include participants who would bring to the coalition complementary *resources* (Hinckley 1979). While Riker & Ordeshook (1973) suggest that these coalition theories conflict, the theories can be largely reconciled by considering how they differ by structural context. A key dimension (discussed below) is the degree to which one considers a more public good (like clean air), or a more private good (like a patronage job). Size theory better explains systems operating with pure private goods, while distance and range theories are better for those stressing public goods (Clark 1972, 1975).

CITIZEN PREFERENCES AND PARTICIPATION

Citizens have grown more politically salient, thus increasing interest in populist theories. In the US and abroad, government programs in the late 1960s stressed citizen participation; the 1970s taxpayers' revolt reinforced these trends. Citizen surveys are increasingly used by political leaders, lending direct policy implications to work in this area.

Economic theories have long stressed citizens, as in spatial theories of political leaders. A central concern in economic theories is aggregating preferences of individual citizens to characterize their collective preferences. Two major efforts at aggregation to generate "social welfare functions" were Arrow (1963) and Samuelson (1969). Each rigorously stated the problem, but concluded that no solution was available that met their (demanding) conditions. These results seem less nihilistic if one seeks something less than an ordering of "all states of the world;" weaker assumptions about individual preferences can generate reasonable if weaker orderings and consistent social decisions (Sen 1970).

Important lessons for urban policy analysts emerge from this work. One concerns the concept of a public good, such as clean air, which is simultaneously consumed by many persons and for which exclusion costs are high. What level of a public good do citizens prefer? Unlike private goods for which citizen demand can be gauged through the marketplace, demand for public goods is hard to assess. In contexts where preferences are revealed through voluntary payments by individuals, this creates an incentive to understate one's preferences and be a "free rider." Much effort has been spent devising schemes to discourage such strategic behavior, while preserving the rich information content of individual citizen preferences via characteristics like transitivity, asymmetry, multidimensionality, intensity, and knowledge level (e.g. Fishburn 1970, Tideman 1976).

Many urban policies, and citizens' willingness to support them, can be productively assessed in terms of a public-separable-private goods continuum. Citizen support for more separable policies can be measured with a "revealed preference" method like user fees, while measurement of more public goods like air pollution usually requires a more active effort, such as a survey. Many surveys ask simply "how satisfied are you with (a service like) police," and "would you like more, the same, or less of it?" Citizens regularly want more. If one asks in the same survey whether citizens prefer more, the same, or fewer taxes, most prefer fewer. These ostensibly conflicting responses for services and against taxes have generated much confusion in public officials and even many survey analysts. Many officials asked just about services in the 1960s and early 1970s; they then often increased services, responding to apparent citizen demand. But in the late 1970s, when their citizens increasingly voted for tax cuts, the problem with the question format became clear. The ideal solution is to impose a precise *budget constraint* on service questions. A format such as a budget pie can limit the size of service slices to the total the respondent is willing to pay. Clark (1974) and Wilson (1983) discuss budget pies; Scott (1976) compares their results to card sorts, ordinal rankings, and self-ordering scales for several public services; McIver & Ostrom (1976) compare budget pies and open-ended items. Ladd & Wilson (1985) analyze the degree to which service and tax items each explain support for the Massachusetts tax reduction referendum (Proposition 2 ½). Slovak (1980) analyzes intercorrelations between different spending and tax items. No format is clearly superior. The budget pie is conceptually more desirable but difficult to interpret for some less educated or informed respondents. A partial solution is to ask several items about both services and taxes and the trade-offs between them.

Related work is that of Converse (1975) who assessed citizen surveys for "constraint"—how much did preferences on one topic constrain (correlate with) those on a related topic? He concluded that less than 10% of the American population held such constrained preferences—a shock to the populist democratic ideal. He has repeatedly been challenged. Nie et al (1976) argued using more recent data that his findings were specific to the complacent Eisenhower years. But they were undercut in turn by reanalyses suggesting that most of their reported changes were just artifacts of changes in questionnaire items (Sullivan et al 1978). Converse has also been criticized for a focus on national issues, thus ignoring structured views on local or other issues salient to the individual (Lane 1962, Bennett 1975). Converse (1975:83–94) accepts the importance of studying citizen preferences in local context.

Indeed the local context is central when citizens evaluate their leaders and city services. Yet, citizens do not just reflect "objective" characteristics of local services—as is implicitly assumed in many surveys by city governments (Clark 1976). An ostensibly simple item like "how satisfied are you with police services" is substantially affected by citizens' personal characteristics (education, race), their neighbors (who may generate more or less crime), service providers (who may be friendly but inefficient, or the converse), and even the style of elected officials (with no changes in police service, socially responsive mayors increased citizen satisfaction with police!). Indeed each factor can explain as much variance in citizen satisfaction as does the actual service delivery (cf Rossi et al 1974, Hoffman & Clark 1979).

The disparity between current policy and that preferred by a citizen is a *loss function* in the public choice tradition of Davis, Hinich, Kramer, and others (e.g. Riker & Ordeshook 1973). Related empirical work on *policy responsiveness* to citizens finds contextual differences by issues, constituencies, and the vulnerability of leaders to electoral defeat (Schumaker 1981, Kuklinski 1978; Schumaker & Getter 1977). Citizen preferences have also been compared to those of leaders on issues like budget allocations, service delivery patterns (Baldasarre & Protash 1982), and similar items (Schumaker, Getter & Clark 1983, Ostrom et al 1978). Citizen participation is simpler to measure than preferences and is often studied. But most studies use individual characteristics to explain participation and ignore the social context. The "standard" individualistic model thus estimates participation rates from respondent's income, occupation, education, age, etc. The standard result, from national surveys of 1500 individuals, is that higher status persons participate more in voting and quasi-political groups (Verba & Nie 1972).

Several hypotheses consider participation in social context, but they remain largely untested. For example, Coleman's (1957) community conflict ideas, his (1971) book on alternative strategies for mobilizing blacks, and his (1973) collective action model all stress participation as resource activation that varies with actions by others in the same system. Similar notions of slack and pyramiding resources in Dahl (1961), political mobilization in Deutsch (1963), and resource inflation and deflation in Parsons (1969) demand system-level data.

To permit cross-city comparisons, several studies employ indirect participation measures. Crain et al (1969) thus used the form of government and holding a referendum, and Turk (1977) the number of voluntary association headquarters. Others survey actual citizen participation, but for just one or a few cities (e.g. Ostrom et al 1978, Warren et al 1974). Gamson's provocative hypotheses about coalitions and mobilization have been tested using only disparate protest groups (1975). A single study surveyed voting turnout in local elections with a national sample of cities (Alford & Lee 1968). It impressively contradicts the standard individualistic model: the higher the educational level in a city, the lower the voting turnout. This seems due to the greater homogeneity of small and middle-sized suburbs where more-educated persons live; suburbs thus have fewer fundamental divisions, less social conflict, and less voter participation.

Contextual factors like a critical local election or political conflict can dramatically affect individual participation. Voting turnout approached 80% in cities like Cleveland, Gary, and Chicago when they first elected a black mayor (Nelson & Meranto 1977). "Community control" school boards were enthusiastically introduced in New York in the late 1960s in an effort to shift control to low-income parents. But voting turnout soon fell to about 10% and elections became dominated by the teachers union. Such contextual effects are dramatic in case studies, but integrating them with the more general theories and comparative empirical work remains a future task.

STRUCTURAL CONTEXTS AFFECTING CITIZENS, POLITICAL LEADERSHIP, AND POLICY OUTPUTS

While much work on political leaders and citizens remains individualistic, contextual characteristics are increasingly stressed. Still the predominance of case studies has usually led to ad hoc introduction of contextual characteristics in considering specific processes like voting turnout.

Several analysts turned to political culture in the early 1980s to systematize contextual characteristics. Political culture includes values and norms defining policy preferences and political rules of the game. The importance of political culture grew clearer as long-accepted norms were shaken, from the 1960s riots through taxpayer revolts and retrenchment. But these patterns differed by type of city. Empirical findings thus often take the form of statistical interaction effects. An essentially similar approach has been used in related fields under such headings as "contextual analysis," "structural effects analysis," and (in organization studies) "contingency theory."

Political culture initially emerged from comparing sociocultural support for different political systems across nations (e.g. Almond & Coleman 1960) and cities (e.g. Banfield & Wilson 1963, Elazar & Zikmund 1975). Recent works include Lipset (1979, 1981), Knoke (1981); Douglas & Wildavsky (1982); Kincaid (1982); Clark & Ferguson (1983); and Maddox & Lilie (1984).

Table 1 illustrates how political cultural elements define distinct urban contexts. Across the top are five dimensions from the theories discussed. Two key dimensions of citizen and leader policy preferences are fiscal and social liberalism. Then organized groups and citizens appear as alternative sources of policy in group and populist theories. Finally come public goods consumed by the "whole community" versus separable goods like jobs and contracts that can be targeted to specific constituents. These five dimensions, "deep structures" of all democratic political systems, variously combine to generate distinct political cultures. While other combinations are logically possible, four are most important for American society today: Democratic, Republican, ethnic, and new fiscal populist. The four differ in their policy preferences and rules of the game and thus define contexts where general theories differentially apply. The conflict between group and populist theory is resolved by recognizing that in Republican (e.g. San Diego) or new fiscal populist (Pittsburgh under Mayor Flaherty) political cultures, citizen preferences play a more critical role, while groups are less legitimate—except those that act with concern for the "whole community." By contrast, in traditional Democratic (Boston) or ethnic (Gary) political cultures, parties, unions, churches, and other organized groups are key actors; networks joining leaders and groups should explain more variance in policy outputs in such cities. While both citizens and groups provide inputs in most political systems, different political cultures encourage alternative input patterns. For example, the taxpayers' revolt had to become explosive before traditional Democratic leaders responded (e.g. in Boston), while populist leaders conduct polls to monitor subtle attitude changes of individual citizens.

The political culture approach is relativistic, resembling Marx's contrast of how processes vary under capitalism or socialism. Yet Marx's deterministic emphasis on the economy as prime mover is not shared by current political culture writers, nor do they advocate a cultural determinism common to the

Table 1   General characteristics generating four types of political culture

	Policy preferences		Legitimate sources of input to the political system:		Public goods emphasized as resources
	Fiscal liberalism	Social liberalism	Individual citizens	Organized groups	
New Deal Democrat	+	+	−	+	−
New Deal Republican	−	−	+	−	+
Ethnic politician	+	−	−	+	−
New fiscal populist	−	+	+	−	+

German idealists. The political cultural approach is multicausal, but goes beyond this general statement to specify how and where specific causal dynamics operate.

The Table 1 transformation rules illustrate an approach that could incorporate other dimensions and contexts. Its general message is to codify specific processes by identifying their critical elements and how they combine in empirically important cases. It can thus be used like the chemical table of elements. By defining where distinct theoretical models hold, and matching them with empirical cases, the framework becomes a sociology-of-knowledge–type map. The four political cultures characterize different types of cities and leaders, but many cities include elements of all four types. Local policy debates, then, often focus on appropriate rules of the game.

The four are also historical residues from past developments. Some critical past developments highlighted distinct aspects of political culture. The developments were initially overinterpreted; more balanced assessments followed. Black social protests in the late 1960s were initially seen by some, especially neo-Marxists, as revolutionary. Protests were followed by marked increases in numbers of black elected officials, and ethnic politics won new respectability in programs like affirmative action. Karnig & Welch (1980) and Nelson & Meranto (1977) consider how black politics emerged as a new ethnic political culture when the civil rights movement backed candidates for city elections. Fiscal policies in such cities shifted dramatically as social services expanded (Browning, Marshall & Tabb 1984).

Social movements for peace in Vietnam, women, gays, and ecology flourished in the late 1960s and early 1970s. Movement activists mobilized behind George McGovern at the 1972 Democratic Convention, defeating traditional Democrats like Richard Daley and later making important rule changes—e.g. abolishing seniority in the Democratic Party and the US Congress. As the parties weakened, movement-based "special interest groups" grew more powerful. Lipset (1981) and others saw an expanding "New Class" of liberal college graduates generating these developments, while Douglas & Wildavsky (1982) saw them as flowing from a "sectarian" tradition in American political culture. From nineteenth century utopian communities to 1970s social movements, this sectarian culture has been much committed to its movement goals, strictly egalitarian in treating members, and hostile to nonmembers—continuing a quasi-religious view of politics that originated in the Protestant sects (Lipset 1979; Elazar & Zikmund 1975). This culture sees coldly bureaucratic or market-defined rules as illegitimate and calls for strict moral accountability in populist manner. In the past it encouraged "reform" politics, which redirected urban fiscal policies (e.g. McDonald & Ward 1984); more recently it has encouraged citizen advisory panels, public hearings, sunset laws, more disclosure of budgeting and auditing, and freedom of information acts.

The taxpayers revolt was another critical development. Soon after California's Proposition 13 in 1978, some concluded that a New Right had succeeded the New Left (e.g. Howe 1978). But the taxpayers revolt was not simply New Right—conservative on both social and fiscal issues. Most Americans support lower taxes yet are liberal on social issues, i.e. their views are consistent with those of neither Republicans nor New Deal Democrats. Support for both parties fell as citizens grew more liberal on social issues, but conservative on fiscal issues—and found that neither party supported this policy combination. The number of Americans who considered themselves Independents rose until in 1980 they equaled the number of Democrats (38 percent). The New Left or New Class interpretation of increasing liberalism thus holds for social but not fiscal issues, while the New Right interpretation holds for fiscal but not social issues.

Local political leaders responded better than national leaders to these new preferences, because local parties are weaker. Socially liberal but fiscally conservative mayors came to office in increasing numbers over the 1970s, including Peter Flaherty in Pittsburgh, Edward Koch in New York, William Green in Philadelphia, Kathy Whitmire in Houston, Dianne Feinstein in San Francisco, and many less well-known mayors in smaller cities. These New Fiscal Populists have been changing American political culture. Their new combination of fiscal conservatism and social liberalism leads them to oppose special interest groups, especially municipal employee unions, and to appeal directly to individual citizens in a populist manner offering public goods policies (Caraley 1982). They often support procedural changes like citizen hearings to overcome union pressures and incremental bureaucratic routines (Clark & Ferguson 1983, Clark 1983).

Faced with fiscal austerity, leaders in (New Deal) Democratic political cultures search for less visible revenue sources, like short-term debt or inter-fund transfers, since a constant flow of jobs and favors for constituents is critical to continuing success. Ethnic leaders are similar but seek to protect their ethnic supporters. Republicans emphasize cutting taxes and expenditures with less concern for service effects. New fiscal populists seek instead to improve productivity, since this allows them to respond to the disadvantaged—that is, to be socially liberal—while they remain fiscally tight. Mollenkopf (1983) considers how such Democratic and Republican local policies are reinforced by intergovernmental grants and regulations.

BUREAUCRATIC PROCESSES AND SERVICE DELIVERY

Political leaders record their preferences in laws and budgets. Yet bureaucratic processes shift actual service delivery. Several theories of bureaucratic processes stress one factor, but structural contexts relativize them. First the theories.

Incrementalism

The belief that bureaucrats do the same this year as last but with an increment has long been a central bureaucratic theory (cf Wildavsky 1964, Crecine 1969). The standard operating procedures of professional administrators were correspondingly central in several studies of service allocation across neighborhoods and classes of service recipients (e.g. Levy et al 1974; Lineberry 1977). Most studies stressing incremental procedures are case studies of one city over a short period (but cf Lyon & Bonjean 1981). In studies comparing cities differing in political and social contexts, bureaucratic processes vary in import and specific effects.

The Dynamic Bureau Head

The mirror image of the rule-frozen bureaucrat is the aggressive bureau head driven by direct personal interests: a larger budget, more staff, a better office, and similar amenities. These concerns may be clothed in public interest arguments and groups may be mobilized to support them, but managerial amenities remain the driving force in a theory which Downs and Tullock initiated but Niskanan (1971) elaborated, thus inspiring a volume of papers extending it (Borcherding 1977). Economists have usually developed this approach still further; they find congenial a maximizing framework with a single argument, and they consider immediate personal gain to be sufficient motivation.

If we accept self-aggrandizement as one motivating factor, is it sufficient? What of similar motivations of political leaders, organized group leaders, or even taxpayers? The theory fared less well after the mid-1970s, when top staff more often were promoted for cutting back. Orzechowski (1977) contains a detailed critique of Niskanan, which stresses the specific market or environment (i.e. structural context) as an influence in shifting bureaucratic behavior.

Professionalization and "Reform" Government

Several other factors affecting bureaucratic processes have been studied, but mostly ad hoc. Professionalization is a classic theme. Considerable descriptive information is available about job training and promotion criteria of municipal staff (Greisinger et al 1979), but it has seldom been used more interpretively. Classic "reform" government writings stress professionalization via adoption of a city manager, a civil service, and nonpartisan elections. Such "good government" has been taught in many public administration schools over the last half century. But as political culture assumptions behind reform ideology were critiqued (e.g. Banfield & Wilson 1963; Hawley 1973), they were increasingly recognized as consistent with a Republican or new fiscal populist style but inconsistent with Democratic or ethnic political cultures. Public policy schools have grown more circumspect about ethical training, emphasizing instead more technical or social scientific tools. The increased awareness of social science in the general population (and especially in elected officials) has similarly encouraged professional sophistication. Important vehicles for this are continual workshops, seminars, and professional publications of groups like the International City Management Association, Government (previously Municipal) Finance Officers Association, and various consulting firms. Professionalization has clearly increased, but important differences persist across cities.

Contextual Characteristics Affecting Service Delivery

Unions influence services, but the context shifts their effects. Unionization emerged powerfully in the 1960s. It was previously illegal in most states since civil service implied job security and public officials were considered too integral a part of the "public good" to permit collective bargaining. Yet surprisingly, unionization has had no effect on fiscal strain or even total spending on personal services per capita. Unionization is not unimportant, but its effects shift by context. Ethnic and Democratic cities differ most dramatically from each other. Democratic cities often have unionized, politically influential, and highly paid workforces. By contrast, ethnic, especially black-dominated cities, have weaker unions and pay employees less. Paying less permits hiring more staff, desirable in cities with numerous underemployed. Gary thus paid less than half the compensation of New York but hired more staff (adjusting for population size and functional responsibility). Cities varying in political culture differ considerably in these trade-offs between compensation and numbers, and similarly in capital versus labor, which in turn affect many aspects of service delivery (Clark & Ferguson 1983).

Contracting for services with other governments or private firms has dramatically increased in the last decade. For new fiscal populist leaders confronted with intransigent bureaucracies, contracting is a real weapon. Even if leaders do not contract for refuse collection or police, the threat that they may has often shifted the balance in collective bargaining from municipal employees to citizens (cf Savas 1982).

Thirty-three strategies—some innovative, some less so—by which local governments adapt to austerity are being analyzed in the Fiscal Austerity and Urban Innovation Project. Contracting out, joint purchasing agreements, and laborsaving productivity techniques are among the strategies being adopted by cities whose political and administrative contexts are favorable to them (Walzer 1985, and draft Project papers listed in Project *Newsletters* 1982–1984).

Parks & Ostrom (1981) studied police departments for trade-offs between service delivery of bureaus and the amenities of the bureau heads; they found that departments that experience more competition with cities nearby provide better services. Peterson & Wong (1985) show how education and housing policies are constrained when they assume a more redistributive emphasis.

Chan, Clark & Troha (1983) show how organizational slack varies across cities.

Wildavsky, who contributed much to bureaucratic and incremental interpretations of service delivery, has recently stressed broader political variables. He points to social movements and special interest groups as destroying the bureaucratic and rational rules of the game upon which incrementalism depends. In his history of budgeting, incrementalism is only sometimes preeminent; the dominant political culture redefines appropriate management, budgeting, and finance procedures (Wildavsky 1985). From roughly 1945 to the late 1960s, elements of rational, bureaucratic political culture were more widely shared than was generally articulated in the US and much of Europe. But a political culture of "chronic instability" has come to characterize many national and local governments in more recent years, leading to a breakdown in many norms like incrementalism, the balanced budget, and comparing costs and benefits across programs (Rose & Page 1982). When disturbances to a political system increase, heightened by social heterogeneity, incrementalism is less likely and leaders and organized groups are likely to play more active roles (Clark & Ferguson 1983; Galaskiewicz 1981).

POPULATION REDISTRIBUTION AND LOCATION OF ECONOMIC ACTIVITIES

Research is sparse that joins specific urban policies to the location of population and economic activities. Consider first some major population trends affecting cities over the last decade. These include a decline in the birthrate, fewer school-age children, and more older persons. *Ceteris paribus* these imply less demand for urban public services. Yet two countertrends weaken such effects: smaller average households and immigration from abroad, especially by Spanish-speaking persons. Metropolitan areas in the South and West have been growing, and many in the Northeast declining. Nonmetropolitan areas have been growing, but not farming areas. Central cities are declining relative to suburbs, but this trend has slowed and does not hold in many smaller SMSAs. "Gentrification" proceeds in many downtown neighborhoods independent of other trends (See US Census, Current Population Surveys and 1980 Census reports).

These descriptive results assume greater policy interest if their causes and consequences are specified, but causal modeling requires more data and time. This is an exciting moment for work of this sort, as past approaches are being fundamentally questioned. Standard migration theory explained population movement by firm location: people moved to jobs, and once in the area, sought to minimize their travel from the job. Most rural to urban migration around the world has been explained by less demand for farm labor due to technological advances, and location of industry near transportation nodes. Then the central city decline relative to suburbs was explained by the telephone, automobile, airplane, and lower costs of single-story assembly and warehouse areas (e.g. Shaw 1975, Berry & Kasarda 1977).

The shift of population and job growth to the US Sunbelt, and similar patterns in several European and Asian countries, has led to much public debate over the causes. Past models seem inadequate and are further weakened by three recent research findings.

First is the critical role of small service firms. From 1969 to 1976, 80% of new jobs in cities were in firms with 100 or fewer employees, and 66% in those with 20 or less. About 70% of new jobs are in service firms, from accounting to computer programming to fast food. But these little firms are born and die rapidly; their differential birth and death rates across cities thus explain overall job changes (Birch et al 1977, Vaughan 1977, Kasarda 1983). The image of major corporations moving thousands of jobs from New York to Houston is consequently incorrect; relatively few jobs shift this way.

The second trend builds on the first: people increasingly move and then create jobs once in an attractive location. This was quietly reported in simultaneous equation studies of job and population changes (Muth 1971, Greenwood 1975). Detailed work on the Cleveland area shows similar results (Bradbury et al 1982). Moving small service firms is clearly simpler than moving huge factories, so personal location preferences can play a larger role.

The third trend is the heightened effects of public policy on job and migration decisions. One basic policy measure is the tax burden, which earlier studies often found unrelated to migration and employment. Better measures of the total tax burden show clear effects. Clark & Ferguson (1983: 204–219) report that a 10% increase in tax burden decreases net migration by about 2% (controlling 22 other variables). Similarly important policy effects emerge in careful modeling of zoning (Shlay & Rossi 1981), environmental controls, social service benefits, and schools (Tolley et al 1979, Katzman 1978). Numerous economic development incentives like tax abatements emerged in the last decade (Clarke & Rich 1985), but their effects are still largely undemonstrated (Clark 1981a). As people can increasingly make location decisions as residents rather than as employees, amenities and public services may grow in explanatory power.

It is unclear how much all three newly documented trends reflect change or simply more careful research. Proponents of the established theories remain active, so critical assessments continue. What seems at stake is not the existence of these new trends, but their importance compared to traditional factors. The new trends have already redirected research and led public officials to reassess their policies.

Distinct employment and population patterns encourage distinct political cultures. Cities with numerous industrial plants and blue collar workers are more often unionized and support Democratic political culture. If Catholics, blacks, or Hispanics are also numerous, ethnic political culture is more likely. Cities with more service jobs and highly educated citizens have more new fiscal populists, while those with high income residents are more often Republican. Correlatively, specific causes of migration and employment change probably vary across cities by political culture and associated contextual characteristics. Bradbury et al (1982) document some, but this remains more a future task.

CONCLUSION

Urban policy analysis has seen many new approaches over the last decade, but many were launched overenthusiastically. As proponents of new approaches— e.g. neo-Marxists, network analysts, public choice theorists—refine their views, they often develop more overlap with other traditions. Analytical coherence can be maintained if processes identified by these approaches are located within appropriate structural contexts. Much specific work also proceeds independent of these theoretical concerns, especially by persons working closely with policymakers. But advice can have policy impact only if it is politically and administratively feasible. Explicit analysis of the structural context thus can both join alternative theories and help define policy feasibility. This distinctly sociological approach to urban policy analysis continues the tradition of Marx, Weber, and Durkheim. Recent work, as reviewed above, is rediscovering these roots.

ACKNOWLEDGMENT

This is research report No. 148 of the Comparative Study of Community Decision-Making.

Literature Cited

Alford, R. R., Lee, E. C. 1968. Voting turnout in American cities. *Am. Polit. Sci. Rev.* 62:796–813
Almond, G. A., Coleman, J. S. 1960. *The Politics of Developing Areas*. Princeton, NJ: Princeton Univ. Press. 591 pp.
Arrow, K. 1963. *Social Choice and Individual Values*. New York: Wiley. 2nd ed.
Baldasarre, M., Protash, W. 1982. Growth controls, population growth, and community satisfaction. *Am. Sociol. Rev.* 47:339–346
Banfield, E. C., Wilson, J. Q. 1963. *City Politics*. Cambridge, Mass: Harvard Univ. Press/MIT Press
Bennett, W. L. 1975. *The Political Mind and the Political Environment*. Lexington, Mass: Heath
Berry, B. J. L., Kasarda, J. D. 1977. *Contemporary Urban Ecology*. New York: Macmillan
Birch, D. L. et al. 1977. *The Behavioral Foundations of Neighborhood Change*. Cambridge, Mass: Joint Ctr. Urban Studies Harvard and MIT
Borcherding, T. E., ed. 1977. *Budgets and Bureaucrats: The Sources of Government Growth*. Durham, NC: Duke Univ. Press
Bouinot, J. 1984. Les villes americaines face a la crise economique, lecons pour la France. *Revue Francaise de Finances Publiques* 5:165–172

Bradbury, K. L., Downs, A., Small, K. A. 1982. *Urban Decline and the Future of American Cities*. Washington, DC: Brookings

Brieger, R. L. 1979. Toward an operational model of community elite structures. *Qual. Quant.* 13:21–57

Browning, R. P., Marshall, D. P., Tabb, D. H. 1984. *Protest is Not Enough*. Berkeley: Univ. Calif. Press. 317 pp.

Burt, R. S. 1981. Spatial models of community leadership. See Clark 1981b, pp. 103–122

Caraley, D. 1982. *Doing More With Less*. New York: Columbia Univ. Program in Publ. Policy and Admin.

Castells, M. 1972. *La Question Urbaine*. Paris: Maspero

Castells, M. 1983. *The City and the Grassroots*. Berkeley: Univ. Calif. Press

Chan, J. L., Clark, T. N., Troha, M. A. 1983. Organizational slack in municipal governments. *J. Urb. Aff.* 5:95–108

Clark, T. N. 1972. Structural-functionalism, exchange theory, and the new political economy: institutionalization as a theoretical linkage. *Sociol. Inq.* 42:275–311

Clark, T. N. 1974. Can you cut a budget pie? *Policy Politics* 3:3–32

Clark, T. N. 1975. Community power. In *Ann. Rev. Sociol.* 1:271–96

Clark, T. N., ed. 1976. *Citizen Preferences and Urban Public Policy*. Special issue of *Policy and Politics* (4). Also Sage Contemporary Soc. Sci. Iss. Series 34. Beverly Hills, Calif: Sage

Clark, T. N., ed. 1981a. *Community Development. Urban Affairs Papers,* Vol. 3, no. 3. Beverly Hills: Sage

Clark, T. N., ed. 1981b. *Urban Policy Analysis: Directions for Future Research. Urban Affairs Annual Reviews,* Vol. 21. Beverly Hills, Calif: Sage. 296 pp.

Clark, T. N. 1983. The new fiscal populist. *Public Opinion* 6:50–52

Clark, T. N. 1985. The fiscal austerity and urban innovation project. In *Research in Urban Policy*, ed. T. N. Clark, 1:355–362. Greenwich, Conn: JAI Press. 393 pp.

Clark, T. N., Ferguson, L. C. 1983. *City Money*. New York: Columbia Univ. Press. 440 pp.

Clarke, S. E., Rich, M. E. 1985. Making money work. See Clark 1985, pp. 101–116

Coleman, J. S. 1957. *Community Conflict*. New York: Free

Coleman, J. S. 1971. *Resources for Social Change*. New York: Wiley. 118 pp.

Coleman, J. S. 1973. *The Mathematics of Collective Action*. London: Heinemann. 191 pp.

Converse, P. E. 1975. Public opinion and voting behavior. In *Handbook of Political Science*, ed. F. I. Greenstein, N. Polsby, pp. 75–170. Reading, Mass: Addison-Wesley

Crain, R. L., Katz, E., Rosenthal, D. B. 1969.

The Politics of Community Conflict. Indianapolis: Bobbs-Merrill

Crecine, J. P. 1969. *Governmental Problem Solving*. Chicago: Rand McNally

Dahl, R. A. 1961. *Who Governs?*. New Haven, Conn: Yale Univ. Press

DeSwann, A. 1973. *Coalition Theories and Cabinet Formations*. San Francisco: Jossey-Bass

Deutsch, K. W. 1963. *The Nerves of Government*. New York: Free

Douglas, M., Wildavsky, A. 1982. *Risk and Culture*. Berkeley, Calif: Univ. California Press

Downs, A. 1957. *An Economic Theory of Democracy*. New York: Harper & Row

Eberts, P., Kelly, J. M. 1985. How mayors get things done. See T. N. Clark 1985, pp. 39–70

Eberts, P. 1985. Fiscal austerity and its consequences in local governments. See Clark 1985, pp. 365–384

Elazar, D. J., Zikmund, J. II, eds. 1975. *The Ecology of American Political Culture*. New York: Crowell

Fiscal Austerity and Urban Innovation Project, *Newsletters* No. 1–10 (1982–1984)

Fishburn, P. C. 1970. *Utility Theory for Decision-Making*. New York: Wiley

Friedland, R., Bielby, W. T. 1981. The power of business in the city. See Clark 1981b: 133–51

Friedland, R., Piven, F. F., Alford, R. R. 1977. Political conflict, urban structure, and the fiscal crisis. *Int. J. Urban Regional Res.* 1(3):447–71

Friedland, R. 1983. *Power and Crisis in the City*. New York: Schoken. 248 pp.

Galaskiewicz, J. 1979. *Exchange Networks and Community Politics*. Beverly Hills, Calif: Sage

Galaskiewicz, J. 1981. Interest group policies from a comparative perspective. *Urb. Aff. Q.* 16:259–80

Gamson, W. 1975. *The Strategy of Social Protest*. Homewood, Ill: Dorsey

Greenwood, M. J. 1975. A simultaneous-equations model of urban growth and migration. *J. Am. Stat. Assoc.* 70:797–810

Greisinger, G. W., Slovak, J. S., Molkup, J. J. 1979. *Civil Service Systems*. US Depart. Justice, LEAA and NILECJ. Washington, DC: GPO

Groennings, S. et al, eds. 1970. *The Study of Coalition Behavior*. New York: Holt, Rinehart & Winston

Hawley, W. D. 1973. *Nonpartisan Elections and the Case for Party Politics*. New York: Wiley-Interscience. 202 pp.

Hinckley, B. 1979. Twenty-one variables beyond the size of winning coalitions. *J. Polit.* 41:192–213

Hoffman, W. L., Clark, T. N. 1979. Citizen preferences and urban policy types. In *Fiscal*

Retrenchment and Urban Policy, ed. J. P. Blair, D. Nachmias, 85–106. Beverly Hills, Calif: Sage

Howe, I. 1978. The right menace. *The New Republic* 9:12–22

Hunter, F. 1953. *Community Power Structure*. Durham, NC: Univ. NC Press

Karnig, A. K., Welch, S. 1980. *Black Representation and Urban Policy*. Chicago: Univ. Chicago Press

Kasarda, J. D. 1981. Entry level jobs, mobility, and urban minority unemployment. *Urb. Aff. Q.* 19:21–40

Katzman, M. T. 1978. *The Quality of Municipal Services, Central City Decline, and Middle-Class Flight*. Research report R78-1. Cambridge, Mass: Depart. City & Regional Planning, Harvard Univ.

Kincaid, J., ed. 1982. *Political Culture, Public Policy, and the American States*. Philadelphia: Inst. Study Hum. Issues. 241 pp.

Knoke, D. 1981. Urban political cultures. See Clark 1981b, pp. 203–25

Kuklinski, J. H. 1978. Representations and elections. *Am. Polit. Sci. Rev.* 72:165–77

Ladd, H. F., Wilson, J. B. 1985. Proposition 2½: explaining the vote. See Clark 1985, pp. 199–244

Lane, R. 1962. *Political Ideology*. New York: Free

Laumann, E. O., Pappi, F. U. 1976. *Networks of Collective Action*. New York: Academic

Levine, C. H., Rubin, I., eds. 1980. *Fiscal Stress and Public Policy*. Beverly Hills: Sage

Levy, F., Meltsner, A., Wildavsky, A. 1974. *Urban Outcomes*. Berkeley: Univ. Calif. Press

Lineberry, R. L. 1977. *Equality and Urban Policy*. Beverly Hills, Calif: Sage

Lipset, S. M. 1979. *The First New Nation*. New York: Norton. 2nd ed.

Lipset, S. M., ed. 1981. *Party Coalitions in the 1980s*. San Francisco: Inst. Contemp. Stud.

Lyon, L., Bonjean, C. M. 1981. Community power and policy outputs. *Urb. Aff. Q.* 17:3–22

Maddox, W. S., Lilie, S. A. 1984. *Beyond Liberal and Conservative*. Washington, DC: Cato Inst.

Marsden, P. V., Laumann, E. O. 1977. Collective action in a community elite. In *Power, Paradigms and Community Research*, ed. R. J. Liebert, A. W. Immerschein, pp. 199–205. Beverly Hills, Calif: Sage. 343 pp.

McDonald, T. J., Ward, S. K., eds. 1984. *The Politics of Urban Fiscal Policy: New Approaches to Social Science History*, Vol. 5. Beverly Hills: Sage. 176 p.

McIver, J. P., E. Ostrom. 1976. Using budget pies to reveal preferences. See Clark 1976, pp. 87–110

Mollenkopf, J. 1983. *The Contested City*. Princeton: Princeton Univ. Press

Mueller, D. C. 1979. *Public Choice*. Cambridge, England: Cambridge Univ. Press

Municipal Finance Officers Association. 1982. *Indicators of Urban Condition*. Washington, DC: MFOA

Muth, R. F. 1971. Migration: chicken or egg? *South. Econ. J.* 37:295–306

Nelson, W. E., Jr., Meranto, P. J. 1977. *Electing Black Mayors*. Columbus: Ohio State Univ. Press

Newton, K., ed. 1981. *Urban Political Economy*. London: Pinter. 223 pp.

Nie, N. H., Verba, S., Petrocik, J. R. 1976. *The Changing American Voter*. Cambridge, Mass.: Harvard Univ. Press

Niskanan, W. N. 1971. *Bureaucracy and Representative Government*. Chicago: Aldine-Atherton

Orzechowski, W. 1977. Economic models of bureaucracy: survey, extensions, and evidence. See Borcherding 1977, pp. 229–59

Ostrom, E., Parks, R. B., Whitaker, G. P. 1978. *Patterns of Metropolitan Policing*. Cambridge, Mass: Ballinger

Parks, R. B., Ostrom, E. 1981. Complex models of urban service systems. See Clark 1981b:171–200

Parsons, T. 1969. *Politics and Social Structure*. New York: Free

Peterson, P. E., Wong, K. K. 1985. Toward a differentiated theory of federalism. See Clark 1985, pp. 301–324

Riker, W. H., Ordeshook, P. C. 1973. *An Introduction to Positive Political Theory*. Englewood Cliffs, NJ: Prentice-Hall

Rose, R., Page, E. 1982. Chronic instability in fiscal systems. In *Fiscal Stress in Cities*, ed. R. Rose, E. Page, pp. 198–245. Cambridge, Eng: Cambridge Univ. Press. 245 pp.

Rossi, P. H., Berk, R. A., Eidson, B. K. 1974. *The Roots of Urban Discontent*. New York: Wiley

Samuelson, P. A. 1969. Pure theory of public expenditure and taxation. In *Public Economics*, ed. J. Margolis, H. Guitton, pp. 98–123. New York: St. Martin's

Savas, E. S. 1982. *Privatizing the Public Sector*. Chatham, NJ: Chatham. 164 pp.

Schumaker, P. D., Getter, R. W. 1977. Responsiveness bias in 51 American communities. *Am. J. Polit. Sci.* 21:247–280

Schumaker, P. D., Getter, R. W., Clark, T. N. 1983. *Policy Responsiveness and Fiscal Strain in 51 American Communities*. Washington, DC: Am. Polit. Sci. Assoc. SETUPS Series

Schumaker, P. D. 1981. Citizen preferences and policy responsiveness. See Clark 1981b, pp. 227–44

Scott, D. 1976. Measures of citizen evaluation of governmental service. See Clark 1976, pp. 111–28

Sen, A. K. 1970. *Collective Choice and Social Welfare*. San Francisco: Holden-Day

Shaw, R. P. 1975. *Migration Theory and Fact*. Philadelphia: Regional Sci. Res. Inst.

Shlay, A. B., Rossi, P. H. 1981. Putting politics into urban ecology. See Clark 1981b, pp. 257–86

Slovak, J. S. 1980. Property taxes and community political structures. *Urb. Aff. Q.* 16:189–210

Sullivan, J. L., Pierson, J. E., Marcus, G. E. 1978. Ideological contrasting in the mass public. *Am. J. Polit. Sci.* 22:233–9

Tideman, T. N. 1976. The capabilities of voting rules in the absence of coalitions. See Clark 1976, pp. 23–44

Tolley, G. S., Graves, P. E., Gardiner, J. L. 1979. *Urban Growth Policy in Market Economy*. New York: Academic

Turk, H. 1977. *Organizations in Modern Life*. San Francisco: Jossey-Bass

Urban Affairs Quarterly. 1983. Symposium: Urban Theory and National Urban Policy. *Urb. Aff. Q.* 19:1–143

Vaughan, R. J. 1977. *The Urban Impacts of Federal Policies*. Report R-2028-KF/RC. Santa Monica, Calif: Rand

Verba, S., Nie, N. H. 1972. *Participation in America*. New York: Harper & Row

Von Neumann, J., Morgenstern, O. 1944. *Theory of Games and Economic Behavior*. Princeton: Princeton Univ. Press

Walzer, N. 1985. Fiscal austerity in mid-sized cities. See Clark 1985, pp. 161–74

Warren, R. L., Rose, S. M., Bergunder, A. R. 1974. *The Structure of Urban Reform*. Lexington, MA: D. C. Heath

Whitt, J. A. 1982. *Urban Elites and Mass Transportation*. Princeton, NJ: Princeton Univ. Press. 231 pp.

Wildavsky, A. 1964. *The Politics of the Budgetary Process*. Boston: Little, Brown

Wildavsky, A. 1985. Budgets as social orders. See Clark 1985, pp. 183–90

Williams, J. A., Zimmermann, E. 1981. American business organizations and redistributive preferences. *Urb. Aff. Q.* 16:453–64

Wilson, L. A. 1983. Preference revelation and public policy. *Public Adm. Rev.* 43:335–42

Zimmermann, E. 1981. *Interest and Control in Community Decision-Making*. Bern/Frankfurt/Las Vegas: Peter Lang. 235 pp.

Ann. Rev. Sociol. 1985. 11:457–83

ORGANIZATIONAL CULTURE

William G. Ouchi

Graduate School of Management, University of California, Los Angeles, California 90024

Alan L. Wilkins

Graduate School of Management, Brigham Young University, Provo, Utah 84602

Abstract

The contemporary study of organizational culture reflects mainline concerns of the organizational sociologist. Though anthropology and cognitive psychology have made significant contributions to this new field, the study of organizational culture may be seen as a return to some of the most basic concerns about the nature of organizations and the appropriate methods for analyzing them. We review current work on theory, empirical studies, and contributions—both theoretical and empirical—to the understanding of planned change of organizations. The contemporary study of organizational culture reflects several hotly contested concerns, among which are the following: Can culture be intentionally managed? Must culture be studied using the tools of the phenomenologist or the ethnographer, or does the use of multivariate statistics also have a place? Which social science paradigm is most appropriate for understanding organizational culture: phenomenology, symbolic interaction, semiotics, structural-functional anthropology, cognitive psychology?

INTRODUCTION: THE CONTEMPORARY STUDY OF ORGANIZATIONAL CULTURE

During 1983 three major collections of articles on organizational culture appeared. Since 1979 no fewer than seven review articles have been published on aspects of this topic, and the outpouring of work shows no signs of abatement. Few readers would disagree that the study of organizational culture

457

0360-0572/85/0815-0457$02.00

has become one of the major domains of organizational research, and some might even argue that it has become the single most active arena, eclipsing studies of formal structure, of organization-environment research, and of bureaucracy.

What is perhaps most unusual about this development is that several books and articles by academics have been widely read by nonacademics, and a few have appeared on best-seller lists. At the same time, studies of organizational culture often compare western organizations to Japanese or other national organizations, thus bringing an unusual comparative international flavor to organizational research.

Indeed, some might observe that the rise of research on organizational culture came about because Japanese firms were during the late 1970s and the early 1980s widely considered to have superior operating characteristics, but the forms of organizational research dominant then emphasized formal structure and so failed to uncover any difference between Japanese and western firms. As a consequence, scholars began to examine the possibility that the different national cultures might have penetrated modern corporate forms, thus creating differences in organizational culture between, say, Nissan and General Motors. Several early studies gave credence to this approach, which led next to the possibility that even within a single national culture there might be local differences in the culture of firms, e.g. between Hewlett-Packard and ITT.

A casual inspection of the contemporary literature suggests that most of those who study organizational culture trace their intellectual roots to a few key anthropologists. Both the point of view and the method of the anthropologist might seem to have been heavily borrowed by the student of organization. It is undeniable that anthropological style and method have been a great, perhaps the single greatest, influence on these contemporary studies, but this new work owes a very major debt to the sociology of organizations as well.

We offer the view that the contemporary study of organizational culture may be best understood as a continuation of the main line of organizational sociology, which has always focused on the normative bases and the shared understandings that, through subtle and complex expression, regulate social life in organizations. Many younger scholars, trained to study those problems most easily subjected to multivariate statistical analysis, may have the impression that the study of organizational culture through participant observation is an aberration or a departure from the tradition of organizational sociology. Such a view does not withstand historical review.

As we trace the development of organizational sociology since Max Weber, we find a constant tension between those who prefer to study what is explicit about organizations and those who prefer what is implicit; a tension between those who emphasize the capacity of organizations to create order and rationality versus those who are struck by the sometimes chaotic and nonrational features of organizational life. The study of organizational culture grows out of that tension and represents, we believe, but the most recent stage of the intellectual cycle.

The preparation for writing a review article mostly involves reading a large number of books and articles, many of them not yet published. In many domains of scholarship that can be a chore. To read in organizational culture is more nearly a pleasure, in large part because the contemporary study of organizational culture relies upon bringing to life the richness and the vitality of people living and working together. The equations and statistics are few, the attempts to capture an ineffable essence are many. These studies recall the excitement, the passion, and the drama of social life, which were and continue to be central to the reason for the study of organizations.

THE INTELLECTUAL FOUNDATIONS OF ORGANIZATIONAL CULTURE

Heterogenous Intellectual Roots: A Citation Analysis

The contemporary study of organizational culture appears to amalgamate several points of view, rather than to constitute one branch of a single disciplinary family of scholarship. There is no single dominant point of view or method but rather a rich mixture of ideas and of approaches. We attempt to characterize the most important of these. Our review is limited to the study of formal economic organizations, primarily business firms.

During 1983, three collections of articles on organizational culture appeared: an anthology on *Organizational Symbolism* (Pondy et al 1983) and special issues of *Administrative Science Quarterly* (Vol. 28, No. 3) and of *Organizational Dynamics* (Vol. 12, No. 2). In all, these comprise 32 articles. A citation analysis reveals something of the diverse intellectual roots of this new field. Those sources cited six or more times are listed in Footnote 1.

These works, which provide the foundations of the field, are as heterogeneous as are most other aspects of the study of organizational culture. Of the seven most frequently cited works,[1] one was written by an anthropologist, three were authored or coauthored by sociologists, and three by management scholars (categorized by place of employment, rather than by training).

---

[1]Most frequently cited works: C. Geertz, *The Interpretation of Cultures,* 1973—ten citations; P. Berger, T. Luckman, *The Social Construction of Reality: A Treatise in the Sociology of Knowledge,* 1966—seven citations; Burton Clark, *The Distinctive College: Antioch, Reed, and Swarthmore,* 1970—seven citations; Terrence Deal, A. Kennedy, *Corporate Cultures,* 1982—seven citations; William G. Ouchi, *Theory Z,* 1981—six citations; A. M. Pettigrew, "On Studying Organizational Culture," *Admin. Sci. Q.* 24:570–81, 1979—six citations; Karl Weick, *The Social Psychology of Organizing,* 1979—six citations.

In all, a total of 103 works are cited in the 32 articles. Eleven authors are cited for three or four separate works each. Of these eleven, ten hold appointments in graduate schools of management.

The Influence of Sociology on Studies of Organizational Culture

Many students of organizational culture would assert that their primary intellectual debt is to the anthropologist rather than to the sociologist. Most would also assert a debt to the social psychologist. Although this review will focus on the debt of organizational culture studies to sociology, we will begin with a brief review of the impact of anthropological tradition on this field, and end the section with the briefest of acknowledgments to social psychology as a coda.

The Influence of Anthropology on Organizational Culture

Most of the currently "popular" work on organizational culture (Ouchi 1981; Pascale & Athos 1981; Deal & Kennedy 1982; Peters & Waterman 1982) as well as other work written for management audiences and management scholars (Dandridge et al 1980; Dyer 1982, 1984; Schein 1983a, 1983b; Martin & Siehl 1983; Wilkins 1983a, 1983b; and Wilkins & Ouchi 1983) draws upon the spirit if not the details of the functionalist tradition in anthropology. This influence can be further divided between two rather distinct forms of contemporary work.

Radcliffe-Brown (1952) and Malinowski (1961) represent a school of thought in anthropology that encourages the scholar to consider a group or society as a whole and to see how its practices, beliefs, and other cultural elements function to maintain social structure. Although organizational scholars rarely cite these sources, their work describes such cultural elements as employment practices, corporate ceremonies, and company legends in structural-functional terms. Malinowski and Radcliffe-Brown might be appalled by the explicitly promanagement and change-oriented bias of many contemporary scholars, but the impact of their organic, whole view of the structure and functioning of social systems on the contemporary study of organizational culture is undeniable.

Benedict (1934) and Mead (e.g. 1949) also represent an interest in groups or societies as a whole but tend to describe society as a large complex personality. This "configurationist" position suggests that a culture "selects" from a virtually infinite array of behavioral possibilities a limited set that may be interpreted as a particular configuration of related patterns. For example, Benedict (1934) described the Apollonian discomfort with excess and orgy and the Dionysian encouragement of psychic and emotional excess (see Sanday 1979) as opposing patterns found in many cultures. Some contemporary work on culture describes patterns of assumptions within organizations (Dyer 1982) in this tradition.

A second school of thought in anthropology is perhaps best represented by Clifford Geertz (1973), the most frequently cited of any scholar in the foregoing citation analysis. Along with other contemporary anthropologists such as Goodenough and Lévi-Strauss, Geertz emphasized the importance of discovering the "native's point of view." This approach has been called "semiotic" for its focus on language and symbols as the principal tools for apprehending the native's perspective.

Geertz (1973:24) suggests that "the whole point of a semiotic approach to culture is to aid us in gaining access to the conceptual world in which our subjects live so that we can, in some extended sense of the term, converse with them." Accomplishing this purpose, according to Geertz, requires that the anthropologist be immersed in the complex clusterings of symbols people use to confer meaning upon their world. Anthropology is thus not a matter of precise method but requires instead that the anthropologist engage in an intellectual effort that is "an elaborate venture in, to borrow a notion from Gilbert Ryle, 'thick description' " (pp. 5–6).

By contrast, Goodenough (1971) and others have developed an approach labeled "ethnoscience," "componential analysis," or "cognitive anthropology." While their aim is similar to that expressed by Geertz they differ considerably in method. Culture for ethnoscientists is the system of standards or rules for perceiving, believing, and acting that one needs to know in order to operate in a manner acceptable to the members of the culture. Anthropologists in this tradition have been strongly influenced by linguists (e.g. Chomsky 1972). They have in mind that just as a learned, and usually implicit, grammar helps people generate acceptable sentences, so cultural rules and categories and principles help people to generate acceptable behavior. Cultural description, according to Goodenough and others in this tradition, requires the discovery and writing out of systematic rules or algorithms that members of the culture implicitly use to generate acceptable behavior.

While most scholars currently working in the area of organizational culture refer to Geertz to suggest the need for "thick description," it appears that those who engage in empirical work instead use some variant of the methods suggested by Goodenough. Perhaps this is because the methods suggested by Geertz require a great deal of artistic ability and intuition while Goodenough's methods are more systematic and thus easier to learn. Sanday (1979) notes a similar tendency among practicing anthropologists to quote and admire Geertz but to follow the methods of Goodenough. Contemporary organizational scholars who have been influenced by the semiotic school include Pondy (1978), Smircich (1983), Gregory (1983), Barley (1983a), Evered (1983), Van Maanen (1979), and Frost & Morgan (1983).

The elements that comprise a culture to an anthropologist, such as language, ritual, and social structure, develop over decades or centuries. These cultural elements represent specific solutions to what often are universal problems or needs of social life and of survival, and in this sense culture is to the anthropologist both a dependent variable (shaped by a unique time and place) and an independent variable (shaping the beliefs and behavior of individuals). As we shall see, the contemporary student of organizational culture often takes the organization not as a natural solution to deep and universal forces but rather as a rational instrument designed by top management to shape the behavior of employees in purposive ways (Lammers 1981). The study of organizational culture typically takes culture as the independent variable, rarely attending to the environmental forces that have shaped the culture of, say, IBM or Sony and instead concentrating on a description of those critical elements of the firm's culture and on the patterns of employee behavior that they guide. Despite these differences, the study of organizational culture owes a great debt for point of view and method to anthropologists.

THE INFLUENCE OF ORGANIZATIONAL SOCIOLOGY ON ORGANIZATIONAL CULTURE

The influence of sociology on the study of organizational culture has been broad and direct. As a consequence, it is difficult to characterize a few main streams of effect. The several streams of work that have been most influential—the study of myth and ritual, symbolic interaction, ethnomethodology, and the study of organizations as institutions—are so interrelated that we have chosen to recount their effects in the form of an interpretive history rather than as separate schools of thought.

This historical approach leads us to conclude that the contemporary study of organizational culture is perhaps best understood as only the latest turn in the struggle between explicit and rational views of organization on the one hand and implicit, nonrational views on the other. This tension has long been a central feature in the sociology of organizations, and we can expect that the approach of organizational culture will have its day and then recede in importance, to rise yet again in modified form.

The Explicit Versus the Implicit Features of Organization

Perhaps the most pervasive effect has been Durkheim's emphasis on the importance of myth and ritual as the counterpoint to the study of social structure. Durkheim asserts that concrete symbols, such as myths, are necessary for solidarity because ". . . the clan is too complex a reality to be represented clearly in all its complex unity" (1961:220, from French). This suggestion that simple, symbolic representations of a complex social reality are fundamental to collective life has had a pervasive effect on the study of organizational culture. Durkheim suggested that this symbolic structure can be apprehended through the study of those myths and rituals that lie on the surface of social life and that provide clues to the deeper strains and forces. This method has also become a central feature of the study of organizational culture. Finally, Durkheim (1893), like Weber (1968) and Toennies (1957), drew a distinction between the explicit and the implicit features of social life and regarded the study of both as essential. This dual interest in the objective and the subjective features of organizational life has consistently been a central theme in the sociology of organizations and has become central to the study of organizational culture.

A later school of sociology came to emphasize not only that the objective and the subjective features of social life are separable, but that the two sides may be disconnected from one another more often than was supposed, and even that commonly understood symbols may be manipulated for the purpose of deceiving a social partner. Thus Goffman (1959) found more meaning in what is implicit than in what is explicit in the presentation of self, and Garfinkel (1967) asserted that juries engage in sense-making of their decisions only after the fact and that this constitutes a form of social deception. Berger & Luckman (1966) offered a legitimating sociology of knowledge to which many students of organizational culture resort in emphasizing ethnographic method in a field that has in recent years been dominated by multivariate statistics.

This line of work was also characterized by a critical antiestablishment tone that sought to expose the taken-for-granted social reality that, it was argued, had been largely fostered by the ruling classes for their own benefit (Gouldner 1970). A remnant of that critical strain remains in the contemporary study of organizational culture, but it has found an inhospitable environment in schools of management.

Rational versus Nonrational Features of Organization

A brief historical review suggests that the current managerial view of organizational culture is only the latest in a series of pretenders vying for control of how organizations shall be understood. During the 1950s and the 1960s, organizational sociologists sought to explore the informal relations that regulate organizational life. However, they never strayed very far from ideas of bureaucratic administration. They sought to understand how informal relationships and beliefs modified the demands of the formal system or provided a means to cope with its pressures. Furthermore, their search was strongly motivated by an underlying belief that the fundamental contribution of large-scale economic organizations is to bring "rationality" to an otherwise overwhelmingly complex reality. This predisposition can be attributed to the emphasis by Weber (1968:223) on the rational properties of bureaucracy:

> Experience tends universally to show that the purely bureaucratic type of administration . . .
> is, from a purely technical point of view, capable of attaining the highest degree of efficiency

and is in this sense formally the most rational known means of exercising authority over human beings. It is superior to any other form in precision, in stability, in the stringency of its discipline, and in its reliability . . . The choice is only between bureaucracy and dilettantism in the field of administration.

While the ethnomethodologists and symbolic interactionists of the 1950s and 1960s sought to emphasize the nonrational aspects of organizational life, the mainstream organizational sociologists tried instead to discover the rational basis of organizational life (thus choosing to ignore Weber's emphasis on the importance of charismatic leadership), and the next twenty years of scholarship reflected this tension. We shall describe that contest in some detail because it contains the central forces that today motivate the various approaches to the study of organizational culture.

In 1937 Gulick & Urwick published their *Papers on the Science of Administration* and established the school of "Administrative Rationality." Among the collected papers in that 1937 volume was one by Graicunas which pointed out that as the size of a small group increases, the number of possible interactions grows so rapidly that no manager could oversee more than five or six workers effectively. Thus was born the study of formal organizational structure and the attempt to discover the bases of organizational rationality.

In 1938 Chester Barnard published *The Functions of the Executive*. He emphasized the overwhelming ambiguity of organizational life and suggested that it is the role of the executive to provide the overarching point of view that brings meaning and order to corporate life. In 1939 Roethlisberger & Dickson published the Hawthorne Studies, in which they described the informal norms of workers that successfully frustrated the productivity goals of the management. Each of these themes—organizational rationality, formal structure, leadership under ambiguity, and informal organization versus formal purpose—was subsequently developed. For example, though he wrote of leadership in a slum, Whyte (1943) described how informal leadership always formed within a social group and influenced group behavior. However, the predisposition that dominated the field was to find that large, complex organizations can be made orderly, responsive to top management, and "rational" in serving the purposes of their owners. The problem was that, as anyone could see, no large organization was in fact so orderly. How could we believe that organizations can be rational?

The legitimation for combining a belief in organizational rationality with the empirical observation of organizational nonrationality was offered by Herbert Simon in 1945. Simon argued that human behavior that appears contrary to organizational goals is in fact quite rational if one takes into account the imperfect and limited information-processing ability of human beings, who cannot understand all of the far-flung organizational consequences of their current actions. With this idea of "bounded rationality," Simon provided the basis for the coupling of the rational and the nonrational views of organizations. With that, the study of organizations exploded. It grew in part because large public and commercial organizations proliferated rapidly in the west during the twentieth century, and it grew because Simon had supplied the last necessary piece of a paradigm within which most features of organizational life could be understood.

For the next twenty years (roughly 1945–1965), the main line of research juxtaposed the objective against the subjective, the formal purpose against the informal purpose, the explicit against the implicit in organizational life. The principal method of inquiry was the case study written from the point of view of the social scientist rather than of the native and interpreted to demonstrate why apparently irrational behavior was, in fact, rational or in concert with the goals of the owners and managers of the organization under the circumstances. The method was crystallized by Homans (1950), who interpreted the Hawthorne Studies to great effect. It was employed by Selznick (1949), Trist & Bamforth (1951), by Gouldner (1954), Blau (1955), Lipset, Trow & Coleman (1956), and by Crozier (1964). It must be said that these studies remain among the most informative, penetrating, and lively of all organizational literature.

The tension between rational and nonrational views of organization continued, but the rational view steadily gained the upper hand. Observing that executives, managers, technicians, and workers seem not to share a common purpose, Parsons (1956) offered a mainline theoretical rationale to explain why this was perfectly consistent with prevailing norms of rationality. Udy (1962), on the other hand, maintained that there must always be a tension between the rational goals of economic organizations and the nonrational goals of their social milieu and that this prevents organizations from ever attaining full rationality. Blau & Scott (1962) took perhaps the most trenchant position of all and produced a book that defined the field for more than a decade; it established the interpretation of a formal organization as a purposive aggregation of individuals who exert common effort towards a shared and explicitly recognized goal. In hindsight, it appears that the dominance of this view may have been but one expression of the major shift then taking place in the culture of US social science towards explicit, quantitative, computer-aided analysis.

The Period of Comparative Multivariate Analysis

In 1944 the first computer, Mark I, was developed, and in 1946 the first commercial prototype, ENIAC, was introduced. By the late 1960s, 20,000 computers were in use worldwide (Ouchi 1984). This development had a great impact on the metaphor with which social scientists thought about organizations. For the first time, organizations were construed as information-processing systems rather than as status systems or systems of domination or of ritual.

Computers also had a great impact on the methodology of organizational research. In 1955 Terrien & Mills followed up the logical implications of Graicunas's (1937) article on the span of control. They found that the administrative ratio in school districts was positively related to number of employees and thus conjectured that this relationship would severely limit the maximum feasible size of such organizations. Anderson & Warkov (1961) found that organizational complexity mediates this size–administrative ratio relationship, and at that point a "true science" of organization was off and running. For the first time, students of organization not only could adopt norms of rationality, they could subject their hypothesis to the sort of protorational test using the computer that had previously been accessible only to physical scientists. Subsequent studies by Hage & Aiken (1967), by Hall et al (1967), Blau (1968), Blau & Schoenherr (1971), and a host of other organizational sociologists explored every subtlety of the paradigm. Particularly notable were the studies by the Aston Group in England: Pugh et al (1969), Hinings & Lee (1971), and a steady stream of similar work, most of which involved the application of factor analysis to the study of organization. All of this research on the structure of formal organizations was done in the name of Max Weber, all of it represented attempts to represent operationally the elements of bureaucratic administration that Weber had described, but in the end it was an effort dominated by a methodology and by a computer rather than by a point of view.

The September 1974 issue of *Administrative Science Quarterly* included a letter to the editor from Cornelius Lammers, a Dutch sociologist playing the role of friendly uncle. Lammers visited 18 US campuses, talked to faculties of 16 sociology departments and of 12 schools of management, and tabulated the responses of 20 leading scholars (including Aiken, Aldrich, Blau, Evan, Laumann, Selznick) to questions concerning the state of their field. The research trend mentioned most often as being strong at the time was "comparative studies of organizational structure." The trend most often evaluated as being "bad" was "comparative studies of organizational structure" (Lammers 1974:423). What had seemed a few years earlier to be the continuation of the mainstream of organizational sociology turned out instead to be an epiphenomenon, driven as much by the new computer technology as by any underlying conceptual force.

While this development in organizational sociology was dominating the attention of many sociologists, the principal heirs of Herbert Simon's (1945) work were following a path that had a similar history but a quite different ending. March & Simon (1958) attempted to place the study of organization within an explicitly rational metaphor, adopting a propositional form modeled on the hierarchy of operating systems and application systems of computer software. They developed the view that organizations economize on the bounded rationality of human beings, thus producing what, in the end, is a system in which goals and behavior are connected in a manner that is quite rational. Cyert & March (1963) took the computer metaphor to its logical if austere conclusion, while Thompson (1967) attempted a formal theory of organizational rationality. Although this approach seemed for a while to have the kind of promise that had been hoped for in the comparative study of organizational structure, it too subsided.

The period of the mid-1950s through the 1960s was marked not only by the dominance of the rational point of view in the study of organizations but also by a cleavage in method that clearly set apart organizational ethnographers from the multivariate statisticians of the Terrien & Mills (1955) school and from the applied mathematicians of the Simon (1945) school. The academic ethos of the time quite clearly granted the nod to those who were more quantitatively oriented, but the qualitative social scientists did not entirely disappear. In organizational sociology, the main line that had been represented in an earlier period by Selznick (1949) was carried forward in studies of construction firms by Stinchcombe (1959), of utopian communities by Kanter (1968), of "skid row" communities by Spradley (1970), and of colleges by Clark (1970). All of these chose as their subject something other than large public or private organizations. They were substantively as well as paradigmatically on the fringes of organizational sociology, but they preserved a link to Durkheim's (1961) tradition while the Weberian (1968) point of view temporarily took center stage. This small but hardy family of scholarship was later to become a focal point for the development of organizational culture studies.

Also during this period, the method of ethnography and the point of view of symbolic interaction developed within the sociology of occupations. The work of Becker & Carper (1956), of Gouldner (1957), of Roy (1960), Janowitz (1960), and of Gertzl (1961) had barely penetrated the organizational sociology of the period, but it too was to become a central feature of the later study of organizational culture. Consider next how this intellectual setting gave rise to the contemporary study of organizational culture.

Anomaly Leads to Evolution

Every scholar in the field may legitimately point to a book or article that he or she favors as the beginning of the study of organizational culture as we now see it. The beginnings, however, came not in the putting forward of a new scheme but rather in the form of several stirrings, none of which seemed at the time to be consequential for organizational sociology.

It was the resistance of school systems to bureaucratic interpretation that provided the major anomaly and brought an end to the study of formal organizational structure. Cohen, March & Olsen (1972) found that even the idea of bounded rationality failed to capture the weakly rational properties of school systems; these authors describe them instead as "organized anarchies".

Dornbusch & Scott (1975) had a similar befuddling experience in applying the bureaucratic study to school districts and delayed the publication of their book for several years while they attempted to make sense out of the experience. Weick (1976) could describe them best as "loosely coupled systems", and Meyer & Rowan (1977) saw in their formal structure nothing more than myth and ceremony, detached from the "real" activities of teachers and of students. Becker & Gordon (1966) attempted to apply the paradigm, by then well developed, of comparative organizational structure to the analysis of hospitals but found that it did not effectively capture their essence.

Another significant anomaly at this time occurred as organizational sociologists attempted to apply the size-complexity-administrative ratio model to business organizations in Japan. Abegglen (1958), Dore (1973), McMillan et al (1973), Tracy & Azumi (1976), Marsh & Mannari (1976), and Cole (1979) found that some stable results replicated in Japan, while others did not. Lincoln et al (1978), in a study of Japanese-owned businesses in the United States employing expatriate Japanese and Japanese-Americans, found little difference in structure related to the ratio of Japanese ethnics to whites, but the authors were quite clearly frustrated at their inability to capture statistically what they experienced as a major organizational difference: "We cannot describe adequately how different is the atmosphere in an organization where 50 to 80% of the personnel have Japanese origins, where Japanese is widely spoken and certain Japanese interpersonal customs are observed, from one employing few or no Japanese or Japanese-Americans" (1978:834).

The ground was thus prepared for a new approach to the study of organization. The paradigm of formal organizational structure had been found incapable of encompassing the anomalous forms of hospital and of school organization, nor could it effectively encompass the modern Japanese industrial firm, which had come to prominence in scholarship as well as in public affairs. The attitude among many organizational scholars was one of despair. If organizations are anarchies, if their social structure is a myth that is entirely disconnected from everyday behavior, then there is little that the mainline social scientist can bring to the study of them.

Groundwork for a solution came from the extensive sociology of careers and occupations. Kuhn (1970) observed that a socially constructed point of view strongly influences the behavior of scientists, and it tends to be consistent within professions and across organizations. Lodahl & Gordon (1972) demonstrated that this view was entirely compatible with mainline sociological tradition, and Imershein (1977) suggested that the idea of scientific paradigm might be applied to the organization rather than the profession as the unit of analysis, thus creating the idea of an organizational paradigm. Van Maanen & Schein (1978) described how the processes found in occupational socialization were also at work in organizations. Van Maanen (1973) reported on his year of living with a police force, thus bringing the method and point of view of the ethnographer squarely into the mainstream of management literature. Pfeffer (1981) elaborated the idea of an organizational paradigm and fleshed out the possibilities of the study of management as symbolic action.

The study of organizational culture is rooted more deeply in sociology than in any other intellectual tradition. Critical both to sociology and to the study of organizational culture is the idea of an organization as a social phenomenon that has its own features which distinguish it from an environment on the one hand and from the individual desires and predispositions of its members on the other. Whereas the sociologist will typically emphasize the organization as a dependent variable with respect to macrosocial forces, it seems organizational culture has instead treated the organization as an independent variable almost exclusively, paying attention to the effect of organizational culture on employee participation and morale.

At the moment, the study of organizational culture is dominated by behavioral scientists working in the 600 schools of management in the US. These management schools now produce a good deal more organizational work than do departments of sociology, which surely must be a reversal of the situation of twenty years ago. The sheer growth in numbers of management schools is largely accountable for this difference, but there is a difference of intellectual domain as well. When sociologists became disenchanted with the multivariate studies of organizational structure in the 1970s, they simply took their intellectual curiosity and methodologies and migrated to the study of community structure, of occupational structure, of the structure of health care, and so on. Those who are employed in schools of management, however, are rather permanently committed to the study of business firms. As a result they maintained their focus on business organizations but sought new points of view and new techniques with which to revitalize the study of those specific institutions. In that transition was created the study of organizational culture. Perhaps it is through culture, rather than formal structure, that large firms can be bent to the will of their masters and rendered predictable, "rational."

It was a curious turnabout, to say the least, in which the study of informal organization as the opponent of organizational rationality was thus transformed into the study of organizational culture as the basis for organizational rationality.

We should mention at least briefly some developments in social psychology that have had an important bearing on the development of the study of organizational culture. Many organizational scholars have been influenced by the tradition in psychology of studying the disjuncture between expressed intention and observed behavior (e.g. Festinger 1957, Kelley 1977). Variously developed as the study of cognitive dissonance, of persuasion, and of attribution, this tradition has consistently drawn attention to the nonrational features of individual behavior. For example, cognitive psychologists have shown systematic biases in the way people assess causality and make decisions (Kahneman & Tversky 1979). People tend to use story or single-case information more than multiple observations to make judgments (Borgida & Nisbett 1977). They also engage in self-serving rationalizations of the past, attributing success to their own efforts and failure to external forces beyond their control (Weiner et al 1971). Apparently, organizations similarly attribute success to managerial skill and poor performance to a poor economy or other external forces (Staw et al 1982).

The import of these ideas for organizational scholars has been to bolster the view that decision making in organizations is not consistently rational. Goals are often discovered or created after the organizational activities they are supposed to direct (Weick 1979). Popular stories may have more influence on decisions and commitment than rules and statistics (Martin & Powers 1983).

A second significant line of social psychology for the study of organizational culture has been the study of organizational climate (Forehand and Gilmer 1964, Tagiuri 1968). Studies of climate have been sometimes indistinguishable from some current studies of organizational culture. The method of those studies, however, was that of survey research rather than of ethnography, and survey methods were under heavy attack within social psychology as lacking in the precision of experimental method. Two broad critiques of the climate studies appeared in one year (Hellriegel & Slocum 1974, James & Jones 1974) and effectively diminished the activity in that area of study. We shall also see that the use of survey methodology is seen by many current scholars of culture as being too much the product of the social scientist's rather than the participant's point of view and therefore inappropriate as a method for measuring culture. There are thus many scholars who are aghast that anyone would label climate studies as studies of culture even though some of the underlying ideas are the same.

A REVIEW OF CURRENT THEORY, EMPIRICAL RESEARCH, AND PRACTICE IN ORGANIZATIONAL CHANGE

The historical review just concluded attempted to relate some older themes to the contemporary work, thus providing an ordering of the contemporary approaches. In this section, we offer a second and more complete attempt to bring order to this new work, making use of categories that occurred to us as we sifted through several score books, articles, and working papers.

We begin with current theoretical work on organizational culture. Then we consider current empirical work. Finally, we consider work on the planned change of organizational culture. The interested reader may also wish to pursue other recent reviews by Burrell & Morgan (1979), Sanday (1979), Smircich (1983), Gregory (1983), Louis (1983), and Morgan et al (1983).

Theoretical Studies of Organizational Culture

The currently developing theory may be assigned in a rough way to the category of either macroanalytic or microanalytic approaches to culture in organizations. The macroanalytic theories have in common an attempt to understand the culture of a whole group or subgroup, the functions that culture performs in maintaining the group, or the conditions under which the group and its culture and subcultures develop. The microanalytic theories present culture as something that resides within each individual and can be understood through the cognitive processes of sense-making, learning, and causal attribution, or by probing the unconscious mind.

MACROANALYTIC THEORIES OF ORGANIZATIONAL CULTURE   Most of these exhibit a functional logic reminiscent of the anthropologists Malinowski and Radcliffe-Brown. For example, in studying the rites and ceremonies of organizations Trice & Beyer (1984, see also Trice 1983) developed a typology of rites (rites of passage, of degradation, of renewal, of integration, etc) and suggested that these rites fulfill both manifest and latent social functions (e.g. to socialize, integrate, assign social identity). Wilkins (1983a) suggests that popularly told stories about founders and other key organizational actors in some organizations perform integrative and control functions by serving as persuasive and instructive exemplars of managerial paradigms.

A second group of studies has adopted the view that the study of organizational culture should be closely related to some aspects of institutional microeconomics. In this view, both the form and content of culture are interpreted as consequences of the needs of the firm for efficiency. Wilkins & Ouchi (1983) argue that a homogeneous corporate culture performs organizational control functions but that it will develop only under certain conditions (e.g. long and stable membership, interaction across functional/hierarchical boundaries, and an absence or discrediting of institutional alternatives). In a similar vein, Jones (1983) suggests that the content of an organizational culture results from the particular economic conditions (property rights structures, etc) in which organizational participants find themselves. He suggests three types of cultures that may result: production, bureaucratic, and professional. Barney (1984) extends these ideas to suggest that in some organizations culture can become a "firm-specific asset," which can produce "supernormal returns."

The study of occupational groups as cultural forms is now a lively and active field for both theory and empiricism. Van Maanen & Barley (1984) review an extensive occupational literature and assert that we are much more likely to find shared understandings and values among members of a same occupational group than among the functionally differentiated and spatially dispersed members of an origanization. Others who have raised this problem of subcultures or lack of shared organizational culture—though with differing suggestions for subunits and how to select them—include Louis (1983), Martin & Siehl (1983), Gregory (1983), and Wilkins (1983b).

By and large, these studies attempt to describe the purpose and function of patterns of belief, language, and symbol in organizations. They tend to present these elements of organizational culture as necessary to order and stability, and to regard them as resistant to explicit attempts at manipulation owing to their natural or evolutionary character. Rarely, however, do they attempt to explain the relationship between an organization's internal culture and its larger cultural or socioeconomic environment. At this moment, the diversity of approach seems to be vigorously wide.

MICROANALYTIC THEORIES OF ORGANIZATIONAL CULTURE   Attempts to develop theories of organizational culture from a psychological point of view are small in number and tend to be mid-range rather than grand abstractions. Existing works can be separated into two general categories—one for those that tend to use psychological notions of attribution or social learning and one for those that point to the unconscious or underlying assumptions that give meaning to the surface manifestations of culture.

In the first category, Pfeffer (1981) exemplifies the use of theories that emphasize the lack of coupling between attitudes and behavior. He suggests that organizational symbols are decoupled from actual outcomes, which are primarily mediated by environmentally determined, resource-dependency relationships. Schein (1983a) argues that culture is the sum of what individuals have learned of their organizational world, based on (a) the observed consequences of past action, and (b) the success or failure of attempts to cope with needs for anxiety avoidance. This learning ultimately yields a few commonly shared organizational beliefs. A similar approach is taken by Martin et al (1983), who present a typology of organizational stories that serve to resolve or express psychological tensions.

The second class of psychological theories suggests that culture is best understood by going beyond surface manifestations. Some follow Freudian or Jungian psychoanalytic approaches, while others subscribe to a more linguistic, "deep structure" approach (Chomsky 1972). Mitroff and his colleagues (see Mitroff 1983, Mitroff et al 1983, and Dandridge et al 1980) present a Jungian concern for archetypes or other meaning-structures to help them characterize deeper layers of meaning in organizational life. Walter (1983), following Lasch (1979), points out the neurotic aspects of organizational culture in a psychoanalytic vein. Pondy (1978, 1983), on the other hand, uses a linguistic approach to "uncover meaning." He sees leadership as a language game, the meaning of which can only be understood by getting at underlying "grammar" or rules and standards in people's minds from which they generate appropriate behavior.

It seems natural to seek the cognitive analogues of organizational belief, as some of this work does. What is more interesting, however, is that this line of work seeks explicitly to join the psychology of individual cognition with the organizational setting that provides much of the cognitive field. When studies of formal structure dominated organizational research, there were few obvious opportunities for developing the social psychology of organizations, and the distance between organizational sociologists and organizational psychologists grew. Through the study of organizational culture, that distance may be diminished.

Empirical Studies of Organizational Culture

The issues, problems, and methods of research on organizational culture have been discussed in several recent reviews (e.g. *Administrative Science Quarterly* 24:4; Spradley 1979; Martin 1983; Van Maanen 1979; Louis 1984; Burrell & Morgan 1979). Each of the reviews presents a unique view of the field. Some argue that quantitative techniques have no place in empirical studies of culture, while others assert that multiple methods, both quantitative and qualitative, are necessary. The range of methodologies is broad, with much borrowing from linguistics, survey research, participant observation, ethnomethodology, and symbolic interaction.

We have divided the empirical work into categories that follow from the principal intellectual traditions described above. These are: (1) *holistic studies* in the tradition of Radcliffe-Brown and Malinowski; (2) *semiotic or language studies,* which follow Geertz and Goodenough; and (3) *quantitative studies,* which use surveys or experimental manipulation.

HOLISTIC STUDIES OF ORGANIZATIONAL CULTURE   The exemplar in this category is the work by Rohlen (1974), who presents an ethnographic description of his participant observation in a Japanese bank. More recent examples of ethnographic descriptions of organizations include Krieger's portrait of a San Francisco rock music station (1979), Van Maanen's (1973) description of the socialization of police recruits, Manning's (1979) study of the world of detectives, Dyer's (1982) description of a computer company, Wilkins's (1983b) study of subcultures in an electronics company, the examination by Trice & Beyer (1985) of two social movement organizations routinizing the charisma of their founder, and Barley's (1983b) study of the evolution in organizational roles accompanying the introduction of CAT scanning technology in two hospitals.

These studies vary greatly in their degree of overt analysis and of theorizing. For example, Krieger (1979) avoids theoretical interpretation while Trice & Beyer (1985) use their observations of contrasts between the two organizations over a the 20-year period to generate a rough theory of routinization of charisma. While some of these studies employ quantitative methods such as content analysis (Martin et al 1984) or surveys (Barley 1983a), most rely upon field observation for periods of 6 months to 20 years (off and on). They tend to be rich and interesting descriptions of organizational life and provide a sharp contrast to the statistics typical of the structural view of organizations.

One major subset of holistic studies relies on archival, historical, or other public documents rather than field observation to arrive at an understanding of a social group. One example is Clark's (1970) study of organizational "sagas" at Antioch, Reed, and Swarthmore colleges; he relied upon historical documents supplemented with interviews to recreate the past. Similarly, Dyer (1984) studied cultural evolution at "Brown Corporation" during the years 1922–1983 through a combination of interviews, public records (e.g. annual reports, minutes of stockholder meetings), internal reports (e.g. minutes from Board of Directors meetings, financial and personnel records) and industry reports.

Boje (1983) has used public histories combined with field observation to study changes in the folklore of the commercial printer since 1400. He finds that with recent rapid technological change the previously traditional and longstanding culture has been virtually destroyed. Kanter (1968) and Martin & Siehl (1983) relied upon secondary histories or other books as their primary sources. While the potential limitations and biases associated with such sources are obvious, the use of public and historical documents has encouraged a longitudinal perspective that is otherwise almost impossible to obtain. While these holistic studies embody the spirit of Radcliffe-Brown and of Malinowski, they employ an amalgam of methods both old and new to study the modern business firm and are thus quite distinct from any earlier body of work.

SEMIOTIC STUDIES (FOCUS ON LANGUAGE AND SYMBOLISM)   The ethnoscience approach mentioned earlier is exhibited clearly in recent studies by Gregory (1983) and Barley (1983a). Gregory interviewed 75 professionals from several companies and studied several companies in depth in Silicon Valley. Her analysis of the language of these professionals suggested several taxonomies that enable the natives to make sense of their multifaceted and rapidly changing industry. Barley (1983a) studied the language of funeral directors to understand the implicit categories and taxonomies they use to make sense of their work. He spent some time observing a funeral home and then conducted several in-depth interviews, which were transcribed and later used for the linguistic analysis.

Other studies have focused on language but without the overtly ethnoscience approach. Pondy (1983) used ethnographic accounts of Communist China and of an African tribe (the Nuer) to illustrate the role of metaphor in helping participants in a culture to use the past to understand the uncertain or complex future. Huff (1983) examined public documents in a graduate school of management to show how the language of different subgroups was first couched in terms preferred by a new dean but then changed as the groups became increasingly independent. Pondy & Huff (1983a) have also traced the decline of one frame of reference used by policy makers and the rise of another by following the language used in public documents and recorded interviews over a several year period. They have documented (Pondy & Huff 1983b) the use of rhetoric by an administrator to prepare the way for a goal of computer literacy in public schools.

These semiotic studies appear to have been quite directly influenced by the tradition in anthropology. They typically require painstaking effort both in the collection of transcripts and in analysis, and they sometimes resemble exercises in methodology as much as anything else. As the techniques become more widely disseminated, however, the approach seems likely to expand rapidly.

QUANTITATIVE STUDIES   Some studies of culture seem to be very much like the previous studies of organizational climate as we noted earlier. For example, Ouchi & Johnson (1978) employed questionnaires to characterize the differences in the cultures of companies "A" and "Z" (see also Ouchi 1983). O'Reilly (1983) distributed questionnaires in seven high technology companies in Silicon Valley to test the association between the presence of a "strong culture" and employee identification with the firm. He found general support. Bowditch et al (1983) used a standard climate survey with an original culture survey to study the effect on culture and climate of the merger of two banks. Friedman (1983) reports on the use of content analysis of projective measures to reveal subcultures in one particular firm. He is careful to note that the procedure requires qualitative observation and data collection to assist in the interpretation of results. Beck & Moore (1983, 1984) report studies that use a variety of projective measures in order to illuminate the relationship between broader social norms and the firm-specific culture of Canadian banks.

Meyer (1982) used both questionnaires and content analysis of stories collected through open-ended interviews to examine the creation of shared ideologies. Finally, Zucker (1977) subjected the theme of institutionalization to laboratory experimentation, and Martin & Powers (1983) report the use of experimental manipulation to demonstrate that facts embedded in organizational stories are more vivid and persuasive than are quantitative summaries.

SUMMARY: EMPIRICAL STUDIES   The empirical studies of organizational culture involve a combination of the technology of the organizational social scientist with the interests of the cultural anthropologist. Since the organizational scholars of management schools have highly developed skills in the multivariate analysis of survey and experimental data, it is not surprising that they approach the study of organizational culture with these techniques. However, most of these studies also employ to varying degrees the techniques of participant observation, which have long been absent from organizational research. An ethnographer might assert with some justification that this new line of work is nothing but a mongrelization of the study of culture, and perhaps in the end the studies of this sort will be evaluated as having been a fad. At the moment, we can only observe what appears to be new "hybrid energy" flowing from the confluence of several established methodologies with a variety of approaches to the idea of organizational culture. This confluence is producing a quite novel form of organizational scholarship.

Work on Planned Change Related to Organizational Culture

The prescriptive work in this area can be conveniently divided into two general categories: (*a*) case descriptions of planned change efforts; and (*b*) advice to executives. Both are natural developments in the milieu of a school of management.

CASE DESCRIPTIONS   Although management scholars may seek to find useful prescriptions that can guide managers, their inquiry is nonetheless guided by more traditional rules of science, and their predisposition towards claims of simple organizational change is one of skepticism. The descriptions of efforts to change culture are not encouraging to those who believe culture can be a tool for management control. For example, Van de Ven (1983b) documents, with pre- and post-interview and survey data, the failure of a charismatic black minister to integrate into a single organizational culture several semiautonomous entities. Bowditch et al (1983) describe how the attempted cultural merger of two banks resulted instead in the domination of one culture by the other. Trice & Beyer (1985) point out that the founder of Alcoholics Anonymous was able to institutionalize his organization through a set of quite unique circumstances, which another similar organization was unable to duplicate. These studies might properly be regarded as a subset of holistic studies of organizational culture, particularly because they are few in number. However, these studies have typically found that organizational cultures are not easily altered in intentional ways, and they have often turned to an examination of environmental factors to explain this result. Studies of change are thus typically more inclined to see organizational culture as a dependent variable than are the other approaches, and they are of particular interest for that reason.

ADVICE TO EXECUTIVES   Much of the advice to executives seems quite distant from the detached tone of typical academic writing. This area seems to proceed directly from the popular success of descriptions of already successful corporate cultures (Ouchi 1981, Pascale & Athos 1981, Deal & Kennedy 1982, and Peters & Waterman 1982) to general recommendations about how to influence corporate culture. Most authors in this genre present the view that the culture of a successful company can be emulated, although with difficulty.

Some of the most popular advice to executives comes from consultants or business school professors who offer recommendations about how to influence attitudes, opinions, and beliefs. Peters (1978, 1980) suggests that executives can effectively signal changes in values by the way they spend their time, what they ask questions about, and what they include on their agenda. Sathe (1983) uses a social psychological model to suggest how managers can help partici- pants interpret events and can use hiring and training to influence beliefs.

Other approaches in this area follow the lead of Selznick (1957). For example, Van de Ven (1983a) suggests that the primary role of executives should be to articulate and embody a mission and role for the organization. Ouchi & Price (1978) suggest that executives should articulate a philosophy of management that describes organizational goals.

Some are less sanguine about the possibility of changing an organizational culture but suggest that it is useful to have culture in mind because it delimits efforts at change. For example, Schwartz & Davis (1981) suggest that execu- tives should consider the "cultural risk" of proposed new strategies. In their view, the organizational change implied by new business strategies should be compared to the cultural orientations of the organization in order to determine the degree of potential resistance.

Schein (1983a), as noted above, has forcefully argued that much of an organization's culture represents the ways people have learned to cope with anxiety. Thus attempts to change culture are tantamount to asking people to give up their social defenses. We should consider the ethics of such a course, according to Schein. We should also be aware that threats to such social defenses are only likely to meet with success when the culture is under considerable challenge.

CONCLUDING THOUGHTS

The large commercial organization is a recent phenomenon, which developed only after the introduction of rail transport and telegraphy. It is therefore to be expected that scholars will continue for some time to try one intellectual template after another before finding one that adequately captures its essence. On the other hand, the business firm is just one special case of a much older class of large and complex social structures, and it is therefore to be expected that many inherited scholarly tools will be useful in studying it. This review suggests both that the study of large firms is in a period of experimentation and that it draws upon many insights that anthropologists, sociologists, and psy- chologists have developed in the study of other forms of social organization.

We have treated the contemporary study of organizational culture as a cultural phenomenon as much as a scholarly development. As a cultural phenomenon, this field exhibits two facets of particular interest. First is a struggle among academics over which of many points of view will dominate the study of organizations, and second is the impact of multivariate statistics on the study of organizations.

Several points of view are now in active contention for dominance among students of organizational culture. One contest is over whether culture is a dependent or an independent variable. Among those who prefer to study organizational culture as a dependent variable, some take a natural-systems point of view and conclude that the culture of a firm is the natural outgrowth of its particular time and place and is not subject to human attempts at manipulation, while others assert that critical features of organizational culture may be systematically altered by a determined management. Those who view culture as an independent variable tend to ignore these possibilities and instead seek to explicate the variety of forms through which the subtle and implicit features of organization influence the thoughts, feelings, and behavior of individual participants.

A second contest is over the appropriate methods of study. Some hold that the method of lengthy field observation must be employed, while others assert that the whole point of the contemporary study of organizational culture is to go beyond the method of the anthropologist by applying multivariate statistical analysis to these issues. Although rarely written in journal articles, it is often said by those who are statistically inclined that organizational culture has become the refuge of the untrained and the incompetent, who will degrade this new field if they are not rooted out.

This review has consistently taken a historical point of view in attempting to achieve perspective on the study of organizational culture, and it is with a historical perspective that our review will conclude. The study of organizations, like any field of study, grows only through a constant intellectual tension that yields thesis and antithesis. During the 1960s, the multivariate studies of complex organizations had just begun to invade a domain that had long been dominated by field studies. The sociology of prisons, armies, slums, and gold coasts had been rich with the participants' point of view. Those who first championed the "comparative" (that is, large-sample) point of view were passionate about the inherent superiority of intellectual rigor in their approach. The struggle often produced research that manifested elements of various approaches, research that raised scholarship to new heights.

During much of the 1970s, the struggle ceased. The multivariate approach dominated the leading journals, and those who preferred qualitative approaches established their own journals, meetings, and subculture. In the absence of conflict, there was a flowering of subbranches and of sub-subbranches dealing on the one hand with abstract representations of networks of interorganizational relations and on the other hand with Jungian archetypes of corporate personality. Neither, as of this moment, has amounted to much. It is difficult to resist the interpretation that conflict and confrontation are good for research and that they are essential for good research. It is on these grounds that the contemporary study of organizational culture shows promise. This new field is rich with confrontation between those who feel that the statisticians continue to be too powerful and those who feel that the phenomenologists have sapped the scientific rigor of the field. Those who study occupational cultures argue passionately that any attempt to describe the culture of a firm with its many occupational subcultures is superficial, simpleminded, and cheap. The disputes are deeply felt and hotly contended, as are the more basic intellectual commitments on which they rest.

In a way, the study of organizational culture is a return. Much of the contemporary writing on organizational culture is accessible to the educated layman and is of interest even to the press. This was true of an earlier period of urban sociology, of industrial social psychology, and of cultural anthropology. There is in the field a return to a concern for the whole of the organization, an interest in knowing not only about that which can be captured in a standardized regression coefficient, but in knowing also what can be described only in a lengthy quotation that reveals the native's point of view. There is a return to a dual interest in description and in prescription, which typified the social sciences after World War II but which became unbalanced in a single-minded allegiance to description 20 years later. With the return to these earlier, perhaps more complete, approaches to organization come also the old tensions between points of view, tastes, and methods that do not make natural bedfellows. For the moment, at least, we can expect the study of organizational culture to be marked both by dissension and by creativity.

ACKNOWLEDGMENTS

We would like to thank several people whose thoughtful comments have improved this paper. They include Jay Barney, W. Gibb Dyer, Jr., Connie Gersick, Mitchell Koza, Barbara Lawrence, J. B. Richie, Harrison Trice, and the members of the UCLA interdisciplinary organization discussion group (Lynne Zucker, chair).

We are grateful for the financial support of the Office of Naval Research and the Hank Marcheschi Entrepreneurship Fund.

Literature Cited

Abegglen, J. 1958. *The Japanese Factory,* Glencoe, Ill., Free Press
Administrative Science Quarterly. 1979. 24(4):519–671
Administrative Science Quarterly. 1983. 28(3):331–502
Anderson, T., Warkov, S. 1961. Organizational size and the functional complexity: A study of administration in hospitals. *Am. Sociol. Rev.* 26:23–28

Barley, S. 1983a. Semiotics and the study of occupational and organizational cultures. *Admin. Sci. Q.* 28:393–413
Barley, S. 1983b. *The evolution of roles in a technological subculture: A case from CAT scanning.* Presented at the Conf. on Interpretive Approaches to Study of Organ., Alta, Utah
Barnard, C. 1938. *The Functions of the Executive.* Cambridge, Mass: Harvard Univ. Press

Barney, J. 1984. *Economic profit from organizational culture.* UCLA Grad. School Mgmt. Working Paper

Beck, B., Moore, L. 1983. *Influence of corporate image on manager's styles: The example of five Canadian banks.* Presented at the Conf. Organ. Folklore, Santa Monica, Calif.

Beck, B., Moore, L. 1984. *Linking the host culture to organizational variables.* Presented at the Conf. Organ. Culture and Meaning of Life in the Workplace, Vancouver, Canada

Becker, H. S., J. W. Carper. 1956. The development of identification with an occupation. *Am. J. Sociol.* 61:289–98

Becker, S., Gordon, G. 1966. An entrepreneurial theory of formal organizations, Part I. *Admin. Sci. Q.* 11:315–44

Benedict, R. 1934. *Patterns of Culture.* New York: Houghton-Mifflin

Berger, P., Luckmann, T. 1966. *The Social Construction of Reality: a Treatise in the Sociology of Knowledge.* New York: Anchor

Blau, P. 1955. *The Dynamics of Bureaucracy.* Chicago: Univ. Chicago Press

Blau, P. 1968. The hierarchy of authority in organizations. *Am. J. Sociol.* 73:453–67

Blau, P., Schoenherr, R. 1971. *The Structure of Organizations.* New York: Basic

Blau, P., Scott, W. R. 1962. *Formal Organizations: A Comparative Approach.* San Francisco: Chandler

Boje, D. 1983. *The fraternal spirit and folklore of the commercial printer.* UCLA Grad. School Mgmt. Working Paper No. 83–27

Borgida, E., Nisbett, R. E. 1977. "The differential impact of abstract vs. concrete information on decisions." *J. Appl. Soc. Psychol.* 7:258–71

Bowditch, J., Buono, A., Lewis, J. III. 1983. *When cultures collide: The anatomy of a merger.* Presented at the Acad. Mgmt. Mtgs. in Dallas, Tex.

Burrell, G., Morgan, G. 1979. *Sociological Paradigms and Organizational Analysis.* London: Heineman

Chomsky, N. 1972. *Language and Mind.* New York: Harcourt, Brace, Jovanovich

Clark, B. 1970. *The Distinctive College: Antioch, Reed, and Swarthmore.* Chicago: Aldine

Cohen, M., March, J., Olsen, J. 1972. A garbage can model of organizational choice. *Admin. Sci. Q.* 17:1–25

Cole, Robert. 1979. *Work, Mobility, and Participation,* Berkeley, Calif: Univ. Calif. Press

Crozier, M. 1964. *The Bureaucratic Phenomenon.* London: Tavistock

Cyert, R., March, J. 1963. *A Behavioral Theory of the Firm.* Englewood Cliffs, NJ: Prentice-Hall

Dandridge, T., Mitroff, I., Joyce, W. 1980.

Organizational symbolism: a topic to expand organizational analysis. *Acad. Mgmt. Rev.* 5:77–82

Deal, T., Kennedy, A. 1982. *Corporate Cultures.* Reading, Mass: Addison-Wesley

Dore, Ronald. 1973. *British Factory, Japanese Factory.* Los Angeles, Calif: Univ. Calif. Press

Dyer, W. G. Jr. 1982. *Culture in organizations: a case study.* MIT Sloan School of Mgmt. Working Paper

Dyer, W. G. Jr. 1984. The cycle of cultural evolution in organizations. In *Managing Corporate Culture,* ed. R. Kilmann et al. San Francisco: Jossey-Bass. In press

Dornbush, S., Scott, W. R. 1975. *Evaluation and Authority.* San Francisco: Jossey-Bass

Durkheim, E. 1893. *The Division of Labor in Society.* Transl. G. Simpson, 1933. New York: Free. (From French)

Durkheim, E. *The Elementary Forms of Religious Life.* Transl. J. Swain, 1961. New York: Collier (From French)

Dyer, W. G. Jr. 1982. *Culture in organizations: a case study.* MIT Sloan School of Mgmt. Working Paper

Dyer, W. G. Jr. 1984. The cycle of cultural evolution in organizations. In *Managing Corporate Culture,* ed. R. Kilmann et al. San Francisco: Jossey-Bass. In press

Evered, R. 1983. The language of organizations: the case of the Navy. See Pondy et al. 1983 pp. 125–44.

Festinger, L. 1957. *A Theory of Cognitive Dissonance.* Stanford, Calif: Stanford Univ. Press.

Forehand, G., Gilmer, B. 1964. Environmental variation in studies of organizational behavior. *Psychol. Bull.* 22:361–82

Friedman, S. 1983. *Cultures within cultures? An empirical assessment of an organization's subcultures using projective measures.* Presented at the Acad. of Mgt. Mtgs., Dallas, Tex.

Frost, P., Morgan, G. 1983. "Symbols and sensemaking: the realization of a framework." See Pondy et al 1983, pp. 207–36.

Garfinkel, H. 1967. *Studies in Enthnomethodology.* Englewood Cliffs, NJ: Prentice-Hall

Geertz, C. 1973. *The Interpretation of Cultures.* New York: Basic

Gertzl, B. G. 1961. Determinants of occupational community in high status occupations. *Sociol. Quart.,* 2:37–40

Goffman, E. 1959. *The Presentation of Self in Everyday Life.* New York: Doubleday

Goodenough, W. 1971. *Culture, Language, and Society.* Reading, Mass: Addison-Wesley Modular Publ., No. 7

Gouldner, A. W. 1954. *Patterns of Industrial Bureaucracy.* Glencoe, Ill: Free

Gouldner, A. W. 1957. Cosmopolitans and locals: toward an analysis of latent social roles, Parts I, II, *Admin. Sci. Q.* 2:281–306, 3:444–80

Gouldner, A. W. 1970. *The Coming Crisis of Western Sociology.* New York: Avon

Graicunas, V. A. 1937. Relationship to organization. In *Papers on the Science of Administration,* ed. L. Gulick, L. Urwick, pp. 183–87. New York: Columbia Univ. Inst. Publ. Admin.

Gregory, K. 1983. Native-view paradigms: multiple culture and culture conflicts in organizations. *Admin. Sci. Q.* 28:359–76

Gulick, L., Urwick, L., eds. 1937. *Papers on the Science of Administration.* New York: Inst. Publ. Admin., Columbia Univ. Press

Hage, J., Aiken, M. 1967. Relationship of centralization to other structural properties. *Admin. Sci. Q.* 12:72–92

Hall, R., Haas, E., Johnson, N. 1967. An examination of the Blau-Scott and Etzioni Typologies. *Admin. Sci. Q.* 12:118–39

Hellriegel, D., Slocum, J. Jr. 1974. Organizational climate: Measures, research and contingencies. *Acad. Mgt. J.* 17:255–80

Hinings, C. R., Lee, G. 1971. Dimensions of organization structure and their context: replication. *Sociology* 5:83–93

Hirsch, P. 1972. Processing fads and fashions: An organization-set analysis of cultural industry systems. *Am. J. Sociol.* 72:639–59

Homans, G. C. 1950. *The Human Group.* New York: Harcourt, Brace, World

Huff, A., 1983. A rhetorical examination of strategic change. See Pondy et al 1983, pp. 167–83

Imershein, A. W. 1977. Organizational change as a paradigm shift. *Sociol. Q.* 18:33–34

James, L., Jones, A. 1974. Organizational climate: a review of theory and research. *Psychol. Bull.* 81:1096–1112

Janowitz, M. 1960. *The Professional Soldier.* Glencoe, Ill: Free

Johnson, R., Ouchi, W. G. 1974. Made in America (under Japanese management). *Harv. Bus. Rev.* 52(5):61–69

Jones, G. 1983. Transaction costs, property rights, and organizational culture: an exchange perspective. *Adm. Sci. Q.* 28:454–67

Kahneman, D., Tversky, A. 1979. "On the psychology of prediction." *Psychol. Rev.* 80:237–51

Kanter, R. 1968. Commitment and social organization: a study of commitment mechanisms in utopian communities. *Am. Sociol. Rev.* 33:499–517

Kanter, R. 1977. *Men and Women of the Corporation.* New York: Basic

Kelley, H. 1977. Attribution in social interaction. In *Attribution: Perceiving the Causes of Behavior,* ed. E. Jones, et al. Morristown, NJ: General Learning

Krieger, S. 1979. *Hip Capitalism.* Beverly Hills: Sage

Kuhn, T. 1970. *The Structure of Scientific Revolutions.* Chicago: Univ. Chicago Press

Lammers, C. 1974. The state of organizational sociology in the United States: Travel impressions by a Dutch Cousin, *Adm. Sci. Q.* 19(3):422–30

Lammers, C. 1981. Contributions of organizational sociology Part II. Contributions to organizational theory and practice—A liberal view. *Organization Studies* 2(4):361–76.

Lasch, C. 1979. *The Culture of Narcissism.* New York: Warner

Lawrence, P., Lorsch, J. 1967. *Organization and Environment.* Cambridge, Mass: Harvard Grad. School Bus. Admin.

Lincoln, J. R., Olson, J., Hanada, M. 1978. Cultural effects on organizational structure: The case of Japanese firms in the United States. *Am. Sociol. Rev.* 43:829–47

Lipset, S., Trow, M., Coleman, J. 1956. *Union Democracy.* Glencoe, Ill: Free

Lodahl, J., Gordon, G. 1972. The structure of scientific fields and the functioning of University Graduate Departments. *Am. Sociol. Rev.* 37:57–72

Louis, M. 1981. A cultural perspective on organizations: the need for and consequences of viewing organizations as culture-bearing milieux. *Hum. Syst. Mgmt.* 2:246–58

Louis, M. 1983. Organizations as culture-bearing milieux. See Pondy et al 1983, pp. 39–54

Louis, M. 1984. *An investigator's guide to workplace culture: assumptions, choice points, and alternatives.* Presented at the Conf. on Organ. Culture and Meaning of Life in the Workplace. Vancouver, Canada

Malinowski, B. 1961. *Argonauts of the Western Pacific.* London: Routledge, Kegan Paul

Manning, P. 1979. Metaphors of the field: varieties of organizational discourse. *Admin. Sci. Q.* 24:660–71

March, J., Simon, H. 1958. *Organizations.* New York: Wiley

Marsh, Robert, Mannari, Hiroshi. 1976. *Modernization and the Japanese Factory,* Princeton: Princeton Univ. Press

Martin, J. 1983. *Breaking up the mono-method monopolies in organizational research.* Stanford Grad. School Bus. Working Paper

Martin, J. 1984. *The elusiveness of founder effect on culture.* Stanford University Grad. School Bus. Working Paper.

Martin, J., Feldman, M., Hatch, M., Sitkin, S. 1983. The uniqueness paradox in organizational stories. *Admin. Sci. Q.* 28:438–53

Martin, J., Powers, M. 1983. Truth or corporate propaganda: the value of a good war story." See Pondy et al 1983, pp. 93–108

Martin, J., Siehl, C. 1983. Organizational culture and counter-culture: an uneasy symbiosis. *Organ. Dynam.* 12(2):52–64

McMillan, C., Hickson, D., Hinings, C.

Schneck, R. 1973. The structure of work organizations across societies. *Acad. Mgmt. J.* 16:555–69

Mead, M. 1949. *Coming of age in Samoa.* New York: New Am. Lib.

Meyer, A. 1982. How ideologies supplant formal structures and shape responses to environments. *J. Mgmt. Stud.* 19(1):45–61

Meyer, J., Rowan, B. 1977. Notes on the structure of educational organizations. In *Studies on Environment and Organization,* ed. M. Meyer, San Francisco: Jossey-Bass

Mitroff, I. 1983. Archetypal social systems analysis: on the deeper structure of human systems." *Acad. of Mgmt. Rev.* 8:387–97

Mitroff, I., Kilmann, R., Saxton, M. 1983. *Organizational culture: collective order-making out of an ambiguous world.* Univ. Calif. Working Paper

Moore, L., Beck, B. 1983. Leadership among bank managers: A structural comparison of behavioral responses and metaphorical imagery. In *Managerial Work and Leadership: International Perspectives,* ed. J. Hunt et al. New York: Pergamon

Morgan, G., Frost, P., Pondy, L. 1983. "Organizational symbolism." See Pondy et al 1983, pp. 3–38

O'Reilly, C. 1983. *Corporations, culture and organizational culture: lessons from Silicon Valley firms.* Presented at the Acad. of Mgmt. Mtgs. Dallas, Tex.

Organizational Dynamics. 1983. 12(2):80 pp.

Ouchi, W. G. 1980. Markets, bureaucracies, and clans. *Admin. Sci. Q.* 25:129–41

Ouchi, W. G., 1981. *Theory Z.* Reading, Mass: Addison-Wesley

Ouchi, W. G. 1983. Theory Z: An elaboration of methodology and findings. *J. Contemp. Bus.* 11:27–41

Ouchi, W. G. 1984. *The M-Form Society,* Reading, Mass: Addison-Wesley

Ouchi, W. G., Johnson, J. 1978. Types of organizational control and their relationship to emotional well-being. *Admin. Sci. Q.* 23:293–317

Ouchi, W. G., Price, R. 1978. "Hierarchies, clans, and theory z: A new perspective on organization development." *Organ. Dynam.* 7(2):25–44.

Parsons, T. 1956. Suggestions for a sociological approach to the study of organizations, Pt. I, II. *Admin. Sci. Q.* 1:63–85, 1:225–39

Pascale, R. T., Athos, A. 1981. *The Art of Japanese Management.* New York: Simon Schuster

Peters, T. 1978. Symbols, patterns, settings: An optimistic case for getting things done." *Organ. Dynam.* 7(2):3–23

Peters, T. 1980. "Management systems: The language of organizational character and competence." *Organ. Dynam.* 3–27

Peters, T., Waterman, R. 1982. *In Search of Excellence: Lessons from America's Best-Run Companies.* New York: Harper, Row

Pettigrew, A. M. 1979. On studying organizational culture. *Admin. Sci. Q.* 24:570–81

Pfeffer, J. 1981. Management as symbolic action: the creation and maintenance of organizational paradigms. In *Research in Organizational Behavior,* ed. L. Cummings, B. Staw, 3:1–51

Pondy, L. R. 1978. Leadership is a language game. In *Leadership: Where Else Can We Go?,* ed. M. McCall, M. Lombardo. Greensboro, NC: Duke Univ. Press

Pondy, L. R. 1983. The role of metaphors and myths in organization and in the facilitation of change. See Pondy et al 1983, pp. 157–66

Pondy, L. R., Frost, P. M., Morgan, G., Dandridge, T. C. 1983. *Organizational Symbolism.* Greenwich, Conn: JAI

Pondy, L. R., Huff, A. 1983a. *Achieving routine.* Univ. Ill. Dept. Bus. Admin. Working Paper

Pondy, L. R., Huff, A. 1983b. *Budget cutting in Riverside: Emergent policy reframing as a process of analytic discovery and conflict minimizing.* Presented at the Acad. of Mgmt. Mtgs. Dallas, Tex.

Pondy, L. R., Mitroff, I. I. 1979. Beyond open system models of organization. In *Research in Organizational Behavior,* ed. B. Staw, Vol. I. Greenwich, Conn: JAI

Pugh, D., Hickson, D., Hinings, C., Turner. C. 1969. An empirical taxonomy of work organizations. *Admin. Sci. Q.* 14:115–26

Radcliffe-Brown, A. 1952. *Structure and Function in Primitive Society.* London: Oxford Univ. Press

Rohlen, T. 1974. *For Harmony and Strength: Japanese White-collar Organization in Anthropological Perspective.* Berkeley: Univ. Calif. Press

Roethlisberger, F., Dickson, W. 1939. *Management and the Worker.* Cambridge, Mass: Harvard Univ. Press

Roy, D. 1960. Banana time: job satisfaction and informal interactions. *Hum. Organ.* 18:156–68

Sanday, P. 1979. The ethnographic paradigm(s). *Admin. Sci. Q.* 24:527–38

Sathe, V. 1983. Some action implications of corporate culture. *Organ. Dynam.* 12(2):5–23

Schein, E. 1983a. *Organizational culture: A dynamic model.* MIT Sloan School of Mgmt. Working Paper No. 1412–83

Schein, E. 1983b. The role of the founder in creating organizational culture. *Organ. Dynam.* 12(1):13–28

Schwartz, H., Davis, S. 1981. Matching corporate culture and business strategy. *Organ. Dynam.* 10(1):30–48

Selznick, P. 1949. *T.V.A. and the Grass Roots.* Berkeley, Calif: Univ. Calif. Press

Selznick, P. 1957. *Leadership in Administration*. Evanston, Ill: Row, Peterson

Simon, H. 1945. *Administrative Behavior: a Study of Decision-making Processes in Administrative Organization*. New York: Free

Smircich, L. 1983. Concepts of culture and organizational analysis. *Admin. Sci. Q.* 28:339–58

Spradley, J. 1970. *You Owe Yourself a Drunk: an Ethnography of Urban Nomads*. Boston: Little, Brown

Spradley, J. 1979. *The Ethnographic Interview*. New York: Holt, Rinehart, Winston

Staw, B., ed. 1981. *Research in Organizational Behavior*. Greenwich, Conn: JAI

Staw, B., McKechnie, P., Puffer, S. 1982. The justification of corporate performance. Unpublished manuscript, Univ. of Calif. Berkeley

Stinchcombe, A. 1959. Bureaucratic and craft administration of production. *Admin. Sci. Q.* 4:168–87

Tagiuri, R. 1968. The concept of organizational climate. In *Organizational climate: explorations of a concept*, ed. R. Tagiuri, G. Litivin. Boston, Mass: Grad. School Bus., Harvard Univ.

Terrien, F., Mills, D. 1955. The effects of changing size upon the internal structure of an organization. *Am. Sociol. Rev.* 20:11–23

Thompson, J. 1967. *Organizations in Action*. New York: McGraw-Hill

Toennies, Ferdinand. 1957. *Community and Society*. Transl. C. P. Loomis, East Lansing, Mich: Michigan State Univ. Press (From French)

Tracy, P. K., Azumi, K. 1976. Determinants of administrative control: a test of a theory with Japanese factories. *Am. Sociol. Rev.* 41:80–94

Trice, H. 1983. Rites and ceremonials in organizational culture. In *Perspectives in organizational sociology: Theory and research*, Vol. 4, ed. S. Bacharach, S. Mitchell. Greenwich, Conn: JAI

Trice, H., Beyer, J. 1984. Studying organizational cultures through rites and ceremonials. *Acad. Mgmt. Rev.* 9:653–69

Trice, H., Beyer, J. 1985. The routinization of charisma in two social movement organizations. In *Research in Organizational Behavior*, Vol. 7, ed. B. Staw and L. Cummings. Greenwich, Conn: JAI

Trist, E. L., Bamforth, K. W. 1951. Some social and psychological consequences of the longwall method of coal-getting. *Hum. Rel.* 4:3–38

Udy, S. H. Jr. 1962. "Administrative rationality, social setting, and organizational development," *Am. J. Sociol.* 68:299–308

Van de Ven, A. 1983a. *Creating and sustaining a corporate culture in fast changing organizations*. Univ. Minn. Working Paper

Van de Ven, A. 1983b. *An attempt to institutionalize an organization's culture."* Presentation at the Acad. Mgmt. Meeting, Dallas, Tex.

Van Maanen, J. 1973. Observations on the making of policemen. *Hum. Organ.* 32:407–18

Van Maanen, J. 1979. The fact of fiction in organizational ethnography. *Admin. Sci. Q.* 24:539–50

Van Maanen, J., Barley, S. 1984. Occupational communities: culture and control in organizations. In *Research in Organizational Behavior*, Vol. 6. ed. B. Staw, L. Cummings. Greenwich, Conn: JAI

Van Maanen, J., Schein, E. 1978. Toward a theory of organizational socialization, In *Research in Organization Behavior*, ed. B. Staw. Greenwich, Conn: JAI

Walter, G. 1983. "Psyche and symbol." See Pondy et al 1983, pp. 257–72. Greenwich: Conn: JAI

Weber, Max 1968. *Economy and Society*. Berkeley, Calif: Univ. Calif. Press

Weick, K. 1979 *The Social Psychology of Organizing*. Reading, Mass: Addison-Wesley. 2nd ed.

Weick, K. 1976. Educational organizations as loosely coupled systems. *Admin. Sci. Q.* 21:1–19

Weiner, B., Frieze, I., Kullea, A., Reed, L., Rest, S., Rosenbaum, R. 1971. *Perceiving the Causes of Success and Failure*. Morristown, NJ: General Learning

Whyte, W. F. 1943. *Street Corner Society*. Chicago: Univ. Chicago Press

Wilkins, A. 1978. *Organizational stories as an expression of management philosophy: implications for social control in organizations*. PhD thesis. Stanford Univ. 202 pp.

Wilkins, A. 1983a. Organizational stories as symbols which control the organization. See Pondy et al 1983, pp. 81–92

Wilkins, A. 1983b. The culture audit: a tool for understanding organizations. *Organ. Dynam.* 12(2):24–38

Wilkins, A., Ouchi, W. G. 1983. Efficient cultures: exploring the relationship between culture and organizational performance. *Admin. Sci. Q.* 28:468–81

Zucker, L. 1977. The role of institutionalization in cultural persistence, *Am. Sociol. Rev.*, 42:726–43

SUBJECT INDEX

CUMULATIVE INDEXES

CONTRIBUTING AUTHORS, VOLUMES 1–11

A

Aldous, J., 3:105–35
Aldrete-Haas, J. A., 7:157–75
Aldrich, H. E., 2:79–105
Alford, R. R., 1:429–79
Anthony, D., 5:75–89
Aponte, R., 11:231–58
Atchley, R. C., 8:263–87

B

Bahr, H. M., 9:243–64
Baldassare, M., 4:29–56
Barchas, P. R., 2:299–333
Baron, J. N., 10:37–69
Bechhofer, F., 11:181–207
Ben-David, J., 1:203–22
Berg, I., 4:115–43
Berger, J., 6:479–508
Berk, R. A., 9:375–95
Berk, S. F., 9:375–95
Bertaux, D., 10:215–37
Bielby, W. T., 3:137–61
Billy, J. O. G., 11:305–28
Blalock, H. M., 10:353–72
Block, F., 7:1–27
Boli-Bennett, J., 1:223–46
Bonacich, P., 4:145–70
Boocock, S. S., 4:1–28
Boorman, S. A., 6:213–33
Boruch, R. F., 4:511–32
Bottomore, T., 1:191–202
Braithwaite, J., 11:1–25
Branch, K., 10:141–66
Brinkerhoff, D., 7:321–49
Brint, S. G., 11:389–414
Burstein, P., 7:291–319
Burt, R. S., 6:79–141

C

Canak, W., 7:225–48
Caplow, T., 9:243–64
Carroll, G. R., 10:71–93
Catton, W. R. Jr., 5:243–73
Chadwick, B. A., 9:243–64
Chase-Dunn, C., 1:223–46
Cheng, L., 9:471–98
Cherlin, A., 9:51–66
Chirot, D., 8:81–106
Choldin, H. M., 4:91–113

Cicourel, A. V., 7:87–106
Clark, T. N., 1:271–95; 11:437–55
Cohen, E., 10:373–92
Cohen, E. G., 8:209–35
Collins, H. M., 9:265–85
Cook, K. S., 9:217–41
Coser, L. A., 2:145–60
Crittenden, K. S., 9:425–46
Cunnigen, D., 7:177–98

D

DeLamater, J., 7:263–90
Demerath, N. J. III, 2:19–33
DiRenzo, G. J., 3:261–95
Dobratz, B. A., 8:289–317
Dobson, R. B., 3:297–329
Dunlap, R. E., 5:243–73
Dynes, R. R., 3:23–49

E

Eckberg, D. L., 6:1–20
Elder, G. H. Jr., 1:165–90
Elder, J. W., 2:209–30
Elliott, B., 11:181–207
Emerson, R. M., 2:335–62; 7:351–78
Erickson, M. L., 1:21–42
Evans, P. B., 7:199–223

F

Feagin, J. R., 6:1–20
Featherman, D. L., 4:373–420
Fine, G. A., 10:239–62
Fischer, C. S., 1:67–89
Fisher, G. A., 11:129–44
Fishman, J. A., 11:113–27
Flacks, R., 4:193–238
Foley, D. L., 6:457–78
Foner, A., 5:219–42
Form, W., 5:1–25
Fox, R. C., 2:231–68
Frank, A. W. III, 5:167–91
Freese, L., 6:187–212
Freidson, E., 10:1–20
Friedland, R., 1:429–79; 10:393–416
Frisbie, W. P., 3:79–104
Fuguitt, G. V., 11:259–80

G

Galaskiewicz, J., 4:455–84; 11:281–304
Garrison, H. H., 8:237–62
Gecas, V., 8:1–33
Gelles, R. J., 11:347–67
Gerstein, D., 11:369–87
Gibbs, J. P., 1:21–42
Giele, J. Z., 5:275–302
Glasberg, D. S., 9:311–32
Glenn, N. D., 3:79–104
Goldstein, M. S., 5:381–409
Goldstone, J. A., 8:187–207
Gottfredson, M. R., 7:107–28
Gordon, C., 2:405–33
Gordon, G., 1:339–61
Greeley, A. M., 5:91–111
Gusfield, J. R., 10:417–35

H

Hall, T. D., 8:81–106
Hannan, M. T., 5:303–28
Hare, A. P., 5:329–50
Harris, A. R., 8:161–86
Haug, M. R., 3:51–77
Hauser, R. M., 3:137–61
Heer, D. M., 11:27–47
Hegtvedt, K. A., 9:217–41
Heilman, S. C., 8:135–60
Henshel, R. L., 8:57–79
Hermassi, E., 4:239–57
Hill, G. D., 8:161–86
Hindelang, M. J., 7:107–28
Hirschman, C., 9:397–423
Hollander, P., 8:319–51
Holz, J. R., 5:193–217
Horwitz, A. V., 10:95–119

J

Janson, C.-G., 6:433–56
Jaret, C., 9:499–525
Jenkins, J. C., 9:527–53
Johnson, M. P., 2:161–207
Jones, R. A., 9:447–69

K

Kalleberg, A. L., 5:351–79
Kandel, D. B., 6:235–85

494

CHAPTER TITLES, VOLUMES 1–10

Annual Reviews Inc. | ORDER FORM

A NONPROFIT SCIENTIFIC PUBLISHER

4139 El Camino Way, Palo Alto, CA 94306-9981, USA • • (415) 493-4400

Annual Reviews Inc. publications are available directly from our office by mail or telephone (paid by credit card or purchase order), through booksellers and subscription agents, worldwide, and through participating professional societies. Prices subject to change without notice.

- **Individuals:** Prepayment required on new accounts by check or money order (in U.S. dollars, check drawn on U.S. bank) or charge to credit card — American Express, VISA, MasterCard.
- **Institutional buyers:** Please include purchase order number.
- **Students:** $10.00 discount from retail price, per volume. Prepayment required. Proof of student status must be provided (photocopy of student I.D. or signature of department secretary is acceptable). Students must send orders direct to Annual Reviews. Orders received through bookstores and institutions requesting student rates will be returned.
- **Professional Society Members:** Members of professional societies that have a contractual arrangement with Annual Reviews may order books through their society at a reduced rate. Check with your society for information.

Regular orders: Please list the volumes you wish to order by volume number.
Standing orders: New volume in the series will be sent to you automatically each year upon publication. Cancellation may be made at any time. Please indicate volume number to begin standing order.
Prepublication orders: Volumes not yet published will be shipped in month and year indicated.
California orders: Add applicable sales tax.
Postage paid (4th class bookrate/surface mail) **by Annual Reviews Inc.** Airmail postage extra.

ANNUAL REVIEWS SERIES		Prices Postpaid per volume USA/elsewhere	Regular Order Please send:	Standing Order Begin with:
			Vol. number	Vol. number
Annual Review of **ANTHROPOLOGY** (Prices of Volumes in brackets effective until 12/31/85)				
[Vols. 1-10	(1972-1981)	**$20.00/$21.00]**		
[Vol. 11	(1982)	**$22.00/$25.00]**		
[Vols. 12-14	(1983-1985)	**$27.00/$30.00]**		
Vols. 1-14	(1972-1985)	**$27.00/$30.00**		
Vol. 15	(avail. Oct. 1986)	**$31.00/$34.00**	Vol(s). _____	Vol. _____
Annual Review of **ASTRONOMY AND ASTROPHYSICS** (Prices of Volumes in brackets effective until 12/31/85)				
[Vols. 1-2, 4-19	(1963-1964; 1966-1981)	**$20.00/$21.00]**		
[Vol. 20	(1982)	**$22.00/$25.00]**		
[Vols. 21-23	(1983-1985)	**$44.00/$47.00]**		
Vols. 1-2, 4-20	(1963-1964; 1966-1982)	**$27.00/$30.00**		
Vols. 21-23	(1983-1985)	**$44.00/$47.00**		
Vol. 24	(avail. Sept. 1986)	**$44.00/$47.00**	Vol(s). _____	Vol. _____
Annual Review of **BIOCHEMISTRY** (Prices of Volumes in brackets effective until 12/31/85)				
[Vols. 30-34, 36-50	(1961-1965; 1967-1981)	**$21.00/$22.00]**		
[Vol. 51	(1982)	**$23.00/$26.00]**		
[Vols. 52-54	(1983-1985)	**$29.00/$32.00]**		
Vols. 30-34, 36-54	(1961-1965; 1967-1985)	**$29.00/$32.00**		
Vol. 55	(avail. July 1986)	**$33.00/$36.00**	Vol(s). _____	Vol. _____
Annual Review of **BIOPHYSICS AND BIOPHYSICAL CHEMISTRY** (Prices of Vols. in brackets effective until 12/31/85) (Formerly Annual Review of Biophysics and Bioengineering)				
[Vols. 1-10	(1972-1981)	**$20.00/$21.00]**		
[Vol. 11	(1982)	**$22.00/$25.00]**		
[Vols. 12-14	(1983-1985)	**$47.00/$50.00]**		
Vols. 1-11	(1972-1982)	**$27.00/$30.00**		
Vols. 12-14	(1983-1985)	**$47.00/$50.00**		
Vol. 15	(avail. June 1986)	**$47.00/$50.00**	Vol(s). _____	Vol. _____
Annual Review of **CELL BIOLOGY**				
Vol. 1	(1985)	**$27.00/$30.00**		
Vol. 2	(avail. Nov. 1986)	**$31.00/$34.00**	Vol(s). _____	Vol. _____
Annual Review of **COMPUTER SCIENCE**				
Vol. 1	(avail. late 1986)	**Price not yet established**	Vol. _____	Vol. _____
Annual Review of **EARTH AND PLANETARY SCIENCES** (Prices of Volumes in brackets effective until 12/31/85)				
[Vols. 1-9	(1973-1981)	**$20.00/$21.00]**		
[Vol. 10	(1982)	**$22.00/$25.00]**		
[Vols. 11-13	(1983-1985)	**$44.00/$47.00]**		
Vols. 1-10	(1973-1982)	**$27.00/$30.00**		
Vols. 11-13	(1983-1985)	**$44.00/$47.00**		
Vol. 14	(avail. May 1986)	**$44.00/$47.00**	Vol(s). _____	Vol. _____

ANNUAL REVIEWS SERIES	Prices Postpaid per volume USA/elsewhere	Regular Order Please send:	Standing Order Begin with:

Annual Review of **ECOLOGY AND SYSTEMATICS** (Prices of Volumes in brackets effective until 12/31/85)

[Vols. 1-12	(1970-1981)	$20.00/$21.00]
[Vol. 13	(1982)	$22.00/$25.00]
[Vols. 14-16	(1983-1985)	$27.00/$30.00]
Vols. 1-16	(1970-1985)	$27.00/$30.00
Vol. 17	(avail. Nov. 1986)	$31.00/$34.00

Vol(s). _____ Vol. _____

Annual Review of **ENERGY** (Prices of Volumes in brackets effective until 12/31/85)

[Vols. 1-6	(1976-1981)	$20.00/$21.00]
[Vol. 7	(1982)	$22.00/$25.00]
[Vols. 8-10	(1983-1985)	$56.00/$59.00]
Vols. 1-7	(1976-1982)	$27.00/$30.00
Vols. 8-10	(1983-1985)	$56.00/$59.00
Vol. 11	(avail. Oct. 1986)	$56.00/$59.00

Vol(s). _____ Vol. _____

Annual Review of **ENTOMOLOGY** (Prices of Volumes in brackets effective until 12/31/85)

[Vols. 9-16, 18-26	(1964-1971; 1973-1981)	$20.00/$21.00]
[Vol. 27	(1982)	$22.00/$25.00]
[Vols. 28-30	(1983-1985)	$27.00/$30.00]
Vols. 9-16, 18-30	(1964-1971; 1973-1985)	$27.00/$30.00
Vol. 31	(avail. Jan. 1986)	$31.00/$34.00

Vol(s). _____ Vol. _____

Annual Review of **FLUID MECHANICS** (Prices of Volumes in brackets effective until 12/31/85)

[Vols. 1-5, 7-13	(1969-1973; 1975-1981)	$20.00/$21.00]
[Vol. 14	(1982)	$22.00/$25.00]
[Vols. 15-17	(1983-1985)	$28.00/$31.00]
Vols. 1-5, 7-17	(1969-1973; 1975-1985)	$28.00/$31.00
Vol. 18	(avail. Jan. 1986)	$32.00/$35.00

Vol(s). _____ Vol. _____

Annual Review of **GENETICS** (Prices of Volumes in brackets effective until 12/31/85)

[Vols. 1-15	(1967-1981)	$20.00/$21.00]
[Vol. 16	(1982)	$22.00/$25.00]
[Vols. 17-19	(1983-1985)	$27.00/$30.00]
Vols. 1-19	(1967-1985)	$27.00/$30.00
Vol. 20	(avail. Dec. 1986)	$31.00/$34.00

Vol(s). _____ Vol. _____

Annual Review of **IMMUNOLOGY**

Vols. 1-3	(1983-1985)	$27.00/$30.00
Vol. 4	(avail. April 1986)	$31.00/$34.00

Vol(s). _____ Vol. _____

Annual Review of **MATERIALS SCIENCE** (Prices of Volumes in brackets effective until 12/31/85)

[Vols. 1-11	(1971-1981)	$20.00/$21.00]
[Vol. 12	(1982)	$22.00/$25.00]
[Vols. 13-15	(1983-1985)	$64.00/$67.00]
Vols. 1-12	(1971-1982)	$27.00/$30.00
Vols. 13-15	(1983-1985)	$64.00/$67.00
Vol. 16	(avail. August 1986)	$64.00/$67.00

Vol(s). _____ Vol. _____

Annual Review of **MEDICINE** (Prices of Volumes in brackets effective until 12/31/85)

[Vols. 1-3, 5-15, 17-32	(1950-52; 1954-64; 1966-81)	$20.00/$21.00]
[Vol. 33	(1982)	$22.00/$25.00]
[Vols. 34-36	(1983-1985)	$27.00/$30.00]
Vols. 1-3, 5-15, 17-36	(1950-52; 1954-64; 1966-85)	$27.00/$30.00
Vol. 37	(avail. April 1986)	$31.00/$34.00

Vol(s). _____ Vol. _____

Annual Review of **MICROBIOLOGY** (Prices of Volumes in brackets effective until 12/31/85)

[Vols. 18-35	(1964-1981)	$20.00/$21.00]
[Vol. 36	(1982)	$22.00/$25.00]
[Vols. 37-39	(1983-1985)	$27.00/$30.00]
Vols. 18-39	(1964-1985)	$27.00/$30.00
Vol. 40	(avail. Oct. 1986)	$31.00/$34.00

Vol(s). _____ Vol. _____

Annual Review of **NEUROSCIENCE** (Prices of Volumes in brackets effective until 12/31/85)

[Vols. 1-4	(1978-1981)	$20.00/$21.00]
[Vol. 5	(1982)	$22.00/$25.00]
[Vols. 6-8	(1983-1985)	$27.00/$30.00]
Vols. 1-8	(1978-1985)	$27.00/$30.00
Vol. 9	(avail. March 1986)	$31.00/$34.00

Vol(s). _____ Vol. _____

serving science · Annual
since
1932
Reviews · Annual

R **Annual Reviews Inc.**
4139 EL CAMINO WAY
PALO ALTO, CALIFORNIA 94306-9981, USA

A NONPROFIT
SCIENTIFIC PUBLISHER

FROM

NAME

ADDRESS

ZIP CODE

PLACE
STAMP
HERE

For over half a century Annual Reviews Inc. has produced high quality books for use by the worldwide scientific community. Timely, comprehensive, and affordable, Annual Review publications are your best value in scientific review literature. We are particularly proud of the three newest additions to our collection:

ANNUAL REVIEW OF IMMUNOLOGY, Volume 4

Editor: William E. Paul **Associate Editors:** C. Garrison Fathman, Henry Metzger
Available April 1986 • Price: $31.00 USA/$34.00 elsewhere, postpaid

ANNUAL REVIEW OF CELL BIOLOGY, Volume 2

Editor: George E. Palade **Associate Editors:** Bruce M. Alberts, James A. Spudich
Available November 1986 • Price: $31.00 USA/$34.00 elsewhere, postpaid

ANNUAL REVIEW OF COMPUTER SCIENCE, Volume 1

Editor: J.F. Traub
Available late 1986 • Price: to be determined

ANNUAL REVIEWS SERIES		Prices Postpaid per volume USA/elsewhere	Regular Order Please send:	Standing Order Begin with:

Annual Review of **NUCLEAR AND PARTICLE SCIENCE** (Prices of Volumes in brackets effective until 12/31/85)

[Vols. 12-31	(1962-1981)................$22.50/$23.50]		
[Vol. 32	(1982)......................$25.00/$28.00]		
[Vols. 33-35	(1983-1985).................$30.00/$33.00]		
Vols. 12-35	(1962-1985)................$30.00/$33.00		
Vol. 36	(avail. Dec. 1986)............$34.00/$37.00	Vol(s). _____	Vol. _____

Annual Review of **NUTRITION** (Prices of Volumes in brackets effective until 12/31/85)

[Vol. 1	(1981)....................$20.00/$21.00]		
[Vol. 2	(1982)......................$22.00/$25.00]		
[Vols. 3-5	(1983-1985).................$27.00/$30.00]		
Vols. 1-5	(1981-1985)................$27.00/$30.00		
Vol. 6	(avail. July 1986)............$31.00/$34.00	Vol(s). _____	Vol. _____

Annual Review of **PHARMACOLOGY AND TOXICOLOGY** (Prices of Volumes in brackets effective until 12/31/85)

[Vols. 1-3, 5-21	(1961-1963, 1965-1981)........$20.00/$21.00]		
[Vol. 22	(1982)......................$22.00/$25.00]		
[Vols. 23-25	(1983-1985).................$27.00/$30.00]		
Vols. 1-3, 5-25	(1961-1963, 1965-1985)........$27.00/$30.00		
Vol. 26	(avail. April 1986)............$31.00/$34.00	Vol(s). _____	Vol. _____

Annual Review of **PHYSICAL CHEMISTRY** (Prices of Volumes in brackets effective until 12/31/85)

[Vols. 10-21, 23-32	(1959-1970, 1972-1981)........$20.00/$21.00]		
[Vol. 33	(1982)......................$22.00/$25.00]		
[Vols. 34-36	(1983-1985).................$28.00/$31.00]		
Vols. 10-21, 23-36	(1959-1970, 1972-1985)........$28.00/$31.00		
Vol. 37	(avail. Nov. 1986)............$32.00/$35.00	Vol(s). _____	Vol. _____

Annual Review of **PHYSIOLOGY** (Prices of Volumes in brackets effective until 12/31/85)

[Vols. 19-43	(1957-1981).................$20.00/$21.00]		
[Vol. 44	(1982)......................$22.00/$25.00]		
[Vols. 45-47	(1983-1985).................$27.00/$30.00]		
Vols. 19-47	(1957-1985)................$27.00/$30.00		
Vol. 48	(avail. March 1986)............$32.00/$35.00	Vol(s). _____	Vol. _____

Annual Review of **PHYTOPATHOLOGY** (Prices of Volumes in brackets effective until 12/31/85)

[Vols. 2-19	(1964-1981).................$20.00/$21.00]		
[Vol. 20	(1982)......................$22.00/$25.00]		
[Vols. 21-23	(1983-1985).................$27.00/$30.00]		
Vols. 2-23	(1964-1985)................$27.00/$30.00		
Vol. 24	(avail. Sept. 1986)............$31.00/$34.00	Vol(s). _____	Vol. _____

Annual Review of **PLANT PHYSIOLOGY** (Prices of Volumes in brackets effective until 12/31/85)

[Vols. 13-23, 25-32	(1962-1972, 1974-1981)........$20.00/$21.00]		
[Vol. 33	(1982)......................$22.00/$25.00]		
[Vols. 34-36	(1983-1985).................$27.00/$30.00]		
Vols. 13-23, 25-36	(1962-1972, 1974-1985)........$27.00/$30.00		
Vol. 37	(avail. June 1986)............$31.00/$34.00	Vol(s). _____	Vol. _____

Annual Review of **PSYCHOLOGY** (Prices of Volumes in brackets effective until 12/31/85)

[Vols. 4, 5, 8	(1953, 1954, 1957)............$20.00/$21.00]		
[Vols. 10-24, 26-32	(1959-1973, 1975-1981)........$20.00/$21.00]		
[Vol. 33	(1982)......................$22.00/$25.00]		
[Vols. 34-36	(1983-1985).................$27.00/$30.00]		
Vols. 4, 5, 8	(1953, 1954, 1957)............$27.00/$30.00		
Vols. 10-24, 26-36	(1959-1973, 1975-1985)........$27.00/$30.00		
Vol. 37	(avail. Feb. 1986)............$31.00/$34.00	Vol(s). _____	Vol. _____

Annual Review of **PUBLIC HEALTH** (Prices of Volumes in brackets effective until 12/31/85)

[Vols. 1-2	(1980-1981).................$20.00/$21.00]		
[Vol. 3	(1982)......................$22.00/$25.00]		
[Vols. 4-6	(1983-1985).................$27.00/$30.00]		
Vols. 1-6	(1980-1985)................$27.00/$30.00		
Vol. 7	(avail. May 1986)............$31.00/$34.00	Vol(s). _____	Vol. _____

ANNUAL REVIEWS SERIES	Prices Postpaid per volume USA/elsewhere	Regular Order Please send:	Standing Order Begin with:

Annual Review of **SOCIOLOGY** (Prices of Volumes in brackets effective until 12/31/85)

[Vols. 1-7	(1975-1981) . . . . $20.00/$21.00]		
[Vol. 8	(1982) . . . . $22.00/$25.00]		
[Vols. 9-11	(1983-1985) . . . . $27.00/$30.00]		
Vols. 1-11	(1975-1985) . . . . $27.00/$30.00		
Vol. 12	(avail. Aug. 1986) . . . . $31.00/$34.00	Vol(s). _____	Vol. _____

Note: Volumes not listed are out of print

SPECIAL PUBLICATIONS	Prices Postpaid per volume USA/elsewhere	Regular Order Please Send:

Annual Reviews Reprints: **Cell Membranes, 1975-1977**

(published 1978)   Softcover . . . . $12.00/$12.50   _____ Copy(ies).

Annual Reviews Reprints: **Immunology, 1977-1979**

(published 1980)   Softcover . . . . $12.00/12.50   _____ Copy(ies).

History of Entomology

(published 1973)   Clothbound . . . . $10.00/$10.50   _____ Copy(ies).

Intelligence and Affectivity:
Their Relationship During Child Development, by Jean Piaget

(published 1981)   Hardcover . . . . $8.00/$9.00   _____ Copy(ies).

Some Historical and Modern Aspects of Amino Acids,
Fermentations, and Nucleic Acids: Proceedings of a
Symposium held in St. Louis, Missouri, June 3, 1981

(published 1982)   Softcover . . . . $10.00/$12.00   _____ Copy(ies).

Telescopes for the 1980s

(published 1981)   Hardcover . . . . $27.00/$28.00   _____ Copy(ies).

The Excitement and Fascination of Science, Volume 1

(published 1965)   Clothbound . . . . $6.50/$7.00   _____ Copy(ies).

The Excitement and Fascination of Science, Volume 2

(published 1978)   Hardcover . . . . $12.00/$12.50
Softcover . . . . $10.00/$10.50   _____ Copy(ies).

TO: **ANNUAL REVIEWS INC.,** 4139 El Camino Way, Palo Alto, CA 94306-9981, USA • Tel. (415) 493-4400

Please enter my order for the publications checked above. California orders, add sales tax. Prices subject to change without notice.

Institutional purchase order No. _____

Amount of remittance enclosed $_____

INDIVIDUALS: Prepayment required in U.S. funds or charge to bank card below. Include card number, expiration date, and signature.

Charge my account ☐ VISA

☐ MasterCard   ☐ American Express

Acct. No. _____

Exp. Date _____   _____
Signature

Name _____
Please print

Address _____
Please print

Zip Code _____

_____ Send free copy of current **Prospectus** ☐

Area(s) of Interest